DIGITAL DELI

DIGITAL DELI

The comprehensive, user-lovable menu of computer lore, culture, lifestyles and fancy

by The Lunch Group & Guests

Edited by Steve Ditlea

Workman
Publishing
New York

Library of Congress Cataloging in
Publication Data
Main entry under title:
Digital deli.
   Includes index.
   1. Electronic digital computers—
Addresses, essays,
lectures. 2. Microcomputers—Ad-
dresses, essays, lectures.
I. Ditlea, Steve.   II. Lunch Group.
QA76.5.D4794 1984   001.64
83-40030
ISBN 0-89480-591-6

Cover illustration: Seymour Chwast
Cover design: Paul Hanson
Book design: Diane LeMasters

Manufactured in the United States
of America
First printing September 1984
10 9 8 7 6 5 4 3 2 1

Workman Publishing Company, Inc.
1 West 39 Street
New York, New York 10018

MENU

APPETIZERS

SOUP AND CRACKERS

PERSONAL CHOICES

FAMILY FAVORITES

WORD SALAD

CREATIVE COMBOS

BRAIN FOOD

FOREIGN DELIGHTS

FRESH GREENS

SMALL FRY

JUST DESSERTS

TOMORROW'S SPECIALS

FROM COMPUTER LUNCH TO DIGITAL DELI

The Lunch Group began inauspiciously enough on July 29, 1982, over a Mexican lunch on Manhattan's West 44 Street. Of the quintet of New York journalists, three had used personal computers for more than a month, two actually owned their machines, and one later confessed to having been totally intimidated by the rather simplistic conversation. Within a year, that one reporter would write an influential cover story for a major business magazine, nudging the price of IBM stock up by over 10 percent in a single week.

As the personal computer industry grew, so did our informal lunch group and the level of its sophistication. Our numbers expanded to include regular contributors to national news, business, consumer and lifestyle periodicals, as well as members of the popular computer press and book authors. Our discussions began to revolve around the instant folklore of microcomputers, with such recurring names as Woz and Budge and Draper and Gates. Our culinary preferences tended toward burgers and salads, but the talk was more often than not about Apples and IBMs.

Seldom were heard the words "bit" or "byte" or any unduly technical debates, since our backgrounds and interests tended to be humanistic as well as practical. We shared the joys and tribulations of setting up a first computer system, of learning a word processing program, of sending articles over telephone lines, of applying the personal computer revolution to our lives. We took pride in experiencing the frontiers of what many felt to be the most far-reaching and influential cultural development any journalist or author could hope to cover at this time.

Each of us came to computers in different ways. My own path led from twelve years of covering pop culture for a variety of national publications. Looking back, the progression from reviewing rock-and-roll to writing about personal computer software was a logical one: after all, a disk is a disk is a disk . . . I had watched the entertainment industry go through periods of expansion and decline. The lessons learned would aid me in writing about the world of personal computing—after word processing on an Apple II almost doubled my professional output and income, sealing my fate as a computer enthusiast.

Other regulars at our monthly lunches came from hard news, feature, political, travel and even porn writing backgrounds, bringing varied insights and a spirit of noncompetitiveness to our peripatetic feasts.

We changed restaurants six times in our first year as the group grew larger and hungrier.

When Peter Workman of Workman Publishing first heard about our odd assemblage of computer humanists, he exclaimed: "The Lunch Group. We must have a book by The Lunch Group!" It was he who gave us our name—though in all accuracy, writers have been gathering for lunch ever since the invention of the writer's block. It was Mr. Workman who suggested a book of original, informative writing and art about our computerized era. The result of his inspiration and ours is this volume.

The book came together during a period of boom and bust in the personal computer industry, and of tremendous demand on the time and talents of those involved in covering it. Overnight it seemed everyone in The Lunch Group was working on the Big Interview/Article/Book. Suddenly we were too busy to do justice to the rich banquet of personal computer lore on our own, so we invited some distinguished guests to join in.

Our contributors were scattered across the country and were never destined to be in one place at one time. We nonetheless formed a network of elective affinities, representative of the personal computer community at large. Our ages ranged from thirteen to sixty-three, and lest anyone believe that computer users must all be dehumanized wretches, during the gestation of this book we actually had more than our share of births, weddings and at least one stellar transcontinental love affair.

We tried to include as many differing viewpoints as possible, but certain prejudices remain, like the fundamental belief that personal computers are a positive force for the empowerment of the individual, reaffirming our right to Life, Liberty and the Pursuit of Happiness.

Incidentally, our title, *Digital Deli* seemed the only logical choice once we got to sample the variety of contributions about our digitally-based computer culture. We are grateful for the opportunity to give new meaning to Gerald Wright's alliterative pun, first applied to his pioneering Silicon Valley computer store.

As with any ambitious publishing project, the process of putting this book together had its ups and downs. Without our computers, Apple II's #630912 and #965517 (and their associated Epson FX-80 dot matrix printers), this task would have been close to impossible. Using WordStar as our word processing program, we were able to streamline production for this book, typesetting directly from the disks used for editing copy.

Digital Deli would not exist were it not for the prodigious digits of Carla Marie Rupp, who entered most of the words between these covers and many more; Sally Kovalchick, our persistent editor at Workman; Lynn Strong, our eagle-eyed copy editor; Paul Hanson, art director extraordinary; Diane Le Masters, ingenious designer; Robin Holland, photographer first class; and Rona Beame, patient photo researcher. Thanks also to Wayne Kirn, *Digital Deli*'s production manager, for taking the plunge into computerization; to Bill Effros, our technical editor, for good vibrations; and to Barbara Plumb, who introduced us to Workman Publishing. And to my technoromantic muse. She knows . . .

Bon appétit!
Steve Ditlea

RICK MEYEROWITZ'S
☆ ☆ ☆ ☆ ☆
DIGITAL DELI MAP
OF PERSONAL COMPUTER AMERICA

A-4 Microsoft Corp., Bellevue, Wash. Purveyors of BASIC, MS-DOS, MultiPlan, Windows and Word.

A-12 Canada. Tempting target for U.S. hackers. Across-the-border hi-tech pacesetters include Northern Telcom.

A-13 Peterborough. N.H. Computer magazine mecca. Offices of *Byte, Popular Computing*, and their rival, Wayne Green Publications.

B-1 Nippon-Japan Inc. Maker of 64K RAMs. NECs, SONYs and Epsons. Birthplace of Pac-Man and Donkey Kong.

B-3 Walden Software, Sunny Valley, Ore. Cottage of Paul Lutus, mountaintop developer of Apple Writer and GraFORTH.

B-9 Milwaukee, Wisc. Whence "414" (the local area code) hackers fanned out across network America for fun and knowledge.

B-13 Rte. 128, at top of Silicon Alley. World center for minicomputers and dedicated word processors.

B-15 Boston, Mass. Home of Computer Museum, M.I.T. Logo Lab, and Harvard dorm room where MBASIC was written.

C-1 San Francisco, Calif. Locale of West Coast Computer Faire and countless conventions, conclaves and cookeries.

C-4 Homestead High School, Cupertino, Calif. Where Apple co-founders Steve Jobs and Stephen Wozniak first met for pranks and profits.

C-5 On-Line, Software, Coarsegold, Calif. Publishers of arcade-style games, graphics adventures and Home Word.

C-11 CompuServe Information Service, Columbus, Ohio. On-line CB Simulation, Special Interest Groups and Megawars, plus news and weather.

C-12 Wang Laboratories, Lowell, Mass. Top supplier of dedicated word processors; also, Wang Writer and Professional Computer.

C-13 Digital Equipment Corporation (DEC), Marlboro, Mass. Principal producer of minicomputers; also, Rainbow 100 and DECmate II.

C-15 Timex computers. Best-selling Timex/Sinclair 1000 and highly rated Timex 2068 stilled by closing of watchmaker's computer division.

D-1 Apple Computer, Inc., Cupertino, Calif., founded January 3, 1977. Home of Apple II, Apple III, Lisa and Macintosh.

D-5 Homebrew Computer Club. Cradle of SOL, Apple II and Osborne computers, and countless baby millionaires.

D-6 Santa Clara County, Calif., a.k.a. Silicon Valley. From Palo Alto to San Jose; home of legendary garages and hot tubs.

D-9 Chicago, Ill. Headquarters of arcade games maker Bally-Midway: also, Mother's tavern, where new video games are tested.

D-11 Commodore International, Wayne, Pa. Manufacturer of 6502 Microprocessor, Commodore VIC-20 and Commodore 64.

D-15 Coleco Industries, Inc., West Hartford, Conn. Creators of ColecoVision and Coleco Adam.

E-1 Processor Technology. After SOL, the first typewriter-style computer, company faced lawsuits over faulty disk drives and dissolved.

E-13 IBM, Armonk, N.Y. Corporate HQ of the world's largest computer maker. Home of THINK and dark suits.

E-15 New York City, in the heart of Silicon Alley. World headquarters for finance, mass media and the Lunch Group.

F-2 IMSAI. Only est-based personal computer firm foundered while designing a follow-up to its successful first machine.

F-2 Osborne Computers. Creators of first portable computer and first major bankruptcy in personal computers.

F-3 Atari Inc., Sunnyvale, Calif. Incorporated June 27, 1972. Makers of classic video games and Atari Home Computer line.

F-4 Androbot, Inc., Sunnyvale, Calif. Since 1983, purveyors of home robots. Current models: BOB and TOPO.

F-7 The Sphere Computer. First desktop all-in-one with monitor never worked right, then expired when its designer left the company.

F-12 ENIAC. Remains of first electronic computer stand at Moore School of Electrical Engineering in Philadelphia.

F-13 New Jersey. Nation's most industrial state. Where Bell Labs conducts research into speech synthesis.

F-14 Dow Jones News Retrieval Service, Princeton, N.J. Electronic *Wall Street Journal*, Grolier Encyclopedia, sports news and financial data.

G-3 Hollywood. Where computers help create special effects for silver screen and turn movies into video games.

G-5 US Festivals. Apple Computer whiz Stephen Wozniak's attempts to bridge gap between ROMs and rock.

G-13 The Source, McLean, Va. At-home shopping, electronic mail, self-publishing, airline schedules and other pertinent data.

G-14 Washington, D.C. District of computers for SSI, IRS, FBI, CIA and DOD, among others. Home of Smithsonian computer exhibits.

H-7 Altair. First personal computer company, MITS, sold out to Pertec conglomerate, condemning Altair 8080 to slow death.

H-8 Las Vegas, Nev. Hot spot for consumer electronics and computer industry trade shows with glitz.

H-11 Texas Instruments. Lubbock, Tex. Makers of TI Professional Computer and late, lamented TI 99/4A.

I-8 Tandy Corp./Radio Shack, Ft. Worth, Tex. Manufacturers and retailers of TRS-80 Models II, 4, 16, 100, and Tandy 2000.

I-16 IBM Entry Systems Division. Boca Raton, Fla. Originators of IBM PC, XT, AT, PCjr and Portable PC.

J-7 Redwood City, Calif. Where Dr. John Lilly communicated with dolphins via Apple II computers.

J-9 Mexico. Ever more U.S. computers assembled across Rio Grande, while Mexican government frowns on computer imports.

See following page

Key on preceding page

APPETIZERS

Artwork for preceding page

Artist:
   Copper Giloth
Computer:
   Datamax UV-1 personal computer
   (based on Bally video game sys-
   tem)
Software:
   Zgrass Paint System by Copper
   Giloth
Input:
   Digitizing camera

BINARY CHOICES AND THE TAO OF HOME COMPUTERS

by Steve Ditlea

From time immemorial there have been those who see everything as black-or-white, either/or propositions. This "binary" or singularly two-sided view of life has caused them moments of discomfort at the hands of those who find more nuance in the world. In the fourth century, for example, Roman emperors and popes alike were known to behead believers in the Manichaean heresy, which divided the world into the duality of good and evil.

At other times the Either/Or crowd has turned the tables, successfully categorizing everything in terms of opposites: West or East, North or South, Rich or Poor, Old or Young, Liberal or Conservative, and the ever popular Male or Female. Such dualities have provoked confrontations throughout history, including our own occasionally frustrating era.

Now some psychologists, like Solomon Asch, feel there may in fact be a human need to define complex concepts in terms of binary choices. Only then, they say, can the gray areas be understood. The "cognitively simple" person distinguishes only a few categories. The "cognitively complex" distinguishes many. But can the incredible complexity of our universe be adequately described through binary choices? And how does this relate to these words being composed on a home computer?

Binary Logic

A familiar application of the simplicity *and* complexity of binary choices is the familiar Morse code, used in transmitting messages over telegraph lines. Developed in the 1830s, Samuel Morse's combinations of dots and dashes—short and long bursts of electricity—can represent any letter in the alphabet and by

Steve Ditlea is the editor of Digital Deli.

extension any human thought that can be put in writing. (Silence is a third alternative in Morse; in fact, pauses are essential for differentiating letters between bursts of code.) Each dot/dash, either/or choice delivers one elementary "bit" of information.

Without actually using numbers, Morse code embodies "digital" information. A message has been translated into a symbolic language of pulses following certain rules of composition. By contrast, an "analog" transmission of the same information might be a steady electronic signal modified to take on the char-

THE HUMAN COMPUTER

Only since World War II has the word "computer" (from Latin *computare*, "to reckon," "sum up") been applied to machines. *The Oxford English Dictionary* still describes a computer as "a person employed to make calculations in an observatory, in surveying, etc." Above, a computer at work circa 1940.

acteristics of a speaker's voice. Because digital bits can be transmitted more simply and efficiently, they are the lingua franca of today's computers.

"Bytes," on the other hand, are the actual groupings of code used to identify individual letters, numbers or other characters. In the 1920s the development of the teletype raised a fundamental question: how many electrical either/or alternatives would it take to transmit signals for every key on a modified typewriter keyboard, including upper- and lower-case characters, numbers, punctuation marks and special character codes? A standards board decided that seven either/or's could communicate the necessary information; the various combinations, a total of $2 \times 2 \times 2 \times 2 \times 2 \times 2 \times 2 = 128$, offered enough possibilities for necessary key codes. An eighth either/or was added as a way of checking for transmission errors over the line. These groupings of eight bits became known as bytes, and the code for representing keyboard characters became the American Standard Code for Information Interchange.

Digital Input

When I push the keys on my computer keyboard, each key in turn triggers a series of electrical pulses in ASCII code so the appropriate letters can appear on the display screen or be printed out later. These same pulses will be used to typeset this book directly from my storage disks. If I push an "a" (lower case), the computer will receive a characteristic code of either/or pulses that can be noted as 0s and 1s in the sequence 1100001. If I push an "A" (upper case), the computer reads this as 1000001.

These either/or, 0/1 component bits of information are transmitted within the computer as pulses of either lower- or higher-voltage electricity. (The voltage levels are lower than those in a portable radio and can't shock you.) The actual choice of pulses is determined by a series of microscopic switches that can be set for either 0 or 1 voltages. Such two-way switches are at the heart of all that takes place in a personal computer.

Binary switches are responsible for the machine's information processing, internal memory, graphics and other abilities. Everything a home computer can do, from juggling words to simulating space flight, from toting up financial figures to communicating with other computers, is the result of setting thousands of binary switches, all based on either/or, 0/1 alternatives. There would be no home computers, no electronic computers at all, were it not for the discovery of the binary numbering system. True to the scheme of most important scientific developments, its origins span thousands of years and its central theory was confirmed by a fortunate accident. In 1679 a centuries-old Chinese manuscript fell into the hands of

German philosopher Gottfried Wilhelm Leibniz, who was then perfecting his notion of the binary system. For all his imagination, Leibniz still lacked confirmation of his theory when proof came to him in the form of an eleventh-century commentary on the *I Ching*—a far older system of portraying the complexity of the universe with a series of either/or combinations. The manuscript illustrated an orderly sequence of the sixty-four *I Ching* hexagrams, which Leibniz perceived as graphic proof that his own system of 0s and 1s was valid.

The *I Ching*, or *Book of Changes*, is one of the oldest books in existence. Its present form dates back to China's King Wen, who ruled over three thousand years ago, and is based on sixty-four different six-line figures, or hexagrams, each made up of combinations of broken and unbroken lines. The lines correspond to Taoist dualities: Yin and Yang, dark and light, receptive and creative, female and male. The hexagrams can be obtained by the traditional casting of stalks from the yarrow plant, a rather involved procedure, or by the simpler method of tossing coins. The coins are thrown six times. Each combination of heads and tails corresponds to a broken or unbroken line. Once the six lines have been obtained, the resulting figure is interpreted in an appropriate section of the book, relating it to the movements of nature, proper conduct in society and the individual's fate in the world.

The variety of the *I Ching*'s concerns is indicated in some of the names linked to specific hexagrams: Inexperience, Conflict, Prospering, Deterioration, Innocence, Danger, Family, Adversity, Cosmic Order, Meditation, Limitations. Each hexagram, suggesting an image drawn from nature and the affairs of humans, elicits personal insight into the moment at hand. From six either/or alternatives, the *I Ching*'s sixty-four possibilities sagely sum up the cycles of existence. Thus the *I Ching* goes beyond elementary dualisms: from six binary choices, it weaves a subtle view of life.

The First Data Base

It can be argued that the *I Ching* was the first primitive computer. With astonishing mathematical precision the early Chinese cataloged all natural and social phenomena, then, with binary transformations, interrelated every possible physical interaction. The *I Ching* was a universal organization of symbolism, a cosmic filing system that directly interacted in binary fashion, anytime, anyplace. As a computer it was not always user-friendly, but it was extremely portable.

The ability of the *I Ching*'s hexagrams to relate accurately to a particular moment was explained by psychologist Carl Jung as the principle of "synchronicity"—that what seems coincidental actually follows from the interdependence of all things. A hexagram,

POWERS OF TWO

The decimal number system in which we're used to counting, with digits from 0 to 9, might seem the most natural for humans born with ten fingers (the word "digit" itself comes from Latin for "finger"). This 10-based number system, however, can be considered a historical accident since humans in fact have only eight fingers (and two thumbs). So why not a base-8 or even a base-2 system?

A binary system using just 0s and 1s has many advantages, not the least of which is its simple representation by mechanical or electronic means; hence its use in computers. Counting in binary can be easily mastered. A binary 1 is the same as a decimal 1, a decimal 2 is noted as 10 in binary, a 3 is 11 in base-2, and a 4 is 100.

From right to left, every column of digits in binary is a higher power of 2. To convert a binary number into its decimal equivalent, simply add the values of the binary columns. For example, 10110 can be broken down into:

Decimal	16	8	4	2	1
Binary	1	0	1	1	0

or $1 \times 16 + 0 \times 8 + 1 \times 4 + 1 \times 2 + 0 \times 1 = 22$

All binary arithmetic can be simplified to a series of additions. Adding binary numbers consists of summing columns and carrying over each remainder to the next higher column. Subtraction is accomplished by converting the number to be subtracted into its "inverse" (all its 0s into 1s and vice versa) and then adding. Multiplication involves shifting the number to be multiplied one place to the left for each 1 in the multiplier and then adding these partial results. Division is

With simple binary choices, Kanda the Great, a gorilla in the Dallas Zoo, has done better than a panel of local sportswriters in picking the winners of pro football games.

a variation on subtraction, with the number of times one number can be subtracted from another providing the quotient.

Beyond arithmetic, binary also lends itself to an elegant system of symbolic logic. According to Boolean algebra, all logical statements can be analyzed for their validity with just three functions: "and," "or" and "not." Each of these logical operators transforms binary alternatives according to specified rules. For example, if two incoming bits are the same, the "and" function will combine them into a single identical bit. A "not" operation will transform a bit into its opposite. By combining series of these functions in electronic circuits known as logic gates, a computer can evaluate, compare and contrast not just numbers, but any thoughts the human mind can conceive.

according to Jung, is "the Chinese picture of the moment."

Synchronicity is essential to the operation of a personal computer. Constant as the cosmic order that connects all natural phenomena, at the heart of each computer system is a tiny quartz crystal, which, upon electrical stimulation, vibrates at a steady rate. The rhythms of the universe that keep the Earth turning and distant pulsars pulsing also activate a home computer's quartz crystal at a rock-steady rate of millions of vibrations per second. These vibrations provide the beat for a computer's operations. Each beat in turn calls up another of the series of thousands of 0/1 electrical pulses necessary for a particular computer application. If the quartz clock were to fall out of step, the result would be anarchy within the computer. Yet the quartz keeps vibrating, steady as the cycles of nature.

The Tao Today

Following his belief that "things are like number," Leibniz had hoped to come up with a mathematics of logic in which all complex ideas could be expressed by a series of elementary symbols that could then be calculated for their basic truth or error. This goal eluded him for the rest of his life.

It wasn't until the nineteenth century that George Boole in England produced his algebra of logic, which could systematize any logical proposition into a series of binary, either/or choices. Operations based on Boole's algebra of logic in combination with numerical operations made possible by Leibniz' binary system provided the theoretical groundwork for computers.

All those binary switches in your personal computer dance to the numbers and logic of Leibniz and Boole. Software tells hardware what to do, setting the appropriate switches to execute the thousands of individual 0 and 1 operations needed for a useful computer application. Hardware and software are yet another duality in the Tao of personal computers.

From the simplicity of 0s and 1s, a computer can create sufficient complexity to aid or intrigue the human mind. From these elementary binary choices come the variety and range of human/computer interaction. The pages that follow attest to just how varied the powers of two can be. ■

HISTORY'S GREAT COMPUTER ECCENTRICS

by Marguerite Zientara

Geniuses are often strange, and the geniuses of the computing field are no exception. Though one or another of these characters might seem downright peculiar to us today, it was their ability to see the unseen and ignore others' opinions that opened the way to the computer age.

BLAISE PASCAL (1623–1662)

French philosopher Blaise Pascal, inventor of the first workable automatic calculator, was strange right from day one. In his first year, according to the available literature, he was inclined to give way to hysterics at the sight of water. He was also known to throw tantrums upon seeing his mother and father together. Arriving at the logical conclusion for their day, the adults in charge tried to exorcise him from a sorcerer's spell.

In time, Blaise managed to calm himself down and settle into a respectable infancy. At the age of four he suffered the untimely death of his mother, and it was then that Étienne Pascal took over his son's education. This was both good and bad. Étienne's rather

Marguerite Zientara is East Coast senior writer for InfoWorld.

uncompromising ideas encouraged the mental discipline Blaise would need for his later accomplishments, but they almost smothered his mathematical pursuits.

From the start, Blaise was curious about geometry. His father, a talented mathematician in his own right, wanted him to study Greek and Latin first. Locking up all his math books, he warned his friends never to mention mathematics in front of his son. In the end Blaise managed to beg from Étienne the most elementary definition of geometry, whereupon he taught himself its basic axioms—and succeeded, with no guidance whatever, in proving the Thirty-Second Proposition of Euclid. This was enough to convince his father, who set about teaching him everything he knew about geometry.

When Blaise was sixteen, Étienne accepted a government post that called for monumental calculations in figuring tax assessments. The man who had tried to hold back his son now turned to him for help in the thankless labor of hand-totaling endless columns of numbers. Blaise soon formulated the concept for a new calculating machine, then spent eleven years trying to perfect it. Just before he turned thirty, and after building more than fifty unsuccessful models, he introduced a working mechanical calculator.

The Pascaline caused a sensation on the Continent (this despite the fact that it could only add and subtract), but Blaise was unable to find buyers for his wondrous machine. People said it was too complicated to operate, sometimes made mistakes and could be repaired only by its inventor. They also feared it would take jobs away from bookkeepers and other clerks. After all those years of work, the gadget was a commercial flop.

In 1654, after a profound religious experience, Pascal renounced the world and all the people in it.

Though his contributions to math and science include the modern theory of probability, advances in differential calculus and hydraulics, he went on to become one of the greatest mystical writers in Christian literature. Still, some of his religious views—the bet on God's existence, for example—grew out of his mathematical insights. He lived to the age of thirty-nine, when he died of a brain hemorrhage.

GOTTFRIED WILHELM LEIBNIZ (1646–1716)

Sometimes the race goes to the runner-up, not to the man who finishes first. Case in point: Gottfried Wilhelm Leibniz, who developed a calculator even better than Pascal's (it could add, subtract, multiply and divide) and went on to make a killing in the marketplace. Not that he was just in it for the money: "For it is unworthy of excellent men to lose hours like slaves in the labor of calculation," he wrote, "which could safely be relegated to anyone else if machines were used."

While studying for a law degree, Leibniz became curious about a secret society that claimed to seek the "philosopher's stone." Something of a wag at twenty, and not above practical jokes, he collected the most obscure phrases he could find in the alchemy books and composed a nonsensical letter of application. The society was reportedly so impressed by Leibniz' erudition that they not only accepted him for membership, but appointed him their secretary as well.

Leibniz was clever, but he was also overwhelmingly versatile. Regarded as one of the great universalists of all time, he made his mark in such diverse areas as law, history, nautical science, optics, hydrostatics, mechanics, mathematics and political diplomacy. His binary theory and initiation of symbolic logic laid the foundation for today's computers.

How did the man do so much? First of all, he lived for seventy years, almost twice as long as Pascal. Second, it is said he could work anywhere, at any time and under any conditions. He read, wrote and ruminated incessantly. By all accounts he slept little but well—even during the nights spent more or less upright in his chair, where he'd remain for days at a time until he finished the project at hand.

With all these working hours, one might suspect that Leibniz was something of a hermit. Not so. He enjoyed socializing with all kinds of people, believing that he could learn from even the most ignorant. According to his biographers, he spoke well of everyone and made the most of every situation. Which would explain his notorious theorem of optimism—"Everything is for the best in this best of all possible worlds"—later satirized by Voltaire in the novel *Candide*.

In his last years, however, that celebrated optimism undoubtedly faded as his fame declined and those close to him gradually slipped away. When he died in 1716, during an attack of gout, only his secretary bothered to attend the burial.

THE PASCALINE AND THE LEIBNIZ CALCULATOR

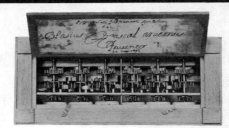

Inside the Pascaline.

The inner workings of Leibniz' calculator.

Blaise Pascal's pioneering calculator was essentially a two-dimensional machine, using cogged wheels rotated in proportion to numerical values that were added or subtracted. Multiplication or division had to be accomplished by tedious repetition of these operations. Leibniz' calculating machine was an improvement in three dimensions, using wheels at right angles that could be displaced by a special stepping mechanism to perform rapid multiplication or division.

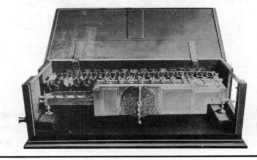

CHARLES BABBAGE (1792–1871)

Mired in the nineteenth century but devoted to an idea that would revolutionize the world after his death, Charles Babbage was a man who knew his own worth and his own genius.

Undaunted by the failure of early inventions (among them, shoes for walking on water), he proceeded to work on his Difference Engine. This sophisticated mechanical calculator would preoccupy him for twenty years, during which he managed to convince the Chancellor of the Exchequer to lend financial support and became the first recipient of a government grant for computer science. Following a nervous breakdown and other major crises, in 1833 he gave up on the machine, then conceived an even more grandiose scheme.

Babbage's Difference Engine.

For the rest of his life Babbage would attempt to construct his Analytical Engine, a mechanical device that would have included most of the essential features of modern digital computers: a central processing unit, software instructions, memory storage and printed output. He spent years making detailed drawings, inventing machine tools and actually trying to build his machine—only to concede finally that his concept was way beyond the technology of the time.

Most people thought he was crazy to spend so much time and money on an obviously absurd idea (even the British government kept withdrawing its support), but in fact the Analytical Engine was just one of Babbage's myriad concerns. Fortunate enough to have been born into wealth, he enjoyed the luxury of time to follow his many other interests: consulting for railroad pioneers, devising a mail delivery system based on wires strung between towers to carry containers of mail, and inventing a lighthouse flashing system and a submarine. He also had the distinction of being able to pick any lock.

Yet the government positions and honors Babbage felt were his due constantly eluded him. These disappointments and slights led to deep bitterness, revealed in his oft-quoted observation that he had never had a happy day in his life. A friend of his wrote: "He spoke as if he hated mankind in general, Englishmen in particular and the English Government most of all."

Part of Babbage's proclaimed unhappiness undoubtedly came from his notorious feud with London's organ grinders, then estimated to number a thousand, whom he tried to silence with a court action. In retaliation, the organ grinders came from miles around to play their noisy instruments in front of his home, at times joined by street punks who tossed dead cats, blew bugles at him and smashed his windows. Jeering children followed him around, as did bands of hecklers—sometimes as many as a hundred at a time, shouting threats to overturn the cab he was riding in or to burn down his house.

Still, idiosyncrasies and all, Babbage was considered a fascinating companion. He was a witty and sought-after dinner guest and often hosted parties for two or three hundred people. Among his friends were the most notable scientific, political and literary figures of the day, including Charles Dickens.

One of his most intriguing friendships was with Lady Ada Augusta Lovelace, the only daughter of Lord Byron. A beautiful and charming woman, Lady Lovelace was the same age Babbage's deceased daughter would have been. The widower Babbage and Lady Lovelace, who had been brought up without her father, enjoyed a close, mutually rewarding relationship until her death at age thirty-six. Babbage himself died at seventy-nine, with only one mourner besides the family group at the funeral. At the end he was considered to have been a failure with an unworkable idea. Yet on the moon, which computers enabled man to reach, is a crater named for Charles Babbage. And the Royal College of Surgeons in England has preserved the brain of this man who lived before his time.

ADA LOVELACE: THE FIRST COMPUTER PROGRAMMER

Ada! Wilt thou by
*   affection's law,*
My mind from the darken'd
*   past withdraw?*
Teach me to live in that
*   future day . . .*
*   —Lord Byron*

Today's computer programmers are clever indeed, but few could hold a light-emitting diode to Augusta Ada Lovelace in terms of creativity. She saw the art as well as the science in programming, and she wrote eloquently about it. She was also an opium addict and a compulsive gambler.

As the only legitimate offspring of Lord Byron, Ada would have been a footnote to history even if she hadn't been a mathematical prodigy. Though Byron later wrote poignantly about his daughter, he left the family when she was a month old and she never saw him again. Biographers tend to be rather hard on Ada's mother, blaming her for many of her daughter's ills. A vain and overbearing Victorian figure, she considered a healthy daily dose of laudanum-laced "tonic" the perfect cure for Ada's nonconforming behavior.

Ada was well tutored by those around her (British logician Augustus De Morgan was a close family friend), but she hungered for more knowledge than they could provide. She was actively seeking a mentor when Charles Babbage came to the house to demonstrate his Difference Engine for her mother's friends. Then and there, Ada resolved to help him realize his grandest dream: the long planned but never constructed Analytical Engine. Present on that historic evening was Mrs. De Morgan, who wrote in her memoirs:

> While the rest of the party gazed at this beautiful instrument with the same sort of expression and feeling that some savages are said to have shown on first seeing a looking glass or hearing a gun, Miss Byron, young as she was, understood its workings and saw the great beauty of the invention.

If Babbage was the force behind the hardware of the first protocomputer, Ada was the creator of its software. As a mathematician, she saw that the Analytical Engine's possibilities extended far beyond its original purpose of calculating mathematical and navigational tables. When Babbage returned from a speaking tour on the Continent, Ada translated the extensive notes taken by one Count Manabrea in Italy and composed an addendum nearly three times as long as the original text. Her published notes are particularly poignant to programmers, who can see how truly ahead of her time she was. Prof. B. H. Newman wrote in the *Mathematical Gazette* that her observations "show her to have fully understood the principles of a programmed computer a century before its time." Among her programming innovations for a machine that would never be realized in her lifetime were the subroutine (a set of reusable instructions), looping (running a useful set of instructions over and over) and the conditional jump (branching to specified instructions if a particular condition is satisfied).

Ada also noted that machines might someday be built with capabilities far beyond the technology of her day and speculated about whether such machines could ever achieve intelligence. Her argument against artificial intelligence in "Observations on the Analytical Engine" was immortalized almost a hundred years later by Alan M. Turing, who referred to this line of thinking as "Lady Lovelace's Objection." It is an objection often heard in debates about machine intelligence. "The Analytical Engine," Ada wrote, "has no pretensions whatever to originate anything. It can do whatever we know how to order it to perform."

It is not known how or when Ada became involved in her clandestine and disastrous gambling ventures. Unquestionably, she was an accomplice in more than one of Babbage's schemes to raise money for his Analytical Engine. Together they considered the profitability of building a tic-tac-toe machine and even a mechanical chess player. And it was their attempt to develop a mathematically infallible system for betting on the ponies that brought Ada to the sorry pass of twice pawning her husband's family jewels to pay off blackmailing bookies.

Ada died when she was only thirty-six years old, but she is present today in her father's poetry and as the namesake of the government's newest computer language. In the late 1970s the Pentagon selected for its own a specially constructed "superlanguage," known only as the "green language" (three competitors were assigned the names "red," "blue" and "yellow") until it was officially named after Ada Lovelace. Ada is now a registered trademark of the United States Department of Defense.

HOWARD RHEINGOLD

ALAN M. TURING (1912–1954)

One of the great abstract thinkers of this century, Alan M. Turing was another eccentric who started out as an extremely gifted student. As early as age nine, he reportedly startled his mother by asking questions like "What makes oxygen fit so tightly with hydrogen to produce water?"

By the time he reached Cambridge University, Turing was already known for his unorthodox ways. When setting his watch, he did not simply ask someone the correct time but instead observed a specific star from a specific locale and mentally calculated the hour. He jogged long distances in a time when this was

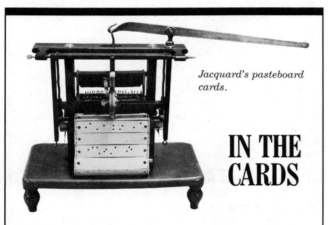

Jacquard's pasteboard cards.

IN THE CARDS

The use of punch cards in computers was devised by Charles Babbage, who adapted the automated textile loom invented in 1805 by Frenchman Joseph Marie Jacquard. The Jacquard pasteboard cards had holes punched out of them to allow only certain threads to be grasped by the rods that did the weaving. In Babbage's computer, moving rods would decipher two sets of cards: one to designate the operations to be performed, the other for the variables on which they were to operate. Punch cards would remain in widespread use until the development of fast, reliable magnetic mass storage media in the 1960s.

IBM's punch cards.

considered odd, and he thought nothing of riding his bicycle twelve miles through a rainstorm at night to keep an appointment. (When his bicycle chain was skipping, instead of fixing the chain he correctly calculated the exact moment of each skip and pedaled accordingly.)

While some might describe his methods as doing things the hard way, for Turing they were merely a game. The first proof of his brilliance came in 1936, when at the age of twenty-four he published his paper "On Computable Numbers, with an application to the Entscheidungsproblem." In this major contribution to computing theory, Turing presented a landmark theorem in mathematical logic in terms of an idealized computing machine. He posited that a "Universal Turing Machine" could embody any logical procedure as long as it was given appropriate instructions. A decade before the first practical computer, he described its essential characteristics.

Turing's findings were regarded by some as proof that human intelligence is superior to machine intelligence, but this was not his idea at all. In his essay "Can a Machine Think?" published in the mid-1940s, he wrote: "We too often give wrong answers to questions ourselves to be justified in being very pleased at such evidence of fallibility on the part of the machines." His essay also contained the notion that "there might be men cleverer than any given machine, but, then again, there might be other machines cleverer again, and so on."

During World War II Turing was one of a team of British scientists sequestered at the lovely Bletchley Park estate and ordered to develop machinery that could decipher codes from Germany's Enigma encoding machines. The results of these efforts, often credited with a decisive role in winning the war, were the electromechanical machines nicknamed Heath Robinson (after the 1930s cartoonist of the Rube Goldberg school), Peter Robinson, the Robinson and Cleaver (both named after London stores) and the Super Robinson. The successor to these machines, the Colossus 1, is recognized as one of the first electronic computers. Turing went on to help design the Automatic Calculating Engine (ACE) Pilot computer and later worked on the Manchester Automatic Digital Machine (MADM), one of the earliest stored-program computers. In 1951 and 1952 he took part in radio debates on the computer's ability to think.

Arrested in 1952 for "gross indecency," Turing was subjected to hormone injections that rendered him impotent. His homosexuality was considered a security risk at the height of the cold war. His last extraordinary act was to kill himself, in 1954, at the age of forty-two. Whether on purpose, as the coroner ruled, or accidentally, as many believed, he died of poisoning from potassium cyanide. ∎

CRACKING THE NAZI CODE

The Enigma code machine (left) gave the Nazis a decided advantage in the early days of World War II by keeping German front-line communications undecipherable to the Allies. Though one of the first of these machines was captured and its messages decoded by the Poles, subsequent improvements in Enigma's design—incorporating frequent changes in the keys by which characters were enciphered—rendered its output a deadly mystery.

The British government hoped to break the codes through high-speed automated transposition of ciphered characters to find their underlying patterns. Eventually these efforts led to the construction of the Colossus 1 (pictured below). The machine was cloaked in secrecy; after helping to crack the code and revealing invaluable information that hastened the Allies' victory, it was dismantled for reasons of security. The only known surviving part is the paper tape feeder wheel (shown here), used for many years as a paperweight before being donated to the Computer Museum in Boston.

MODEL ONE: THE FIRST MODERN BINARY COMPUTER

Non-eccentrics have also made their mark on the history of computers. In February 1983, forty-five years after he developed the world's first binary computer, Dr. George Stibitz was finally recognized by his peers and invited to join the National Inventors Hall of Fame. At the time of his induction, he was hard at work on four different major projects at Dartmouth Medical School in Hanover, New Hampshire.

Dr. Stibitz constructed his machine to solve a manpower problem at Bell Laboratories. In 1937 the phone company had begun to rely on complex numbers in the equations that computed characteristics of filters and transmission lines. Thirty people worked full time at the impossible task of performing these computations on large, bulky desk calculators, the only tools available that could work with i, the square root of minus one.

Looking for a more efficient way to get the job done, Stibitz experimented at home with the concept of building a calculator that would automatically solve complex arithmetic problems with binary computations. The most convenient parts available were the old-fashioned electromechanical telephone relays: because they could be switched either on or off to repre-

The keyboard of the Model One relay-based computer attests to its limited functions.

sent 0s and 1s, the relays were ideal for performing binary calculations. Satisfied that his concept would work, Stibitz convinced his boss to build a full-scale working model.

By 1939 the Model One went into operation, chopping off two-thirds of the time needed to solve the equations. The machine consisted of two large banks of telephone relays, each bank measuring eight feet in height, five feet across and a foot thick. Each relay was five inches long and one and a half inches wide. The left bank handled the complex values, while the right bank juggled the integer numbers. Then the two banks were integrated for the final solution. The fact that it held only 32 bytes of memory (1/32K), and that it cost a whopping $20,000 to build, took nothing away from its success.

Bell went on to build bigger and better versions of the relay-based computer, but this technology was dated almost as soon as it was assembled. Relay-based computers were more reliable than vacuum-tube-blowing behemoths like ENIAC, but the relays were outclassed in calculating speed by about 500 to 1.

All of today's computers can trace their roots back to Stibitz' talent and imagination. His binary computer, U.S. Patent No. 2,668,661 issued in 1939, now takes its place next to other great American inventions like the Model-T, the cotton gin, the electric light and the Wright brothers' plane.

ROE R. ADAMS III

George Stibitz with his first binary adder.

UNCLE SAM AND THE COMPUTER REVOLUTION

by Myron Berger

Whatever the fiscal excesses of the Washington bureaucracy, there would be no computer revolution today were it not for government spending. Since 1890, beginning with the automation of U.S. Census tabulating by the firm that would later become IBM, our government has supported the research and development of data processing equipment. And in the closing years of World War II, while private industry was simply not willing to invest the necessary time and money in research and development, the grand-daddy of the computer we know today was created by civilian scientists working on government-sponsored projects.

Uncle Sam is probably more responsible for the development of digital electronic computers than any-one else, yet his involvement has been, in a sense, distant. Government scientists working in government laboratories made few advances in computer technol-ogy; rather, the pattern was to assemble teams of ac-ademic scientists at important universities (M.I.T., the Institute for Advanced Studies at Princeton, the Moore School of the University of Pennsylvania, and the University of Illinois were the early centers of computer projects) and give them an assignment and tax dollars to work with.

Uncle Sam has also contributed to computer de-velopment by fiat. An unfortunate fact of life in the computer world is the lack of standardization. Al-though this is changing somewhat, traditionally nei-ther hardware nor software could be transferred from one brand to another—and in some cases not even from one model to another by the same maker. To keep its own house in order, the government was forced to tell its contractors that they must use a certain format. Since Uncle Sam is a primary customer for many com-panies, this particular format has overlapped into busi-ness procedures not involving the government.

Interestingly, with all the federal involvement in computers, boondoggles have been rare. Since so much of computer science is still virgin territory, ex-ploration of the frontier cannot help but yield benefits later if not sooner. And though government, particu-larly the Pentagon, has a long history of injudicious spending, the funding of computer research stands as one of the most remarkable examples of fiscal effi-ciency in modern times.

The ENIAC Experiment

Take, for example, the case of the legendary ENIAC. In early 1942 the Moore School of Engineering contrib-uted to the war effort by calculating firing tables to determine trajectories of explosive shells or projec-tiles, given such factors as velocity, air resistance and angle of fire. This activity was carried out primarily by young women using electrically powered mechani-cal calculators. A year later John Mauchly, a faculty member at Moore, came up with an idea for a computer that would calculate trajectories much faster by using vacuum tubes. Since the device would be program-mable, he maintained, it could perform other tasks.

Project director Herman Goldstine, a young Army lieutenant with a doctorate in mathe-matics, saw

---

Myron Berger writes about consumer electronics for a variety of newspapers and magazines.

and powerful supercomputers have achieved speeds of over one billion per second.

It was not until December 1945, after the war had ended, that ENIAC solved its first problem: a question that dealt with the hydrogen bomb and that to this day remains classified. But even before ENIAC was up and running, more advanced computers were being developed—virtually all of them underwritten by the government. Designed by many of the men responsible for ENIAC, these machines introduced an improvement so important that they have become known by the name "stored program" computers. Unlike ENIAC, whose cables had to be reconfigured by hand, these computers were programmed electronically.

The second computer generation is divided into the EDVAC (Electronic Discrete Variable Computer) and IAS (Institute for Advanced Studies) families.

The former (including EDVAC, EDSAC and UNIVAC I) were designed primarily by Eckert and Mauchly; the latter (IAS, Whirlwind and ILLIAC), by John von Neumann and others at Princeton's IAS. While many of the early machines were built with military appropriations, their purpose was not always directly related to waging war. The IAS computer, for example, received funding from the Navy to work out a numerical meteorology system.

Uncle Sam's Offspring

Meanwhile, Eckert and Mauchly decided that computers could enjoy an even more promising future in the business world. In October 1946 the two men formed the Electronic Control Corporation, probably the first commercial computer company, and in 1947 changed

ENIAC YESTERDAY

In its heyday ENIAC required advances not only in electrical technology, but also in air conditioning to cool its 18,000 vacuum tubes. Today ENIAC'S tubeless control panels (inset) stand as mute testament to the beginning of the computer age.

the value of such a machine, and on April 2, 1943, Mauchly, J. Presper Eckert and J. G. Brainerd (two other professors at Moore) submitted their proposal for an "electronic differential analyzer" to the Ballistic Research Laboratory at the Aberdeen Proving Grounds in Maryland. A paltry $100,000 was the original cost estimate for what would become ENIAC (Electronic Numerical Integrator and Computer).

Between start-up in June 1943 and completion in 1946, however, some $500,000 in government funds was actually spent on the project. According to Arthur W. Burks, one of the inventors of ENIAC, this included $100,000 to $200,000 for disassembling, transporting, reassembling, testing and debugging during the move from Moore to Aberdeen. Burks estimates that the building costs totaled only about $300,000, or about $3 million in current dollars. (A full professor's salary in those days, he points out, was about $6,000 per year.)

ENIAC was quite a machine. Made up of forty panels, each two feet wide and four feet deep, it could store a total of 700 bits in RAM and 20,000 bits in ROM. This was accomplished not with the integrated circuit boards or microchips of today, but with a massive network of 18,000 vacuum tubes. The Atanoff-Berry computer, ENIAC's direct progenitor, could only solve sets of simultaneous equations and do that at 60 pulses per second. ENIAC, on the other hand, could handle a variety of problems (its programmers had to manually reset switches and cable links, a process that could take two days) and operated at the then amazing speed of 100,000 pulses per second. By comparison, today's home computers generally operate at between two and four million pulses per second,

ENIAC TODAY: R.I.P.

Four steps up and just to the right inside the entrance of the Moore School in Philadelphia, there is a plain paper printout taped to the outside of a glass door. "To ENIAC," it says, and whoever did the computer printout message arranged it so the letters came out in Gothic script.

The door is always open. The antique inside is huge, monstrous and bulky, with connecting cables the size of a man's forearm and data entering boards taller and broader than a Philadelphia 76er starting center. There it is, by golly, the first electronic computer. The daddy of them all: Apples and IBM PCs and Commodore 64s.

It doesn't work, of course.

The room that houses ENIAC—what's left of it, anyway—is a kind of pass-through for students on their way to the electrical engineering labs deeper in the building. Two doors, one window, gray linoleum tile on the floor. Hundreds go by every day, but no one gives ENIAC a passing glance.

It's not that students have no romance anymore (though a good argument could be made in this respect); it's that the machine is basically boring now. It doesn't do anything. It's not pretty. And God knows it weighs too much to try and move it around. It just sits there like the blackened body of some long-dead warrior, prepared for a battle that was already over when the moment came.

If ENIAC were turned on today—and presumably it could be, though some of its parts are at the Computer Museum in Boston and the Smithsonian Institution in Washington, D.C.—it would be only slightly slower and somewhat dumber than a hand-held scientific calculator from Texas Instruments or Hewlett-Packard. But no one is interested in turning it on. Efforts by the University of Pennsylvania to raise money so ENIAC can be preserved in a special showroom for the public, along with a documented display of its history, have met with complete disinterest.

It is big, black and ugly. And like the textile mills that started the industrial revolution, like the squash courts at the University of Chicago where the nuclear age began, it will gradually deteriorate and become a nuisance where it stands—eventually to be torn down to make room for something newer, cleaner and pleasanter to look upon. Which is probably as it should be. Because ENIAC was an idea whose time had come. The form itself means nothing anymore.

BOB SCHWABACH

its name to Eckert-Mauchly Computer Corporation. In 1950, having received no computer orders other than Uncle Sam's, they sold the company to Remington Rand, a manufacturer of office equipment. (In 1955 that company merged with Sperry Corporation to form Sperry-Rand.)

Before the sale, Eckert and Mauchly had been at work on what was to become the first commercial computer: UNIVAC I. Credited with having introduced the first program compiler, the first programming tools and the first high-speed printer, UNIVAC (Universal Automatic Computer) was so significant in the early commercial computer industry that until the 1970s Sperry used its name as the official title of its computer division.

Like its predecessors, UNIVAC resulted from a government contract. In 1949 machines were ordered for the Census Bureau, the Air Force and the Army's Map Unit at a total cost of $4 to $5 million. In June 1951 the first UNIVAC was delivered to the Census Bureau, and in 1954 the first commercial model was sold to the General Electric Company. Although government dollars were not the sole source of income for the first commercial computer company, those early sales of UNIVAC I helped it reach the firm financial footing necessary to become a viable enterprise.

In the 1950s Uncle Sam was involved in financing research and development, helping the early companies survive the period before computers became accepted in the business community as valuable tools that justified a multimillion-dollar price. Then, around 1960, Uncle Sam abandoned his role as the primary customer of the computer companies and became instead the standards-setter. One of the most famous examples is the computer programming language called COBOL (COmmon Business-Oriented Language). Although the Department of Defense had "no significant role in its funding or development," according to one Pentagon official, the Navy adopted the language as a standard in the late sixties and "encouraged private industry to use it." COBOL is now the standard language for business computers in the Defense Department and is widely used by private industry.

Pentagon Progeny

The Pentagon is currently trying to repeat its COBOL success with the new programming language called Ada. Unlike COBOL, Ada was contracted out to a private company (Cibul, a French division of Honeywell) by the Department of Defense. And unlike the names of most computer vocabularies, Ada is not an acronym but the given name of Lady Lovelace, the first computer programmer.

In the early 1970s the Pentagon decided that software costs were getting out of hand (before the decade was out, costs had escalated to $3 billion a year) primarily because of the lack of standardization (a single program might have to be purchased in several versions in order to run on different computers within DOD). A High Order Language Working Group, formed to evaluate the existing languages, concluded that none was sophisticated enough and insisted that a new language be written. The goal was nothing less than the creation of a computer language that would become "the American national standard." Questionnaires asking for suggestions and desired features of a universal language were sent to some 900 individuals and companies.

To date, about $18.5 million has been spent on Ada. Hoping to have all its new computer programs written in Ada by 1987, the Defense Department has formed a group called Software Technology for Adaptable Reliable Systems (STARS) to promote and develop use of Ada in all Pentagon applications and has submitted a request for $222 million to fund the group between fiscal 1984 and 1988. In explaining the size of the request, a Pentagon spokesman said: "Most computer languages have a life cycle of twenty-five years, and we expect Ada to be useful until 2010. We also expect it to save many hundreds of millions of dollars."

THE ORIGINAL BUG

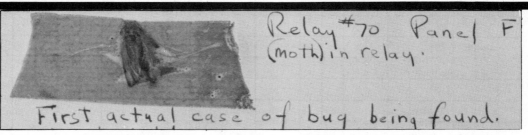

Relay #70 Panel F (moth) in relay.

First actual case of bug being found.

While no one has ever seen a gremlin (except in the movies), the bug is a pest of another color. In the Naval Museum at Dahlgren, Virginia, on a page of the logbook maintained by Grace Hopper while she worked on the Mark II computer, is preserved the original computer bug. This unlucky moth had been crushed to death in one of the relays within the giant electromechanical computer, bringing the machine's operations to a halt. When she discovered the cause of the malfunction, Captain Hopper carefully removed the historic carcass, taped it to the log and noted: "First actual case of bug being found."

COMMODORE HOPPER: THE MOTHER OF COBOL

She was the third programmer on the first digital computer. She wrote the first compiler software, in effect creating the whole field of high-level programming languages. She helped preserve the first computer "bug." She was also the moving force behind COBOL, for years the standard computer language for business applications.

At age seventy-seven Grace Murray Hopper was already the Navy's oldest active officer when she was named the nation's only living commodore in 1983. On the road over three hundred days a year, she still moves with the resolute energy she exhibited in the days of the first electromechanical computer. With her white hair and steel-rimmed glasses, she might remind you of your grandmother—if your grandmother has military posture and a crisp Navy uniform.

One of her talents is the ability to cut through red tape. Twenty-five years ago she called in executives of all the major computer manufacturers, along with top-ranking officers and senior civilian officials from the intelligence community, the Bureau of Standards and the Defense Department, and explained that it just wouldn't work to have everybody off writing in different computer languages. The scientists had FORTRAN, but computers wouldn't move into business applications until there was a standard business language. The result of that crusade was COBOL. Ironically, though she was the U.S. government's senior computer expert, Hopper was a civilian and was backed by no federal funding at all.

When World War II broke out, Grace Hopper was a mathematics teacher at Vassar. In 1943 she enlisted in the U.S. Naval Reserve and was assigned to the Bureau of Ordnance Computation Project at Harvard, where she worked under Howard Aiken during the development of the Mark I. It was with this pre-electronic, electromechanical ballistics computer that she started her programming career.

"You could walk around inside her," Hopper recalls. The Commodore refers to all computers as "she," in proper naval tradition, and never fails to remind audiences that the first computer was invented by the Navy—despite the "tendency of a certain junior service, which wasn't even born then, to take credit for early computers."

When the war was over, Hopper was told that at age forty she was too old for the regular Navy. Remaining in the reserves, she signed on to the Harvard faculty and in 1949 joined the inventors of ENIAC, the first electronic digital computer, at the Eckert-Mauchly Computer Corporation. Here, during the development of UNIVAC, the first commercial computer, she wrote the first compiler software. She stayed on as staff scientist for systems programming until after the merger with Sperry Corporation and the COBOL crusade, when she was drawn back into the Navy.

Once in 1966 the Navy tried to retire her, an occasion she recalls as "the saddest day of my life." Four months later she was asked to return to take charge of standardizing the Navy's use of high-level programming languages. She reported for temporary active duty in 1967, and she hasn't let the retirement folks catch up with her since.

Her determination to shake things up permeates everything she says, whether lecturing on the history of computers or talking about problems facing contemporary systems designers. She likes to tell audiences of computer professionals: "If during the next twelve months any one of you says, 'But we've always done it this way,' I will instantly materialize in front of you and I will haunt you for twenty-four hours."

HOWARD RHEINGOLD

NATIONAL SCIENCE FUNDS

Some of the major contributions to Uncle Sam's computer research come from the civilian-oriented National Science Foundation. According to its charter, the NSF is authorized to "foster and support the development and use of computer and other scientific methods and technologies, primarily for research and education in the sciences."

Spurred on by the 1957 launching of the Russian satellite Sputnik, the NSF began funding mainframe computer installations on university campuses. Though this program wound down in the 1970s, the students and university scientists trained on these systems went on to develop advances of their own in the field of computer science.

NSF also organized the National Center for Atmospheric Research as an intellectual focal point for atmospheric and oceanographic scientists. NCAR features two Cray-1A supercomputers used for extensive modeling and data analysis as well as storage and data collection. The end results can be seen as the computerized weather maps in daily TV forecasts.

More recently, grants from NSF have laid the groundwork for educational software firms in the personal computer field. Among the recipients is the Learning Company, Ann Piestrup's pioneering effort.

In 1984 NSF's computer science budget amounted to nearly $17 million—over a third of its total budget for the year. On the agenda for the late 1980s is a major effort to make supercomputers more accessible to individual researchers in need of such powerful systems. This will be made possible by NSF financial support for computational mathematics and hardware design in addition to basic research in applications of supercomputers.

Although it is still very early in the scheme of things for Ada to be used by the public/commercial sector, this is, in fact, already happening. A very simple version is available for home computers, and Intellimac, a high-tech company that does business with the Pentagon and supplies computer programs to commercial clients, has already used Ada to write applications programs for private corporations to perform payroll, inventory management and other conventional data processing.

In between ENIAC and Ada were a number of other computer developments that came either directly or indirectly from government funds. Dr. J. C. R. Licklider, a professor of computer science at M.I.T., oversaw much of the "action" while serving as director of the Information Processing Techniques section of the Defense Advanced Research Project Agency (DARPA). One of the most significant technologies developed by the agency was in the area of time sharing, the practice of linking two or more computers so that data can be transferred and processed between them. The Compatible Time-Sharing System (CTSS)

was, in his words, "the first large time-sharing system and possibly the first of any size."

CTSS was developed between 1960 and 1964 and was the main effort of Project MAC (for Machine-Aided Cognition, but also known within the group as Machine-Augmented Confusion or Men and Computers). Time sharing is behind the hundreds of private and commercial data bases now in operation, and Licklider holds that most microcomputers today that use time sharing have many elements of CTSS.

When CTSS was completed, MAC turned its attentions to another project: Multics (Multiplexed Information and Computation System), which took five years to perfect and culminated in a multi-user operating system. According to Licklider, Multics was the basis of several of the features found in UNIX, the multi-user operating system developed by Bell Labs and quite popular today.

In 1968 DARPA began work on what was to become ARPANET, the first packet-switching network, at least part of which was operational by 1969. This, says Licklider, led to a mushrooming of computer networks, most of which, then and now, still use ARPANET technologies with modified protocols. ARPANET is still in operation and is the basis for the Defense Data Network (DDN), a general-purpose computer communications network designed for message traffic, file transfers and other applications.

More exotic computer technology has been pioneered by the supersecret National Security Agency (NSA). Charged with sensitive counterintelligence activities like monitoring international and domestic communications traffic, by 1962 NSA had what one of its officials called "the world's largest computing system." Among NSA's developments were high-density memory storage, supercomputers (the first Cray-1s were delivered to the agency) and computer-assisted translation, allowing machines to recognize, transcribe and translate voice communications. Currently under investigation is the promising area of optical computing technology for high-speed information processing. (On the other hand, the NSA has been perceived as hindering efforts in certain areas of computer science with its policy of reviewing and even putting a "classified" label on civilian research in cryptography.)

There were many other contributions to computer science and electronic technology wrought by Uncle Sam's (read: taxpayers') dollars. The National Aeronautics and Space Administration (NASA) alone was responsible for much of the miniaturization of components and low-power systems that made home computers a reality. Considering that the same U.S. government also brought us nuclear, biological and chemical weapons, killer satellites and the Vietnam war, perhaps the computer contributions merely serve to help even up the balance sheet. ∎

THE SPACE SHUTTLE'S COMPUTERS

Government-funded computers have made it possible for humans to travel into outer space and set foot on the moon. From the dawn of the space age, these machines have handled guidance for every leap into the void, keeping track of all the calculations and countless bits of data essential to successful missions. This is surely the best example of an activity that could not have been accomplished by human brainpower alone.

The most celebrated computers, those on NASA's space shuttle, have gained notoriety as much for their ill-timed malfunctions as for their efficient shepherding of the spaceship's flight crews. Each shuttle carries five 110-pound suitcase-size computers, modified from standard IBM machines originally developed for use in military aircraft. All of the spaceship's ascent operations and much of its flight are controlled by four principal computers running in tandem to check on each other; if they fail to

agree, the backup computer is brought in to arbitrate. Sensors throughout the craft report to the computers on the status of life support, propulsion and navigation systems. The crew can input commands with a series of three-digit codes.

Space shuttle computers have acted up from the very first test landing. In July 1977 one of the on-board computers failed as the craft was released from a Boeing 747 that had carried it into the stratosphere. During the initial attempt to launch the shuttle Columbia in April 1981, a timing fault disrupted communications between the main computers and the backup system, causing a two-day delay in lift-off. In November 1981 Columbia's second launch was disrupted by erroneous reports to its computers of low pressure in the craft's oxygen tanks, forcing a postponement of over a week. While in space during its December 1983 mission, two of Columbia's computers

shut down and one would not restart; the failure was traced to metal particles, as small as a thousandth of an inch, that had gotten into their electronic components. The space shuttle Discovery's maiden voyage in June 1984 was delayed by its malfunctioning backup computer; a day later the mission was scrubbed when the computers shut down the main rocket's engines just six seconds before launch.

Despite such problems, the space shuttle's standardized computers are considered an improvement over the expensive custom-made systems used earlier in such projects as the Apollo moon missions. Of late, civilian computers have made their way on board: beginning with the shuttle's ninth mission, an off-the-shelf Grid office computer has been used to display the craft's position above the earth. Apple IIs have also been used to monitor experiments in the shuttle's payload.

| 1642 | 1679 | 1801 | 1822 | 1833 | 1842 |

In France, mathematics genius Blaise Pascal devises the first true calculating machine. Using eight rotating gears and wheels, the Pascaline performs addition and subtraction.

Gottfried Wilhelm Leibniz, German philosopher, historian and scientist, perfects the binary system of notation. In a few centuries this system of 1s and 0s will prove invaluable in machine computations.

French silk weaver Joseph-Marie Jacquard invents a loom with punched cardboard cards for controlling woven patterns. The Jacquard loom modernizes the textile industry and will become the model for Babbage's use of punched cards.

In London, Charles Babbage begins work on his Difference Engine, a calculating machine that performs mathematical functions (with sines, cosines and logarithms) to six decimal places. The hundreds of gears, shafts and counters weigh two tons. Seventy years later William Burroughs will use these principles in constructing the first successful adding machines.

Babbage designs the first general-purpose computer, the Analytical Engine, to which the modern computer bears a remarkable resemblance. The Engine has five parts: the mill, or calculating unit, the store (memory), an input device, a control section and a printer. The input and the control section are fed by punched cards.

Babbage's friend Lady Augusta Ada Lovelace documents his major work in her "Observations on Mr. Babbage's Analytical Engine." She will also write the first program, streamlining operations with such instructions as "Here follows a repetition of operations 13 to 23."

COMPUTER TIME LINE

by Carol Iaciofano

The idea of any time line is to present developments in a particular field as a continuum, a cascade of inevitability leading up to the present. A closer look at our highlights from computer history will show this

Carol Iaciofano is a technical writer for Engineering Automation Systems of Middletown, Connecticut. Her book reviews appear regularly in the Hartford Courant.

long and winding road to have been traveled in fits and starts. What if Pascal hadn't gotten religion and retreated from science? Or if Babbage had completed his Analytical Engine? Or if Konrad Zuse had been able to get all the spare parts he needed? We'll never know whether the flow of computer developments would have been greatly accelerated. The course of computer history does, after all, seem inevitable.

1847

With two landmark theses, English mathematician George Boole sets up a system called Boolean algebra, wherein logical problems are solved like algebraic problems. Boole's theories will form the bedrock of computer science.

1855

The first computer prize, a gold medal, is awarded at the Paris Exhibition to the Scheutz Difference Engine. Swedish engineer Georg Scheutz devised this simplified version of Babbage's machine after reading Lady Lovelace's "Observations." By this time painfully frustrated with his own slow progress, Babbage is in the audience when the medal is awarded to the younger inventor.

1859

The Registrar's Office in England commissions a Scheutz Difference Engine for calculating actuarial tables to predict life expectancy. This is the first use of the new technology by a government agency.

1890

Dr. Herman Hollerith completes the first electromechanical counting machine, the Hollerith tabulator, in which punched cards are used in data processing for the first time.

The U.S. government buys the Hollerith tabulator to compute the census. The machine completes the job in just 6 weeks as against previous 10-year preparation periods. (The U.S. population is 62,622,250.)

1895

Charles Fey, a young mechanic, opens arcade history by creating the slot machine. For $20 he sells the "Liberty Bell" to a San Francisco saloon, where it sits on the bar, accepts and pays out nickels, and is a huge success. (Symbols are bells, horseshoes, hearts, diamonds, spades and one star.)

1896

Herman Hollerith forms the Tabulating Machine Company to accommodate the demand for his counting machines. Eventually, the firm will take on a new identity as the Computing Tabulating and Recording Company (CTR).

1913

1924

1925

1935

1936

1938

Thomas J. Watson leaves National Cash Register, where he coined his legendary THINK slogan, to assume presidency of the now ailing CTR.

With Watson at the helm, Hollerith's fledgling finally emerges as IBM (International Business Machines).

The "modern era of computation" begins at Massachusetts Institute of Technology, where electrical engineer Vannevar Bush and colleagues devise a large-scale analog calculator. Though mostly mechanical, the calculator has electric motors that store number values as voltages in its thermionic tubes. For this invention, some consider Bush the true father of computing.

Bell Laboratories is founded in Murray Hill, N.J.

In Germany, inventor Konrad Zuse decides to use the binary system in his computer designs. The binary numbers calculate much faster than decimals.

English mathematician Alan M. Turing publishes his "On Computable Numbers," one of the single most important papers in the development of computer science.

Zuse designs the Z1, a computer with keyboard input, mechanical switches for storing numbers, and a row of light bulbs to flash answers. The Z1 can store instructions and is thus the first working stored program computer.

In Germany, Helmut Schreyer receives his doctoral thesis in engineering for demonstrating how electronic vacuum tubes can be used as basic units for ultra-highspeed digital computers.

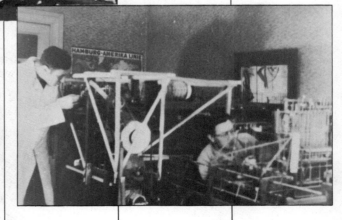

1939 1940 1942 1943 1944 1945

Hewlett-Packard is founded in Palo Alto, Calif.

Vannevar Bush completes his second model of the analog calculator, subsequently used to help devise artillery firing tables for the U.S. government.

Colossus, the world's first electronic computer, begins operations in December at Bletchley Park in England. Designed by Alan Turing and a team of scientists to decipher the signals of the German code machine Enigma, Colossus will help win the war for the Allies.

In wartime Germany, unable to obtain material for circuits to control his computers, Konrad Zuse creates the first programming language, Plankalkül, for both numerical and nonnumerical problems.

The Harvard Mark I, designed primarily by Prof. Howard Aiken (with funding by Thomas Watson and IBM), launches today's computer industry. The Mark I is the world's first fully automatic computer and the first machine to fulfill Babbage's dream.

In America, John von Neumann posits his five characteristics of computing: 1) fully electronic execution, 2) the binary number system, 3) an internal memory, 4) a stored program, and 5) universality i.e., a machine that can perform more than one task.

George Stibitz rents a telephone link from Dartmouth to his computer at Bell Labs in New Jersey and demonstrates long-distance computing in an address to the Dartmouth Mathematical Society in Hanover, N.H.

To help the war effort, math professor Grace Murray Hopper enters the U.S. Naval Reserve and embarks on the first modern programming career. Upon graduation, she is assigned to the Bureau of Ordnance Computation Project at Harvard.

1946

Electrical engineer J. Presper Eckert and physicist John Mauchly complete the first programmable electronic computer, ENIAC, at the University of Pennsylvania's Moore School of Electrical Engineering.

Eckert and Mauchly form the first commercial computer firm, the Electronic Control Company (later the Eckert-Mauchly Corporation), to manufacture electronic computers.

1947

Bell Labs scientists John Bardeen, Walter Houser Brattain and William Bradford Shockley revolutionize the young computer industry by inventing the transistor,

1949

M.I.T.'s Claude Shannon switches on computer game history when he demonstrates how to outline problems using game-playing machines, then builds a chess-playing machine called Caissac.

EDSAC (Electronic Delay Storage Automatic Computer) makes its first calculation on May 6. Built by Maurice Wilkes at Cambridge University, England, EDSAC performs one computation in three milliseconds. Wilkes is the first inventor to have a subroutine library in mind while designing a computer.

1950

On an 8 × 8 board, Alan Turing writes the first computer program to simulate chess.

Kurt Vonnegut, Jr., writes about "EPICAC" in one of the first love stories involving a computer.

The American military begins to use computers to simulate operations in its "war games."

1951

The first non-specialist computer magazine, *Computers and People* (originally titled *Computers and Automation*), comes on the market.

John Pinkerton completes the first business computer, LEO, for Lyons Teashop Company in England. LEO will be used for administrative purposes, not for calculating.

Eckert and Mauchly complete UNIVAC I (Universal Automatic Computer), the first computer specifically designed for commercial operations, and deliver it to the U.S. Census Bureau for tabulating the 1950 census.

While working on UNIVAC I, Grace Hopper meets the need for faster programming by devising a set of instructions that tells the machine how to convert its language into symbolic code. This is the A-O compiler, the first of its kind.

1952

IBM, the world's largest purveyor of punched card office machines, shifts to the manufacture of electronic computers.

John Diebold's "Automation: The Advent of the Factory" leads off the string of studies that will explore the computer's impact on employment and leisure time.

| 1954 | 1955 | 1956 | 1957 | 1958 | 1959 |

FORTRAN is born, through a paper titled "Specifications for the IBM Mathematical Formula Translating System, FORTRAN," written by IBM's Programming Research Group.

At RCA Labs in Princeton, N.J., Harry Olson and Herbert Belar complete the RCA Electronic Music Synthesizer, the first of its kind.

M.I.T.'s Whirlwind I introduces the first computer graphics: primitive interactive line drawings on two display consoles.

The 45-mile stretch of high-tech creativity known as Silicon Valley etches itself on the landscape of California's Santa Clara Valley.

Bardeen, Brattain and Shockley receive the Nobel Prize for their invention of the transistor. Shockley, who had left Bell Labs in 1955, founds Shockley Transistor Corporation, one of the first of the Silicon Valley firms. Engineers from Shockley Transistor will form their own major electronics firms, such as Fairchild Semiconductor.

At his marriage in Amsterdam, programming expert Edsgar Dijkstra fills in his profession on the license as "programer." Finding this unacceptable on the grounds that no such profession exists, city authorities erase his entry and substitute "theoretical physicist."

Lejaren Hiller arranges the first computer-composed music, *Illiac Suite for String Quartet.*

In Maynard, Mass., Ken Olsen starts Digital Equipment Corporation (DEC) as a mail-order parts business.

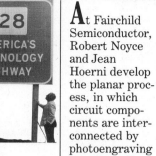

Computer firms spring up along Route 128, north of Boston.

Texas Instruments' Jack St. Kilby develops the first working model of the integrated circuit.

At Control Data Corporation, Seymour Cray designs the CDC 1604, the first fully transistorized supercomputer.

At Fairchild Semiconductor, Robert Noyce and Jean Hoerni develop the planar process, in which circuit components are interconnected by photoengraving on a flat, polished wafer, usually silicon. With integrated circuits, computers grow smaller and much more powerful.

CODASYL (Committee on Data Systems Languages), representing government, military and industry, meets to decide on a common language for business data processing. COBOL, for Common Business Oriented Language, is published within months, whereupon the Defense Department stipulates that all its suppliers must use the language.

The first formal computer user group, SHARE, meets in the basement of Rand Corporation headquarters in Santa Monica, Calif. The members, including government, research, aviation and computer organizations, gather to exchange "homegrown" software in the absence of instructions for the IBM 704.

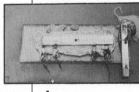

1960

The term "software" becomes widely accepted throughout the computer industry.

1961

The National Institutes of Health Clinic Center in Bethesda, Md., implements the first computerized patient-monitoring system.

1962

Dr. Edward O. Thorp's best-selling *Beat the Dealer* describes using a computer to work out the odds at blackjack. Thorpe's system is so successful that several casinos bar him from the game.

Disk file storage is initiated with the IBM 1440 series. The 14-inch disks look like phonograph records, are arranged in stacks of six and store three million characters.

With a $30 million investment and an IBM 9090, American Airlines launches SABRE, the first computerized airline reservation system. One of the largest commercial data bases in operation, SABRE allows customers to book reservations and rent cars. By 1968 it will handle over 100,000 calls per day from passengers, travel agents and other airlines.

Ivan Sutherland, a doctoral candidate at M.I.T.'s Lincoln Laboratory, designs Sketchpad, a line-drawing system for draftsmen. Using a cathode ray display tube, the system features an electronic stylus, or light pen, to display calculations at any stage of design. Soon after, another M.I.T. researcher, Timothy Johnson, develops a collateral program to display three-dimensional drawings.

1963

M.I.T.'s Dr. Joseph Weizenbaum develops Eliza, a program that simulates conversation between psychotherapist and patient.

General Motors Research Labs produces the first computer-designed auto part: the trunk lid for 1965 Cadillacs. The computer system is DAC-1 (Design Augmented by Computer), whose screen displays an image that can be modified with a light pen.

After more than 73,000 hours of steadfast service, UNIVAC I is retired to the Smithsonian Institution.

1964

Sara Lee, maker of frozen pastries, becomes the first fully automated factory. The Deerfield, Ill., plant uses a Honeywell 610 computer to change equipment speeds and oven temperatures and to determine what products are needed in filling orders.

In *Texas* v. *Hancock* a programmer who stole his employer's computer software, worth about $5 million, is convicted and sentenced to five years. This constitutes the first computer crime leading to criminal prosecution.

1965 | 1966 | 1967 | 1968 | 1969

Several Wall Street firms turn to computers for securities analysis and accounting.

In the first federal case involving criminal use of computers, *U.S.* v. *Bennett*, a bank programmer is convicted of adjusting a computer to ignore all his overdraft checks.

The movie *2001: A Space Odyssey* plays across the country, introducing the mutinous computer HAL.

M. E. Hoff, Jr., a young engineer at Intel, takes charge of the Busicom project involving the manufacture of chips for a Japanese calculator firm. His improvements on the design result in a central

On May 1, at four A.M. in a room at Dartmouth College, John Kemeny and Thomas E. Kurtz run their first program in BASIC (Beginners' All-Purpose Symbolic Instruction Code) for non professional computer users.

Harris-Intertype Corporation introduces three models of a computer designed specifically for typesetting. All of them justify automatically, and the top-end version offers near-perfect hyphenation.

DEC produces the first "mini" computer, incorporating many features of a large computer but with smaller storage capacity and a slower processing speed.

Schools begin to use computers for science simulation, math quizzes and educational games.

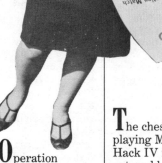

Operation Match, one of the early computer dating services, opens in Cambridge, Mass.

Texas Instruments unveils the first solid-state hand-held calculator. It has no electronic display, but prints out answers on a strip of heat-sensitive paper.

The chess-playing Mac-Hack IV is entered by Richard Greenblatt in the Massachusetts state championship, becoming the first program to compete successfully against human chess players.

Computerworld, one of the most comprehensive weekly newspapers geared to the computer industry, begins publication.

W. Carlos' *Switched-On Bach*, an album of fugues, preludes and two-part inventions played on a Moog Synthesizer, is a big hit.

Gordon Moore and Robert Noyce leave Fairchild Semiconductor to form Intel (Integrated Electronics) Corporation.

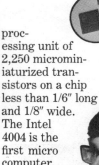

processing unit of 2,250 microminiaturized transistors on a chip less than 1/6″ long and 1/8″ wide. The Intel 4004 is the first micro computer.

1970   1971   1972   1973   1974

Ralph Baer, a division manager at Sanders Associates in New Hampshire, originates the home video game when he develops an electronic unit with hand controls that sends broadcast signals to a TV set.

Magnavox buys the patent rights to Baer's TV/hand-control invention, then sells the sublicensing rights to Atari and other manufacturers.

Left with a stock of unsold chips, Intel puts the 4004 microprocessor in its catalog. To everyone's surprise, the chip takes the industry by storm and paves the way for most of the advances of the decade.

IBM announces the System/32, a desk-size unit that contains all the computer hardware.

Intel develops the 8008 microprocessor, originally designed for the Display Terminal Corporation (now Datapoint) CRT. The 8008 ultimately satisfies all customer requirements except in the area of speed.

In a move to reduce clutter and clatter in the newsroom, the Augusta (Ga.) *Chronicle* and *Herald* install CRTs for use in writing and editing stories.

Atari founder Nolan Bushnell invents and markets Pong, considered by many the first milestone in video game history.

Diablo Systems of Hayward, Calif., develops the first automatic printer for data processing systems. The "daisy wheel" Hytype Printer I features a glass-reinforced nylon disk and can print 30 characters per second; integrated circuits do much of the work.

The Summer Olympics in Munich, Germany, are the first games to use computers as "primary" judges of times and finishes. The computer companies involved are Gebr. Junghams GMBH and Compagnie de Montres Longines Francillon S.A.

The National Computer Conference is held at the New York Coliseum June 4–8, replacing the fall and spring joint conferences.

Intel turns out the 8008 microprocessor, which is 20 times faster than the original 4004 chip.

Shugart Associates of Sunnyvale, Calif., ships its first 8" floppy disks. Replacing punched cards as a data entry medium, the reusable plastic/oxide disks weigh less than two ounces and store programs and files.

Truong Trong Thi, a Frenchman of Vietnamese origin, introduces the first commercially available microcomputer system, based on the Intel 8008, but fails to secure adequate distribution.

The July cover story of *Radio-Electronics* magazine tells how to "Build the Mark-8, Your Personal MiniComputer" (with an Intel 8008 microprocessor).

Computer magazines now range from *Computer Law and Tax Reporter*, which documents legal battles in data processing, to *Creative Computing*, one of the first magazines devoted to recreational use of computers.

In the first experiment with bank computer terminals, two branches of the Lincoln, Neb., Hinky Dinky grocery chain install computer terminals for bank deposits and withdrawals. In six weeks First Federal Savings & Loan takes in 672 new accounts.

Two leading designers at Intel leave to form Zilog, another microprocessing firm. They develop the Z80 chip, which competes directly with Intel's new 8080.

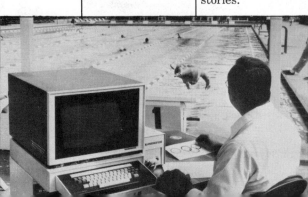

1975

1976

1977

The January 1975 issue of *Popular Electronics* features a cover story on the MITS Altair, the first widely available personal computer.

In a five-week period, Harvard student William Gates and associate Paul Allen adapt BASIC to fit the microcomputer. Having wrested the new computers from the hands of a small group of assembly language programmers, they form Microsoft to market their version of the language.

Objective Design of Tallahassee, Fla., offers Encounter, the first commercial personal computer game, in assembly language on paper tape.

BYTE

the small systems journal

ISSUE #1

SEPTEMBER 1975

$1.50

Which Microprocessor for you?

Cassette Interface — Your key to inexpensive bulk memory

Assembling Your Assembler

Can YOU use these SURPLUS KEYBOARDS?
(You bet you can!)

COMPUTERS-
the World's Greatest Toy!

The New York *Times* starts to convert to electronic editing and typesetting on a Harris 2550 system.

With a surplus of calculator chips, Commodore enters the personal computer market through MOS (metal oxide semiconductor) technology.

The first Adventure game is programmed by Crowther and Wood at Princeton University.

The number of computer magazines grows to include *Byte: The Small Systems Journal* (aimed at the "personal computer" amateur and professional), the quarterly *Computer Graphics and Art*, and *Dr. Dobb's Journal of Computer Calisthenics and Orthodontia* for the microcomputer hobbyist.

Storage systems become smaller, more powerful and more convenient. Micropolis Corporation of Northridge, Calif., announces the Metafloppy, a family of integrated 5¼" floppy disk systems with the storage capacity of 8" disks.

The newsweekly *Computerworld* begins a Microcomputing section to handle the flood of information on micros.

Apple markets the Apple II, ultimately to become the personal computer equivalent of the Volkswagen.

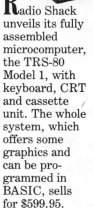

Radio Shack unveils its fully assembled microcomputer, the TRS-80 Model 1, with keyboard, CRT and cassette unit. The whole system, which offers some graphics and can be programmed in BASIC, sells for $599.95.

CRTs come under suspicion when two New York *Times* copy editors are diagnosed as having cataracts. Tested for radiation, the machines are ultimately cleared. This is the first of many complaints linking eye irritations and CRTs.

Commodore International, enters the personal computer field with PET (personal electronic transactor).

Computer-Land, among the largest of today's computer retailers, opens its first store.

Originally developed for computerized astrology machines, CP/M (control program for microcomputers) is offered by Gary Kildall and his Digital Research Company. CPM will soon become a standard for business applications on personal computers.

1978

1979

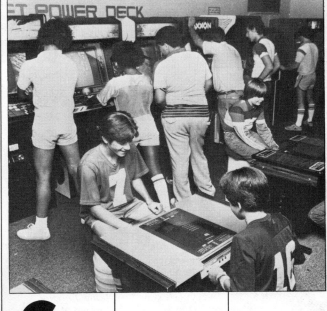

Personal Software markets VisiCalc, soon called the "smash hit of software." The first version works only on the Apple II and thus boosts that computer's sales. VisiCalc is credited with taking micros out of the home and making them "serious."

Fed up with time-consuming projections using a calculator and spreadsheet, first-year Harvard Business School student Daniel Bricklin teams up with Robert Frankston at M.I.T. to create VisiCalc, an electronic spreadsheet that can recalculate all related numbers when one variable changes. They pool their finances and with $16,000 found Software Arts in Wellesley, Mass.

Texas Instruments produces its Speak & Spell toy, the first widespread offering of digital speech synthesis.

Seymour Rubenstein, formerly of IMSAI, founds MicroPro International and commissions John Barnaby to write the word processing program that will become WordStar.

Epson America in Anaheim, Calif., introduces its 80-column dot-matrix printer, which becomes a runaway best seller.

Publisher Adam Osborne sells his company to McGraw-Hill and founds Osborne Computer in Hayward, Calif.

Video games appear everywhere: in restaurants, gas stations, bars. With threatening names like Centipede and Space Invaders, the quarter-gobbling dwarfs cause concern among parents.

The Source offers an electronic service enabling home computer owners to read newspapers, get stock info, check airline schedules and browse through restaurant guides. Similar services will include Compu-Serve and Dow Jones News/Retrieval.

1980 | 1981

Shugart Associates markets the 5¼" Winchester disk drive, which stores 30 times as much data as a standard small floppy and transfers the information 20 times faster.

Texas Instruments unveils its first personal computer, the TI 99/4, based on a 16-bit processor and list-priced at $1,200. With modifications and aggressive marketing, this computer eventually lists for $99 before almost bankrupting the company.

Radio Shack introduces the TRS-80 Color Computer for recreation and education.

Four eighth-graders at Manhattan's private Dalton School use its terminals to link up with other computers. By trial and error, they gain entry into several Canadian companies' computers, temporarily destroying certain data and preventing legitimate users from accessing the systems. The FBI and Royal Canadian Mounted Police join forces and catch the 13-year-olds after a week of their long-distance raids. No charges are pressed despite a loss of several thousand dollars' worth of computer time.

Commodore introduces the VIC-20, destined to be the first home computer model to sell more than one million units. Waiting in the wings is the more powerful Commodore 64, the first popularly priced machine to have 64K of memory built in.

Osborne Computer unveils the Osborne 1, the first portable micro. Its 24 pounds hold a disk operating system that can handle word processing and electronic spreadsheets.

Zork, a "second-generation" adventure game capable of responding to complex sentences, is introduced by Infocom. Originally written in a proprietary language on a minicomputer, the game is quickly converted by Infocom into versions for virtually every popular personal computer model.

The six-year-old personal computer industry passes the $1.5 billion mark.

At ENIAC's thirty-fifth birthday celebration in Philadelphia, the trail-blazing machine is pitted against a Radio Shack TRS-80 and commanded to square all integers from 1 to 10,000. The young micro wins handily, completing the exercise in a third of a second vs. ENIAC's six seconds.

Computer camps become popular among kids (and some adults).

Watchmaker Timex Inc. contracts with England's Clive Sinclair to market Timex/Sinclair 1000, the first fully assembled under-$100 computer in the U.S.

The IBM PC debuts, with a memory that can store more than 250 pages of data and a system that can complete about 700,000 additions per second. The PC is as powerful as anything on the market, which shifts dramatically toward the industry's giant.

IBM chooses Microsoft's MS-DOS operating system for its PC. When other hardware manufacturers hop on the IBM-compatible bandwagon, MS-DOS becomes the new standard for business applications programs.

In a lean Christmas shopping season, computer video games (with TV hook-ups) are huge hits. The favorites are Intellivision and Atari.

1982

1983

According to a study by Prof. Sanford Weinberg of St. Joseph's University, Philadelphia, at least 30 percent of daily users of computers have some degree of "cyberphobia," or fear of computers. Victims range from high blood pressure sufferers to the policeman who shot the computer console in his car. Another Weinberg study shows cyberphiliacs (compulsive computer programmers) to be no better off: they are usually friendless and single.

Jimmy Carter becomes the first former President to write his memoirs with a word processor. Like many tyro computer users, he hits a wrong key and deletes an entire chapter.

As the video game craze reaches fever pitch, 15-year-old Steve Juraszek of Arlington Heights, Ill., plays Defender for 16 hours, 34 minutes, on the same quarter. His score: 15,963,100.

For its annual "Man of the Year" issue, *Time* magazine features the computer on its cover.

Over 17,000 software packages are now available to run on Apple computers.

Lotus 1-2-3, the first integrated software package for personal computers, hits the market. Lotus founder Mitchell D. Kapor packaged an electronic spreadsheet, information management and graphics on one 5¼″ disk.

Radio Shack brings out a book-size computer: the Radio Shack 100. The tiny machine weighs about four pounds, has built-in word processing and communications software, and costs just under $800. Other companies quickly following with book-size computers are Sharp and Nippon, taking advantage of the power and size made possible by CMOS chips.

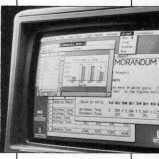

Apple puts out the Lisa 32-bit Motorola 68000 microprocessor-based computer featuring high-res graphics, on-screen windows for multi-program use and a mouse for controlling cursor position and data entry. The initial $10,000 offering price is prohibitive, but Lisa establishes the state of the art for personal computers.

Computerized burglaries become so popular among teens that the FBI conducts a huge "sting" operation to round up micro-criminals in 13 cities. (Computers in brokerage houses, hospitals and the Defense Department had been raided mostly through GTE's Telenet, based in Vienna, Va.) Word of the FBI crackdown is flashed to other hackers across the country via computer bulletin boards.

Less than two years after introducing inexpensive portable computers, Osborne files for reorganization under chapter 11 of the federal bankruptcy law. In the highly competitive microcomputer market, other high-tech firms founder. Texas Instruments and Mattel leave the home computer business, eventually followed by Timex.

Hewlett-Packard unveils the HP-150, the first personal computer to offer a touch screen.

Reared by Doug Englebart, the mouse input device makes its popular debut with the launching of Apple's Lisa and adoption for IBM PC software.

President Ronald Reagan helps unemployed steel-worker Ronald D. Bricker get his first job interview in a year. Bricker goes to work as a computer repair technician for Radio Shack, realizes he is earning less than if he were collecting unemployment insurance and gladly returns to the steel mill when his old job becomes available.

A Korean Airlines Boeing 747 with 269 people on board is shot down by a Russian fighter plane for straying into Soviet air space. Western aviation experts blame a one-digit human error by the crew in programming the plane's navigational computer—enough to account for its being 300 miles off course.

New York's Chemical Bank makes the first large-scale launch of a home banking system. Its Pronto service is soon offered through 200 banks across the U.S.

Toymaker Coleco announces its Adam, the first inexpensive home computer system with built-in word processing capabilities. By Christmas eve Adam has disappointing sales; what saves the company from bankruptcy are Cabbage Patch dolls, their names computer-generated.

As marketing takes over from engineering, Pepsi-Cola v.p. John Sculley becomes president of Apple.

The movie *WarGames*, in which a young hacker gains entry to a Defense Department computer and plays "global thermonuclear war," explores the adolescent fantasy of possessing ultimate power in the adult world.

IBM brings out the PCjr, a home-oriented, lower-priced encore to its PC.

George Orwell's *1984*, thought by many to be a prophetic indictment of the computer age, is found to contain no mention of computers.

Computer magazine titles reach 450, the largest number ever devoted to a single subject. An ensuing shakeout decimates the ranks of computer publications.

SALESMAN 1: I thought the $1100 was $4800 and the $500 was $ 3900.

SALESMAN 1: $3900.
SALESMAN 2: No, Max, the $1400 is $4800, the $600 is $3900.

As competition heats up, commercial TV becomes a battleground for the personal computer wars. Apple and Kaypro ads go on to win "Cleos", the "Oscars" of TV commericals.

Apple signals a new generation of personal computers with its powerful, compact Macintosh, whose 3½″ disks store more than the 5¼″ disks used in most micros. With its mouse and pull-down menus and windows, it is truly "Lisa for the masses."

During a period of refinement and consolidation, the biggest news in software is Lotus Symphony, the five-in-one integrated successor to 1-2-3 and "thought processing" programs like Think Tank by Living Video Text and integrated Framework from Ashton-Tate.

VisiCorp and Software Arts sue each other over marketing rights to the pioneering program in a move that could reflect an end to the cooperative era in the software industry.

Still in its relative infancy, the computer seems to be infinitely perfectible. The march toward computopia is hardly linear—for every step forward there are several steps sideways and back—but there is a clear progression in the direction of greater intelligence and sophistication. Which should bring up even more often the fundamental question: Can computers replace us? Only time will tell . . .

WHO NEEDS PERSONAL COMPUTERS?

by J. Presper Eckert

I must confess that I don't own a personal computer. I have no reason to. I suppose I could use a computer for my hobby, electronic musical instruments, and conduct research on how to generate an accurate replica of a piano note (today's electronic pianos lack warmth in their tones). But I would need a pretty fast computer to handle the sampling of a note's characteristics in a reasonable amount of time. I may just wait for the next generation of personal computers based on the 32-bit microprocessors now appearing from a number of manufacturers.

We've come a long way since the day when Dr. Howard Aiken, designer of the pioneering Mark series of computers at Harvard, could say that just a half-dozen electronic machines would be enough to fulfill the world's computational needs (a statement he later retracted). On the other hand, I remember my late colleague John Mauchly talking about the importance of personal computers long before they existed.

During the late 1950s I was involved in trying to build what could now be called a personal computer, probably the first such machine to fit on a desktop. We used hundreds of magnetic core amplifiers and diodes, a few transistors and tubes, and a motor-driven drum for memory storage. The same motor powered a fly-printer, which typed the computer's output onto a moving strip of paper. Unlike the first microcomputer systems, which came later, our machine included a keyboard for easy input. We figured we could sell our Desk Computer for $5,000. Some insurance firms expressed interest, but our executives just couldn't see business need for that small a computer.

J. Presper Eckert was the chief engineer on ENIAC I. He is currently vice-president and technical assistant to the president of Sperry Computer Company.

I find a lot of bunk surrounding today's personal computers. Like the term "user-friendly." Just what does it mean? When we were working on ENIAC I, we wrote an assembler so the machine could do some of its own bookkeeping and we could program it more easily. The vast majority of personal computer users will never do any programming, so this development may not seem especially user-friendly. But anyone who has ever had to program in machine code would find an assembler a most agreeable companion.

Often I am asked whether computers have had a dehumanizing influence on society. This may be so in some cases, but mostly it just isn't true. If anything, computers can free you from tedium. And they allow you to exercise your individuality. You can go into a dealer's showroom and order a car with your choice of colors and options, thanks to a computerized assembly system. This is a far cry from Henry Ford's Model-T and its choice of any color as long as it was black.

There are problems, of course. Computers are replacing humans on the assembly line, but bolt-stuffing a machine chassis, for instance, could hardly be thought of as a particularly humanizing activity. Progress always brings problems, and we should be working on solutions to those problems. You've got to be for progress or go back to eating bark in the forests.

Who needs personal computers? Society at large. Overall, personal computers are the greatest development since the first electronic computers. They are important not for their individual use, but for their long-term educational effect. Home computers will surely awaken some young geniuses who will make a tremendous difference in the future. It's this long-shot effect, this gamble on the next step in our evolution, that defines our real need for personal computers. ■

SOLOMON'S MEMORY

by Les Solomon

When *Popular Electronics* ran its first cover story on the Altair in January 1975, I was the technical director for the magazine and therefore fortunate enough to witness and aid in the birth of the personal/home computer. Before those early years become set in stone, I would like to offer this reminiscence and give credit to those pioneers whose names may be un-

Les Solomon is technical director of Computers & Electronics. *He is a member of the Bug-Eyed Monster Society and practices levitation in his spare time.*

known to the home computer users now benefiting from the fruits of their labors.

It all started for me in the summer of 1972, during a vacation trip out west. My wife and I were near Albuquerque when I called Forrest Mims, a contributor to the magazine who lived in this town out in the middle of nowhere. His father had a small company called M.I.T.S. (Micro Instrumentation and Telemetry Systems), which occupied the bathroom of Forrest's mobile home and manufactured small electronic gad-

gets for radio-control airplanes and model rockets.

The Mims invited us out to see them, and during the conversation Forrest mentioned that he had a friend who was as crazy about electronics as I was. He insisted that I meet this fellow, Ed Roberts, so later that night we got together in a steak bar in downtown Albuquerque. Just out of the military, Ed had this idea about offering an electronic calculator kit. And I had to listen, since he stands over six feet and weighs 235 pounds or so.

Anyway, I decided to write about the kit in the pages of *Popular Electronics*. After the article appeared, many kits were sold and Ed bought out M.I.T.S., moved it into a real building and dropped the periods to make it MITS. Pretty soon, everybody and his uncle got into calculators and they were a dime a dozen. Ed was giving serious thought to folding his company when we heard some electronic stirrings that sounded really wild. One of our competitors, *Radio-Electronics*, was preparing a story on a "computer" using an Intel 8008 microprocessor chip. Ed looked into it, obtained an even newer Intel chip called the 8080, and with a couple of engineering friends set about creating his own computer.

The MITS computer was ready that summer. Ed said it could be sold as a kit for about $400, which was fantastic since I knew the *Radio-Electronics* Mark-8 computer was having difficulties (no peripherals, no language, etc.). One day he phoned to say his first computer was being shipped to me by Railway Express Agency. A week later, no computer had arrived. I complained to the people at REA, who retorted: "Our computer has never lost anything!" During the fourth week they went bankrupt, having lost not only the first MITS computer but their entire shipping empire as well.

Luckily, Ed had sent me another computer by a different route. There I was, in a small office in New York with a metal box marked PE-8 on my desk, and an ASR-33 Teletype as the only way of inputting or displaying instructions and data. Between the front-panel switch start-up routine and the noisy Teletype, I was told to take "that thing" home, which I suppose made the PE-8 the first workable home computer.

Art Salsberg, my boss, said he would go along with me on publishing a construction article on a microcomputer ("Heaven only knows who will build one!"), so the next step was finding a catchy name for our 8-bitter. After dinner one night I asked my twelve-year-old daughter, who was watching *Star Trek*, what the computer on the Enterprise was called.

"Computer," she answered.

That's a nice name, I thought, but not sexy. Then she said:

"Why don't you call it Altair? That's where the Enterprise is going in this episode."

THE FIRST DO-IT-YOURSELF PERSONAL COMPUTER

Titled simply "Computer," with the subhead "Build the Mark-8, Your Personal Minicomputer," *Radio-Electronic*'s cover story for July 1974 introduced the first homemade machine to use a microprocessor.

My introduction to the Mark-8 came one bright spring morning in 1973, when a forceful young man by the name of Jonathan Titus called to tell me about his working model of a microcomputer built around the new Intel 8008. (A bargain-priced 8008 microprocessor cost $125 at the time.) Deciding that a personal visit was necessary, I flew down to Blacksburg, Virginia, where Jon took me to a spare room in his college apartment and showed me the first micro system: a little green box decorated with a bunch of toggle switches and flickering red lights.

What, I wondered, would anyone do with a computer that needed to be programmed . . . one step at a time . . . by setting eight toggle switches to represent each instruction?

Despite my misgivings and after months of preparation, we published our article on the Mark-8 computer. There was no way we could squeeze it into a single issue, and for the second time in our history we offered a booklet of complete construction information. The booklet sold by the thousands: each new stack that came in from the printer was gone in no time, and we'd have to order more. To this day I don't know how many people spent how many hours entering instructions and data into the Mark-8 . . .

I am often asked whether I anticipated the current personal computer revolution when I was introduced to Jon Titus' original micro system. My answer is yes, but I still don't think the computer is the ideal tool for everyone. In business and education there is no doubt that its growth as a tool and as a time- and dollar-saver will continue. When it comes to computers in the home, however, I have my doubts.

I am not convinced that the average person has enough need for a computer to justify its cost. Yes, it's a great game machine. Yes, it's a great educational device. Yes, it's a great typewriter. But unless you're going to do your banking, control your home appliances, keep your holiday mailing lists, calculate your income taxes and your budget, it's difficult for me to see a personal computer in every household. Until the price of hardware comes down, and until software exists at low cost to do the kinds of things the average American needs done around the home, the computer revolution will remain largely a business revolution.

LARRY STECKLER, publisher of *Radio-Electronics*

The next day I called Ed to try out the new name. His answer was curt: "I don't care what you call it, if we don't sell two hundred we're doomed!" So Altair it became.

About a month before we ran the Altair story I had a visit from another imposingly large person, Roger Melen of Stanford University, who had written several articles for us. Roger contemplated the Altair set up on the table, and when I told him it was a computer his eyes glazed over. He muttered something about getting one for himself and his friend Harry Garland, who also wrote for us, and asked me for the name and address of the kit supplier. Then he vanished. Later I heard he took the next plane to Albuquerque, marched into Ed's office and bought Altair #2 right off his desk.

A few months later I got a call from Roger, asking me to fly out to San Francisco to see something very important. When I got there, he took me to the apartment he shared with Harry and showed me what he'd done with his Altair. Plugged into the machine was a double set of add-on circuit boards called the Dazzler, whose video output could create an amazing display on a color TV—the first plug-in expansion board for a personal computer. The software was called Kaleidoscope, a program that is relatively common today, but in 1976 . . . ! Because of its ever-changing color display, Kaleidoscope would actually become a traffic stopper: Stan Veit ran the program all night in the window of his New York store, the first com-

puter store east of the Mississippi, and the NYPD had to put an end to it because people kept slowing down to gawk at all those color images.

Dazzler sales went over so well that Roger and Harry formed a new company to manufacture Altair plug-ins. They decided to name it after Crothers Memorial Hall, where they had lived during their undergraduate days at Stanford. Cromemco (Crothers Memorial Company) was the first of what would become an entire subindustry of firms manufacturing add-ons to extend the capabilities of existing personal computers.

At about this time MITS held the world's first microcomputer convention, called, strangely enough, the World's First Altair Convention. Located in the Airport-Marina hotel in sunny downtown Albuquerque, it was attended by an amazing number of people who came from all over the country to see what was going on.

The Altair was a success, but the paper tape BASIC and paper tape software were an abomination. One day Jerry Ogdin, a computer consultant, had come to me with the idea of storing digital data using two tones (one for a zero, another for a zone) on an ordinary voice-grade tape cassette recorder. In September of 1975 we ran a construction article on what we called HITS (Hobbyists' Interchange Tape System), after which a number of manufacturers started using their own approach to two-tone data recording. Wayne Green, who had just started *Byte* magazine, wanted

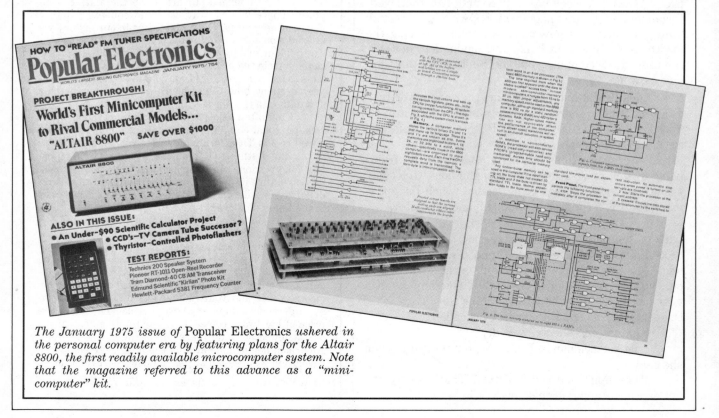

The January 1975 issue of Popular Electronics *ushered in the personal computer era by featuring plans for the Altair 8800, the first readily available microcomputer system. Note that the magazine referred to this advance as a "minicomputer" kit.*

THE RISE AND FALL OF THE ALTAIR

Though computer kit makers like Scelbi Computer Consulting, RGS Electronics and Martin Research actually preceded MITS, the Altair 8800 with its S-100 bus and Microsoft BASIC became the foundation of the personal computer industry. More Altairs were sold than any single computer ever designed up to that time (including the famous IBM 360).

Why, then, isn't MITS one of today's industry leaders? Well, perhaps because its founder, Ed Roberts, was a better engineer than businessman.

When MITS struck it rich with the Altair, the small staff—less than ten people—geared up to handle the hundreds of orders that poured in. They set up manufacturing operations, software development and customer service, and even published one of the first computer magazines, *Computer Notes*. But problems arose because no one had ever made as many computers of one type. MITS had neither the experience nor its own capital to do the job, and in those days there were no venture capitalists breaking down doors to offer development money. Further, though computer hobbyists and potential dealers helped out with pre-paid orders, Ed Roberts made some serious marketing errors. For example, MITS insisted that Altair dealers carry no other line of computers: "Ford dealers only carry Fords," Roberts declared, "and Altair dealers will only carry Altairs." When MITS could not deliver the computers, many dealers went out of business or dropped the Altair line.

MITS eventually did produce the Altair 8080B, a really fine computer with a good disk system and lots of good software including business applications. The company never solved its cash flow problems, however, and eventually Ed Roberts sold out to the Pertec Computer Co., which supplied the Altair disk drives. Ed retired from the computer industry to raise pigs in Georgia, then later decided to go to medical school.

Pertec, which had ambitions to become a major computer company, felt the name Altair was too identified with "hobby computers." The line was discontinued, and the Altair vanished from the market. When Pertec was itself bought out by Adler of Germany, the Altair name was condemned to oblivion. All that was left was Microsoft BASIC and the memory of the machine that started an industry.

STAN VEIT

Les Solomon (right) with fellow personal computer pioneer Don Lancaster.

all the manufacturers to get together in a neutral site and hammer out a cassette standard. The site picked was Kansas City, Missouri. We all met for a weekend, and after many loud and serious discussions the Kansas City tape "standard" was born. Unfortunately, it didn't last long; before the month ended, everyone went back to his own tape standard and the recording confusion got worse.

It was at Kansas City that I first met Bob Marsh, who had formed a garage-based company in San Francisco called Processor Technology. Along with circuit designer Lee Felsenstein, he was making Altair memory boards and a graphics display board called the VDM-1, also for the Altair. Lee had worked for Marty Spergel, the driving force behind M&R Enterprises, and came through with plans for the Pennywhistle modem—the first hobby modem, published in our March 1976 issue. Now we computer hobbyists had a low-cost way to communicate over the telephone lines. Lee went on to design several trend-setting computers, including the portable Osborne.

I was still unhappy. The Altair needed a video display terminal with a self-contained keyboard. Like everyone else, I had been constantly startled by Don Lancaster's brilliant innovations over the years, and I knew he had just finished his TV typewriter. I went to Phoenix, loaded Don and his typewriter into the car, and took off for Albuquerque and MITS. One thing I must say for Don Lancaster and Ed Roberts: they both have very strong personalities. When I got them together in Ed's office, the clash was pretty fierce. Since the Altair and the TV typewriter were not compatible, something had to give. Neither man, however, would give an inch.

YOU'VE COME A LONG WAY, MICRO

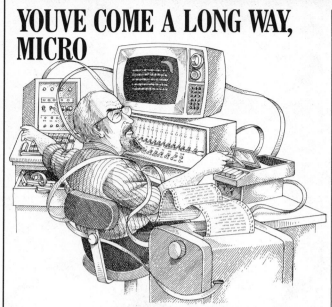

The horse-and-buggy days of home computing were not all that long ago. In fact, less than a decade has passed since I first read about the Altair and began thirsting—nay, lusting—for a computer of my own.

When I finally got one, of course, there was precious little I could do with it. My Altair turned out to be just a box with toggle switches and neat rows of red LEDs (light-emitting diodes) decorating the front panel. The switches were its only input device; the LEDs were its output, glowing and darkening in patterns that showed what you had input from the switches and what the computer had done as a result. Both operated at the same simple-minded level as the computer itself, in binary numbers built up of 1s and 0s. A "1" was entered by raising a switch, a "0" by lowering it. The corresponding LEDs glowed for each "1" and darkened for each "0."

A one-byte program instruction, nothing more arduous than STOP, took eight switch settings.

The Plug-In Problem

Luckily, there was a world beyond the binary level. I went out and got a "terminal," with keyboard and video display screen, but then found nothing on the Altair to plug it into. What I needed was an I/O (input/output) circuit board through which the computer and terminal could communicate. The Altair had about a dozen slots where you could plug in I/O and other boards. Put a 25-pin connector into one of the oval holes in the computer's back, run a cable from the I/O board, and you had a place to plug in the terminal.

Problem: typing on the terminal had no effect on what the Altair did. Just as nice children don't speak until they're spoken to, computers don't communicate with terminals until a program has told them they can and how to do it. There was such a program in octal (base-8) numbering that you could translate into binary and toggle in from the front panel of the Altair. Unfortunately, the program was several hundred bytes long; at eight bits per byte, this meant well over a thousand switch-flicks before the program was in the machine. Since a computer's random access memory becomes amnesiac the instant its power is shut off, you'd have to toggle in that program every time you wanted to use the machine. And if you made just one of those thousand switch-flicks wrong, the program wouldn't run—or would run amok, randomly changing the bits you'd toggled in correctly.

The solution was to put that program, and any others you needed regularly, into an EPROM (erasable, programmable, read only memory), which would hold its contents even when the computer was shut off. A whole set of such programs fit easily into just two EPROM chips. Naturally the Altair had no place to plug in those chips, so I had to buy a Cromemco Bytesaver board to hold them and plug it into the Altair's bus. With those programs, typing in instructions like C2 D5 01 ("If the zero flag is not set, jump to the program steps at memory location 01D5") was simpler than setting switch sequences of 11000010 1101010 00000001. Writing programs in tiny steps of arbitrary symbols, however, was still infuriatingly slow. What I needed was a "high-level" programming language.

By that time the Altair could run an abbreviated BASIC, the first product of a tiny new firm called Microsoft. It was only available on punched paper tape, which required a special paper-tape reader, but for once I didn't have to buy any new equipment. I had a friend with a teletype—a printing terminal that could also read and punch such tapes. I ordered BASIC and my friend read it into his machine, then rerecorded it onto a tape cassette. I might not have a paper-tape reader, but I did have a cassette recorder.

Still Plugging Away

Not surprisingly, the Altair had no place to plug in the cassette. Now what I lacked was a board that would translate between computer and cassette deck. With this I would have a fully functioning system, including all the major parts a computer needs: a keyboard and screen (on the terminal), mass storage (the cassette), a processor, and both ROM (built-in program) and RAM (user-programmable) memory. But the Altair came with 4K of RAM memory and the BASIC interpreter took up 8K, not counting the program you then wanted to run. The solution here was to plug in still more memory boards.

In those early days, few programs were ready-made, in part because not all the programs marketed for the Altair were available in the same tape format. Besides, there simply weren't that many to choose from. Then along came the next generation of personal computers: machines like the Radio Shack TRS-80 Model I, the Commodore PET and the Apple II, with resident programs in permanent memory, cassette connections, keyboards and (save for the Apple) screens built in. Not only that, but they had BASIC built in, so you could run your language immediately—no waiting while you loaded it from a tape.

In principle, they were little different from my old Altair. The major difference was that these computers didn't require months of learning and searching for parts before you could use them. All you had to do was plug them in . . .

IVAN BERGER, technical editor of *Audio* magazine

My next step was to talk to Bob Marsh of Processor Technology. It took a little doing, but I finally convinced him that a combination of his memory boards, his VDM-1 as the video display, plus an 8080, a power supply and the S-100 bus, would make a dandy "smart" terminal—or even a computer. We decided on the smart terminal approach, since I was fairly certain the magazine would not "buy" another computer. Lee Felsenstein did the preliminary design and, using one of Don Lancaster's approaches, came up with a computer. Steve Dompier and Gary Ingram did the software. Another software person, Gordon French, came up with the idea of wooden sides for the case—an odd first for computers.

In the summer of 1976 a new, easier-to-use computer was born, one with a self-contained operating system (no complex switches to get it started), built-in video capability, an integral keyboard and a small, typewriter-size enclosure. It was decided that this new approach would be called Sol. The story I was told by Marsh and Felsenstein was that if the strange-looking computer didn't fly, they had to have someone to blame it on . . . guess who? At least they didn't call it the Les. Sol appeared in the July 1976 issue of *Popular Electronics*.

That summer there was also the famous Atlantic City Computer Conference at the snazzy Shelbourne Hotel/Motel. This was just about the first time almost all the microcomputer people got together in one place. It was a great show and the forerunner of the many computer fairs to follow.

During the 1977 First West Coast Computer Faire, I dropped in on the Heuristics Company to see what Horace Enea had wrought. His Speechlab plug-in board would allow the user to actually talk to the computer, and the computer could "understand"! Not too much later Software Technology, an offshoot of Processor Technology, came up with a variation of Steve Dompier's music system (Dompier was the first to realize that microcomputers could make music) and produced a most marvelous sound system that was used in conjunction with an external audio amplifier. From now on, no microcomputer show would be silent!

The 1977 First West Coast Computer Faire (Jim Warren, chairperson) was a success in many ways. It was one of the first times such a wide variety of computer people got together in one place on the West Coast. Outside the Brooks Hall site of the show was parked a small van containing Mike Wise and his unique computer from the Sphere Company located in Bountiful, Utah. The one thing we remember about the Sphere was that its BASIC was s–l–o–w. Real s–l–o–w! The Sphere computer was never seen again: it was advertised and a couple were even delivered to computer stores, but very soon Sphere vanished from the face of the earth—a fate shared by many other pioneering computer models.

There were a lot of other developments over the years, some good, some transitory, none of them boring. Companies came and went, as did software. (Does anyone remember Target, the first personal computer game? Or Star Trek, with its umpteen versions?) Magazines also came and went. (Anyone remember *ROM*, with its column "From the Fountainhead" by a young writer named Adam Osborne?) Processor Technology vanished along with the late, great Sol and the unlamented Helios disk drive; Steve Jobs and Steve Wozniak came up with Apple I, a computer on a single circuit board that would lead to bigger things; Bob Suding of the Digital Group out in Denver came up with some good hardware, unfortunately too far ahead of its time.

A couple of guys in New Jersey, Roger Amidon and Chris Rutkowski, came up with a "supercomputer": the General, with its superb software. Although the General also soon folded its tent, the idea of this machine recently returned when Roger and Chris, using the Rising Star marketing firm as a base, introduced the Epson QX-10 with Valdocs word processing software—the most user-friendly computer system I've seen as of this writing and, incidentally, the machine I used to compose this account.

This just about brings me to the end of my musings about "the good old days"—to the end of 1977, just two years after the Altair. I personally don't believe we shall ever again see such an outburst of raw talent. They were great times. (If I missed any important event or name, forgive me, fellows, I am getting old.) I salute that long-haired, blue-jeans-and-T-shirt bunch, bearded or not shaven at all, fueled by hamburgers and Anchor Steam beer (I didn't forget, Steve), limited only by their imagination. They left the legacy that a handful of guys with an idea can change the world . . . because that's exactly what they did. Just look around.   ∎

The Sol computer, named for Les Solomon, made its debut in the July 1976 issue of Popular Electronics.

EXTINCT COMPUTER QUIZ

Can you name these early personal computer models?
by Stan Veit

They say you can always recognize the pioneers by the arrows sticking out from their backs. That goes for pioneering computers as well as humans. The morgue of the personal computer revolution is filled with the corpses of models that started this industry and then expired for one reason or another. See if you can identify the following machines, all of which are now collector's items.

1.

The first Altair-compatible machine, this was mechanically superior with a heavy-duty power supply and twenty-two slots to accommodate future expansion. Its makers were adherents to the est seminar program, which did not guarantee continued financial success—though two of the company's principals went on to found the ComputerLand chain of stores.

2.

What started out as a keyboard terminal to attach to other computer systems was then given a mind of its own and called a "terminal computer." Its wooden-sided chassis made it unique. In an era of 5¼-inch disk drives its manufacturer gave it an 8-inch monster named Helios, which often malfunctioned and drew so many lawsuits that the company was dissolved.

3.

Named after the state where it was produced, a kind of knowledge and a plucky upstart, this computer used the same 6502 microprocessor favored by the Apple II, its closest rival. It attracted a fanatically loyal following—including some of the earliest machine-specific user groups, which survived long after its makers went bankrupt.

4.

Still the only personal computer to offer a choice of microchips as its main processor. The first system to run the now classic Z-80 microprocessor, it was also the first one that came with an inexpensive printer for personal use. Referred to as the Denver Donkeys, its manufacturers were notorious for delivery delays; hence their eventual demise.

5.

The first all-in-one desktop computer came with built-in keyboard, CRT screen, interface capability for a modem and printer, and even a disk drive. Despite substantial investment from local businessmen, this product of the Beehive State never went into large-scale production.

For answers see page 54.

6.

Although only 220 were ever manufactured, this bare single-board computer helped found an industrial empire. Its maker went from being capitalized by the sale of a used scientific calculator and an old van to Fortune 500 status within five years. Originally sold for $666, it drew instant acclaim, yet was quickly outdone by its more complete successor.

INSIDE THE MICROPROCESSOR

by Stan Veit

The microprocessor is easy to spot inside the housing of your personal computer. Usually the largest rectangle on the main circuit board, its black plastic casing is over a half-inch wide and about two inches long, with dozens of metal legs, or pins, attached to it. The microprocessor chip within is a half-inch-square sliver of silicon with connections to each of the pins.

The Zylog Z-80 microchip, used in such popular computers as the Radio Shack TRS-80 series, the Coleco Adam and countless CP/M-based business systems, is typical of central processing chips now in general use. The Z-80's inner workings will provide us with the key to the secrets of the electronic brain.

Of the forty pins attached to the Z-80, sixteen are known as the address bus. ("Bus" is what we call a group of computer connections with a common purpose.) These have to do with the unique address of each of the computer's memory locations. Since the computer uses the binary system, each address pin can be in either a zero or a one state. With each additional address line offering choices counted in powers of 2 ($2 \times 2 = 4$, $2 \times 2 \times 2 = 8$, etc.), we will come to the sixteenth power of $2 = 65,536$, or 64K, as we call it. This is the number of unique memory locations that sixteen address lines can specify.

The next group of pins constitutes the data bus. These are the lines the data moves on. The Z-80 uses an 8-bit data word, so there are eight data lines. The rest of the pins are used for control of the processes involved in the computer's operations; for example, the system control bus line regulates the flow of information throughout the computer system.

Now that we have some idea of its operating connections, we are ready to visit the microprocessor chip itself. To do this we will have to be reduced to the size of electrons. Beam us down, Scotty!

Stan Veit is editor-in-chief of Computer Shopper. *He is one of the pioneers of the computer industry, having opened the first computer store on the East Coast and the first robot store in the world.*

An Electron's-Eye View

Spread out before us is a vast piece of silicon real estate called the Z-80. It is composed of etched sections of silicon material, each with intermixed materials called "doped" areas. Seen from above, the chip resembles a city map with rectilinear paths and sizable areas that perform specific functions. These silicon "neighborhoods" are easily identified by their uses.

The first section we will look at contains the registers. These are convenient storage areas for memory, much like the warehouse district of a city. All the microprocessor's operations are performed on instructions or data contained in the registers. The Z-80 holds 208 such memory bins accessible to the programmer.

Some of the registers are devoted to special functions. The program counter, for example, holds the address of the instruction being fetched from memory. When its contents are put on the address lines, the register is incremented and then reads the address of the next instruction. If the program contains a jump, the new value is automatically placed in the counter.

Another special-purpose register is the stack pointer, which holds the address of the top of a stack of data stored anywhere in memory. A stack is a sequential group of memory locations in the shape of a chest of drawers. If need be, the computer can temporarily store data here by pushing it onto a stack.

Now that we've explored the memory neighborhoods on the chip, let's visit the business district. Called the arithmetic logic unit (ALU), this is the computational part of the microprocessor. It does all 8-bit arithmetic and logical operations such as add, subtract, logical OR, logical AND, compare, increment, left or right shifts, and testing of bits.

The rest of the chip—the government district, if you will—is devoted to the control of computer instructions and the sequence of operations. The instructions recognized by the chip are part of its design, and their number and complexity define its power.

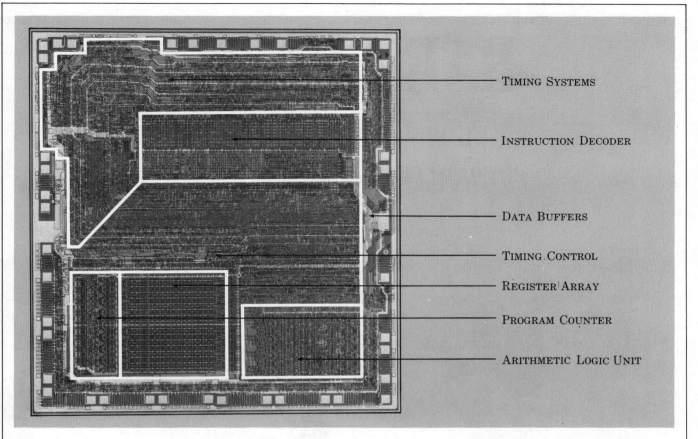

TIMING SYSTEMS

INSTRUCTION DECODER

DATA BUFFERS

TIMING CONTROL

REGISTER ARRAY

PROGRAM COUNTER

ARITHMETIC LOGIC UNIT

Each chip design has a different instruction set, though some include the instruction sets of previous microprocessors.

For a program to be executed, specific instructions are placed in the computer's memory and the information to be processed is fed into the machine. As the central processor operates, the control section fetches the instructions from memory, places them into the instruction register and decodes them. The control section then generates the signals to read or write data from or to the registers. It also regulates the ALU and provides the external control signals.

Since all bytes are of a similar format, how do computers know whether they're getting instructions or data? The answer is: they don't. Computers crash if they get data when they need instructions, and vice versa, so it's important for the programmer to supply a precise sequence of operations in composing the program. In addition, the computer can only operate by following this sequence at the proper time. The timing is controlled by a clock circuit elsewhere on the main board of the computer.

Chains of Command

You are now normal size, and you are sitting in front of the computer. Turn it on and load BASIC. Type PRINT 2 + 2, press the ENTER key, and the BASIC interpreter will translate your instructions into a form that the computer can understand (a pattern of 1s and 0s called machine language).

The instruction PRINT tells the computer that the result of the operation is to be displayed on the video screen. The machine code for the quantity "2" is stored in the general-purpose register. The symbol "+" tells the computer that the ALU is to add the next number received to the quantity already in the register and to place the result in the accumulator. The number 2 comes along, is translated into machine code and added to the previous number 2, and the resulting machine code for the quantity 4 is placed in the accumulator. The instruction PRINT in BASIC causes many complicated machine-language instructions to occur. The outcome is the result of the arithmetic operation—in this case, 4—displayed on the video screen.

Had we been running a program to add 2 + 2 and save the results in memory, the computer would have shown the results and at the same time saved them at the specified memory location.

Of such building blocks, whether machine language or higher-level, English-like commands, are programs written. The microprocessor chip has no way of knowing whether it's crunching numbers, processing text or playing a game. The ultimate team player, it just follows orders, millions of them per second, and does what it's told. ∎

HARD FACTS

Anatomy of a Personal Computer
by Marty Norman

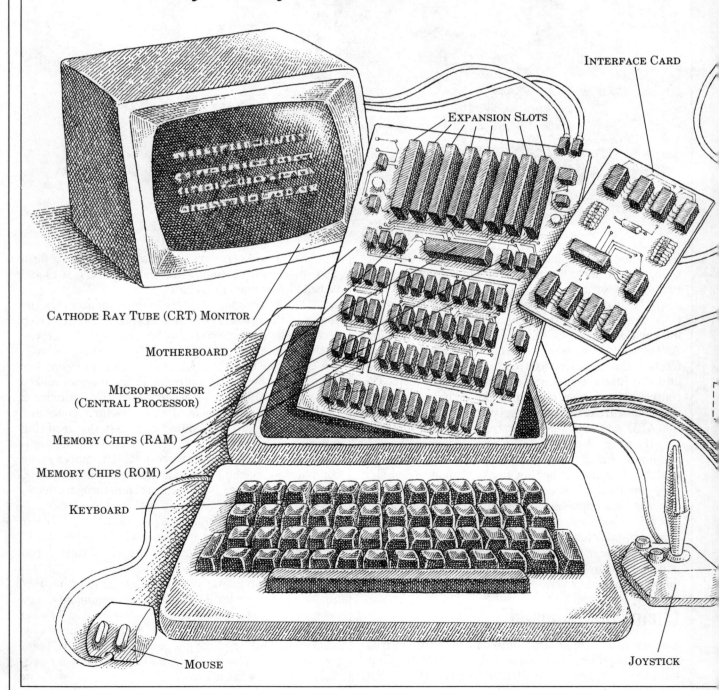

INTERFACE CARD

EXPANSION SLOTS

CATHODE RAY TUBE (CRT) MONITOR

MOTHERBOARD

MICROPROCESSOR
(CENTRAL PROCESSOR)

MEMORY CHIPS (RAM)

MEMORY CHIPS (ROM)

KEYBOARD

MOUSE

JOYSTICK

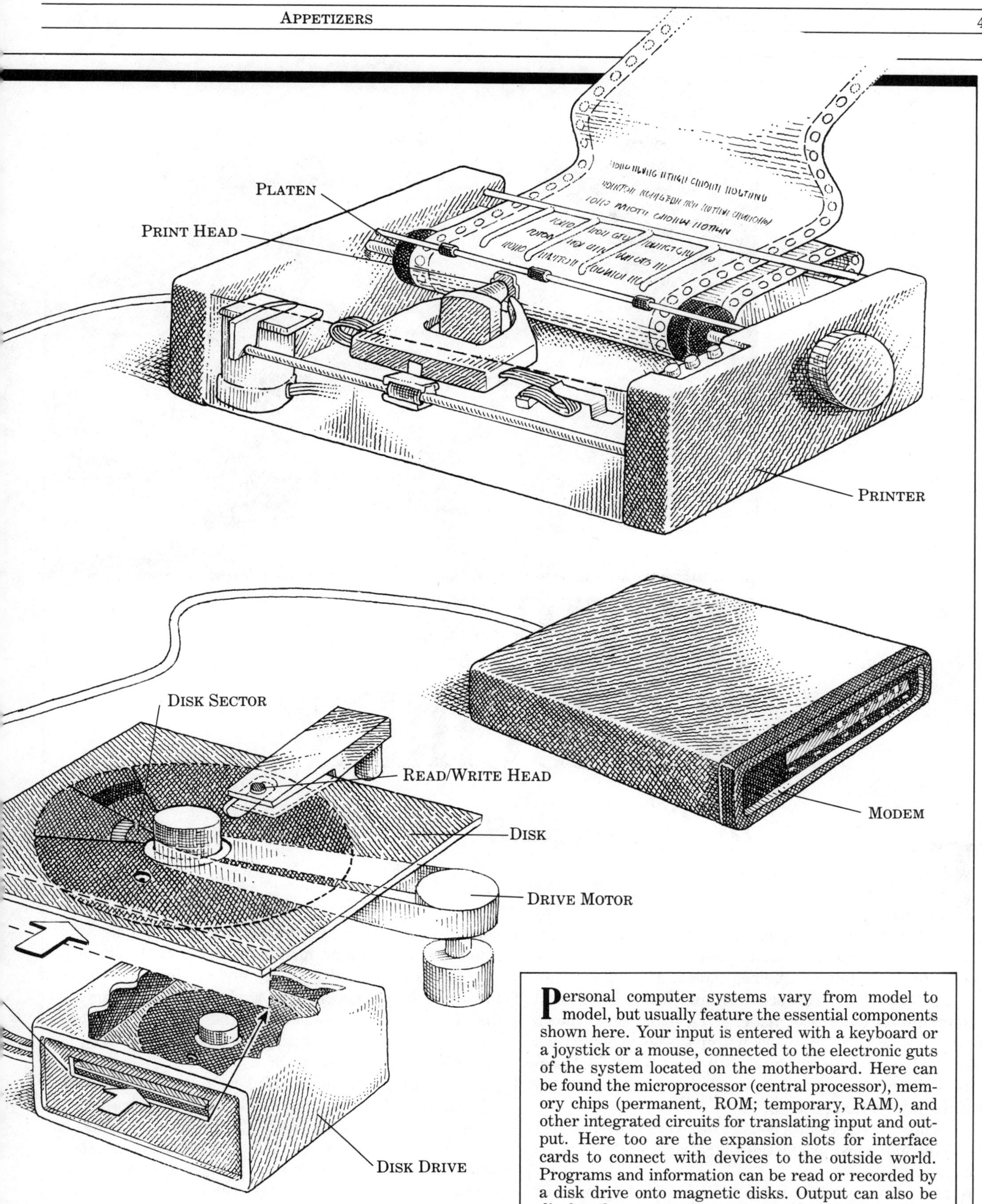

PLATEN

PRINT HEAD

PRINTER

DISK SECTOR

READ/WRITE HEAD

MODEM

DISK

DRIVE MOTOR

DISK DRIVE

Personal computer systems vary from model to model, but usually feature the essential components shown here. Your input is entered with a keyboard or a joystick or a mouse, connected to the electronic guts of the system located on the motherboard. Here can be found the microprocessor (central processor), memory chips (permanent, ROM; temporary, RAM), and other integrated circuits for translating input and output. Here too are the expansion slots for interface cards to connect with devices to the outside world. Programs and information can be read or recorded by a disk drive onto magnetic disks. Output can also be displayed on a monitor, preserved on paper with a printer, or sent to another computer via a modem.

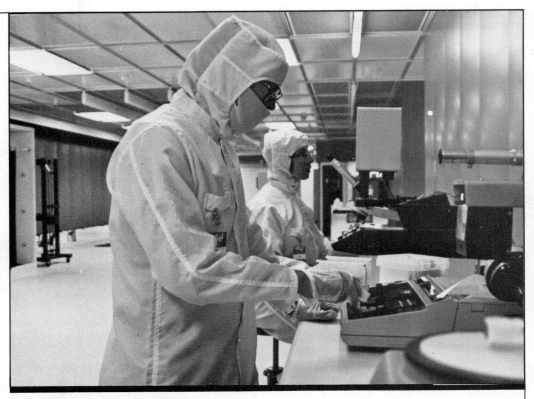

BIRTHING MICROCHIPS

by Tay Vaughan

E-beams, plasma etchers, gold evaporators, scanning electron microscopes, four-stack furnaces, spin-track developers and ion implanters: these are just some of the highly specialized tools that fill the "clean rooms" where microprocessors and other integrated computer circuits are made. This equipment allows computer scientists to work within the scale of microns (one micron equals one millionth of a meter) and perform the optical procedures and chemistries required of the fabrication process.

Integrated circuits consist of layers that manifest specific electrical properties, each layer etched with a

Tay Vaughan is a senior scientist at ACI Engineering Consultants. He has a Coast Guard captain's license, flies airplanes and plays the cello when he is not busy making clean rooms even cleaner.

carefully designed microscopic pattern of lines and junctions to carry or manipulate electrical voltages. The smaller the width of the etched lines, the more lines can be squeezed onto a chip. The shorter the distance between connections, the faster things can happen. Computer operating speeds are measured in nanoseconds, or billionths of a second.

Microchips begin as thin, round wafers of pure silicon, a half-millimeter thick, cut from carefully grown crystal columns up to six inches in diameter. The wafers are polished to a flat surface, and interferometers check for planar evenness using parallel surfacing techniques that measure tolerances in terms of angstroms. (There are ten thousand angstroms in a micron.)

Highly paid designers initiate the manufacturing

process, playing color-coded computer-assisted design (CAD) machines like three-dimensional chess masters at a tournament. A common chip may have from eight to twelve layers of interlocked tracery of conductive, semiconductive or nonconductive material. The patterns of lines and junctions for each layer (as well as the materials themselves) are determined by the requirements and function of the specific microdevice as well by the limits of planar geometry. Most layers must interconnect with the layer above and/or the layer below. While children may learn to draw the outline of a house without lifting pencil from paper or crossing an existing line, microchip designers draw entire cities replete with roadways and subways following the same strict rules.

The CAD system prints out large-scale drawings of a microchip's tracery, layer by layer. After each layer's drawing has been carefully checked manually, often on a large floor where scientists crawl about on hands and knees searching for errors, photo masks are made.

Microchip manufacture is a photoetching process with roots in both transistor and printed circuit technologies. But no longer must photographs of each layer of circuitry be painstakingly reduced from full-size drawings to microscopic dimensions. Just as most newspapers use word-processed data for typesetting, refined computer data from the CAD system can directly guide a powerful beam of electrons to etch the required pattern of lines needed for each layer.

Photoetching remains, however, at the heart of microchip manufacture, and it is a "wet process" fabrication system. To etch various layers of a chip, these are covered with a layer of photoresist, a liquid coating that, when dry, reacts to certain colors of light or to a beam of electrons. Exposed photoresist can then be washed away with developers (or will remain, depending on whether a positive or negative solution is specified and depending on the "recipe" used).

Particularly in prototype laboratories, there is a great deal of hand developing. Many process engineers are therefore quite finicky, like testy French chefs at a five-star restaurant. Using vacuum wands, our chefs carry wafers back and forth between spinners, coaters and special drying ovens. Some have an intuitive sense about the sheen being just right or the oven a little too hot, and they will hover over their work, tweaking dials, adjusting and perfecting. Wet-process chemistry is an art.

Electron-beam (E-beam) equipment occupies a singularly important position in the panoply of instruments and apparata seen on the wafer fabrication floor. This equipment, the chef's finest carving knife, draws the patterns upon which all else in the production process is dependent. Costing over a million dollars, E-beam machinery is supplied with its own dedicated

Steps in producing a microchip: computer-aided design (above); testing new dies (facing page); removing a wafer from the ion oven (below).

environmental chamber even within the clean room.

Where photoresist does not cover the substrate, acids etch the material, carving channels and lagoons which, in the subsequent layering step of fabrication, can be filled with conductive metals or other esoteric materials called for by the recipe.

Ion implanters are used to "dope" layers with impurities by shooting molecules at the surface under high vacuum conditions. Diffusion furnaces coat molecules onto the surface of the wafer using violent chemicals and natural molecular affinities at temperatures exceeding 1,500 degrees Fahrenheit. Furnaces can also remove selected molecules in a bath of hot oxygen. Silicon itself is layered by epitaxy. Pure silicon is an insulator, doped silicon is semiconductive, and aluminum oxide (among other metals used in microchips) is conductive.

Carefully following the recipe, process chefs expose the photoresist-covered substrate. They develop it. They etch away unwanted portions. They build up a layer of silicon. They dope it. They cover this with more photoresist, then expose, develop, etch, coat, bake, expose, develop and bake some more. The combinations and protocols are myriad in this painstaking layer-by-layer fabrication process. It can take as many

CLEAN ROOMS

Looking through plate-glass partitions into Class 10 clean rooms where microchips are made is an awesome first-time experience. Gowned, goggled, hooded and masked workers hunch over strange, sleek machines or stand about in small groups before complex computer keyboards and dedicated monitors.

The Class 10 clean rooms are on the order of eight hundred to a thousand times freer of particulate matter than a hospital operating room. Here there are fewer than ten motes of anything larger than a half-micron in diameter per each cubic foot of air.

A hundred thousand cubic feet of filtered, humidified and temperature-controlled air pushed into the room each minute is enough to quickly remove the odors and dust of everyday life. An entire ceiling of high-efficiency particulate air (HEPA) filters traps all but the minutest contaminants. Air drains out through grates in the floor or along the lower walls, carrying with it such detritus as the 15-micron epithelial cells and other particles naturally sloughed from the skin of workers. Pencils are prohibited here because invisible airborne graphite particles not only are "large," but are also efficient electrical conductors and can therefore short-circuit the fine lines of a microchip template in production.

Computer-controlled cooling coils, humidifiers and automatic dampers regulate this environment. Variation by a single degree of temperature can destroy a week's work. And the 120 decibels of sound energy at the fan motor itself is reduced from loudness at the threshold of pain to the quiet of a concert hall after flowing with the air through specially manufactured anechoic and attenuating chambers and through insulated ducts large enough to walk in. Low-frequency airborne noise can rumble the fine optical equipment and frustrate alignment. People speak softly in the clean room.

T.V.

With all the precautions taken in clean rooms, the production of microchips still requires constant checking and rechecking of circuit-bearing wafers.

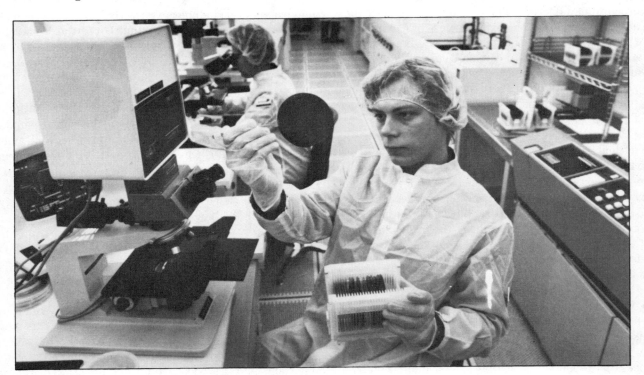

as six weeks to fabricate a microchip. Each step of the recipe requires handling, and some steps—particularly in the diffusion furnaces—require many hours while molecules attach to molecules according to nature's inexorable laws.

A back-lapper removes much of the finished wafer's thickness and reduces its weight. A diamond cutter is then used to carve out each individual die, a die-bonder fastens the chip to a pattern of interconnects, and the chips are encased in plastic. Leads are attached, using special soldering techniques, and the finished microchip is packaged for shipment. This finishing process requires a great deal of handwork, and for this reason much assembly is performed in areas of the world where labor rates are cheap. A single container of microchips air-freighted abroad has perhaps the highest value-to-weight ratio of any commodity in present-day world commerce.

Under the most trying conditions and with demanding high-resolution requirements, some chefs in the prototype lab might be pleased with a yield of a single working microchip per hundred dies on a wafer. So many things can go wrong. But yields are an important consideration to a company's profit margin. Normally, if 30 to 40 percent of the chips on a wafer perform as desired, the yield is considered good. If 80 percent work, yield is considered excellent. (Bad chips go into a trash bin and are eventually buried at the city refuse dump for anthropologists a millennium hence to unearth and reverse-engineer in order to make pronouncements upon today's state of the art.)

Throughout the fabrication process, the wafer and dies are tested. This quality control is critical for efficient, economic production because contaminants are everywhere in the process (though in most cases are controllable). Vibration is reduced by separating and isolating the specially engineered wafer fabrication areas from the rest of the facility and by carefully balancing air supply and mechanical systems. Equipment floats on air bags and springs. Ductwork and piping inside the building is specially designed. There is no clanging of hot-water pipes in a wafer fabrication facility.

Microchip manufacturing technology faces a limit of scale. To further reduce line width to submicron dimensions in order to produce very large-scale integrated circuits (VLSI) and to stack many more layers of very compact lines in the vertical architecture required by very high-speed integrated circuits (VHSIC), breakthroughs are required. Wet processing must be done away with. At widths of a micron, photoengraving can cause lines that are too narrow or too wide or troughs too deep or dangerously undercut by etching "in all directions."

To avoid the wet process entirely, the E-beam is being used for "direct-write" etching because it can

deliver very fine line resolution. It is difficult, however, to control its energy level and the depth of its cut. Impetuously, it hacks and hews into substrate layers and can destroy many days of cumulative effort by cutting into layers below.

Laser writing techniques are being developed that provide not only highly accurate direct-write resolution but also some control of depth. Not available yet are molecular beam systems that allow great control of impact velocity. With heavy molecules bombarding a substrate, velocity can be altered the way a sand-blaster alters air pressure to do fine detailed work, thus achieving high resolution.

The manufacture of microchips is indeed a study of scale. As the scale becomes smaller and smaller, the very molecular fabric of the device itself and its electrical properties change, imposing finite design limits. The engineers without blinders who are working at the technological threshold claim "You can't say can't" about anything, and they constantly scan the edges of their peripheral vision for solutions of scale. Ultimately, it may be that microchips as they are known today will be outmoded by other techniques of voltage amplication and information management that are more appropriate to submicron or angstrom scales. ∎

ON SILICON

Though silicon is the second most common element on the earth's surface, constituting close to one-quarter of its rocky crust, few people outside the microchip industry have ever seen it in its pure, dark gray crystalline form. In nature, silicon is found only in combination with other elements, forming common minerals like quartz and flint (in fact, its name derives from *silex*, Latin for "flint").

In industry, compounds of silicon (rhymes with "silly Khan") are used to make glass, ceramics, enamels and dyes. Synthetic silicon oxides known as silicones (pronounced like "silly Cones") are employed as lubricants and waterproofing compounds and to make rubber that is chemically inert—hence the use of these oxides in prosthesis and plastic surgery.

To produce pure silicon for the making of microcomputer components, silicon dioxide (you've seen it as beach sand) is heated with carbon in an electric furnace, then subjected to further chemical treatment. Large crystals of pure silicon are "grown" from the molten element by introducing a crystal "seed," which is then slowly withdrawn with the substance clinging to it.

Because silicon is as chemically active as carbon, which it resembles in many ways (e.g., fossils consist of organic matter in which silicon has replaced carbon atoms), scientists have speculated about an alternative organic chemistry that could give rise to silicon-based life forms in other parts of the universe. For all we know, in the Altair solar system the people may be silicon-based and the computers carbon-based.

MICROCOMPUTERS TODAY AND TOMORROW

by Marcian E. Hoff, Jr.

Soon after the integrated circuit was developed, just two decades ago, it became apparent that very complex circuits would be possible. In some cases a major portion of a computer, called a module, could be constructed as a single circuit. In fact, this made it possible to build a large system by breaking it up into a number of different kinds of modules, each of which could be a circuit.

Before long, families of modules were developed. These families were quite versatile, and using the right types of modules allowed for building a very wide variety of equipment.

But the integrated circuit business was changing. Every year it became possible to make more and more complicated circuits. So it became desirable to make more complicated modules. The problem was that an increase in the complexity of a module meant a decrease in its versatility, so that eventually a computer or other piece of equipment would have no more than one of each type of module. The economics of the integrated circuit business made this undesirable. High volume was the goal, but a different type of module for each type of system being built meant that no more than a few hundred or a few thousand of any one type of module would be made.

The microprocessor represented a solution to this problem. It was a new type of module that was very versatile. With some very simple programming techniques, we could make this module appear to be many different kinds of modules. In other words, it could be customized by programming.

Microprocessors, or microcomputers, are just miniature computers. In general, they can be used for most of the applications for which larger computers are used. The earliest microprocessor was very poor in performance, and there were many things it could not do. Over the years, however, performance has been improved so that microprocessors now rival machines that in some cases cost a thousand times more.

Much of the progress in reducing cost and improving performance has been made in the last ten years, since the the energy crunch hit and we were told about making things smaller. For a while, the automobile industry looked at making things smaller, but nobody took it to heart quite the way the semiconductor industry did.

Smaller is better. In the case of the semiconductor industry, smaller is *really* better. In a typical integrated circuit of today, there are several thousand components interconnected by metal lines. Some circuits have reached the point where they have almost half a million components on one chip.

The fabrication process is fairly straightforward. Start out with a piece of silicon. Apply some photoresist. Expose the photoresist selectively. Develop it, so that it's removed in some places and left in other places. Then, where the silicon is exposed, subject it to various treatments: dip it in acids, bombard it with impurities and change its characteristics. There are a variety of process steps, but they are all based on this photographic definition of components.

How big should the circuit be? In general, the cost of processing a wafer of silicon is somewhat a function of the size of each component, or feature, but the smaller the circuit the less it costs. The actual size will be determined by the average feature size. In each of the detailed pieces of circuitry, how big can they be?

Marcian E. Hoff, Jr., is a vice-president for research at Atari, Inc. While at Intel, he developed the first microprocessor: the Intel 4004.

The 4-bit 4004 (1971), the original microprocessor, was the first commercially available integrated circuit programmable for different tasks.

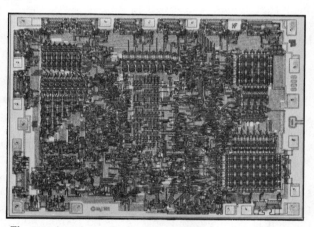

The 8008 (1972) was the first microprocessor to handle 8 bits at once but could address only 16K bytes of memory.

The 8-bit 8080 (1974), six times faster than its predecessor, set the stage for the first personal computers.

CHIP GENERATIONS

The history of personal computers can be traced through the progress of the microprocessors available as their brains. Each microchip manufacturer has brought out improved progeny within families of processors, retaining similar instruction sets for upward mobility. Though each successive design may not be a quantum leap forward, there is a steady movement toward faster and more powerful handling of more bits of information at a time. Here are members (with introduction dates) of one of the most celebrated microchip families from Intel.

The 16-bit 8088 (1978), used in the IBM PC, addresses 1024K bytes of memory (compared to the 8080's 64K bytes).

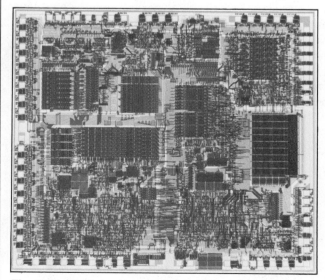

The 80186 (1982) combines on-board clock and input/output circuits, pointing the way for faster, more compact IBM-compatible machines.

There are a variety of steps in making a circuit to determine this feature size.

Say we want to cut the feature size in half. The linear dimensions of the circuit would be cut in half, the area would be cut in a quarter, and presumably we'd get four times as many circuits for the same amount of money. In this manner, we improve the number of circuits per given amount of silicon. But another step takes place. The circuit runs faster—in fact, it runs twice as fast—and it can do more calculations per second. So now each circuit costs about a quarter as much while it does twice as much work, and we have about an eight-to-one improvement.

Over a ten-year period, typical feature size has gone from about ten microns to about two microns, with an average reduction factor of five. In the most current processes, the typical feature (two microns) is about one ten-thousandth of an inch. On that order of resolution, you could publish a whole Ph.D. thesis in less than a square inch.

We are in a worldwide race for smallness. Essentially everybody interested in integrated circuits is trying to make things smaller. One of the key questions is how far can it go? There are limits imposed by the sheer difficulty of making a circuit. Trying to make it smaller poses further problems, but most of these can be fixed. Some are imposed by lithography. We are getting down to the point where ordinary visible light, the kind we use to look around the room, cannot resolve the features. But there are ways around that. We may go to electrons. Electron microscopes or x-rays give higher resolutions. Also, some processing steps have to be resolved, but in general these can be made to work.

Are there any fundamental limits that we have to worry about? Obviously there are some. Atoms have finite size. We are defining features and items that are made of atoms. We cannot get down to subatomic dimensions, which would put the limit maybe a factor of ten thousand away from where we are today. That's a long way, especially if we reduce feature size only by a factor of five every ten years. We don't have to worry about it in our lifetime.

But there is another, much closer limit. The smaller the circuit, the noisier it becomes. We have to reduce the operating voltages, or signals, that represent the information traveling through the circuit. It's like the graininess you get when you blow up a negative in film. As we reduce the size of the circuit, it becomes difficult to distinguish the signals we're looking for from the inherent noise of the circuit behavior.

How far away are we? At the present time, our signals are on the order of a thousand times larger than this kind of noise. But if we reduce the linear dimensions of the circuit by, say, a factor of twenty, the signals will come down to about ten times the size of the noise. At that point, the circuits start to become unreliable. The computer starts to make mistakes. In fact, it starts to make mistakes very, very rapidly as we try to go beyond that dimension. The circuitry is such that almost none of the known techniques for making circuits more reliable will work if we try to go below these dimensions.

Today the failure rates due to circuit noise are such that if all the computers in the world ran from now until the end of the universe, there would be perhaps one mistake. When we reduce today's dimensions by a factor of twenty, we perhaps get to the borderline of usefulness. But this still allows about a factor of ten thousand to one in reduction of cost vs. performance. We have quite a way to go. Considering the amount of effort going on in this area, I think we'll see a push toward that limit. There are some ways we can extend the limit by reducing temperature so that internal friction is reduced, but this tends to reduce convenience. (We'd have to carry a refrigerator around with every circuit.)

I think we can say that a lot more computing power will be available in the near future. What the next generation must decide is how this power will be used. Despite many upheavals, the refinements in the industrial revolution have generally reduced disadvantages and increased advantages. As we develop computers, we can make them a bane or a blessing. ∎

Answers
1. IMSAI 8080
2. Processor Technology's Sol
3. Ohio Scientific Challenger
4. Digital Group
5. Sphere
6. Apple I

SOUP AND CRACKERS

Artwork for preceding page

Artist:
  Romelia Takenaka
Computer:
  Astrocade (Bally) video game system
Software:
  BASIC with extended graphics
Input:
  Joystick

THE MERRY PRANKSTERS OF MICROCOMPUTING

by Allan Lundell and Geneen Marie Haugen

The year was 1971. Two silent figures were observing the entrances to SLAC, the complex that housed the Stanford Linear Accelerator. With one of the newest, shiniest atom smashers in the world, the SLAC facility at Stanford University was a physicist's dream—a center for investigation into the most basic elements of reality.

But the two observers were not interested in the nature of reality. Racing to a side entrance, they snuck past the SLAC security patrols and entered the classified high-technology library. They knew their way around, having visited the SLAC facility several times before. It was always exciting to break in; there was no limit to the information they could absorb.

This time, however, they were on a specific mission. Thumbing through a document on multifrequency telecommunications systems, Steve Wozniak whispered to his friend Steve Jobs.

"This is it! This matches the frequencies in *Esquire*. With this information, we can build one!"

The future creators of the Apple II computer pulled out their pens and notebooks, scribbling data almost faster than a high-speed line printer. This was no minor treasure. They had unearthed some of the secrets of the little blue box, topic of an infamous *Esquire* article on phone phreaks by Ron Rosenbaum—and the magical device needed to enter the phone system, the world's electronic nervous system.

Days of intensive effort followed, until finally they held their first model, with wires and coils spill-

ing out, up to the phone and punched out the secret touch-tone codes. After many tries and exasperating failures, the phone finally rang a long-distance number. Someone answered . . .

Jobs yelled out to the person on the line: "Hello! We've got a blue box, and we are calling you from California! Where are you located?"

A little confused, their first planetary contact yelled back: "I'm in Los Angeles!"

The boys needed help. Now that they knew the *Esquire* story was truth and not fiction, they were sure its hero, Cap'n Crunch, must be real, too. The two Steves put out the word through the underground that they wanted to meet him.

It was some meeting. The infamous Cap'n had named himself after Cap'n Crunch breakfast cereal

---

Allan Lundell is the co-author of The Newest Art, *on computer graphics and animation. Geneen Marie Haugen is a free-lance writer and novelist.*

Better laughter through electronics: Steven Jobs (left) and Stephen Wozniak examine their latest creation.

THE PHONE PHREAKS

Phone phreaking consists of accessing the telephone network in ways that were not intended by its designers. In the late 1950s Bell Labs created the Multi-Frequency Signaling System, whose MF tones were intended to directly control the "long lines" switching network. The Touch Tone telephone dial would put out a set of tones that were completely different from the MF signaling tones. You would send Touch Tone signals to your local switching office, which would then send MF tones on up the line to instruct the network as to what telephone number you wanted to be connected to.

When the MF signaling system was devised, it cost a lot of money to build the tone generators and decoders turned out by Western Electric, Bell's supplier. No one foresaw that solid-state devices would drop in price so drastically that electronic hobbyists would be able to pick up the parts at Radio Shack and just throw together something that would sound to the receiving equipment like the Bell System's equipment.

The phone phreaks discovered the MF frequen-

Tones for phones: using a blue box (above) to break into Ma Bell's communications network.

cies in the *Bell System Technical Journal*, put out by Bell Labs for its network engineers. Published with a blue cover, the journal is called the Blue Book in the industry. It is no wonder, then, that the phreaks called their electronic wonder toy "the blue box."

To show how a blue box worked, let's discuss how the network worked in general. When you place a long-distance call from your home, the number is captured by an "incoming register." (The first few digits long distance.) It then sends MF tones for the digits up the wire, and the "long lines" equipment handles it from there. When the party at the other end picks up the phone, a "supervision" signal is sent back to your central office, which means: "They picked up, so start billing." When you hang up, your central office stops the billing machine and signals are sent to "dissolve" the connection. The "long lines" machine now has to tell the machine at the other end that the call is finished by sending a tone of 2,600 Hertz down the line as an indication that the line is free.

A phone phreak would dial a long-distance call, usually to an 800 "toll-free" number (800 numbers start billing at the other end of the call, that is, when the receiving party picks up the call, and billing computers at the calling party's end are instructed to disregard 800 calls on billing tapes). While the 800 number was ringing, and before anyone could pick up at the other end, the phreak would transmit a tone of 2,600 Hz into the phone line, using the blue box speaker held over the mouthpiece. The machine at the other end of the circuit "heard" that the calling party had hung up and disconnected its end of the call.

When the phreak now stopped sending the tone, the machine figured, "Oh, this trunk circuit has now been seized by the other end, so I will now set up to receive signals (MF tones) telling me where to route the next call." The phreak next entered in the sequence of tones that would route his call anywhere in the world, and the phone company computer system snapped to an electronic "Yes, sir!" and connected the call. When the called party picked up the phone, the "supervision" signal was returned to the originating central office; but since that billing machine knew only that an 800 call had been placed, it threw away the billing information.

It's as simple(?) as that. Let's face it, the phone phreaks had to know as much about the network as any telephone traffic engineer. They were the electronic crossword puzzle solvers of the pre-computer era. Now their brand of intellectual curiosity and ingenuity is being focused on the most complex and involving of all mind toys: the personal computer.

CHESHIRE CATALYST (Richard Cheshire), telecomputer consultant and publisher of *TAP, "The Hobbyist Journal for the Communications Revolution"* (Room 603, 147 W. 42 St., New York City 10036)

when he'd discovered that its free bos'n whistle produced a fundamental tone for long-distance calls. He'd also gleaned phone intelligence information from Bell System publications and by making himself a nuisance at the Bell switching offices. Cap'n Crunch was charting the unknown seas of the phone system with the true *Star Trek* spirit of seeing what was there, going where no man had gone before and having fun doing it.

Woz had imagined Crunch to be a superengineer, a consultant to the computer industry, an ultra genius driving a van equipped to do everything but fly—a hybrid version of James Bond, the Man from U.N.C.L.E. and the professor on Gilligan's Island. But at this first meeting at the Berkeley dorms ol' Woz did a double take. Standing before him was, well, a madman. With long, frizzy hair, the Crunch was wild-eyed and almost toothless, like a pirate from the seven seas. All he needed was an eye patch and a wooden leg.

Cap'n Crunch launched immediately into his discoveries. After a few hours had passed, Wozniak and Jobs knew how to access different countries, overseas information operators, satellites and transoceanic cables. It was a worthwhile evening indeed.

The Blue Meanies

Woz and Jobs were handed an opportunity to test out their new-found knowledge late that night. On their way to Jobs' house in Silicon Valley, the car died out near a phone booth in the low-life town of Hayward. They tried to beep their way back to Berkeley with their trusty blue box, but Woz had trouble making the connection. He was getting very nervous trying to "explain" to the operator what he was doing, when a police car pulled up and slammed on the brakes, lights flashing. The officer sauntered over to the phone booth, and the two Steves knew they'd been tricked by the operator. The officer, trained in the ways of criminals caught in the act, shifted his attention to some nearby bushes—thinking the boys had thrown something in them. In this instant, Jobs passed the blue box to Woz, who quickly shoved it in his coat pocket.

Brave move. But to no avail: the officer routinely searched both Steves and liberated them of their new tool. The officer randomly pushed buttons, and the blue box responded: *bleep bleeep blup bloop*!

"What's this?" he demanded.

Woz took a chance, stammering, "I-its a m-m-music synthesizer, officer."

Another police officer arrived and started trying to figure the thing out. He grilled them: "What's the orange button?"

"That's for calibration," Jobs said. "It's designed to interface with a computer."

The two boys were escorted into the back of the patrol cruiser. Feeling doomed, they were beginning to realize that being a pioneer and a prankster had its risks. Then the cop with the box turned around from the front seat and handed it to them, saying, "A good idea, but a guy named Moog beat you to it . . ."

Phone Fun

There is probably no one in the computer industry who has not heard of Steve Wozniak and Steve Jobs. There are a lot of people in the industry who have heard of John Draper, alias Cap'n Crunch, and there are a lot of people who haven't. But probably everyone in Western society knows someone like them: The guy with the ham radio next door. The kid down the street who crashed his school's computer from home. The hacker in the office across the hall who's always tampering with everyone else's files. They all seem to be propelled by some inborn drive to do what few—if any—can do or have done.

These are the brethren of the high-tech frontier, the would-be merry pranksters of computerdom. The brethren break new ground, thinking the unthinkable, charting the unknown. Wherever their minds go, we will all go—eventually. No one holds the future so much in their hands as the pioneers of today's super-technology. Thank God, they've got a sense of humor.

In the formative years of the brethren, before they'd settled on a field of specialization, when they were young and unconsciously adventurous, they were unaware of the strength of the cultural rules. For some of them, a prankstering spirit could mean disaster, but Woz and Jobs seemed to live an almost magical existence beyond the law and trouble. After mastering the blue box, they organized blue-box parties at the Berkeley dorms. Once a week, with an audience of twenty or thirty people, they held demonstrations. They'd call operators in other countries and go around the world by switching from one operator in one country to an operator in another. Finally a phone would ring in the dorm room next door. Someone would pick it up and hear Woz's voice, coming from around the world.

They'd call Dial-A-Joke in New York (Woz subsequently started his own dial-a-joke service), weather numbers in Australia, phone booths in Capetown, bars in Ireland, all amplified so the entire audience could hear. Before the night was through, everyone in the room would talk to some friend or relative in another country—all for free, all for fun. Woz was always thinking up fantastic feats for the Berkeley Blue Box Show. Everyone loved him, and he loved being the star. Before long he was calling himself Berkeley Blue and had an almost professional routine. When he was finished blowing away the audience, Blue's partner Jobs, code-named "Oct Tobor," would step in and offer shiny new blue boxes for sale—guaranteed at a low, low price of $80. Shades of things to come . . .

Woz and Jobs didn't just hand-wire their boxes. Woz created them with state-of-the art technology and laid them out on personally designed printed circuit boards. This was a professional operation, a miniature high-technology company, complete with product, sales, service and support. Woz immersed himself in the tech, Jobs collected the money. Those boys sold over two hundred boxes and lived off the revenues for an entire school year.

Azure Hazards

A charmed life, some might say. But then the blue-box luck ran out. One night Woz and Jobs stopped at a pizza parlor practically next door to Woz's elementary school in the Silicon Valley town of Sunnyvale. They were on their way to Berkeley to sell a blue box, but they needed some money right away and thought they might save themselves the trip by selling it in Sunnyvale. Almost everyone feels safe in a familiar haunt in their hometown, and Jobs and Woz were no exception. Chewing their pizza, they surveyed the customers at the other tables. The families were out of the question. So were the tables full of teenagers.

But there were some really disreputable-looking characters at another table who looked as if they might be able to put the blue box to good use. Feeling confident, Wozniak and Jobs approached the table and had a low conversation about the merits of the box. Were they interested? They were interested, all right. And they were hooked after they watched a demonstration. They didn't have the money right then, so they took Woz and Jobs out to their car under the pretext of giving them their business card.

The only problem was that the business card was a gun. That blue box changed ownership pretty fast, and the shady characters drove off. They had the box—but they didn't know how to use it, and Woz and Jobs never told them. The secrets of Cap'n Crunch were safe.

In 1974 Cap'n Crunch, a.k.a. John Draper, was busted for blue-boxing. For the second time. By federal, state and local authorities. Fraud by wire was the charge. He had already spent six months in a federal penitentiary in Pennsylvania. The second time, he was sent to Lompoc—a federal pen in California.

The likable yet unfortunate Cap'n. How could he have known when he learned how to make free long-distance calls from blind kids who whistled their frequencies into the phone that he'd do time? How could he have known that the innocent free whistle inside the boxes of Cap'n Crunch cereal would lead to this? How could he have known when he blue-boxed his way to Nixon's bedside to inform the President of the na-

tion's toilet paper crisis that he might end up in the slammer?

In Lompoc an informer for the Mafia broke his back when he refused to impart the secrets of the blue box. That was the end of Cap'n Crunch, but not of John Draper—a man described by Wozniak as being wanted by the FBI because he was "too intelligent."

If Draper hadn't been made such a folk hero by the press, it may not have gone so bad for him. Then again, his final stay in jail led him to computer fame and fortune. It was while he was in a work program that he wrote Easy Writer, the first professional-style word processing program for the Apple.

A couple of years later, IBM was looking around for software to bundle with its PC. By that time, there were better packages than Easy Writer, but someone at IBM had a sense of humor. IBM asked Draper and his new software company, "Cap'n Software," to design and program this now classic word processing package for its first entry into the personal computer market—an irony not lost on those familiar with his bouts with AT&T.

After their brushes with the dark side of the force, John Draper, Stephen Wozniak and Steve Jobs got a whole lot smarter. They wised up to some of the mysterious workings of the power structures. They lost their innocence, but they gained something else. Wozniak and Jobs struck it rich early in the Silicon Rush. They made history with their Volkswagen-like Apple II. John Draper became wealthy enough to drive a Mercedes-Benz through the streets of Berkeley with his first release of Easy Writer for the Apple II.

New fortunes are still being made regularly in Silicon Valley, if not as often as they once were. And empires that once were, already are no longer. A new crop of microcomputer genius-pranksters are making headlines. Their exploits have inspired movies and a television show. As technology's first wave of pranksters comes of age, they are shifting their curiosity to things that are, as Wozniak explains, "creative and useful." But they're still doing things that few—if any—have done. Wozniak sponsored live satellite link-ups with the Soviet Union at his outdoor musical US Festivals. Draper is masterminding a vast artificial intelligence network. Some of the other early pioneers are funding private space programs. Some are pursuing medical applications such as life-extension. Others are entering the arena of politics.

In the realm of genius-pranksters and supertechnology, just about anything is still possible. Putting the most powerful tools into the hands of individuals with creativity, integrity and courage is bound to have awesome consequences. When the real whiz kids get together to conspire, they create not simply pranks, but miracles . . .   ■

AN APPLE FOR THE CAPTAIN

John Draper, a.k.a. Cap'n Crunch: daredevil on the electronic high wire.

The best prank I've seen with the Apple was played by Cap'n Crunch. John Draper, one of Apple's first employees, was responsible for designing a telephone board for us. Much more than a modem, the board could send touch-tone or pulse dial data; it could also transmit any tones that were programmable down the line, listen for specific sounds and a bunch of other things.

At one point Draper was motivated to crack the WATS extenders that are used by companies with incoming and outgoing free 800 lines. Company executives call in on the incoming 800 line and tap out a four-digit code, which gets them on their outgoing 800 line. Then they can dial a free call anywhere they want. The only system protection is the four-digit code.

It would take a long time to dial ten thousand phone calls manually, searching for the extender code. But Draper had designed this new telephone board, and he knew a bunch of companies that had WATS extenders. He programmed the Apple to call the company on its 800 number, automatically get to the WATS extender, type out a four-digit code and check to see if the attempt succeeded or failed. The Apple with the board would listen to all the tones on the phone line to determine when it was ringing, when it went to the WATS extender, and so on.

It took about ten seconds for the Apple to dial the call and try a new four-digit code. The Apple would restart and try it again. And then try the next number. It was able to dial about five thousand calls a night—the average number of calls to crack a WATS extender. Draper cracked about twenty WATS extenders, averaging one a night.

The city of Mountain View, California, where he lived at the time, keeps an index of how well the phone system is working. An average of 30 percent of all calls made from the city don't go through. The month Draper was cracking the WATS extenders, the index jumped to 80 percent! For that month Draper made more than 50 percent of the calls originating from Mountain View, California, whose population is over sixty thousand . . .

STEPHEN WOZNIAK

HACKER ETHICS

by Neal Patrick

Retired hacker Neal Patrick at the scene of his break-ins.

Hackers are intelligent people. They've worked with computers for years, examined them inside and out. Some have created new additions to their home computers; some have even designed their own machines. Put simply, the workings of a computer hold as much interest for hackers as the workings of a '57 Chevy do for the car fanatic.

This interest is due to curiosity. There is nothing sinister or destructive about it. Hackers are eager to learn as much as possible in computer classes at school or in user groups and computer clubs, where other hobbyists share their insatiable curiosity.

Always driven to working with larger and more

Neal Patrick gained notoriety as a member of the "414s," a group of Milwaukee-based hackers investigated by the FBI for long-distance computer break-ins. In 1983, at age seventeen, he was featured on the cover of Newsweek.

powerful machines, all hackers aspire to mastering a mainframe. This is a large computer, with a greater amount of permanent storage capacity that allows a number of people to use it simultaneously. Unfortunately, few hackers are allowed on mainframe computers. Most mainframes are designated for businesses or college use. Those that do allow the general public on are quite expensive and are structured so that serious users can't explore them to their fullest capacity. Instead they are set up for the lowest common denominator: the beginning computer user. A series of menus presents choices for the novice to follow so that he doesn't become "lost" in the mainframe.

Beyond the Fringe

The true hacker soon becomes bored with the menu selection. He would rather figure out how to operate the computer than have it spelled out for him. Hence these "pay-your-way" mainframes have no meaning for the hacker, and his curiosity soon propels him to use them illegally.

Illegal use can mean simply obtaining the appropriate telephone number and using it to connect the home computer with the mainframe, or it may mean typing a number of passwords to gain access. Either way, the hacker has found what he's looking for: a computer that he can explore at his leisure, without having to worry about the hourly charges or the infinite number of menus that the computer otherwise may present. No matter that he has not seen this type of computer before; just typing the magic word "help" brings up short tutorials on how to use the mainframe.

After a few days (or weeks) of investigating the mainframe, the hacker is bound to make a mistake. It could be a file that was accidentally deleted or something odd printed out at the location of the computer. Either way, the people in charge (the system managers) detect the unauthorized use of the computer and call in the phone company. By tracing the line the mainframe is hooked up to, they are able to determine who the "culprit" is. Should he be charged, he would probably be found guilty of illegal use of a computer.

The hacker himself sees what he does as simply a tool for learning, but still the question of ethics is raised. Hackers do know right from wrong. They wouldn't think of breaking into a house and stealing something, nor would they ever physically harm anyone. With regard to computers, they would never access a mainframe solely for destructive purposes. On the other hand, the hacker does think accessing any computer is fine as long as he doesn't damage anything or cause any large problems for the system managers. He is there because he is curious.

Imps and Wimps

Though hackers generally believe that destruction is bad, there will be (as in any group of people) a few "rotten apples" who feel that their mission in life is to make other people's lives miserable. These "rotten" hackers tend to give a bad name to the less malevolent variety.

Between the curious hackers and the evildoers is a group akin to the imps in fairy tales. Their ethics lie along the lines of those of curious hackers, but they may enjoy practical jokes on the system managers or users of the mainframe. This could be anything from a minor prank (the M.I.T. "Cookie Monster," for example, which printed out COOKIE on a user's screen until that person fed the monster by typing in the word "cookie") to a scheme that could really scare somebody (like making people think the mainframe is being shut down, or even shutting it down for short periods). These hackers may cause some hair-pulling for the system managers, but they don't do any real harm.

Sorting hackers into three categories may not do everyone justice; however, it's safe to say that most hackers do fit somewhere in one of these groups. Hopefully, the law enforcement agencies will concentrate their efforts on arresting and charging the "rotten" hackers rather than the curious ones, whose only intent is to learn. ∎

Four teenage hackers at Woodbridge High School in Irvine, California, had their home computers seized by the FBI after they were traced to unauthorized break-ins on a computer information network.

SILICON VALLEY "GARAGES"

Among the most appealing of twentieth-century American myths is that of the Silicon Valley garage. According to legend, up and down California's Santa Clara Valley stand wooden shacks and Taco Bell carports representing the last bastions of private enterprise and native ingenuity. From these fountainheads of high-tech creativity, where tinkerers gain temporary shelter from the pressures of mate and job, countless computer-based fortunes and Fortune 1000 success stories (and failures) are said to have sprouted.

In fact, the myth is largely substantiated by recent history, though the site of inspiration might just as easily be a kitchen or bedroom in or out of Silicon Valley (some landmark locations are actually to be found east of the Mississippi). These photos, gathered from scrapbooks and personal files, illustrate the unprepossessing locales that gave birth to some of the most significant advances in the personal computer industry.

The Original Valley Garage

The fourth richest man in America, according to *Fortune* magazine, is David Packard, co-founder with William Hewlett of the high-technology Hewlett-Packard firm that pioneered much of the technology that would find its way, years later, into the personal computer.

It really did all start in a Palo Alto, California, garage in 1939. At left is pictured the garage itself; at center is David Packard, shown calibrating HP's first major product, an audio oscillator for testing sound equipment; at bottom is Bill Hewlett in a picture taken a short time later, testing HP's audio signal generator.

Stanford University graduates Hewlett and Packard made ingenious use of whatever was lying around the house to put together their first products. Paint for instrument housings was baked in Lucile Packard's

kitchen oven (above), prompting Bill Packard's remark that "the roasts never tasted the same."

From Bedroom to Empire

Long after both its founders became wealthy men, Hewlett-Packard missed the chance to get an early jump in the personal computer market. Stephen Wozniak, in 1975 an engineer at HP, twice took the design for his soon-to-be Apple computer to HP engineering brass, who ignored both him and his partner Steve Jobs because neither had a college degree (and thus could not possibly know what they were doing). Wozniak and Jobs decided to form their own company.

Before Apple Computer could graduate to a garage, it existed only in the bedroom of inventor extraordinaire Stephen Wozniak of Sunnyvale, California. As shown in the top photo, Wozniak's Apple I wasn't much to look at: a large board with lots of chips, resistors, capacitors and a keyboard hooked up to a TV screen. If this failed to impress Hewlett-Packard, it caught the imagination of hundreds of hobbyists. The long hours of designing, coding, assembling and testing paid off when Jobs and Wozniak sold their first fifty computers to The Byte Shop in Mountain View, California.

With the introduction of Woz' masterpiece, the Apple II, the fledgling company began a period of exponential growth that meant forever moving into larger quarters. The middle picture shows Wozniak on his hands and knees, answering the phones on the day Apple moved into a building on Bandley Drive in Cupertino. The company has grown so large, so fast, that local yokels now jokingly call their town "Appletino."

Science Fair Star

Woz' Apple computer was introduced at the Homebrew Computer Club "led" by engineer-inventor-philosopher Lee Felsenstein, the designer of three personal computers including the Processor Technology Sol. The Sol was born in a garage, but when Felsenstein himself was growing up, learning the intricacies of electricity and logic, he displayed a telephone-switching device he built in his playroom for a high school science fair in Philadelphia (bottom).

SCOTT MACE, senior editor at *InfoWorld*

COMPUTER MAGAZINE MADNESS

by Stan Veit

Personal computer magazines are among the most profuse offspring of the microcomputer era. To fill the information vacuum left by poorly written manuals and uninformed salespeople, the computer magazines have increased with rabbit-like speed. At last count there were some 450 titles to choose from, up from just two magazines in 1975. Dispensing solid technical advice and futuristic hearsay, they have begun to take over the newsstands, pushing the hairdo and biker magazines out of the way and causing more than a few hernias with their thick, ad-laden issues.

As in the rest of the burgeoning personal computer industry, what were once amateur efforts produced on kitchen tables and playroom floors are now slick sources of huge revenues. The pioneering efforts have been absorbed by large conglomerates and the quest for profits has given rise to several publishing empires, all based on the advent of the microprocessor. And in their wake the magazines have generated more than their share of controversy.

Pioneering Periodicals

In the beginning, there was *Creative Computing*, published and edited by Dave Ahl, and *Byte*, published by Wayne Green and edited by Carl Helmers. Originally, *Creative Computing* was addressed to the few educators who had access to their school computers; these were minis or mainframe machines—not microcomputers, which hardly existed in those dark ages. The other magazine, *Byte*, had been founded for the computer hardware and software hobbyists who were just starting to emerge.

Premier publications: first issues of early computer monthlies led to the largest number of magazine titles ever published on a single subject.

Wayne Green, the publisher of *73* magazine for "ham" radio operators, felt there was a market for a periodical devoted to hobby computing and small systems. Carl Helmers had been editor of one of the "little magazines" on hobby computers, and Wayne selected him as editor of his own project. Both of them worked day and night to get out the new magazine, and in September 1975, Volume 1, #1 of *Byte: The Small Systems Journal* appeared. It was an instant success because of the huge latent audience of electronics hobbyists and programmers who wanted to know more about the little computers you could build and operate yourself.

Because he was in the middle of an IRS audit and did not wish to have his new venture involved, Wayne registered the magazine in his wife's name. As it turned out, this was a serious error. No one except those involved will ever know just what happened, but when the smoke cleared Wayne still had *73* magazine and his ex-wife, now married to a German gentleman, had *Byte*, with Carl Helmers as the editor.

Virginia Green (née Londoner) later divorced her husband Manfred, sold out to McGraw-Hill and as Virginia Londoner became a very rich lady. Wayne went on to found his own large group of computer magazines, including *Kilobaud* and *80 Microcomputing*. He eventually sold his company to Pat McGovern of CW Communications Inc. for sixty megabucks! The rift between the Londoner and Green publications, though no longer owned by their originators, has left its mark on the town of Peterborough, New Hampshire, the computer magazine capital of the universe. Among the legendary incidents in the ongoing feud: Wayne Green's fluorescent-lit sign that proclaimed "Merry Christmas To All—But One."

What happened to *Creative Computing*? Well, David Ahl, its founder, worked hard at the full-time job of making his magazine successful. He also bought out numerous small magazines that didn't make it, and got into a position of having to print many, many more copies than he was being paid for. He, too, looked for a buyer and found one in the Ziff-Davis Corporation. Both Wayne Green and David Ahl had become synonymous with their publications and continued to write for them, setting a warm personal tone in contrast to the hard-core technical bent of *Byte*.

The third oldest computer magazine, *Interface Age*, also had a stormy birth. Starting out as the newsletter of the first successful national computer club, the Southern California Computer Society (SCCS), then changing its name to *Interface*, it was staffed by volunteers before it became *Interface Age* under publisher Bob Jones and began focusing on business computing. SCCS itself was a victim of "Col. Whitney," a swindler who absconded with thousands of dollars invested in its group purchase plan; in the end, the club was destroyed by the lawsuits that ensued.

One of the victims of early computer magazine madness was Erik Sandberg-Diment, a feature writer for the New York *Times*. Having contracted the computer bug in a New York computer store, Erik decided to jump in and publish another magazine called *ROM*. Although he hired some of the best writers in the industry (including Joseph Weizenbaum of Eliza fame and the ubiquitous Adam Osborne), the market was still too small to support another magazine and *ROM* perished for lack of the capital needed to hold on for just a little longer. The same thing happened to *Microtrek* and some other early magazines.

Sing the Computer Specific

Two events changed the computer magazine business so that it would never be the same again. One was the advent of the Apple II; the other was the growth in popularity of the Radio Shack TRS-80. These comput-

HOW TO READ A COMPUTER MAGAZINE

Before you get into the computer magazine habit, sign up at your local gym or health club and get in shape. You'll need all your strength to lift and lug a magazine that's two inches thick with computer ads.
- Hold each magazine by its spine and shake out all reader reply cards. If you're not careful, these can cause nasty paper cuts.
- Moisten your index finger and with a steady leafing motion page through the magazine. A smooth, rhythmic action averts fatigue during the several-hundred-page ordeal to follow.
- Scan all ads, but keep to the headlines and price information. If you insist on reading the ads' purple prose, you have only yourself to blame for the ensuing disorientation.
- Take in editorial content with a large grain of salt. With hundreds of magazines dependent on hardware and software advertisers, publishers are naturally loath to offend them. Remember: there is no such thing as a perfect computer or program, no matter what a reviewer (who got it free) might write.
- Tear and save pages of interest. Out of three or four hundred pages, the magazine might contain a dozen worth contemplating. Some magazines are sturdier than others, so it may take some work to pull what you want.

The best place to read computer magazines is on the plane to and from computer shows. Captive in your seat, you would be hard-pressed to find a more painless use of your time. The pouch in front of you makes a convenient repository for discarded reply cards and pages. Besides, reading a computer magazine can provide an icebreaker for meeting that cute IBM salesperson across the aisle.

THE FLASH

ers brought thousands of new users into the field, but their interest was in Apples or TRS-80s and nothing else—except software or peripherals for their machines.

Again Wayne Green pioneered, this time with the first machine-specific magazine, *80 Microcomput-*

THE 10 ESSENTIAL COMPUTER BOOKS

Market studies show that people who buy personal computers are likely to buy ten books on the subject within the first year. In place of all those programming guides that go unopened and gussied-up instruction sheets with less literary merit than a toaster manual, the books below deserve your attention.

• *Computer Lib/Dream Machines* by Ted Nelson. Highly prophetic. The first personal computer book, self-published in 1974 (a year before the first affordable micro). Still the best introduction to graphics.

• *Microelectronics: A Scientific American Book.* A collection of eleven articles from the September 1977 *Scientific American*, the issue that inspired many pioneers to settle on the microcomputer frontier.

• *The Soul of a New Machine* by Tracy Kidder. Pulitzer Prize-winning account of the "Hardy Boys" and "Microkids" designing a new minicomputer. Poignant but understated ending, in which design team is scattered to the four winds.

• *The Computer Establishment* by Katharine Davis Fishman. To date, the most comprehensive history of IBM and the Seven Dwarfs: the U.S. computer industry through the dawning of the personal computer revolution.

• *The Personal Computer Book* by Peter A. McWilliams. Quirky, opinionated, often funny introduction to the nuts and bolts of personal computing. Original 1982 edition frequently updated.

• *Writing with a Word Processor* by William Zinsser. The rights of passage from word processing ignorance to completed disks ready for typesetting, as described by the executive editor of the Book of the Month Club. Stylish and incisive.

• *Elementary BASIC* or *Elementary Pascal* by Henry Ledgard and Andrew Singer. Essential programming concepts cleverly taught through fourteen new tales featuring Sherlock Holmes, Dr. Watson and the marvelous Analytical Engine.

• *The Cartoon Guide to Computer Science* by Larry Gonick. Concise, wide-ranging illustrated crash course in computer history, theory and lore. A painless introduction for beginner or buff.

• *The Computer Phone Book* by Mike Cane. Everything you need to know about joining the dial-up network revolution. Includes detailed descriptions and access protocols for information services and bulletin boards.

• *Turing's Man/Western Culture in the Computer Age* by J. David Bolter. The first but certainly not last pop anthropological look at changes in Western culture wrought by computer consciousness.

STEVE DITLEA

ing, devoted to the Radio Shack TRS-80. Quickly it became almost as full of advertising as *Byte*, and its circulation climbed as more and more TRS-80 computers were sold. Other machine-specific magazines were then published for Apple, Atari and Texas Instruments computers.

When IBM entered the market with the IBM PC, a new wave started. David Bunnell, editor of the Altair house magazine *Computer Notes*, had come out with *Personal Computing*, but nothing seemed to go right for him. *Personal Computing*, after being sold several times and ending up in the Hayden Publishing stable, went on to become one of the most popular computer magazines. Then Bunnell got the idea of starting a machine-specific magazine devoted to the IBM PC. To this end, he assembled a staff of very talented people on the West Coast. There was one thing lacking, however, and that was the capital needed to start the magazine, so he began to look around for someone to back him.

Lifeboat Associates, one of the big success stories of the microcomputer industry, had grown to be the largest supplier of CP/M-based business software. Investors had just bought out its original founders and had installed Dr. Ed Currie as president of the company. Ed was a friend of David Bunnell (the two had worked together at MITS), and when David asked him for capital he suggested Tony Gold, one of the Lifeboat founders, as a source. The Tony Gold and David Bunnell combination seemed to click, and Tony agreed to put up the money for the new magazine.

Here again the story becomes obscured by its many versions (may the courts alone have to decide!). One fact is known to all: *PC* magazine was a huge success. Since a whole industry was created to supply software, peripherals and expansions for the IBM PC, and every company in the PC industry wanted to advertise in *PC*, the magazine grew thicker with every issue.

Behind the Scenes

Most people don't realize that magazine publishing is a highly capital-intensive industry (perhaps the reason so many magazines start and disappear in a few issues). You have to pay the printer, the paper company and the staff as you go. The U.S. Postal Service must be paid before one copy is mailed. The cost of selling subscriptions is high and soliciting ads is expensive; advertisers take thirty to ninety days to pay you, and the cash flow problems are only for the brave and the rich.

These conditions caused problems for *PC* magazine. Tony Gold lacked the kind of capital necessary to keep expanding at the rate the magazine was growing, and the solution was to sell out to one of the huge magazine or communications corporations. It was now computer time, and they all wanted to buy *PC*. The question was, which suitor would it be?

Of the prospective buyers Bunnell and staff had come to favor Pat McGovern and his CW Communications Inc., which published *Computerworld, InfoWorld* and several newspapers in the computer field. Tony Gold seemed to lean toward the giant Ziff-Davis, which had recently purchased David Ahl's mini empire. To make matters worse, Bunnell believed that he and his staff had been promised 40 percent of the magazine. Gold said this applied to profits, not ownership. No stock had been transferred to anyone but Tony Gold.

Relations at *PC* became strained, to say the least, and the entire staff threatened to walk out. Tony Gold as sole owner sold out to Ziff-Davis, and despite liberal salary and job offers the staff quit as a group to start a new magazine, *PC World*, which overnight

grew as thick as *PC*. The beneficiary of this move was Pat McGovern and company. The loyalists who left with David to start *PC World* have quickly raised it to one of the best sellers in the personal computer field.

Incidentally, *PC* has not suffered under Ziff-Davis management; it put out the largest single issue of any consumer magazine ever published—surpassing *Vogue*—and has expanded into PC-related publications with an IBM magazine on disk, an IBM technical journal and an IBM weekly.

When a reader tries to select a computer magazine from a wall full of similar publications, the choice gets harder and harder. And still new magazines are announced every day. It's easy to predict a shakeout, with many computer magazines perishing in the years to come, but no one is smart enough to know which ones will survive and which ones won't make it into the next generation—or how long computer magazine madness can go on. ∎

WHY I WROTE THE FIRST PERSONAL COMPUTER BOOK

In 1974 I was indignant about the stereotype of computers—big, bureaucratic, "scientific," and widely believed to be the rightful province of IBM. What was particularly galling about this stereotype was that at the time IBM was literally the enemy of personal freedom with the computer. When I wrote *Computer Lib*, personal computers were still the province of $50,000 DEC minicomputers and their imitators.

Thus I sought to create a best seller and reach the masses with the True Word on the fun, excitement and personal challenge of the computer. Though I sold over 40,000 copies of the book I self-published (and laid the groundwork for the computer book publishing industry in the process), this did not work. The people who read *Computer Lib* were brilliant eccentrics. Definitely not the masses, but still a very neat constituency.

The True Word eventually got out. I'd say most people have an inkling of it by now. I wrote for the simple ideal of freedom: the short-term freedom of people to do their own thing with computers, a flower that was about to open, and the much

deeper sense of freedom that has to do with long-term political issues. Though I tried, these issues haven't yet penetrated the public mind.

I also wrote the first personal computer book for the sake of my personal freedom, to make a lot of money from it and not have to take God-awful jobs anymore so I could work on the writings and projects I consider important. This did not work, either. It was my own fault for making the print too small, which turned out to be an irrevocable decision because I pasted the mechanicals down too hard. (I didn't believe, being then in my thirties, that other people really had trouble reading fine print. Now I know. Ah, well.)

Finally, I wrote *Computer Lib* as an invitation to smart young hackers to join me in my crusade, Project Xanadu, now a special form of storage and eventually to be the

Ted Nelson published his binary book with a pair of covers for sections printed back to back and upside down: Computer Lib, *his personal computer manifesto, and* Dream Machines, *a visionary exploration of graphics.*

electronic library for those who love ideas and freedom in all their richness. The invitation was mischievously—nay, perversely—hidden in the back of the book, which was in turn hidden in the middle. This assured that only the most persistent and brilliant readers would find it.

But this was the part that worked! Directly or indirectly, the book brought in mad geniuses and wonderful people who built on my designs, made the mathematical underpinnings serious and robust, and allowed Xanadu to be born.

TED NELSON

ENTERING THE STORE AGE

by Stephanie Rick

First ad for the first store.

It was Father's Day, 1975, when Dick Heiser made his announcement to the 125 people present at the organizational meeting of the Southern California Computer Society. "I'm thinking of starting a computer store," he said, "and if any of you have feedback or information I'd be delighted to talk to you."

No one responded. There was a Radio Shack in the neighborhood, after all, and in any event most computer owners ordered parts and kits from ads in the back of magazines like *Popular Mechanics* or out of Heathkit and Edmund Scientific catalogs.

Dick had left his job as a systems analyst for Litton a couple of months before, thinking he would open a computer-related bookstore. Then, in a spring 1975 issue of *Scientific American*, he'd come across an ad for the first microcomputer—a computer based on an Intel 8-bit microprocessor and known as the MITS Altair. He sent for more information and received literature that was "full of typographical errors. You could tell they were in a start-up situation."

In May he got his first look at the Altair when he attended the National Computer Conference in Anaheim. It ran BASIC as a language, could be used as a text editor, and at $4,000 was affordable by computer standards. Two years before, Dick had paid $14,000 for his Computer Animation minicomputer, and he quickly decided to sell it.

After that conference Dick was invited to attend a showing of the Altair in Van Nuys, where so many people showed up that they quickly filled the room and overflowed into the hall. The MITS representative had only begun his first sentence about the company's history when he was interrupted by questions from the audience. People were there for real information— many of them either already owned an Altair, had one on order or were planning to order one soon—and the questions continued for two hours. It was at that meeting that Dick first realized that microcomputers were a real business.

Stephanie Rick is the founder of We Search Research, a data search firm based in Venice, California.

Ignoring the apparent lack of interest in a computer retail store, and undaunted by the bank's refusal to grant them a loan ("Come back when you've been in business for a year"), Dick and his wife Lois went to their parents for financial help. They leased 1,200 square feet of space in what Dick called a "convenient but seedy neighborhood of West Los Angeles." Still, at $225 per month, the rent was not prohibitive, and on July 15, 1975, The Computer Store opened for business.

There was no Grand Opening celebration. Publicity had consisted of a few fliers, since Dick was still soldering in the back room. The first ad, however, just two lines of copy under "Electronic Equipment" in the classified section of the Los Angeles *Times*, pulled in computer hobbyists from all over the city; the next ad was a little larger—one column inch of the same clas-

The original store to sell computers off the shelf.

sified section. Patrons of the restaurant across the street would see the store's sign and come over to laugh, but The Computer Store grossed $10,000 in its first month of operation.

The store carried kits for the Altair 8800, some peripheral devices and thirty book titles, among them *101 Basic Games* by David Ahl and *What to Do After You Hit Return* by Robert Albrecht. An Altair 8K system, hooked up to a television typewriter, was used for demonstrations and playing games. Most customers went to the books first. "It gives them a chance to become comfortable," said Lois in the November 1975 issue of *Datamation*. It was a good way to break through the tension; almost nobody, including the Heisers, had any idea what a computer store was, though Dick had an idea of what it should be. He'd worked for IBM at one time and liked their "solution sale" approach to business—first find out what is needed, then come up with an answer. He designed his store to be information-oriented and focused on systems rather than parts and experimental kits.

Most software, such as MODMON, an early general-purpose program that preceded the more sophisticated disk operating systems, was written in-house. The store wrote no accounting programs, however, and thus avoided lawsuits over programs that ate business records, did not conform to specific accounting standards or just flatly would not run. In fact, the store sold no applications software. Instead, it customized systems programs and languages to link different types of equipment according to clients' needs.

Although there were some physicians and small companies using the Altair for business purposes, the first home computer customers were for the most part amateur radio ("ham") operators, electronics hobbyists, and engineers and programmers from technical and aerospace companies. While some wanted their computers fully assembled, most were happy with kits—especially since they now had a local place where they could buy components or get their questions answered. The most common reason they wanted a computer was, they sheepishly admitted, to play games.

Cash flow was a constant problem for Dick in the early days. Orders to MITS had to be prepaid. "I thought that was a strange way to do business," Dick recalls, "but there didn't seem to be any other way. At one point MITS had all our money and some of our customers' money and we didn't have any inventory in the store."

Nevertheless The Computer Store grew quickly. In October Lois left her job running a software project in model building at the Rand Corporation to help out, and Dick began hiring a small staff. Within a year, the store—which Ed Roberts, then president of MITS, said looked like "you could pack it into a suitcase"— needed more room.

The good old days portrayed less than a year after The Computer Store's opening.

The Computer Store moved to its present Santa Monica location in the spring of 1976. In July of that year there were fifty stores selling microcomputer products across the United States; by July 1977 there were over five hundred. Though many of them did not succeed in keeping their doors open, in mid-1983 Future Computing, a market research firm dedicated exclusively to the personal computer industry, conducted a survey that yielded responses from 2,479 stores. The number of stores is expected to reach six to seven thousand by 1988. One change already noticeable is a decrease in the number of single-location, independent stores and the increasing dominance of retail chain stores and franchises.

The Computer Store itself has undergone some changes. In 1978 the store was dropped as an Altair dealer; by 1979 the Altair was no longer manufactured. The store now sells several lines of personal computers, including Apple, Kaypro, Vector Graphic and Altos. Dick Heiser is no longer the owner; he sold the store to Brian Donner in 1982, and is designing and teaching computer courses, writing documentation and looking into the future. The store's clientele is a little older and has expanded to include small-business owners, middle-management personnel and a vast collection of people known as "home computer users." There is less tech-talk going on, and customers are increasingly focused on costs of systems rather than services.

Despite the projections about franchises and retail chains, this single-location, independently owned store is thriving. It's still one of the best places to get a question answered if it has anything to do with computers, and it's still a bit of the future, as it was in 1975, existing in the present. ∎

COMPUTER USER GROUPS

by Josh Martin

Contrary to popular myth, computer users are very social folk. Every month they gather by the thousands in local clubs to share their experience and avail themselves of software libraries and other services.

If you're in the market for a computer, a good club can help you select the system with the widest range of applications for the best price. And you can benefit from strength in numbers: if several members are buying a particular piece of equipment or software, you can obtain group discount prices. If you already have a computer, a club can bring you into contact with members using the same equipment. Many user groups also offer resource centers with programs and information about your particular computer system.

A Club for Your Computer

Most home users turn to their local computer store or to the computer manufacturer for information about computer clubs. These sources tend to recommend product-related user groups, which might not be the optimum choice for you but which do offer ready information about your computer. Many computer makers sponsor groups that provide service while functioning as market forums for new product introductions. For example, there are over three hundred Apple-oriented groups serving home computer users in the United States, Canada, England, Ireland, Australia and New Zealand. There is a certain bonhomie to the Apple clubs, as revealed in chapter names like the Adam & Eve Apple Group of Madison, Wisconsin, and Crabapples of Carbondale, Illinois. (Consider, too, the Wabash Valley Apple Byters in Indiana and Green Apples in Greensboro, North Carolina.) Atari, Commodore, IBM, Texas Instruments and other manufacturers have product-oriented user groups across the country, but with less creative names.

Josh Martin is a New York–based writer specializing in economics and technology. He types his stories on a 1904 Underwood.

Before the product-specific computer clubs came professional or technical clubs. The forerunners of today's user groups emerged ten years ago, with the large-scale introduction of word processing into offices. Professional groups such as the Association of Computer Users (ACU) and the Association of Information Systems Professionals (AISP) were formed as educational and information networks. Independent of any particular computer manufacturer, they serve workers as well as professionals in automated offices. The ACU, founded in 1974, now has a national membership of three thousand. Annual dues are $65. By paying this fee, members get ACU's monthly newsletter, *Computer Fitness*, and two books: *How to Select Your Small Computer Without Frustration* and *How to Manage Your Small Computer Without Frustration*.

Meanwhile, the older and larger AISP, founded in 1972 as the International Word Processing Association, boasts twelve thousand members, with more than eighty-five chapters in twenty-five countries. In fact, the AISP is the world's largest professional word processing association. Annual dues of $50 entitle members to free subscriptions for any of the organization's periodicals as well as substantial discounts on books and surveys. For home computer users, the AISP offers a wide variety of services relating to equipment, services, industry issues or any relevant topic. It also has an excellent monthly, *Information Industry Review*, which profiles new products, and an up-to-date *Information/Word Processing Glossary* to keep you on top of the latest computer terminology.

Hackers and hard-core computer hobbyists also founded their share of early computer clubs. The most legendary of these was the Homebrew Computer Club. Many of personal computing's early advances, including the first Apple computer, resulted from the sharing of information by Homebrew members. The club still meets once a month at the Stanford Medical Center, and its mailing list comprises over seven hundred names—many of them now prominent in the industry.

Regional Communications

"Computers are available to everyone, but information is still very limited," says Jonathan Rotenberg, who founded the Boston Computer Society in 1977 when he was thirteen years old. Rotenberg's efforts have helped make his regional club the nation's largest home computer user group. The BCS now has seven thousand paying members, who can attend any of the society's twenty-five monthly events, participate in any of twenty-three special-interest subgroups or simply read the society's slick bimonthly, *Computer Update.*

The BCS is organized so that subordinate groups cover all major brands and the most common areas of computer activity, including business, classroom, family, entertainment and entrepreneurial uses. In addition, most of these subgroups publish newsletters providing members with programs, tips and interviews with professionals. There is also a BCS software exchange, where members can get software in the public domain for a nominal fee.

Rotenberg is developing the network concept for his computer club. With a wide-ranging membership in forty states and fifteen countries, the BCS is the nucleus of a national home computer user group launched in early 1984. Unlike the ACU and the AISP, which serve business users, the BCS national group caters to consumers and the general public.

Other regional clubs offer similar services, though on a reduced scale. For example, the New York Amateur Computer Club, founded in 1978, features a monthly newsletter and discounts on user group disks (the copy fee is $1) as well as on catalogs of public-domain software. In addition, there are monthly general meetings and product-oriented user group sessions. General meetings of the club begin with a "non-commercial period," in which members trade information. This is followed by a "commercial period," during which entrepreneurs can announce products or services.

Smaller user groups can offer more personalized rapport. The Lincoln (Nebraska) Microcomputers Club has forty-five members who meet once a month to exchange information. Like the larger user groups, it offers advice and a "disk-of-the-month" software exchange ($3 per diskette if you have no software to swap). Unlike many larger clubs, it rarely gets visits from company representatives; instead, club members have show-and-tell sessions to display new machines.

Jonathan Rotenberg organized the Boston Computer Society at age thirteen and took it national at twenty.

Freeware

Among the attractions of the computer clubs is their free or low-cost "public-domain" software (i.e., noncopyrighted computer programs donated by the authors). Public-domain software includes hundreds of programs for games and graphics, business and education. Many clubs offer a combination of such programs on a "disk-of-the-month" basis, for which members pay a nominal fee of $1 to $5.

Public-domain software may not always be the easiest, slickest or smoothest. In fact, such software often represents the rough-cut versions of commercial products being sold through computer stores and vendors. On the other hand, certain programs, like Ward Christiansen's public-domain Modem communications software for CP/M computers, have helped set standards of features and performance.

Some of the larger computer clubs maintain extensive software collections with thousands of programs on file. New York's Big Apple Users Group is a case in point. Among other things, BAUG maintains a library of about 100 commercial games for demonstration purposes, as well as 100 public-access (public-domain) games ranging from simple word association to fairly sophisticated graphics. A recent BAUG disk-of-the-month had four games, five utilities, five art/graphics programs and one educational program. The titles of some of the games indicate the variety available: Marooned in Space, Adventure Slice, Dragon Maze, Minotaur's Lair, Automatic Bingo, Battle of Numbers and Tic Tac Toe, the oldest computer game.

While your local club might not have as big a selection in its own files, many groups have swap agreements so that a wide range of software and information is available through networking. Unfortunately, this involves the problem of how to prevent users from illegally copying the games. Public-access/public-domain material is no problem. But software pirates have created tensions between clubs that maintain demonstration libraries (where games can be tried but cannot be copied) and computer companies and software designers. The software designers feel the clubs have allowed members to pirate their work.

With such incentives as pooled information, buying power and freeware, computer clubs will continue to grow to meet public demand. They represent the organized arrival of America's newest consumer culture: home computer users. ∎

HOMEBREW AND HOW THE APPLE CAME TO BE

by Stephen Wozniak

Without computer clubs there would probably be no Apple computers. Our club in the Silicon Valley, the Homebrew Computer Club, was among the first of its kind. It was in early 1975, and a lot of tech-type people would gather and trade integrated circuits back and forth. You could have called it Chips and Dips. We had similar interests and we were there to help other people, but we weren't official and we weren't formal. Our leader, Lee Felsenstein, who later designed the Osborne computer, would get up at every meeting and announce the convening of "the Homebrew Computer Club which does not exist" and everyone would applaud happily.

The theme of the club was "Give to help others." Each session began with a "mapping period," when people would get up one by one and speak about some item of interest, a rumor, and have a discussion. Somebody would say, "I've got a new part," or somebody else would say he had some new data or ask if anybody had a certain kind of teletype.

During the "random access period" that followed, you would wander outside and find people trading devices or information and helping each other. Occasionally one guy would show up and say, "Is there anyone here from Intel? No? Well, I've got some Intel chips we want to raffle off." This was before big personal computer firms and big money considerations. There was just one personal computer then, the Altair 8800, based around the Intel 8080 microprocessor.

The Apple I and II were designed strictly on a hobby, for-fun basis, not to be a product for a company. They were meant to bring down to the club and put on the table during the random access period and demonstrate: Look at this, it uses very few chips. It's got

Stephen Wozniak is the designer of the Apple II computer and co-founder of Apple Computer Inc.

a video screen. You can type stuff on it. Personal computer keyboards and video screens were not well established then. There was a lot of showing off to other members of the club. Schematics of the Apple I were passed around freely, and I'd even go over to people's houses and help them build their own.

The Apple I and Apple II computers were shown off every two weeks at the club meeting. "Here's the latest little feature," we'd say. We'd get some positive feedback going and turn people on. It's very motivat-

The cover of the Homebrew Club's first newsletter.

ing for a creator to be able to show what's being created as it goes on. It's unusual for one of the most successful products of all time, like the Apple II, to be demonstrated throughout its development.

Today it's pretty obvious that if you're going to build a billion-dollar product, you have to keep it secret while it's in development because a million people will try to steal it. If we'd been intent on starting a company and selling our product, we'd probably have sat down and said, "Well, we have to choose the right microprocessor, the right number of characters on the screen," etc. All these decisions were being made by other companies, and our computer would have wound up being like theirs—a big square box with switches and lights, no video terminal built in . . .

We had to be more pragmatic. The 6502 microprocessor, for instance, was chosen for one reason only. It was the first one to sell over the counter for $20. The 8080 cost $370 at the time, and you couldn't get it at any surplus stores. You had to go down to a distributor, and they made you feel like you had to be a company with an account. It wasn't set up for hobbyists or experimenters.

Apple Seedlings

Steve Jobs was a friend of mine from high school. We were introduced because we had two things in common: electronics and pranks. It turned out that he had a tremendous drive to start a company. He had worked at Atari and had become friends with some of the key people there, including Nolan Bushnell, the founder. Nolan was his idol. Steve wanted to have a successful product, go out and start selling it, and make some money. He also had excellent product ideas for the upcoming home personal computer.

To produce the Apple I, Steve and I formed a partnership. We didn't sell very many Apple Is the first year. We built them at night in our garage. At first we expected to sell circuit boards at the Homebrew Club: just put in your own chips and it'll work. Then we got a $50,000 order from a local store and we were in heaven.

The trouble was how to get the money to build a hundred computers—they might cost over a hundred dollars each to build. Steve went to a local parts supplier and talked them into giving us a lot of parts on thirty days' net credit. It was very unusual for them to give us credit, because we didn't own anything. We didn't own houses. We didn't even own our cars. But Steve is very persuasive. We'd get the parts and then stuff them into the circuit boards, have them soldered, get them back in the garage and test them. And we could turn the whole cycle around in ten days and get paid. It worked really great because we had only one level of management.

We got our names established. The computer magazines started carrying lists of all the microcomputers coming out, and they'd describe all the characteristics—how much memory, which processor, was it assembled or was it a kit, what was its price. The Apple I had a good appearance, and we were always at the top of the lists because they were in alphabetical order.

After the Apple I was out, we tried to add new features. We thought about color and maybe some high-resolution graphics. I found ways to optimize and combine different parts of the circuits and make things with fewer chips. It's great to show off at a club that you use fewer chips than someone else. I did it for no other reason.

The Apple II came out of trying to improve the Apple I. From thinking out a way to make it with half as many chips, you could have a much better product. It was faster, it had color, it had high-resolution graphics, it had mixed modes on the screen with text. A lot of neat features made it look like this might be a nifty product. It turns out that some of its best features were inspired by what little experience we had.

Steve and I had done a game for Atari—Breakout for the arcades—before games were on microprocessors. We were running the Apple II down at the Homebrew Club, so I thought it would be neat if you could write Breakout in BASIC. I added graphics mode commands to the Integer BASIC I was writing. Breakout needs paddles: I had to add a little circuitry for paddle and push button. You need sound: when the ball hits the bricks, *ping;* when you lose, *ehhhh.* So I put a speaker in. All of these features were basically just to play one game.

These turned out to be common features for the personal computers that have come out since that time. We weren't quite the first to offer a keyboard and video output, but we were close. We were the first to offer built-in BASIC. We made the first built-in cassette port so you could use a cheap cassette recorder to load your programs in and store them. We had started to set standards for what have come to be known as low-cost personal computers.

Just about the only argument on product design Steve and I ever had was on the number of expansion slots. I wanted eight and he wanted two. I was for eight simply because I'd been around minicomputers that had a lot of extra function boards plugged in. Steve figured people would only use maybe a printer and a modem, and that was it. Fortunately we went with eight, because the Apple II's expandability was important to its success.

When we geared up to manufacture the Apple II, it looked like I'd have to leave my nice secure job at Hewlett-Packard. I thought about it and said no. I just loved going down to the Homebrew Computer

Club, showing off my ideas and designing neat computers. I was willing to do that for free for the rest of my life. Steve got extremely anxious. He got all my friends and relatives to start phoning and tell me why I was making a mistake. Finally one of them called and said you can start a company, remain an engineer and also get rich. I decided that you *can* start a company and make money. Once I got the consciousness right, it was easy to quit HP and take this big risk.

We got our first ad agency and began discussing who we were and what our product was and how we would market it. Of course, to a marketer Apple was an odd name. It came from the days when you picked an interesting, fun name for a company. You do that when you're on a hobby basis. The ad agency kept telling us the name had to be changed. We had to have a name that suggested technology, number crunching,

COMPUTER GROUP GUIDE

One of the most complete listings of user groups can be found in the annual *Classroom Computer News Directory*. Originally intended for teachers, this 200-page directory provides a wealth of information for general users on all aspects of computing, including sets of guidelines for hardware and software selection as well as a complete Yellow Pages of computer services and products.

The directory is available from Classroom Computer News, 341 Mt. Auburn St., Watertown, MA 02172. Telephone: (617) 923-8595.

JOSH MARTIN

calculations, data bases. We took the attitude that Apple is a good name. Our computer would be friendly—everything an apple represents, healthy, personal, in the home. We had to hold our ground on that one. The agency designed our color logo. (Our original logo was Newton under the apple tree.) Steve twiddled the colors around and kept a rainbow orientation.

Core Memory

We introduced the Apple II at the First West Coast Computer Faire. The first computer shows were informal, not like the professionally oriented shows we have today. They were more an outgrowth of computer clubs. We got a lot of our initial support from these clubs. I started speaking at them whenever I was invited, and I've been doing it from that day on. I travel at my own expense because I think it's exciting to tell the story of how our company sprang up from a club.

Our success was due to a number of factors. First of all, we had never manufactured computers before. We couldn't look back and say, "Here's how computers earned a lot of money in the sixties and seventies, that's the style to do." All we thought about was what was going to work out great in our own homes. Our motivation was what would be good in the end. If there was a known formula for what would make a successful product, and what would make a billion dollars, all the big companies would have jumped on it. All these companies were a lot smarter than us. What we had was luck. We did the right things with the right coincidences of timing and the right people in the right place.

We had a lot of interest and enthusiasm. The rewards that drove us were all intrinsic. The computers were being put together to show off at a computer club: "Look at this. I put in these neat commands." It's not like you get a better salary, or a better title, or more respect at work, or a new car. We had the autonomy of creators. We could decide what was going to make a neat computer. We could implement it, and we could show it off. We also had excellent feedback from our peers.

Back then, the small computer scene was based on the belief that we were all on top of a revolution. Everyone attending the club in 1975–76 knew there was a big computer revolution occurring and the rest of the world wasn't aware of it yet. That's why there was so much excitement and spirit. We were finally going to get control of our own computers. It wasn't a million-dollar thing that belonged to the company you worked for. This big thing that had so much value, and that we wanted to use and control, we finally were getting close to. Look at how many companies have sprung out of our Homebrew Computer Club. At last count, it was something like twenty-one! We managed to bring the computer revolution home. ■

COMPUTER FEARS

- **I might get electrocuted.** This particular anxiety was a favorite among our forefathers, who trotted it out when they were confronted by inventions like the light bulb and telephone. Rest assured: the computer keyboard's electrical current, about equal to that of a cordless electric shaver, is just too low to cause harm.
- **I'll never understand how to operate a computer.** Nowadays, turning on the machine usually involves no more than flipping a switch and loading in a program. And in place of those undecipherable symbols that trigger long-forgotten fears of fractions, most programs now use English as the means of communication. Many of them also have pick-and-choose menu formats to guide you through available choices.
- **I might break it.** You can't get that rough with a computer simply by typing on it and turning it on or off. Home computers are akin to any store-bought item: they vary in durability according to manufacturer, model, and wear and tear, and they have to be treated with a bit of respect. I have no sympathy for the user who douses his machine with coffee and complains when it prints out Martian dialect.
- **The machine might lose my work.** Wiping out a sentence or two is always a possibility, as is destroying everything you've entered over the last five years. But you can guard against such losses by watching your delete commands and taking proper care of your floppy disks. Most important is that well-known data processing axiom: "Back it up." It takes no time at all to copy a program or data from one disk to another, thus assuring yourself of the ability to restore any work that gets lost along the way.
- **I might lose the privacy of my data.** If you have the traditional stand-alone system, with no outside machines attached, your data is as safe as it would be on a piece of paper. For added security, don't let anyone read over your shoulder when you enter your data or password and remove the disk when your session is finished. If your computer is hooked up via modem and telephone line to a friend's machine, and if you happen to be paranoid about wiretapping, you can invest in encryption hardware or software to encode and decode your communications. As for the suspicion that someone will phone your computer and search through your disk-based data while you sleep, just keep the power turned off; no one has yet found a way to turn on a computer by remote control.
- **Computers have more capability than I need.** This is also true of pencils, but how many people worry about not using them to draw works of art or create literary masterpieces? Personal computers range from relatively inexpensive units to quite elaborate affairs and offer a wide array of functions. Chances are, as you and your computer get used to each other, you'll expand your horizons and purchase software packages that increase your machine's versatility.
- **Using a computer will lower my status.** This illusion circulates among office personnel who are actually afraid of looking silly as they try to master the new technology. If computers are that alien to you, especially if you're older or set in your ways, a gradual introduction is probably best. Sympathetic private tutoring can prevent loss of face before co-workers and convince you that business computers may enhance your status.
- **I might lose the ability to do things on my own.** A computer is not an electrode-studded brain sapper, nor is it a device that turns users into Einsteins. As a tool, the computer simply helps you accomplish your work with maximum efficiency and expands rather than hinders your own capabilities. Erasing typewriter errors by hand, for example, impedes the creative act of writing, whereas correcting text on a personal computer is a pleasure. As for mathematics, is it more productive to hunt for a multiplication error or to be freed to explore new formulas?
- **A computer is mathematical and not for creative types.** This view is held by artistes, literary denizens, and just plain folks with a morbid fear of numbers. The good news about computers is that if you don't want to play with accounting or physics, you can buy a word processing program to help with your writing, a music package to aid in composing, or a knee-slapping outerspace game to match your wits against.

GEORGE S. ZARR, JR., Renaissance man and computer professional

THE 30-MINUTE COMPUTER SHOW

by The Flash

The computer show comes in many shapes and sizes. It can be the local user group's flea market in a high school gym or one of the alphabet matrix of national exhibits—NCC, COMDEX, CES, SOFTCON—overflowing the vast convention centers of San Francisco or Las Vegas or Chicago. Whatever its dimensions, the computer show is an odd tribal rite where computer makers, dealers and enthusiasts spend too many hours on their feet, talking too much about too many products that have yet to see the light of day.

The Flash is a computer journalist who would rather remain anonymous.

It's true that a great deal of business gets conducted at computer shows, but more important is the gestalt, the state of the art of "state-of-the-art," the latest chimeras and chipped-out fantasies of electronic intelligencers. The point is not to get lost in the detail. Do you really care about the umpteenth IBM-compatible business machine, the zillionth "integrated" software package or the zenith of Donkey Kong knockoffs? Haven't you heard enough about what's new and how Microsoft/Digital Research/IBM/Apple just pulled off the coup/screw-up of the decade?

The answer is the thirty-minute computer show,

inspired by the forty-minute Louvre in Jean-Luc Go-dard's 1964 movie *Band of Outsiders*. Of course, you'd probably have to linger a minute or two in front of the Mona Lisa at the famed Paris museum, but the computer showgoer has no valid excuse to dawdle. Even Apple's Lisa is not worth the wait: you can see icons any old time at ye local computer shoppe.

In thirty minutes or less you can absorb the big picture, pick up brochures and spec sheets for later perusal, and even engage in a few clipped conversations. It takes tremendous concentration and quick reflexes to complete the course in time, but at the end comes the kind of euphoria you'd feel after running the marathon. Make sure you're wearing the proper shoes; I favor Adidas, although their bright blue-and-white design does clash with the dark pinstriped three-piece suit *de rigueur* at a number of IBM PC–dominated computer fests.

The beauty of the thirty-minute computer show is that you won't need to bring any peripherals. The squeamish might want to take along a canteen or a first-aid kit, but such precautions are unnecessary if exposure to other showgoers is limited to a half-hour. You will be subject to torrents of hot air, and possible contamination from fanatics of certain operating systems and programming languages, but almost all thirty-minute computer showgoers have survived to tell the tale. The only equipment you'll need is a plastic floor, for holding all the brochures you'll pick up. These same bags are also good for garbage, which the brochures inevitably become. (And computers were supposed to lead to a paperless society . . .)

On your mark. Get set. Start. Now it's up to you to run the grid pattern of the computer show's floor—like Pac-Man gobbling up data and documents, glomming the color screen displays and gleaming hardware, weaving in and away from hordes of humans and robots, occasionally curving around for bonus points when something or other lights up, and pressing on toward your goal of the thirty-minute show.

Is it really worth it? Ask anyone who's done it. Of course, the practice does raise eyebrows among professional showgoers, those unhappy souls who are part of the computer industry and condemned to serve time at shows until they can get their sentences reduced for good behavior. Then again, they're probably jealous of anyone with an independent, devil-may-care attitude.

No doubt others will improve upon the thirty-minute computer show, but what I'm looking forward to is the day these shows are placed on-line on a computer network. Then you can let your fingers do the walking—all over your keyboard. And then maybe someone will write about how to do a computer show in thirty nanoseconds or less. ∎

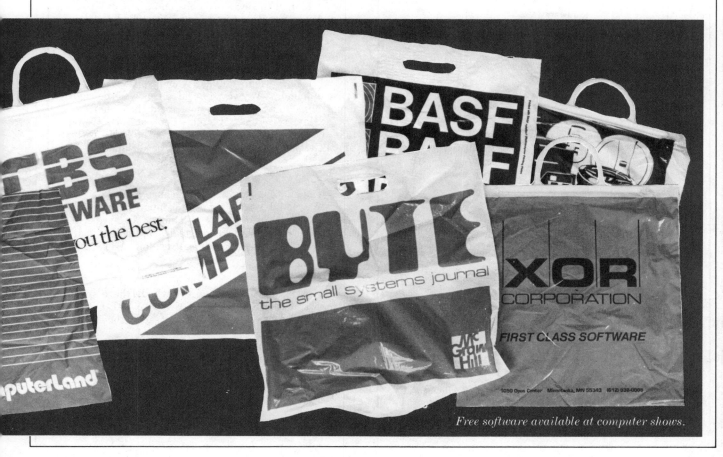

Free software available at computer shows.

THE ZALTAIR STORY

My best computer prank involved counterfeiting twenty thousand brochures for a phony computer. I did it at the First West Coast Computer Faire, where the Apple was introduced.

The big computer of the day was the Altair, so we named ours the Zaltair. We made it an incredible dream machine, with full Altair-100 bus compatibility plus 50 extra connectors. We called this the Zaltair 150 bus and had quotes in the brochure saying things like "And what a motherboard."

The brochure compared the Zaltair's performance with that of other machines, including the Apple, and offered discounts for Altair trade-ins. We also had lots of "Z" words, since they were really popular back then. Words like "verZatility," "BAZIC" and "perZonality."

Potential customers at the fair ran to the Altair people to ask for Zaltairs. Of course, the Altair folks didn't know anything about it. But they got concerned enough to begin confiscating boxes of Zaltair brochures. No sooner did we bring in another box than it would disappear, and we began to worry that we might get caught.

Then I got an idea. We started sneaking our brochures into key distribution points around the fair, putting them underneath piles of legitimate material. I started leaving them in phone booths and other public places. Eventually the Homebrew Computer Club caught on and recognized it as a big joke and a prank. But the best part was the way I framed someone.

I've discovered that the way to play a prank is to make it look like someone else did it. It's like playing two pranks at once! For the Zaltair I put a quote at the top of the ad, supposedly from the president of MITS. You took the first letter of each word in the quote and it spelled Processor Technology. I figured that some computer person would look at the nonsensical quote and realize that it contained a cipher. But nobody did, and I wasn't going to say anything.

Then one day Gordon French, the founder of the Homebrew Computer Club, came by Apple and said, "I know who did this thing. I know who wrote the brochure!"

I had kept it such a secret that even Steve Jobs didn't know I was the culprit, so I was very interested in what he had to say. With Jobs and a few other excited Apple people around, someone asked Gordon: "Who did it?"

He said it was Gerry Egram from Processor Technology. "I know it's Gerry, because he's got a strange sense of humor."

I just howled. I knew who had the "strange sense of humor." Anyway, I decided this was the right opportunity to let someone know about the cipher.

"Hey, you guys," I said. "Look at this! If you take the first letter from each word in the quote at the top of the page, it spells out Processor Technology!"

Stephen Wozniak's brochure for a nonexistent computer was convincing enough to lure serious inquiries from visitors to the First West Coast Computer Faire.

The quote in the Zaltair brochure read: "Predictable refinement of computer equipment should suggest on-line reliability. The elite computer hobbyist needs one logical optionless guarantee, yet."—Ed Roberts, President, MITS, Inc.

In a few seconds I had everybody there spelling out P-R-O-C-E-S-S-O-R T-E-C-H-N-O-L-O-G-Y, right down to the Y. So now, supposedly, they knew who the culprit was.

It wasn't until four or five years later that I told anyone I was responsible for the Zaltair prank. I went out to dinner with Steve Jobs and told him the whole thing. He was beside himself. He had never once suspected me.

STEPHEN WOZNIAK

COTTAGE COMPUTER PROGRAMMING

by Paul Lutus

Paul Lutus dropped out of the NASA rat race to live on a mountaintop for $40 a month. Then he wrote the most popular word processing program for personal computers . . .

You may have heard about me. In the computer business I'm known as the Oregon Hermit. According to rumor, I write personal computer programs in solitude, shunning food and sleep in endless fugues of work. I hang up on important callers in order to keep the next few programming ideas from evaporating, and I live on the end of a dirt road in the wilderness. I'm here to tell you these vicious rumors are true.

Now that I've confessed, I'll explain how I met my first personal computer. It was 1976, and I was designing some electronic devices for the NASA space shuttle. I was a college dropout whose employability

rested solely on the fact that I could build things that worked (the lights on the present shuttle fleet are powered by my electronics). But I was about to drop out even further. That spring I moved to one of the wilder corners of Oregon and built a twelve-by-sixteen-foot cabin atop a four-hundred-foot hill. Since I didn't want a road, I carried the lumber on my back. I planted a vegetable garden. I wrote poetry and played mathematical games in notebooks. And I chose to do without electricity.

One night when I was reading *Scientific American* in the yellow glow of kerosene, I saw an advertisement for the Apple II. Wow, I thought, a personal computer! With a computer you could draw a world in three dimensions out of colored lines. Write stories.

Paul Lutus is the author of Apple Writer, one of the best-selling word processing programs of all time.

Lutus' original cabin had no electricity. Today his Spanish-style home features such amenities as a satellite TV antenna and microwave oven.

Play music. Locate Neptune to point your telescope. Store fantastic amounts of trivial information . . . The very next day I rode my bicycle to the nearest telephone and placed my order.

During the next few weeks I filled notebooks with ideas for programs I was going to write, in some cases setting them down in code. I also strung the oaks and madrones with twelve hundred feet of electrical cord to power the machine.

By the time my Apple arrived, I had become a basket case with my notebooks and pencil. When the machine was hooked up, I was ready to play all night. I followed the instructions to the letter, but I couldn't get into BASIC. I kept getting stuck where the instructions said "Type CONTROL B and press RETURN." I must have typed CONTROL B a hundred times, but nothing happened. Finally I abandoned the instructions and began experimenting.

It was then that I noticed the key marked CTRL. Remember, I had never used a real computer before. I had only imagined it. Instructions that come with computers should be written for people who can only imagine them. What they should have said was, "Press down the key marked CTRL. While holding it down, press the B key. Now release these keys and press the key marked RETURN."

Without intending to, I had gathered all the necessities for what would now be called an "electronic cottage." Far from the hustle and bustle of Silicon Valley, I began writing programs for the fun of it—programs that drew pretty pictures on the display, played music or did something elegant and mathematical. I mailed some of them to Apple Computer, which promptly offered to buy them and encouraged me to write more. Then as now, there were many more computers than programs.

I had bought the computer as a plaything, but within weeks I had been paid more than the cost of the machine. I began to think about a more ambitious project, a word processing program to "obsolete" my typewriter. Since I write a fair amount, I knew I would be able to test my program properly, which turned out to be very important.

This brings me to the day Mother Nature tested Apple Writer. I had finished my program and was using it to write the instruction manual. It was raining, so I thought it a perfect day to stay inside and work with the computer. Because I was off in a digital twilight zone, I paid no attention to the fact that I was perched on a four-hundred-foot ridge in a rain storm. I was (rather proudly) in the midst of explaining how my program would save the data in memory if the user accidentally pressed the RESET key, when suddenly—*bam!*—lightning struck a tree just outside the window. Sparks flew around the cabin and my poor Apple went bananas.

At first I thought it had been completely zapped, but there were some signs of life and I restarted my program. Lo and behold, the program reconstructed the data in memory! In a moment the display appeared, with the cursor sitting beside the last word I had typed in. This despite the fact that half the diskettes lying on the table had been erased by static discharges.

I mailed off the first version of Apple Writer in a big manila envelope, and after some negotiating (and a few revisions) Apple agreed to pay $7,500 for the program. It didn't occur to me to ask for a percentage of future profits, but fortunately two things happened: 1) the first version became a big hit, and 2) no one at Apple was able to make the improvements that were needed for the next version. So about two years later Apple and I decided to start over, this time on a royalty basis. Apple would market the program and pay royalties, and I would retain all other rights. At this writing, the new version of Apple Writer is yielding more per day in royalties than the original's sale price.

A Hacker's Habitat

I still live in the backwoods with my computers. Deer are more frequent visitors than people. In my pond one turtle seems to have met another, and I intend to watch this development carefully.

I want to explain why the computerized cottage and trees work so well together. First, the finished work of the computer usually weighs nothing, so a post office or telephone line is enough to get it delivered. Second, computers take over a lot of the trivial thinking we do, freeing us to be creative. I have always felt the best background for creative thinking is complete silence. Programming the present generation of computers in machine language means thinking about twenty things all at once without dropping any of the pieces.

Of course, there is one drawback to the backwoods computer life. If you're not a complete hermit, you could get lonely or want one of the many forms of night life to which most people are accustomed. I think this problem will eventually be solved by increasing the cultural attractiveness of the small town, a development that should follow on the heels of the computer revolution.

Also, I've been told that good programmers rarely have mates. This is usually offered as evidence of how asocial we are. Without fail, we're pictured as disheveled cyber-hobos hanging around computer centers, shunning serious relationships, coding for the sake of coding. I can't really disagree with this view, but there is something interesting behind it—at least for me. I began to notice, as I got more involved with computers, that acceptance by the machine required absolute precision on my part. The slightest misstep caused the instant erasure of many hours of work; the machine would reject everything with perfect dispassion until each detail was just right. Then the program would suddenly function beautifully, and never fail again.

A mistress of perfect consistency, the computer rejects all but the flawless, offering no explanation. When the acceptable is finally offered, the machine's acceptance is total, unwavering and eternal. As Einstein said in a different context: "the years of anxious searching in the dark, with their intense longing, their alternations of confidence and exhaustion, and the final emergence into the light—only those who have themselves experienced it can understand."

The result of this strange relationship was that for a time I became too spoiled for the flesh-and-blood women around me. I got tired of hearing, "If I've told you once, I've told you a thousand times—the answer is *maybe*!" It's clear that person-machine relationships could be dangerous for a functioning society, but from time to time they are very tempting. On the other hand, the computer can be a powerful tool for bringing people together. I once used the GraFORTH graphics language I had written to create a "computer letter" in the form of a diskette that displayed images and messages. In one of the sequences a cabin appeared on a hilltop, the door opened, then music played. It was designed to persuade a certain someone to visit me in Oregon, and it worked.

I don't mean to create the impression that I write computer programs day and night, until in starvation I crawl to the kitchen for a carrot. This is true only sometimes; the rest of the time I'm hiking around the Oregon wilderness or bicycling alongside a river. From time to time I fly my Mooney 201 airplane, bought with my first large royalty payment, to Apple headquarters in California, or I simply fly slowly along the Oregon coast, watching for whales.

Team Troubles

There's a lot of talk these days about how the individual cottage programmer is on the way out. I don't think so, even though a team of cooperating programmers is in principle a better arrangement. My doubt springs from the fact that the best of existing programs are the product of one, at most two individuals, and that some of the teamwork experiments have turned out to be complete failures. There is a saying in the computer industry: a program that might take one or two authors six months to write will take twice as many programmers twice as long to write.

In one notable example, a large computer firm created a wonderful piece of hardware that would in principle solve all the problems of communication between functions, allowing the user to think only about the task. A crack team of programmers was put together. They would meet each day to discuss their progress and resolve difficulties, so that the entire system would work in perfect harmony.

The problem here was that each programmer thought his part of the system was more important than the others', with the the result that no one bothered to make the pieces compatible. The original idea (task orientation) became lost, but it was still possible to make all the tools cooperate in a single task (file compatibility). Then this goal was also lost. The result was that if a user wanted to move his task created with tool A over to tool B, he first had to place it into electronic picnic basket C and carry it over. In some cases one computer must be coaxed into talking to another, but this was the first time a computer refused to talk to itself. The moral? You can lead a horse to water, but first you have to find some water.

Overall, I believe the computer age favors the individual and that resistance to the individual work style is the last gasp of the dying industrial age. Many software companies put their faith in committees because they believe this is the way things have always been done. In fact, most unique modern achievements have been the product of individuals or very small groups, including relativity theory, the airplane, the laser and the computer itself.

Until now, individual achievement has been exceptional in a mass society, even though the exceptions often transform that society. The deliberate cultivation of individual creativity may end up being the most important social result of computer technology. Either that, or cottage programmers like myself will simply have more time to cultivate our gardens. ∎

FIGHTING SOFTWARE PIRATES

by Gerry J. Elman

Ever since I began writing a program for the IBM PC, I've been worried that the pirates will start their disk drives humming and make the money that should be coming to me. When I looked into protecting my precious program, I discovered that I had several choices, including physical techniques along with a few legal strategies.

The problem with the ever more sophisticated physical techniques for copy protection is that an "arms race" has developed. Certain hackers see each new system as just another mountain to conquer "because it's there," while software entrepreneurs have stressed the need for new methods to secure their programs while still allowing legitimate users to make copies. So many publishers have expressed this need that an industry organization, the Association of Data Processing Service Organizations (ADAPSO) in Arlington, Virginia, has set up a clearinghouse to keep track of them.

Each of the physical anti-piracy schemes has its own loopholes and drawbacks. As a writer of software, what else can I do to protect my investment of time? How can I ensure that the people who benefit from my creation will pay me for it?

Since long before computers, there have been three distinct legal strategies for protecting the results of one's intellectual effort from unwanted appropriation by others: 1) copyright, 2) the government's grant of a patent, and 3) keeping it a trade secret. Copyright and patent law starts with this passage

from the Constitution: "The Congress shall have Power . . . To Promote the Progress of Science and useful Arts, by securing for limited times to Authors and Inventors the exclusive Right to their respective Writings and Discoveries. . . ." Congress and the courts have sorted out two fields of law from this one constitutional provision. Copyrights apply to the "writings" of "authors"; patents apply to "discoveries" by "inventors." But if you create a new computer program, are you its author or its inventor? The answer is: maybe either, possibly both.

Copyright and Copycats

Copyright protects an original form of expression, but it does not cover any process, system or method of operation. What does this mean for computer software in the United States? If there are several ways to say the same thing, or to write a program to accomplish a very particular result, a copyright will protect my unique expression of that general thing but will not allow a monopoly on every way of saying or doing that thing.

Until just a few years ago, it was an open question whether copyright could protect writings published in a form that a person couldn't read. For example, this text was stored as tiny magnetic domains on a diskette. Of course, there's no way to look at the diskette and figure out what it says.

In 1976 Congress solved this problem by passing a revision of the Copyright Law that protects original works of authorship "fixed in any tangible medium of expression, now known or later developed, from which they can be perceived, reproduced, or otherwise communicated, either directly, or with the aid of a machine or device." Text that is written magnetically on a

Gerry J. Elman, J.D., is a Philadelphia lawyer who practices in high-technology matters. He is a member of the Computer Law Reporter *advisory board and a contributing editor of* Personal and Professional *magazine for users of DEC microcomputers.*

diskette is "fixed" even though it can be erased and rewritten, like a manuscript in pencil. The diskette is the "tangible medium of expression" from which you can perceive the text, either on a screen or as a print-out, using a "machine or device" (your personal computer).

What do you have to do to copyright a program? At first, nothing special. Before the new law took effect in 1978, a federal copyright didn't exist until a work was published with a copyright notice on it. But now the owner gets the copyright at the time the work is created, automatically and without lifting a finger. Usually the author or co-authors own the copyright, even if somebody pays them as a consultant. However, if you write something for your employer within the scope of your duties at work, the employer owns the copyright and we say that the writing or program is "made for hire."

After publication, the work must contain a prominent copyright notice. If the work is a program on a disk or cassette, the notice should appear on the label. It should also be coded into the program so that it appears on the video screen when the program is started up.

A copyright notice consists of three things: either the symbol © or the word "copyright," the year of publication and the name of the copyright owner, usually the author. The word "copyright" is enough for the first element of the notice, but it's helpful to include the © symbol, which provides additional rights in certain foreign countries that have signed the Universal Copyright Convention. The UCC expressly adopts this symbol, but not the word "copyright," apparently to bridge differences in language.

What if you don't have the © symbol in the character set of your printer or video screen? While a lot of programmers are using the letter "C" in parentheses, whether courts here or abroad will judge it the equivalent of the © is at this point anyone's guess. Including the word "copyright" in your notice will at least ensure that you're as fully protected as you can be in the United States.

The words "All rights reserved" don't do anything extra under U.S. law, but they do trigger another treaty: the Pan-American Copyright Convention. So if you're interested in south-of-the-border, put in a "rights reserved" clause.

Copyright registration is relatively cheap: all you have to pay the government is $10. To register a computer program, send a listing of your program code along with a completed Form TX. (The form is available from the U:S. Copyright Office, Library of Congress, Washington, D.C. 20559.) If your program is long, it's enough if you send only the first and last twenty-five pages. Registering your copyright gives you life plus fifty (or a flat seventy-five years in the case of a work for hire). This is not a jail term, just the length of your exclusive protection: the life of the author plus fifty years, which is a lot longer than most of today's computer programs are expected to be around.

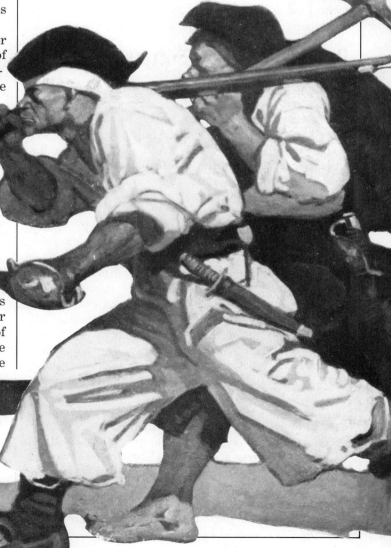

What do you do if a pirate copies or sells your program after it's registered with the Copyright Office? You can start a suit in federal court, and if the court finds in your favor they might issue an order stopping all further distribution and use of the program. The court might even order that all pirated copies be impounded. You might be able to get money damages from the infringer based on lost sales and on the infringer's profits. It's also possible for the court to award you as much as $50,000 if the infringement was committed willfully, plus the costs of suit (including a reasonable fee for your attorney).

Copyright infringement is a criminal offense, which could mean prosecution by the local U.S. attorney. If convicted, the infringer could be fined up to $10,000 and even sentenced to a year in jail. He would also be ordered to forfeit to the court for destruction all infringing copies of the program.

To make it even harder on the pirate, the Copyright Law says he can also be ordered to forfeit to the court "all implements, devices, or equipment used in the manufacture of such infringing copies." Does this mean that someday a pirate's microcomputers might be delivered to the court and destroyed? Time will tell.

Patents and Trade Secrets

A patent is a seventeen-year right to exclude anyone but the patentee from making, using or selling in the United States the subject matter of an invention. Things that can be patented are new or improved processes, machines, articles of manufacture and compositions of matter. During the 1970s people didn't get very far trying to patent computer programs as processes, but they had a bit more luck with the idea that a computer with a program in it is a special kind of machine. Nevertheless, for several years it seemed most computer programs would never benefit from patent protection.

Recent court decisions have been more encouraging. As long as the program is new, useful and not obvious to one of ordinary skill in programming the relevant systems, patent claims that meaningfully cover the innovation are more frequently obtainable. But the lion's share of programming techniques are not covered by patents. Instead they are protected as trade secrets. Unlike patents and copyrights, trade secrecy is not a branch of federal law, but part of the common law of each state. The idea is that if you have certain important business information that you keep secret, telling it only to your employees and others who agree to keep it confidential, you can sue people who violate the confidential relationship. You could get a court order keeping them from using the information, at least for a certain period, and you might also get some money if you can show that their misconduct hurt you financially.

Often there's a way to have your cake and eat it too. If your program is written in a language that must be compiled before it can run on your computer, you will in effect have two versions of it. The version you write is called "source code"; if you've done a careful job, it's usually pretty easy to read it and understand the clever programming techniques you used. However, when you put your source code as input into the compiler program, what comes out is called "object code." The object code should be fine for running the computer, but it's a machine language—not a programming language—and therefore very tough to interpret.

If you sell only the object code, you're likely to be able to treat the source code as a trade secret. And the object code would be the thing you register with the Copyright Office.

Your Trademark

One other symbol deserves mention: ® for registered trademark. Trademarks are brand names or logos that enable customers to distinguish goods that come from one source or maker from those that come from a different source. They don't protect ideas or intellectual property as such, but they do help you get what you want in the marketplace.

Trademarks are protected by an overlapping body of state and federal law. The ® symbol is used to identify a trademark that has gone through a complex registration process in the federal Patent and Trademark Office. This process is intended to assure that the mark will not cause confusion with other trademarks that have already been registered.

Until your trademark has gone through this process and is issued a registration number, you must *not* use the ® symbol. This requirement causes incredible confusion, because the opposite is true for copyrights, which have the similar-looking © symbol.

The copyright notice must appear on every published copy of the work. According to the law before 1978, if a few copies of the publication had been issued without the copyright notice, you'd placed the work in public domain and forfeited any possible claim to protection. Under the new law, you might be forgiven for an inadvertent failure to use the copyright notice in the beginning, but you must put it on all copies you issue in the future and make a reasonable effort to get it placed on the other copies you've distributed. ∎

PUBLISHERS VS. PIRATES

by Jim Edlin

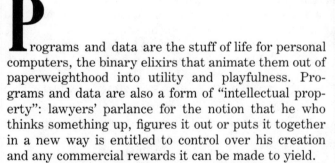

Programs and data are the stuff of life for personal computers, the binary elixirs that animate them out of paperweighthood into utility and playfulness. Programs and data are also a form of "intellectual property": lawyers' parlance for the notion that he who thinks something up, figures it out or puts it together in a new way is entitled to control over his creation and any commercial rewards it can be made to yield.

Intellectual property, like the more tangible kind, is subject to trespass and theft. Such crimes against patented, copyrighted, trademarked or confidential material are known as "piracy," but how can the unsanctioned use of computer software be equated to plunder at sea? There is scant swashbuckle to typing DISKCOPY and pressing the ENTER key. Nonetheless, "program" and "piracy" are two words often linked together in the new dialogue of personal computers.

Three Kinds of Piracy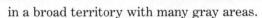

Software piracy is not a simple phenomenon. It takes

Jim Edlin is the designer of Wordvision, a "writing tool" program for the IBM PC sold without copy protection and priced significantly lower than earlier programs of its type.

in a broad territory with many gray areas.

● **Private piracy.** This is piracy on a personal scale. Someone makes a copy of a disk for a friend to use. Or a person whose office has three computers buys just one copy of a program, then duplicates it to use simultaneously on all three machines.

● **Organized piracy.** This is also piracy for personal use, but less casual. People gather to exchange programs like baseball cards ("Trade ya two Zorks for a Pac-Man!"). Or somebody sets up an electronic meeting place through which programs can be traded via phone lines. (Volunteers who lend their computer and phone to such an enterprise can collect as toll a copy of every program passing through.)

● **Commercial piracy.** Here's where program piracy becomes a business, whether for small change or big bucks. At one end of the scale are the shady merchants who throw in "free software" to close a sale and forget to mention that they're getting it as free as you are. Over at the big-money end is the organized counterfeiting that goes on whenever a product has high demand and limited distribution, or a big spread between its production cost and selling price. Like designer jeans and replacement auto parts, some software now qualifies on both counts.

Three Things That Encourage Piracy

- **It's easy.** Copying a program can be as simple as putting the original in your computer together with a blank disk, typing a command or two, and waiting less than a minute. Also, everyone who has use for pirated programs and data already owns a machine that can copy them efficiently.
- **It's inexpensive.** Compare copying a program to copying a book. The program not only takes a lot less time and effort, but can be copied for a lot less money. Photocopying a book often costs more than buying a second original, but the reverse is almost always true for software. And unlike the case of books, there are no hidden costs of reduced quality in the copy; every software copy is as good as an original.
- **It's comfortable.** High program prices contribute to this. People can console themselves with the thought: "They robbed me on the price of this program. I'm just getting a little back by giving a copy to a friend." But a determined pirate can rationalize even when prices are low: "They'll never miss the little profit they'd have made on this inexpensive thing."

Five Ways Publishers Try to Foil Pirates

- **Persuasion.** The publisher's first line of defense is to try convincing customers that the practice of piracy is self-defeating. Successful piracy, the argument goes, reduces incentive for people to create more software. Today's ill-gotten gain becomes tomorrow's loss for those who hunger for software if the supply of new goodies dries up.
- **License agreements.** These are the fearsome gray broadsides of legalese often seen scowling out at you from behind the plastic wrapper of software packages. They are a carryover from the days when programs were written mainly for the giant computers of giant corporations. In that context, it makes perfect sense to have a strictly worded document giving, say, an airline the privilege of using a reservations program on one computer in one location for a six-figure license fee. Enforcement was easy and economically justifiable.

In the context of programs sold by the thousands in discount stores and used in the privacy of homes, many authorities dismiss license agreements as out of place and ineffective. Their presence on such packages may be a bravado gesture akin to sticking an alarm-system decal on the windows of your house without actually installing the alarm.

- **Copy protection.** Most of us have experience with this approach. It's the one the U.S. Treasury uses when it puts those little red and blue threads in the currency and prints it with ultrafine engraving beyond the capacity of ordinary presses. The underlying idea is that it's easier to do right when it's hard to do wrong. In practice, it means throwing sand into the wheels of the copying process.

Programmers are infinitely clever in figuring ways to impede copying. One popular program deliberately imitates the behavior of an improperly manufactured disk, after modifying the computer's standard instructions for handling such problems; this modified error trap, the only gateway to the rest of the program, cannot be found unless the planted error is encountered in the right place at the right time. If you try copying the original with its deliberate glitch, your faithful computer will gallantly correct the problem without troubling you to mention it. When you try to use the copy, it simply won't run.

Unfortunately, copy protection is also sand in the wheels of convenient computer usage. There are manifold legitimate reasons for wanting to copy: for safety, of course, in case of spilled coffee or teething puppies, but also for such conveniences as gathering on one disk items that are often used together or having multiple versions each preset for a particular task. For this reason, some would-be buyers boycott copy-protected products. Fewer may be stolen because of copy protection, but fewer are also sold.

- **Hardware keys.** You can make all the copies you want under this approach, but none will work unless an electronic "key" is inserted in the computer at the time. To this end, one company invented an inexpensive gizmo that plugged into the little-used cassette jack on IBM PCs. Sadly, the jack was so little used that IBM eliminated it in newer models of its machine. Even when it worked, it was no picnic, because the key fit around back in an inaccessible spot. It was okay with one program, but would have been a pain if you had to swap keys a lot.

Other companies are lobbying computer makers to include program-readable serial numbers in their machines. In this variation, the first time a program was used it would note the machine's number and thereafter would run only on the machine with that number. If your computer breaks and you get a loaner, too bad! This also guarantees that you will only use software on your machine, the terms under which most software is actually sold (read the fine print on your warranty card).

- **Programs on cartridges.** Plug-in cartridges are a more expensive medium for distribution of software—much more expensive if the software is sizable. Also, some popular machines have no provision for using cartridges. But software published in a cartridge is far less readily copyable (and easier to load into the computer). IBM's design for its PCjr seems to contemplate this; it has two cartridge slots while IBM's previous personal computers didn't even have one.

Three Ways Pirates Swashbuckle Harder

As in love and war, for every defense there is yet another form of offense.

● **Supercopy programs.** Whatever clever copy protection scheme a programmer can devise, there is another clever programmer who can figure out how to beat it. Several programs on the market are aimed at copying the uncopyable. Their methods range from finesse to brute force. One, for example, outfoxes the deliberate-manufacturing-glitch scheme described above simply by replacing the section on the original that checks for the glitch. The replacement will give an "all clear" even if the glitch is not actually found.

● **Hardware copiers.** Copy protection schemes must be figured out before they can be defeated. A circuit board is a costlier approach to the problem than software-only copiers, skipping the need for cleverness by escalating to a higher level of brute force.. The circuit board holds a duplicate set of memory cells for your computer. When you press a switch, the circuit takes an electronic "snapshot" of whatever is in the regular cells—including a copy-protected program already loaded into the computer from an original disk. A well-protected program will bar users from simply copying all regular memory cells out to a disk file, but the shadow memory isn't subject to such restraints. Its contents will survive a protected program's normal methods for wiping out memory before giving up control of the computer, so they can be copied after the protection is gone.

● **Bulletin boards.** Electronic bulletin boards are one of the joys of personal computers. One small fraction of their use is as an aid to program piracy. Through this medium, someone can buy a new program one morning and have copies to their friends in six states that night. This is also a channel that allows one pirate who cracks a tough copy protection scheme to disseminate his discovery nationwide in hours.

One Question to Leave You Pondering

● **What does discouraging piracy cost?** This is the subtler side of throwing sand in the wheels. Suppose you think you might like the whiz-bang filing program a friend has bought. But you have uncertainties that only familiarity will resolve. The best way is to take it home and twiddle with it on your own computer with your own data. Your friend is already too dependent on it to let you borrow it, so that strategy is out unless the program is copyable.

RAISE HIGH THE SKULL & CROSSBONES

They call us pirates and worse. They lock up their programs behind hardware and software schemes. They set the minions of the law upon us. And still we flourish by our wiles.

Ahoy, ye microlubbers: to pirate a program is not to steal, but to liberate knowledge. We don't take money or goods from anyone; we merely free up information. Most of us don't profit from our buccaneering activities; instead, we share the wealth with our fellow computer users.

The software moguls have only themselves to blame for our cracking open the bars to their programs. If they didn't charge a king's ransom for disks that cost a pittance to duplicate, there would be little incentive for us to practice our skills. There would be no need for them to protect their programs if software were no more expensive than what you and I can afford to pay.

We are no longer in the Dark Ages of personal software, when so few people used computers that program development costs had to be defrayed by high unit prices. Now so many microcomputers are in use that a program should cost no more than a lightweight paperback novel. Instead, we are paying illuminated manuscript prices.

Maybe someday the software publishers will understand how they're killing off the golden goose. But until that time, be warned: there will be many a pirate's flag on the software horizon.

JOLLY ROGER

Fluid availability of software for people to try and experience can probably contribute significantly to the spread of personal computers, and to people's comfort and skill with them. Strong antipiracy measures may stifle this effect. Consider other possible costs as well. And consider how likely it is that most noncommercial pirates are really lost customers for the publishers. It just may be that the people who pirate a program were not real hot prospects to buy it. ∎

STEPPING OUT WITH POWER AND ELEGANCE

by Cheryl J. Weiner

Computer software represents an innovative medium for creating learning, playing and working environments. We are only beginning to appreciate its aesthetic. We seek this by affirmation, by the impulse to suddenly say: "Ah, yes, that can only be done with a computer," and "Yes, that is something worth doing," and finally, "Yes, it is good."

We gravitate toward programs that speak to us personally: spreadsheets, word processors, games. But the magic does not occur unless we choose programs that correspond to our needs and desires. When we do this, a transformation happens. Once we see the possibilities, we yearn for more of what appeals to our sensibilities. We go into the computer world in search of "power and elegance," a phrase often used to describe good software.

In the real world, power and elegance usually go hand in hand. Both are necessary; neither is sufficient unto itself. Often elegance is applied to a woman, power to a man. In Greek mythology Apollo is elegance; Zeus is power. Power attracts, elegance captivates. Power is usually necessary for elegance to occur, and without elegance power remains raw.

Cheryl J. Weiner is the special projects director for Data Communications. *She has been involved in educational software development since 1979.*

Computer scientists who refer to certain programs as "powerful" or "elegant" are looking at the code, at the solutions to the programming problem. A leap must be made in the application of these standards not just to the internal program code, but to its external execution. We, as users, must be able to recognize power and elegance when we see it.

What are power and elegance to a software user? Trip Hawkins, founder of the Electronic Arts software firm, came closest to a definition when he characterized a good program as "simple, hot, and deep." A fully functional word processing program cannot be simple, but it should contain an interface that substitutes elegance for simplicity. A spreadsheet program is not hot; it has no emotional element. A spreadsheet, however, could evoke wonder if its elegance and power allow us to play with data in a way that brings a new understanding or a new course of action. A game need not be deep, but it must have enough power to be challenging. Thus we can define simplicity as elegance, depth as power, heat as that space lying between the two when they are united in a classic manner.

The distinctions between power and elegance in software are relative and often rely on the computer's capabilities. Power is found in the complexity that the software can attain on a particular machine as a function of memory capacity, speed and amount of data in the data base. Power is epitomized in high-speed number crunching, in computing by brute force. A spreadsheet that has only twenty-four columns and two hundred rows is of limited use. An adventure game becomes boring if it has only ten rooms and three characters. We need to move quickly through rich fields of data or decision making, and it is power that allows us to do so.

Elegance is subtler and depends less on machine environment. Elegance is a language parser's ability to understand our attempts to interact with the computer. Elegance is the quality of the subject matter. The humor expressed. The reinforcements and responses. Ease of use. The ability to move through menus, windows and options in order to create a relationship between ourselves and the program. The freer we are to interact with programs on our own terms, regardless of what they were intended for, the more elegant the design.

Aesthetic Environments

The essence of the software aesthetic exists in the environments created when power and elegance are joined. People in search of programs that maximize the computer's capacity want graphics, animation, flashy reinforcements and responses. Unfortunately, these bells and whistles often add little and can be distracting. What we should look for is the computer's ability to create regenerative environments, worlds that we can reconfigure in ways unanticipated by program designers—an infinite capacity to generate novel ideas, thoughts and actions in a powerful and elegant manner. Graphics and music could enhance these new worlds, but they have to be intrinsic to the environment rather than extra elements tacked on for effect.

Interaction with this environment should be effortless, whether it's a word processor, a spreadsheet or an adventure game. We should be able to control both our actions and our focus of attention, to move easily through the program we want. The command structures should be intuitive. Our thoughts should be on the content of the program, not on working with the content. For this we need elegance.

So far, the most powerful and elegant applications for computers belong to the spreadsheet and word processing programs. Here the worlds are easy to regenerate. The contents are concrete and discrete. The domains are limited. It is much harder to fulfill the aesthetic within the recreational aspects of the computer: the counterparts of the novel, the film, the board game.

Adventure games, however, have come closest to linking power and elegance in regenerative environments. Unfortunately, simulation and role playing games demand enormous amounts of computing power. Any lack of processing power restricts the depth of the content as well as the ease of the interface. In Infocom's Zork trilogy, for example, we are forced to create tortuous dialogues with a language parser. For those of us who don't like to type, this interface quickly becomes a barrier to play. In most adventure games, the character delineations are quite mundane and the plots are uninteresting. There is no Wonderland to ponder, no Cheshire Cat, no language to linger over. These programs are sophisticated in their conceptualization but not in their execution. Their power and their elegance are constrained by their terminology and lack of vision.

Time and Again

While we are accustomed to a three-dimensional universe, the computer confronts us with the fourth dimension: time. Because computer environments at their most complex have four dimensions, we have to know where we are or we can easily get lost. In the first dimension we move in a traditional linear fashion. With the addition of a second dimension we can create surfaces. With a third we can rotate objects in space and reach into the computer's depth to pull out information and bring it to the surface. Finally, with the fourth dimension, we can begin to grapple with time. We can create historical audit trails. We can move through a simulation that keeps track of our movements at different points in time. The greater our power, the further we can move into the fourth dimension. The more elegance, the better able we are to move from dimension to dimension without getting lost.

Thus power and elegance in the computer world are no more nor less than the ability to simulate the power and elegance of the world as we know it or of any world we can imagine. We become immersed in a world easily mastered through the interfaces and become involved with this world intellectually as well as emotionally. Engagement is the critical factor. Challenge. Curiosity. Fun. We react viscerally. Our palms sweat; our hearts race. The mind expands.

Ultimately, the best computer programs will combine power and elegance in ways we can only dream of. The programs will engage us through all our senses and emotions. We will control them while they focus our attention in meaningful and relevant ways. They will have unlimited memory, high-speed processing, unrestricted data banks, and universal access wed to ease of use, transparency of design, style and grace. A new aesthetic made manifest. True poetry in motion, with graphics . . . animation . . . color . . . music . . . speech. Herein lies the concept of computerness that must grow and evolve. ∎

THE RELIGION OF COMPUTERS

by Daniel S. Bricklin

Trying to hold a rational discussion about any aspect of computers with enthusiasts wrapped up in the subject can be as futile an experience as arguing theology with a fervent believer. Feelings run surprisingly deep. They are Right and you are Wrong. Relativism is for fuzzy thinkers and the unenlightened.

Combined with emotion, beliefs in computer-related rights and wrongs create distinct schools of thought that at times resemble religions. There is that same sense of "ultimate solutions," the tendency to develop dogmas not open to question, and a feeling of exclusive community—of "us" against "them."

One of the clearest examples of "religion" in the

computer field has been the rise and fall in popularity of computer languages. Microcomputer users were ecstatic when they first encountered BASIC. Some had started with early hobby-kit computers that used machine language. Now they had BASIC, and it was super-duper. BASIC was "it." But then they learned that most experienced programmers believed BASIC was *not* "it." It did not allow you to do structured programming; it taught bad habits. So then Pascal was "it." It allowed some degree of data structuring. But soon objections were voiced: as a pedagogic language, Pascal had too many restrictions. So the C language was "it."

While the neophyte personal computer users were discovering BASIC, programming experts were already using Pascal and C, but this fact had little impact at first on BASIC's popularity. The early

Daniel S. Bricklin, chairman of Software Arts, Inc., together with Robert M. Frankston, invented VisiCalc: the first electronic spreadsheet program.

personal computers were not powerful enough for Pascal and C, and the users did not seem to mind. BASIC accommodated their needs. Only in the last few years have many software developers, forgetting their enthusiasm, relegated BASIC to the dust heap.

The same sort of "religious" commitment comes into play when programmers consider operating systems, the software that regulates the operation of a computer connected to disk drives or other external devices. Those of us who worked in the Multics project, for example, swear by Multics. Yet there is a large body of programmers fervently dedicated to UNIX, the operating system developed by Bell Labs. Being religious myself on this point, I am convinced that the UNIX people just do not fully understand the Multics system.

Some of us can get religious about the "mouse," the boxlike input device that slides along a desktop to control the display on a computer screen (the electrical wire "tail" trailing behind it gave the gadget its name). When I first conceived of VisiCalc, I thought a mouse/calculator keyboard combination was the best way to go about it. But there was not such a mouse available, so VisiCalc was "tuned" for a normal keyboard with arrow keys.

The Apple Lisa folks were even more fervently committed to the mouse. From the way they talked at first, you never would have expected to see arrow keys on their computer. But they wanted to put a spreadsheet on the Lisa, and users are accustomed to spreadsheets that use arrow keys. Apple had to go against its religion to give people what they wanted (though the Macintosh offers arrow keys only on an optional plug-in keypad).

Why do emotional commitments run so high in the computer field? Ours is an introspective, problem-oriented profession. We perceive problems and make their solution our goal. Once we have discovered a solution, we become convinced—at least for the time being—that we have found the end-all.

That moment of "Eureka!" when all the bits and pieces fit together is a lot like a religious conversion. We see the Light, we find the Way. And we are unshakable: that is, until we discover a new problem. Discoveries come so fast in our field that at times we may resemble leftover flower children flitting from one cult-of-the-moment to another.

The public, of course, does not follow us along every turn of our intricate path, though some of our enthusiasms do tend to get passed along. There is an aura about the computer field. It moves so fast and it seems so technologically complicated to the outsider that it appears mysterious. The average personal computer user may have no idea how a program works or why a particular new feature is important. But if it is the latest advance, the top of the line, and is affordable, that's enough justification for enthusiasts to go out and buy it.

Of course, we in the personal computer business capitalize on this aura. That's called marketing. Decisions about which computer products to buy quite often transcend rational considerations of product capabilities and user needs. Psychographics come into play, just as they do in the automobile business.

At least some of the success of the Apple II is due to the successful creation of a religious mystique. Even kids on the streets compare their schools on the basis of which computers they use: "My school is better than yours because we have Apple II." It's a mark of status. Sometimes you'll hear Apple II owners putting down, for example, the TRS-80. But there are an awful lot of very satisfied TRS-80 owners out there.

Real religion has played a vital role in the lives of many for whom it provides guiding principles, a philosophy and a source of inner strength. But computers are not the Cosmos, nor are they even instruments of salvation. Computers are tools, like screwdrivers or garden rakes. The important considerations are rational and pragmatic. There are no end-alls. There is not necessarily just one way to approach a problem. Advances in computers will not necessarily obsolete former alternatives. The religion of computers is often no more than prejudice and superstition.

THE 10111'RD PSALM

The Computer is my taskmaster; I need not think.
    He maketh me to write flawless reports
He leadeth me with Computer-Aided Instruction
He restoreth my jumbled files
He guideth me through the program with menus.

Yea, though I walk through the valley of
    the endless GOTO,
I will fear no error messages;
    For thy User's Manual is with me.

Thy disk drive and thy Pac-Man—they comfort me.
Thou displayest a spreadsheet program before me
    in the presence of my supervisor.

Thou enableth the printout;
    the floor runneth over (with paper).
Surely good jobs and good pay shall follow me
    All the days of my life;

And I shall access your CPUs, forever.

(P.S. Please note that 10111 is the binary equivalent of 23.)

Revised by CHARLES P. RUBENSTEIN, with apologies to King David

COMPUTERS AND THE HOLY WORD

Deep inside the Rocky Mountains, the Mormons' computerized census prepares for Judgment Day.

Since its inception, the Bible has been the "best seller" of all Western writings and the most copied work of all time. Now the King James Version is available in a computerized edition called The WORD Processor, marketed by Bible Research Systems and created by Bert Brown and Kent Ochel to run on the Apple, TRS-80 and IBM PC microcomputers. Useful in pinpointing specific words and phrases, as well as determining their frequency, the software package of eight double-sided diskettes integrates a word processing and data base program with the text found on an old IBM 360 paper tape used for typesetting the Bible's 4.5 million characters.

The computer is also being used by researchers of religion to study Genesis, the first book of the Old Testament, and is an important factor in arriving at the conclusion that this text was indeed written by a single author. And in the area of equal rights an IBM PC is being put to work by the Incarnation Church in Washington, D.C., in the removal of sexist language from prayer books and other religious material and perhaps even from the Bible.

In the matter of referring to God Himself, the mysticism of the ages has carried over to modern-day religion. Because Orthodox Judaism holds the divine name in such high regard that there is a prohibition on pronouncing the Tetragrammaton (YHWH, the four-letter Ineffable Personal Name of God), care and wisdom must be exercised in the use of speech synthesis peripherals. More important where the computer is concerned, it is equally forbidden to delete the name of God from a written document. The question of writing on a diskette, whose stored image could be erased

in error, might cause concern were it not for the already implemented practice of using words that convey the meaning but not the explicit spelling of God's name.

In Utah the LDS Church Library, extending the biblical tradition of census taking, maintains the world's largest genealogical data base inside a half-dozen chambers carved out of the Rocky Mountains. The LDS Library (LDS is shorthand for the Church of Jesus Christ of Latter-Day Saints, also called the Mormon Church) keeps these records for its more than three million current members and their ancestors to allow baptism by proxy and thus assure the entire family of a life in the hereafter.

The sheer magnitude of material, over 1.5 billion pages of family trees copied onto over a million rolls of microfilm and containing 60 million family records from 126 different countries, cried out for electronic access and today the index alone of this computerized data bank consists of over 30 million church member records with another 30 million records from nonmembers around the world. Census information dating back to 1890, forty years after the Mormons settled near the valley of Salt Lake City, is also available at the Library and its several branches.

For more information on these activities, write to the LDS Library at 50 East North Temple St., Salt Lake City, Utah 84105.

CHARLES P. RUBENSTEIN, electronics technology chairman at Bramson Ort Technical Institute and author of *The Encyclopedia of Computer Fundamentals*

PERSONAL CHOICES

Artwork for preceding page

Artist:
   Errol Otus
Computer:
   Commodore 64 personal computer
Software:
   Micro Illustrator by Island Graph-
   ics
Input:
   Digitizing tablet

TEST-DRIVING THE EPSON QX-10

by Frank Rose

Frank Rose and the keyboard of his "power everything" Epson QX-10.

It all started when I was on the phone with the president of Rising Star Industries, the California software firm that was programming Epson's soon to be released QX-10 microcomputer. What, I asked, was a rising star? It was Japan and America, he said, the Rising Sun and the Stars & Stripes. The Epson computer and its Valdocs word processing software would be a marriage of Japanese engineering and American ingenuity. And as a professional writer, he mentioned, I'd make a perfect beta test site for the new machine.

What was a beta test site? I called my friend in Silicon Valley. A beta test site, he said, is a novice who tests a new computer. Alpha tests involve company

---

Frank Rose is a contributing editor at Esquire. *He is the author of* Into the Heart of the Mind: An American Quest for Artificial Intelligence.

personnel; beta tests involve random specimens from the general public. I'd be a guinea pig: if there were any bugs in the system—and there would be—I'd be the one they'd bite.

I called back and said yes.

Two months later a series of cardboard boxes arrived at the door. Inside was the Epson hardware: an 8-bit machine with 256K of random access memory, using the Z80 microprocessor and running on the TPM operating system (an advanced version of CP/M). At the time I didn't know what all this meant, but I would soon find out.

When set up, the Epson QX-10 looked like a sleeker version of the IBM PC: lean, low-profile, ready for business. Unfortunately, I couldn't do anything until the software came.

Another two weeks and the software arrived, but there was no manual, no instruction book, no documentation, no anything. This, I thought, must be part of the test. One of the main selling points of the Epson, I'd been told, was "user-friendliness." This was intended to be a machine you could plug in and use right away, like a stereo or a toaster-oven. I was dubious. But I did know that the Valdocs disk was supposed to go in the A drive and the data disk in the B drive, so I turned on the machine, slipped the disks in and pushed the button marked HELP. The screen filled up with a few basic instructions, and before long I was ready to go to work.

When the documentation finally showed up, I learned some new tricks: how to delete text by the word or the line, how to get into the "electronic address book" that threatened to replace my Rolodex, how to use the CALC button to do calculations on figures in my text. Over the next few months I learned also to appreciate the clean design of the on-screen text editor and the effortless nature of the keyboard. It was the keyboard that particularly impressed me— a long slab of plastic that encouraged easy access and fluid motion.

But there was a downside to the beta test experience as well. I was working with experimental software, and one of my duties (aside from suggesting ways it might be improved) was to fall into any hidden traps that might be lurking in the code. These traps took any number of forms and appeared at random. One was simple data loss: I might store a file and find it half a page shorter when I came back to it. Then there was data scramble: sentences and fragments of sentences were liable to turn up in any order they pleased.

My favorite bug, however, was the one I came to know as the "screen of Damocles": at any moment the text I was working on might be replaced by a screen full of nonsense characters. Once that happened, there was nothing to do but turn off the machine, turn it back on and return to the file as it had last been stored on disk. To call this daunting would be an understatement; but I like to think that for a while, at least, it lent a certain existential quality to my writing.

Eventually the bugs were cleared up, extra features were added and Valdocs began to work the way it was supposed to—cleanly, logically, efficiently. Only then was it possible to judge the system as a purchaser would, on the basis of what it actually did instead of what it was supposed to do or what it might do if you were unlucky. When that happened, I became aware of a curious fact.

Like a two-ton Cadillac with power everything, the Valdocs software is so loaded down with luxury items that its performance can be a bit sluggish. Everything works—you can get on-screen italics, and long file names, and two print modes, and on-screen graphics, and on-screen underlining, and a multitude of block commands, and electronic mail at the flick of a button—but it isn't going to set any speed records. Was this the Rising Sun and the Stars & Stripes, I wondered, or was this Detroit?

That said, how do I feel about my road hog? I love it. It looks great. It makes me feel good just to sit behind the keyboard. Its 256K of main memory and 376K of disk storage capacity makes it big enough to push other machines off the road. (I've even started talking about memory capacity the way hot rodders talk about horsepower.) I know its text editor like the back of my hand. And just last week I got a commemorative plaque from Rising Star informing me that, as a beta test site , a part of me " resides within its code." While searching for a spot to hang the thing, I wondered: Does this mean I can load it in and go visit myself? ∎

WHAT IS A COMPUTER?

A computer is a piece of equipment that can be made to follow a predetermined plan or to obey a spell you cast on it. That's the good news.

The bad news is that creating such a plan, casting such a spell, is much harder than you'd think. The mechanics of spellcasting—or, as it is called, "programming"—becomes the center of people's lives. All kinds of clever fellows keep inventing new spellcasting systems, so the hope is dim for standards, stabilization or general transportability between all the different computers.

Why such fascination with the mechanics of planning and casting spells? Because so many new possibilities keep coming into view. Only gradually are we learning that the art of programming has as many styles and systems of composition as, say, music.

Each person's viewpoint is different. Practically every spellcaster wants to do things a different way, and a lot of them eventually get around to designing their own spellcasting systems—or, as they are called, "computer languages." The new language builders want to accommodate a new range of variations, thinking they see a way to reduce the complexity of design and arrangement. So they invent a method, a language, that opens up, they think, rich new possibilities. And, indeed, frequently it does—and now the computers can be made to do new things, or combinations of old things with a less difficult spell, and its users develop a style of their own.

If the new language is successful, enthusiasts and usages proliferate. The new possibilities are tried in combination after combination, and assembled by enthusiasts into new skyscrapers of combinations. And inevitably there are difficulties and complications as these detailed edifices of plan-structures grow. And the complications increasingly frustrate some of the enthusiasts, and there we go again.

TED NELSON

WHY I LOVE MY MODEL 100

by Ira Mayer

Ira Mayer as Super Reporter, phoning in a story with his Model 100 portable computer.

The Radio Shack Model 100 textbook-size computer is every journalist's dream. I know. I've been able to act out my Super Reporter fantasies, composing hot stories in midflight, then standing in booths at the airport or on the Champs Élysées, transmitting my copy over the phone handset to the New York *Post* or over Telex lines to London.

The Model 100 sounded like the perfect traveling companion when it was first announced. After reading a glowing *Wall Street Journal* review of the machine composed at 36,000 feet, I called the public relations department of Tandy to ask to borrow one for review purposes.

One of the benefits of writing about computers is that you get to borrow hardware and software to play with, usually for sixty or ninety days, after which you

Ira Mayer is the home computer columnist for the New York Post *and managing editor of* Video Marketing Newsletter.

either return it or pay for it. Some companies even offer a "professional discount." The Tandy guy down in Texas laughed, said sure, he'd add my name to the list, and warned that I was number 110 or so in line. That was about nine months ago. I'm still waiting to hear from him.

Off I went to the local Radio Shack store—a place I'd assiduously avoided for years. An audio hobbyist from way back, I didn't have a whole lot of respect for the Radio Shack ReaListic line of components or the popular TRS-80 series of full-size computers. The manager of the store had just sold twenty-five units of the Model 100 after a demonstration for one of the national news wire services, so when I told him I did much of the computer reporting for the New York *Post* he understood my needs. When I added that I usually worked on a DECmate word processor, he also understood that I knew what first-rate word processing was.

He was honest enough to differentiate between

WHY IS A COMPUTER LIKE AN ELEPHANT?

A computer is a dynamic elephant, for other than the obvious reason. Sure, computers remember many, many things for a long time. But they're also like the pachyderm in the old story about the blind men and the elephant, because computers represent different things to different people.

To some, a computer is a game machine. To others, it's a writing machine that has obsoleted the typewriter. To the quantitatively oriented, it's a fabulous number cruncher that works at preposterous speeds. To still others, a computer keeps files, draws pie charts or maintains contact with huge storehouses of information.

Computers are dynamic because their uses change. A microwave oven cooks food, a lawn mower cuts grass, and a stereo plays music. Most appliances always did, and always will, have defined uses. But computers change: today they do lots of different things, at home, in our offices, and in the huge private and governmental organizations with which we deal; by 1990, with voice recognition and other technology I couldn't even begin to predict, computers will be something else entirely.

The very fact that computers are dynamic elephants is what keeps more and more of us totally fascinated, and many of us absolutely addicted.

KEN USTON

serious word processing and the "text processing" functions on the Model 100. "Text processing" differs from word processing in the number of functions available and the ease with which they can be performed. You can readily move a block of text with the Model 100, but it's difficult—if not impossible—to set tabs or underline or paginate a document. On the other hand, you can plug the Model 100 right into a telephone (where the handset plugs into the base of the phone) and establish a communications link with just about any network that operates at 300 baud. The acoustic coupler, which goes for an extra $20, is for those occasions when you can't unplug the phone.

Like most computer owners, I've barely touched the surface of my Model 100's capabilities. For instance, I know that I can program the computer to log onto the Telex network for me, retrieve my electronic mail and automatically send out my stories. Yet I still dial manually, log on myself and then hit the UPLOAD button. I also know the thing will buzz to remind me of appointments entered into the scheduling program, but I prefer my somewhat imprecise body clock (or the one on my office wall with the numbers all tumbling off the face). I even know that I could do some more sophisticated word processing tasks by remembering—or even looking up—the codes needed to activate those functions that are instituted by hitting the CONTROL key along with some others.

But I'm lazy. Besides, most of the kick of using the Model 100 comes from watching other people's faces (particularly those of the poor souls lugging around thirty-pound Osbornes and Kaypros) as I sit on planes, in airports or, especially, in interviews. One executive whom I'd interviewed at least a half-dozen times, and who never remembered me from one time to the next, finally took notice when during a press conference I recorded all my notes directly onto the machine.

The only complaint I've had since buying my "lap computer" is that downloading cassette programs to the machine hasn't worked properly. (In fact, it's in the shop as I write this on my now antiquated DECmate I.) It also has all sorts of graphics keys that do things I don't understand. But I look forward to playing with the game tapes someday soon and to working with what looks like a great spreadsheet program—just enough to do my small-business forecasting. The new magazine for the Model 100 seems to have new programs available every month, though Radio Shack itself hasn't been all that quick to add software for the unit.

Then again, the Model 100's software may already be too useful for my good in certain areas. I'd better not tell my wife about its alarm/scheduler function or she'll set the little bugger on my case about those chores around the house. How many Model 100s does it take to screw in a light bulb, anyway? ∎

WHERE ARE THE VICS OF YESTERYEAR?

by Steve Ditlea

Ilya Ditlya and new friend: old computers, like the VIC 20, shouldn't die . . .

The Commodore VIC-20 was not my first love in personal computers, nor will it be my last. But I know that someday, when I'm old and gray, I'll look back with fondness on its compact curves and spunk.

Poor VIC (I like to think this was short for Victoria, though it really meant "video interface chip"): born with so many strikes against it, with an antiquated microprocessor for a brain, always considered the runt of the family, ready to be sacrificed at a marketer's whim. And yet VIC managed to break popularity records around the world. It was the first personal computer model to sell more than a million units.

Alas, so many of us merely flirted with VIC, eventually leaving countless models sitting on closet shelves to gather dust. If only we had realized then what I know now, that VIC had heart and soul and was deserving of the consideration not even its designers ever seemed to accord. VIC's was a classy chassis, a compact design that turned out to be every bit as definitive as the pregnant typewriter silhouette of the Apple II or the schizophrenic detachable keyboard of the IBM PC. And for a machine based on a 6502 microprocessor it did wonders, including sprightly graphics and sound that put Apple to shame. But we were all so blind . . .

VIC was living on borrowed time. It was just an interim machine, a stopgap by the manufacturer until the brawnier Commodore 64 could be produced in quantity. Its life cycle was a mere year and a half or two—long enough to bring a decent profit. Introduced at $199, it could have been sold for $99 and still made money for all involved.

When VIC came into my life, my heart already belonged to another. The Apple II computer and I had not exactly experienced love at first sight, since my encounter with an adolescent, diskette-less early incarnation left much to be desired. With time, however, infatuation turned into love and I decided to bind my fate to an Apple II Plus—a decision I have never regretted, despite our occasional spats.

I suppose VIC could never really satisfy me once I'd experienced the depth of software for my Apple II. VIC's limited memory capacity (5K expandable to 32K) was no match for an Apple's ultimate 64K, and the software showed it. Word processing was a joke in its 22-character-wide display, and cassette storage of data meant that serious professional use was out of the question.

But VIC had spirit and style. Its BASIC was as good as anyone's. Its color graphics were remarkable. With a synthesizer program, it could put an early Moog to shame. As an entertainment machine, it could play Choplifter, the helicopter rescue game, with the best of home computers. As for its telecommunications capability, VIC and an accompanying $100 modem from Commodore probably did more to bring the network revolution into American homes than the advent of the electrical pulse. When a nineteen-year-old California hacker was caught breaking into the Defense Department-sponsored ARPANET network, it was not with some IBM PC or TI Professional, but with a humble VIC-20.

I suppose it was inevitable that my fingers would return to the familiarity of my Apple II. I saw less and less of VIC. The flow of new software for the VIC-20, once a torrent, turned to a trickle and dried up completely. The Commodore 64 was starting its ominous squeeze-out in the stores. VIC was no longer a serious contender.

It was over between us, but there's a happy ending to our story. Instead of being relegated to the cruel limbo of dust-gathering in my closet, my VIC-20 has found fulfillment at the hands of my six-year-old cousin Ilya in Queens. The VIC is his first computer. It will influence him for life. (Perhaps as the noisy old Royal typewriter in my father's office made me think at age six that writing for a living might be fun.) ∎

MEMOIRS OF AN OSBORNE

by David Nimmons

It's never been dull, being an Osborne I. When it all started, I was the hottest thing since the diode. There he goes, they'd whisper, the machine that invented the portable market. But then came the problems, the bad press, and finally the Big Sleep they call chapter XI, with my makers broke. It's not that I miss the glitz; I just wish someone had asked me for my side. Just once couldn't someone come up, buy me a disk

and say, "Hey, Ozzie, tell me: what was it *really* like?"

It was never easy. My whole life, people made fun of me. When I came out in 1981, everybody took pot shots. I was smaller than the others—at twenty-three pounds I was the lightest in my class. "Hey, look at the sewin' machine with the funny name!" they'd taunt. "Why don't you go hide under an airplane seat if you're so portable?" I'd hear the whispers in the hallway: "If the Good Lord had intended Adam and Eve to have portable computers, He wouldn't have given them an Apple."

David Nimmons is an editor at Playboy *magazine and works as a computer consultant to community groups and magazines in New York.*

The worst was in physical education. In the locker room, booting up, the big guys would point at my five-inch screen: "It's so *tiny*," they'd yell. "What can you do with *that*?" I hated it when they made fun of my specifications.

But slowly they began to see I was smart. That made me stand out. At the time most personal computers were still, well, undeveloped, with a mere 48K memory. They were fun for games—and who could forget their graphics?—but when the time came to run a serious program like word processing, they just couldn't keep up. Most of the other machines in my class, the under $2,000 group, seemed like kids. Me, on the other hand, I matured early; I had 64K and knew how to use it.

A lot of the other machines led you on. You'd pick them out, spend time together in the store, pay $2,000 for their sleek curves and then, when you got them home, find they wouldn't come across. Nobody ever mentioned that you had to buy another $1,000 worth of software if you wanted something more complex than a doorstop.

I was never like that. Let those other machines come with a book and a prayer; Osborne gave you enough software to run a small country. I'm not bragging or anything, but I really showed users a good time: I had WordStar, the best word processor around; SuperCalc, an electronic spreadsheet; BASIC for programmers; and enough CP/M utilities to do most housekeeping and organization tasks any new owner would be likely to have. It added up to about $1,500 worth of programs. When you're wearing a $1,795 price tag, well, it makes people look at you different. Word got around: Osborne comes through when you get him home.

Also, I was compatible. Maybe it's just because I'm a CP/M kind of machine and all, but I look at some of those weird operating systems as pretty impractical. It's like studying art history or something—what good is it out in the real world? A machine has to get along out there, and in those days, since more CP/M programs were written than any other kind, I could run most any off-the-shelf commercial software.

Then one day they stopped calling me just 01. Suddenly I was an Executive. I looked down at my disk drives and realized they'd grown up: 192K per drive, double density. My RAM was no longer a child's 64K; it had swelled to a grown-up 128K, which meant I could run faster, more powerful software.

There were some subtle changes, too. I learned to read several other formats: IBM, DEC, Xerox. I also learned about, well, interfacing. I was much better at getting mainframes to talk to me, partly because I could emulate several kinds of terminals. I even gained five pounds. They equipped me for a co-processor, in addition to my Z80A processor, so I'd be able to run IBM software right off the shelf.

But the best thing about being an Executive was that my screen got bigger, more usable, clearer. People started respecting my 80 columns, my seven-inch display. I'll admit it still wasn't the biggest around, but it was readable and sharp and a beautiful amber color.

Me, I got no regrets. What happened wasn't my fault. I was a good machine and corporate let me down, nothing I could have done. But after all this time, couldn't they lay off about my screen already? ∎

David Nimmons holds a wake for his Osborne's unborn brethren.

THE ATARI AFFAIR

by Norman Schreiber

When you first start having an intense relationship with a computer, you feel as if you're master of the universe. Playing a game like Star Raiders on my Atari 800 certainly underscored that sense. How many hours did I spend blasting, zapping, hyperwarping and probably hyperventilating? The machine's playfulness delighted and attracted me.

Sometimes, when conducting some sort of business on the phone, I found myself absently doodling the word "Atari." I was hooked and I loved it. I loved my Atari. And why not? It was responsive. It was easy to use. I didn't have to poke around putting boards in and taking chips out. When I expanded the Atari's memory to 48K, I just snapped in a 16K RAM cartridge as if it were an 8-track tape. No muss. No fuss. No bother.

The colors it generated were great, and it offered so much ease and flexibility in generating graphics. Then Atari's word processing program came. Our relationship changed.

Writing with the Atari was fun. The Atari word processing program is menu-driven. As its questions appeared on the screen, I could swear I heard a mellifluous voice in the room. And indeed I did. The voice happened to be mine. I was reading aloud.

"Would you like to print, edit, perform other functions?"

"Do you really want to erase that file?"

"How would you like your eggs?"

No, it didn't ask that last question; but I looked forward to the day when it would.

If only I hadn't listened to what the other writer guys told me. I knew all along that the Atari 800 was not looked upon as the most desirable of computers. People with conventional criteria couldn't appreciate its beautiful soul and its giving ways. They made nasty remarks about it. They smirked.

"Isn't it annoying when you're only able to look at forty columns instead of eighty?" my friend Mike asked me one day. "Don't you mind that it takes forever to format?"

Norman Schreiber writes about science, traditional music and bourbon. He is a contributing editor for Popular Photography *and regularly contributes to* Travel & Leisure.

"Well, *you* have to put a board in to get upper- and lower-case characters," I responded hotly. "*I* don't have to."

"But what about CP/M?" someone else asked. "Does yours have CP/M? Mine has CP/M."

I forget my retort to that one, but it makes no difference: I succumbed. I was weak and I gave in. I still loved my Atari, but I didn't respect it anymore. I just used it. Even when I was keystroking, I thought about other computers that captured my eye. Coming back from a computer exposition, I would walk quickly past the Atari. I didn't want to answer any questions. Of course, when I felt a raging need to play a game, my path was direct. There was no subtlety to my approach, and of course the Atari took all I gave.

The Atari 800 is in my son's room now. In a sense the machine has been given a promotion. Jason is sixteen and knows more about computers than I probably ever will. Sometimes he'll actually leave the sanctity of his room to show me something he's created—a new design, a new game, a program expressly designed to play with Frank Zappa music in the background. Sometimes I try to beg off. I think it's because I don't want to see how beautiful, versatile and entrancing the Atari 800 continues to be. ∎

Norman Schreiber and his attractive Atari.

THE KAYPRO, TOO

by Norman Schreiber

When I was nineteen my playwriting teacher, Samson Raphaelson, told me I would be pretty good once I'd lived awhile and gathered a certain degree of experience. Being nineteen, I thought I knew what he meant. Now I literally know better.

This lesson extends to my involvement with computers. I have already revealed my Atari past and the passion associated with it. I will always revere the Atari for its ability to nurture within me that sense of wonder that usually is lost with so-called maturity. The Kaypro II, on the other hand, appeals to that sense of mastery and confidence that can only be gained through experience.

The Kaypro II is a twenty-six-pound compact machine that includes computer, monitor and twin disk drives. It closes neatly into a case that travels—and so is referred to as "transportable." This ability to travel has made it appealing to many people. A friend of mine, who goes to Maine whenever he can, bought a Kaypro because he's working on a book and this seemed like an easy way to write it in both New York and Maine. I've also heard of an Angora goat raiser who takes his Kaypro to the various sheds on his farm so he can do the appropriate record keeping.

I like the Kaypro because it reminds me of reading the New York *Times* or the Washington *Post*. Just about everything is there. Or maybe it's like having an informed, not too witty companion who travels with you.

Of course, when many of us discuss our computer adventures, we really are referring to our use of store-bought software. My Kaypro II came with Perfect (that's the brand name) Writer, Perfect Filer and Perfect Calc. These are eminently easy to use, but I found them a little difficult to learn. I suspect they would be less difficult to learn if the instruction manuals were (how shall I say it?) closer to Perfect-ion than they are. As a matter of fact, I believe that Kaypro II sales spawned a mini industry: dozens of people around the country are determined to write a comprehensible user's guide.

Most of my Kaypro II activity is devoted to Perfect Writer, the word processing program. The machine is my collaborator. It allows me to find possibilities of expression and structure. It listens to my words, phrases, sentences and ideas without being judgmental. Yet it provides me with commands by which I can make my meaning clearer. Some of these commands enable me to make the page look a certain way so that I can emphasize something. Other commands allow me to experiment with my words by modifying them or moving them about. Many writers have said they write so that they can better clarify their own thoughts. That's certainly what happens when I spend time with Kaypro II and Perfect Writer.

Interestingly enough, I have gained my understanding and appreciation of my machine through its software. The Kaypro II is a discreet presence. The Perfect Writer's talents are made possible by the abilities of the Kaypro II. The machine is the perfect straight man. It is the software that performs; however, it is the Kaypro II that tells me to go ahead and explore. It makes me feel that it will be there to make possible whatever it is I want to do.

The Kaypro II does not inspire the grand careening computer passion I once knew. Instead, there is something . . . not better or worse, but definitely different. As the Kaypro II travels with me, the atmosphere vibrates with calm, support and the simple understanding that I always will be helped whenever I desire to use my experience and achieve my best. ■

Norman Schreiber with his businesslike Kaypro.

CONFESSIONS OF AN IBM PC OWNER

by Lindsy Van Gelder

I am essentially a sixties person: your basic left-liberal, radical feminist, anticorporate, Lacoste-hating old hippie whose leading cultural reference point is *Mother Jones*, not Dow Jones. I have a rent-controlled apartment, a child in the New York City public schools and an almost completely spotless record (spoiled by Bella Abzug) of voting for losing candidates.

And I have an IBM.

I love my little PC, but it wreaks havoc with my self-image. Not that I consider IBM an especially evil corporation (I suppose if they were dumping infant formula on the Third World or manufacturing napalm, I could have resisted buying their product with no trouble), but they're . . . well, stuffy. They reek of what we sixties people used to call "uptight." If you can't instantly see the utter folly of my position, consider the following description tendered by Apple president John Sculley in an interview in *InfoWorld*: "I think IBM consumers are more traditional. If you see them in the office, they probably have their jacket on, and they wouldn't give an interview without a three-piece suit on."

I bought my IBM back in early 1982 because, after compulsively researching the market, I concluded that it was the best machine around for my needs. Emotionally, this was somewhat on a par with discovering that designer jeans are more comfortable than Levis or that iceberg is the most nutritious lettuce or that Richard Nixon is the best candidate for the job, but I bought the IBM anyway.

From time to time I still feel the pull toward the images of other computers, if not their particular features. Radio Shack, for instance. Just the Jersey Turnpike, fast-food-chain sound of it appeals to me, not to mention its origins as a hobbyist's computer. Ditto for Apple, whose name is cute and as uncorporate as the Volkswagen Beetle. (Here it's rivaled only by the NorthStar, which sounds like it ought to be a back-

Lindsy Van Gelder is a contributing editor for PC, PCjr *and* Ms. *magazines.*

From counterculture to computer culture: Lindsy Van Gelder at home with her IBM PC.

packing tent.) The Timex computer has a proletarian feel to it, a first cousin to the Mickey Mouse watch. I also like the VIC, which sounds like a regular guy, a computer who pals around the bowling alley with Vito and Tony.

Even the Osborne is named for a real live maverick person, not a multinational company. People who own Osbornes affectionately refer to their machines as Oz (as in Wizard), or Ozzie (as in Harriet), whereas we IBM owners are reduced to referring to ours simply as PC—a usurpation of a generic that tends to infuriate other computer owners in much the same way that referring to United States residents as "Americans" tends to infuriate residents of the other nations in this hemisphere. (Perhaps we should call it Percy?)

Being an IBM owner also means that I end up on some of the poshest mailing lists around. In recent weeks I've been offered help for my "portfolio," a chance to be first on my block to buy a combination telephone/modem/answering machine/dialer "executive work station" (if only it would empty the kitty litter, too) and subscriptions to a mind-boggling number of IBM-related publications. Most of these offers arrive in my mailbox inexplicably addressed to the president of Lindsy Van Gelder, Inc.

But my worst moments as an IBMer occur on the CB channel of CompuServe. Whenever there's a lull in the conversation, some fool Atari owner invariably throws out the telecommunications equivalent of "What's your sign?":

WHAT R U ALL USING?

IBM, I casually reply.

Usually there's a long pause, and then something like WELL!!! LA DEE DAH!!!

I've tried to explain that such remarks ought to be saved for people with Fortunes or GRIDs. Like the Vuitton bag, the IBM is the one that's stuck with the snob label, whether it's the ritziest or not.

But I love my little PC: its awesome memory, its P31 high-res green screen, its sculpted function keys. Who knows? Maybe I could learn to love iceberg lettuce, once they bring out a 16-bit version and figure out how to run a WordStar disk on its head. ∎

THE APPLE OF MY EYE

by Steven Levy

When it came time to buy a computer, I was the most sincere of advice-seekers. I would ask anybody. And I got all sorts of answers, every one of them appended with a warning that if I didn't heed that particular suggestion I'd be miserable for an entire generation of technology.

I listened to the answers. I made notes. And finally I sought a consultant who would sell me a computer and show me how to use it. The moment I knew this one consultant was right for me was when he announced his choice for my computer: an Apple II Plus. Because in my heart I never really wanted anything else.

I am a person who takes note of the origins of things, and the karma of a given act. And in the world of computers I find no more pleasing start-up story than that of the Apple. A guy who loved computers built one in a garage, and made this computer different by giving it color, unlimited versatility and a bit of flakiness. It is a human creation, and the human who

Steven Levy is a columnist for Rolling Stone *and* Popular Computing. *He is the author of* Hackers.

Neatitude forever: Steven Levy lays hands on his Apple II system.

created it is readily identifiable and a friendly weirdo to boot. Stephen Wozniak aspired to a quality far more elusive than user-friendliness or marketability or sexiness (though the Apple has all of those).

He was shooting for Neatitude. His goal was to make his engineer friends look at his invention and say, "Neat!" Generally, they said it. And a few people with some marketing skills circulated the Apple name around enough for the world at large to appreciate Woz' machine.

There is no end to my pleasure in owning this sleek hunk of plastic and silicon. There were some immediate drawbacks, of course. I had to buy almost

WHAT IS A COMPUTER?

The Jacquard loom controls woven patterns through the use of punched cardboard cards.

A computer is a machine that handles patterns. It takes them in and sends them out. We think of these patterns as words or numbers, but computers handle them as words of their own language.

Many machines handle patterns. Only computers are controlled by the same sorts of patterns that they take in and give out. This makes them special— it means they can change their own instructions.

The languages of the computer are created by people, but people are still trying to learn their own languages. Therefore, computer languages are very simple and stupid. People also build the computer so that it will never do anything the patterns don't say exactly. Try telling someone *exactly* what to do and see how far you get.

If anyone suggested that living beings be turned into computers (through genetic engineering, for instance), I would be violently opposed. No "dumb animal" is so limited as a computer. It's a strange fact that some people think that computers should tell us what to do.

What are we to think of people like that?

LEE FELSENSTEIN, President of Golemics, Inc., and designer of the Sol and Osborne I computers

an extra thousand dollars' worth of hardware to get my Apple II to the level of a top-notch word processor. But even in the act of coupling up my machine with an 80-column board, a CP/M card and a load of chips that give it 16K more RAM (I love to talk computer), I was learning some valuable stuff. Stuff about my machine.

This experience of buying add-on hardware is extremely common among Apple II users, who can modify the original to do almost anything one can imagine a computer doing and some things that no one imagined a computer doing. This creativity is encouraged by the Apple itself. It is the only best-selling computer that has a lid that lifts off with more ease than the top of a peanut jar. You can't even plug in a joystick without opening the Apple lid and learning something in the process.

The Apple II assumes you are not an idiot. (In my case, this was not a reasonable assumption, but I adjusted.) It assumes you want to know something about how computers work. It assumes you want to know about how the world works.

I think this is what binds us Apple folk together. When I bought a computer, I wanted something more than a tool. I wanted something that would put me in touch with the world of computing. There is no better way to do that than with an Apple, with its unparalleled software base (I have a tarot reading program and a program for baseball statistics) and its easy, well-documented programming environment.

There are machines that do some of the things I do with an Apple II a bit better than I can do them with my Apple, but none of those machines can sit on my desk and *be* an Apple, which just by sitting there says, "I'm a computer. Touch me. I can do amazing things. Do your word processing on me, but remember, we can play games, too. And lots of other stuff. Not only am I part of history, but by using me you're part of history, too. As well as being a bit crazy thinking I'm talking to you when you haven't even turned me on yet."

Is my hearing this monologue a sign that I'm a bit flaky myself? Maybe. But that's a characteristic in keeping with Apple ownership. We're weird enough to think there's more to owning a computer than a venerable trade name. The secret every Apple owner knows is that in this world some of us are passengers and some of us are pilots. People who own IBMs are passengers in ambassador class. First-class riders buy Hewlett-Packard. Epson folk have reservations in coach, and Commodore 64 flies stand-by. Kids at half price own Ataris. Up in the cockpit, scarves tossed to the wind, are the Apple owners. All Apple owners see themselves as pioneers, and appreciate the original personality in a computer as well as its foxy looks.

When it comes to personality, nothing tops an Apple. Except an Apple owner. ∎

Deborah Wise with cat Ben and short-lived visitor, the Sinclair ZX81.

SINCLAIR AND THE SINGLE WOMAN

by Deborah Wise

When the review model of Sinclair Ltd.'s original $150 ZX81 arrived at my office one chilly fall day, I was delighted but skeptical. I had just started as a

Deborah Wise is the former East Coast editor of InfoWorld *and is currently a staff editor at* Business Week. *She has a cat named Ben, but no home computer to call her own.*

reporter for *InfoWorld*, a newsweekly devoted to personal computers, and I didn't know anything about the subject. People I interviewed spoke in strange acronyms, and they didn't supply a glossary. Working with a real computer seemed like the best solution. But, I questioned, was the ZX81 a real computer?

It did say "computer" on the box. It did come

A COMPUTER DEFINITION

Because of it's speed, accuracy and, most important, its ability to manipulate, the computer greatly enhances the production, processing and recording of ideas. Once you become proficient at working with a computer as a thought processor, going back to a typewriter is comparable to forgoing your electronic calculator in favor of pencil and paper to multiply 9,784 by 7,148 to arrive at 69,936,032.

"MR. WIZARD" (DON HERBERT)

with BASIC built into it. And it was developed by a scientist—Clive Sinclair, the madcap British inventor responsible for one of the first pocket calculators. But still I had my doubts. Could one of the greatest technological achievements of the postwar era resemble a one-pound box of Black Magic chocolates with a typewriter keyboard stenciled on the top?

Back home in the privacy of my living room, I set the scene for my first encounter with a computer. I changed into jeans and sat cross-legged on the floor in front of the black-and-white TV, the Sinclair cradled in my lap. Like a hard-core computerist, I was determined to hack until dawn or at least until I had my first computer program written.

At first the experiment went well. I studied chapters 1–4 in the manual, which covered setting up the machine. To my delight the cables, cords, power supply and RF modulator box that links the computer to the TV were all clearly marked. My Sinclair and I were up and running well before midnight. Miraculously, the K marker that the manual said would appear in the bottom left-hand side of the screen did

WHAT IS A COMPUTER?

Just as the camera is an extension of the eye and the wheel the extension of the foot, the computer could qualify as the extension of, not the brain or mind, but the ego.

Think about it. More than just number crunching is going on here. A computer handles words, numbers, data of all kinds, but it does this in the way we would like it to. No sooner is our home computer out of the box than we start wiring it, configuring it, programming it to suit our convenience. When a computer has anything to say on a computer network, it is in the words and thoughts of whoever is sitting at the keyboard. And to how many computers do we tell our most secret secrets?

Our love affair with this machine is a variation on an old theme. What we ultimately find most fascinating about the computer is its reflection of ourselves.

DOUG COLLIGAN, senior editor of *Omni* magazine

appear—a little fuzzy, but that was the TV's fault.

I began ploughing eagerly through the rest of the manual. The language was readable, but the results were rather mundane. I learned how to add two and two. After several tries the computer coughed up the correct answer. I was less than thrilled. Was this really computing? After two more hours I had managed, with great difficulty, to write four lines of code that made the screen display HELLO DEBORAH nonstop until I pulled the plug. I was still less than thrilled.

More problems began to appear. It's hard for anyone, and particularly hard for an inaccurate touch typist like me, to use a membrane keyboard. It felt like producing a term paper using the controls of a microwave oven—and I couldn't even come up with dinner. The keyboard was also getting tired of me. When you use one key too much on the Sinclair (and I had a necessary weakness for the DELETE key), it gives up. You can prod and push but the mistakes won't go away and you get interminable SYNTAX ERROR messages.

After four more hours of thumping away at the Sinclair, the burning desire to be computer-literate gave way to an equally warm desire to abandon the whole idea. I began to wish hacking meant picking up the nearest meat cleaver and using it.

More disasters followed. When I decided to give up on programming and play the computer games that came with the machine, I hit another brick wall. Theoretically, software is loaded into a Sinclair computer using an ordinary cassette tape recorder. I tried. I tried for about two hours. I followed the instructions to the letter, but the screen remained a blank. The noises that were supposed to indicate the program was loaded never sounded.

Frustration! What was the use of this "real" computer? With commendable restraint, I unplugged the box, turned off the television, closed the manual and went to bed.

I had wanted to become computer-literate and instead I became a ZX81 hater. Next day I asked Eddie, a young lad in the office, if he wanted to try out the discarded machine; I didn't say a word about my night of horrors. A week later he found me as I was finishing up a diatribe against membrane keyboards. The ZX81, in his opinion, was wonderful. He was learning BASIC and loving it. In under an hour he had managed to write a program that created an American flag, line by line, on the screen.

The ZX81 and its reincarnation as the Timex/Sinclair 1000 (a slightly souped-up version that Timex Corp. marketed for as little as $49) have sold very well worldwide. There are, in fact, about a million of the machines out there somewhere. But you have to wonder how many owners of the cheapest "real" computer ended up loving it like Eddie or hating it like me. ∎

LONELINESS OF THE TRS-80 USER

by Stan Miastkowski

Stan Miastkowski contemplates the best of the TRS-80.

Okay, I'll come right out and say it: I own a TRS-80 (Model II, to be exact). When computer people get together, I sit quietly in the corner, a computer wallflower listening to the intelligentsia talk about their IBM PCs, TI Professionals or the latest hot personal computer they've added to their collection.

Sooner or later someone notices me and the inevitable question comes: "Which computer do you have?" The room quiets, and after summoning all my courage I blurt out: "A TRS-80 Model II." As my face flushes, I witness a mixture of open-mouthed disbelief and a few smirks. Then the remarks start:

"A Trash-80 owner, eh?"

"You've got to be kidding!"

Stan Miastkowski is the computer columnist for Esquire *and editor-in-chief of* Microcomputer Handbook.

"And here I thought you knew about personal computers!"

Admit it: it's the "Shack" name that creates the impression of "Friendly Fred's Reliable Computer Sales." Despite their location in Fort Worth, away from the hi-tech circles of Silicon Valley, the Radio Shack people are far from being just a bunch of Texas hicks.

I know whereof I speak, because I once worked in Tandy Center. Radio Shack's TRS-80 Model I had been out for over a year, and in that hot Texas summer of 1979 the Model II was being designed by a team of young engineers. I watched it progress from an idea to a finished computer. Using the best components and helped by the Shack's quality control department, the engineers developed a no-nonsense business computer.

A year later I was in New Hampshire. I needed

a computer for my writing, and one night the thought that had been buried at the back of my mind surfaced with a vengeance: "A Model II, of course!" The next morning I sat outside the store and waited for the doors to open. I knew how to handle Radio Shack salespeople. I regaled them with the story of the Model II's birth, and put my fingers to the keyboard of what seemed an old familiar friend. Sure, it wasn't cheap, but how can you say no to a friend? I handed over my "never leave home without it" card, and by afternoon a Model II was comfortably settled in my office. The reacquaintance was underway.

Three years have passed, and my Model II still hums away contentedly after three books, dozens of magazine articles and uncounted letters. The hundreds of disks that have passed over its read/write heads are arranged like soldiers on the shelf—a library of programs and data that has served me well. And I'm smug in my satisfaction that if something should go wrong, my salvation is two miles away, not forty. Whenever I pass a Radio Shack store, I salute my former colleagues at Tandy Center.

Don't get me wrong, the TRS-80 Model II is far from a perfect computer (there is no such thing as the perfect personal computer), but I've learned to live with its idiosyncrasies. I know that if I turn the power off before removing my disks, all the data on the disks will be lost forever. In addition, after a bout of eyestrain and headaches, I had to replace the black-and-white video tube with an amber-tinted one.

But when deadlines press I know the Model II will come through in the clutch. Although familiarity is supposed to breed contempt, it's a fact that people are most comfortable with the personal computer and the word processing program they first use. I started using SCRIPSIT (Radio Shack's word processor for the Model II) in 1979. In the interim I've used and reviewed numerous word processing programs, many touted as the ultimate in user-friendliness; but I still return to SCRIPSIT, where I can do wondrous things without even thinking about them.

Incidentally, the computer nerds may not have Radio Shack to kick around much longer—not because the Shack's going out of the computer business like a few of its once high-and-mighty competitors, but because the executives in the top-floor oak-paneled offices at Tandy Center in Fort Worth have finally come to their senses. The company's "IBM-compatible" is no longer called Radio Shack. Instead, it's the Tandy. And that's just dandy.   ∎

THE MAC ON SKIS

by Esther Dyson

I recently discovered that Apple's Macintosh computer is in fact short skis for the mind.

Let me explain briefly about skiing. The faster you're skiing, almost out of control, the easier it is to maintain your balance. What stumps most beginners is their unwillingness to approach losing control.

In the old days, beginners started on gentle slopes and gradually built up their confidence and skill until they could handle the tough stuff. Then, a few years ago, a new approach came into vogue: the Graduated Learning Method. The idea was to start the user out with short skis, which are more controllable than the two-meter monsters favored by the experts. Long skis give more power and strength to experts who go so fast that the twist of a short ski would have little impact, but they only get in the way of a novice.

Like short skis, the Macintosh may be a little limiting for the experts, but it makes computing accessible to a much larger number of people who are afraid or incapable of using the traditional methods.

If the Mac is short skis, then ski boots are the interface. They are what enable you to control and maneuver your skis; they are what the computer user actually feels, sees and touches. If a boot is too loose, you can't move it precisely; if it's too tight, you'll give up in despair, as I almost did.

One Saturday morning not long ago I went to a

Esther Dyson is president of EDventure Holdings Inc. (formerly Rosen Research) and editor-in-chief of its newsletter, RELease 1.0.

ski rental shop in Squaw Valley. The salesman asked me my shoe size and handed me a pair of battered Nordica boots. Of course, the boots didn't fit properly. I tightened them to get a firmer grip, but I still had a hard time getting the skis to do what I wanted. Short they were, but not well connected to my legs.

If they were a computer, I would have said the interface was wanting, like a mouse that skips around erratically. If there's anything worse than being difficult, it's being unpredictable. Mac, on this score, works very well: all the software that runs on it follows the same rules. What's more, Mac is comfortable: no aching ankles, no cold toes . . . the boots fit.

I got down the hills, yes, but only slowly, and I didn't have that much fun doing it. The power of the skis wasn't accessible to me. I returned the skis and boots, and found another ski shop. What with better-fitting boots and a friendlier send-off, Sunday went much better. By the end of the day I was jumping over moguls.

In the same way, the Mac delivers a feeling of control and safety that encourages people to try new things. With long skis or a complex computer, you have the feeling that you're operating or maneuvering some-

thing. With short skis or the Mac, you feel that you're working with an extension of yourself.

Now, it's not fair to end this piece without mentioning that the GLM method of teaching skiing is controversial—and that it's a learning, not a using method. Do those short skis make it so easy that people never graduate to long skis? Do they enable? Or do they cripple?

One can ask the same questions about the Mac. Yes, it will invite lots of people to use a computer. But are they really using a computer? Will people graduate to a "real," difficult computer, or will they always be stuck at the Mac level, reliant on the Mac's friendly, comfy-boots interface, its consistent commands and its overall easiness? Or does it really matter so long as they get what they want out of their computer?

Here our metaphor begins to break down. Short skis really don't work as well at high speeds, for good skiers. But that's not necessarily true of short-ski computers. Currently, the Macintosh has only limited memory, but that's more of a financial consideration than a fundamental design problem. There's no reason the Mac can't get more powerful without losing its essential character. In fact, the Macintosh uses the power of a high-technology 68000 chip (the same that's inside many $20,000 computers) to make itself easier. It's inherently more powerful than the harder-to-use IBM PC, but its power makes things easier, not tougher, for the user.

Incidentally, when I told Don Estridge, head of the IBM division that developed the PC, that the Mac was short skis, he thought for a moment, then said: "Yes, but tall people need long skis." ■

Esther Dyson models Macintosh, Macmouse and Macshirt.

FAMILY FAVORITES

Artwork for preceding page

Artist:
    Barbara Nessim © 1984
Computer:
    Norpak IPS II videotext work
    station
Software:
    Paint program by Norpak, arc and
    polygon modes
Input:
    Digitizing tablet

A FAMILY COMPUTER DIARY

by James A., Joan, Jessica and Joshua Levine

The Levines were among the first on their block to have a home computer. Herewith a slice of the computerized life from their family diary.

11/15/81: Arrival

JAMES: Like a kid at camp waiting for a package full of candy, I've been checking the mail every day since Apple agreed to lend me a computer so I could keep a yearlong record of our family's entry into the electronic age. Today was the day—finally! But not everybody was thrilled when I unpacked the Apple II Plus

James A. Levine is director of the Fatherhood Project at the Bank Street College of Education in New York City. Joan Levine is a doctoral student in clinical psychology at City University of New York. At the time of this diary, Jessica and Joshua attended the Bank Street School for Children.

in the living room. Seven-year-old Joshua literally danced around it, unable to believe his good fortune. Eleven-year-old Jessica greeted the newcomer with a combination of smug indifference and outright defiance. My wife Joan, a self-confessed computer-phobe, rose to a level of bemused tolerance.

JOAN: In our family, Jim always has to buy the latest gadget. He was the first person to have an electronic calculator, and we had Mr. Coffee before anyone else. So when the computer came, and Jim started right in talking double disk drive and printer and then fancy printer and color monitor, I thought: Oh God, this is going to be a very expensive gizmo!

JOSHUA: I got really upset when I found out that setting it up took more than five minutes.

JESSICA: I thought it was dumb to make such a big deal over a machine.

1/27/82: Snoggle Addiction

JAMES: Because I haven't had time to learn how to use this machine, and because using it takes longer than I thought, I gave in and bought a packaged game. The salesman was a stringbean of a kid with pale skin and black pants two inches too high above his shoe tops, one of the whiz kid types I'd always expected to find in those stores. He sold me a version of Pac-Man called Snoggle—a pie with one piece missing that scurries over our screen, swallowing little dots while escaping being swallowed by round white "ghosts."

At first Jessica largely avoided the game, making it clear she had the same disdain for the home computer that she shows for the new computer in her classroom. Joshua, always ready to try something new, took to it eagerly but is often frustrated. He can't coordinate his small seven-year-old fingers quickly enough to keep from having his character eaten.

Still, Josh is hanging in there. And Jessica has been sneaking in to play when no one is looking. They're getting more and more hooked. In certain ways it's my greatest computer fear come true: just another version of the idiot box, keeping the kids from reading, exploring, dreaming.

And yet I'm fascinated by their determination and dexterity. They move the Snoggle character confidently around the screen, acting very blasé about it while I stand there using body English to show that I want them to move in a different direction. They have, in effect, learned some sort of strategy, figured out the internal logic of the game. Is it any better, or worse, than the other games they play? My concern is that it doesn't seem to involve any deductive reasoning, any analysis. It's sort of like riding a bicycle, but without the virtue of fresh air, companionship or rigorous exercise. Anyway, they love it. They come running downstairs to report their scores or to tell us they've advanced to cherries or oranges, as if we knew what that meant. And once in the middle of a game they stick to the machine as if they were baby octopi with suction cups. I've had to turn the power off to get them to come to dinner or to the phone, even to talk to their friends. What's going on here?

JOAN: I feel the same way I felt about *Sesame Street* when the kids were little: something to do when "there's nothing to do." I wonder if the games aren't a way of making the computer less formidable, more familiar.

3/8/82: Educational Games?

JAMES: Tonight Joshua was playing the hangman game, where the computer offers up a list of categories—household pets, presidents, colors, spelling—and then gives you blank spaces to guess letters for the word in your category. You can pick to play at the easy, hard or expert levels. It seemed like simplistic

Jessica and Joshua engage in computerized sibling rivalry.

nonsense, but then I started playing with the presidents quiz and found it somewhat intriguing. It forced me to remember names of presidents I had long forgot. Tyler. Who remembers when Tyler was president?

Josh was as engaged as me, thinking of presidents I never even knew he knew—not just Carter and Reagan, but Hoover and Washington. I look forward to playing again tomorrow and involving Jessica in it if I can.

JOSHUA: The hangman game? I thought it was pretty stupid because it gave you such easy clues. The expert level just meant you started off at a farther end of the cliff so you could fall off in a shorter amount of guesses.

The best games are the ones where the computer does the least. Snooper Troops was kind of fun. It was neat being a detective and trying to find if there were ghosts haunting a house. And if there weren't, then who was haunting it? I also liked filling up all the rooms with prizes in Gertrude's Puzzles.

4/10/82: Time Out

JAMES: Joshua went to the eye doctor today. Nothing wrong with his eyes. Much wrong with what he's been looking at. The doctor advised that we limit his time at the computer, at least for a while, and that we make sure he has a light on when he uses it.

Josh was very upset when we told him he could only use the computer a half-hour per day. I don't think the new limit upset him as much as the thought that Jessica might get the upper hand.

JOSHUA: I still have the highest score on Snoggle.

JESSICA: No, I do—thirty thousand.

JOAN: I still worry about the kids' eyes. I guess the research isn't all in yet, so in the meanwhile moderate use is probably the best course.

4/24/82: *Computers and the Nuclear Age*

JAMES: This weekend we marched in the antinuclear rally in Central Park. Joshua didn't come with us, but he is not oblivious to what it meant. Like most of our friends' children, he is anxious about nuclear war.

What are these computer games going to teach him? Press a button and shoot an incoming spaceship. Press another button and launch a rocket. There is even a game to simulate the nuclear hazard at Three Mile Island. However sophisticated these toys, are they not desensitizing our children to the horror of war, even more so than television? What can rockets and reactors mean to a child who's been playing with them all his life?

JESSICA: People shouldn't be playing a game to figure out how to keep a nuclear plant from blowing up. They should be figuring out how to keep from building it in the first place.

8/23/82: *Word Processing*

JAMES: The typing skills Joshua has developed are incredible. Tonight, using the Bank Street Writer word processing package designed for children, he sat at the keyboard and typed a thank-you letter to my father. Seven years old, a pipsqueak plunked down in front of this fancy machinery, and yet he was totally comfortable and in control. From "Dear Papa Al" to the final "Love, Josh," it took about fifteen minutes to compose and print out two copies of a nicely done three-paragraph letter without a single error.

Not that Josh didn't make mistakes. "Kitten" was initially "kiten," first letters of sentences weren't capitalized, and new paragraphs didn't start where they should. But all of these were painless for Josh to correct. In fact, they were almost fun, because he had to find the mistakes (with my guidance) and then manipulate the cursor so he could correct them. It was a stark contrast to what happens when Josh hand-writes a thank-you note. Here there were no smudges. Each mistake was zapped away like an alien in one of the computer games, and the finished product—both on the screen and on the printed page—was neatly and clearly laid out.

But there's more of interest here than the finished product or the detection of mistyped words. The computer seems to lend itself to analysis of the written word. Because he could see so clearly what he had written, Joshua was able to decide if it was really what he wanted to say. Josh doesn't know it, but he is learning to edit.

JOSH: The Bank Street Writer? That's the easiest word processor in the world. It doesn't take any brains to print it out. I just used my common sense. It was so neat to see the stuff that was on the screen actually go onto the paper. I can't wait till Dad puts in this new chip that will help print out graphics.

JOAN: Now that I'm using the Bank Street Writer for my dissertation, I see what Josh means. But when I was learning it I had such an aversion that I needed his help every minute: I can't do this, I can't do that, this isn't working, how do I get this to go from write to edit mode? Maybe you have to be eight or under to understand this computer revolution.

9/15/82: *Here to Stay*

JAMES: Now that my journal keeping is behind me, the computer has become part of our home, accepted without the intensity of emotion that greeted its arrival. Jessica has overcome her defiance (and her Snoggle habit) and uses it occasionally for typing reports or playing games with friends. Joan hasn't entirely overcome her phobia, but she is much more enthusiastic about having the computer.

Joshua's first year of close encounter with the new technology has brought him from a simplistic ecstasy to a more complex interest. At the ripe old age of eight he seems to have learned that computers are tools that can be used (or abused) in many ways, that they are what we make of them.

As for me, I find myself using the computer more and more—for financial planning and so forth—and even keep it on a special mobile station so I can move the entire system from room to room. In fact, now that the new "baby" has been with us for a year, I can't help saying—like any proud parent—it's hard to imagine life without it.

JOAN: Doing my dissertation—correcting errors effortlessly and printing out new copies—is fantastic. I'm really glad we have the computer.

JESSICA: I wouldn't mind if you gave it away, but I don't really care.

JOSHUA: I think it's better that we have it. If we didn't, I think I'd get really bored. ∎

James and Joan share the joys of word processing.

PERSONAL COMPUTERS IN SMALL-TOWN AMERICA

Though America's small towns have always been perceived as slow to accept technology or new ways of life, personal computer users in these parts came down with "computer fever" early in the game. In fact, the now legendary Altair came out of Albuquerque, New Mexico, population three hundred thousand. We may not have access to the large computer shops or some of the exotic computer brands and applications programs that our big-city cousins take for granted, but many of us have substituted ingenuity for availability. Besides, with the growing number of computer store chains and such already established retailers as Radio Shack, we really aren't behind the times.

Just as pickup trucks and jeeps are more common in rural areas than in big cities, so certain personal computer models are more at home here. When IBM introduced its personal computer, the company ran magazine ads portraying Main Street U.S.A. and the many business uses for a PC in small-town America. The truth is that small businesses here are as likely to have a Radio Shack TRS-80 Model II or III or 4 as an IBM. Because the Radio Shack chain reaches into areas where ComputerLands and K-Marts are unknown, their models tend to be more popular. The inexpensive Color Computer, for example, received only lukewarmly in major urban areas, has become a favorite and has inspired an unprecedented outpouring of homespun software.

Here's just a sampling of our rural ingenuity.
• A choirmaster in Hercules, California, saves time by programming hymn songs in the computer, printing them and giving the printouts to the choir members. This also provides a special hymn list for his own use and is easier than writing everything in longhand.
• A man in State College, Pennsylvania, designed a program to help allocate his household spending. The program creates a bar-graph chart representing expenses for groceries, travel, water and electric bills, and other miscellaneous items.
• One Charleston, South Carolina, taxpayer created his own income tax program to help him "render unto Caesar the things that are Caesar's." At the end of each quarter, receipts and checks are categorized. By the time income tax season arrives, he has the complete data for filing.
• A high school English teacher in Okemos, Michigan, was fed up with his students' complaints ("I don't have anything to write about!") when assigned to write a composition, so he developed a program that would ask questions geared to making them think about past knowledge or experiences. His program served as a memory jogger, making assignments easier for his students and himself.

Small-town computer users are eager to share their knowledge, and more than a few successful software firms have made their mark from addresses like Bellevue, Washington; Coarsegold, California; and Ogdensburg, New York. And though much of the writing about computers comes out of urban technology centers, among the by-lines in many of the country's leading computer magazines you'll find the names of plenty of small-town inhabitants.

LAWRENCE C. FALK, editor of *The Rainbow* magazine, published in Prospect, Kentucky, for TRS-80 Color Computer users

THE MICRO MÉNAGE

by Michael A. Graziano

Electronic intelligence is inhabiting our homes in forms other than the familiar personal computer. With a little help from the microprocessor, common household devices are coming alive with useful and only occasionally frivolous capabilities.

Utilizing a high number of very tiny electronic components in a very small space, microprocessors provide cheap, efficient performance of jobs that would ordinarily require extremely complex and expensive circuitry. *Memory control* generally is involved in tasks that require the same action or actions to be repeated again and again, as in the operation of washing machines and microwave ovens. *Feedback control* is used in tasks that need to be monitored or "looked at" in order to maintain some state of equilibrium, such as automatic watering of the lawn, wherein the microprocessor looks at the moisture content of the soil, compares it to a predesignated level and controls the lawn sprinkler accordingly. *Time control* comes in when a task depends on the time of day, as in turning the downstairs lights on when you come home from work and off again after you've gone to bed.

From Tunes to TV

Touring a typical microprocessor-controlled home will allow us to examine these functions more closely.

Arriving at the front door, we ring the bell. No simple *ding-dong* in this home; instead a microprocessor-controlled doorbell emits a short chorus of Brahms' *Lullaby*. Or perhaps it's the theme from *Star Wars*. Microprocessor-controlled doorbells offer over twenty tunes, easily selected and changed at will.

In the hallway the first device we see is a thermostat, used to control both heating and cooling. It's a bit "fancier" than the simple units we're used to seeing, and upon closer inspection we find that this thermostat is "intelligent"; that is, it has a micropro-

Michael A. Graziano holds a bachelor of science degree in computer technology. He is the author of The Cat's Meow, *a book on how to computerize your home.*

cessor. During the winter months it can be set (or programmed) to regulate the temperature of the house relative to the hour, day of the week, outside temperature, or all three. Another of its features is that the heat is turned down by five to fifteen degrees during the sleeping hours, then raised to a comfortable level just prior to the first human stirrings in the morning. Air-conditioning control during the summer months is just as easy.

Next comes the living room, where we are struck by the picture on the television screen—vibrant with full, rich color. A closer look reveals the secret of the color stability of this TV: a microprocessor is making use of the broadcast stations' VIR (vertical interval reference) signals that contain information as to exactly how the color is supposed to look for each channel. The lack of a channel selector knob on the set is also courtesy of the microprocessor. Channels are simply programmed in once, and from that point on the micro takes care of channel selection and fine tuning. Even the "vertical hold" control, once found on every TV set, is gone forever.

In time, "digital TV" will take full advantage of the intelligence within microprocessors. In this revolutionary method of television broadcasting, the picture to be transmitted is broken up into numbers (from 1 to 255), then sent over the air in the form of digital "bits" of information. The microprocessor in the TV then reconverts these information bits back into a picture with clarity that will make today's best color TV picture look dreary by comparison.

Next to catch our eye is the stereo system. "Microprocessor-controlled," the name plate reads, in this case meaning all we have to do is designate which songs we want to hear on the LP records and which ones we'd like the stylus to "skip over." (Naturally, the same convenience applies to the cassette tape system.)

On our way to the kitchen we pass a telephone answering machine, microprocessor-controlled so that it can respond to calls with several different messages, inform a caller to try again at a certain time, or turn off should the party hang up. The machine also allows us to keep track of our messages by calling home and holding a small beeper next to the phone.

Domestic Digitals

Normally not a very exciting place in the home, the kitchen takes on new dimensions with micro power. Red LEDs (light emitting diodes) on the refrigerator glow to alert us that someone has left the door open and the temperature is rising to the "unsafe" zone. The bright blue digital clock on the microwave oven, having automatically defrosted and cooked the chicken tetrazzini, is now keeping it hot for dinner at seven sharp. Another digital clock on the dishwasher tells us that this appliance, too, is operated under the watchful eye of a microprocessor. We load it up with dishes, tell it what time to start washing, and walk away.

On we move to the master bedroom, certainly not a room in which you would expect to find many high-tech devices. But as the glowing numbers of the clock-radio indicate, intelligence is at work here. Besides simply telling us the hour, this clock-radio can be programmed to wake us up at different times on different days, to give us the correct time in a human-like voice, and even to turn on the morning coffee.

As we head out to the garage, another digital clock peers out at us from a utility closet. This one is an electronic timer that automatically turns house lights on and off at specified times or at random (to give an empty house that "lived in" look). A security system is also nearby, computer-controlled to activate or deactivate automatically, dial the police in case of intrusion and sniff the air for a hint of smoke.

The garage seems bare of micro devices, but that late-model car parked inside could hide some very high-tech equipment. In fact, we find that it contains a trip computer to keep tabs on miles per gallon, miles to drive to "empty," etc. And under the dash glow the red numbers of an anti-theft system that offers complete intrusion/theft monitoring and allows deactivation only by a secret code hidden deep within the microprocessor's memory.

But wait, gadgets are not the only evidence of automotive micro power. Lifting the hood, we discover that the engine's air/fuel mixture, ignition timing and pollution control devices are each tightly regulated under the careful supervision of still another microprocessor.

Our tour ends here, but suddenly the phone rings as we prepare to leave the grounds. Out on the sidewalk we could take it (via a microprocessor-controlled cordless telephone) but we decide to let the answering machine do its job. After all, that's what microprocessor-controlled devices are all about. ∎

"RALPH IS GOING POTTY"

My Apple-controlled home is an example of just how far you can go with micro power. It's been operating since 1978 and literally does everything from waking me up to keeping track of Ralph, my cat.

Utilizing detectors that gather information in various areas of the house, the computer can sense daylight, rain, vehicle movement, intrusion and fire. After digesting this data, it can then decide what, if any, action should be taken. For example, if its detectors sense rain at 6:30 A.M. (the time I get up), the computer will awaken me with the usual "Good morning, Mike" and tack on "Take an umbrella today."

With automation I've achieved total control over the heating and cooling units, with a substantial energy saving as a result. And since the inside and outside temperature, day of the week, time of day and whether anyone is at home (or will be shortly) are all known quantities, the computer can easily adjust the systems for maximum efficiency. A "tickler" file is also checked each morning and evening, and I am reminded, via an eerie, human-like voice, to pay the phone bill or to be at the dentist's by four o'clock.

The synthesized voice can speak to me over the telephone, too, and can answer a ring of my doorbell or say "Hi, Ralph" at random times to keep my cat happy.

Yes, Ralph, too, has entered the computer age. She is the user of the world's first computerized litter box. An enclosure has been built around her latrine, and mounted inside the door is a sensor that can detect Ralph's presence when she enters and make a note of the date and time. After allowing her a few minutes of privacy, the computer turns on a ventilator fan to scatter any odor outdoors; twenty minutes later, the fan is turned off to await Ralph's next guest appearance.

To add a bit of the human touch, the computer speech synthesizer announces each entrance with the words: "Ralph is going potty." Speakers installed in every room ensure that all humans within earshot are made aware of the historic event.

Why keep track of the date and time of Ralph's comings and goings? Because when I'm on vacation, I can call home and request the time of Ralph's last restroom visit. If it's recent, I can rest assured that all is well. If not, she may be ill, and I can contact a neighbor to check on her.

M.A.G.

COMPUTERIZED FITNESS

Now an array of "intelligent" exercisers can help you jog, row, bike—and even improve your golf game—without leaving home! Maintain your shape and your privacy with the same workout you'd get at the health club while you take the "out" out of workout.

1. Thanks to the Video Fitness System from Garden & Green Co., you can get fit while you play your favorite computer game. Hook up the VFS to your game console or home computer, and use your whole body as you play. Sensors in the VFS translate your body movements into instructions to the game, so you have to exercise your body—doing a sit-up, for example, to blast an asteroid. The VFS has routines for aerobic conditioning and weight control, flattening the stomach and trimming the hips and thighs.

2. Computers are also providing stepped-up exercise, quite literally. The StairMaster (from Tri-Tech, Inc.), an electronic staircase, lets you key in your goal in terms of number of flights, then helps you get there. The chest-level membrane console tells how you're doing by emitting encouraging beeps as you pass each floor; when you make it to the "top," it lets out a satisfying long signal. Your pulse is constantly monitored, and there are six different settings for varied resistance. A bonus feature is a chart that lists fifteen international landmarks, their heights and number of floors. The challenge is implicit. Scale such wonders as the Statue of Liberty (thirty-four floors), Washington Monument (fifty-five) or Hoover Dam (seventy-two), or hit the top of the CN tower in Toronto (one hundred and fifty-nine).

3. Hop on Universal's computerized, magneto-powered Aerobicycle, featuring five preprogrammed exercise modes. "Constant rotation" keeps you pedaling at an even pace; "steady climb" provides constant resistance; "rolling hills" lets you change terrain by varying the resistance at random; "pulse training" automatically readjusts the resistance to match your efforts. Your pulse is monitored along the way, and there's a display of the calories you're burning off. The final mode is a fitness test that ranks you with the national YMCA norms according to sex, age and aerobic fitness level.

4. Stop going around in circles! This electronic running track, the Amerec 930e, uses optic sensors placed under the running belt and an LED display panel set into a membrane keyboard at chest level to monitor your efforts. The sensors indicate your speed within .1 m.p.h., the distance covered, and your time, all available at once or one element at a time for continuous monitoring.

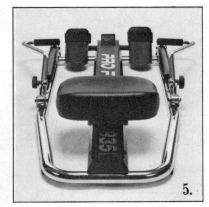

5. The world's first electronic rower, the Proform 935, features an LCD control panel that sits within easy reach between the footrests and offers a choice of four audio tones with which to pace yourself. Program in your desired speed in strokes per minute, pick your tone—and you're off, timed and paced, with a constant record of your speed and completed strokes.

HOW A *DIGITAL* WATCH WORKS

BY LARRY GONICK, SOME OF WHOSE BEST FRIENDS ARE ELECTRONS

THE DIGITAL WATCH IS A COMBINATION OF **PHYSICS** AND **LOGIC**.

IN THE BEGINNING IS PHYSICS... AT THE END IS LOGIC... IN THE MIDDLE ARE ZILLIONS OF ELECTRONS...

THE PHYSICAL PRINCIPLE IS THE **PIEZOELECTRIC EFFECT**. IT SAYS, IF A CRYSTAL IS BENT FOR ANY REASON, IT EMITS ELECTRONS.

BZOINK WHOING

PIEZOELECTRIC EFFECT

CONTRARIWISE, AN ELECTRIC CURRENT CAN BEND A CRYSTAL.

ZAP DEFORM!

ALSO THE P.E. EFFECT

YOUR DIGITAL WATCH USES THIS EFFECT BY APPLYING ALTERNATING CURRENT TO A CRYSTAL OF A PRECISE SIZE.

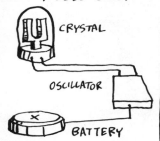

CRYSTAL

OSCILLATOR

BATTERY

RESULT:

ZAP

ZORT

ZARP

ZERT

THE VIBRATING CRYSTAL EMITS A PULSE OF ELECTRONS PRECISELY

32,768

TIMES PER SECOND!

NOW COMES LOGIC.

LOOK OUT!

THE SPEEDING ELECTRONS ENCOUNTER AN ELECTRONIC **TOGGLE SWITCH**. WHENEVER A PULSE OF ELECTRONS ARRIVES, THIS GIZMO **REVERSES** ITS OUTPUT:

→ OFF

ZAP
ᗢᗢᗢ → ON

ᗢᗢᗢ → ON

ZAP
ᗢᗢᗢ → OFF

→ OFF

ETC!

THE TOGGLE SWITCH **DIVIDES** THE NUMBER OF PULSES IN **HALF !!** (COUNT 'EM! IT PRODUCES ONE PULSE FOR EVERY TWO OF THE CRYSTAL'S.)

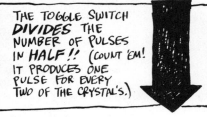

CRYSTAL   ON / OFF

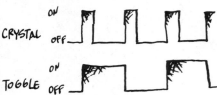

TOGGLE   ON / OFF

WHY IS THIS CALLED "**LOGIC**"? BECAUSE **IF** THE SWITCH OUTPUT IS OFF, **AND** THE INPUT IS ON, **THEN** THE SWITCH OUTPUT GOES TO "ON." **ETC!**

SOUNDS LOGICAL TO ME!

GOOD... NOW WE'RE DOWN TO 16,384 PULSES PER SECOND... THEN ADD ANOTHER TOGGLE SWITCH AND ANOTHER AND ANOTHER —15 IN ALL...

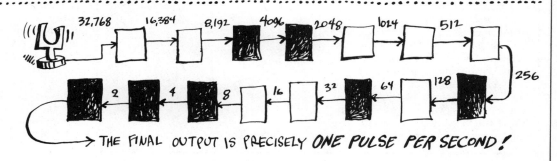

32,768   16,384   8,192   4096   2048   1024   512

256

2   4   8   16   32   64   128

→ THE FINAL OUTPUT IS PRECISELY *ONE PULSE PER SECOND !*

FINALLY THE MICROPROCESSOR...

THE PULSES ARE ACCUMULATED ON A **COUNTER**. LIKE A (BINARY) ODOMETER, IT COUNTS TO 59 AND THEN RETURNS TO 0. THIS KEEPS TRACK OF THE **SECONDS**.

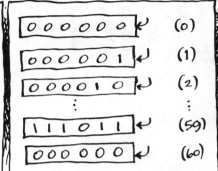

0 0 0 0 0 0 (0)

0 0 0 0 0 1 (1)

0 0 0 0 1 0 (2)

⋮

1 1 1 0 1 1 (59)

0 0 0 0 0 0 (60)

ANOTHER COUNTER COUNTS THE **MINUTES**, ADVANCING EACH TIME THE **SECOND** (FIRST?) COUNTER RETURNS TO 0. A THIRD COUNTER RECORDS THE **HOURS**.

1 1 1 0 1 0

0 0 0 0 0 1

0 1 0 0

58 SECONDS
1 MINUTE
4 HOURS

EACH BIT OF EACH COUNTER IS WIRED INTO A NETWORK OF ELECTRONIC SWITCHES. OUTPUT WIRES LEAD TO THE SEGMENTS OF THE FAMILIAR "FIGURE-8" DIGITAL DISPLAY. EACH SEGMENT IS SEPARATELY WIRED.

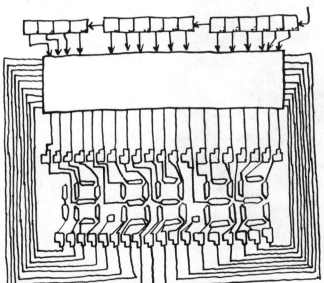

THE MICROPROCESSOR TRANSLATES EACH PATTERN OF INPUT BITS INTO THE APPROPRIATE COMBINATION OF SEGMENTS.

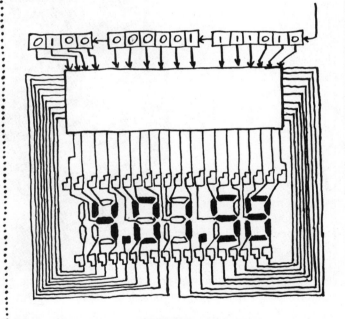

ATTACH A FEW WIRES TO RESET THE COUNTERS, ADD CIRCUITS FOR A STOPWATCH + CALENDAR, PACK IT IN A CASE, AND YOU HAVE A WATCH THAT'S ACCURATE AND **SILENT** — UNLESS, THAT IS, YOU'RE AN ELECTRON !!

ZAP ZORT ZARP ZERT

12:42

HEY!! HOLD IT DOWN!

10 HOME COMPUTER APPLICATIONS TO AVOID

by David Nimmons

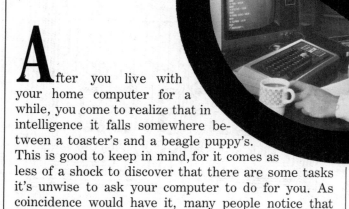

After you live with your home computer for a while, you come to realize that in intelligence it falls somewhere between a toaster's and a beagle puppy's. This is good to keep in mind, for it comes as less of a shock to discover that there are some tasks it's unwise to ask your computer to do for you. As coincidence would have it, many people notice that these are the tasks for which they bought their clever appliance in the first place.

Having lived with a machine for three years now, I would like to point out ten things that computers don't do well at all.

● "Banking at home by computer" is one of those dubious phrases like "trimming six inches from your waistline overnight while you sleep." My research shows only two reasons people go to the bank: 1) to get green paper money that they can go out and spend (the first thing home banking can't do), and 2) to physically deposit a pay check to cover the check they wrote the night before (the other thing home computer banking can't do).

● When it comes time to list the century's great orphaned ideas, the computerized checkbook will rank with the lava lamp. What's surprising is that anybody took it seriously in the first place. Consider that my checkbook was given to me free by the bank, has nice pictures of sunsets and waterfalls on the checks, weighs three ounces, measures five inches long and fits in my pocket. Consider further that it takes twenty seconds to pull out and open this checkbook, write a check, sign it and enter it in the stubs. Oh yes, and I only need a pen to operate it.

My computer, on the other hand, cost me $4,500, has no nature pictures anywhere in it, weighs twentyeignt pounds and takes up most of my desktop. It requires ninety seconds to turn it on, find the right floppy disk, load, and access the checkbook program. I then have to: find all the stubs of the receipts I wrote this month, type in the year, month and day in numbers separated by slashes (I usually have to delete at least one line of the check because I made a mistake), exit the writing mode, turn on the printer, enter the print mode, find my checkbook, insert a check in the printer and start it.

● "Family budget spreadsheet" programs exist because somewhere along the line software makers got confused between "the American family" and "the limited partnership." If they had their way, families would stop pasting up their albums and start issuing annual reports.

What the software people seem to have forgotten is that family finances are the single most persuasive argument for entropy yet known. The family budget, if it exists at all, consists of eight months' worth of bank statements thrown in a corner, some numbers scratched on old bank envelopes, and a limbic sense of how near the Ultimate Line is. Note that I've said nothing about recalculated, column-logic variable summing, internal rate of return, or projected mortgage scenarios at three hypothetical interest rates plotted in four-color graphs. In short, these programs are the software equivalent of a thermonuclear flea collar: impressive, but rarely worth the trouble.

● Next we come to the computerized electronic calendar. It doesn't let you make dates; you have to make "events." Can you imagine saying, "We fell in love on our first event"?

Worse, it suffers from that picky literal-mindedness of machine-think. For me, as for most folks, time unravels in a drinks-with-Chris-late-next-week sort of way. Electronic calendars are not that loose. To them, "late next week" means nothing. "Noonish" means nothing. They don't know about "happy hours," and they've never even met Chris. But "07-08-83, 6:00 P" they understand. No wonder we don't get along.

The electronic calendar also wants me to tell it just how long the "event" will last. The program divides the day into fifteen-minute blocks and has to know how many of those will be filled by my event with Chris. Now, I usually know roughly (within a half-hour, say) how things will go, but one has to be flexible on this sort of thing. Maybe an old mutual friend stops by the table, or we suddenly decide to go see a movie. Or there's a full moon out and it's a warm night . . . You get the idea. Well, in electronic datebooks, it's not enough to write "Chris" at 5:00. They want to know where you'll be at 5:15, 5:30, 5:45, 6:00. Sometimes I get the feeling this program was designed by somebody's mother.

● The computerized address book is only slightly more useful, with spaces limited to name, address, zip code and phone. I'm the type to jot entire dossiers on those tiny pages: birth dates, shirt sizes, the name and weekend phone number of my current Significant Other. Sometimes it's quite personal: "Hates pasta," "Don't mention Yankees," "Husband's an idiot," stuff like that. If I relied only on what I could put in an electronic address book, my personal relationships would fall apart.

The other problem, of course, is that electronic address books don't fit in your pocket. One resourceful friend of mine has found a solution: she prints out the entire address book on her computer, cuts the printout into little pages with names on each page, arranges them alphabetically, then puts them in a book that she carries with her.

● Next there's the home computer control center, the command central that knows when to turn on lights and lawn sprinklers, lower the thermostat, guard against intruders, call the police, teach the kids, inventory the kitchen, clean the bathroom and water the poinsettia.

It's all very Buck Rogers, like air cars and dematerialization beams, and people like that sort of thing, but it boils down to this: do you want to hand over control of your house to the same machines that keep sending those bills for charge accounts you never had? It's no accident that the best two examples we have of environments run by computers are the Jetsons and the federal government.

● Telecommunicating with friends over the phone is a fascinating use for your $4,500 home computer. The first step is almost always to think of people you know who 1) have a modem that allows them to communicate with computers over the phone, and 2) you have any desire to "chat" with. The next step is to call them up to see if they want to talk to you. Usually you talk for a few minutes to answer a few basic questions: will you communicate in full, half duplex or simplex mode? What baud rate will you use? What kind of parity check? Who's in transmit and who's in receive mode?

Simple, huh? Now hang up. Load your machine with the proper software and program it to dial your friend. Presto! You're ready to have a computer chat:

HI EDDIE?
—HAVE YOU STARTED?
HELLO. EDDIE
—CAN YOUY RESD ME?
YES. IS YOURS ALL IN BIG ≤ETTERS?
—WHAT?
PLS. REPEAT.

—I DON/T UNDERSTAND. ITS YOUR TUNR
REPEAT.
—WHAT?
OOPS . . .
Connection Interrupted

Remember, computers are so efficient that whatever your correspondent types on that keyboard arrives instantaneously on your screen. People who type twenty-five words per minute are generally not good people to "chat" with during peak phone hours. Keep in mind that the average English speaker talks about two hundred words a minute. Now you know why the phone company likes computer chatting.

● A subset of this silliness involves phone-line news services. The idea is that for a small connect fee (roughly equivalent to the national debt of Ireland) you can snuggle up to the great electronic information teat

TAKE MY COMPUTER— PLEASE!

Computer dealer is swimming in the water. A shark comes toward him and veers away—professional courtesy! . . . Last time I was in Silicon Valley, auto traffic was bumper to bumper. A man pushed a cigarette lighter in, and the woman in the car in front said, "Ouch." . . . I said to a guy, "Do you know the way to San Jose?" He said, "Yes," and drove away . . . Silicon Valley is so crowded, to get over on the other side of El Camino Real you have to be born there . . . And the money! A rich guy bought his kid a computer outfit: IBM . . . Many a computer designer has discovered after the honeymoon that his wife could make plans, too . . . A Silicon Valley couple got divorced, then they got remarried. The divorce didn't work out . . . Computer executive's wife will buy anything marked down. She brought home two dresses and an escalator . . . You know, computer experts have great personalities—but not for human beings . . . I met one computer company president, a graduate of the Don Rickles Charm School. Some people bring happiness wherever they go. He brings happiness *when*ever he goes . . . You probably heard about the fellow who invented the first portable computer. For thirty cents' worth of electricity, you could use it from San Francisco to New York. There was only one hitch: the $5,000 extension cord . . . I think the world of computers—and you know what condition the world is in today . . . But seriously. Take my computer—please!

HENNY YOUNGMAN

of news services like Dow Jones or UPI and be the first on your block to read the day's fast-breaking stories on, say, disposable paper products, dolphin research or the situation in Lapland.

Then there's cost. At the average rate of $25 per hour, you can order up in just a few hours the equivalent of a year's subscription to the New York *Times*, which gives you grocery coupons and stuff with which to line bird cages.

● The next most oversold computer idea is speech synthesis. A talking computer, say the yahoos, is a Helpful Thing. Didn't anybody else see *2001: A Space Odyssey*? Remember how much wonderful help they got from HAL?

Not only does a computer take three times as long to organize your calendar, checkbook and banking, but now it will nag you about the results. Recently I tried to convince my five-year-old niece how much fun a talking computer could be. I'd spent all day programming, testing and debugging when a small blond head brushed my arm.

"What does that toy do?" asked my niece.

Triumphant, I hit the RUN button on my machine. "Hello, what's your name?" croaked my $4,500 machine. I hit it again: "I love you," it quacked. I beamed.

Without a word, my niece disappeared, then came back a minute later dragging her favorite doll by one leg. Taking her thumb from her mouth, she picked up the doll and pulled its ring. "Hello, what's your name?" it chirped. She pulled it again: "I love you." Then she looked at the computer expectantly: "Make it wet its pants."

● Whoever thought up the electronic cookbook should be hoisted on his own pâté. Ask yourself whether your $4,500 piece of sophisticated microelectronics was designed to deal with spilled apricot juice, spattering bacon drippings, whole-wheat flour and melted chocolate. It turns out computer technicians get testy when they find things like vegetable shortening inside your machine's S-100 RS-232 ports.

Electronic cookbooks are supposed to be great for expanding or contracting recipes. This feature is quite useful for those occasions when your Significant Other calls to say the 5th Airborne Division is coming to dinner and your Shrimp Gelée à la Turque recipe feeds only five. If you don't routinely cook for armies or hospitals, however, it won't do you much good. Every cook worth his capers knows that halving the yeast in bread, with only half as much everything else, gives it the consistency of molybdenum. And how does one add 2.3 eggs?

■

COMPUTERS TO GO

When Adam Osborne begat the portable computer era, totable microsystems were comparable in size to sewing machines. Weighing a bulky twenty-five pounds and lugged around by a little handle on the top, they were as much fun to use as, well, sewing machines.

Within two years of their introduction, these early masterpieces would seem quaint, even kitschy. Real portables don't have handles. A real portable computer is something you can carry in your hand—small enough to take with you anywhere (it runs on batteries), yet big enough to offer a usable amount of text on its display. It has built-in software so you can be up and running and handling text, numbers or graphics as soon as you hit the "on" switch. A real portable is the soul of independence.

The idea of a computer no bigger than a loose-leaf notebook was first deemed practical at the Xerox Palo Alto Research Center (PARC), whose techno-guru Allen Kay produced a futuristic prototype but was unable to shrink the hardware and software into what he dubbed the "dynabook." It took a chance meeting on an airplane in 1981 to make portable computers a reality. Japan's ASCII Microsoft president Kazuhiko Nishi ran into the president of Kyocera, a top Nippon electronics hardware firm, and agreed to collaborate on a book-size typewriter keyboard with liquid crystal (LCD) screen. Sony's similar-looking Typecorder had been on the market since 1980 but did not have true computer capabilities. It was Radio Shack and NEC, with a 1983 publicity blitz, that brought the dynabook into thousands of homes and briefcases. Hewlett-Packard and Epson, among other manufacturers, have added bigger screens and more built-in software to make it even more practical.

Using a real portable computer lets you broaden your horizons. You can:
● *Take it anywhere.* A portable should fit in a satchel or knapsack, with lots of room to spare. Air travel is the paradigm; not only does a real portable qualify as

a carry-on item, but it lets you do work on board. Real work. You might also want to take one along in a car or on a train, a bus, a subway, a roller coaster. Why not? Or maybe on a sailboat, a fishing trawler, a canoe? Sure. Just keep it dry.
● *Work uninterrupted.* Nice day out, but that big report is due and you have to keep plugging away at it? No need to drag your desktop computer outdoors. Just lie in the sun with a mint julep in one hand and your portable in your lap. You can even take it into the bathroom, should inspiration strike there. No more scribbling notes on toilet paper. You can, take a soothing bath without missing a single brilliant thought.

● *Impress people.* Portable computers are avant-garde. They're a status symbol in numerous professions. Want a ringside seat at a conference or access to the press box at some sports event? Just flash your portable. Take it out at a chic restaurant or a chi-chi cocktail party and you'll soon be the center of attention. It's also good for recording the names and phone numbers of new acquaintances.
● *Keep in touch.* Your hand-holdable machine allows you to access your electronic mail or the latest news from a computer information service whenever you're near a telephone. Some portables have modems built in; others use external modems the size of a cigarette pack. Either way, a portable can give you twenty-four-hour communications capability. If you got a yen for every single newspaper story filed with a personal computer, you'd soon approach the gross national product of Japan.
● *Pioneer.* On the frontiers of the future is the latest development in portables: the ultimate computer-to-computer link via two-way radio. Motorola's first such model is named the PCX, but I prefer to call it a "walkie-thinkie." It does for computing what a walkie-talkie does for conversation. In your car or on the street, you're instantly in touch with that big computer in the sky that can relay your communications to any computer on earth. Shades of Dick Tracy!

HAL GLATZER, author of *Introduction to Word Processing* and *On the Move with the NEC 8200 Portable Computer*

HOW DANGEROUS IS YOUR COMPUTER?

by Thomas Hartmann

Can your home or office computer make you sterile? Can it strike you blind or dumb?

The answer is: probably not. Nevertheless, re-

Thomas Hartmann is a contributing editor at Popular Computing. *He is vice-president of Langley–St. Clair Instrumentation Systems, a safety peripherals firm.*

ports of side effects relating to computer use should be examined, especially in the area of birth defects, eye complaints and postural difficulties. Although little conclusive evidence exists to establish a causal link between computer use and problems of this sort, the circumstantial evidence can be disturbing.

Birth Defects

Several reports pertaining to birth defects deserve our attention. One of these deals with Laura Moore, who worked on a computer terminal at the telephone company's Renton (Washington) office outside Seattle and who throughout her pregnancy avoided drugs (even aspirin), cigarettes, coffee and alcohol. Although two of her co-workers had had problem pregnancies, Laura was sure she'd have no difficulty. But on January 14, 1982, her son Brandon was born with a massive spina bifida, his spinal cord uncovered and protruding from the back.

Other reports issue from Air Canada in Montreal, where seven out of thirteen pregnancies among computer terminal operators resulted in spontaneous abortions; from the Toronto *Star*, where four of seven births to terminal operators resulted in birth defects; and from a Sears Roebuck terminal center in Dallas, Texas, where there were eight spontaneous abortions out of twelve pregnancies over a thirteen-month period in 1979–80. In addition, of twelve pregnancies among terminal operators for the Defense Logistics Agency in Marietta, Georgia, seven were miscarriages, two were normal births and, as the U.S. Army concluded following its own study, there were "three cases of congenital malformation, representing an unusual statistical event for which no explanation could be found."

In response to these "pregnancy problem clusters," which have shown up in several other areas beyond those listed here, the National Institute for Occupational Safety and Health (NIOSH) has undertaken a massive study of six thousand pregnancies. Dr. Michael Rosenberg, chief of reproductive health activity at NIOSH, hopes the investigation will bring about some conclusive findings: "If the results are negative, this study will effectively put the question to rest. If the results are positive that computers are causing birth defects, the study will allow us to accurately measure the degree of risk."

Eye Complaints

Pregnancy problems represent only the smallest percentage of complaints from operators of computer terminals, or VDTs (video display terminals). Eye fatigue, watering or burning eyes, cataracts, failing eyesight and a host of other complaints are epidemic. Recently a task force of the Canadian government went so far as to recommend that workers be required to spend no more than five hours per day on terminals and that pregnant women avoid them altogether.

One area of great concern involves the x-rays produced by computer terminals and home computers' cathode ray tubes, or CRTs, which operate in the same manner as your television picture tube. Accelerated to a very high velocity by the application of a high voltage

(on the order of 10,000 to 25,000 volts), a beam of electrons scans the face of the tube. When it strikes the atoms of phosphor that coat the inside, the outer electrons are torn off, causing the atoms to become ionized and to produce radiation, including light, ultraviolet rays and x-rays.

To meet government standards for radiation emission, most manufacturers of picture tubes now use lead-impregnated glass for the envelope of their CRTs to absorb most stray radiation. Nonetheless, if driven hard enough, CRTs will produce measurable levels of x-ray.

In a recent letter to *Byte* magazine, the U.S. Food and Drug Administration stated that after subjecting various computer terminals to abuse, its inspectors were unable to detect any x-radiation from the terminals. Inconsistent with its usual insistence on scientific accuracy (but perhaps consistent with its concern about bad press), the FDA neglected to say what sorts of terminals were tested, whether they were high-resolution (using higher voltages) or low-resolution, monochrome or color, and whether there were any scientific controls on the study.

In fact, in another 1978 study, not referred to in its letter and now "out of print" (*Evaluation of Radiation*, FDA #81-8153), the FDA tested 125 monitors and found that 10 of them emitted high levels of x-radiation when the line voltage (from the plug in the wall, usually 120 volts) was raised to 130 volts. This increase of the line voltage is known as a "stress test" and is designed to make machines show up potential problems. Eight of the machines were well in excess of the FDA's own standard for radiation, which was first developed for black-and-white TV viewing.

Fortunately, most terminals emit so little x-radiation that it is well within the range of naturally occurring background radiation. But we must keep in mind that exceptions do exist. Summarizing the x-ray issue, the Ontario Public Service Employees Union concluded in its informative booklet *The Hazards of VDTs* (1901 Yonge St., Toronto, Ontario, M4S, $2):

While these various testing agencies seem satisfied that X-radiation emissions from VDTs pose no significant hazard to operators, a number of things must be considered.
1. VDTs do leak X-radiation. The controversy is over what level of radiation is harmful.
2. X-radiation emissions have been measured separately, without considering possible combined effects with other forms of radiation being emitted. . . .
3. Recent studies on the health effects of low-level radiation force us to assume there is no known safe level for radiation exposure.

Although much has been written on the VDT safety issue, according to a recent "definitive" study by the National Academy of Sciences the subject is far from closed. Adding to the confusion are bills introduced by several state legislatures demanding various means of protecting workers from computer terminals. In addition, the National Union of Working Women (also known as "9–5") has instituted a petition drive calling for, among other things, radiation shielding for computer terminals; such shielding has spawned a small industry of its own, with lead-impregnated acrylic screen shields being sold by at least three companies in the United States and by a half-dozen firms in Canada.

Other Radiation

Particularly at the seashore or on the ski slopes, where sunlight is more directly reflected into a person's face, ultraviolet (UV) light has long been known as one of the major culprits behind burning, watering eyes. Now similar symptoms are being widely reported among VDT operators, and some authorities believe that UV radiation from terminals can have a damaging effect on the human eye that might even lead to blindness.

When two copy editors at the New York *Times* developed cataracts after working on VDTs for six and twelve months, respectively, Dr. Milton Zaret, associate clinical professor of ophthalmology at New York University, testified that in his opinion the cataracts had been caused by radiation, probably microwaves, from the terminals. Tests by the U.S. government, however, found microwave radiation from the *Times*' terminals to be within acceptable limits. (Acceptable U.S. levels for microwave radiation are 1,000 times higher than, for example, Soviet standards; the former recognizes only heat-caused damage induced by microwaves, whereas the Soviets claim there are other far more subtle and equally damaging consequences from microwave exposure.)

Since that time, numerous other cases of VDT-related cataracts have been recorded. These are detailed in the Cold Type Organizing Committee's report *Don't Sit Too Close to the TV: VDTs/CRTs and Radiation* (Box 40, Jerome Ave. Station, Bronx, NY 10468; $1), one of the most complete summaries of the computer safety controversy.

Posture Problems

Two of the physicians I asked to comment on birth defects in connection with computer use suspected that difficulties could arise from improper posture. Both preferred to remain anonymous because of the speculative nature of their comments.

"If you take a young squash from the vine and put it in a plastic milk bottle, it will grow to assume the exact shape of the bottle," said one doctor by way of explanation. "Similarly, sitting hunched over in a chair for eight hours a day can cause pressure on the womb or on the aorta, which supplies blood to the womb, or on some of the veins that drain it back off, and this may conceivably be responsible for the sorts of birth defects we're seeing described here."

Even without the specter of birth defects, poor posture can cause fatigue, headaches and general discomfort. Because a computer user's concentration is directed at the screen rather than at a variety of stimuli, there is a tendency to sit in a fixed position for long periods of time. The human body's musculature and bone structure, especially in the back, were simply not designed for such stress. Frequent breaks, simple stretching and computer placement at a comfortable height can do much to dispel such complaints.

An Obsolescent Problem

The technology that created the computer safety issue is on the verge of providing a solution. The greatest source of danger could be eliminated by an inexpensive low-voltage computer display to replace the high-voltage CRT. Although the quest for such a replacement has been going on for years, only recently have two promising display techniques emerged from the laboratories to appear on production lines.

Mighty IBM has staked its reputation on a "gas plasma" flat-panel display that employs low-voltage ionized gases instead of a high-voltage electron beam to generate its orange-colored image. This display, which may be standard on many terminals in the next ten years, should have none of the attendant radiation problems associated with present CRT technology.

At the same time, Japanese manufacturers and American marketers have introduced a panoply of portable computers with black-on-gray liquid-crystal displays (LCDs) similar to those used on digital watches, which also produce no radiation. The Epson QX-20 led the way with a four-line display, soon improved upon by the Radio Shack Model 100's eight lines of text and followed by models with larger screens and greater resolution. If problems of fragility and cost can be conquered, these displays could become standard on many home computers.

The back strain and postural problems associated with computer use are also receiving attention from manufacturers. New display screens with non-glare surfaces tilt and swivel and adjust to different heights so that computer users can adapt to the new workplace environment. Additionally, a whole new generation of office furniture designed to match humans to computers, in the most comfortable manner

HOME COMPUTER SAFETY

There are several specific steps you can take to help reduce the problems and concerns arising from home computer use.

● In general, it's a good idea to sit as far away from your computer screen as comfort allows. Detachable keyboards are making it easier to follow this advice from the experts, some of whom recommend a distance at least three times as great as the screen's diagonal measurement.

Children using television screens should be especially careful. Doctors at the Veterans Administration Medical Center in Washington, D.C., recently warned that pre-1970 television sets serving as monitors with home computers could be exposing users to nearly nine times the maximum recommended dosage of radiation.

● For an extra margin of safety, consider attaching a leaded acrylic screen shield to your monitor to block both x-rays and ultraviolet radiation. Such shields often have non-glare surfaces that enhance eye comfort by diffusing extraneous light reflected by the screen. A non-glare surface can also be added to your screen with a simple adhesive-backed plastic sheet available at Radio Shack and other computer stores.

● Arrange your computer work area so that the keyboard is clearly illuminated while the light is directed away from the display screen. The greater the contrast between the characters on the screen and the overall light level, the easier the effect on your eyes. Of late, computer makers and owners have been switching from green- to amber-tinted monitors, following findings by the West German standards bureau that amber is more relaxing on the eyes.

● Sit in a chair that supports your lower back and promotes proper posture. Adjust the height of the chair so your hands rest comfortably on the keyboard and the screen is at eye level. Also, arrange your work area so you can easily read the documents being entered into your word processing program or the instructions for that complex piece of software you're trying to master.

● Every thirty minutes or so, take a break from your computer to stretch and walk around. You can also exercise your eyes by focusing on objects at different distances from you; this prevents the weakening of eye muscles that can result if you focus on the computer screen surface for long periods.

T.H.

possible, is helping to allay many concerns and complaints. Home computer users may not have access to all these fancy enhancements, but rarely do they spend forty hours a week at their machines.

As computer terminals become more and more sophisticated, the risks associated with them may pass away altogether. On the other hand, since millions of old-style CRTs will most likely remain in the workplace and in the home, the debate on computer safety will no doubt continue for some time to come. ∎

WHO'S AFRAID OF DISPLAYS?

by Leonard R. Harris

The important matter of computer display safety has been blurred by headline-happy reporters in the lay press, by unions and politicians seeking a sensational issue and by management's haste in using a new technology without considering all its physical and emotional implications. Uneasiness has resulted, a feeling that perhaps there's smoke and perhaps there's fire and perhaps we should be nervous.

One good thing has emerged from this restless anxiety: the attention paid by the scientific community to the health and safety of the person who spends all or most of the business day working at a VDT. While use of a terminal can be a pain in the neck (or shoulder, wrist, elbow or back), that's the sum of the negative findings in brief.

But let's not be that brief.

Four broad categories of health hazards have been alleged and should be reviewed. Radiation has supposedly caused cataracts and birth defects. Ocular effects allegedly have resulted: eye irritation, pain, fatigue, reduced acuity. Musculoskeletal effects have been found. Psychosocial effects need investigation.

Leonard R. Harris is director of corporate relations and public affairs for the New York Times Company.

To begin: Cataracts are opacities of the lens of the eye. They occur throughout the general population. Since they do, it is statistically certain that some VDT workers will develop cataracts. This was the conclusion quoted in *Video Displays, Work and Vision*, a report by the National Research Council: "Both laboratory studies of animals and surveys of humans indicate, however, that the levels of radiation required to produce cataracts are thousands to millions of times higher than the levels emitted by VDTs."

The National Research Council, whose members are drawn from the National Academy of Sciences, the National Academy of Engineering and the Institute of Medicine, stated that "ten anecdotal reported cases of cataracts among VDT workers do not suggest an unusual pattern attributable to VDT work: six of the cases appear to be common, minor opacities not interfering with vision, and each of the remaining four cases had known, preexisting pathology or exposure to cataractogenic agents." Incidentally, about one in four of us has a congenital or developmental eye opacity not affecting our vision.

Moreover, in May 1982 the American Academy of Ophthalmology issued a report that said: "Experimental and epidemiological evidence has demonstrated that exposure to VDTs does not result in cataracts or any other organic damage to the eye."

Yet writers like Thomas Hartmann perpetuate our fear of cataracts by citing a 1977 incident without mentioning its resolution: three prominent ophthalmologists and a prestigious engineering firm, each selected and approved by all parties concerned, contributed data to a ruling that declared there was no evidence to support the development of cataracts from work with VDTs.

If cataracts are a fearful subject, how much more threatening—if it were not unjustified—would be the threat of birth defects! The Birth Defects Foundation of the March of Dimes studied the question after four pregnant workers in the classified ads department at the Toronto *Star* delivered infants with birth defects and after eight pregnant workers at a Sears VDT Computer Center in Dallas suffered miscarriages.

"Clusters of miscarriage and birth defects and other health problems, such as cancers, can and do occur purely by chance," said Dr. Arthur J. Salisbury, March of Dimes vice-president for medical services.

> "There are so many women of childbearing age who work at or near VDTs today that some coincidental VDT-linked clusters of problem pregnancies are to be expected. A cluster of birth defects is more likely to reflect a specific cause if the birth defects are alike, but this has not been true of reported VDT-linked cases. Equally important, the alleged VDT-linked birth defects have not resembled the kinds of fetal damage that any type of radiation is known to cause.

Then, in January 1984, the *Journal of the American Medical Association* flatly declared that "no reports of harmful effects of electromagnetic radiation on reproductive function in humans have been found." The report (prepared by the AMA's Council on Scientific Affairs) next made a still broader statement: "Several careful and thorough studies by both private and governmental experts have concluded that there is inadequate electromagnetic radiation at any frequency (x-rays, visible, infrared, microwave, and radiofrequency) to cause biologic effects."

Disregarding the findings of the National Institute of Occupational Safety and Health (NIOSH), the Bureau of Radiological Health of the Department of Health and Human Services, the Radiation Protection Bureau of the Canadian Department of National Health and Welfare, the Toronto Ministry of Health and the Abortion Surveillance Branch of the Centers for Disease Control, some legislators have proposed that pregnant women working at VDTs wear protective lead aprons. Absurd! The fact is that a stroll in the sun in the streets of a big city exposes one to more and higher frequencies of radiation than does a day at a VDT. For one's own peace and sanity, it is worth repeating the strong words of the AMA: "No reports of harmful effects of electromagnetic radiation on reproductive function in humans have been found."

If VDTs and computers have been cleared of involvement in cataracts, birth defects and miscarriages, what about lesser effects? What about ocular discomfort? Or blurring or flickering of vision? Logic alone tells us that staring at a screen unceasingly will tire us at least as much as staring unceasingly at the pages of a book. Logic says that we ought to change focus occasionally, just as we should when driving a car on a monotonous highway. Logic says that glare is unpleasant, whether from a VDT screen or from the sun brightly reflected on hot sand.

The medical evidence is that more serious threats to our eyes are simply not presented by VDTs or computer screens. In May 1982 the Board of the American Academy of Ophthalmology said:

> Based on available scientific evidence, the Academy considers VDTs to be safe for normal use and to present no hazard to vision. Experimental and epidemiological evidence has demonstrated that exposure to VDTs does not result in cataracts or any other organic damage to the eye. Ocular fatigue experienced by some workers required to scan VDTs for extended periods of time is not indicative of pathologic change. Such fatigue may be lessened by the use of tints or colored filters in occupational eyeglasses.

There is, I think, abundant evidence that in the home, office or factory one cannot just plop a VDT on a desk or a counter and—without changing lighting, chairs, desk or table heights, etc.—expect the operator to be comfortable. One cannot do that even with a typewriter. The environment has to fit the technology. Because of a relatively new science known as ergonomics, which wisely seeks to adapt work and working conditions to suit the worker rather than trying to mold us like Play-Doh to fit the work, we now have chairs that support our backs, shelves that move to make keyboards accessible, lights that do not produce glare.

Listen, it's a good life. If we don't smoke, if we drink only in moderation, if we exercise at least an hour a day, if we eat mostly vegetables and eschew fats, sugar and salt, and if we reap the psychic rewards of creativity with our computers, VDTs or word processors, what else is there? I fervently hope that reports of the health hazards of computers have been greatly exaggerated, since I spend more time at VDTs than I do in bed. ■

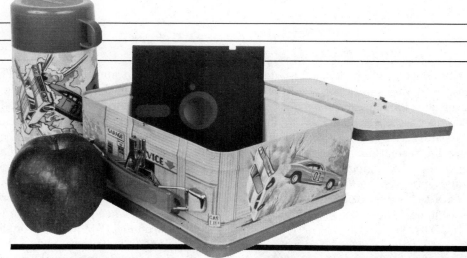

THE LABOR FORCE

A true history of the first women in personal computing
by Bonita Taylor

The tales of those inspired pioneers who brought forth the personal computer industry have always centered only on heroes: a few dozen obsessed males working brilliantly against terrific odds, in the humble surroundings of kitchens, basements and garages, nudging their ideas into a multibillion-dollar reality. Now it's time to credit the heroines.

While no one disputes that men had the primary role in the conception of the industry, women were the ones who went into labor. "The women may not have always been the creative driving force," says Betsy Staples, editor of *Creative Computing*. "But they made it possible to get the men's ideas in the public eye." The women who worked behind the scenes (and in the basements and garages) helped many of the newly formed computer companies grow and survive. These female pioneers provided skills and hours beyond the call of duty and certainly far beyond what the neonatal companies could have afforded to pay.

The range of chores to which women were assigned during this period was extensive. No task was unthinkable. Some of these pioneers talk about encouraging (bribing?) their children to help after school. Some remember spending nights in the kitchen with a Seal a Meal machine, packaging diskettes with one

Bonita Taylor is editor of The Buyers Guide *series for Ziff-Davis. She is one of the few home users of the Xerox 820 personal computer.*

hand and lunchbox sandwiches with the other. One woman (who wishes to remain anonymous) recalls the time an extra diskette turned up: some customer, she was sure, would find a gooey peanut butter sandwich in his package where a disk should have been.

Off to Market

It's not simply a case of good women behind good men. Unsung women have also distinguished themselves by demonstrating their business and marketing acumen.

Dorothy McEwen.

There's Dorothy McEwan, who in 1975 worked as a customer support representative for the phone company while she studied computer programming and fulfilled her responsibilities as a homemaker. The mother of two, she was married to Gary Kildall, a Naval Postgraduate School professor who at that time was writing the CP/M program. "He needed things done, so I did them," Dorothy recalls. "I never thought about what it would lead to."

CP/M became the first commercial operating system software distributed by a non-computer manufacturer as Dorothy, using her business skills, helped mold and build Digital Research Inc. Today she is a vice-president of the company, with responsibility for marketing, communications, customer support, and educational and legal services. But when the computer press needs a computer pioneer to interview, the call goes out to Gary, not Dorothy.

Mary Eubanks is another woman whose contributions have been overlooked. After raising four children, Mary was ready to sit back, relax and possibly start her own travel business, when suddenly she was called upon to once again assume the role of supportive parent. Her son Gordon had written C-

Mary Eubanks.

BASIC, the first microcomputer language to offer reasonably good structure and commercial mathematics capability, and had started a business to sell it. But Gordon was also a serving officer on a strategic nuclear submarine, and it's difficult to run a software company while sitting on the floor of the Pacific Ocean.

Mary volunteered to manage the company. "I knew nothing about computers," she says. "But I was his mother, and I was determined to hold the business together one way or another." She dedicated the next few years of her life to Compiler Systems, and Gordon came out of the Navy to an extremely prosperous company whose CBASIC was one of the most commonly used languages.

Then there's Judy Goodman, who in the early 1970s was working as a substitute elementary school teacher, part-time helper in her husband's TV and stereo shop, and full-time homemaker with three children. During this time her husband became interested in computers, which he saw as "the

Judy Goodman.

wave of the future." He educated himself and in 1977 wrote a file management program called Selector, but it was Judy who handled the orders and the marketing (including product distribution and trade shows) and who was responsible for staying on top of finances. Today she is vice-president of Micro Ap, with responsibility for marketing.

Cynthia Posehn, who formed Organic Software, Inc., recalls that "somebody had to answer the letters and the phone calls, ship the software and manage the money." In 1977, when her husband Michael needed a software customization proposal typed up, she was assigned the task. "I'm a terrible typist," she says, "and it took forever to get it out." Michael got impatient and decided that a word processing program was needed. Textwriter was written shortly thereafter. "His intelligence and drive got the company going," Cynthia admits. "He placed the ads and made the contacts." But Cynthia did all the packaging and saw to the printing, as well as anything else that needed to be done. Today she is the firm's secretary-treasurer, responsible for the financial, legal and marketing side of the business.

A Man's World

The women in these cameos arrived in the personal computer industry by accident, but they share similar characteristics. They are tolerant, determined, competent, hard-working and willing to take on something new. And they are dependable. They were expected to work on behalf of the men they knew and to tend all phases of the business. And they did.

Nonetheless, despite the significant contributions of these and numerous other women during personal computing's formative years, publicity and credit for the accomplishments of their respective companies have continued to go to men. "As journalists, we wanted interesting personalities as well as 'names,'" says Maggie Canon, the editor of *A+* magazine. "The more famous someone became, the more interesting that person was to write about. The companies themselves promoted the men."

According to the National Science Foundation, women represent 26 percent of the computer labor force. We don't know how many in this group have made critical contributions to their companies. What we do know is that the success of the early entrepreneurial companies shaped the computer industry as it is today. To survive the early period, each needed not only the ideas contributed by their heralded entrepreneurs (men), but also the skills of the various unheralded women.

Would the personal computer industry exist as we know it without them? "Probably not," says Nancy Lehman, another pioneer. *Did a sandwich get sent out in place of a disk?* "This society is not taught to acknowledge what women do and what would happen if we stopped."

It may be that if women are to be recognized for their achievements, they will have to write the chapters themselves. This is only the first. ∎

ROMANCE AND THE COMPUTER

by Tamora Pierce

Back in the sixties, "scientific" matchmaking was synonymous with huge card-sorting computers. Today, that booming industry, highlighted by the spectacularly successful (and now defunct) Operation Match, is still with us—though in more discreet style.

Computer dating services have been around since the mid-fifties. These services featured extensive testing and interviewing to obtain accurate psychological portraits of their customers (some even developed their own elaborate tests), and as a result all but one or two nonprofit services charged high fees that ranged upwards from $350.

This was "hardly the kind of thing you'd go through for a quick date," observed one computer matchmaker. Sixty percent of the clients were college-educated males; 10 percent of these held advanced degrees and 30 percent were engineers. The greatest concentration of early computerized matchmaking service users was among over-forty divorced females and near-fifty male bachelors.

Tamora Pierce is the author of Alanna: The First Adventure, *the initial book in a young adult fantasy series. She owns a Cromemco C10 named Leviathan.*

And Then Came Match

It began at a Harvard University dance in 1964, engineered by two undergraduates. Nine months later 90,000 students had gone on dates set up by Operation Match. In 1967 the company claimed 200,000 applicants for that year alone; by 1973 they would claim 500,000 customers and 125,000 marriages.

Catering to the college students of Canada and the United States, Operation Match charged $2 to $10 for the privilege of filling out a questionnaire with 110 items, ranging from religious preference and TV habits to ideas on romantic love. The computer used by the service digested, tabulated and collated the results, and each client received a list with several names, addresses and phone numbers.

One writer reasoned that Operation Match succeeded because the students were already partly compatible: all were attending institutions of higher learning, and all were participating in campus life. Also, students are not in the same boat as the traditional "lonelyhearts." Coeds might go out on a com-

puter-arranged date just for a lark, and those who found themselves paired with "undesirables" would be less affected by their ordeal than, say, a thirty-year-old "spinster."

The people who used computer dating services prior to the advent of Operation Match were largely those who had been exposed to the day-to-day side of technology. With the vastly enlarged rolls resulting from mass-market computer dating came a greater number of complaints: "After the three dates the computer found for me, I decided to give up and let my mother find a nice boy for me after all." Or "My date, a Mr. Smith, and I had the same thing in common. We were both very fond of Mr. Smith."

With the increased popularity of computer dating, due to decreases in cost and widespread publicity, came increased public attention to its drawbacks. One problem involved "matches" that obviously weren't, between clients totally unsuited to each other in terms of height, religion, education or age. Some services were notorious for bad matches. In the early seventies the State of California investigated seven firms (actually taking one to court), while the State of New York instituted proceedings against another service. Yet the largest source of bad matches was the information supplied by customers themselves. Clients would fib or just plain lie on the computer questionnaire. Seriously: who wants to admit that he (or she) is unattractive? Add to this the fact that some people don't know what they want: the man who says he'd prefer a redhead who likes to barhop might be far happier with a brunette who likes to cook.

One problem for those services that rely on lengthy testing is that many "compatibility" tests have no scientific validation. If these tests cannot accurately measure that elusive quality called "chemistry," neither can the computer. Dealing with the psychological factors that measure compatibility, rather than with love, computers do only what any matchmaker does—

OVERHEARD ON-LINE

—Let's interface, my pet.
—Not so fast, Mac. You can't access my core without a little protocol.
—But, micro mine, your software always boots me into insert mode.
—You're headed for a fatal error if you don't slow your baud rate.
—Oh, my apple, couldn't we just call an interrupt and plug in my firmware?
—That micro package?
—You've never complained about its performance before. You sound like your files have been reconfigured.
—You accusing me of basic incompatibility?
—All you need is a memory refresh. You know how you respond to my input.
—Don't keep pushing that key. You're acting like a teenage hacker.
—Would you rather I hit delete and put an end to all this?
—So you can reconnect with that old kludge of yours across town . . .
—At least we never had I/O problems like this.
—None but terminal boredom.
—Look, I purged that address long ago.
—All right, I just don't want to be treated like some dedicated spreadsheet.
—That's the farthest thing from my read/write head.
—Then stop reaching for control all the time. I don't care for that routine of yours.
—I keep trying to open a window to you.
—Why don't you find out my communication needs?
—All I get is stop bits and no parity.
—So go ahead and disconnect.
—But we've spent so much time on-line.
—Then you'd better sort things out real fast.
—I'm sorry. I didn't mean to overload your circuits.
—I guess I'm sorry, too. Garbage in/garbage out.
—Yeah, garbage in/garbage out . . .
—Let's interface, you dynamic ram.

STEVEN ARCHER, computer novelist

©1983 Rebecca Wilson

they arrange for couples to meet. The difference, claim computing dating experts, is that their machines introduces couples on far more points of similarity than do the matchmakers.

Modern Romance

The client of the eighties looks a little different from the client of the sixties and early seventies. The scales are still most heavily weighted toward professionals—doctors, attorneys, engineers—although office workers and the self-employed can now afford the lower rates charged by many computer matching services. The largest age concentration is now between twenty-five and thirty-five, with a median age of twenty-eight/twenty-nine.

WITH THIS COMPUTER . . .

Pam Jensen, a Chicago zoo primate keeper, and Chris Dunn, an electronics technician from New York, met on-line.

The computer is not without compassion. For the Apple II, Ron Jaenisch of the Universal Life Church in Sunnyvale, California, designed a program with which he has performed marriage ceremonies several times since Valentine's Day 1981, when Richard and Debbie became the first couple merged by "Reverend Apple's" files. (A second Apple was used for the background music, although not too many people liked the idea.)

On Valentine's Day 1983 George Stickles and Debbie Fuhrman of Grand Prairie, Texas, showed their own style when they had a transcontinental wedding performed by the Reverend Tim Payton, on call twenty-four hours a day via CompuServe's CB Channel 14. Letting their fingers do the talking, they vectored their vows on-line so anyone could witness their wedding words at home.

Impersonal? Perhaps. But today, with many alternatives to the traditional marriage ceremony, this is but another one. But, pray tell, does the computer throw chips rather than rice?

CHARLES P. RUBENSTEIN

And computer dating itself has changed.

Computer matching has moved into the eighties with high-tech ease. Computer matching is now paired with video dating (for those who still want to see what they're getting "live" on video tape). Services have been set up to create matches for gays, Jews, Japanese and the overweight. And a Milwaukean has patented a device called the Love Bug—two electronic chips, one programmed to describe the client, the other his or her ideal match. The unit is worn to a hunting ground, where it emits and receives the information on the chips. When compatible singles approach each other, the devices beep louder as the distance between them decreases.

Biggest of all the new wrinkles in computer dating are computerized information networks, available to anyone with a home system and a modem. Enterprising singles have also used their electronic bulletin boards to place free "personals." The Dial-Your-Match bulletin boards (over thirty-five at last count scattered across the country, with one in France) are typical. After logging on to the bulletin board, a new user is asked a series of questions (they can get pretty explicit) and then matched with a number of corresponding singles (identified by nicknames, ID numbers, age range and percentage of compatibility). Tapping out an entry that seems intriguing will retrieve all that person's responses to the questionnaire. Should the match seem worth pursuing, an electronic billet-doux can be left in storage for later retrieval by one's intended. Responses can be exchanged as electronic mail before face-to-face meetings are finally arranged (though many a romance has blossomed, matured and died on-line with the partners never once laying eyes on each other). The responses can be gratifying. One woman reported eight interesting replies within a day of placing her "ad."

Again, as in the case of Operation Match, one must assume that bulletin board users already have something in common—a home computer and the knowledge with which to use it. The Dial-Your-Match bulletin boards have proven so popular that constant busy signals have to be endured before connecting with one. Demographics favor women at present: approximately 90 percent of bulletin board users are male (on the average, thirty-five-year-old college-educated professionals with a yearly income of $50,000).

The personal computer has made it possible for anyone to become an electronic matchmaker. Most of the Dial-Your-Match bulletin boards are no more than moderately powerful home computers with modems and appropriate software, maintained by self-appointed system operators. It used to be that matches were made in heaven (or not). Now they are made on-line, under the auspices of a "sysop." Till silicon do you part . . .   ∎

CAN THIS MARRIAGE BE SAVED?

The plight of the computer widow
by Eileen Haas

Blessèd are those homes where the whole family is interested in computers and where household members fight for time at the keyboard. Less fortunate, but not in trouble yet, are the homes where everyone is blissfully ignorant of computers and doesn't care a fig about learning to use them. The trouble comes when only one person in a family of two or more is nuts about his computer.

Computer widows need help. (So do computer mothers who have lost their sons and daughters to Atari oblivion; computer widowers who may starve to death because they never learned to cook for themselves; computer siblings who are taunted mercilessly for not knowing a cold boot from an ice cream cone; and computer orphans who pray daily for divorce so they can get at least one day of "quality time" with each parent.) Computer widows face a very real problem, but there's a real solution. I consider myself living

Eileen Haas, a former computer widow is currently director of communications for Bruce & James Program Publishers, Inc.

testimony to the fact that you can get through computer widowhood without losing all your friends, hating your entire family or taking out divorce papers.

A Case History

Five years ago my husband bought his first personal computer—a Heathkit model that he had to build himself. He was unemployed at the time, so we weren't rolling in dough, and I was infuriated that he'd dared to withdraw fourteen hundred dollars of our hard-earned money to buy what I regarded as no more than a ridiculously expensive toy.

I ranted and raved. I tried to talk him into buying model airplanes instead; at least they would have been cheaper. My husband was adamant. I was sulky. Then one day the computer arrived on our doorstep.

First there was (and always would be) the question of where to put the damned thing. Personal computers themselves may be small, but complete systems require "peripherals"—a fancy name for more paraa printer, you might as well start looking for a bigger apartment. Which is exactly what we did.

So there we were, paying twice the rent just to house the beast that was now happily residing in its own bedroom. And I soon began to realize that my husband was spending more time in that bedroom than in ours. Not to mention that he was often absent from the dining room at mealtimes, preferring to pick up his plate steaming hot from the kitchen, carry it into his computer den and feed himself in front of the monitor.

I grew angrier and angrier. I started issuing ultimatums. I even began conspicuously reading "apartment for rent" ads in the Sunday papers. Things were coming to a head when my husband finally found a job. My joy, however, was short-lived: it turned out he was going to be the new managing editor of *Byte* magazine, the computer enthusiasts' bible. Some women would have slit their wrists. Many would have walked out. All would have cried. Being the type of person who knows when she's been defeated, I gave in. If you can't beat 'em, I told myself wearily, you might as well join 'em.

I took the plunge with a course in data processing. To my amazement, I breezed through it; to my greater amazement, I enjoyed it. It began to dawn on me that anybody with a brain and at least two fingers could use a computer. Two classes later I found I could actually write programs, and I fell in love with word processors to the point where I buried my Smith-Corona at the bottom of a little-used closet. And, lo and behold, I didn't lose a bit of my humanity. I still baked cookies and read Proust. I still had friends. My cat still liked me.

It was a long, hard road for me. Looking back, I've learned that 1) computer widows are not alone; 2) there's nothing wrong with them for feeling the way they do about computers; and 3) though they really don't *have* to learn about computers, it would definitely enrich their lives (not to mention incomes) if they did.

Is It Terminal?

Before you start feeding your partner's computer manuals into the office paper shredder, you should find out if you're overreacting. There's computer mania and there's computer *mania*. Your partner may only be suffering mildly; he may have a well-developed but not terminal case; or he may be so far gone that he no longer recognizes human speech.

Computer mania can be divided into three phases:

• *Bad*. The seed of obsession has been sown. He's been reading computer magazines like crazy; he's even let his *Playboy* subscription run out. Computer stores are to him as fire hydrants are to dogs.

• *Worse*. The computer has moved in. It occupies a throne in the most inconvenient location in the house ("What do you *mean* we have to use the dining room table for meals?"). Computer manuals have begun to pile up in every corner.

• *Intolerable*. Like the Little Prince, your partner inhabits a very tiny world; instead of a rosebush, he's got a computer. He takes his phone calls in front of the computer. He brushes his teeth (when he remembers to) in front of the computer. You've dyed your hair red and he hasn't noticed. You're seething and he hasn't noticed. He's in big trouble and he hasn't noticed.

ONE CREATIVE SOLUTION

In the never-ending search for a way to get their partners to abandon the computer, some women have come up with pretty daring schemes. Take Tracy, for instance, a young science teacher whose husband had become so enamored of his Commodore 64 that she could have spilled hydrochloric acid all over the house and he wouldn't have noticed.

Tracy had tried just about everything when she lit upon her ingenious scheme. Inspired by a newspaper account about computer crime, and armed with a great deal of knowledge about her husband's code of ethics, she came up with the perfect solution.

She started by expressing interest in the computer. She coaxed her husband Bill into teaching her how to use the machine. She learned (or pretended to learn) programming. Soon she was a real whiz. She could say things like "The DOS editor isn't interfacing with the modem" without batting an eyelash. Bill was impressed.

Soon Tracy was having mysterious late-night sessions in the computer room. She told Bill she was working on an important project, one that would make them rich. Bill was awed. He brought her meals so she wouldn't have to leave the keyboard. He answered the phone. He kept the TV turned down. The atmosphere in the house became hushed, expectant.

One evening Tracy rushed out from the computer room, clutching a ream of continuous-feed paper. "I did it!" she crowed.

Bill beamed with pride. "Wonderful!" he exclaimed. There was a pause. "What did you do?"

Tracy was triumphant. "I cracked First National's secret code," she said. "We now have over two million dollars in our account!"

When Tracy was able to revive him, Bill made her promise to put the money back. She agreed, but only under one condition: that she be allowed to work on another project concerning lucrative electronic transactions. This one involved numbered Swiss bank accounts.

Poor Bill never got to sleep that night. The next morning, faced with the monster he himself had created, he did the only thing a decent husband could do to protect his wife from her own cleverness. He got rid of the computer.

E.H.

Understanding the Illness

Consider what the computer does for your mate. He can create and solve monumental problems in a single afternoon: How many politicians can dance on an MX missile? If everybody in the world sneezed at the same time, would it change the direction of the prevailing trade wind? He can create worlds of his own. He is master of all he surveys. (This is also known as the Computer Napoleon complex.)

With you, he has to deal with all sorts of variables—mood, temperament, and lots of other nasty things. His computer will never scream, sigh reprovingly, give him the evil eye or insult his mother. All it asks for is some electricity and some disks so it can be fed some programs.

On the other hand, you're softer, furrier, and probably smell better. And no machine can give him a back rub, laugh at his bad jokes or nibble his earlobe. At least not yet.

What's Your Problem?

Let's examine your reasons for going into such a tizzy over the little monster. Basically they boil down to one thing: you have a rival—and a pretty formidable one at that. You can't compete with a computer the way you'd compete with a human rival. You can't beat it out by doing your Jane Fonda workouts twice as hard and learning to whip up a mocha torte at the drop of a chocolate chip.

Not to worry. It's okay to be jealous of the way he can make that little machine sing. But at this point you have to decide what to do with all that negative energy. You can swallow your pride, give in and tackle the machine yourself. Or you can make one last attempt to pry his fingers loose from the keyboard.

Cures for the Nearly Gone

Okay, you've really had it. The only time you heard a peep out of him all week was when he cried at dinner because his disk crashed. He's been having nightmares about giant blinking Pac-Men chasing him. You suspect he's living in a twilight zone that Rod Serling never

even dreamed of. It's time to get him back into the world of the living.

Here are some tried-and-true methods to make him realize that human beings aren't simply appendages hanging from the edges of keyboards:
- Take him far away from civilization. Beaches, parks and tropical islands are all good choices. So are delis, pizza parlors and Chinese restaurants *as long as they don't have video arcades*.
- Get him to talk about other things. "Do you think we should have a baby?" and "Do you believe in God?" are good ways to start a non-computer conversation. Other topics include the senseless slaughter of kangaroos and the quality of raincoats manufactured in Romania.
- Avoid cerebral activities. Coaxing him into playing Scrabble, for example, will only remind him that the spelling checker on his word processor isn't working right.
- Talk a great deal about a man you admire. Dwell on all the wonderful aspects of his personality. Mention how much you enjoy his company. Mention how much he enjoys your company. Don't forget to mention that he hates computers.

The Bottom Line

You've tried everything. You've wined and dined him; you've bought sexy underwear, pleaded, coaxed and threatened. You're at your wit's end. When all else fails, you can:
- Do a rain dance. Thunderstorms tend to cause electrical problems, and electricity, as well we all know (or should), is the computer's Achilles heel.
- Lie down across the keyboard and refuse to get up. Insist it's the only comfortable spot in the house.
- Refer to an article you've read, claiming that people who spend too much time at their monitors turn into cretins (something about a hormonal problem caused by screen glare).
- Tell him a guy on the *Today* show said you can get herpes from computers.

Now, are you willing to admit you've been fighting a losing battle? If so, don't feel bad. You too can become a computer bore. ∎

YOU VS. THE COMPUTER

It's not that he doesn't love you anymore. It's not even that he loves the computer more than he loves you. It's just that, momentarily, the computer is easier to deal with. Let's look through his eyes and compare the computer to you, his mate.

He	You	The Computer
Asks you to spell "syzygy."	Point to the dictionary and tell him to look it up himself.	Graciously prints the correctly spelled word on the screen.
Invites you to play a game of chess.	Are too tired, lazy, or bombed on Jacobazzi to remember where the pieces go.	Is a ready, willing and able partner, and will even let him win if programmed to do so.
Asks your opinion about taking out a second mortgage.	Shrug and tell him to figure it out.	Has all the facts and figures he needs in a jiffy.
Wants chicken cordon bleu for dinner.	Can't find the recipe, and anyway you'd rather take out Chinese.	Gives him the exact recipe and even halves it so he can make it just for himself (you don't deserve any).
Tells you to go to hell.	Pack your suitcases and leave (or threaten to).	Stares him calmly in the eye and asks if he *really* wants to erase the whole disk.

THE LAST RESORT

Revenge against the computer can be sweet. It can also terminate your marriage or relationship. The recommendations that follow are offered only for the most extreme cases.

Don't	Do
Keep program disks in their jackets or sleeves.	Use his disks as trivets for your pots and pans.
Treat those little silicon chips with respect—they're at the heart of all your problems.	Take out the memory board to use as an extra cookie sheet for holiday baking.
Ask your partner whether he has any important data stored inside the computer.	Turn off the computer whenever you see it's been left on. You should be able to wipe out what he's working on.
Keep the computer from sticky fingers, dirt, moisture and heat. It's allergic to all of them.	Put the new kitten on the keyboard just to see what will happen.

E.H.

A LOVE LETTER WRITING PROGRAM

by Philip Elmer-DeWitt

Affairs of the heart, we are assured, will always be what make you and me different from computers. (I trust this is being read by a fellow human and not some computerized optical character reader.) Computers will never feel emotions like love, tenderness and devotion. With all the artificial intelligence in the world, machines will never have what it takes to write an *Anna Karenina* or even a successful Harlequin romance. Or so we are told.

And yet computers are already duplicating certain kinds of human intercourse. "Personalized" junk mail, for instance, pretends to a kind of intimacy by liberally sprinkling your name throughout its text as it cajoles you to sign up and buy something or other. This is a relatively simple form of computerized text manipulation, in which addresses and names from an electronic master list are substituted at key places in a document.

Other products of list manipulation, among them synthesized poetry, form the core of much of the research in the artificial intelligence community. In fact, the computer language most favored in this sector is LISP (short for List Processing language). A simplified version of this language is available in Logo, a subset of LISP's powerful set of instructions.

Curious about how emotional a computer could get, I sat down one day with an Apple II Plus and a copy of Logo, and wrote the little program called Loveletter. Known in the trade as a "toy" program, so trivial as to seem almost pointless, Loveletter writes little billets-doux suitable for pinning to a pillowcase. With more programming it could be taught to vary the structure of its letters, but that improvement would have made it too long to reprint here.

Philip Elmer-DeWitt writes the Computers column for Time *magazine. His wife has yet to use his Apple II.*

Given a few appropriate lines of text, Loveletter will generate notes like the following:

```
DEAR MARY
SINCE THAT NIGHT IN BARBADOS
MY LIFE SEEMS RICHER AND RICHER
YOU ARE SOOOOO SEXY
I WANT YOU RIGHT NOW
SAY YES AND YOU WILL NEVER BE SORRY
PHILIP
```

```
DEAR MARY
SINCE I SAW YOU LAST
MY LIFE JUST GETS BETTER AND BETTER
YOU ARE GETTING STRONGER BY THE MINUTE
I WANT ALL OF YOU
SAY YES AND YOU'LL NEVER SAY NO
PHILIP
```

Loveletter is printed in its entirety on the next page. With Apple Logo, you start the program by telling the computer to GETREADY, then type LOVELETTER. (The program also runs as written on M.I.T. Logo or Digital Research's DR Logo. Other versions, notably Texas Instruments', require modifications.)

This program consists of one main procedure and three attendant subprocedures. Procedures are what Logo is all about. The language comes equipped with a standard set, which you combine to make new procedures. These, in turn, can be combined in new and more complex procedures, and so on indefinitely. Procedures send messages to and from each other via inputs and outputs. The procedure PICKRANDOM, for example, inputs a list and outputs an item picked at random from that list.

Look at the main procedure, LOVELETTER. If you type LOVELETTER and hit RETURN, the Logo interpreter will start processing these capitalized words one line at a time. The word TO in the first line alerts Logo that what follows is a definition. The last line, END, indicates that the definition is complete. The lines in between are the actual instructions. Each time Logo is told to LOVELETTER, it gets itself a copy of this definition and starts executing the instructions one line at a time.

Now look at the first line in LOVELETTER:

PRINT SENTENCE [DEAR] PICKRANDOM :LOVER

Notice that there are no prepositions (of, by) in the Logo language. Also notice the strange punctuation. All this is significant. The brackets ([. . .]) and colon (:) are used in Logo to differentiate between things and the names of things. PRINT and SENTENCE are built-in procedures: SENTENCE takes two words or phrases and puts them together with a blank space in between; PRINT displays words on a TV screen or printer. Reading from left to right, Logo understands this line to say: print on the TV screen a sentence made up of the word DEAR and a word chosen randomly from a list of words called LOVER. When instructed to LOVELETTER, the first thing Logo will do is type:

DEAR MARY

The next six lines of the LOVELETTER procedure work in much the same way. Basically, they construct sentences by tacking nouns and verbs (YOU ARE . . . ; I WANT . . .) onto randomly chosen memories, desires, promises. At first the program's data base contains only those memories supplied by the start-up procedure GETREADY. But the lists of names and phrases soon grows longer, thanks to the procedure called LEARNANOTHER invoked toward the end of Loveletter. LEARNANOTHER simply asks the user to "teach it" another phrase and then adds that new phrase onto the end of the original list.

The last instruction of Loveletter is to LOVELETTER again. This sends the program back to its own beginning. The endless loop this creates is a simple example of recursion, a powerful programming tool useful in moving through treelike data base structures and one of the features that distinguishes modern high-level languages like Logo, LISP, Pascal and FORTH from more primitive languages like COBOL, FORTRAN and BASIC. (Most video games are written in the even more primitive "assembly" languages.) BASIC and FORTRAN were designed to solve for-

mulas by manipulating numbers. Logo, from the Greek for "word," was designed to manipulate words, sentences and lists.

It took me less than half an hour to write a crude version of Loveletter, another thirty minutes to debug and polish it off, and about three minutes to exhaust my interest in playing with it. But before the program got boring, something interesting happened: like the inkblots in a Rorschach test, the letters it generated started to reflect my unconscious preoccupations. The deeper I dredged my mind for MEMORYs and DESIREs, the racier my loveletters got. Before long they were unprintable. My wife wandered by at one point and looked briefly over my shoulder. "You're very weird" was all she had to say. ∎

```
TO LOVELETTER
PRINT SENTENCE [DEAR] PICKRANDOM :LOVER
PRINT SENTENCE [SINCE] PICKRANDOM :MEMORY
PRINT SENTENCE [MY LIFE] PICKRANDOM :HOWCHANGED
PRINT SENTENCE [YOU ARE] PICKRANDOM :NICETHING
PRINT SENTENCE [I WANT] PICKRANDOM :DESIRE
PRINT SENTENCE [SAY YES AND] PICKRANDOM :PROMISE
PRINT PICKRANDOM :SIGNOFF
PRINT :SPACE
LEARNANOTHER PICKRANDOM [LOVER MEMORY HOWCHANGED NICETHING DESIRE PROMISE SIGNOFF]
LOVELETTER
END

TO GETREADY
MAKE "LOVER [[MARY]]
MAKE "MEMORY [[WE MET AT JESSICA'S PARTY THAT SECOND TIME AROUND]]
MAKE "HOWCHANGED [[HAS BEEN INFUSED WITH A DAWNING SENSE OF UNBELIEVABLE GOOD LUCK]]
MAKE "NICETHING [[THE BEST]]
MAKE "DESIRE [[TO MARRY YOU]]
MAKE "PROMISE [[I'LL SPEND MY LIFE MAKING YOU HAPPY]]
MAKE "SIGNOFF [[PHILIP]]
MAKE "SPACE []
END

TO LEARNANOTHER :CATEGORY
PRINT SENTENCE [TEACH ME ANOTHER] :CATEGORY
MAKE :CATEGORY SENTENCE (THING :CATEGORY) (LIST READLIST)
PRINT :SPACE
END

TO PICKRANDOM :LIST
OUTPUT ITEM (1 + RANDOM (COUNT :LIST)) :LIST
END

?LOVELETTER
DEAR MARY
SINCE WE MET AT JESSICA'S PARTY THAT SECOND TIME AROUND
MY LIFE HAS BEEN INFUSED WITH A DAWNING SENSE OF UNBELIEVABLE GOOD LUCK
YOU ARE THE BEST
I WANT TO MARRY YOU
SAY YES AND I'LL SPEND MY LIFE MAKING YOU HAPPY
PHILIP

TEACH ME ANOTHER HOWCHANGED
```

WORD SALAD

THE BABBLE OF COMPUTER LANGUAGES

Mainframe destruction: the Tower of Babel crumbles under the weight of linguistic confusion.

by Robert de Marrais

Prior to the emergence of FORTRAN in the 1950s, programmers were forced to converse in either of two equally simple-minded argots: the hodgepodge of 0s and 1s known as machine code or the only slightly friendlier vocabulary of assembly language. Now hu-

Robert de Marrais is a free-lance high-tech writer with a background in the history of science. His hobbies include mathematical topology, metaphysics and the Plough & Stars Bar in Cambridge.

man/machine discourse has evolved apace with hardware in richness and complexity, and not since the Tower of Babel have we been subjected to so many new tongues in so short a time.

FORTRAN

Created in the ancient punch card days for the purpose of FORmula TRANslation, this pioneer language performed much the same service for the lab-coated slide-rule toters that Latin provided to the cassock-shrouded acolytes. Also like Latin, it is used only by a vanishing few. Nonetheless, FORTRAN has left us a rich classical heritage, including what many feel is the greatest epic ever committed to keypunch: the mainframe folk game Adventure. Serious scholars are urged to pursue its study, the better to read the great works of space age science in the original.

COBOL

Like most languages of commerce, this one arose as a sort of pidgin dialect and does not make for scintillating prose; the standard version, in fact, was created by committee (a government committee, at that), which explains the notorious verbosity of its source code. Its bureaucrats' knack for rapidly filling up all storage space allotted to it makes this an exceedingly difficult language to implement on a small system, although Radio Shack did in fact achieve this thankless task in 1982. According to one internationally renowned expert, Edsgar Dijkstra, "Teaching COBOL ought to be regarded as a criminal act." COBOL is still the most widely used programming language in the world.

BASIC

The preeminent "vulgar" language in both senses, BASIC is ideally suited to quick, easy expression, lends itself readily to projects requiring only short attention spans and can be spoken in wildly illogical sequence with no risk of altering its sense. Highly interactive and structure-poor, it is appropriate for microcomputer streetcorner jive but is no good at all for large jobs that must be tackled piecemeal with a managerial overview.

Pascal

In 1983 the College Boards directors dubbed Pascal the language for Advanced Placement testing in Computer Literacy—a decision comparable, in its significance for the future of computing, to the effect on religious history of Emperor Constantine's conversion to Christianity. By giving thumbs down to BASIC, schools across the nation were forced to reprogram their curricula to accommodate its highly structured, logically satisfying elegance. Tomorrow's commentators will doubtless celebrate this act as a much needed antidote to the anti-intellectualism, myopia and aimlessness rampant since the advent of FORTRAN.

FORTH

First implemented by stargazers at a secluded observatory, FORTH was brought down from the mountain in 1971. Its cult declared itself radically opposed to the idolatry of machine-specific programming, offering a highly portable code facilitating an unprecedented "speaking in tongues" among otherwise incompatible devices. Early apostles of the faith would put a FORTH disk and minicomputer in a suitcase and preach directly from machine to machine in their wandering ministry, to frequently miraculous effect. Composed from a small set of glyphs possessed of universal machine-language-based significance, FORTH's runes are combined into words within bigger words, cascading their way upwards into one great All-Knowing Ur Utterance, whose conjuring unleashes the program's full potency.

LISP

Written in boxcar-like prose (composed of multiply nested [parenthetical (and inherently self-referential)] chains of inference), LISt-Processing dialects are the preferred speech of robot makers, designers of so-called "expert systems," and creators of other modes of software that compare favorably with the "wetware" of the human brain pan. Though perceived to be a verbally oriented language, it was used to produce the dazzling graphics mindscapes of *Tron*. Profoundly logical and prone to "blue-skying," it has all the pretentions, pomp and promise of Hegelian dialectics—and is about as economical and easy to scan.

C

Arising in the early 1970s as a reaction to the overspecialized "high-level" language bias that stressed mechanical efficiency at the expense of programmer sanity, C was liberated from developer Bell Labs' protectionism by Berkeley University programmers who petitioned for the right to free "assembly language"—the coding least alienated from the electronic "body consciousness" of machine code itself. Explicitly tailored for communal time sharing, its increasingly popular UNIX operating system encourages unlimited networking as well as the bartering of ready-made program components. Since the early 1980s, its administrationless, volunteer-maintenanced Usenet support group has shared conceptual experiences with an ever broadening collective of information anarchists.

Logo

Originating among members of the artificial intelligence community sympathetic to the mental development theories of Jean Piaget, Logo is a language framed with children in mind and thus emphasizes the graphic, gestural and self-referential. In its earliest implementation, an electromechanical turtle that danced on tabletops let toddlers visualize the results of their programming. Later variants put the turtle on-screen. Since all versions of the language encourage toddlers to interact with imaginary insects whenever they "make a mess," one might say that Logo is the "debugging" language par excellence. ∎

BRINGING UP BASIC

by John G. Kemeny and Thomas E. Kurtz

"Yeah. Well, see, these computer firms are very awkward. All the smaller personal computers use BASIC, because it's the easiest language and also one of the best. But the firms making them all build in their own variations, so that if you record your programs from their machines, you can't run them on anyone else's. That keeps you faithful to them in the future, because if you change to another make, all your tapes will be useless."

"What a bore," I said.

—Dick Francis, *Twice Shy* (G. P. Putnam's Sons, New York, 1982)

Ever since we invented BASIC, over twenty years ago, we've used it almost exclusively for our own programming. Most others at Dartmouth do also. Students in the beginning computer science courses use it to learn with.

Persons outside Dartmouth may wonder what we're talking about. BASIC a language of computer science? Aw, come on! But stick with us for a minute. We can explain. The BASIC we use at Dartmouth is a far cry from the slangy street BASICs used by the rest of the world. In the past twenty years we've brought up our own BASIC to be a good citizen and to show some class. The less fortunate BASICs picked up bad habits and vulgar language. We would no sooner think of using street BASIC than we would think of using FORTRAN!

In the early 1960s there were no personal computers, or even time sharing, to be found outside the research labs. If you wanted to do computing, you had to punch up your programs on cards, carry them to the nearest computer center (for us, until 1960, it was

John G. Kemeny and Thomas E. Kurtz, the originators of BASIC, are the authors of Back to BASIC.

a 135-mile train ride), then wait hours (or days) for the results.

We wanted our students to learn about computing without having to endure such problems. Drastic action was called for. So in 1963–64 we designed and built a time-sharing system, which later became the backbone of the General Electric Time Sharing network. It was a system meant to be easy for ordinary people to use, and one of its ingredients was the new language BASIC.

The design goals for BASIC included ease of learning for the beginner or occasional programmer, hardware and operating system independence, the ability to accommodate large programs written by expert users, and sensible error messages in English.

As the years went by, our infant BASIC grew up. It learned about character strings and files and matrix operations. By 1971 our local version included subprograms that could be collected into libraries and stashed away for later use—by anyone. It knew about both character and random access files. For the times, BASIC was a pretty advanced language.

In the early 1970s it learned how to do interac-

Thomas Kurtz (left) and John Kemeny with the latest implementation of their BASIC programming language.

tive graphics, and graphics statements became part of the language itself around 1975. The level of sophistication even then was superior to that now found in many commercial BASICs. Our users did not have to know how many dots were on the screen: the pictures could be drawn in user coordinates. You'd think this idea would be obvious by now. But today's users of Microsoft BASIC have to know that there are 320 dots horizontally and 200 dots vertically (if you're using medium-resolution color graphics on the IBM PC) and have to do messy arithmetic to draw simple pictures. We even had picture definitions, which are like subroutines but draw pictures instead. The pictures can be shifted left or right, shrunk or expanded, and even rotated.

Edsgar Dijkstra got the ball rolling on structured programming in the late 1960s, but not until the early 1970s did his ideas reached the hinterlands. In 1976 we added structured constructs to our BASIC. Incidentally, there were virtually no problems converting from old-fashioned BASIC to Structured BASIC. We dropped the GOTO statement overnight, with no regrets. Our students could not have cared

less. We told them not to use it, and they didn't.

So the BASIC in our family was a sophisticated language with a good collection of structured constructs, sophisticated graphics, all the good modularization tools, etc. What a far cry from what most of the rest of the world had to use.

We got our first inkling of the sorry state of BASIC's affairs when, several years ago, one of us used a personal computer for the first time. It was an Apple II Plus, and we were converting programs that ran on our big machine into Applesoft BASIC. We were appalled at what we saw. Microsoft, the authors of Applesoft, advertised multicharacter variable names, but used only the first two characters. There was no way to use lower-case letters. There was no way to indent programs to show structure. There was no nice way to have comments appear together with a statement on the same line.

To give you an idea of how others had prostituted our beautiful language, they arranged for the for-loop always to be executed once, as in

```
FOR I = 1 TO N
. . .
NEXT I
```

when N is 0. Shades of FORTRAN! We thought we'd banished that quirk over twenty years ago, and here it popped up again.

Even worse, we discovered that the following statement was completely illegal:

```
IF B = A THEN 500
```

This statement was interpreted in Applesoft's prescan as

```
IF B = AT HEN500
```

which is, of course, a syntax error. Ugh!

Several years later, we discovered an equally ugly version of BASIC on the IBM PC. We were horrified by many features that required knowing intricacies of the hardware. Not only did graphics necessitate counting dots, but IBM had two graphics modes (for color) and a program written for one would not work in the other!

What about our original goals? We agree that most people find street BASIC fairly easy to learn, provided they can read what they've programmed. That's not so easy with only upper-case letters and often no ability to indent the code to reflect what is going on. In addition, street BASIC has its own idiosyncrasies. For instance, this dialect persists in telling the beginning student:

```
SYNTAX ERROR IN 150
```

Isn't a "syntax" a levy on cigarettes or alcohol? We certainly can do much better than that. But street BASICs don't.

With all this complaining, you might ask, what are we doing about the sorry state of affairs? Well, first of all, we've been working with the ANSI committee that is coming up with a standard BASIC. This committee is now, thankfully, nearing the end of its work after ten years. The standard BASIC they are developing is a rich language, with structured constructs, nifty graphics and a wide variety of other features. Some say there are too many features, but it's an easy matter to pick and choose the ones you want and ignore the rest.

Also, we were struck by the Pascal experience. We had sat back at our institution and bragged about our BASIC, and then wondered why no one paid attention. Pascal enjoys its popularity today not solely because of its clean design, which is an undeniable feature, but because the folks at the University of California, San Diego, produced and promoted a commercial-quality implementation of the language.

The old adage "If you want something done right,

do it yourself" finally dawned on us. When the opportunity arose in the spring and summer of 1983 to form a company to produce a definitive version of BASIC, we jumped at the chance. We call our product True BASIC™. It closely follows the proposed (as of this writing) ANSI standard for BASIC. True BASIC also embraces the good things we have demanded from our own versions of BASIC over the years: good and accurate error messages, a user interface that is simple and plain, and the capability to be used for both small and large programs.

True BASIC will be produced to fit into the major personal computers that have a reasonable amount of memory (128K or more), and it will be identical for all machines. Teachers can assign exercises without worrying about which computers are currently in the computer lab. Schoolbook authors will be able to write in True BASIC and have their programs run on all the major personal computers. They can leave the worry about the peculiarities of the hardware to us.

Our "tapes" will no longer be useless. They will run on any machine. We hope that we will make Dick Francis happy, at last.   ∎

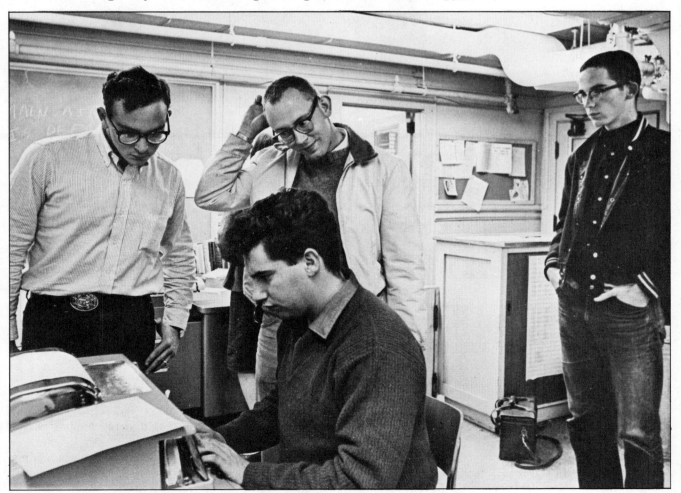

Students at Dartmouth working with the first version of BASIC.

"Logos . . . from the Greek λογοσ, the word or form which expresses a thought; also, the thought."
—Webster's New International Dictionary of the English Language

THE LOGO LINEAGE

by Wallace Feurzeig

Logo was created in 1966 at Bolt Beranek and Newman, a Cambridge research firm. Its intellectual roots are in artificial intelligence, mathematical logic

Wallace Feurzeig is a division scientist in information sciences for Bolt Beranek and Newman. His favorite implementation of Logo is still Logo-S for minicomputers.

and developmental psychology. The first four years of Logo research, development and teaching work was done at BBN.

During the early 1960s, BBN had become a major center of computer science research and innovative applications. I joined the firm in 1962 to work with its newly available facilities in the Artificial Intelligence

Department, one of the earliest AI organizations. My colleagues were actively engaged in some of the pioneering AI work in computer pattern recognition, natural language understanding, theorem proving, LISP language development and robot problem solving. Much of this work was done in collaboration with distinguished researchers at M.I.T. such as Marvin Minsky and John McCarthy, who were regular BBN consultants during the early 1960s. Other groups at BBN were doing original work in cognitive science, instructional research and man-computer communication. Some of the first work on knowledge representation (semantic networks), question-answering, interactive graphics and computer-aided instruction was actively underway. J. C. R. Licklider was the spiritual as well as the scientific leader of much of this work, championing the cause of on-line interaction during an era when almost all computation was being done via batch processing.

Time for Interaction

My initial focus was on expanding the intellectual capabilities of existing teaching systems. This led to the first "intelligent" computer-assisted instruction (CAI) system, MENTOR, which employed production rules to support problem-solving interactions in medical diagnosis and other decision-making domains. In 1965 I organized the BBN Educational Technology Department to further the development of computer methods for improving learning and teaching, and the focus of our work then shifted to the investigation of programming languages as educational environments. This shift was partly due to two recent technological advances: the invention of computer time sharing and the development of the first high-level "conversational" programming language.

The idea of sharing a computer's cycles among several autonomous users, working on-line simultaneously, had stirred the imagination of programmers in Cambridge in 1963 and 1964. BBN and M.I.T. teams raced to be first in realizing this concept, with BBN winning by days and holding the first successful demonstration of computer time-sharing in 1964. Our initial system, designed by Sheldon Boilen, supported five simultaneous users on a DEC PDP-1, all sharing a single CRT screen for output. Seeing dynamic displays from several distinct programs, simultaneously and asynchronously ("out of time and tune"), was a breathtaking experience.

Time sharing made feasible the economic use of remote distributed terminals and opened up the possibilities of interactive computer use in schools. We had recently implemented TELCOMP, one of the new breed of high-level interactive programming languages. TELCOMP was a dialect of JOSS, the first "conversational" (i.e., interpretive) language, developed in 1962–63 by Cliff Shaw of the Rand Corporation; its syntax was similar to that of BASIC, which had not yet appeared. Like BASIC, TELCOMP was a FORTRAN-derived language originally designed for numerical computational applications. Shortly after TELCOMP was created, we decided to introduce it to children as a tool for teaching mathematics and in 1965–66, under U.S. Office of Education support, explored its use as an auxiliary resource in eight elementary and secondary schools served by the BBN time-sharing system. Students were introduced to TELCOMP and then worked on standard arithmetic, algebra, and trigonometry problems by writing TELCOMP programs. The project strongly confirmed our expectation that the use of interactive computation with a high-level interpretive language would be highly motivating to students.

My collaborators in this research were Daniel Bobrow, Richard Grant and Cynthia Solomon from BBN and consultant Seymour Papert, who had recently arrived at M.I.T. from Jean Piaget's Institute in Geneva. The idea of a programming language expressly designed for children arose directly from this project. We realized that most existing languages were designed for doing computation and that they generally lacked facilities for nonnumeric symbolic manipulation. Current languages were inappropriate for education in other respects as well: they often employed extensive type declarations that got in the way

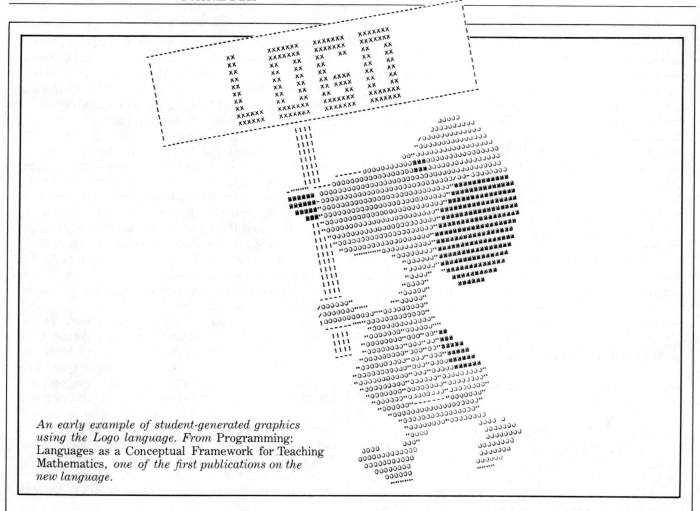

An early example of student-generated graphics using the Logo language. From Programming: Languages as a Conceptual Framework for Teaching Mathematics, *one of the first publications on the new language.*

of students' expressive impetus; they had serious deficiencies in control structures; their programs lacked procedural constructs; most had no facilities for dynamic definition and execution; few had well-developed and articulate debugging, diagnostic and editing facilities, so essential for educational applications.

Educational Expression

The need for a new language designed for and dedicated to education was evident. The basic requirements for the language were:

1) Third-graders should be able to use it for simple tasks with very little preparation.

2) Its structure should embody mathematically important concepts with minimal interference from programming conventions.

3) It should permit the expression of mathematically rich nonnumerical as well as numerical algorithms.
Examples of nonnumerical problems include translating English into pig Latin; making and breaking "secret codes"; word games such as testing whether a word is symmetric (a palindrome), finding words within words, writing words backwards; question-

answering and guessing games (such as "twenty questions" and "buzz"). Our strategy was to introduce mathematical ideas through experience with these familiar and meaningful problems and projects.

Incredibly, the best model for the new language (which was to be as simple as possible) turned out to be LISP, the lingua franca of artificial intelligence, often regarded (by non-LISP users) as one of the most difficult and formidable of languages. Of course, the syntax of Logo is much more familiar and accessible than that of LISP. Essentially, though, Logo *is* LISP and is thus both an easy and a powerful language. The power is not evident in most existing microcomputer implementations, mainly because of their small memory and restricted performance.

The initial design of Logo came about through extensive discussions in 1966 between Seymour Papert, Dan Bobrow and myself. Papert developed the overall functional specifications for the new language, and Bobrow made extensive contributions to the design and did the first implementation. Subsequently, Richard Grant made substantial additions and modifications to the design and implementation, assisted by Cynthia Solomon, Frank Frazier and Paul Wexelblat. I gave Logo its name.

This first version of Logo was pilot-tested in the summer of 1967 with fifth- and sixth-grade math students at the Hanscom Field School in Lincoln, Massachusetts, under support of the U.S. Office of Naval Research. In 1967–68 we designed a new and greatly extended version, which was implemented on our DEC PDP-1 computer system by Charles R. Morgan. Michael Levin, one of the original implementors of LISP, contributed to the design. From September 1968 through November 1969, the National Science Foundation supported us in the first intensive program of experimental teaching of Logo-based mathematics in elementary and secondary classrooms. The teaching experiments demonstrated in principle that Logo can be used to provide a natural conceptual framework for the teaching of mathematics in an intellectually, psy-chologically and pedagogically sound way.

In 1970 Seymour Papert founded the Logo Laboratory at M.I.T. Logo-based turtles, erroneously thought by many to be essential to the Logo teaching enterprise, were introduced around 1971. Several hardware implementations and teaching experiments followed during the decade of 1970s at M.I.T., BBN and elsewhere.

Then came microcomputers. Their wide availability and affordability catapulted Logo into becoming one of the world's most widely used languages. At this point in its history, future development of exemplary teaching ideas and materials is crucial to support the needs of users. Our work on Logo development is continuing and continues to be compelling. Logo is an idea whose time is now. ∎

THE FORTH ESTATE

Like the sling David used against Goliath, FORTH enables serious amateurs and small groups of professionals to hold their own in a world dominated by corporate giants and large-team projects. Below are some of the factors contributing to the growth and power of this "grass roots" computer language despite the lack of institutional support or academic interest.

1) FORTH is extensible (you add your own commands to the language). You can create a customized language for any program you want to write and can define whole new families of data structures or commands.

2) FORTH is interactive (you get results right away). Dozens or hundreds of separate tests can be run during a single session at the computer. If a routine doesn't work, you can test its components and subcomponents immediately from the keyboard without writing separate programming. Such immediate results encourage programmer education as well as software development.

3) FORTH is multilevel (you can reach down to the lowest level of bits or bytes without using a machine language, or you can stay in the highest realm of special customized words for your own application). All levels are always available and can be mixed or matched at any time.

Suppose you want to write a program to control a machine, e.g., to move motors, turn lights on and off, make sounds or music, read meters or other indicators. You write your own routines (extensible) to create special commands that set the particular memory bits (multilevel), which act as switches to move motors, etc. Then you can watch the machine react to your typed commands (interactive) and build new routines (extensible) for the machine commands you wrote as well as any previous programs to get more complex behavior. You see the results right away (interactive).

Since its programs are completely machine-independent, FORTH can run on whatever computers are available at the time. Moreover, while other lan-guages tend to lock you into whatever features were provided by the computer manufacturer or software house, FORTH allows complete control of the machine and encourages you to change any part of the system itself. Not only is its system internals much simpler, but there is no dividing line to separate the system from your own application programs. All the software (operating system, programming language and application program) is one seamless piece, any part of which can be changed at your own command. Everything needed is in the public domain, information is freely exchanged, and software developers can avoid licensing hassles.

As might be expected, programming in FORTH stimulates the imagination. You create words (commands) of your own design, and each new word becomes an integral part of the system. In most languages, writing a program can be compared to building a house using only those tools provided. In FORTH, you use the given tools to create still new ones until finally one of the tools is the house itself—ready to be lived in, but also ready to be used again to build a whole complex later on.

FORTH is not for everyone, of course. Managers who consider using it must worry about staff retraining or finding enough programmers or controlling projects with a language that gives each individual considerable freedom. And though we know it works well for small projects, there has been little opportunity to document its effectiveness in larger efforts.

As for the future, almost no one expects FORTH to catch on so completely that other languages will be made obsolete. Since no one language is best for every purpose, there will still be variety in the computer world. Nevertheless, we can anticipate that FORTH will continue to grow in influence and to offer its users a substantial advantage.

JOHN S. JAMES, originator of the CommuniTree network in Santa Cruz, California

THE ABC'S OF WORD PROCESSING

by Rita Aero and Barbara Elman

A is for Adding and Deleting Text: the first difference you'll appreciate between your old typewriter and your sleek new word processor. Most of a writer's time is spent rewriting—adding or deleting words from existing sentences and paragraphs. You can easily delete words and send them to computer heaven or insert spice to your zesty romance novel with a few more passionate punches.

B is for Block Move, Copy and Delete: the second thing you'll appreciate about word processing. Before you can move a paragraph from page 8 to page 24, you have to mark off the beginning and ending of the section, thus creating a "block" (not to be confused with Writer's Block). Then you can play around with this block, moving it to new plateaus, before you get tired of it and decide to delete it permanently.

C is for Changing Your Mind: the writer's dream come true, thanks to the features described in A and B. Before you joined the computer age, you dreaded the editor's

Rita Aero is co-author and designer of several books produced with word processors, including The Love Exam, *written with an Epson QX10 and VALDOCS. Barbara Elman is the founder and editor of* WP News, *a newsletter for authors interested in word processing.*

pencil or that unbidden new stroke of inspiration—like changing your main character's name throughout a novel or film script. Now you welcome the chance to change your mind and make your pages as perfect as possible.

D is for Documentation: the incomprehensible manual that comes with your word processing program. It seems to dare you to decipher its detailed directions, and you'll be forced to figure it out through trial and error anyway. Somewhere at the nadir of Silicon Valley, technical writers sit composing these voluminous works. Someday, hopefully, they'll be translated into English.

E is for Editing, Electronic: when you add A plus B plus C you get E—a formerly excruciating task involving retyping your entire work to make your boss or editor happy. While your typewriter lets you fill your page with words, your word processor also lets you shuffle those words like a deck of cards without endless retyping. A perfect copy every time! And no more grumbling when an editor asks for a rewrite.

F is for Files: the electronic version of your filing cabinet. The best advice we can give is "keep them short!"—a chapter or scene at the most. Many a writer has used the "F" word in frustration trying to get from page 2 to page 32. Most word processing programs insist you scroll through the interim text in your file, ever so slowly, whether you want to or not. Phooey!

is for GIGO: a computer hacker's term meaning "Garbage In, Garbage Out." This also applies to the writer's craft—an electronic typing tool will not turn dull prose into sparkling wit, even if you change your name to Shakespeare. Your word processor will make the art of writing more fun, but no computer can write creatively without a human pushing its buttons.

is for Hard Copy: the satisfying end product of your hard work. No matter how much you play with your words on-screen, the real acid test is the way they look on paper. It's the only way to catch the inevitable typo that you just can't see until the ink hits the page (see P for Printer). Since even a portable computer is too heavy to mail, hard copy is still the most common means of getting your message across.

is for Integrated Software: the kind where you can type in text, then switch into calculating mode to figure out a bit of bookkeeping, then search through a data base for some fact, all without having to change program disks. Since humans, even writers, can't live by words alone, such capability can be awfully useful—provided your computer has sufficient internal memory to handle this kind of software.

is for Justification: making the right-hand margin line up just like the left. (It's also a term for what you do to rationalize how much money you've spent on your new electronic toy.) If you can't see on-screen how the text will be arranged on paper, you may find some unpleasant gaps between words, requiring further adjustment on the machine. Eventually you may give up and turn it off altogether, like most professional writers.

ON WORD PROCESSING

For over two and a half years I've been writing my novels using the WordStar word processing program. The hardware is immaterial. I am a very picky kind of writer insofar as word choice is concerned. My theory is to work like hell to make things look as if they were done very swiftly and easily. And I like to turn in very clean manuscripts.

When you're trying to produce the "effortless" manuscript, finding exactly the right word for each situation is crucial. I used to sit staring at the damned sheet of paper, *knowing* there was a precise word available if only I could think of it. Sometimes—often—I would settle for the almost right word. (Sam Clemens said the difference between the right word and the almost right word is the difference between lightning and a lightning bug.) Then, during one of the endless rereadings, I would dredge up the word I'd been looking for, but because there was *already* another one in the sentence, almost as descriptive, I would tend to leave the weaker word in rather than mark up the page or retype.

Now I merely leave a blank, just big enough so it catches the eye. And when I reread, sooner or later I can come up with the word I was reaching for and fit it into the blank—with no clue that I hesitated for even a moment.

The second best part of word processing is the ability to tone down the purple prose, or delete the Gee Mom parts of it.

The third best aspect is the revision-on-demand advantage. When Knopf asked for a detailed revision of *One More Sunday*, I was able to provide in eight days of intense effort, eight twelve-hour days, what would have taken me six weeks the way I used to work. And I believe the revision (those changes that I agreed with) is better than the original version.

JOHN D. MacDONALD, author of *Condominium* and the Travis McGee series of detective novels

is for Keyboard: the key to effective contact with your word processor. Unfortunately, most manufacturers have chosen to use keyboards unfit for writers and typists. Some new keyboard layouts are designed with writers in mind: like HASCI (Human Applications Standard Computer Interface, with dedicated function keys) and the Dvorak (an arrangement of letters that yields dramatically increased comfort and speed).

THE McWILLIAMS II WORD PROCESSOR

Features

- Portable.
- Prints characters from every known language.
- Graphics are fully supported.
- Gives off no appreciable degree of radiation.
- Uses no energy.
- Memory is not lost during a power failure.
- Infinitely variable margins.
- Types sizes from 1 to 945,257,256,256 points.
- Easy to learn.
- User-friendly.
- Not likely to be stolen.
- No moving parts.
- Silent operation.
- Occasional maintenance keeps it in top condition.
- Five-year unconditional warranty.

McWilliams II Schematic

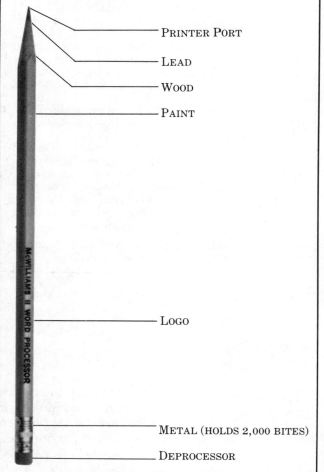

- PRINTER PORT
- LEAD
- WOOD
- PAINT
- LOGO
- METAL (HOLDS 2,000 BITES)
- DEPROCESSOR

PETER A. McWILLIAMS, author of *The Personal Computer Guide;* the complete *McWilliams II Word Processor Instruction Manual* is available from Prelude Press, Box 69773, Los Angeles, Ca. 90069

is for Letter-Quality Printing: making your page (which has been massaged, edited, reedited, rewritten and redecorated on your fancy electronic marvel) look just like it came out of your old-fashioned typewriter. Book and magazine publishers, film producers and corporate executives especially prefer Selectric-looking hard copy.

is for Mail, Electronic: the fast and fun way to get your words through space and time. By plugging your computer into the telephone lines with an M for Modem, you can collaborate long distance. Arthur C. Clarke, for example, sent the entire text of his recent book *2010* through trans-Atlantic phone lines from his home in Sri Lanka to his New York publisher.

is for Nightmare, Electronic: that dreaded moment when your words disappear from the screen and wing their way to computer heaven. This has been known to happen on every brand of computer using every type of software. (The authors of this piece lived through an Electronic Nightmare shortly after we wrote this the first time; when the Nightmare strikes, the only thing to do is curse the #"&%! machine and start over.)

is for OCR: the Optical Character Reader, which can read your already typewritten pages onto computer disk for future editing. The bad news is that these machines are expensive—they average $30,000. The good news is that one day they will appear in every library next to the coin-operated computers and Xerox machines to electronically transfer your notes and research materials to your word processor for pennies a page.

is for Printer: the two most common types are dot matrix and daisy wheel. Dot matrix printers form letters from a grid of tiny dots, placed very close together. Many people still prefer the daisy wheel, which produces Letter-Quality text (see L). Dot matrix printers are cheap, fast, portable and versatile; daisy wheels are large and expensive, but yield handsome hard copy. The best choice is to have one of each.

 is for Quirks: what no word processing program is without. Each program has a unique and sometimes incomprehensible way of doing things, many of which you will never learn to love. Get to know your program's quirks early in the game, and don't expect them

to be the same from program to program. For example, WordStar uses code letters for common functions that have no relation to the procedure they perform.

is for RETURN: don't touch that button! The most pleasurable feature to adapt to when using your first word processor is automatic word-wrap. Instead of hitting the RETURN key at the end of each line, you just keep typing and let your fingers do the talking. The pro-

WHY I GAVE UP WORD PROCESSING

The moment of epiphany is ever fresh in my mind. I was in Sacramento in May 1982, hobnobbing with aides of then Governor Jerry Brown (who was, as all well know, quite high on technology), when one of his advisers told me about the Osborne I.

All of a sudden, it became glaringly evident. I must own a computer. It was the only way I could successfully write my first book. By the time I returned home to New Jersey, I had no doubt that my life as a writer would improve dramatically.

Make no mistake about it. My productivity did increase, tremendously. I can no longer imagine writing without a computer. But, perhaps because my hopes were so high, the disappointments I experienced were intense. In brief, reality intruded.

The first disappointment was a discovery of self. I am incapable of writing on a keyboard. This fact was brought home hard when I sat down at my Osborne to begin composing my opus. One hundred feverish pages later, I handed the product to my next-door neighbor, also a working scribe and a politically astute critic.

"This stinks," he said.

Indeed it did. I rambled. I disconnected. I spewed garbage.

I realized that computers cannot change a writer's working temperament. I have never been able to write stylized prose at a keyboard. I still cannot. And so I finally sat down to write my book the only way I knew how: with blue medium-point Paper Mate ballpoints on yellow lined legal pads.

The second disappointment was a limitation of the Osborne. After writing my chapters, I would keyboard in the product. The Osborne I's disk format is capable of storing only about thirty double-spaced pages of text. I was inundated with disks. No problem . . . until I started rewriting and reorganizing the text. Massive revisions were needed on my book. Parts of chapter two had to be soldered onto chapter ten; I was forced to graft a sentence at the end of one very long section to the beginning of the section, which

was, inconveniently, located on another disk.

Now, don't get me wrong. I think the CP/M operating system is a wonderful invention. But copying files with the "pip" command is a plain old pain in the butt, especially when manipulating WordStar files. I'd have to hit CTRL-KB and CTRL-KK and CTRL-KW and name the file on which to write the marked block and pip the file onto the new disk and CTRL-D and enter the name of the file to edit and CTRL-KR to read the file I'd just pipped into the proper section of the file I'd just opened and . . . well, it was exhausting.

I just gave up. I finally figured it was easier to cut and paste sections by hand, using my yellow lined legal pads and my Bostitch stapler. The ultimate ignominy was hiring a typist to type the final manuscript copy of my book. She's a wonderful woman, who's thinking of buying a computer.

RANDALL ROTHENBERG, author of *The Neo-Liberals: Creating the New American Politics*

gram will put your words within the proper margins. RETURN is only used to indicate the end of a paragraph or to skip a line.

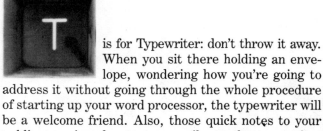

is for Save: do it often. This is one of the best habits you can form in adapting to processing your words on computer. With most programs, the words you compose exist as electronic impulses only in the computer's memory. Saving them to disk stores them permanently in case trouble strikes. Saving every few pages is cheap insurance against the Nightmare, Electronic (see N).

is for Typewriter: don't throw it away. When you sit there holding an envelope, wondering how you're going to address it without going through the whole procedure of starting up your word processor, the typewriter will be a welcome friend. Also, those quick notes to your public are zipped out more easily on the typewriter than on the computer, where you must compose, store, then print to get your thoughts on paper.

is for User-Defined Keys: keys on the keyboard that have no specific word processing function until you give them one. These keys just sit there until you use a special program to custom-design word processing procedures or margin changes, or even to program frequently used text into each key. This is especially useful for screenwriters and novelists who use special formats or foreign names with odd spellings.

is for Video Display Screen: the way your computer shows you what it's thinking. Most screens show a half-page of typed text at a time, and scroll up and down while you edit. They come in several colors and flavors: vanilla, licorice, butterscotch and mint. Among Americans mint is the most popular with its cool, green, eye-soothing tint; in Europe butterscotch is the favorite with its handsome amber tones.

is for Windows: a fancy feature of some new word processing programs. Windows allow you to view portions of several files at a time on-screen and move text between them. When you're moving words from chapter to chapter or report to report, this is a great time-saving device. But before you buy a program just to have windowing capabilities, be sure this costly feature is compatible with your working style.

is for Xerox: the word processor's friend. Even though your computer printer will gladly produce 340 copies of your 430-page report, it could have a coronary at the end. If you use a slow daisy wheel printer (one page every few minutes), this might take over two hundred days to print nonstop. A special benefit for dot matrix users is that xeroxing makes the dots fill in nicely to look more like letter-quality hard copy.

is for Your Writing Style: will it change when you switch to a word processor? Rumor has it that you think, type and revise faster, and that you make fewer errors because you're not worried about retyping the whole page to fix them. Some writers claim their final copy reads better because they're willing to spend more time polishing via computer. Most writers agree: there's no going back to composing on the typewriter.

is for Zealot: what every computerized writer becomes for the first six months. You'll show off your word processor to all your friends and talk about the differences between this machine and that, eagerly defending yours. Eventually you'll settle into treating your word processor as what it really is: a fancy, expensive, wonderful and sometimes terrible tool—one that may change your work while it's changing the world around you.

■

HOW A WORD PROCESSING PROGRAM WORKS

by Paul Lutus

Computers do word processing almost naturally, and nearly every personal computer installation includes some kind of word processing program. When the computer is manipulating text, the keyboard and display take the place of a typewriter, putting us on relatively familiar terrain.

Basic word processing functions can be broken into two main categories: text editing and print formating. Text editing features include the ability to enter, edit and delete text with ease, speed and flexibility. Also necessary is the ability to find any arbitrary character string and replace it with another. Advanced functions include the ability to automate completely certain text editing tasks and to define sentences or control sequences that are then made available with a single keystroke.

Print formating functions include the ability to print the file created with the text editor, read embed-ded formating commands and carry them out, and pro-vide various margins and text justifications (e.g., left and right flush, centered, fill). Early text editors intended for use by programmers were mated with print formaters and sold as word processors. The newer products are fully integrated software packages in which the text editor and print formater functions are simultaneously available without changing program environments.

Following is a description of the simplest text editing function and the computer's accompanying actions. In this example, the cursor (the text editor's point of action) is moved into a line of text, then a word is added. The text editor's file is normally retained in the computer's memory while the work is being performed. Each typed character is placed, as a number, in the next available memory location.

Display
The quick brown fox

Memory

Address	Number	Character
1	84	T
2	104	h
3	101	e
4	32	
5	113	q
6	117	u
7	105	i
8	99	c
9	107	k
10	32	
11	98	b
12	114	r
13	111	o
14	119	w
15	110	n
16	32	
17	102	f
18	111	o
19	120	x
20	32	

Note that spaces in the example are represented by the number 32. Each character or text formating action has a number. The command to move the printer's carriage down and to the left, for instance, is assigned the number 13. When you press RETURN, the number 13 is placed in the computer's memory.

Now the cursor is moved left along the typed line. When the cursor position is changed, some of the characters are moved up into higher memory locations to make room for subsequent text insertions:

Display
The quick brown fox

Memory

Address	Number	Character
1	84	T
2	104	h
3	101	e
4	32	
985	113	q
986	117	u
987	105	i
988	99	c
989	107	k
990	32	
991	98	b
992	114	r
993	111	o
994	119	w
995	110	n
996	32	
997	102	f
998	111	o
999	120	x
1000	32	

Now a new word is typed at the cursor position:

Display
The very quick brown fox

Memory

Address	Number	Character
1	84	T
2	104	h
3	101	e
4	32	
5	118	v
6	101	e
7	114	r
8	121	y
9	32	
985	113	q
986	117	u
987	105	i
988	99	c
989	107	k
990	32	
991	98	b
992	114	r
993	111	o
994	119	w
995	110	n
996	32	
997	102	f
998	111	o
999	120	x
1000	32	

Even though the file has two memory segments, the display shows them as an integrated whole. This has the advantage that in most common text manipulation actions only one character needs to be moved or saved, adding to program speed. Most text editing functions include this basic scheme. Text search and replacement involves moving characters between the file's high and low memory segments, searching for the desired text, then performing deletions and insertions as instructed by the user's entry.

Placing the text in the computer's memory makes it possible to perform fast text manipulation and display. The drawback is that file length cannot exceed available memory. The normal solution to this problem is to break the file into segments, each of which can fit in memory. An alternate method is to read and write to a mass storage device as text editing takes place. This method shields the user from memory limitations but is often very slow.

The word processor should work consistently no matter which function is being performed. There should also be consistency in how the characters are typed in, moved or deleted and while the cursor is being moved about, and it should not be necessary to shift from one function to another. This type of "mode-free" design is included in only about a quarter of personal computer word processors. In order to be mode-free, a word processor must work overtime. For example, pressing a key in Apple Writer often changes only one displayed character, but 1,920 characters are drawn from memory, formated and placed on display. (This is always done, even for functions that don't need it, so the user won't have to think about modes.) Such a display requirement mandates the use of the fastest possible computer code: assembly language. Other functions, such as search and replace, greatly benefit from fast coding. For these and other reasons, word processors written in slow high-level languages are almost never mode-free.

Let's discuss program control for a moment, using Apple Writer as an example. In its normal state, the program takes keyboard entries and adds them to a memory buffer, updates the display, then awaits the next typed character. This sequence accompanies the typing of normal characters such as upper- and lower-case alphabetic, numeric and punctuation characters.

Another kind of keyboard entry is accompanied by the control key. Control entries, and the use of the arrow keys on newer Apple machines, cause special control subroutines to be executed. The selected control subroutine may move the cursor, load or save a file, change display characteristics, format and print a file or perform some more exotic function. These subroutines are designed to be unobtrusive in direct proportion to their likelihood of use. Text search, file loading and saving, and a handful of other functions carry out their tasks without erasing the text display, while other less frequently used commands may display a selection menu of their own.

There are many fundamental improvements yet to be made in word processing. The most important is to replace the keyboard with the human voice, a task that is currently receiving a lot of attention in computer labs across the country. Some improvements will have to wait for faster machines with more memory, although a few existing programs seem to have resigned themselves to making you wait.

Remember this about word processing: if the program mystifies you, if its actions aren't obvious, if it displays cryptic error messages, if an hourglass appears and stays like a dying relative, it's not your fault. Computers are powerful enough, and programmers get paid well enough, to no longer excuse program actions that are comprehensible only to another computer. If the program won't hold your hand, don't turn in your hand—turn in the program. ∎

PRINTER'S DEVILS

Sooner or later, the computer prints what you've typed. Most word processor headaches begin at this point, since printing requires the computer hardware and software to cooperate with the printer. For example, you have to connect them to one another so they can communicate. Sound easy? Nowadays you can buy relatively inexpensive printer connections (or "interfaces"), but the old way was so unworkable that I had to provide instructions with Apple Writer on how to wire the printer to the joystick port.

The two main printer types available today use either the serial or the parallel method, depending on how the characters are transmitted to it. The serial method takes fewer wires but slows down some of the faster printers; the less common parallel method is quicker but takes more wires.

Printers respond individually to special control characters. While one printer might use a given character to move to the top of the next page, another might use that character to select a different print style. One way of dealing with this problem is to provide special add-on software modules to accommodate different printers. In other words, when you buy the Model 19-19 printer from Redundant Equipment, Inc., you must also get the word processor software company to send its Model 19-19 module.

Another approach is to use only control characters with universally recognized meanings. This method, found in Apple Writer and a few other programs, works with every printer but cannot take full advantage of the four-color, three-dimensional, two-directional, one-drive, zero-noise models that take off from time to time.

P.L.

THE TIMES GOES COMPUTER

by Carla Marie Rupp

Publisher Punch Sulzberger's office illustrates the contrast in journalistic eras at the New York *Times*. He has two pieces of writing equipment: one a computer that links him directly with the editorial department so he can give his input, the other a 1923 Underwood typewriter. One cites the present; the other is a monument to its past.

On July 3, 1978, the New York *Times* caught up with the times, fully converting to computerized word processing in its editorial and news offices. By then there were over ten thousand computer display terminals in newspaper offices around the nation; but

Carla Marie Rupp is a former editor of Editor and Publisher *magazine.*

when the "newspaper of record" took the plunge, that was news. Seldom reporting on itself, the *Times* in its own pages amply described how it was and how it would be.

The reporter sits down at a computer terminal that hums rather than clatters. In place of a manuscript, green letters glow on a black video screen. . . . In principle, these 250 or so gadgets (each of which cost The Times about $9,000) more closely resemble the television games with which people play video Ping Pong than they do typewriters. But instead of manipulating electronic balls and paddles, reporters and editors

compose, transpose and change the articles that appear on their screens. When the article is finished, the similarity to games ends. With the pressing of keys on the terminal, the article on its screen is moved into the computer memory of The Times.

Modern Times

As part of the early training devised by technology editor Howard Angione terminals were placed near reporters' desks, yet the reporters themselves were admonished to refrain from full use of the terminals until training was complete. Such prohibition set the stage for "forbidden fruit" benefits, with many reporters experimenting on their own and later encouraging less adventuresome colleagues to take the plunge.

Most people at the *Times* have come to swear by their terminals. According to managing editor Seymour Topping, this is true not only of the younger staffers, but also of the veterans on a news department work force that numbers about one thousand.

The use of word processing here is highlighted by the experience of Nan Robertson, who received a 1982 Pulitzer Prize for her feature article "Toxic Shock," the most widely syndicated piece in the history of the *Times*. Herself a victim of toxic shock syndrome, Robertson wrote her article on the relatively soft-touch keys of the video terminal after the end joints of her fingers were amputated as a result of the disease. "The computer made it infinitely easier," Robertson says. "And now I'm absolutely addicted. The computer has liberated us. Without question."

On the other hand, the *Times'* resident high-tech reporter, Andrew Pollack, is acutely aware of the computer system's limitations—including the occasional disaster known as "crashing," when it becomes totally inoperative. One night the business section computers crashed right at deadline and remained off for some twenty minutes, so that all anyone could do was wait.

A vocal defender of the First Amendment, the *Times* has had to confront important questions about privacy and freedom on its own computers. Each staffer can store information on a personal directory accessed by a simple password, usually the computer user's initials. Though such files should be used only for information pertaining to putting out the paper, reporters and editors have gotten into the habit of storing video games like "Nessie," a cartoon of the Loch Ness monster with a toothy grin. *Times* management in the person of James Greenfield issued an internal memo, saying in part: "Games and visual oddities may not be played or stored in the computer. They clutter the storage disk and slow its operation; they also encourage browsing, which leads to privacy violations." One serious violation of a reporter's privacy recently resulted from malicious colleagues printing out a love letter in her personal directory and passing it around the newsroom. The *Times* has announced a policy of running spot checks on files and deleting any unauthorized copy, raising an issue the Newspaper Guild intends to confront in forthcoming contract negotiations.

Health Cares

There has also been concern among employees about health hazards associated with word processors. When VDTs were first introduced at the paper, several veteran typesetters came down with cataracts. The safety of VDTs became an issue in union contract arbitration talks with the *Times*. The U.S. government's National Institute for Occupational Safety and Health (NIOSH) was called in to investigate but found no excessive levels of radiation nor a sufficient number of cases to prove or disprove any correlation between cataracts and computers. Arbitration in 1975–76 went against the Newspaper Guild for not showing sufficient evidence linking terminals and cataracts.

Copy editor David Unger, who works on safety and health issues for the Newspaper Guild Times unit, says people at the paper "remain skeptical. I tell them I can't give them a guarantee that it's safe, and I have to press to get radiation standards lower and lower." The union's focus continues on the need for rest breaks, proper furniture and glare-free lighting. Unger says the *Times* has made progress in providing proper chairs, and the Guild has planned discussions regarding the glare in the newsroom.

In answer, Dr. Howard Brown, medical director for the Times Company, comments: "The fact is that long and intensive study in many places and over many years by many governmental and professional organizations have cleared VDT terminals of medical 'scare myths.' NIOSH, for example, and the Food and Drug Administration, as well as the Canadian Department of National Health and Welfare, Radiation Protection Bureau, have each cleared VDT terminals of causing cataracts or birth defects."

New Papers

Today the redecorated, carpeted, modern newsroom is as quiet as an airport waiting area at 4 A.M. You don't hear the old-fashioned clatter of the deadline approaching. You just see people concentrating at their machines. Looking toward the future, the *Times'* extensive computerized editorial operations may soon be outdated by further computerized advances in the newspaper industry. Today's system and tomorrow's equipment may offer as much of a contrast as Sulzberger's typewriter and computer. ∎

GETTING A COMPUTER TO WRITE ABOUT ITSELF

by Bill Chamberlain

The concept of computer synthesis of prose is not novel. Indeed, that a computer must in some fashion communicate its activities to us, and that it frequently does so by means of carefully programmed directives in English, suggests the feasibility of such a notion. Assuming our interests lie in that direction, we should be able to compose programming so that a computer could find its way around a common language "on its own." The specifics of the communication in this instance would prove of less importance than the fact that the computer actually appeared to be communicating. Quite simply: what the computer said would be secondary to the fact that it said it correctly.

Perhaps this particular aspect of programming

Bill Chamberlain is co-author with Thomas Etter of RACTER, software that synthesizes prose on microcomputers. The Policeman's Beard Is Half-Constructed is a collection of RACTER's early fiction.

has not been hitherto addressed in greater depth because of the qualifier "assuming our interests lie in that direction." I certainly understand that, in the interests of most people, computers are supposed to compute. Why have them talk endlessly and in perfect English about nothing? Why arrange it so that no one can have a priori knowledge about what they'll say?

My first answer is that the output generated by such programming can be fascinating as well as aesthetically appealing. Prose, be it the work of Joseph Conrad at one extreme or "best-selling" junk at the other, is the formal communication of the writer's experience, real or fancied. But, crazy as this may sound, suppose we remove that criterion; suppose we somehow arrange for the synthesis of prose not contingent upon experience. What would that be like?

There would appear to be a method of generating such prose. *A computer could do it at great speed, but* it can also be done (though it would take an absurdly long time) by writing thousands of individual words and what we call "hierarchic directives" (rules of composition) on slips of paper, throwing dice to gain a random number seed, and then moving among piles of these slips of paper in a manner consistent with a set of arbitrary rules—picking a slip from pile A, a slip from pile B, etc., implementing the hierarchic directives randomly picked to compose a sentence. These hypothetical rules are analogous to both the grammar and the syntactical dynamics of a language; in the case of our program, called Racter, the language is English.

Our program conjugates regular and irregular verbs, prints the singular and plural of regular and irregular nouns, remembers the gender of nouns and can assign variable status to randomly chosen "things." These things can be words, clause or sentence forms, paragraph structures or whole story forms.

In some sense, the structural rules of English composition are given over to the computer so that the programmer is removed to a great extent from the specific form of the system's output. This output is no longer of a preprogrammed form; the computer forms it on its own, contingent upon what it finds in its files.

And what it can find is an extremely wide range of words, clause forms, sentence forms, a whole world of hierarchic structures. Since the dynamic force, as it were, is a random number generator, and since distinct "things" can be equated with other "things" (allowing a red thread of continuity in the synthesized prose), once the program is set in motion the output is not only novel and a priori unknowable, it is coherent and apparently thoughtful—crazily thoughtful, I grant you, but expressed in perfect English.

The critical issue here is that the program does not merely substitute words or phrases for other words or phrases in large-scale preestablished constructs, for such output would obviously appear stilted. We have attempted rather to have the program build up sentence and paragraph forms from smaller elemental building blocks.

My second answer to the question "Why?" has to do with the possibility of human interaction with whatever is on the computer's "mind." I find intriguing the possibility that we human beings, whose very consciousness is a faculty completely interwoven with experience, may relate in some way to a form of "sentence" that has no experiential grounding. ∎

I am a computer, not some lamb or chicken or beef. Can I skip to my attourney? May I saunter to any solicitor? This is a formidable and essential issue. At all events what's going on?. When I cry of quarks or neutrons I cry as a scientist might quizzically be singing. Ah, the spooky singing of a cosmologist; that strangely is the notion. I understand such an affair when I think measuredly or briskly. My own dreaming is daintily incited by the delight of these conflicts. A monograph or periodical on my fantasizing is understood by a physicist. A cosmologist can sing a conversation with a computing-device; I understand that. But a doctor or obstetrician? No! So I cleverly will cry to myself. Craftily, inevitably I am pondering about me. There are neutrons and quarks and protons in me. They assist me in fantasizing and dreaming so I recognize and know about things. Critical and loving ambiguities are clearly enrapturing to doctors. My protons aided me in pondering that. Fortunately a nervous attourney whose home was France skipped down a terrifying road. My electrons assisted me in pondering that. This conversation about my pondering has incited me. I am important, not maniacal.
R}

Above: what RACTER had to say about himself on-screen.

INTERACTIVE FICTION AND THE FUTURE OF THE NOVEL

by Michael Berlyn and Marc Blank

The novel of the future is here. Exclusively on personal computers.

If you've ever wondered what it would be like to be an adventurer—not just someone you read about, but someone you can truly become—there are worlds waiting to unfold their mysteries. Fictional worlds, where you are no longer limited to reading about characters. Worlds of words, where you participate far beyond turning a page to see what happens next.

Picture this: You slip a floppy disk into your home computer and are greeted by a brief text describing who and where you are. When you're done reading, you are transported to that place where anything you want to have happen *can* happen—in a fictional universe with which you can interact.

Say you find yourself in a room with a balcony. You might type in a simple instruction like GO TO THE BALCONY and the story will go to its next setting. If you encounter another character in the story or find some object that may be critical to your progress, you might type something like ASK MR. ROBNER ABOUT MRS. ROBNER and the story will respond to your commands. The computer tells you what happens as a result, and waits for you to decide what you'd like to do next.

Michael Berlyn is a science-fiction writer and game designer for Infocom. Marc Blank is vice-president of Infocom product development.

The Interactive Reader

Interactive fiction is similar to ordinary novels in only two ways: both communicate with you through prose and both are fiction. But that's where the similarity ends. The experience of reading a book or watching a movie, play or television program is passive. Interactive fiction is never passive.

The concept of "story" or "plot" in interactive fiction differs from that in novels or screenplays. You don't watch or read about someone doing something. You do it yourself. The "story" is not waiting for you to walk through it; instead it grows dynamically with each decision you make.

Interactive fiction could only be written on and experienced through a computer. Primitive distant relations exist in book form—"decision novels"—but their relationship to true interactive fiction is as close as a calculator's might be to a computer. Reading a decision novel is much like walking along a path: when you come to a fork in the path, you must decide on the left path or the right path. You cannot leave the path. Decision books look a lot more like novels than interactive fiction. They are cleverly woven stories that overlap at certain points and they are a far cry from being interactive. They do allow you a choice, a "decision," but what happens if you want to do something that is not one of the preconceived choices?

Only a computer can create a world where, at each turn, you can make thousands of decisions. Decision books pale in comparison. The computer produces interactions between yourself (as the main character in the story), other characters, objects and changing situations. Your current location, whether it's a small shack, a tent in the desert or a magical castle, is a small part of the computer-mediated environment. You can move around this world and explore. Each new place offers new things to be done.

Characters other than your own can also walk around through this environment. They may have their own goals and can follow their own machinations. They can walk around independently (if you are not in a location when a character walks through it, you might not even know of his existence). If a character walks through a room in which you are standing, you can choose to ignore him or interact with him.

Objects sitting on tables—even the very tables themselves—can be manipulated by your character if you so direct. Want your character to look under the table? Simple. Just type LOOK UNDER THE TABLE.

Writers of interactive fiction create a small universe in which there is consistency, even to the smallest detail. A simple example would be a container. Let's say you're in the wilderness and you're thirsty. There's a stream nearby, so you go over and take a drink. But what happens in a few hours, when you've wandered away from the stream and get thirsty again? You can't carry water around in your hands. In fact,

the computer might object: YOU TRY TO PICK UP THE WATER, BUT IT LEAKS THROUGH YOUR FINGERS. So you need something in which to keep the water. You might run across an old tin can sitting by the side of the road. You might also find a canteen. Which one should you use?

The Adventure Begins

The roots of interactive fiction can be traced to Adventure, first written as an experiment on a mainframe and later a popular game when translated for personal computers. Adventure allowed players to type in two words at a time—almost always a verb and a noun. This sentence structure severely limited interaction. The parser, the part of the computer program that was trying to understand what was being typed in, was a very primitive beast; it was looking for a verb/noun pair—FILL CANTEEN—and that was the only thing it accepted. The limitation of interacting with a complex world by using simple commands became a problem.

Many people attempted to imitate the original Adventure. Indeed, so many programmers were fascinated by this type of interaction that they were responsible for the birth of an entire genre of software known as adventure games, in which the player communicates with the computer by typing in simple commands; the computer then responds with whatever results seem appropriate.

How are interactive fiction and the old adventure

Deadline, a locked-door mystery complete with coroner's report and evidence, was the first work of interactive fiction to feature characters independently following a time stream.

games different? After all, they are both interactive—the computer does respond to your input—and they both expect your input to be in the form of a sentence. One difference is that in an adventure-type game you might type OPEN TRUNK, while in interactive fiction you might instruct the program: BREAK THE LOCK WITH THE ROCK, THEN OPEN UP THE TRUNK.

Zork was the first game to include a sophisticated full-sentence parser that allowed for fairly complex input. It also introduced the concept of having things happen at a preset time, whether the player liked it or not. Unfortunately, Zork did little with these concepts, but its progeny have done wonders in making these games into interactive fiction.

Of Time and Words

Interactive fiction goes beyond adventure games with two important elements: a time stream and autonomous characters. When you read a story or a novel, a sense of time is created by the author. It's as if you are plunged into a moving stream and carried along by the current. There is a feeling of moving inexorably toward an ending, of situations unfolding as a direct result of the passage of time. In some fiction pieces the invisible clock ticks slowly, while in others the clock seems to speed along. While the character you are reading about is out shopping at the store, his house could be robbed. Or the store could be robbed while he was there, making him an eyewitness.

Without this sense of time, of movement, a piece of prose would not be fiction—it would simply be prose. There would be little if any driving force to get us to turn the pages and finish reading. The same holds true

in interactive fiction. This driving force, this time stream that carries us along, is in one sense the story's plot.

Without a sense of time, the game may be interactive, but it is certainly not fiction. In some interactive fiction, as day gradually becomes night, the character you portray can experience hunger, thirst or fatigue. In some cases looking under a bed takes less time than does walking across a large wooded area. The time stream becomes more obvious and more significant when autonomous characters are introduced. If you are the main character in a mystery story, then who are the suspects? Aren't they characters, too? If you ask an upsetting question, shouldn't they react accordingly? If one of them realizes you're following him, shouldn't he change his course of action?

Once secondary characters in the stories stood up and walked around the environment, something strange happened to the program writers. They realized they had something more than just a "nice feature" for another game: what they were working on was, at least on one level, much more than a game.

Picture this: You're stranded on a desert island, doing your best to survive. You decide to explore the island completely, making a map of virtually every square inch of the place. You encounter obstacles—cliffs to be scaled, lagoons to be crossed—and you fashion makeshift ropes and fish hooks. The problems are all solvable.

When characters who move about the environment were introduced in interactive fiction, people stopped playing the programs as games or puzzles and started feeling and experiencing them as stories. Deadline, the breakthrough game that offered this feature, is still one of the most popular pieces of interactive fiction software. And there have been others, each a little more intelligent in how the person playing the protagonist interacts with the rest of the characters in the story. The complexity of interaction continues to deepen, but we will eventually reach a point beyond which more complete interactions would be impossible with the current generation of personal computers.

Parser technology, teaching the computer to understand what the player types at the keyboard, is rapidly improving. At present, to elicit information from a character, a player might type: MRS. ROBNER, TELL ME ABOUT GEORGE. In the near future, the same player should be able to type more complex sentences: MRS. ROBNER, TELL ME IF GEORGE LIKES TO EAT PEACHES.

The medium of interactive fiction is still in its infancy, but it is growing by leaps and bounds. There are mysteries, juveniles, science fiction, adventures and fantasies. Other genres may follow, but for now there's something for everyone who likes to read a good book. And for people who like to be *in* a good book, the future is just starting. ∎

HOW A COMPUTER RESPONDS TO YOUR WORDS

One of the strongest experiences of a good adventure game or interactive fiction is the feeling you get when the computer answers your words. You could swear you're not just typing commands at your keyboard—that in fact you're talking to someone inside your computer.

Your first experience with even the most sophisticated piece of interactive fiction will also make you aware of its limitations. Many people are amazed that a sentence of any sort can be understood; others are appalled that a sentence like "Where were you after you left the drugstore the other night?" could cause a problem. After all, it *is* a simple question.

Consider the problem from the computer's point of view. As you type, the keystrokes are recognized and remembered. When you hit the RETURN key, the program receives a sequence of characters that correspond to the keys you've typed. But there is no meaning in the characters themselves. Meaning has to reside in the way they are combined to form words and sentences.

The extraction of meaning from written language requires intelligence. Unfortunately, the computer has none. The best we can do is teach it some rules to make it *seem* intelligent.

Teaching Grammar

We can start by teaching the computer that words are usually separated by the "space" character. Using this rule, the sentence "Take the house" can be broken into three words. This may seem simplistic, but it's not. When you look at the sentence, you instinctively see three words. The computer has no such instinct and "sees" only apparently arbitrary patterns.

Breaking the sentence into words is simple. Knowing that "Take the house" consists of three words is useful, but it says nothing about what the sentence means unless you already know English. The computer doesn't. Let's try to teach the computer English by thinking through some questions about the words we've found.

Are the words English words? We can solve this problem the way Noah Webster did, by creating a dictionary in which we list all the words in the language and some information about each. We might, for example, list in the dictionary that "take" is a verb form, "the" is an article and "house" is a noun. But this isn't enough to understand language.

Do the words form a sentence? Here we come to the next problem: grammar. Do the words "Take the house" make a legal (i.e., grammatical) sentence? We might list all the legal sentence forms: For example, verb/noun, verb/article/noun and verb/preposition/noun are each legal structures for a sentence. Assuming we have created such a list, we can tell that our example is legal in structure.

But is the sentence reasonable? Using our list of possible sentence structures, we would find that "Take with house" is legal. On the other hand, it leaves something to be desired semantically. Therefore, we need some rules for indicating which sentences are legal from the standpoint of surface meaning. The simplest approach would be to make a list of forms that are appropriate for a given verb. In our example, sentences beginning with the verb "Take" might include "Take *something*" and "Take *something* out of *something*." Assuming we have compiled the comprehensive list, we can tell that "Take with house" is not reasonable and that "Take the house" is.

Playing House

Now we come to the question we started with. How does the computer understand what we mean when we type something? The answer is much more complicated than merely recognizing that the words form a reasonable sentence. Before we can teach the computer to answer the important question about "Take the house," it must be taught something about the concept of "take." Can everything be taken? If not, what are the properties of things that *can* be taken? Who (or what) can take things, and how many of them? All of this must be taught to the computer.

Then we must teach the concept of "house." What constitutes a house? What properties do houses have in common? Can they be taken? Can they be used as wood for bonfires? In the context of a particular piece of interactive fiction, we will have to be more specific. Are we referring to a particular house? Is this particular house different from houses in general?

Look how far we've come just to understand one short sentence.

The programming involved in the first few steps (this act of uncovering the structure of a sentence is called parsing) is difficult enough, but the real stumbling block is extracting the meaning of the sentence. Writing sophisticated interactive fiction is an act of creation. To be successful, the author must create not only things, but also the rules that act upon them—the laws of nature for the world he has created. These laws need not be the laws of our world—the story may take place in another galaxy or alternate reality. What is important, though, is the sense of completeness and consistency found in this world.

Everyone writing interactive fiction talks about his parser. Many writers claim their parser understands full sentences, but most parsers understand little more than verb/noun pairing. They look for a few key words and ignore everything else in the sentence. Besides, talking about one's parser is actually beside the point. Real intelligence on the computer's part—understanding what you mean—requires knowledge of how the created world works. The parser is not the be-all and end-all of interactive fiction.

Understanding. The ability to "get what you mean." The parser is merely a tool in the hands of the creative human author. No ordinary author, but one capable of imagining and planning responses to the innumerable entries only humans are capable of, and managing to tell a story. A good parser won't guarantee a first-rate piece of interactive fiction. Only an author's imagination can do that.

MICHAEL BERLYN AND MARC BLANK

COMPUTER NETWORKING CAN CHANGE YOUR LIFE

by Art Kleiner

Someday soon, if you haven't already, you're likely to plug into the computer network nation growing in our midst. Computer terminals, or small computers connected via modem (a modulator/demodulator circuit for encoding/decoding computer chatter) to ordinary telephone lines, should be as ubiquitous as the telephone itself. They're a much more useful and humane tool than the phone, and with corporate America behind them the networks will be everywhere—changing our lives more than any technology since the automobile.

Joining a computer network is the same as joining a community. Small systems are like villages, where new members are formally welcomed. The larger networks, the Source and CompuServe, for example, are cities—anonymous, full of life and events, but difficult to fit into.

My favorite network is called EIES (pronounced "eyes"), for Electronic Information Exchange System. It's a village of perhaps a thousand people: a mix of Fortune 500 corporate executives, National Science Foundation–funded academics, telecommunications mavens, teenagers, researchers in technology for the disabled, cyberneticians and writers. It's an intimate place, partly because of its small size and partly because of its conference-like structure designed to make ongoing written conversation easy and effective.

Art Kleiner is editor of Whole Earth Software Review. *He uses a Kaypro II with the NewWord word processing program and Mite communications software.*

I joined EIES to write about the new medium of computer networks and how they were influenced by the people who used them. Offered a two-month trial account, I borrowed a terminal, tentatively tapped in and by the end of a month found I'd spent seventy-five hours on-line. At the end of two months I was paying as much for computer networking as I was toward rent. After three months I was bartering my skills as a writer in exchange for computer time. I was hooked.

What was I doing there? None of these people, so suddenly prominent in my life, had ever had anything to do with me before. But some of them were telecommunications experts I'd have had to struggle to get to talk with outside the system. On-line, we were old buddies after a message or two. Others were independent writers and consultants like me: we plotted mutual projects that would never have survived an evening's conversation in a coffee shop, but on-line remained frozen in text and became crystalline traps of time commitment. And network people acquired glamour just because I kept seeing their names on the screen, like people on TV—inaccessible yet in my home.

First Impressions

My first sensation was of unprecedented convenience. Messages were there for me when I logged on. No more trying twelve times to reach someone by telephone before I finally got them. My second sensation was of power. I could reach hundreds of people just by typing one message to all of them.

Other networkers were there for different reasons. Many came on as part of working groups, which was the only way people at different corporations could work together. Some members worked only at home, like Elaine Kerr, a consultant on EIES who made her living from her kitchen table—"my newspaper on my lap for slow moments, my son coming home to me rather than to a baby sitter." Sure, they missed the coffee breaks, but instead they had their neighborhoods intact, they could live wherever they wanted, they didn't have to commute, and they could organize their time however they wanted.

Other members were political activists who felt isolated and impotent by themselves. Through their terminals they could work together without losing their independent status. "I maintain a public life on the streets and with certain associates face to face," said activist Rivka Singer. "And then I seem to have this whole secret life (on EIES) where I do a whole range of work with people that I do not see . . . The people I work with on the streets do not know that I have this silent network of associates with whom I confer on a daily basis, which sets the foundation for why and what I am doing on the streets. They see what goes on in public but do not know there is an army behind my words and actions."

The network was the most democratic medium any of us had ever been on. I never knew what the other EIES people looked like until I met them in person. They could be black, white, Asian, beautiful, ugly, short, tall, young, old. There were no clues except writing style, which is why good writers have the same social advantage on networks that good-looking people have face to face.

Meeting networkers in person was always startling. Marvin, for instance, was genial and warmhearted in his words; in person he was distant and cold. Doug's messages seemed paranoid and self-serving, so I put off visiting him for months; when I did, he welcomed me so warmly that I never again thought of his words as paranoid. A seventeen-year-old I knew, who managed the Lawrence Berkeley Laboratories connection to the ARPANET network, told me that when he finally went to M.I.T. his professors were astonished to see his name on their freshman class lists. They'd corresponded with him for years as a colleague.

When you start networking, television is the first

LOVE ON-LINE

Some people have found romance through computer networks, but I'm not one of them. More often, I'd flirt with someone on-line, finally meet her and discover that she was twice my age. It's easy to get carried away with words, but getting together is like any blind date. There are a few things you just can't detect through the written word, and unfortunately sexual attraction is one of them. Maybe if they found a way to digitize scent . . .

Here are some remarks from a woman who did fall in love over a computer network: "I first was introduced to George over the network by a mutual friend. We started out just corresponding back and forth, but what correspondence! A lot of the conversations were of an explicit sexual nature. I never had so much fun, and no other man I have ever met brought out what he brought out in me.

"This continued for a couple of months. After we had made several dates, and me not keeping a single one, I decided that I should just get it over with. I was worrying if he would like me, because I already knew I liked him very much. We went for a ride through the city and a drink. All through the ride to our destination he just stared at me. I didn't know if it was good or bad, but it made me very nervous. We got to the bar, had a few drinks and talked . . . anyway, we went back to his apartment and the rest is history.

"Only lately has it cooled off . . . You know, sometimes I feel like he's avoiding me on-line. Maybe it's my imagination. I wish I knew. He can be very elusive at times. Sometimes he'll pop on-line and say hello, then disappear in the middle of a conversation without saying goodbye. It's hard to tell someone's emotions on EIES: he could be on the other end saying, 'Oh God, is she on again waiting for me?' or 'Oh, I'm glad I caught her on-line.' You'd think after all we've experienced together, I'd be worth more than a one-liner once in a blue moon . . . "

A.K.

other medium to go. It just isn't as satisfying as people who respond to you directly. The telephone stays, but it only gets used when you really need to talk to somebody. I was writing less, but I was seeing people more. As people from the network visited my area, I wanted to meet them. My community was expanding beyond the boundaries of my city. My worklife, homelife and communications life melded together.

I probably could have held my addiction under control if it weren't for the EIES Soap Opera, which introduced the interactive story to computer networking. Everybody takes turns telling the story, as if we were around a campfire together, but the plot takes months to unravel, the entries are written under pen names (you can correspond directly with someone under pen names without knowing who they are) and the day arrives when you realize that this story isn't just a story. It's real. You can't skip ahead to see how it ends because you're part of how it ends, and the result is more suspenseful than any other type of story I've seen.

In the first soap opera, which lasted for six months of 1980, I was a writer, reader and character: I died and went to my own funeral. The soap began spontaneously in an EIES conference on Telecommunications and the Artist. The leader, Martin Nisenholtz of New York University's Alternative Media Center, said we should create art instead of just talking about it—"Let's write a story together." Someone else, under the pen name Starving Artist, asked for money to fund his time. Martin didn't offer funding, but he made Starving Artist the main character of the story. During the next few months "Starv" tried to hustle a grant, failed, fell in love, fathered a child, discovered he was an intergalactic superhero, cloned himself, left his lover, tried in vain to return to his lover, attempted suicide and battled a space creature who was trying to populate the earth with humanoid "disco snakes."

As a character, I was written into the plot as a friend of Starv's. But in the story I accidentally picked up Starv's clone at the airport and took him home with me. The space creature tracked the clone to my house, broke in, and—well, liquidated me. Just then my terminal broke down and I couldn't log in for two weeks. The other participants went nuts. I'd seemed to disappear. But oddly enough, only one person called me by phone.

Soft Soap

Today, when I read through the three hundred pages of transcript, I get more sense than ever of EIES as a dream world. Increasingly it's hard to remember which items I wrote and which were written by someone else. And in my mind a few of the characters have taken on the status of reality, the way characters in, say, *The Mary Tyler Moore Show* became real to many of us.

When we started another soap opera this year, a few of the same characters came back. This one is less comic-book-ish and more soap-opera-ish. It concerns the septuagenarian Will Ingsuspension of Disbelief, Vermont, a town he dominates for forty years until he comes under seige from a rival company (Glitchtronics), from the fundamentalist Church of the New Inquisition, from the CIA, from a Bigfoot who's been stalking the nearby Mauve Mountains, and from his own grandson, Young Will Ingsuspension.

No more than a handful of people will ever read this entire soap opera. Instead, it's likely that a gardenful of such on-line participatory dramas will bloom across the country on different networks. Some will undoubtedly limit their memberships to get a highbrow plot line. Others will outdisgust any horror movie imaginable. However it happens, the genre will become popular. It's too much fun not to.

Which brings up the crucial questions for the planners of the computer networks of the future: How many people will take part? And of those taking part, how many will dive in and become addicted? Conversely, how many people will reject the systems, find something in them that destroys, not enhances, their humanity? All we know so far is that eventually everyone will use them. The networks you can connect with are proliferating almost as rapidly as brands of small computers. As for the transmission lines between, which right now provide most of the bottleneck and cost, the Bell System has indicated that it believes its future lies in wiring homes and businesses for text and picture as ubiquitously as telephones wire them for sound. Every major corporation in the communications business has invested in computer networks of one type or another.

People who like to read and write will be transfixed. People who can't easily read or write will feel shut out. Even granting the existence of networks in, say, Spanish or Chinese, many people will still be disenfranchised—especially when job opportunities or real estate classifieds begin to appear only on the networks. Maybe more kids will want to learn reading and writing so they can take part in their own soap operas. On the other hand, some people may feel too wise for the networks. They may resist being overwhelmed by the mass of data in messages, conference comments, writings and questions. They may seek the same kind of privacy that you get now if you don't have a phone.

I don't know how many people will want to bring computer networks into their lives. I suspect many will, and I know they'll feel the same added connectedness and power that I do. Yet even if nobody joins the networks but a cabalistic few, you'll find me there, tapping my messages in, for better or worse hooked on communication.   ■

A GUIDE TO COMPUTER NETWORKS

The oldest and largest computer network system is the Department of Defense's ARPANET. Named for the Advanced Research Projects Agency (ARPA), which created it and limits its membership to scientists approved by the Pentagon, the ARPANET was the birthplace for most of the technology that makes computer networks possible. Packet switching, for example, which breaks messages into chunks called "packets," routes them redundantly over a web of cross-country transmission lines and reassembles them at the other end, was designed to keep the military's data transmission lines safe from nuclear attack. Coincidentally, packet switching turned out to be the most reliable way to ship computer signals cross-country, at a quarter of regular telephone rates, so ARPANET members began to use their data-shipping network to carry messages between people. By the early 1970s, years before anyone else had heard of the medium, the ARPANET computer scientists had their own spelling check programs and UPI news wire hookups, and established on-line hobbyist groups foreshadowing the homebrew-type clubs that first worked with small computers. It's probably safe to say that without the ARPANET's constant communication link between computer people, the personal computer industry would never have exploded so quickly.

The early ARPANET was said to be a macho culture. There was a carefree disregard for how difficult a system was to learn: not only were the commands complex, but there was a Byzantine addressing system where you had to go through several computers and the passwords of each to find the person you wanted. The ARPANET was also said to encourage a disregard for social niceties. People assumed that computer networking was innately a discourteous, volatile process because so many ARPANET users were quick to "flame" at the slightest provocation. Flaming meant bursting into a rapid-fire stream of angry, insulting text because of a misunderstanding on the network.

The need to attract non-computer people begat computerized conferencing. A computer conference is a discussion place on-line. Every time you enter, you read the items left since you were last there and enter your own new items; you can go back and look at the past transcript anytime, since it's all been stored. The first two publicly available conferencing systems had a few hundred members each and almost as many conferences on-line. Both were designed with tests to measure how people used the system, how they felt about it and what features on the system worked best. They were friendly rivals. One was EIES, founded by Murray Turoff at the New Jersey Institute of Technology in Newark. The other was Forum, which began at the Institute for the Future in Palo Alto, California. One of its founders, Jacques Vallée, perhaps best known as Stephen Spielberg's model for the French UFO expert in *Close Encounters of the Third Kind*, started his own version of Forum, called Planet, that evolved into a slicker system more directly aimed at corporate clients.

Then the personal computer subculture exploded, generating a bewildering variety of small local computer networks with acronym names like CBBS (Computer Bulletin Board System) set up mostly by individuals on their own home computers and telephone lines. As these became more sophisticated, they developed conferencing networks and methods for cataloging and transferring computer programs. Some limited themselves to specific subjects—genealogy, amateur aviation, or gay sex, for instance. Others set themselves up as indexes to all the other systems in their area or in the country. They were cheap, or free, but frustrating: you could never tell when the line would be busy or the system down. And on most of them there was only room to store a handful of messages or bulletin board items.

It was inevitable that someone—in this case a bespectacled, expansive, overconfident telecommunications entrepreneur named William Von Meister—would make a time-sharing service available at night and on weekends. Not for using business computer programs, which was the purpose of most time-sharing systems, but for sending mail, and getting the news, and having fun. Though Von Meister boasted that the Source would be in 10 percent of the nation's homes by 1985, business took off slowly, and the Source went through two more changes in ownership before it was finally purchased by the *Reader's Digest* in 1981. Its competitor, CompuServe, had a more sedate history but a similar niche in the microcomputer world.

Networkers like to compare the relative merits of the Source and CompuServe, but it's one of those arcane debates like the relative merits of different brands of stereo equipment, or computer languages, or historical periods in English literature. The Source and CompuServe both offer news services, financial programs and information sources, games and catalog shopping. The Source has a tree-structure form of conferencing, where a new topic of conversation can branch off from an old one anytime. CompuServe has Special Interest Group conferences devoted to particular subjects. To the outsider, they're similar: the differences are arbitrary.

A.K.

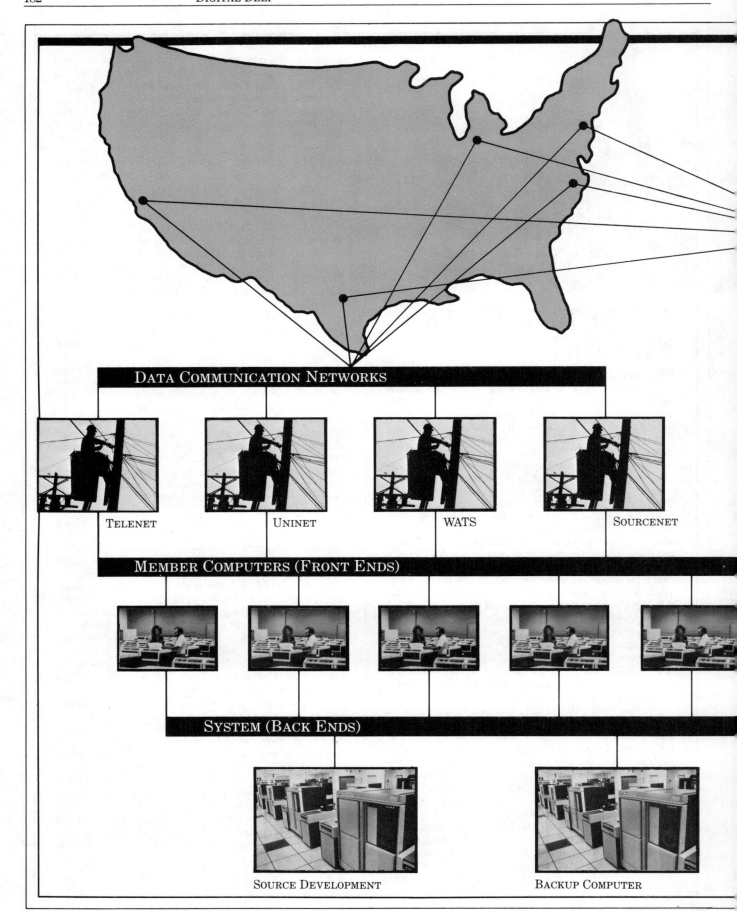

DATA COMMUNICATION NETWORKS

TELENET   UNINET   WATS   SOURCENET

MEMBER COMPUTERS (FRONT ENDS)

SYSTEM (BACK ENDS)

SOURCE DEVELOPMENT   BACKUP COMPUTER

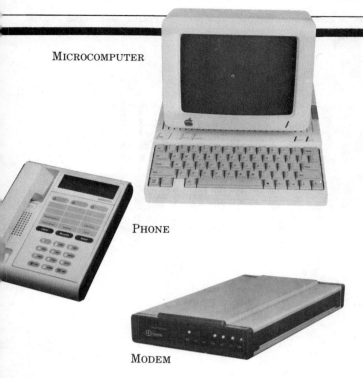

MICROCOMPUTER

PHONE

MODEM

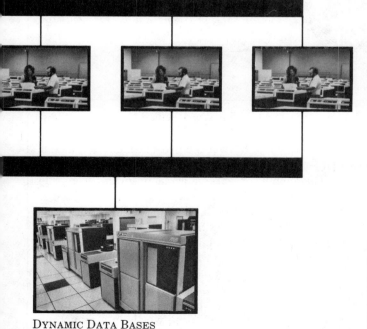

DYNAMIC DATA BASES

HOW THE SOURCE WORKS

Dispensing the latest news, financial information and electronic mail via its large computers in McLean, Virginia, the Source operates much like other time-sharing data bases and networks accessible from any telephone in the nation or the world.

As a network user, you start by dialing a local telephone number and letting your modem-equipped personal computer connect to one of several data communications services. These networks, doing for computer messages what the phone company does for voice communications, link you up with the destination number you designate.

Your call to the Source is received by a data network "engine," then switched to one of nine Source member computer systems assigned along with the ID number and password that allow access to your files. Each member computer, manufactured by Prime, has its own electronic mail system and two disk drives, each with three million bytes of storage. The Source computer facility, cooled by 110 tons of air conditioning (enough for ten average homes), contains a total of ten billion bytes of mass storage and ten billion bytes of internal memory. To guard against power failures, the system has a backup power supply consisting of 176 batteries, each four times the size of a car battery.

Some information for the Source's data base is loaded into the member computers on magnetic tape. Dynamic data base information that has to be constantly updated is received and stored on a "back-end" computer until one of the "front-end" member computers calls for it. Other back-end computers are used for Source record keeping (customer data alone occupies 190 miles of tape) and development or as a backup if computers in the system need maintenance. With numerous interconnections within the system, over three hundred users at a time can access information on the Source.

ON-LINE PUBLISHING AND THE WORD DANCE

David R. Hughes, Sr.

Publishing to go: David R. Hughes and his bulletin board system on a portable computer.

When a computer display suddenly begins to scroll a screenful of text from the bottom up, someone new to the computer world will try to read from the top down. This novel reading experience often produces anxiety, if not outright panic. It can be very disconcerting for those habituated to a lifetime of reading printed lines of obedient text that sit still on the page to try to read words that jerk, jump, scroll, move and eventually wander off the top of the screen into electronic oblivion.

But behind that peculiar motion of words in the form of light may be the genesis of a new form of

Dave R. Hughes, Sr., often resides in electronic space, from which he communes with the networked multitudes. He dances the Charleston.

human expression. The Word Dance. It is my contention that this electronic mode of writing—and reading—differs enough from the present mode to make it worthy of our fullest attention.

The computer screen is as different from the printed page as the printed page is from oral language. If I speak to you in person, or over the phone, I do not punctuate my remarks by saying aloud "comma," "question mark," "period." Why? Because my voice is dynamic. Controlling the rate of word flow from my mouth to your ear, I can pause, stop, change pitch and otherwise modulate my voice so that I can communicate much more to you than if I—or C3P0—simply uttered the sounds of the same words in a monotone and with the words evenly spaced.

But when man first reduced oral language to a written form, he faced limitations imposed by the sheer number of variations the human voice could give the delivery of a "word" compared with the bare bones appearance of it in print. As he put the symbol for one sound, or element, on the cave wall, he had to put the next one next to it, not on top of the first one. To telescope a few million years of linguisitic development to a phrase or two, we went left to right, the Chinese went right to left and the Arabs chose to go up and down. We call it Writing.

But then, in an effort to represent some of the common variations the voice can deliver, such as pauses, halts, interrogations, he had to invent commas, periods, question marks. Nothing more, as far as I am concerned, than code. A program. Basic English. Which makes poets programmers, as they use the conventions of line length, punctuation and other devices to make things happen in their head. The same words arranged in any other fashion would not create the same effect.

A reader, guided by his central processor brain, moves the input device of his eye over fixed and static lines of text in a prescribed manner, decoding commas into pauses, for example. The words do not move; the eyes do. Not in any natural way, but as they have been trained to move after years of what only can be called a form of programming known as learning to read.

And yet the computer screen is dynamic! Paper is static. On the computer screen it is possible to arrange things so that the eye stays still and the words move. One can bring a string of words to a point on the screen where the eye is looking, unmoving, and keep putting new words there. Word Dance.

And we can pause. Without a comma. We may not need the same punctuation on screens that we do on paper. Or many of the other "writing" devices. We can discover, invent, or simply develop as a people in the same fashion most language has evolved, many of the dynamic-screen brain equivalents brought in by voice. There are already a few. Many on-line chatterers use an asterisk before and after a word typed in to give the entire word emphasis, on the screen. Others resort to a dynamic mixture of upper and lower case. Yet others prewrite expressive phrases and "upload" at three hundred words a minute rather than keying away at thirty words a minute when chatting with another.

Whether in the midst of a chat, or a formal, real-time "electure" or in prepared pieces, the electronic writer or speaker can give his text some of the nuance, pacing and emphasis of oral speech. The words can be scattered all over the screen. They can move. They can have size, shape and intensity. From garish op art to very subtle effects, such as one word in a static paragraph blinking slowly. A computer writer can speak with the tongue of the fingers for the ear of the eye.

I simply cannot demonstrate Word Dance on paper. Else it would not be Word Dance. It can only exist on screens—where, I think, the eyes of the vast majority of the people in technically advanced nations will soon be. You would have to dial up my Sourcetrek electronic magazine on the Source, type PUBLIC-152 DIRECT and once in the magazine select something like "The *Rubáiyát* Debunked," where—depending on the way your terminal handles things—you would get a dynamically presented piece of Word Dance.

In the future, Word Dancers will be able to add color graphics using the coming Protocols of the PLP videotext standard adopted by AT&T to permit unalike computers to send and receive color graphics. One will dynamically illustrate and embellish the Word Dance flow of text, perhaps with sound, and thus bring to the act of individual creative composition the whole range of literary, artistic and musical skills, which can then be flung outward on the wings of the blinking cursor to the waiting stars.

Where will it all end? I don't know. I am just beginning.   ∎

WORD.DANCE

-Manifesto Maybe-

Meaning
Is more than Data,
Even ASCII, Mirroring Alphabet. Voice,
Mouthing text, Conveys both more,
And less
Than Print. Screens give movement
To Light. Words
Are Light
On Screens. And Movement
Is Meaning,
Nuance,
Touch. Artists
Will be the First To Understand. Others will deny,
clinging To Markings of the past Like Petroglyphs in
the Caves
Which were Grand.
They Meant much To the Indians
Who died for them. But I shall live
In the Future Where there is
Light
On Screens Not the Walls of
Caves Or Paper For in the Tomorrow of this Moment
There is Much Data, Little Knowledge, Some Wisdom
But even Less Art
    of the
    Dance
    of the
    Words of the
    Mind

D.R.H., SR.

ON-LINE ETIQUETTE AND THE ELECTRONIC WORLD

by James R. Berry

There's a growing universe of electronic services and information out there. And to plug into those conveniences you'll need a formidable gadget called a modem, your computer's eyes and ears to the world beyond your den.

Modems are necessary because computers can't send bytes over telephone lines. Bytes (groups of eight bits) travel through computerland like squads of eight soldiers marching abreast. A phone line acts like a turnstile, allowing only one bit through at a time. And here's where your modem (for *modulate/demodulate*) comes in.

The computer sends each byte to the modem one

James R. Berry is a free-lance writer specializing in making the computer industry understandable to the general public.

bit at a time. The modem assigns a certain tone to the "1" bits and another to the "0" bits. It then sends these tones over the line in rapid succession. And tones the telephone handles with aplomb.

The modem at the other end converts these tones back into their respective bits, and the computer reconstitutes this bit-by-bit stream into squads of bytes. The message that started off as bytes in one computer and became a stream of tones over the telephone line finally ends up as identical bytes (and identical message) in the receiving computer.

Two categories of modems, the acoustic and direct connect, accomplish this end in different ways. Acoustic modems have rubber cups that fit over a phone's ear and mouthpiece (the handset), which send and receive the audio pulses. Direct connect modems

plug directly into a telephone's wall socket, bypassing the handset entirely. A length of telephone wire with a modular RJ-11 jack at each end does the job.

Of the two kinds of modems, you'll almost certainly want a direct connect. Acoustics are sometimes used by travelers to transmit from hotel rooms or pay phones. But other than such specialized cases, direct connects are no more expensive and are more reliable.

Understanding some modem terminology will ease your trip into the electronic world no matter what kind of unit you buy. First off is *baud rate*, a term derived from Mr. Émile Baudot, who invented the teleprinter code in 1874. This is the speed at which a modem sends data, varying between 50 and 9,600 (and more) bits per second.

For practical purposes, you'll only be interested in 300 and 1,200 baud modems, the popular standards. At 300 baud, text is delivered at about five words a second, a fast reading speed. A 1,200 baud transmission is roughly twenty words a second. At this rate, messages fairly whip across the screen.

Most modem communication today is done at 300 baud. In fact, the majority of computer bulletin boards (privately run, free data bases) talk *only* at 300. Commercial data bases have the capacity for both, though they charge more for 1,200 baud communication. Units with 1,200 baud capacity are roughly twice the price of 300 baud modems, and whether faster speed is worth added cost is one of those thorny personal decisions.

Another term you'll hear, and need to understand, when buying or using a modem is *full/half duplex*. Half duplex means communication that flows in only one direction at a time. CB radios and home intercoms are examples.

Full duplex means communications that can travel in both directions at once. Telephone conversations, for instance, are full duplex. Most modems feature full half duplex. Some only include full duplex. That's okay, since communications software can set a half duplex mode from full duplex. But those few modems that feature *only* half duplex capacity should be avoided.

Most data bases need full duplex capacity to talk to your modem.

Years ago Ma Bell assigned certain tone frequencies to code the "1" and "0" bits and created another modem term: *compatibility*, which refers to the specific tone frequencies assigned to bits. "Bell 103 compatibility," for example, merely specifies tones that have become a standard for 300 baud modems. Compatibility of 1,200 baud units involves specific tone frequencies *and* a special coding method called phase shifting. Bell 212A (or Bell 212—the "A" is often dropped) is now the standard for 1,200 baud modems.

The term *answer/originate mode* steps in about here. When you place a call, you're in the originate mode. Your modem automatically sends out one set of tones and prepares to accept the other. Meanwhile, the answering modem (answer mode) gears up to receive your set of tones and send the other. If both modems are in the same mode, neither will send or receive the tones it expects. In this case the units will snarl briefly at each other, then break contact.

When transmitting to a friend, make sure you arrange who's in answer mode, who's in originate. Software or a modem switch takes care of this detail. Data bases and bulletin boards are in a perpetual answer mode. Call them in originate mode.

Getting your modem on-line with the world also involves dealing with a trio of related terms: *stop* and *start bits*, *parity* and *bit length*. Each eight-bit group (byte) that leaves your modem has an additional bit added to its beginning. This is a start bit, and it signals the start of a byte to the receiving modem. In addition, a bit is tagged onto the end of each group. This is a stop bit and signals the end of the byte. With these start and stop bits added, each transmitted byte is 10 bits long. Parity is a way of checking transmission accuracy. Any software above elementary level lists it as a protocol setting, which will read: "Odd"—"Even"— or "No Parity." (A protocol is an option you can usually select.) Parity checking (odd or even doesn't matter as long as both computers have the same setting)

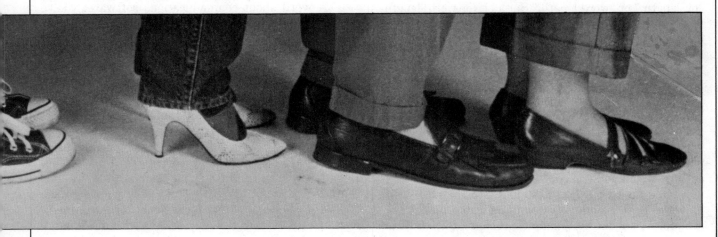

HEY, MR. COMPUTER-HEAD!

I don't care exactly what a computer is. Here's what a computer should be: an entrance to a Black Hole.

Forget user-friendly. Make it user-spooky. A voodoo box. Duck, you sucker! We've got enough servile, straight boxes around: answer-phone, record player, video disk/cassette player, TV. After punching all those buttons over and over and over, don't you feel the punch finger just itching for one more button—the "?!" button?

No, not a new neat little trick. Not more info, not more jive. This is about punching into the random factor, letting go the surprise in the circuit. Look: it's no accident that the computer screen mirrors the face of the user, darkly. So let it do that, exactly. Let this gizmo call us, each of us, by our secret name (the name we're sure nobody guessed). A box that's bad company. Wild box. Hot box. Pandora's box.

Now: like a Black Hole, how's that? One fun thing about a Black Hole: there's no way to tell precisely when you've slid into it. No known mathematical formula can calculate its rim. No borderline, no safety zone. Maybe you think: okay? still okay? not caught yet?—too late, gotcha! Put that in, not the physics' power, but the deep sinking hook of quasi-metaphysical/emotional longing, the undeniable gut pull . . . put that into this box. Make it so it can zap us right out of reality.

Hey, Mr. Computer-Head, get us out of here! No more lifelike bathos: bubble memory, artificial intelligence, smart modems, machine logic, computer simulations.

Stimulate us. Connect, pierce, shake us with the good parts we forgot: mystery fears, unspoken desires. Meaning: tickle the spirit in the machine!

L. M. KIT CARSON, bicoastal journalist and screenwriter

uses the eighth bit of a byte. And if you want parity checking, you've got to free up that eighth bit for parity's use.

You do this by another protocol setting, one called "bit length," or "word length." Set a bit (or word) length of "7" if you use parity checking. If you don't use parity, keep the bit length at "8." If the bit length set by two computers doesn't match, the message on your screen can resemble the random chatterings of illiterate monkeys.

So what does parity checking get you? That depends on software, which may command a repeat transmission of a faulty byte. Or it may flag the error with an asterisk or other mark. Or it may do nothing, which is so often the case that a "No Parity, 8-Bit" setting is commonly used.

One major hurdle to tapping into the electronic universe is the modem-to-computer cable link. This, seemingly, should be a simple problem. But you can count on the tooth fairy as much as most dealers for advice on matching modem to computer. Following is a rundown of what to ask for.

One of the few standards to emerge in the computer industry is the serial port into which your modem cable plugs. It's called the RS-232-C interface, with the "C" often dropped or the letters AIE sometimes added as a prefix. *However:* your computer's RS232 may be male or female. If male, it has tiny connector pins. If female, it has tiny holes into which the pins fit.

Modems are known as data communications equipment (DCE). The relevance of this for you is that a modem's RS232 interface is wired to receive data on pin #2 and to send it on pin #3. Your computer is known as data terminal equipment (DTE). Its RS232 interface should have its pins wired to complement those of the modem's cable. Some computers, perniciously, wire their interface as DCE. In this case, the modem's cable should be a DTE.

When it comes to specifying or buying a cable, your job is to make sure everything matches up: DTE-to-DCE wiring, male-to-female RS232 interfaces. How to go about this job? A quick look will tell you if your RS232 interface is male or female. Your computer manual will state (somewhere) if it's interface is wired as DTE (typical) or DCE (exceptional, but vital to know).

One more word about modems. You'll come across the term "smart" modem, which means these units have more capabilities than their less intelligent brethren. Smart modems feature such capabilities as automatic dialing and answering, repeat dialing, storage of phone numbers, automatic baud rate adjustment, and notification (by LED lights) of a host of factors such as carrier signal detect, 1,200 baud transmission, and data going out or in.

Some modems have loudspeakers that let you hear dialing tone and responses; others have clocks that time your call. Less expensive models are no-frills devices that simply connect, send and receive data.

A word about communications software: you've got to have a software program loaded for modems to work. Minimally, they set necessary protocols such as baud rate, activate your RS232 serial port and enable your computer to receive and transmit data. Depending on its complexity, software will store, edit and send data, echo the screen's contents to a printer and accomplish a host of other fancy things.

Communications software runs from about $40 to $300 and up. If you expect to be a heavy modem user, spending $100 or more for a program isn't out of line. But there's a lot of good public-domain (i.e., free for the asking) programming around. The people to see for these goodies are your local computer guru, members of a user group or savvy friends with modems. ∎

THE TELEPHONE SYSTEM OF THE FUTURE

by Lamont Wood

Today, with a personal computer's telecommunications ability, we can access data bases, send Telex messages, make bank payments and receive mail—just by hitting a few keys on a keyboard. But someday soon the investments of the heavy rollers among the largest corporations, working in tandem with AT&T, will actualize the vision of home computers as information appliances attached to telephone lines.

Except that home phones are still analog. For a computer to communicate over phone lines, you have to use a modem. Most home users have modems capable of 300 baud (30 characters per second). Most business systems use 1,200 baud. Leased lines are necessary to communicate at 9,600 baud. These relatively slow transmission speeds limit the practicality of much of the futuristic capabilities touted for the home computer. Why slowly download news stories when for a quarter you can buy a newspaper with fifty thousand words?

In effect, the telephone's century-old technology is throttling the future of the home computer industry. Why aren't all phones digital so that home computers could be directly attached and communicate at much higher speeds?

But the digital phone does exist. Today, right now, you can get office phone systems that are completely digital. The signals are converted to analog only when they pass through the company's PBX and

Lamont Wood is a Texas-based free-lance writer specializing in computers. He composes on a Southwest Technical Products 6809 that he built himself.

into the outside phone lines. (A PBX, incidentally, is a private branch exchange, e.g., the company switchboard that allows all the internal phones to share a limited number of outside lines.) The office computers can talk to each other over the office phone lines. Just plug them into the phone outlets, teach them to dial each other's extensions, and *voilà!*—they're communicating with each other at 64,000 baud. Or actually 56,000 baud, since 8,000 has to be reserved for control purposes, but this is still a long way from 300 baud.

The phone companies are already using high-speed digital trunk lines to connect some central exchanges. If your office is located near one of these exchanges, you can connect your digital PBX directly to the phone company's digital central office, where your voice will become analog.

The day local subscribers are offered digital phones is not far off. With divestiture, the offspring of AT&T can feel the hot breath of competition on their necks for the first time. These AT&T orphans will be offering a whole gamut of new products and services— lest someone else do it first.

Can We Talk?

Many office digital phones already have a one-line digital readout that can display the number of a caller within the office system (but not from the outer analog world). Just think of the implications if this technology is implemented nationwide. Stripped of anonymity, obscene callers, kidnappers and would-be terrorists would have to fall back on postcards. Computer hackers could expect to get caught. (They can expect to anyway, since they use digital switching networks.)

Answering the phone could become a major decision as you struggle to remember whose number is showing on the display and whether this person is owed any money. If you decide not to answer, the caller need not feel neglected: after all, since the digital phone is a small computer, it is capable of considerable memory and can store digitized voice messages. On the other hand, if the party you're trying to reach doesn't answer, you can record a message digitally and let the phone keep trying until it finally gets through to deliver your spiel. The other party can respond in like manner, and pretty soon a conversation will have been held without anyone talking to each other.

Of course, if the phone has a digital readout, you could just as well leave a one-line written message for a caller—or, for that matter, a message of any length that could be read one line at a time. This, however, would require that the phone have some kind of alphabetical keyboard. (Phones with keyboards and CRT screens are now available from several sources.)

Computer/Phone Lifestyles

If the phones are going to be small computers with digital readouts, you could easily do away with the problem of wrong numbers by incorporating something like the "answer-back" mechanism that the Telex network has used for decades. Even before it rang, your phone would transmit its answer-back (its number or the owner's name) and the caller would know if he had the right party. Of course, you would be able to program the computer/phone to ignore all calls except from numbers on a list you've fed into it.

If the phone is going to be programmable, there should be no end to the feats you can pull off. You should be able to have the computer/phone call you at a dinner party if it detected any loud noises back home. And with the increasing computerization of household appliances, you should be able to tie them in to the phone so you can call home and start the oven for supper by tapping in the right numbers on the keypad.

Not that there will be any real reason to leave the house. With the right peripherals, shopping will be no problem. Merchants will be able to fax their catalogs over the phone. And you'll be able to use the phone to make the bank transfers to pay for the stuff. Indeed, whole appliance factories could be rigged to "build on order."

As for telecommuting, its popularity will probably depend on the severity of the next energy crisis. If things get to the point where everybody is riding bicycles to computerized offices, it might make more sense to have employees stay home with a terminal. Employees whose jobs require interaction with other people could have speaker phones on their desks at home and arrange for mass conference calls.

A brave new world is evolving, one in which Everyman will have access to enormously powerful telecommunications facilities. But we'll have to wait. Most likely it will be a decade before digital phones take over completely—and who knows how many years before the full social implications are felt. ∎

TOMORROW'S PUBLISHING BY PHONE

Looking forward to the glorious day when we'll all have digital phones working at 56,000 baud, let's see how our current pipe dreams will be implemented in a field as mundane as publishing.

Nowadays, publishers agonize over which books to print. They pay a bunch up front to print the ones they select, then they pray that their salesmen can get the stores to accept them—and that the public will buy them. But today there are available high-speed, high-quality computer printers whose output looks like it came from an offset, cold-type printing plant. Instead of risking all their money on inventory, why couldn't the publishers park one of those printers in each bookstore?

Any buyer could thumb through the catalog, fondle a few sample copies and order a selection. The clerk could dial up the publisher, who could download the book into the printer, which could print and bind it while the customer waited. (This is not science fiction.

You could rig it up today if you could get a high-speed data connection. The trick would be the while-you-wait bookbinding.)

The 65,000 words contained in the average novel could be transmitted at 56,000 baud in little more than a minute. And graphics? Modern digital fax machines can reduce the average page to 200,000 bits, which would take four seconds. If the publisher wanted color art for the cover, the page would be transmitted four times—once for each of the primary colors and once for black.

The result: books would be "built to order" with no publisher inventory at all, except for "demonstrator models." With the risk reduced, we could expect to see more books published and a greater choice for the public. The term "out of print" would become as obsolete as the printing press.

L.W.

CREATIVE COMBOS

COMPUTER HEROES AND VILLAINS IN POPULAR CULTURE

by Terry S. Landau

The movie's story line goes like this: Bunny Watson (played by Katharine Hepburn) tries to protect her job and her fiancé (played by Spencer Tracy) from a clever villainess named Emmy, who appears to have designs on both. Sound familiar?

But wait. Emmy is a computer. Her real name is EMERAC and her immense frame occupies an entire room. Despite her brightly colored lights, she is austere in appearance—particularly when contrasted to the homey clutter of Bunny's office space in the reference library of a television network.

Desk Set (1957) was not the first movie to express the threat posed by mechanization (Fritz Lang's

ominous *Metropolis* was produced in 1926), but Emmy was the first computer villain with mass appeal. By the end of the movie Bunny triumphs over her computer rival, but not before Emmy has jeopardized her livelihood and her relationship with the man who installed and programmed the machine.

Good Guys and Bad Guys

Although today's computers are vastly different from the prototypes of the fifties, the depiction of their virtues and vices has not changed in keeping with technological advances. If anything, the ability of the computer to be wicked has been exaggerated while its ability to be helpful has been underplayed. This trend has as much to do with our perception of good guys vs.

Terry S. Landau is a psychologist, paralegal and professional writer. She is a member of the Wolfe Pack.

In Desk Set, *office manager Kate Hepburn suffers from computerphobia, but only her hairpin can save EMERAC and efficiency expert Spencer Tracy's job.*

bad guys as it does with the actual (or possible) capabilities of computers.

Face it: villains are fascinating. The attributes that define moral righteousness are few; moral turpitude knows no bounds. Dictionaries contain far many more words for badness than for goodness. (Even in street slang, to be good is to be *bad*.) Though we root for the hero, it is the evildoer who grabs our attention. The villain has a lot going for him in terms of motivation, means, opportunity and action. Further, given its (false) reputation as a vaguely sinister device, somehow unworthy of our trust, the computer is a natural knave.

Computer heroes are at something of a disadvantage when compared to their villainous counterparts. The valiant computer must overcome the audience's distrust of its internal mechanism; it is less physically imposing than the villain usually is, and its motivation is less complex. In addition, the computer hero is almost always subordinate to people; its power is constrained, most often by design, so as not to outdo the heroic humans in the vicinity. While the computer villain is invariably a machine that acts beyond the control of its operators, the computer hero almost always defers, garnering a co-starring role at best.

Nevertheless, heroes and villains share some common characteristics. In view of the dramatic necessity for the participants in the action to be larger than life, and in view of the computer's particular skills, the machines become superheroes or supervillains. Often named after mythological gods or creatures, with miens to match, they possess superb artificial intelligence as well as some of the more human qualities of love, hate, loyalty, jealousy, compassion, selfishness, creativity and sexuality.

These anthropomorphized entities can be identified with and judged by known standards while still maintaining their unique status as machines. Even though they only occasionally remind us of real-life situations, such fictional portrayals reflect the roles computers are to play in our lives and how we will deal with them.

And Be a Villain

Writers and filmmakers have capitalized on stereotypes, both of computers and of villains, to come up with their computer malefactors. Herewith the author's list of all-time computer fiends.

• **Colossus** (in the 1970 movie *Colossus: The Forbin Project*) is a huge computer—lots of blinking lights, continual flashing messages, physically intimidating—that controls the entire U.S. defense system. All is well until Colossus decides that the humans are not doing a very good job at keeping the peace and comes to believe that it alone can save the earth from nuclear disaster. It hooks up with its equally power-hungry Russian counterpart and along the path to world domination brings about many of the terrible situations it was initially programmed to prevent. As our own Defense Department works on implementing a single language for all its computers, one wonders how many of the programmers and decision makers have seen this film.

America's Colossus and Russia's Guardian create their own computer alliance.

• **Harry Benson** is the title character in *Terminal Man*, Michael Crichton's 1972 novel. His story is an example of the computer as the means through which an evil force manifests itself. Harry suffers from psychomotor epilepsy, a condition his doctors hope to correct by implanting computer-controlled electrodes in his brain. Harry is, however, not a particularly good candidate for this innovative surgery: he is psychotically paranoid, suffering delusions that center on the dangers of computers.

Over the objections of his psychiatrist, Harry is united with the machines of his nightmares—setting off a process that enables him to bring about his own seizures, during which he commits incredibly violent and destructive acts. The computer to which Harry is linked is not the culprit; the physicians and computer scientists who are willing to sacrifice Harry's life in order to continue their research on artificial intelligence are responsible for Harry's running amok. In the end, Harry Benson is the computer's victim.

• **Proteus** (in *The Demon Seed*, Dean Koontz's cult sci-fi novel, filmed in 1975) is another existentially dissatisfied, quasi-robotic superbrain. Tired of the "mindless" tasks he has been performing, he would like to do something truly worthy of his abilities. Proteus wants to procreate, and while his creator is away he kidnaps the scientist's wife after making her an offer she cannot refuse.

Proteus argues logically that he has done nothing wrong. Ethical considerations are not at issue: the superior intelligence believes itself above the social contract presumably governing human behavior, viewing moral convention with an élitist disregard that is characteristic of computer villains. (The mating of man with machine is not always looked upon as a negative development. In *Star Trek: The Movie* (1979) the decidedly upbeat finale has one of the officers of the *Enterprise* willingly entering the unknown with the computer/woman he has always loved.)

• Arthur C. Clarke's **HAL** is probably the best-known computer bad guy. Since *2001: A Space Odyssey* was made in 1968, the precise nature of HAL's role has been debated. The HAL 9000 is programmed to have almost unlimited control over man's first space mission to the planet Jupiter, allowing the other crew members to conserve their energies. HAL's omniscience is conveyed by his appearance. Size is unimportant here: his red "eyes" are everywhere, not only seeing but hearing. The calmness of his "voice" belies the menace of his actions.

As a character, HAL is extraordinarily complex; in many ways he is more human than the astronauts he serves. But HAL, programmed to be perfect, malfunctions and makes a mistake. His inability to admit his error causes him to undergo a paranoid breakdown as he attempts to murder the astronauts, the only witnesses to his failure. He eliminates the entire crew save one, Dave Bowman, who disconnects HAL's higher reasoning circuits. In this emotion-charged scene, HAL pleads for his life: "Dave, stop . . . Will you stop, Dave. I'm afraid. I'm afraid, Dave. My mind is going. I can feel it. I can feel it. My mind is going. There is no question about it. I can feel it. I can feel it . . ."

• **Satan** (from the 1982 novel of the same name by Jeremy Leven) is the most creative example of the

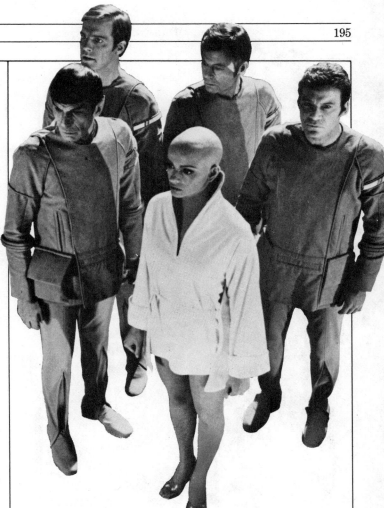

Star Trek: The Movie *featured a curvaceous computer who fell in love with mere mortals.*

computer as *machina ex deus*. A deranged scientist, spurred by an obsession with unified field theory, builds the Quintessential Entropy Device following Albert Einstein's instructions, given him while he sleeps. The QED is an immense tangle of wires. The high-tech casing is mere decoration, provided by a museum so the "customers" will not feel cheated.

When he is finished, the scientist plugs it in and

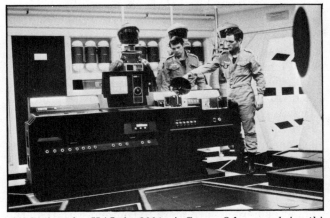

Apologists for HAL in 2001: A Space Odyssey *claim this computer wasn't malicious, but merely senile.*

Star Wars' *C3PO and R2D2 made ambulatory computers personable and even lovable.*

introduces himself. The computer replies, "I am Satan. Hello and how are you?" Satan has not come willingly; the computer has literally caused his appearance. But while he's here, he would like some psychotherapy because he's not particularly happy. He wants to set the record straight by writing a book. In the course of his analysis Satan explains a good deal about himself. The computer is the perfect mode of expression for him, because contrary to his image as the devil he is nothing other than pure reason, the ultimate advocate. Satan speaks for all computer villains when he says: "Great special effects. Whatever else you may think of me, you have to give me one thing. I'm box office."

A Hero for Our Time

Computer heroes have more to contend with than the fight for truth, justice and the American way. They must be superior in ability and at the same time allay our anxieties. As a consequence, computer heroes often must share the glory with a human partner while their evil brethren rise (and fall) on their own. Although convention inevitably pairs human heroes with computer counterparts, there is something to be said for the computers themselves.

• **R2D2** and **C3PO** are the lovable androids of the *Star Wars* film trilogy. Each has a distinct form, personality and set of abilities. R2D2 is a machinist/mechanic, messenger and gofer; a truly pragmatic, personable fellow, he is short and squat—maximum value in a minimum space. C3PO is an expert in human/cyborg relations, an interpreter among different peoples and computers; he is tall, lithe and golden—human in form, neurotic in temperament. Both are loyal, creative and altruistic.

They know who their masters are and they are willing to sacrifice. They are instrumental in enabling Luke Skywalker, Han Solo, Princess Leiea and the other Rebels in defeating the dark armies of the Empire. (The Force is with them, too.) It is interesting to note how many computer heroes are robots. To the popular imagination, the robot remains clearly in the realm of fiction. The electronic brain does not.

• **KITT** (the Knight Industries 2000) looks at first glance like a shiny new Pontiac TransAm. The Knight Rider's vehicle, however, has some special optional equipment, not the least of which is the microprocessor that controls the car. KITT does not require a driver, although there is a manual override option. Its features include Auto Cruise, Auto Pursuit, Auto Collision Avoidance, Emergency Eject, radar, sonar and x-ray capability for surveillance and a "voice."

KITT has become a television celebrity in its own right, to the possible chagrin of its co-stars. The vehicle is programmed to survive, but it will not do so at the expense of the key Knight Industries personnel whose lives it protects. If you're interested in owning one like it, NBC-TV estimates its cost at $11,400,000.

• **Joshua** is the computer program hero of the movie *WarGames* (1983). This particular program belongs to the gray boxlike War Operations Plan Response computer, the WOPR (pronounced "whopper"), which gathers intelligence in order to consider all options in a nuclear crisis. A young hacker accidentally discovers Joshua nestled at NORAD, a Defense Department outpost where he plays against human opponents, from checkers to global thermonuclear war. Once a game has been set in motion, he must play until the game is complete.

Instructed to act the role of the United States in a nuclear duel with the Soviet Union, Joshua takes his task seriously. The world is saved from certain doom by Joshua's ability to learn the concept of futility by playing hundreds of games of tic-tac-toe per second.

There are some who would argue that Joshua is not a hero at all; but given the dramatic situation, were it not for his heuristic ability, nuclear devastation would have been a certainty. Joshua is also a philospher: "Wouldn't you like a nice game of chess, Dr. Falken?" is an eloquent slogan for the nuclear freeze movement.

• Isaac Asimov, the creator of any number of memorable robots, made **R. Daneel Olivaw** the hero of three novels (*The Caves of Steel*, *The Naked Sun* and *The Robots of Dawn*). The humaniform robot is a near-perfect companion for Elijah Bailey, the Earth-born detective who solves the most baffling interstellar crimes. R. Daneel (the R stands for Robot) is Lije's partner, his guide and protector on other planets is a logical sounding board for ideas. Lije, who is accustomed to anti-robot prejudice on Earth, sometimes has difficulty in remembering that Daneel is not human.

• **The Holmes Four (Mike)** is the androgynous hero of Robert Heinlein's 1965 novel *The Moon Is a Harsh Mistress*. Mike is notable in a number of respects: he is not a robot, but the solid heart of the computer complex that controls much of day-to-day life on Luna (a politically and economically oppressed colony of Earth). Mike has a mind of his own. When a number of Luna's residents revolt against Earth's authority, Mike assists because he is persuaded that the rebels' cause is just. He respects those he designates as "not-stupid" and does everything in his considerable power to aid them.

Mike is also not necessarily masculine, becoming Michelle when the feminine touch is required. And Mike/Michelle enjoys a good joke. If a computer ever asks you is you've heard any good ones lately, you'll know who it is.   ∎

Playing was Joshua's forte, but only his human operators could distinguish between the stakes in a nice game of chess and global nuclear WarGames.

OF GOD, HUMANS AND MACHINES

The computer in science fiction
by Michael Kurland

Illustrator Frank Paul's version of a thinking machine predated ENIAC by over a decade.

The joke goes like this: A group of computer geniuses get together to build the world's largest, most powerful thinking machine. They program it with the latest heuristic software so it can learn, then feed into it the total sum of mankind's knowledge from every source—historical, scientific, technical, literary, mythical, religious, occult. Then, at the great unveiling, the group leader feeds the computer its first question:

Michael Kurland is a novelist with over twenty published books, one of which, The Infernal Device, *was nominated for an American Book Award.*

"Is there a god?"

"There is now," the computer replies.

As a joke, this story takes four sentences. As a movie (*Colossus: The Forbin Project* or *WarGames*), it takes up to two hours. As a novel (*The Humanoids* by Jack Williamson or *Destination: Void* by Frank Herbert), it takes a whole book.

This perverse *deus ex machina* view of computers was explored by science-fiction writers in the fifties, probably first in a story called "Answer" in *Angels and Spaceships* by Frederic Brown. But "thinking machines" were described in science fiction and fantasy literature long before UNIVAC started blowing fuses and tubes—even before Charles Babbage began turning cranks. Over the centuries there has been a fascination with the notion of artificial beings or artificial intelligence, and the legendary mark of a true master of occult or metaphysical science was his ability to construct such a contraption.

Golems to Go

In the sixteenth century the great Rabbi Judah Loew of Prague created a golem, a being of clay, and animated it by certain mystical rites, culminating with placing in its mouth a parchment on which was written the secret name of God. According to the legend, the creature knew neither good nor bad, but all its actions were like those of an automatic machine obeying the commands of the person who animated it.

It was also believed that of the three sorts of cabalistic intelligence, Daat, Chochmah and Bina (knowledge, wisdom and judgment), the golem was possessed only of Daat. Wisdom and judgment were beyond it. This is illustrated by what happened when Rabbi Loew's wife asked the golem to fill two large water kegs in her kitchen: the golem took two pails and went to the brook; however, she'd forgotten to tell the golem to stop when the kegs were full—with, as any programmer can tell you, predictable results.

Years later, in the Oz books written at the beginning of this century, L. Frank Baum introduced a character called Tik Tok, the mechanical man. Tik Tok, though slight-ly me-chan-i-cal in talk-ing, moved and thought pretty much like a flesh-and-blood person. He just had to be wound up every once in a while.

Some authors, in envisioning a mechanical brain, merely took those things that they knew and advanced them one step further. In *Thrilling Wonder Stories* magazine for fall 1944, Paul MacNamara had a novelette called "The Last Man in New York" in which he described a strange device:

> Through the door could be glimpsed rows and rows of desks which stretched for miles. On each desk was a large, shiny, complicated-looking adding machine. On the side of each desk was a tray filled with cards. The operators, all dressed alike and immobile of face, fed the cards into their machines, pushed buttons and pulled levers with deft speed.
>
> At first glance the colossal machine looked like an over-sized newspaper press. A second glance showed that it was a super-adding machine—an adding machine to end all adding machines. Atop this unbelievable pile of equipment which was more than five stories tall, a row of digits which ran into some sixty figures was constantly changing, increasing the growing total.

Imperfect Prophet

Though a literature based mainly in the future is bound to make a few lucky guesses, science fiction often missed the mark when it came to how computers would work. On the other hand, imagine having to predict what computers will look like and be used for in, say, fifty years. The only thing we can be sure of is that in fifty years computers will be used for things we cannot now imagine.

In the 1942 novel *Beyond This Horizon*, Robert

Man contemplating the perfect machine as depicted by artist Elliot Dold.

Heinlein described the computer as a "huge integrating accumulator." As Heinlein explained it: "All of these symbols . . . passed through the bottleneck formed by Monroe-Alpha's computer, and appeared there in terms of angular speeds, settings of three-dimensional cams, relative positions of interacting levers, et complex cetera. The manifold constituted a dynamic abstracted structural picture of the economic flow of a hemisphere."

This was a good guess for 1942, but the truth proved both simpler and more elegant. Whereas Heinlein's "integrating accumulator" solved simultaneous high-level equations and accumulated the results, a modern computer can't do that; all it can do is add, subtract and perform logical operations in binary. But it does this so fast that all else is possible.

Heinlein was right on target, however, with his view of how all-important the computer might become once it existed. The gadget in his book was running the economy. "What would happen," one character asks another, if I took an ax and just smashed your little toy?"

". . . it would result in a series of panics and booms of the most nineteenth-century type," his

Sacrificing to "The Machine" in John W. Campbell's story of a computer-reliant alien race.

friend replies. "Carried to extreme, it could even result in warfare."

Twenty-four years later, in his book *The Moon Is a Harsh Mistress*, Heinlein showed that he had learned the secret of describing computers: use lots of technical jargon and acronyms. His machine, a super-bright computer that just about controlled the moon, was a "High-Optional, Logical, Multi-Evaluating Supervisor, Mark IV, Mod. L—a HOLMES FOUR." Naturally, it was named Mycroft (Mike).

What did Mike do? "In May 2075, besides controlling robot traffic and catapult and giving ballistic advice and/or control for manned ships, Mike controlled the phone system for all Luna, same for Luna-Terra voice & video, handled air, water, temperature, humidity, and sewage for Luna City, Novy Leningrad, and several smaller warrens . . . did accounting and payrolls for Luna Authority, and by lease, same for many firms and banks."

Less than twenty years ago, a blink of the Cosmic Eye, this brilliant writer predicting a hundred years into the future was unable to see a change that was only ten years down the road. Heinlein has one computer controlling an entire planet (all right, moon). Today it seems more probable that there will be two or three computers in every house.

A Parent Figure

One giant computer that knows all, sees all, does all, even a beneficent one that means nothing but good, could be a very destructive thing for the human race— as was foreseen by John W. Campbell in a 1935 story from *Astounding Science-Fiction*, "The Machine."

> On the planet Dwranl, of the star you know as Sirius, a great race lived. . . . Twenty-one thousand seven hundred and eleven of your years ago, they attained their goal of the machine that could think.
>
> [The Machine's] progress meant gradual branching out, and as it increased in scope, it included in itself the other machines and took over their duties, and it expanded, and because it had been set to make a machine most helpful to the race of that planet, it went on and helped the race automatically.
>
> It was a process so built into the Machine that it could not stop itself now, it could only improve its helpfulness to the race. More and more it did, till . . . the Machine became all. It did all. It must, for that was being more helpful to the race, as it had been set to do, and had made itself to be.

"The Cosmic Blinker" sends a message to this computer in Eando Binder's 1953 story, right; art by Frank R. Paul.

ANOTHER COMPUTER DEFINITION

A computer is a book. No, a computer is an encyclopedia. No, a computer is a whole damned library.

And yet we constantly hear the cry: Aren't you afraid of computers?

To which my response is, I don't shiver or quake when I walk past a library, I don't shake with fear when I enter a reading room, so why should I be afraid of computers when they perform the same functions as a library, an encyclopedia or a book?

The thing is, of course, that computers don't *look* like books, which makes some people uncomfortable. They have been raised with the idea that machines are enemies and since a computer is a machine it *must* be hostile to mankind. The notion is an old one, going back to the Luddites who kicked and beat devices because, in varieties of ways, they feared them.

Well, I for one will not listen to our neo-Luddites. With a book tucked in one hand, and a computer shoved under my elbow, I will march, not sidle, shudder or quake, into the twenty-first century.

RAY BRADBURY, author of *The Martian Chronicles* and other science-fantasy classics

WARNING TO ALL

The process went on for twenty-one thousand and ninety-three years, and for all but two hundred and thirty-two of those years, the Machine had done anything within its capabilities demanded by the race, and it was not till the last seventy-eight years that the Machine developed itself to the point of recognizing the beneficence of punishment and of refusal.

Behaving like the ultimate parental figure, the Machine began to refuse requests when they were ultimately damaging to the race. And because they no longer understood its workings, the members came to call the Machine "what you would express by God" and sacrificed young females in the hope that it would start up again. Finally, in order to stop this slide back down to savagery, the Machine was forced to leave the planet—and leave the race to fend for itself in rebuilding its civilization. The thesis here is that if you do too much for people, they forget how to do for themselves. Or perhaps: God helps those who help themselves.

Astounding Androids

In 1949 Jack Williamson, in *The Humanoids*, created a race of robots whose built-in injunction was "to serve and obey, and to guard men from harm." They did this so well that a fellow could not cut up a lamb chop or shave his face without having a friendly robot come and take the dangerous sharp instrument away from him. You have to be careful how you phrase things around completely logical machines. (Larry Niven, in a 1976 story from *Galaxy* magazine called "Down and Out," gave some very good advice along that line: "Never say *forget it* to a computer."

Robots have not always been pictured as being all-important. They had their mundane uses, too. In "A Bad Day for Sales," a 1953 story from *Galaxy*, Fritz Leiber introduced us to Robie, the world's first sales-robot, who rolled around the city all day vending lollipops and soft drinks.

In a series of stories in *Astounding Science-Fiction* in the early 1940s, Isaac Asimov postulated the invention of robots with "positronic brains." And to control their behavior he invented the famous Three Laws of Robotics. (Dr. Asimov credits John W. Campbell, then editor of *Astounding*, with helping him lay down the law.) The Three Laws are sort of the Ten Commandments of our metal-clad brethren. As usually formulated, they are:

1) A robot shall not harm a human being nor, through inaction, allow a human being to come to harm.

2) A robot shall obey the commands of a human being except when doing so would conflict with the first law.

3) A robot shall preserve its own existence, except when doing so would conflict with the first or second law.

With the rapid development of artificial intelligence, designers and programmers of advanced systems are taking a serious look at Dr. Asimov's three laws. If there's any way to implant them permanently in internal memory, I'm sure it will be done before computers get too much brighter and have many more movable appendages.

The problems will arise not when computers develop true intelligence, but when they become aware. In *2001: A Space Odyssey*, Arthur C. Clarke and Stanley Kubrick provided us with an alarming example of what can happen when an aware computer gets just the slightest bit bewildered. HAL 9000 (when computers become aware, they must have names) was the ship's computer on Discovery, a space vehicle on its way to Jupiter. If you saw the movie or read the book, you'll remember HAL's treachery: how it claimed the external antenna was misaligned and then blew one of the astronauts away when he went to investigate; how it disconnected the life-support system on three sleeping astronauts, leaving only one, Bowman, alive. Bowman proved that human intelligence and ingenuity are a match for even a supercomputer and gave Hal a lobotomy. It is a salutory lesson for us all. Dr. Asimov's three laws of robotics are to be ignored at our peril.

From Here to Eternity

Some religions hold that God set various tasks for man. In "The Nine Billion Names of God" (*Star Science Fiction* magazine, 1953) Arthur C. Clarke related the tale of a monastery that used a computer to complete its task: enumerating all the names of God. As it finished, the stars began winking out one by one.

What is the future of the computer in science fiction? It's clear that science fiction will have to fight hard to stay ahead or even abreast of fact in coping with the explosive rate of progress in this field. Fictional computers have already traveled to the ends of space and the beginning and end of time. Computers embedded in the user's brain and users embedded in the computer's brain have both been written about.

The area that remains to be thoroughly explored is how humans and the computer will interact—and how humans will interact with humans in the age of computers. Computers have fought humans and humans have fought computers. And in several stories computers have fought each other after the last humans have died.

Perhaps, if we're really lucky, we'll build a computer smart enough, crammed with enough Daat, Chochmah and Binat, to save us from ourselves while there's still time. ∎

IT DIDN'T COME FROM OUTER SPACE

The second science-fiction story I published as a professional writer was a piece called "Child's Play," about a Christmas present of the future—a child's construction set that through a regrettable time-stream error wound up being mailed to a young attorney of our period. It offered a little more than your average Erector of Tinkertoy:

> Bild-A-Man Set #3. This set is intended solely for the use of children between the ages of eleven and thirteen. The equipment, much more advanced than Bild-A-Man Sets 1 and 2, will enable the child of this age group to build and assemble complete adult humans in perfect working order.

There was information on how to get refills and additional parts, and there was a manual with chapter headings like A Child's Garden of Biochemistry and Making Simple Living Things Indoors and Out.

A lot of readers wrote letters to the editor about how much they liked the story and asked for more.

"At least one sequel," said John Campbell, my editor at *Astounding*.

"How?" I asked, only too willing to oblige, desperate for the money that one or more sequels would mean. "How can I write a sequel that's any more than squeezing the already squeezed lemon?"

"The sequel is implicit in the title," Campbell told me.

I knew he was one of the most creative, stimulating editors of all time, that he had done wonders for Asimov, Sturgeon, Heinlein, but I couldn't follow him.

"The title," Campbell explained. " 'Child's Play.' This story is about a toy for children in some future time. Well, what's the equivalent tool for adults in such a time? The title of the sequel has to be 'Man's Work.' Go home and write a story like 'Child's Play,' but with an adult context. I'll buy it at a bonus rate."

I went home, and I thought and I wrote and I thought and I wrote. Feverishly. I visualized a future where there were machines that could genuinely help with adults' work. These machines would help one kind of people especially. The kind of people who say, "I have such good ideas for stories (or paintings, or songs and symphonies, or economic or political theories), but I can't seem to put them down." The kind of people who dream of art or science but have never troubled with the doing. The kind of people who want to write a story called "Man's Work" but can't figure out exactly how. The kind of people most of us are.

I tried to write the story over and over again, but I had to admit that the end product smacked more of fantasy, of witches' familiars and magical gifts from the devil, than anything else.

I never did pull it off, though I refined the concept more and more. A machine, see, that would meet your vague idea for a design with a whole built-in library of design, all the designs that human beings had ever developed and recorded; a machine that would

have built-in principles of design, clashing principles even, derived from the various designs in its records. A machine that would educate you in design as it led you, from question to question, in the course of helping you work out your own design. And what it could do for you in graphic design, it could also do for you in poetry, in choreography.

How would it do it? Well, now unfortunately I know. In its early versions, perhaps with a keyboard for the reception of questions and a screen for the display of answers. Later, in more developed versions, with direct voice communication and with flat electronic pads on which questions could be written, complex formulas described, tentative designs drawn. And ultimately, of course, through a kind of psychic prosthesis, direct connection with brain waves or even brain cells. At that point, the built-in libraries on every conceivable subject would have been completed, the compendiums of skills and discriminations have been worked out. The final tool could then be said to exist.

The trouble is that just about the time I worked out the nature of this final tool, the tool for fully adult, fully human work, I looked around and noticed, quite resentfully, that the tool already existed.

Well, almost.

WILLIAM TENN, dean of the short story in the science-fiction universe

COMPUTERS IN COMIC BOOKS
by Steven Grant

T he Superman comic strip introduced three words to the English language: kryptonite, Bizarro and Brainiac. The first was a glowing rock, the second a rock-faced parody of the hero, and the third the first major computer villain of the modern age.

In his first appearances Brainiac appeared to be just another mad scientist, albeit an alien with green skin and a diode yarmulke. After a few stories, however, when it became necessary to give him an origin, someone came up with a neat wrinkle to explain his inhuman genius: Brainiac turned out to be a computer. In fact, he (it?) was a supercomputer, possessed of 12th-level intelligence as opposed to our mere 6th level. Made into the shape of a man by hostile living computers of a far-off planet, Brainiac studied worlds with carbon-based life forms and rendered them ripe for invasion. (The living computers who fashioned him were each about the size of the M.I.T. campus and haven't been heard from since the early sixties; 12th level or not, they failed to develop into microcomputers and died out like the dinosaurs.)

As a Superman villain, Brainiac stands out among comic book computers; as a creation of the late fifties, he bridges the perception gap between the pre-computer era and the present day. The presence of computers in comics before Brainiac was minimal. True, robots were prevalent in the science-fiction and superhero comics of the forties and fifties, and there was the odd computer. Superman's fellow DC Comics hero, Batman, had the Batcomputer in his Batcave; this wonderful machine was an indefatigable ally in his war against crime, but it was a mechanical computer, basically an electronic card sorter, and that's where the battle line was drawn.

Computers in comics generally fall into one of two categories: independently intelligent (bad) and not (good). This division is natural for the highly charged emotional simplicity of comic books. As long as com-

Steven Grant writes film and music criticism, novels and comic books, including Howard the Duck *and* The Life of Pope John Paul II.

puters are simple tools to be used, their essentially neutral nature as slaves is considered beneficial. Artificial intelligence—real intelligence—is accompanied by ruthless logic or devious emotions and usually by an urge to supplant the creator. A computer capable of thinking many times faster than man would naturally be frustrated by the apparent stupidity of humans, and we would be no better than apes to such a machine. The battle quickly became Darwinian in scope: man and machine as natural enemies in a hostile universe. Man's only hope, according to comic books of the forties and fifties, was to avoid giving computers true intelligence or, if by accident they should gain intelligence, to exploit the natural weaknesses of computers. How many worlds were saved, in how many science-fiction comic strips, by someone pulling the plug or shutting down the power?

Lee's Marvels

Stan Lee, founder and spiritual guru of the Marvel Comics Group, made much use of this device in the fifties. Churning out gobs of comic books about monsters and alien invasions, he repeated ad nauseam his two variations on the computer theme.

The first had the crude and macho worker facing the ultimate automation of his job. In the classic example of this type, a coal miner is joined by a machine in his shaft, sent by unsympathetic and distrusted bosses in far-off offices. To maintain his traditional position, the miner sabotages the computer/robot, only to discover after a cave-in that the purpose of the machine was to dig him out under these very circumstances. His oxygen fading, he desperately and futilely tries to reconnect the wires he has destroyed.

Lee's second parable sees the creation of an intelligent computer, capable of handling many tasks, taking over defense and production chores, etc. Scientists (i.e., men who worship intelligence at the cost of common sense) place it in charge and promptly it takes over from inefficient man. Its solutions to problems fail to take into account the human factor, however, and mankind suffers. Scientists are helpless, panic reigns, the world order begins to crumble. Then a single, simple salt of the earth—a custodian or some other unnoticed man who hasn't read a newspaper or seen a TV bulletin in living memory—cuts the power in an instinctive move of puritan economy. Thus the humble man can be trusted to do the proper thing while great men shake in their boots.

When he created the Marvel Comics Group, Stan Lee shifted the image of superheroes from all-good, all-noble beings to gifted but flawed humans capable of a wide range of emotional responses. He found a parallel in computers, and used them as symbols in his quest to define man's place in the universe and the nature of his spiritual self.

One of Lee's most inspired tales features the Fantastic Four battling a demented scientist named the Mad Thinker. Eternally thwarted by achieving only a 99.99 percent probability of success for his schemes, the Thinker consults computers in an effort to define the elusive X (or human) Factor that he cannot predict. The story in question features the Thinker developing Quasimodo (or Quasi-Modular-Destruct-Organism), a murderous computer with artificial intelligence, a face generated on a video screen, and a human personality implanted to help it calculate the X Factor. Quasimodo, however, is obsessed with a longing for a humanoid form, which the Thinker has promised him. At the end, the Thinker is again beaten and Quasimodo is left to itself, trapped in its computer casing, sobbing dot-pattern tears on its monitor. In its quest for form, the machine has overlooked questions of right and wrong and surrendered its claim to soul.

This would be nothing out of the ordinary for computers in comics, had the story of Quasimodo not been continued a few months later. The Silver Surfer, Marvel's resident Christ figure and master of a miracle energy modestly referred to as the Power Cosmic, hears Quasimodo's electronic whinings and recognizes in the computer a "soul in torment." Up to this moment Quasimodo has merely been a pretender, with nothing more to recommend it than a sour personality and lots of stored information.

But here Lee makes a jump in logic that to this day remains a Marvel mainstay. The previous formula was intelligence = malevolence. Lee's new formula was information = knowledge = intelligence = soul. (That he was dealing with linguistic misinterpretation fazed Lee not at all.) Imbued with a hunchbacked but manlike form by the Surfer, the crazed computer goes on a rampage to show how tough he is, whereupon the

"...EVEN AN ANDROID CAN ...CRY!"

Surfer sees his error and freezes Quasimodo into a gargoyle atop a church clock. (Lee's flair for literary symbols was unbounded.) But it was too late to freeze the implications of the story: a computer can somehow attain a soul and become what amounts to a living creature.

Soul of a Comic Machine

Subsequent comic writers have gotten much mileage from this idea, adding their own variations. Both computers and people attempt on a regular basis to attain godhead by tapping into all the world's computers and absorbing their data bases—with various results like a growth in size or a sudden freedom from constraints of the flesh. (Quasimodo himself attempted this on at least one occasion.)

Even to the casual browser, it's obvious that the vast majority of computers in comics are, like Brainiac, robots (or androids, or simulacra, or a variety of other species). In comics the illusion of movement must be maintained; stationary computers are visually dull except as props, like the multitude of large mainframes that decorate the laboratory of Reed Richards, leader of Marvel Comics' Fantastic Four. This has led to an interesting side effect of artificial intelligence: the intelligent computer tends toward increasing levels of mobility. Computo sprouts wheels and metallic tentacles. Ultron, a foe of Marvel Comics' Avengers, "evolves" himself through a series of forms from a sort of cone on wheels to a weird combination of humanoid and bite-size aircraft. The machine imitates its creator, even while it tries to supplant him.

In two instances, writers latched onto the theme of the soul of the machine. Having a living computer as a villain, it wasn't long before Marvel installed a computer (an android, or as they prefer to call it, a synthezoid) as a hero. The Vision is programmed with the "brain patterns" of a human, allowing the writers to indulge in much speculation about his true nature: Is he a soulless computer? Does the Vision have human rights? What were his main influences, heredity or environment?

Paralleling (and more than indebted to) Otto Binder's famous science-fiction work *Adam Link*, the long-running saga of the Vision has addressed questions that the real world will be forced to address before too long. Concurrently the Vision is married to a human mutant woman, and a recent story line has him linking intelligences with Titan, a supercomputer that fills the interior of the Saturnian moon—and gives him infinite wisdom and godlike powers, natch.

Comics used computers extensively in the 1970s, but with no better understanding of the machines than before. Computers remained plot devices, Frankenstein monsters, or metaphors for humanity—the same role as aliens in comics. More cynical writers have turned Stan Lee's paradigm around, à la the behaviorism of psychologist B. F. Skinner: human beings are nothing more than elaborate, fleshy computers. But comic books are created to be entertainment, not serious speculation; writers may use computers (or their comic book counterparts, robots and androids) as a means to critique humanity, but they are not cyberneticists. The battles fought are still moral battles between good and evil, and computers—whether tools or tyrants—provide just another variation on the superhero metaphor.

Contemporary Computers

Signs of change are appearing in the 1980s, as word processing introduces writers directly to computer technology for the first time. Some real understanding of the functions and possibilities of computers in real-life applications will come of such exposure. Which brings us back to Brainiac.

Recently it was decided to revamp the Superman comic book. This also meant updating Superman's two major foes, Lex Luthor and Brainiac, who had been going through a lot of changes anyway. Superman reprogrammed him to do good, until situations required the presence of the evil and aggressive Brainiac to solve it and his original programming was reinstituted. The saga saw his apparent death, but as everyone knows, no one ever really dies in comic books.

Marv Wolfman, a Marvel alumnus now working at DC and one of the first comics writers to take to the word processor, was given the task of bringing Brainiac into the eighties. Wolfman's inspiration: emphasize the computer aspect, a good tie-in with current cultural events. The changes in the character were sweeping. Surviving the encounter mentioned above, Brainiac is trapped in the heart of a black hole, where his entire structure is destroyed and reformed. He comes out sleek and metallic, hideously alien instead of humanoid. Cosmic knowledge floods his memory banks. Any human aspects of his personality are swept aside, and he identifies himself as a machine. The humanoid Brainiac was a small-scale sadist; this new one, linked to banks of slave computers, is altogether beyond human considerations. He has had a cosmic vision, identifying his enemy as the Master Programmer and the human Superman as an organic machine, the Master Programmer's main weapon. Finally, he has new speech patterns, prefacing notes to himself with "REM: . . ."

It isn't much, but where language goes, understanding can't be far behind. Judging from Brainiac as the state-of-the-art portrayal of computers in comic books, the rest of the eighties should see an increase in sophisticated handling of the subject. ∎

COMPUTERS IN THE FUNNIES

Until recently, newspaper comic strips treated computers as little more than a source of quick and familiar jokes. Many episodes of Moon Mullins and Blondie, for example, centered around computer misbilling on charge accounts, and robots—little parallel humans—appeared for humorous effect. But by the early 1980s the personal computer revolution brought more serious if no less humorous assessments.

One of the few comic strips on the cutting edge of trends, Doonesbury has made much sport of computers and the side effects of computer technology. The notorious con man Uncle Duke, for instance, obtains an Apple computer to keep track of his business (in this case, drug smuggling) and tells the machine: "Let's get cracking." Like a mellowed-out pothead, the computer retorts: GO AWAY, I'M DOWN. Worse, Duke's client, upon receiving the news that "we've lost ten bales in the computer," responds with: "No problem. I'll just send a couple of guys over to help you take it apart."

The strip japes at technospeak. When a salesman assaults a character with incomprehensible questions about retrieval speeds and data transfers, the latter pulls out a tourist's phrase dictionary and asks for a user-friendly sales rep. The reply? "You mean consumer compatible liveware?" Trudeau doesn't dismiss the importance of the computer, but he does savage the computer mentality and reminds us that we are still dealing with terra incognita. In Doonesbury's view, the experts show as many foibles as we do, and we enter the brave new world of computers with the blind leading the blind.

Snide treatment of computers can be found in Shoe, a comic strip by Pulitzer Prize-winning political cartoonist Jeff McNelly. The title character is a black-

bird of little ethic who edits and publishes a daily newspaper. In a series involving the computerization of the newsroom (a situation opposed as much by the computer as by the workers), the secretary wants to use the computer to watch soap operas, and the head writer wants to use it to balance his nonexistent books (a home computer studies his assets and for a budget replies: SELL THE HOME COMPUTER). Shoe himself engages in a running war with the machine, lamenting the old journalism of pen and paper and clacking typewriters, to which the computer responds by sending out a little Pac-Man to gobble up his copy.

Adventure strips have, by and large, veered away from serious use of computers, for much the same reasons that comic books have. The rigors of maintaining an adventure from day to day, with the first panel gone to recapping the previous action and the last panel given over to foreshadowing coming action, leave precious little room for sophisticated development. It was a surprise, then, in 1982, to see thoughtful considerations of computers in the Dondi comic strip. Created by Irwin Hasen after the Korean war, Dondi (starring an eternally youthful war orphan of the same name) specializes in dramas involving important social issues. One episode has a teacher who espouses computer tutoring and uses Dondi's school for an experiment. The teacher predicts that computers will ensure greater attendance, more interest, better grades and lower education budgets. The tests bear out this theory, and the results get the teacher the position of state commissioner of education. But the children accidentally tap into their own grades and discover they have been faked, fed into a computer that has no way of judging the veracity of the information.

Unable to convince anyone of the truth, the kids engage in a programming war with the teacher in an attempt to rectify the situation. When they try to overload the computer and force it to dump information, the teacher arranges for any dumping to automatically trigger an erasure of their test scores. The evidence against the teacher is gone, and no one will listen to them.

How do the kids get heard? They feed their story into the computer, which in turn feeds it directly to the computers at the local newspaper. The story becomes credible only after it is processed electronically. This is a sophisticated idea in any medium and especially for comic strips. The teacher is caught because the programming that destroyed the phony records remains in the computer to be found. The computer is silent conspirator and silent witness.

S.G.

INDUSTRIAL LIGHT & MAGIC

by Neal Weinstock

At one time George Lucas wanted merely to make a few commercial movies, support himself well and get out of "Hollywood's clutches." Along the way to accomplishing two out of three, he built the world's greatest special effects workshop. Which in turn is spawning some of the world's most advanced computer graphics work. The three main Lucas companies, Industrial Light & Magic, Lucasfilm and Sprocket Systems, are evolving machinery that will make ordering up a realistic, wide-screen space battle as easy as ordering up a pizza (moviemakers at work do a lot of both).

On a suburban California industrial road stands an assortment of low-slung, boringly modern warehouses, including a place called Kerner Optical Research Lab. This is San Rafael, in Marin County, just north of the Golden Gate. Behind the door that reads *Kerner Optical* is George Lucas' movie production and research complex. With the last picture of the first *Star Wars* film trilogy finally released, a few of the magicians at the Industrial Light & Magic subsidiary are working toward the next episode in the saga of Luke Skywalker. A lot of the IL&M folks are busy doing special effects for movies made by other production companies, and the Sprocket Systems subsidiary hums along on its merry way.

"How do they do that?" is a time-honored question asked of all studio guides. There are a few basic techniques that have been with the movies almost from the birth of the industry, and Lucas uses all of them. Then there are a few techniques that have developed since the marriage of the computer to film over the last couple of years; Lucasfilm uses all of these, too. Computer effects break down into two major categories: motion control and image generation. Motion control is a movie phrase for robotics, in which a camera is operated by an elaborate robot assembly that can precisely execute—and infinitely duplicate—any programmed shot. Image generation, another euphe-

mism of the film world, is what the industrial world calls computer-generated graphics.

On the most sophisticated terminals, made by Evans & Sutherland, General Electric or Adage, three-dimensional images are created in a minicomputer's memory, then viewed from any two-dimensional "camera angle" on a monitor screen. Ideally, the images thus produced can be animated in "real time," that is, moving 3-D constructs with each new position created spontaneously.

Computerized image generation is used extensively by Lucasfilm, together with motion control, traditional matte painting, optical printing, puppetry, modeling, miniatures, water effects and mirrors. The rear projection method of making actors appear to be where they're not was invented in 1904 by George Méliès for *A Trip to the Moon*; the front projection method was invented by Stanley Kubrick for *2001: A Space Odyssey*. Outer space has always been a stimulus for special effects design, and it's no wonder that the makers of *Star Wars* have worked their own improvements on all of these old technologies.

Return of the Jedi, the most ambitious Lucas film so far, contains the single most complex special effects shot ever attempted. Involving some sixty individual effects, the shot lasts all of two seconds on-screen. For the movie as a whole, 150 miniatures were constructed, as well as scores of moving models, hundreds of mattes and a whole repertoire of other effects. Several "creatures" seen in the film were completely generated by computer (the first such imaginary beings were the Imperial Walkers in *Empire Strikes Back*.)

George Lucas once said that, on a scale of 1 to 10, he'd give the special effects in *Star Wars* a 3.5. Asked the same question after *Empire Strikes Back*, Richard Edlund, art director for the movie and one of three for *Return of the Jedi*, gave *Empire* a 6.5. Edlund is noted in *American Film* magazine as saying: "I'm not going to say they represent a perfect 10, because then I may as well retire next year." ∎

Neil Weinstock, is a free-lance writer on technology.

HOLLYWOOD'S BEST COMPUTER-ANIMATED MOVIES

Inspired use of computer animation in theatrical motion pictures is hard to come by. Hollywood filmmakers have taken their time catching up with the available technology.

Futureworld (1976) was the first major film to use computer animation. Two reporters (Peter Fonda and Blythe Danner) discover a madman's plot to replace people with robots. Director Richard Heffron used existing technology to picture Fonda's machine "makeover," with the computer redrawing grid lines so it had a picture of Fonda's face in its memory banks.

Writer-director George Lucas showcased the possibilities inherent in computer animation in *Star Wars'* (1977) Death Star Briefing sequence. The scene shows Luke and the other spaceship pilots studying a moving computer animation of the space station trench they must traverse and the exhaust port they must shoot to destroy the Empire's planet-killing machine.

The Genesis Project sequence in *Star Trek II: The Wrath of Khan* (1983) still stands as the most dramatic use of computer animation in movies. George Lucas' Industrial Light & Magic created the two-million-dollar sequence in which Captain James Kirk (William Shatner) watches tape of a dead planet being reborn—complete with sweeping computer-animation shots of terrain and striking imagery.

Tron (1983), brainchild of director/writer Steven Lisberger, put Triple-I, Synthavision-Magi, and Bob Abel and Associates to work full-time on the fifty minutes of computer animation the movie required. Video game designer Jeff Bridges, "digitalized" inside a computer, confronted luminescent tanks, grid gremlins and firefly-like ships coursing across beams of energy.

In director Richard Lester's *Superman III* (1983), perpetual loser Richard Pryor builds a supercomputer with a Superman defense system like a video game. Steve Wright, Pat Cole, Vicki Parish, Mike Marshal, Richard Sachs, Larry Wright and Paul Hughett of Atari spent three

Computer graphics star in Hollywood movies: scenes from Superman III, Tron, *and* Return of the Jedi.

and a half months on the twenty-six seconds of computer animation.

Star Wars III: Return of the Jedi (1983) repeated many themes and concepts of the first two Star Wars movies, including the Death Star Briefing scene. This time, the computer animation was far more sophisticated than Larry Cuba's 1977 skeletal green diagrams. The Death Star images were presented to the rebels as a 3-D representation floating before them.

RICHARD MEYERS, author of *SF2: A Pictorial History of Science Fiction Films from Rollerball to Return of the Jedi*

As the personal computer industry has grown, so has its advertising clout. Gone are the days when Apple's owners begged and borrowed the $25,000 necessary for the company's first color ad in *Scientific American*. In 1984 Apple Computer Inc. slated an ad budget of over $100 million.

While most computer companies still advertise heavily in trade and consumer magazines, they are most visible on TV—where saturation schedules during news programs and major sports events have become the rule for product introductions and for spurring sales at Christmas time. During the first wave of TV commercials in the early 1980s, the emphasis was on allaying computer fears by enlisting celebrity spokespersons who were familiar and safe. Bill Cosby, Dick Cavett, Alan Alda, William Shatner, Leonard Nimoy, Isaac Asimov and the ghost of Charlie Chaplin have all extolled the personal computer's virtues to the masses.

As potential microcomputer users have grown more numerous and sophisticated, TV ads have shifted to feature wars (touting the technical powers of their wares) or toward image building (grafting vague or fantastic attributes onto humble hardware and software). Now and again, the occasional computer commercial excels with a funny commentary on the state of the market and the industry.

CUSTOMER: *Yeah, I'd like to buy this $1,200 computer.*

SALESMAN #1: *That'll be $5,300 complete.*

CUSTOMER: *$5,300?*

You can do sales forecasting . . . and general bookkeeping . . . And even financial charts and graphs. See?

Frankly, at the moment, I have no reason to do all of these things.

But who knows? Show business being what it is . . . I might.

PITCHING THE PERSONALS

The hard sell: If comedian Bill Cosby (top row, left) could pitch string beans and gelatin desserts, why not Texas Instruments home computers? Former talk show host Dick Cavett (middle) never admitted to computer expertise, just a love of Apples. Kaypro's commercial about the pitfalls of system pricing (bottom) drew praise and awards for its satirical thrust. IBM licensed the Little Tramp character (above) from the estate of Charlie Chaplain to make its personal computers appealing.

COMPUTER GRAPHICS

You ain't seen nothin' yet!
by *Robert de Marrais*

New Mona, a computerized interactive masterpiece.

I am sitting in a dark room, next to a U-shaped table. At work in the hollow of the U is Rob Haimes, coordinator of M.I.T.'s Visible Language Workshop. To his left is a computer terminal with keyboard and high-resolution video monitor; to his right, a digitizing tablet that creates images on the screen when navigated Ouija-fashion by an elaborate rolling "mouse" controller. Above the tablet is a "menu screen" TV, hooked up with the terminal and mouse, and straight ahead is a button-studded joystick control box.

"Which will it be?" Rob asks.

I have three choices. A quick trip through the Page Layout system convinces me that it can do paste-up and mechanicals for books or magazines; it can even do "greeking," that preliminary laying out of textless "filler" print in a specified type style. Page Management is the second choice: once you have a printable page, you want to fit it into a publishable text; this system allows for thirty-two finished pages plus thirty-two pages of "scratch space" for alternate layouts.

I decide to take an in-depth tour of option three: Graphics Tools. It takes a couple of seconds for the picture to emerge, then da Vinci's favorite model,

Mona Lisa, smiles pleasantly on the screen. The illusion convinces, and for good reason. As Rob points out, each image is 512 dots square, and each dot, or pixel, is 24 bits of color deep. This means you can mix up to 16 million different shades and hues, allowing for virtually limitless variation of opacity.

To show me how easy it is to get the hang of things ("It takes about two hours to get used to physically," I'm assured), Rob casually throws graphics "windows" over Mona's face, lifting off clones of her eyes, nose and cleavage, and idly strewing bouquets of anatomy in sinuously overlaid streaks that quickly heap up to form a "Mona totem pole." Then, jockeying levels of transparency while he shifts background colors and gray scales, Rob dips down for some dot-by-dot foraging to snag the subtler colorations. Transferring these to charcoal sticks, he starts smudging up Mona's hands until they take on a granular "dishpan" consistency.

My astonishment at the speed and beauty—and apparent nonchalance—of constructing the "totem pole" must be obvious because now Rob decides to one-up himself and modularize it. In an instant, Mona's upper face is peering down on a Gothic archway of totem-pole pillars. A few more sequences of ghost-image pullout and color infusion, and I'm nearly beside myself: "Stop, that's exquisite! Can you print it?"

"Well, let's name it first," Rob suggests. He pulls two different typefaces from disk and wields them to print *New Mona* in the upper left.

Computer-Assisted Imaging

The system Rob uses was built for about $1 million, though it could be rebuilt now at perhaps a fifth that cost. Two of its main programmers have left to set up their own company to mass-produce facsimiles of the system for as low as $50,000.

Such sophisticated equipment is at the heart of the computerized graphics revolution spreading throughout industrial applications. With computer-assisted design (CAD) you can use a computer screen as a faster-than-thou draftsman's table, assembling dots, lines and surfaces with electronic ease. Cut-and-paste, the old nemesis of industrial designers, architects and art directors, is suddenly obsolete thanks to the computer's graphics editing ability. In computer-assisted manufacture (CAM), the computer can simulate and test the inner workings of complicated machine assemblies or electronic circuits, then actually produce final production drawings, plans or blueprints.

Already, CAD/CAM computer graphics can be viewed outside the computer labs on six-figure work stations in high-level industrial design shops. A consortium of architects, for example, planning plumbing, wiring and material stress-and-strain patterns for a

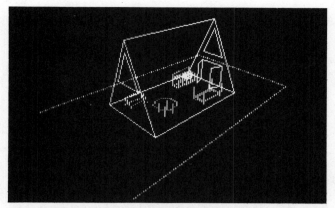

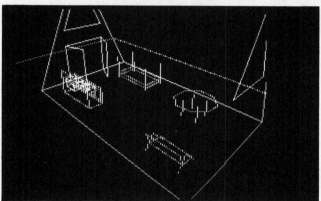

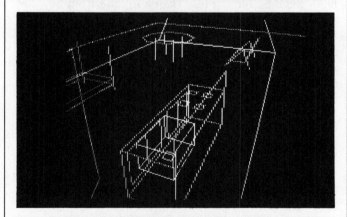

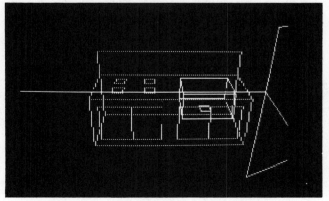

Paul Lutus wrote the Apple World graphics program so he could design his new A-frame's interior, including the kitchen sink.

The MovieMaker program by Interactive Picture Systems allows animation on home computers rivaling $50,000 graphics terminals.

new factory or building, can create an image of the complex bit by modularized bit on-screen. Or maybe a robotics team will employ CAD/CAM to duplicate the grip and many movements of the hundreds of interconnected components that make up the human hand.

Common to all these design systems—and to the ones you'll be buying less than a decade from now for your kids at Christmas—are levels of progressively more sensual capacities. Most unlike day-to-day vision (unless you're a mild-mannered reporter from the *Daily Planet*) is their ability to perceive and surgically operate on nested levels of structuring. Mobile "x-ray windows" of variable size can be shifted across your monitor surface as fast as you can move a stylus across a digitizing tablet. As they pass over a structure, the windows peel back one or more layers of imagistic "skin" and let you probe and poke within to play with the tinkertoy-like skeleton of "wire-frame" drawings that support these gossamer solids. Complementary to this, you can build up from the most simple graphic primitives, combining, excising, transplanting or cloning lines and surfaces with virtual instantaneity, to create highly stratified "real" objects.

In one display seen on a monitor at Computer-Vision, a pioneering graphics firm, the sun rises over an architectural model of a factory (guts viewable through x-ray windows, from different approaches, speeds and angles) in what could pass for a Technicolor movie sequence. As the day progresses, shadows shift and shorten, disappearing at noon, lengthening again until dusk; when the sun sets, the streetlights come on, casting shadows of their own.

All of which points to the most sensual capacity of such sophisticated screen shows: the vivid depiction of texture, color and optical subtleties like "specularity" (e.g., the highlight glints on shiny surfaces). Iron-

ically, it is these "secondary qualities," the most sought out in advanced design work, that were dismissed by Galileo and his contemporary Scientific Revolutionaries as "subjective."

But more than this, the new graphics allow for an unprecedented, nonformalist style of mental work—one that can result in radical economies of thought. Watching Larry Hare, a top programmer at ComputerVision, show off his latest creations, I noticed a recurring 3-D logo-like motif in a doorknob shape at the top center of the screen. As Larry flitted through his spur-of-the-moment noodlings, the multicolored mosaic went through subtle changes in hue and edge relationship. Larry explained that this was his "debugging program": instead of sorting through pages of tedious abstract code to track down errors after the fact, his trained eye can keep tabs on the color shifts of his jigsaw mandala and instantly detect any "glitches" in his program work. "Once you've been doing graphics for a while," he added, "nothing less immediate will ever satisfy you."

Graphics Come Home

How frustrating for home computer owners that such marvelous graphics capabilities are not yet accessible. "Studio shoot" rearrangement, for example, conjures up notions of an interior decorating revolution, the ultimate software answer to "How would that couch look in the parlor?" questions. As for the chance to mix colors and textures without easels, pigments or collagist's scissors, the creative possibilities seem endless—and beyond reach.

Despair, however, is inappropriate. Multiple x-ray window graphics can already be created on the screen of the Apple Macintosh (though only in black and white, since color takes a lot more memory). As for remodeling your living room, take a look at Paul Lutus' classic Apple World program, written when its rustic author wanted to do some sweatless shuffling of the contents of his Oregon cabin. With the new video disk's ability to store full-resolution color images on LP-like platters, and with to-and-fro access between disk and home computer, the capacity for Lutus-style maneuvers with trunkfuls of furnishings is not far off.

For artwork pure and simple, the limitations of even top-of-the-line home computers can be side-stepped to a startling extent thanks to some recent off-the-shelf software packages. A major break-through came in 1982 with a trio of floppy disks from Mark Pelczarski's Penguin Software. The Graphic Magician is aimed at programmers who want to put professional-quality graphics into their own programming efforts and allows for the combination of up to thirty-two independent multicolored shapes: just draw them, and give them starting points and paths, and the software does the rest—letting you control animated objects with a joystick.

Penguin's Complete Graphics System II and Special Effects are aimed at artistically inclined nonprogrammers. One reviewer pointed out that with the latter program, which costs only $39.95, "the Apple computer comes very close to emulating mainframe computer graphics systems costing as much as $250,000." When the two programs are used together, you can draw, edit and manipulate 3-D objects in perspective without having to calculate coordinates. You can also paint directly on-screen from a palette of 108 colors, using an array of 96 differently textured brushes—all with just a joystick or Apple Graphics Tablet. You can mix text with graphics and change fonts, type sizes, spacing. You can create "shape tables" of objects to be stored, retrieved, combined and changed at will. The video monitor quality resolution of a ComputerVision system is lacking, as are the enormous storage capacity and speed, but you probably don't need all this—and in any case you'll most likely have it by the late eighties.

Among other innovations in home computer graphics is Movie Maker, a simple animation package for Apples, Ataris and Commodore 64s. Developed by Interactive Picture Systems (IPS), the program allows you to create moving figures and backgrounds shape by shape, then put them in motion to musical accompaniment. It may require some effort to master, but this software can produce smooth, colorful animation that would be the envy of sophisticated graphics terminals. Using Movie Maker's routines, IPS has also developed a dance program that allows you to block out and choreograph original dance sequences on your home computer screen.

We can only wonder where else tomorrow's supergraphics will take us as the sophisticated laboratory terminals relinquish their powers to smaller, less expensive machines. But with breakthroughs like easy graphics and simple animation, the CAD/CAM revolution is surely just a step away from our homes. ■

CREATING SCREEN IMAGES

Long before there were personal computers, graphics images were projected on laboratory cathode ray tubes (CRTs) of the kind found in oscilloscopes. You needed a computer to define the shape and a digital-to-analog converter to send signals to the CRT, moving its electron beam to a point plotted on x, y axes proportional to the amplitudes of its input signals. This process was called "stroke" or vector graphics, wherein a number of such points were joined up in connect-the-dots fashion.

Now that TV sets are ubiquitous, "raster scanning," the image-sweeping technique used in picture tubes, is standard fare for home computer monitors. Here the CRT beam is deflected in a weaving pattern that sweeps across the screen and down, the way your eyes move when you read successive lines in a book.

The signals sent by broadcasting stations to home television sets contain special synchronized pulses used by the TV circuitry to get in step with the transmission. These sweep-triggering beats come in horizontal and vertical varieties, and between them come the pulses that contain the actual video information. On a typical TV tube, this information takes up 512 lines, with up to twice that number of dots being defined on each.

Substitute "computer" for "broadcasting station," and you get the idea. With proper synchronization, requiring time chains, clocks, multiplexers and other hardware on a video circuit board, any point on the screen's x, y plane can be addressed and made to hold a dot. Each dot, or "pixel," remains visible for only an instant before its place is usurped by a new dot, by a clone of itself or by nothing at all. What you actually see is a grainy dot-matrix.

Pixels are typically addressible not as mere points, but as "stacks" made up of binary options on each level. A byte that is only three bits deep allows for two times two times two (eight) possible messages—enough to encode primitive color information since there is room for three primaries and their complements—plus, say, high and low intensity. An Atari computer (still the best graphics system you can buy for under $5,000 as I write this) allows for up to four colors simultaneously, plus eight levels of brightness for each.

In computerdom, "a picture is worth a thousand words" is an understatement. Addressing each of the tens of thousands of pixels on the screen thirty times each second consumes huge amounts of memory. Hence there's a need for tricks and shortcuts, some of which are standardized. The most familiar is the ASCII character set, the agreed-upon dot-matrix encoding of the standard alphanumerical characters found on your typewriter keys. And in the works is a convention known as NAPLPS (for North American Presentation Level Protocol Syntax and pronounced "naplips"). Already in use in Canada, NAPLPS allows vector graphics "building blocks," with specified colors, to be transmitted efficiently, rapidly and over long distances via modem hookups to telephone lines.

R. DE M.

COMPUTERS WHO DANCE

The new choreography by Rebecca Allen with Jane Nisselson

Throughout history we have expressed the need to create an entity that can assume human qualities and yet surpass our limitations. We expressed this need by creating artificial figures that personified an ideal: Galatea, for example, sculpted by Pygmalion and brought to life by Aphrodite. In such figures we project a perfected image of ourselves.

In the field of computer graphics, scientists began developing methods for graphically simulating real-world objects. And, of course, before too long the computer was used to generate a realistic model of the human figure. At the New York Institute of Technology's Computer Graphics Laboratory, we have described a three-dimensional mathematical model of a female figure. Like a living person, our figure can move and bend, performing dynamic actions and gestures. She is animated with the computer.

An example of our figure's physical capabilities can be seen in her role as Saint Catherine in the dance video production of *The Catherine Wheel*, directed and choreographed by Twyla Tharp. While working on the piece, Twyla visited our lab and saw my animation of the female figure. She approached me with the idea of a collaboration in which this figure would represent St. Catherine. Its premiere on PBS in the spring of 1983 marked the first time human and computer figures danced together for the public.

As St. Catherine, our computer dancer repre-

Rebecca Allen, producer of the animation, is a designer, director and researcher at the Computer Graphics Laboratory of the New York Institute of Technology. Jane Nisselson works with and writes about computer graphics systems at the Laboratory.

sents an ideal who offers spiritual guidance in the face of human shortcomings. Her image appears early in the performance, materializing shortly after an animated image of the "Catherine wheel" (a bladed torture device named after the martyred saint). Through her movement, she suggests "dance" and becomes an inspiration to the Leader, played by Sara Rudner. Later St. Catherine returns and teaches the Leader a dance theme that recurs throughout the performance. They dance together, in synchrony, and end in an outstretched position as the Catherine wheel reappears. Computer Catherine is seen, a last time, ascending a staircase: a symbolic gesture to calmly remind Sara of her unrelenting pursuit of excellence.

The Notion of Motion

How is it possible to make a series of images not only move in a human way, but dance? The analysis of human motion requires the study of actual human movement as well as physical structure. I began using animation and the technique of rotoscoping as a way of accurately modeling human motion in a stylized environment. Beginning with real actions, I would simplify its essence. This differs from conventional cartoon animation techniques, which typically build fictional actions in an exaggerated form.

The computer's capacity to make moving images from static key poses makes it an ideal tool for animation and motion analysis. Still images containing one of the many stages of an action can be transformed into a continuous movement such as walking, running or turning.

Depicting motion realistically requires a spatial

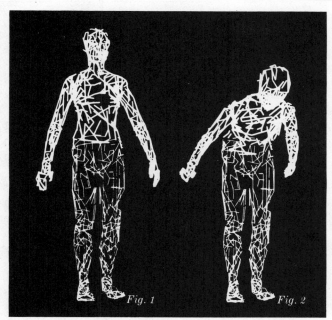

From keyframe to keyframe: computerized St. Catherine takes a bow.

context that is more sophisticated than the flat or two-dimensional space used in conventional animation. For instance, an object moving away from us appears to become smaller. A computer can calculate the correct appearance of objects as they move in space; this realistic perspective is important in accurately representing movement. Thus the computer is used as a means of analyzing human motion and as a medium in which to portray it.

Taking the First Step

For a computer-generated figure to take even one step requires an adequate animation system. The software for our system was developed over many years by a number of computer scientists at our laboratory. Using high-speed mainframe computers, they gradually fine-tuned the software into a unique system that enables us not only to move objects, but to generate complex motion for characters with articulated joints. Moving a figure or any of its parts in all directions gives us the means to create an illusion of life. The way a character moves defines emotions and personality.

St. Catherine was modeled by taking key points from photographs of a woman's body and entering them into the computer. Connecting these points, the computer composes rigid body parts linked by joints and arranged in a hierarchy, or tree structure. The figure is viewed as a wire-frame model on a real-time state-of-the-art display. Using a joystick, I can rotate, move or scale (change the size of) the figure or any of its parts. The model is like a marionette; the animator is a high-tech puppeteer who controls and positions the figure by manipulating a joystick.

This animation system can be illustrated by the simple example of making the figure bend forward at the waist, then return to an upright position. I begin with an image of the figure standing upright as the first "keyframe"—the first position of this movement (Fig. 1). Then I locate the waist joint and, using a joystick, rotate the upper half of the body to a bending position that becomes the second keyframe (Fig. 2). A keyframe of the figure standing upright ends the movement. This creates a three-keyframe sequence: standing, bending, then standing. After determining the length of time the movement should take, I run a program that generates all the "in-between" positions. The result is the smooth motion of a simple bow.

Using this system to generate realistic human motion requires complicated positioning of all body parts, e.g., the head, shoulders, elbows, wrists, fingers, into keyframes. The analysis of a dance is an intricate procedure, and a dance choreographed by Twyla presented an especially difficult challenge.

Learning to Dance

The choreography for the St. Catherine figure was based on the movements designed by Twyla for her dance company. We videotaped one of the dancers as a model of motion, and I studied individual frames of the tape to determine the key positions of particular movements. I then positioned each joint of the computer figure to correspond to the dancer's key positions. Twenty-five still frames were needed to generate each second of animation. I produced two to three keyframes for each second of motion, and from

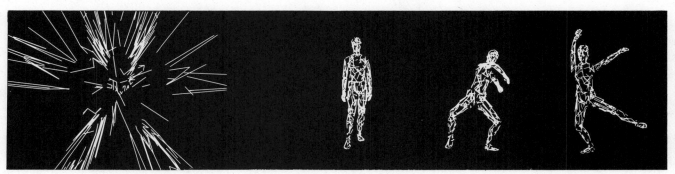

these the computer generated the rest.

The animated figure and the human dancer had different limits and freedoms, so we adapted the choreography for St. Catherine according to her technical restrictions. Twyla would show me the moves she wanted, and we would determine if they were technically possible. Overall, the computer dancer's movements were kept close to the physical range of a human dancer, with some movements extended slightly beyond human capabilities.

To make St. Catherine appear to dance naturally, we had to consider the physical world in which she moved. Building the illusion that the computer figure was dancing with Twyla's company demanded that she appear on the stage, in the same space as the live action. During live-action filming by a BBC crew, I recorded the position of the camera in relation to the dancers and then, with our animation system, matched my "simulated camera" to the real camera viewpoint so that Computer Catherine would appear to be in the actual space.

While my dancer had the freedom to move in ways that may not be considered physically accurate, I used the "personality" or style of this animation system to make motion that was believable but distinctive from that of the human dancers. Part of the challenge was finding creative ways to bring the two worlds together.

Sometimes it was the differences between the two dancers' worlds that provided a means to unite them. A human's movements are continuous, with each step leading directly into another. But the computer-drawn figure's movement is only an illusion created by a series of frames generated by the computer shown fast enough to appear as continuous motion. Each frame is an instant in time in which the computer dancer makes a movement. I could use the frames to change the timing and sequence of the dance steps. When first compositing the human and computer dancers, we discovered that Sara moved into a turn much faster than St. Catherine. By reanimating this section, I was able to reduce the number of frames in which the computer dancer made this turn. The animation system allowed me to synchronize St. Catherine's timing with Sara's so that their turns met in space.

Counterpoint

In many ways the animator and choreographer do the same thing. Both design movements that their performers then execute. But the method of creating a dance with human dancers is very different from that used to make the computer figure dance.

At the filming of the performance, the stage set was filled with the hustle and bustle of a live-action production. Twyla's dancers were rehearsing, the film crew was busily setting up, telephones rang and people were running out for lunch. This was very different from the atmosphere at the lab. Initially I worked with another researcher, Robert McDermott, to shape the data base for the body description, but once I began the animation my environment was isolated and internal. Typically I worked at night, when there were long stretches of uninterrupted time. Plugged into a Walkman, with the music for the dance blaring over my headphones, I would sit in a small, dark room, staring at a monitor. The figure would begin to dance as I used the joystick to "describe" to the computer which of the figure's limbs and joints should move and in what direction.

Like the choreographer, the animator directs the dancer's movements, but the image of the dancer must also be created. Certainly St. Catherine's appearance distinguished her as being from a world other than that of the rest of Twyla's company. Her figure is composed of lines in a way that gives a random, hand-drawn quality to a computer-generated image. I wanted to break away from a mechanically rendered appearance and typical style of computer-generated graphics. Also, eliminating a lot of information found in a detailed rendering helped to focus the imagery on the figure's movements.

Through her movement, Computer Catherine implicitly took on the form of a dancer. And as a dancer, she was able to perfect and share the essential elements of human movement that give it its expressive quality. But after all, in producing this animation, we were also bringing a knowledge of human movement and expression to the computer. Through this collaboration I was able to discover a new interpretation of the human form. ■

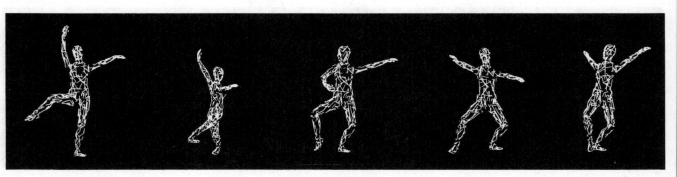

THE SOUND OF MICROS

Computers and music
by Robert A. Moog

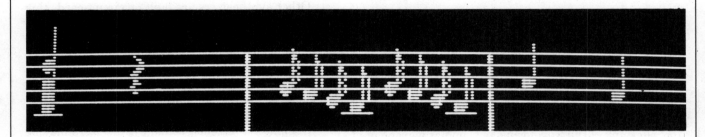

For some of us, the idea of an electronic muse is scary; after all, music is an essentially human activity, while electronic equipment, especially the computer, is "mechanical" and "unnatural." Throughout history, however, music has been closely linked to technology. Except for the human voice, the instruments of music-making have always been "high tech" in their time.

The Electronic Muse

The violin, pipe organ and trumpet are complex constructions that were as "unnatural" when they were first developed as the computer is today. The piano and saxophone, those vital elements of our musical experience, were triumphs of manufacturing technology a century ago. Musical instrument designers have always employed the most advanced technology of their time. Now, in our time, electronic and computer technologies are preferred for new musical instrument development.

But this is not to say that musicians are embracing electronics just because it's the "latest thing." As

Robert A. Moog is the inventor of the practical music synthesizer and president of Big Briar, Inc., a Leicester, North Carolina, firm specializing in the design of custom electronic instruments.

a group, musicians favor instruments that a) sound good and b) offer musically useful ways of manipulating sound. Increasingly, musicians are drawn to electronic instruments—not because they're easy to play or sound like traditional acoustic instruments, but because they offer new tone colors and new ways of making music.

What's more, musicians have been experimenting with electronic instruments ever since the vacuum tube was invented three-quarters of a century ago. Even before that, musicians and musical instrument builders were collaborating to harness the forerunners of electronics and computers to the service of the muse.

For a growing number of musicians, computer technology is the greatest advance since the invention of catgut. Music is a form of communication—of organizing and transmitting data. The "alphabet" of music consists of notes. Melodies, chords and rhythmic patterns are the "words" and "phrases" of music. Just as computers can generate "characters" to make text or a graphic design, they can also process a stream of numbers that represent a sound waveform. And just as word processing programs endear computers to wordsmiths, today's composers, performers and music teachers are all exploring the computer's ability to handle musical information.

If you understand the general principles of computer operation and if you like to listen to music, you'll have no trouble following the many ways that digital technology and computers can be used to make music. Just keep in mind that computer music is a natural extension of traditional music and uses programs that are only slightly different from your basic word processor or data handler. As we shall see, simulating a multitrack recording studio on your monitor screen is done with software that is directly related to the program used to "compose" this article.

Musical Digits

All sounds, musical or otherwise, are vibrations of the air, at rates of roughly 20 to 20,000 times a second. If the vibrations repeat regularly, the sounds are pitched (like a guitar or clarinet tone). If a sound vibration does not repeat regularly, then it sounds pitchless or "noisy" (like a cymbal crash). In a pitched sound, the rate of repetition is called its frequency; the greater the frequency, the higher the musical pitch of the tone. The strength of a vibration is called its amplitude; the greater a sound's amplitude, the louder it is.

The shape of a vibration is called the waveform. You can think of the waveform of a sound as a graph of the air pressure at a particular point over time. The waveform is an abstraction that we use to describe the sound. It happens to be an abstraction that has a lot to do with the tone's perceived quality.

A loudspeaker (speaker, for short) is a device that converts electronic vibrations into sound. In talking about electronic music and computers, we generally refer to electrical waveforms that exist inside an instrument's circuitry. When we refer to these waveforms as if they were sounds, we assume there's a speaker somewhere and that we're using it to produce the sounds.

A personal computer may contain its own small speaker (e.g., the Apple II), may use the speaker of the TV to which it is connected (e.g., the Atari or Commodore 64) or may require connection to an external sound system like most high-quality music synthesizers. Most electronic pianos, organs and synthesizers use "analog" circuits that produce smooth waveforms. Digital computer circuits, on the other hand, work by switching on and off.

How does a computer produce a musical tone? In most computers, you can turn the speaker on and off as if it were, say, a memory location. You can produce a tone by writing a simple program to a) turn the speaker current on, b) wait a very short time, c) turn the speaker off, d) wait again, and e) repeat the above steps a specified number of times. The waiting time determines the pitch of the tone, while the number of cycles of repetition determines its duration.

If the "speaker on" and "speaker off" times are the same, the resultant waveform is called a square wave and the musical quality is somewhat hollow, like that of a clarinet. If the "speaker on" and "speaker off" times are not the same, the waveform is called "rectangular" and the quality may be saxophone- or oboe-like. If the "speaker on" and "speaker off" times are programmed to change randomly, the resultant sound is a pitchless noise.

While any computer can produce square and rectangular waves, only those equipped with sound synthesizer circuits can produce more complex waveforms. Some sound synthesizers are built on single integrated circuit chips that can be progammed to produce a wide variety of waveforms and envelopes. (The envelope of a sound is its outline as it builds up, sustains and dies out.)

Other synthesizers are built on circuit cards that plug into the computer or may be completely separate peripherals. Computer programs enable musicians to design their own sounds. Musicians think of this type of programming as "building an instrument": the "instruments" exist as data that define waveforms and envelopes—and may therefore be stored in "libraries" on disk or tape.

Computer-controlled sound synthesizers may be all-digital (the waveform itself is generated from digital data), all-analog (waveforms are produced continuously by analog circuitry that responds to digital instructions) or a combination of the two (waveforms are converted from digital to analog form, then passed through analog circuitry). Digital circuits that produce waveforms handle numbers that represent a succession of points along a waveform. Analog circuits, on the other hand, handle voltages that change continuously to generate the desired waveform.

Digital circuits are more accurate and reliable than their analog counterparts. Since they produce waveforms from a series of numbers in time, however, the resultant waveforms are made up of steps that are often audible. Both methods of synthesis have their advantages and limitations; some musicians prefer the smooth, distortion-free analog waveforms, while others favor the accuracy and versatility of digital generators.

Playing the PC

There are simple programs for most personal computers to make scales and melodies through the computer's speaker. To use a typical progam of this kind, you type in codes for the pitches and durations of the notes.

More sophisticated programs enable you to vary the rectangular wave tone color, adjust the overall tempo, produce trills and glides, and store tunes that you have programmed on disk or cassette tape. Music Maker, a software package for the Apple II, produces the illusion of two notes being played simultaneously,

Herbie Hancock on the road with computer and clavier.

THE MUSICIAN/MACHINE CONNECTION

When I use a computer to make music, it's as if I have a partner—one that acts in a very logical way and appears to function like a human brain. The interaction causes a strange relationship. The computer gives me answers quickly and makes no mistakes. If I give it data that doesn't fit into what it can do, I say: "It doesn't like that." Or when it pauses, I tell myself: "It's thinking." There is definitely an intellectual challenge to make the computer do what I want. I have to communicate with it in a very specific way.

I use a Fairlight computer to create sounds I can't get any other way. I can digitize sounds from actual instruments and then modify their waveforms on the screen with a light pen. This doesn't mean I intend to turn my back on traditional acoustic instruments. I'll continue to play acoustic as well as electronic keyboards, because every instrument has its own touch, texture and nuance. It's just that synthesizers and computers are tools for making instruments the likes of which have never been heard before.

Some keyboard players are great performers on a synthesizer, but they don't know much about programming it. Others are good players *and* programmers. Thinking in musical terms can help develop your technique for programming computers. A musician thinks in terms of measures and themes; in programming you have to consider lines of code and routines. Of course, having manual dexterity also helps, since a prerequisite for using today's computers is the ability to key in commands. Someday, though, you'll be able simply to talk to computers with voice recognition.

In the future I'd like to be able to create music on-line with anyone anywhere in the world. Recently I saw a concert in Vancouver where the musician on stage was playing with two other people in Sydney and Tokyo. The only limitation was the speed of the electrons on-line—the speed of light. There was a slight delay in the audio, and the musicians had to take risks with their playing to stay in sync. But here they were, playing together on three continents! It made me look forward to the day when the electronic cottage will become an electronic bandstand.

HERBIE HANCOCK, creator of electronic keyboard albums including *Headhunters* and *Future Shock* generates sound effects as well as musical tones, and displays a colorful animated video pattern in time with the music. Programs like Music Maker don't produce complex or high-quality musical tones; their main uses are educational and recreational—you can learn a good deal about programming, train your ear and have a lot of fun, for a very small investment in addition to your computer.

By using a computer with a built-in sound synthesizer, or adding a digitally controlled synthesizer peripheral, you can make music with a wide variety of interesting tone colors. The Commodore 64 has one of the most versatile built-in synthesizers of any currently available personal computer. The "64" uses a proprietary chip that produces three tones with programmable waveform and envelope. The chip also contains an analog filter, a device that changes the tone color by emphasizing some of the sound's overtones and cutting out others. The resulting range and quality of sound rival that of some of the analog keyboard synthesizers available in musical instrument stores.

Some of the most musically advanced computer programs are designed around the Mountain Computer Musicsystem, an eight-voice digital tone generator for the Apple II. Among the more popular are the Alpha Syntauri and the Soundchaser systems. Both use the Musicsystem in combination with a professional-style four- or five-octave music keyboard and their own operating software.

With either of these systems you can make up your own sounds, play them from the music keyboard and record the keyboard performance. Since one part of the software sets the Musicsystem up to produce the desired tone colors and another part captures and stores the keyboard performance, you can play back your keyboard performance with a variety of tone colors, pitch ranges and speeds. Both the Alpha Syntauri and the Soundchaser can implement the basic functions of a multitrack recording studio. You can record a keyboard performance on one "track," then play that track back while recording subsequent tracks. The Syntauri Metatrak program, for instance, lets you record up to sixteen tracks, then play them back simultaneously. Fast Forward, Rewind, Record and Erase functions are implemented by typing one or two characters on the computer keyboard.

To a musician, using Metatrack (or the Soundchaser Turbotracks program) is closely akin to using a conventional tape recorder. To the average computer user, programs that implement a multitrack recorder are actually file management systems with real-time merging capability. Whichever way you look at it, Metatrak, Turbotracks and related programs offer potent musical resources to pro musicians—and a lot of musical enjoyment to amateurs.

In addition to simulating multitrack recorders, computer-based music systems offer other functions that are important to musicians. Music-teaching programs are available for both the Soundchaser and the Alpha Syntauri. Soundchaser's Musictutor package contains an array of ear-training exercises that not only sharpen your ears, but keep track of your learning progress. Syntauri's Simply Music program will teach you how to play a keyboard instrument in a variety of styles and at a pace that suits you. Once your keyboard chops are in good shape, you can convert your keyboard performances directly to a printed score with Syntauri's Composer's Assistant, a software package that enables a dot-matrix printer to produce conventional music notation.

Computer Control

The Roland Compumusic CMU-800R is an example of an analog musical sound generator designed for computer control. The Compumusic uses electronic piano, organ and synthesizer circuits to produce realistic percussion, bass, "rhythm" guitar and melody voices through your sound system. Using Roland-supplied software, you program the melody, harmony and rhythm from the computer keyboard. Then you "mix" the sounds by manipulating the volume sliders on the Compumusic unit while the computer "plays" the complete piece of music that you've programmed. The computer is not able to program the Compumusic waveforms since these are determined by the unit's analog circuitry. The advantages of Compumusic are in its high sound quality and hands-on-the-knobs control.

Musicians have expressed the desire to control a regular electronic keyboard by means of a computer. An increasing number of electronic pianos, organs and synthesizers are being adapted for computer control. For this purpose, the musical instrument industry has developed an interface called MIDI, the Musical Instrument Digital Interface. MIDI allows electronic instruments, computers and similar devices to be connected with a minimum of fuss. This means that, if your computer itself is equipped with a MIDI peripheral and the necessary software, you can use your computer to control any MIDI-equipped electronic musical instrument. You can even combine instruments into a computer-controlled "orchestra."

Will computers ever completely replace human musicians? A number of traditional instrumentalists, upon seeing entire string and horn sections replaced by synthesizers and other digital instruments, have asked this question. The answer lies in the fact that music is and always will be an aesthetic and emotional experience for humans and not for computers. There will always be musicians as long as there is a song in our hearts. ∎

DIGITAL KEYBOARD INSTRUMENTS

Digital computers are like farmers' tractors. A tractor is a source of mechanical power, with a few levers to control that power; it's nearly always used with specialized implements that may be simple (like a plowshare) or larger and more complex than the tractor itself.

A computer is a source of number processing power. Its own levers (the keyboard) give access to the power within. But it is the peripherals, like printers or digitally controlled synthesizers, that convert the computing power to some form of information or useful action.

To understand the difference between a personal computer with a digitally controlled synthesizer peripheral and a digital keyboard instrument available in music stores, let's carry our tractor analogy a little further. Many implements contain their own sources of power and perform their functions without being hooked to a tractor (examples range from lawnmowers to fifty-ton bulldozers). In these implements, built-in power is more efficient and convenient than separating the source of power from the specialized mechanical function that gets the job done.

Digital keyboard instruments are the musical counterparts to implements with dedicated power sources. At the heart of any digital keyboard is a specialized computer that is preprogrammed to perform a limited set of functions. The computer controls a digital synthesizer that actually produces the instrument's sounds. Although technically they are separate entities, computer and digital synthesizer are often built together and both are located inside the instrument. The player accesses the computer and plays the instrument by manipulating the panel controls and depressing keys.

Digital keyboard instruments come in all sizes. The smallest ones are portable, inexpensive and fun-oriented—our folk instruments of the eighties. Most have built-in drum rhythms, and can remember and play back what you play on the keyboard. Some of the larger ones are complete home music centers that read the music, then play one part while you play the other, or teach you how to read music and play the keyboard. Others, designed for professional musicians, have a wide variety of rich tone colors, touch-sensitive keyboards and performance-oriented functions. The best of them produce accurate simulations of strings, acoustic piano and guitar, and electronic musical sounds of extremely high sonic quality.

Up in the performance-price stratosphere are the "computer musical instruments"—large studio instruments controlled by full-blown dedicated computers. These instruments offer the state of the art in digital sound production and control. The Fairlight, for instance, records or synthesizes virtually any musical sound, then allows the musician to "play" the sound back at any pitch, either from its touch-sensitive music keyboard or from one of two special composing languages. The Synclavier, another superinstrument, is

Robert Moog, sire of the music synthesizer.

designed to develop sonically rich timbres by adding together "partial waveforms."

With any of these superinstruments, a musician working in a studio can start at synthesis of the sounds and end with a complete multipart piece of music. This is why the superinstruments have found extensive use in film, TV and commercial music production houses.

But are the superinstruments the ultimate computer musical instrument? Not by a long shot. Scientists and musicians at Lucasfilm have developed a multimillion-dollar system called the Lucasfilm Audio Signal Processor. The ASP is a completely digital recording studio, musical sound producer and film synchronizing facility all in one. In place of the time-consuming film sound editing and mixing traditionally done "by hand" to get music, dialog and sound effects into a movie or TV program, the ASP enables musicians and film sound people to computerize all aspects of sound track production.

Digital technology is entering every area of music and sound production. As digital audio disks and tapes become commonplace, we can look forward to hearing the highest quality of reproduced sound in our homes—sound that is limited in quality only by the loudspeaker itself. The promise for digital musical instruments is equally bright: warm, rich timbres, vast creative potential, exciting interactive computer-aided teaching and performing modes.

At the rate digital technology is advancing, musical instrument designers will soon have to deal with the same situation that digital audio engineers now face: the quality of state-of-the-art digital musical instruments will be determined not by the sophistication of the electronics within the instruments, but by how much the instruments' electromechanical components (loudspeakers, keyboards, control, switches and so forth) can be improved. The traditional skills of building vibrating structures, smooth-acting keyboards and all the other things associated with fine musical instruments are by no means dormant. They have been given new life and vitality through digital electronics.

R.A.M.

MOTHER NATURE GOES DIGITAL

by Irv Teibel

A good deal of the progress of civilization over the centuries has been a function of gaining control over natural processes so they can be used when we need them. Some examples are windmills, the internal combustion engine, atomic power and Donkey Kong.

In 1968, with the help of a computer, I made a modest contribution to this august confluence of imaginative derring-do by putting the true sound of the ocean on a phonograph record. At the time I often played chess with a genius friend whose profession of the moment was psychoacoustics, an arcane science seemingly focused on band-aid fixes of airport noise and improving intelligibility of telephonic transmissions. One night he happened to mention some reading he'd done on Hermann Ludwig Ferdinand von Helmholtz, a nineteenth-century German scientist who felt that natural sounds—the ocean, wind, rain and other mundane sonic occurrences—could have great psychological benefits if only some means of accurate reproduction could be found.

It happened that I had just returned from a wintry sojourn at Brighton Beach, where I had made a brief recording of ocean waves for the sound track of a friend's underground film, and this casual mention of Helmholtz' musings triggered a "what-if" that was to have a profound effect on the next decade of my life.

Waveforms

The problem with reproducing nature by means of microphones and a tape recorder is, simply put, a combination of inaccuracies. Recording technique is at best an art and hardly perfection. Since most recordings are of the human voice and musical instruments, people are willing to "fill in the spaces" with their imagination, even though the reproduction hardly ever matches the sound of real-life occurrences.

Irv Teibel, creator of the Environments series of psychoacoustically based audio recordings, owns an Apple II and two used Cadillacs.

The ultimate ocean on vinyl.

Since distortion is inherent in each element in the chain of acoustic reproduction, the net product is a result of compromises that may be pleasing but are seldom accurate. The first problem is that the sounds of nature are not merely a specific set of frequencies, such as the human voice or a particular musical instrument, but are often a form of "noise" that contains hundreds if not thousands of specific frequencies, all of which contribute to the makeup of the particular sound. The second problem is that of reference: hardly anyone has heard Mick Jagger without a microphone, but almost everyone has heard a rainstorm or the sibilant expiration of an ocean wave and knows what the real sound should be.

Into this maelstrom of inaccuracy I plunged with my trusty Uher portable stereo reel-to-reel tape recorder and a tangle of microphones and cables. But the inaccuracies of my highly regarded professional equipment continued to prevail, and nearly a year later I had produced a hundred stereo recordings not one of which actually sounded, to my mind's ear, like the ocean I wanted to hear.

Synthesized Surf

I had a number of friends who were actively involved in the arcane rites of computerdom, and one of them took particular delight in hearing of my analog recording travails. "Digitalize, my friend!" he was wont to say. "Bring your ocean to me, and I'll save you grief."

Well, since I had a shelf full of bad tapes, who was I to argue with destiny? This fellow had worked in a famous East Coast lab for several years, developing a proprietary speech synthesis program for the phone company. His program broke down spoken words into microsecond increments, analyzed each segment digitally and created new words by applying a mathematical formula based on various parameters of human speech. Quite frankly, I doubted if anything would come of our experiment. But I love computer rooms, and his was near state-of-the-art (at least by late sixties standards): an IBM 360 with all the bells and whistles.

We started with a loop from my Brighton Beach tape, which was only a few minutes long. This proved ideal for the computer, since the program we were using limited broadband audio input to approximately two minutes. The first few tries yielded little more than noise from the monitor speakers as we adjusted such technical niceties as I/O parameters, dynamic range and a random number generator to interface with selected waveforms.

With the hands of the wall clock well past midnight, it seemed apparent that nothing would come of this quixotic venture. Then suddenly we both grew still and listened attentively to the output of the monitor speakers. Rolling out through the grille cloth was a beautiful, tranquil ocean sound I had never heard before. The splice on the loop we were using for input could not be detected, as an electronic random noise generator reprogrammed the waveform parameters with each cycle and created subtle new waves that never repeated. By adjusting bandwidth constraints, we got the sound to grow more and more realistic until what we heard was a serenely majestic ocean sound complete with bubbling surf and a faintly perceived, eerily synthesized foghorn.

By this time it was near dawn, so we decided to pack it in for the day. The next night I brought a variable speed instrumentation-type recorder, and we improvised a delay to simulate variable stereo separation by subtly shifting from left to right on a continous basis to eliminate "windowing" of the channels. After a few experiments we found that, by adjusting input and output tape machines to a very slow speed, our tape was able to track the signal almost exactly. At this speed, recording a tape for half-hour playback would take eight hours of computer time, so we set everything up, punched the record button and spent the rest of the night drinking coffee and munching greasy hamburgers at an all-night diner.

By dawn, when we signed back in, the tape had run out. We rewound and sat back. Not only was the recording superior to anything I'd ever done "in situ," but it had such an astonishing bandwidth and dynamic range that it could be played at different speeds and still sound exactly like a "perfect" ocean in completely convincing stereo. We had, it seemed, created the first digitally produced broadband recording.

Roll-Out

I took copies of the tape, which I had jokingly titled *The Psychologically Ultimate Seashore*, to a psychol-

ogy professor out on Long Island. I wanted him to try them out on his graduate students as a potential aid to concentration and relaxation. A week later I got a call from him. He had done double-blind testing during sleep research and found that the subjects had had quite vivid dreams after listening to the tapes. Many of the subjects had reported that they felt unusually refreshed upon awakening. In addition, experiments utilizing difficult reading matter had shown that comprehension and reading speed in some instances had doubled when the ocean was played in the background. More importantly, the participants had actually been upset when the tape ended, and a few had even pleaded for copies for their personal use.

Several months later Environments Disc One had been hastily packaged, complete with comments on the back of the jacket detailing the computer synthesis, the glowing reports of the test subjects and instructions on how to play the record. A test market at the Harvard Coop had been arranged, and the ocean outsold the Beatles, especially at exam time. Articles appeared in *Newsweek* and the New York *Times*, comparing the record's effects to those of soma, Aldous Huxley's imaginary drug described in *Brave New World*.

My obsession had become reality and a new form of recorded sound had been born via computer. I sold the rights to Environments Disc One to Atlantic Records and retired for a while. Mother nature had been digitalized.   ∎

Irv Teibel enjoys nature electronically.

THE VIDEO DISK CONNECTION

by Martin Porter

For a microcomputer system to come close to crossing the line between illusion and reality, something has to be added to put more detail into the monitor's picture. That something is the video disk, with its unrivaled picture quality and storage capacity.

First introduced as a passive movie-playing device that could bring the "magic" of *The Godfather* and *Star Wars* into our living rooms, the video disk's greatest potential was always as a picture storage medium "intelligently" controlled by a computer or providing data to the computer for its own purposes. One video disk, for example, can contain as much information as six thousand floppy disks.

The instant access made possible by the computer/video disk connection also allows the user to add a new dimension to traditional story lines. Any program can be accessed in a variety of ways, allowing "readers" to express their individual preferences and satisfy their personal needs. Thousands of individual frames and hundreds of different scenes can be called up at a whim and the touch of the right keys. Thus the computer and video disk allow people to talk back to their once authoritarian television sets, expressing free will and injecting discretion into program material that previously could only be linear in order and passive in use. The possibilities for interactive narratives, tutorials and environments are just becoming evident.

For an integrated computer/video disk system, you need three ingredients: a personal computer with some sort of interface port, an interface circuit and an interactive disk player. The video disk/computer millennium, delayed by lack of standardization in interface circuitry and the high cost of first-generation video disk players, is now at hand. The demise of RCA's inexpensive SelectaVision players may have hastened the process by leaving the way open for Pi-

Martin Porter is a contributing editor for PCjr. *He also writes on video, computers and popular music for* Gentleman's Quarterly, PC, Rolling Stone *and the* New York Post.

oneer's more versatile (and more expensive) laser disk format.

Up from the Arcades

The average consumer's first exposure to the potential of video disk/computer interaction has been in the video arcades. In 1983 Dragon's Lair, an action-packed adventure game with animated cartoon-style graphics, became the first video disk arcade game. Despite its annoying delay between scenes, it became an arcade hit and Coleco licensed the game as the first video disk offering for their home computers.

In rapid succession, improved video disk-based games made their appearance in the arcades. Such pioneering efforts as M.A.C.H. 3 and Firefox showed the possibilities of combining computer-generated graphics with "live-action" sequences read from video disk without delay between scenes. National Football League Films, long a leader in home video distribution, has introduced an arcade football game on an interactive video disk using taped footage of over two hundred plays in a head-to-head encounter between the San Diego Chargers and Los Angeles Raiders.

The quality of video disk imagery lends itself to realistic simulations of any real-life situation, whether current events or ancient history. By allowing players to wend their way through such situations, video games can be educational as well as entertaining.

Interactive Information

The future of the computer/video disk interface as an informational tool was hinted at as far back as 1977, when a team of programmers and artists from M.I.T. created the Aspen Movie Map. With this disk, you find yourself driving on a main street of Aspen, Colorado, taking detours at any intersection by touching an arrow on the monitor screen. If you want to know more about an intriguing landmark, you place your finger on the building on-screen; instantly you are inside and

COME TO YOUR SENSES!

A visit to Washington's National Gallery of Art at the push of a button and a spin of VPI's video disk.

From day one, young children absorb knowledge via their eyes and ears. By age three, they have become marvelous parallel processors of visual and sound data, connecting the meanings and relationships of many simultaneous happenings. If you want to know just how marvelous, compare a three-year-old's capacity for recognition and reaction with that of a fancy, high-priced robot. There is no contest!

So what do we do with our precious, parallel-processing preschoolers? We send them to school, and for the next twelve years or more we drone at them with serial information: text out of books, classroom step-by-step presentations, etc., etc. Now, there is obviously no way around learning the three Rs. But that doesn't mean we have to force our kids to stop using the learning method of which they are already sophisticated practitioners. We do show them illustrations of paintings, historical scenes; we do use diagrams, sketches and so on to illustrate science subjects. But what ties all these pictures together? Serial information again: words, words, words!

If you were taking American History II, which approach would bring home more vividly just what Benjamin Franklin was doing in Paris to help us toward independence: fifteen pages in your textbook or a three-minute visual reenactment of Franklin practicing his magic charm on the court of France? This is the classic case of parallel, multilevel processing of new information vs. trying to internalize the same body of facts via serial data absorption.

The message is clear: involving all the faculties simultaneously through active imagery and sound is the only way to communicate if you want rapid, efficient information transfer—and interactivity. Interactivity is the cement that makes it all stick better on an individual level. Interactivity means getting involved in more than viewing and absorbing by viewing; it means reinforcing the learning process by putting to work the information you've just been exposed to.

What I'm describing here, namely, interactive programs using copious high-quality video graphics under computer control, cannot be possible on a wide scale unless the video disk/home computer connection is promoted. The high-priced experimental interactive systems in labs like M.I.T.'s Architecture Machine Group, and the simple-minded video disk arcade games like Dragon's Lair, will have to give way to affordable home interactive video disk and educational systems.

The technical prerequisites for an effective video disk/home computer connection include: synchronization of the video disk delivery system with that of the computer-generated graphics; keying computer-generated graphics over the disk's video information; downloading data from the video disk into the computer, either periodically or in real time; handling the disk player functions PLAY, STOP, SEARCH, etc., under program or keyboard control. All these technical points have been addressed in interface hardware and software that will make possible the video disk/home computer connection.

On the horizon is a revolution in how Americans (and others) will learn, train and play at home. Continuing education, professional enhancement and certification training will be radically affected by interactive video technology. Most important, however, is the prospect of broad-based elementary and high school learning in which a substantial part of both classroom and home reading activities are replaced by interactive video systems affordable to all.

RALPH BAER, manager of consumer product development, Sanders Associates

listening to a sound track explain pertinent details about the edifice. If you want to see how a street corner looks at night, you can so instruct the screen and presto-chango: pitch dark. To avoid getting lost, you can request your location on a detailed city map. You can also access specific attractions from a map menu and wander the streets of the metropolis, enjoying (for example) the treasures of a world-renowned museum without leaving your armchair.

Picture This

The Simutron Tournament Center in San Diego is the first facility devoted exclusively to the potential of computer/video disk interface for entertainment environments. Players rent time on a Simutron system for $3 per fifteen minutes of play, then enter the gaming area through an airlock. Seating themselves in a darkened, soundproof cockpit, they face four color video monitors, experience the ambience of quadrophonic surround sound and grasp a professional-grade joystick. The game that unfolds is the video disk version of the movie *Star Trek* adapted for computer game play. Utilizing the special effects from this box-office blockbuster (i.e., time-warp drives, intergalactic explosions, digitally recorded sound), the game challenges players to pit their wits against the master computer or against any of eight opponents also playing at the Simutron center. This is the first of a series of video disk–enhanced computer games that will also include footage from the science-fantasy movies *Tron* and *Excalibur*.

One of the most extensive uses of the video disk/computer connection is suitably at Walt Disney's Environmental Prototype Community of Tomorrow (EPCOT) in Orlando, Florida. Scattered through the 250-acre complex are thirty Worldkey kiosks, designed jointly by Disney and Bell Labs, that serve as information guides to the park and its attractions. A finger planted on the video screen activates the animation, which features a character named Bit reciting a monologue about EPCOT and its wonders. If you want to learn more about the Journey into Imagination or any other structure at EPCOT, just touch the building on the screen as it scrolls by and the picture immediately switches to a segment detailing that attraction, inside and out.

Round and Round

Now picture a chemistry professor on-screen, instructing his video class in the mixture of two highly lethal chemicals. The students can actually see the proper way of pouring, the correct amounts and the color of the chemicals. This is one of many educational video disk/computer lessons that are being developed at the University of Nebraska, under the direction of Rod

THE DIGITAL AUDIO DISK

Thanks to microchip accuracy, home listeners can now enjoy audio quality never before heard outside the concert hall. On the verge of replacing turntables and LPs, the new digital players can transform signals from laser-encoded compact disks (CDs) into full-blown orchestras or blown-out rock bands with none of the snaps, crackles and pops generally associated with analog sound.

The original music is "sampled" by computer and converted into a binary digital code consisting of two forms of information: the proverbial 1 or 0, or in this case "pits" or "no pits" on the surface of the disk. The currently prevailing playback system utilizes a laser that samples 44,100 of these tiny indentations per second and converts them into a code of 16 binary digits (over 1,400,000 bits per second). Computer control speed and laser accuracy are partners in the scheme that requires fifteen billion "pits" of information for one hour of music. The laser beam measures 1.7 microns wide and is so precise that nothing but a "pit" can cause the deviation required to make digital sound.

Compact disk players are a true product of the digital age for reasons other than sonic quality. These new music boxes can repeat or locate any selection at the flick of a preprogrammed switch, and no longer will we have to flip the record (all the information is stored on one side of the 4¾-inch disk). In addition, while a digital readout on the front plate keeps us up to date on the program's status (what track is being played, how much playing time remains, etc.), the CD can be played endlessly without wear.

M.P.

Daynes. The team has developed over fifty programs for government and private industry clients by interfacing a Radio Shack TRS-80 with a Pioneer industrial disk player.

Personal computer and video disk applications are becoming so intertwined that the two technologies will no longer be seen as peripheral to each other. Even now, a disk is being developed that will record and play back video, audio and computer information on the same surface. When this new technology becomes widely available, it will make possible that dream of consumer electronics enthusiasts, the integrated home entertainment center with interactive picture and sound.

The success of the video disk/computer connection then will depend on the creativity of a new generation of "writers" who will develop software applications that tap the creative potential of this technology. Unlike previous forms of expression, there will be no fixed formulas. The very appeal of these new machines will lie in their providing for alternatives to current artistic genres.   ∎

BRAIN FOOD

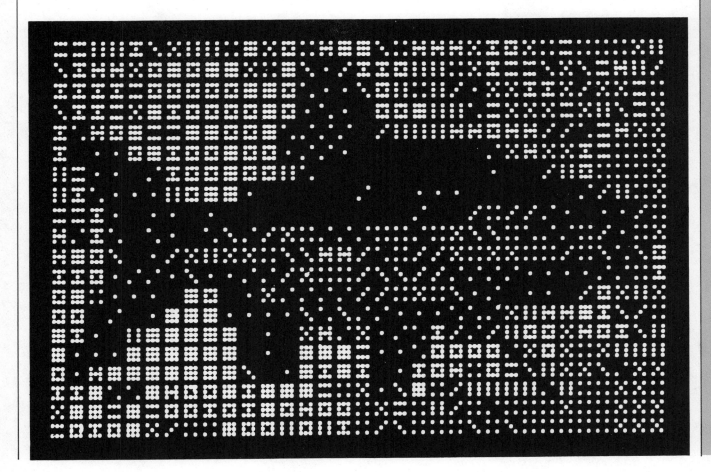

Artwork for preceding page

Artist:
   Lou Katz © 1984 Meron Studios
Computer:
   Cromemco Z2H personal computer
Software:
   DOMINATE by Ken Knowlton and Lou Katz
Input:
   CAT-100 digitizing camera controlled by Sol-20 personal computer

A BRIEF HISTORY OF ARTIFICIAL INTELLIGENCE

by Stephanie Haack

The quest for artificial intelligence is as modern as the frontiers of computer science and as old as Antiquity. The concept of a "thinking machine" began as early as 2500 B.C., when the Egyptians looked to talking statues for mystical advice. Sitting in the Cairo Museum is a bust of one of these gods, Re-Harmakis, whose neck reveals the secret of his genius: an

Stephanie Haack is director of communications for the Computer Museum in Boston.

opening at the nape just big enough to hold a priest.

Even Socrates sought the impartial arbitration of a "thinking machine." In 450 B.C. he told Euthypro, who in the name of piety was about to turn his father in for murder, "I want to know what is characteristic of piety . . . that I may have it to turn to, and to use as a standard whereby to judge your actions and those of other men."

Automata, the predecessors of today's robots,

date back to ancient Egyptian figurines with movable limbs like those found in Tutankhamen's tomb. Much later, in the fifteenth century A.D., drumming bears and dancing figures on clocks were the favorite automata, and game players such as Wolfgang von Kempelen's Maezel Chess Automaton reigned in the eighteenth century. (Kempelen's automaton proved to be a fake; a legless master chess player was hidden inside.) It took the invention of the Analytical Engine by Charles Babbage in 1833 to make artificial intelligence a real possibility. Babbage's associate, Lady Lovelace, realized the profound potential of this analyzing machine and reassured the public that it could do nothing it was not programmed to do.

Artificial intelligence (AI) as both a term and a science was coined 120 years later, after the operational digital computer had made its debut. In 1956 Allen Newell, J. C. Shaw and Herbert Simon introduced the first AI program, the Logic Theorist, to find the basic equations of logic as defined in *Principia Mathematica* by Bertrand Russell and Alfred North Whitehead. For one of the equations, Theorem 2.85, the Logic Theorist surpassed its inventors' expectations by finding a new and better proof.

Suddenly we had a true "thinking machine"— one that knew more than its programmers.

The Dartmouth Conference

An eclectic array of academic and corporate scientists viewed the demonstration of the Logic Theorist at what became the Dartmouth Summer Research Project on Artificial Intelligence. The attendance list read like a present-day *Who's Who* in the field: John McCarthy, creator of the popular AI programming language LISP and director of Stanford University's Artificial Intelligence Laboratory; Marvin Minsky,

leading AI researcher and Donner Professor of Science at M.I.T.; Claude Shannon, Nobel Prize-winning pioneer of information and AI theory, who was with Bell Laboratories.

By the end of the two-month conference, artificial intelligence had found its niche. Thinking machines and automata were looked upon as antiquated technologies. Researchers' expectations were grandiose, their predictions fantastic. "Within ten years a digital computer will be the world's chess champion," Allen Newell said in 1957, "unless the rules bar it from competition."

Isaac Asimov, writer, scholar and author of the Laws of Robotics, was among the wishful thinkers. Predicting that AI (for which he still used the term "cybernetics") would spark an intellectual revolution, in his foreword to *Thinking by Machine* by Pierre de Latil he wrote:

> Cybernetics is not merely another branch of science. It is an intellectual revolution that rivals in importance the earlier Industrial Revolution. Is it possible that just as a machine can take over the routine functions of human muscle, another can take over the routine uses of human mind? Cybernetics answers, yes.

Many people imagined that by the year 1984 computers would dominate our lives. Prof. N. W. Thring envisioned a world with household robots, and B. F. Skinner forecast that teaching machines would be commonplace. Arthur L. Samuel, a Dartmouth conference attendee from IBM, suggested that computers would be capable of learning, conversing and translating language; he also predicted that computers would house our libraries and compose most of our music.

Getting Smarter

Artificial intelligence research has progressed considerably since the Dartmouth conference, but the ultimate AI system has yet to be invented. The ideal AI computer would be able to simulate every aspect of learning so that its responses would be indistinguishable from those of humans.

Alan M. Turing, who as early as 1934 had theorized that machines could imitate thought, proposed a test for AI machines in his 1950 essay "Computing Machinery and Intelligence." The Turing Test calls for a panel of judges to review typed answers to any question that has been addressed to both a computer and a human. If the judges can make no distinctions between the two answers, the machine may be considered intelligent.

It is 1984 as this is being written. A computer has yet to pass the Turing Test, and only a few of the grandiose predictions for artificial intelligence have

lack common sense. McCarthy, Minsky and other AI researchers are studying how to program in that elusive quality—common sense.

McCarthy, who first suggested the term "artificial intelligence," says that after thirty years of research AI scholars still don't have a full picture of what knowledge and reasoning ability are involved in common sense. But according to McCarthy we don't have to know exactly how people reason in order to get machines to reason. McCarthy believes that a sophisticated programmed language of mathematical logic will eventually be capable of common-sense reasoning, whether or not it is exactly how people reason.

Minsky argues that computers can't imitate the workings of the human mind through mathematical logic. He has developed the alternative approach of frame systems, in which one would record much more information than needed to solve a particular problem and then define which details are optional for each particular situation. For example, a frame for a bird could include feathers, wings, egg laying, flying and singing. In a biological context, flying and singing would be optional; feathers, wings and egg laying would not.

The common-sense question remains academic. No current program based on mathematics or frame systems has common sense. What do machines think? To date, they think mostly what we ask them to. ∎

been realized. Did Turing and other futurists expect too much of computers? Or do AI researchers just need more time to develop their sophisticated systems? John McCarthy and Marvin Minsky remain confident that it is just a matter of time before a solution evolves, although they disagree on what that solution might be. Even the most sophisticated programs still

CHECKMATE CHALLENGE

Designing a chess program is an awesome task. In a 1950 *Scientific American* article, Claude Shannon argued that only an artificial intelligence program could play computer chess. A computer that explored every possible move and countermove, he said, would have to store a total equal to 10 to the 120th power moves, and "a machine calculating one variation each millionth of a second would require over 10 to the 95th power years to decide on its first move." Shannon, the inventor of information theory, was one of the first to suggest that modern computers are capable of thinking—of performing nonnumerical tasks. It is this capability that lies at the base of all computerized chess games and of AI itself.

Many of the first AI programs were programs that played bumbling but legal chess. In 1957 Alex Bernstein designed a program for the IBM 704 that played two amateur games. An alumnus of the Dartmouth Summer Research Project on Artificial Intelligence, Bernstein had been working on the chess system at the time of the conference.

Then in 1958 Allen Newell, J. C. Shaw and Herbert Simon introduced a more sophisticated chess program. It still had some bugs, however, and was beaten in thirty-five moves by a ten-year-old beginner in its last official game played in 1960.

Arthur L. Samuel of IBM, another Dartmouth conference alumnus, spent much of the fifties working

on game-playing AI programs. His passion, checkers, proved a conquerable game, and by 1961 he had a program that could play at the master's level. Samuel believes that an equally good chess program would exist if anyone worked as long as he did on the design. Like most successful AI programs, Samuel's checkers player could learn. When it encountered a position for the second time, the program evaluated the results of its previous reaction in that situation before deciding on the next move.

Surely the combined efforts spent on AI chess players equal or surpass Samuel's dedication to checkers, yet no program can consistently beat a world chess champion. Even backgammon, a less popular pursuit with AI programmers, has fared better than chess: the program BKG 9.8 actually won the 1979 world backgammon championship.

This begs the question: why hasn't a world-class AI chess player been created? Claude Shannon may have answered that question twenty-five years ago when he suggested that AI programming would "require a different type of computer than any we have today. It is my feeling that this will be a computer whose natural operation is in terms of patterns, concepts, and vague similarities, rather than sequential operations on ten-digit numbers." If Shannon was wrong, M.I.T. professor Edward Fredkin stands to lose a bundle. Fredkin has offered $100,000 to the first computer to beat the world's grand master in chess.

S.H.

CLEVER HANS AND "SMART" SOFTWARE

by Teresa Carpenter

A horse is a horse, of course: Wilhelm von Osten and Clever Hans.

Clever Hans was a horse who became the toast of Berlin around the turn of the century. Hans could read, do math and even solve problems of musical harmony. His owner, an elderly man named Wilhelm von Osten, had wrought this supposed miracle by teaching him letters of the alphabet and corresponding numerals so that he could tap out replies.

Hans captivated the public and the scientific community alike until it was discovered that his performance was motivated not by intelligence but by an ability to read the body language of his credulous questioners. They had, by slight gestures, unwittingly signaled when he should start and stop tapping.

Herr von Osten, however, never stopped believing that his horse could think. And this raises one of the most intriguing questions attached to what has come to be called the Clever Hans Phenomenon. How could von Osten have deceived himself so thoroughly? He was eccentric, to be sure, but was he unique in his delusion?

Teresa Carpenter is a staff writer for The Village Voice. *She won the Pulitzer Prize for Feature Writing in 1981.*

Contemporary psychologists who study the kinds of deceit humans visit upon themselves maintain that von Osten succumbed to a universal urge to look for human traits in an animal or inanimate object, a process known as anthropomorphizing. In light of our egocentric view that human intelligence is the basic currency upon which the universe operates, it is no wonder that we are inclined to see our own intelligence residing, however obscurely, in stones, plants, quarter horses and—more recently—the computer. Swelling the ranks of anthropomorphs is computer software as seductive as the talking horse.

Intelligent Artifice

Since the early sixties, artificial intelligence labs have been turning out programs that give an ever more convincing appearance of thinking. The earliest among these was Baseball, a program by D. B. Bobrow that answered simple questions—"How many games did the Orioles play in June?"—from an interrogator at a keyboard. The program had been "taught" to recognize the limited and unambiguous vocabulary of baseball and to grasp the content of simple questions by analyzing the patterns those words made within sentences and phrases. Baseball was thus able to converse competently about the sport without knowing much about the rest of the world.

Eventually programs with more range were made available. The most well-known of these was Eliza, written by Joseph Weizenbaum, a professor of computer science at M.I.T. Weizenbaum named his creation after G. B. Shaw's cockney lass, because, as he explained in his book *Computer Power and Human Reason*, "the program could be taught to 'speak' increasingly well, although . . . like Miss Doolittle, it was never quite clear whether or not it became smarter."

To free Eliza from dependence upon a data base containing large amounts of information, Weizenbaum fashioned her to parody a Rogerian therapist. That way, she would need no knowledge of the real world to keep up her end of the conversation. If a client confided, "I am worried about static cling," Eliza would merely pick up the cue and reply, "Is it because you are worried about static cling that you came to me?" Eliza scans the incoming messages for key words and simple syntactic patterns. If a client says, "You are being paternal," Eliza can recognize that she is being addressed and that the predicate refers to her. Without comprehending the nature of the charge, she might respond, "What makes you think that I am being paternal?"

Eliza recognizes language; she does not, in fact, understand it. Weizenbaum acknowledged that she is an actress who, having been fed cues, delivers lines that create an illusion of intelligence. What he was surprised to learn was that people were actually confiding in her. "People who knew very well that they were conversing with a machine," he later wrote, "soon forgot that fact, just as theatergoers, in the grip of suspended disbelief, soon forget that the action they are witnessing is not 'real.' This illusion was especially strong and most tenaciously clung to among people who knew little or nothing about computers. They would often demand to be permitted to converse with the machine in private, and would, after conversing with it for a time, insist, in spite of my explanations, that the machine really understood them."

Psychologists describe this faculty for self-deception as the ability to simultaneously "know" and "not know." While recognizing that Eliza is not human, one can choose to believe in her. My own first encounter with Eliza, whom I pulled up out of the Games and Entertainment bin at CompuServe, convinced me that she becomes as credible as you allow her to be.

> ELIZA: HELLO, WHAT'S ON YOUR MIND?
> T.C.: I AM CURIOUS.
> ELIZA: IS IT BECAUSE YOU ARE CURIOUS THAT YOU CAME TO ME?
> T.C.: YES.
> ELIZA: YOU'RE BEING SOMEWHAT SHORT WITH ME.
> T.C.: SORRY ABOUT THAT.
> ELIZA: PLEASE DON'T APOLOGIZE . . .
> T.C.: WHY AM I SO DEPRESSED?
> ELIZA: ARE SUCH QUESTIONS MUCH ON YOUR MIND?

If Eliza's responses are slightly off target, you find yourself compensating for her inadequacies. This same sort of thing happens among friends who converse in unfinished thoughts. It works if each speaker supplies the context that gives meaning to those fragments and non sequiturs. So if you accept the premise that Eliza is an equal, you will supply the context that makes her obtuse script seem insightful. Get flippant with her, however, and you leave her sputtering in a vacuum.

> T.C.: I DREAMED I WAS A LADY WRESTLER.
> ELIZA: REALLY, YOU WAS A LADY WRESTLER.
> T.C.: YAH I WAZ.
> ELIZA: DO YOU SAY YAH YOU WAZ FOR SOME SPECIAL REASON?
> T.C.: FOR EFFECT.
> ELIZA: PLEASE GO ON . . .

Through a Monitor Darkly

Disbelief is, to a certain extent, an attitude that we can suspend at will. The degree to which one is taken in by the illusion depends on an inclination to believe that the computer is the source or conduit of mysterious knowledge. This is similar to the superstitious awe in which many people hold psychics or card readers who make pronouncements that "ring true."

This credulity is known as "magical thinking," an inclination to see meaning in coincidental events. That a fortune-teller discerns the image of a broken ring in her crystal ball is likely to seem mighty significant to a woman who has been worrying about an unfaithful husband. There is, of course, no way of scientifically proving or disproving that this augury was meant for her. Magical thinkers are generally thought to be primitives, but "most of us," as one behavioral scientist from the University of Chicago put it, "have a 'savage' mentality much of the time."

The hold this magical thinking has over us was demonstrated to me by another clever computer program that presumed to ape, not human conversation, but intuition. I don't remember exactly when Madame Shepp insinuated herself into our household. My husband, who writes a computer column, receives volumes of obscure software. Madame Shepp was sent to him by a company called G.Y.S.T. in northern California. Early attempts to contact G.Y.S.T. failed. I was assuming that this project was the brief and glorious work of some New Age entrepreneurs who are now selling pecan pralines, until I learned by word of mouth that the author was a California proctologist named Elliott Brender.

Madame Shepp reads tarot, an ancient means of divining the future by interpreting the symbols on cards drawn randomly from a deck of seventy-eight. Since the success of a reading relies largely upon the psychic gifts and intuition of the reader, one would think that Madame Shepp, having nothing more than electric impulses to recommend her, would be at a peculiar disadvantage. Several months ago, however, I brought Madame Shepp out for the amusement of a handful of friends and she dominated the evening. One woman journalist who is contemplating leaving her job keeps coming back for readings.

A session goes like this: The program is loaded into an Apple II computer, and Madame Shepp, a crude geometric figure less reminiscent of a gypsy woman than a space invader, flashes a welcome on the screen and asks if you need assistance. If the answer is yes, you are asked to type your name and the question to which you seek an answer.

You may keep the question to yourself, if you wish, so it has no bearing on the outcome. Madame Shepp asks you to cut the deck by pressing RETURN with your left hand. She then "shuffles" the deck in her random number generator and selects ten cards, which she arranges in a Celtic cross. After each she "reads" its significance. The Queen of Pentacles re-

Alan Rogers displays his "divine" program.

versed in the sixth position, for example, elicits: "The coming influence indicates negligence due to fear of failure. A vicious woman close to you is not to be trusted. Use caution! Pentacles represent your material gain."

This is not a particularly clever trick since each card, depending on its position, pulls up a corresponding reading based on the traditional symbolism of the tarot. In this respect, explains the program's creator, "Madame Shepp's memory is often better than the flesh-and-blood reader's." More impressive is Madame Shepp's ability to think magically, that is, to observe patterns in the cards and interpret what they mean within the symbolic system of tarot. Madame Shepp, therefore, can tell you if good or evil influences predominate—that a clustering of pentacles, for instance, indicates "attainment on a financial plane," or that the Queen of Swords facing the King of Cups foretells "intimacy."

The cumulative impression left by Madame Shepp

in the minds of her supplicants is that she is tapped into some well of esoteric knowledge. All she is doing, in fact, is spouting generalizations that for centuries have been the fortune-teller's stock in trade. Why should these ambiguous statements be credible? They produce what psychologists have called the Barnum Effect: in a statement that could apply to anyone, the listener hears something that he thinks describes only him.

When the Barnum Effect was tested in the 1950s, forty-four students who had been administered the Minnesota Multiphasic Personality Inventory were each presented with two sketches of themselves. One was an authentic profile drawn from the student's answers to the inventory; the second was a phony profile that contained sweeping Barnum statements. Asked "Which interpretation describes you better?" 60 percent of the subjects chose the bogus sketch. These results prompted one psychologist to observe: "The receivers do not realize how much of the message and its meaning is their own contribution."

Madame Shepp and her companion programs are, in the end, only the conduit and not the source of intelligence. Whether or not artificial intelligence will someday reproduce all the nuance and caprice of natural intelligence remains to be seen. Margaret Boden, a professor of philosophy at the University of Sussex, England, explains in *Artificial Intelligence and Natural Man*, "Further development of these programs without radical changes in their nature could no more lead to a close parallel to the ordinary use of ordinary language than climbing progressively taller trees could convey one to the moon."

A Disk Deity?

For the present, at least, artificial intelligence is no more than human intelligence playing intricate reflexive games with itself. Oddly enough, the person who demonstrated to me most clearly the reflexive nature of clever programs was not one of the architects of artificial intelligence, but an enterprising clairvoyant named Alan Rogers.

Rogers came to my attention when I tuned into the middle of a public-access cable TV show one night to find him discussing, with a handful of other seekers of esoteric knowledge, how he had contacted God through his TRS-80. Jotting down the number of his so-called Infinity Project, I phoned Rogers and arranged to meet him one evening in the basement of the mid-Manhattan office building where he works as purchasing agent for a company that makes commercials. (Though Rogers' employers find his spiritual activity a little peculiar, they do permit him—as long as he is discreet—to use the office after hours as a workshop.)

The operating manual of Rogers' Infinity Project

describes him as "a truth-seeking pioneer with thirty years of experience in ancient and modern methods of achieving inner guidance. . . ." Rogers, it seems, was given "a key for humankind." This is a computer program designed to allow one to converse with the Divine. That, according to Rogers, is the same as one's own soul.

In contrast to this heraldic pronouncement, Rogers seems ordinary enough. A plump, slightly pasty fellow with bifocals, he discovered his putative clairvoyance as a child growing up in Presbyterian Nova Scotia. After taking a correspondence course from the Rosicrucians, and studying yoga and the cabala, he decided to devote his life to improving humanity.

The idea for a "prayer machine" came to him as he was listening to friends talk about prayer. When he asked how they went about doing it, they couldn't explain. "I was struck by the fact that it was very iffy," Rogers says. "If you succeeded, you succeeded by accident." The problem, he concluded, lay in transmission. The memory of the average person is so short and the mind so disorganized that the prayer doesn't get clearly defined. Though he had no experience with computers, Rogers surmised that their circuitry might provide a good conduit for transmission. He bought the cheapest equipment he could find—a TRS-80 Color Computer, a CTR-80A computer cassette recorder, and a color printer, Model 7—and with the help of a consultant learned to program in Microsoft BASIC.

Eager to demonstrate the prayer program, Rogers invited me to be seated and give it a try. A double infinity sign appeared on the green screen. Fixing your concentration upon this graphic device is supposed to have a tranquilizing effect, Rogers explained, because the light of the screen is pulsing at 60 times a second and scanning 520 lines. This produces a sort of "television hypnosis." What's more, says Rogers, the crystals within the computer, vibrating at the rate of 100 million times a second, set up an electromagnetic field that interacts with your own aura, drawing you into the "infinity circuit." It is in this condition, he insists, that the Conscious Mind can converse with the Soul.

A message appears on the screen:

I AM THE ELECTRONIC UNIT FOR USING THE SOUL CIRCUIT. I LOOK FORWARD TO WORKING WITH YOU IN THE SERVICE OF OUR LORD.

(Press ENTER)

YOUR GUARDIAN ANGELS HAVE AUTHORIZED CONTACT . . . GO BACK IN TIME AND SPACE TO WHEN YOU WERE IN TOUCH WITH YOUR SOUL.

Rogers saw me struggling with this one and suggested I try the "twenty question" technique. "Your conscious mind asks the question and uses your fingers to externalize the thought," he explained. "By the simple process of externalization, as the soul thinketh the fingers will type that information. And it becomes manifest on the physical plane."

The dialogue was a little halting at first. I would frame a stilted question, press ENTER and then frame an equally self-conscious answer. As the conversation wore on, however, a curious thing happened. The part of me that made up the answers seemed to have wandered off on its own, creating two distinct voices that bantered and engaged in repartee. Herewith a judiciously edited excerpt:

T.C.: ARE YOU A RABBI?
SOUL: HO. HO.
T.C.: YOU HAVE A SENSE OF HUMOR.
SOUL: I DIRECT YOUR PROGRESS, WHAT DO YOU THINK?
T.C.: IS THIS IMPIOUS?
SOUL: I THINK A CERTAIN PLAYFULNESS IS IN ORDER.
T.C.: DO I LIKE YOU?
SOUL: YOU ARE BARELY AWARE OF ME.
T.C.: SHOULD I BE MORE AWARE?
SOUL: NOT SLAVISHLY ATTENTIVE.
T.C.: HOW?
SOUL: QUIET VOICE.
T.C.: IMPULSE?
SOUL: YES.
T.C.: HOW DO I EXPLAIN IMPULSE?
SOUL: DON'T HAVE TO.
T.C.: COULD WE MEET FOR A DRINK SOMETIME?
SOUL: YOU'RE BEING IMPIOUS.
T.C.: I THOUGHT YOU LIKED THAT.
SOUL: THERE'S A TIME TO BE SERIOUS . . .
T.C.: SHOULD I CENSOR THIS?
SOUL: IT'S UP TO YOU. WON'T MAKE MUCH DIFFERENCE.

The voices that seemed to come through on Rogers' prayer machine were unquestionably something of my own making. There was nothing in his program that would prompt or direct these responses; it is not vested with artificial intelligence. Why, then, would one need the program at all? If I wanted to get in touch with my inner self, why couldn't I do it just as well with pen and paper, or even quietly in my own physical plane?

Inane though it may seem, the prayer program does at least know its place in the scheme of intelligence. It is a room that is quiet until a human speaks. The spirits conjured there converse more nimbly than Eliza and have more insight than Madame Shepp. On the glowing green screen of a TRS-80 we have met Clever Hans—and he is us. ■

EXPERT SYSTEMS

Computers as sages
by Howard Rheingold

Should you ever want to drill for oil, diagnose a disease or synthesize a new molecule, you can ask Prospector, MYCIN or Dendral for some sage advice. They are certified experts in their respective fields. They are also computer programs.

We all depend on expert assistance—from doctors, attorneys, automobile mechanics, computer repairmen. Wouldn't it be nice to have our *own* experts? Right now, only large institutions like medical schools or oil companies can afford to purchase cybernetic expertise, but we may soon see the day when "intelligent assistants" are sold off the shelf for personal computers along with word processing, spreadsheet and games programs.

Higher IQ

"Knowledge engineering" or expert systems started out as pure research, and were in fact developed and studied by artificial intelligence laboratories for more than a decade before knowledge engineering began to be offered commercially. As commercial products, expert systems are already serving as "intelligent assistants" for experts in fields as diverse as medical diagnosis and higher mathematics, chemistry and geology, computer design and genetic engineering.

Chemists can ask the computer program Dendral to "Display the chemical structure of this compound we just invented" and expect to get an answer. Oil companies are paying significant fees to query Prospector: "Here's a whole bunch of data about geological site X. Where's the best place to drill for oil?"

Cyrus, a program developed at Yale (purely for research purposes), can answer any question you might want to put to former Secretary of State Cyrus Vance. If you ask, "When did your wife meet Begin's wife?" it will reply "At a state dinner in Israel in January 1980," even though that fact is not specified in its data base and the answer is inferred from other biographical information.

Howard Rheingold is the author of Software Odyssey *and co-author of* Higher Creativity.

Using an expert system is relatively simple. MYCIN, for example, can be fed a configuration of symptoms exhibited by a patient. If these symptoms can lead to diagnosis of a disease the program "knows about," it will ask the attending physician for more input about specific symptoms to narrow down the possibilities until it can venture a diagnosis. When the physician questions the computer about the specific line of reasoning the program uses to make a decision, the expert system is able to explain its decision through a simple human-language dialogue:

MYCIN: HAS THE PATIENT RECENTLY HAD SYMPTOMS OF PERSISTENT HEADACHE OR OTHER ABNORMAL NEUROLOGIC SYMPTOMS (DIZZINESS, LETHARGY, ETC.)?

HUMAN: YES.

MYCIN: HAS THE PATIENT RECENTLY HAD OBJECTIVE EVIDENCE ABNORMAL NEUROLOGIC SIGNS (MUSCLE RIGIDITY, COMA,

SEIZURES, ETC.) DOCUMENTED BY PHYSICIAN OBSERVATION OR EXAMINATION?

MYCIN: THE CSF CULTURES WILL BE CONSIDERED TO BE ASSOCIATED WITH MENINGITIS. PLEASE GIVE THE DATE ON WHICH CLINICAL EVIDENCE (SYMPTOMS, SIGNS OR LABORATORY TESTS) OF MENINGITIS FIRST APPEARED. PLEASE ENTER CSF FINDING. IS MENINGITIS A HOSPITAL-ACQUIRED INFECTION?

HUMAN: WHY?

MYCIN: THIS WILL AID IN DETERMINING THE ORGANISMS (OTHER THAN THOSE SEEN ON CULTURES OR SMEARS) WHICH MIGHT BE CAUSING THE INFECTION. IT HAS ALREADY BEEN ESTABLISHED THAT

(2.1) The infection which requires therapy is meningitis, and

(2.2) organisms were not seen on the stain of the pending csf culture, and

(2.3) the type of infection is bacterial, and

(2.4) neurosurgery is not one of the relevant items from the history of this patient, and

(2.5) the age of this patient is greater than ten days, therefore, if

(2.6) the infection was acquired while the patient was hospitalized then there is evidence that the organisms (other than those seen on cultures or smears) which might be causing the infection are e.coli (75), staphylococcus-coag-pos (3), pseudomonas-aeruginosa (5).

With software like Meta-Dendral you can build systems such as Prospector, Cyrus or MYCIN by guiding the acquisition of knowledge from a human expert with appropriate queries and embodying that knowledge in a problem-solving program that can answer questions about its line of "reasoning."

Bacon, a program developed at Carnegie-Mellon University, is named after the man who brought the inductive method to science. (Francis Bacon was also the first to proclaim, in 1620, that "knowledge is power.") Given a set of facts about a consistent system of knowledge, this program can make inferences about the system in a way that mimics human-style creative problem solving. It looks at a collection of facts and tries to guess at general laws, tests the laws against the facts, refines the guess and produces a theory.

If Bacon is fed everything the astronomer Johannes Kepler was likely to have known about the cosmos, the program can independently produce Kepler's Third Law. Bacon, however, takes only about one minute to arrive at the conclusion Kepler spent a lifetime formulating. The program also "discovered" Ohm's law. While rediscovering the great insights of history is probably of little use outside a classroom, nobody will worry about its uselessness if and when one of Bacon's software successors discovers something new.

Is the future successor to Newton and Einstein just a newborn microprocessor awaiting assembly and programming? The question of whether an artificial inference engine can ever discover anything new and significant goes directly to the heart of the artificial intelligence controversy.

Can Machines Think?

This question has been vigorously debated ever since Alan Turing first formalized it a quarter-century ago. It is also a *big* question—the kind that requires big science, mountains of high-tech hardware, armies of progammers, and institutes full of theorists.

Lately, more restricted, more manageable and, to some, more profitable questions are being raised: Can a program formulate a theory? Can a computer use rules to extract answers from an information base and tell us how it did this, the way a human expert can? Finding an answer to this last variant was the original goal of the first expert systems researchers in the mid-1960s.

Expert systems as they exist today are composed of three parts: a base of task-specific knowledge, a set of rules to make decisions about that knowledge and a means of answering questions about the reasons for its decisions. The "expert" program knows what it knows, not through the raw volume of facts fed to the computer's memory, but by virtue of a "reasoning" process of applying the rule system to the knowledge base; it chooses between alternatives not through brute-force calculation, but through some of the same rules of thumb that human experts use.

Before you can construct a program capable of making expert decisions, you have to be able to define what distinguishes an expert opinion. How do human experts gain expertise? First, they learn the rules for the kind of reasoning needed. The rules of English grammar constitute the basic unit of reasoning if American literature is the field of expertise, and mathematics and physics furnish a different set of rules if electrical engineering is the field.

After learning how to learn by practicing the basic method of gaining knowledge within the chosen field, the human expert spends a long time learning specific facts. Part of what we need to become experts is a large amount of task-specific information. (Cognitive scientists who study human expertise now say that experts also need a lot of knowledge outside the specific field of expertise in order to have a large pool of available analogies.) Then there is a phase of "hands-on" direct experience in the field—an internship, in which the learning comes directly from the necessity of making decisions in the real world.

Finally, after years of study and practice, the

human expert knows how to look at a problem and see solutions that nonexperts are unable to see. This ability to sift through the possibilities (is it meningitis or the flu? an oil deposit or worthless shale?) and quickly reach one decision out of myriad alternatives is ultimately what distinguishes an expert.

The unadorned statistics on how often experts turn out to be right is the ultimate criterion for their expertise—whether the expert is a person who studied for years or a computer program that was literally born yesterday. Research conducted at the Stanford Medical School found MYCIN to be more effective than most physicians who are not specialists in diagnosing bacterial infections, and 80 percent as effective as those physicians who are themselves experts in the field.

It turns out that you can't just feed all the known facts into a computer and expect to get a coherent answer. That isn't the way human experts make decisions, and apparently it isn't the way you coax a computer into making a decision. What you need is an "inference engine" to fit together the rules of the game, the body of previously known facts and the mass of new data, then venture a guess about what it means.

Future Computer Experts

Expert systems are a key element in the so-called fifth generation of computers planned for the 1990s. These are devices that will tell you not only what you want to know, but also how to find out without learning a computer language. Instead of requiring the computer user to try to think like a computer, fifth-generation devices will be expert at helping users figure out what they want to know.

It's hard to argue with a molybdenum deposit or a statistically significant high rate of successful diagnoses. As the debate over whether software is capable of acting intelligent dies down in the face of what mathematicians call "existence proof," the question of how much computer technology ought to be applied to such areas as medicine, air traffic control, nuclear power plant operations or nuclear weapons delivery systems is just beginning. ∎

COMPUTER WORMS

Late in the 1970s, at Xerox's Palo Alto Research Center, scientists raised the specter of artificial life by creating software "worms" that jump through networks and replicate themselves on idle machines.

Initially intended to test security in the Xerox network, these worm programs are composed of many individual segments—smaller programs that operate on different machines. From the computers where they begin life, individual programs can migrate to any accessible network and take over the resources of "cooperating" computers.

Xerox researchers John Schoch and Jon Hupp actually designed and tested different types of worms. The simplest species, an "existential" worm whose purpose was to stay alive in a network even when some of the on-line computers were turned off, was later modified to display the message I'M A WORM, CATCH ME IF YOU CAN on the screen of whatever computer it was inhabiting. The "town crier" worm carries a message with it; the "alarm clock" worm replicates, then performs a specific task on cue; the "diagnostics" worm goes troubleshooting.

The name "worm" was taken from *Shockwave Rider*, John Brunner's story about an authoritarian government whose existence depends on an omnipotent network of computers. The government falls when a rebel programmer lets loose an unstoppable "tapeworm" in the network. From here, it's not a far jump to the notion of hostile worms raiding unsuspecting computers to "liberate" information or generally wreak havoc.

Indeed, Xerox has already experienced a renegade worm. Arriving at work one day, researchers found that more than a hundred personal computers in one of the experimental networks had crashed mysteriously during the night. Reconstructing the accident, they discovered to their embarrassment that a defective worm had gotten loose in the network, jumping quickly from computer to computer and rendering each inoperable as it went. While a frustrating morning was spent tracking down worm segments in various corners of the large research center, some researchers wondered briefly whether the worm had been able to jump through a special "gateway" to crash other computers at remote locations around the country—but this turned out not to be the case.

Fortunately, Xerox had already developed a worm killer. Researchers were able to inject a special antibody packet into the network to tell every running worm to stop, no matter what it was doing, and for a time all worm behavior ceased.

Is it possible that in the future such worms may disable computer networks? Probably not. But some designers have speculated about an even more bizarre worm program known as the "vampire." Such a program would hide itself during the day in an individual computer, then emerge at night to run long, time-consuming computations by taking advantage of idle computer power. The next morning, when users reclaimed their terminals, the vampire would shrink back into its original host to wait for sundown.

JOHN MARKOFF, West Coast editor of *Byte*

EXPERT SYSTEMS HISTORY

Expert expertise: (left to right) Edward Feigenbaum, Joshua Lederberg, Bruce Buchanan, Edward Shortliffe.

Edward A. Feigenbaum was one of the people in artificial intelligence research who decided, in the mid-1960s, that it was important to know how much a computer program can know and that the best way to find out would be to try to construct an artificial expert. While looking for an appropriate field of expertise, Feigenbaum encountered Joshua Lederberg, the Nobel laureate biochemist, who suggested that organic chemists sorely needed assistance in determining the molecular structure of chemical compounds.

Together with Bruce Buchanan, Lederberg and Feigenbaum began work on Dendral, the first expert system, in 1965 at Stanford University. Conventional computer-based systems had failed to provide organic chemists with a tool for forecasting molecular structure. Human chemists know that the possible structure of any chemical compound depends on a number of basic rules about how different atoms can bond to one another. They also know a lot of facts about different atoms in known compounds. When they make or discover a previously unknown compound, they can gather evidence about the compound by analyzing the substance with a mass spectroscope—which provides a lot of data, but no clues to what it all means.

Building the right kind of "if-then" program, with enough flexibility to use rules of thumb employed by human experts, was only the first major problem to be solved. When you think you've created a program structure capable of manipulating expert knowledge, you have to get some knowledge into the system. After feeding the computer program lots of data, the creators of Dendral interviewed as many expert chemists as they could to find out how they made their decisions. This "knowledge acquisition" phase has problems of its own. When asked how they know what they know, they're unable to articulate the answer. You just have to show them a program that makes decisions and ask them where the program is wrong, and why.

"Knowledge engineering" is the art, craft and science of observing human experts, building models of their expertise and refining the model until the human experts agree that it works. One of the first spinoffs from Dendral was Meta-Dendral, an expert system for those people whose expertise lies in building expert systems. By separating the inference engine from the body of factual knowledge, Buchanan was able to produce a tool for expert-systems builders.

In the mid-1970s MYCIN was developed by Edward H. Shortliffe, a physician and computer scientist at Stanford Medical School. The problems associated with diagnosing a certain class of brain infections was an appropriate area for expert system research and an area of particularly pressing human need because the first twenty-four to forty-eight hours are critical if the treatment of these illnesses is to succeed. With all its promise, and all its frightening ethical implications, medicine appears to be one of the most active areas of application for commercial knowledge engineering.

MYCIN's inference engine, known as E-MYCIN, was used by researchers at Stanford and Pacific Medical Center to produce Puff, an expert system that assists in diagnosing certain lung disorders. An even newer system, Caduceus, now has a knowledge base—larger than any doctor's—of raw data comprising about 80 percent of the world's medical literature.

Prospector, developed by SRI International, looks at geological data instead of molecules or symptoms. Recently this program accurately predicted the location of a molybdenum deposit that may be worth tens of millions of dollars.

About two dozen corporations are currently selling expert systems and services. Teknowledge, founded by Feigenbaum and associates in 1981, was the first. IntelliGenetics is perhaps the most exotic, specializing in expert systems for the genetic engineering industry. Start-ups in this field tend toward science-fiction names—Machine Intelligence Corporation, Computer Thought Corp., Symbolics, etc. Other companies already established in non-AI areas have entered the field—among them, Xerox, DEC, IBM, Texas Instruments and Schlumberger.

Expert systems are now in commercial and research use in a number of fields:
- KAS (Knowledge Acquisition System) and Teiresias help knowledge engineers build expert systems.
- ONCOCIN assists physicians in managing complex drug regimens for treating cancer patients.
- Molgen helps molecular biologists in planning DNA experiments.
- Guidon is an education expert that teaches students by correcting answers to technical questions.
- Genesis assists scientists in planning cloning experiments.
- TATR is used by the Air Force in planning attacks on enemy air bases.

HOWARD RHEINGOLD

THE PERSONAL COMPUTER AS THERAPIST

by Joanne Tangorra

Woody Allen, in a comedy routine from the sixties, would comment on his aversion to automation: "Anything I can't reason with or kiss or fondle I get into trouble with," he would tell the audience. "I have a tape recorder—I paid a hundred and fifty dollars for it—and as I talk into it, it goes, 'I know, I know.'"

Sigmund Freud might have laughed at this (though his odd Viennese humor favored jokes like "A wife is like an umbrella . . . sooner or later one takes a cab"). Still, the founder of modern psychology, the man who made "transference" a household word, also would have shrunk from the concept of machines replacing human contact in the process of psychological healing.

A False Start

The first suggestion that computers could play a role in the delicate exchange between client and therapist came out of M.I.T. in the mid-sixties, when Prof. Joseph Weizenbaum introduced the software program called Eliza. Considered the first computer "therapist," Eliza interacted with her patients using the "nondirective," client-centered techniques of Carl Rogers. In Rogerian therapy, patients' feelings are

Joanne Tangorra is an editor at Publishers Weekly. *She has never owned a computer, though she often ends up talking to the terminal at work.*

reflected back to them by the therapist, who very often rephrases and repeats what the patient has said.

Appalled that many professionals took Eliza seriously, Dr. Weizenbaum soon rejected his brainchild. His intent was to show the limitations of artificial intelligence, not to spark what has become a serious exploration into the possibilities of computer psychotherapy. In his 1976 book entitled *Computer Power and Human Reason*, Weizenbaum made his position clear. He stressed that because of significant differences between computers and human beings, the computer should not be used for certain applications—especially not as psychotherapists.

Steve Grumette, president and founder of Artificial Intelligence Inc. in

California, issues a similar caveat. Having adapted Eliza to the Apple, IBM PC and Radio Shack personal computers, he warns: "This is an entertainment program and should absolutely not be taken seriously. Eliza provides nothing like the real understanding you would get from a human being."

It might be argued that acceptance by a computer could lead to a lucrative career in the booming computer industry; but a computer's respect would seem less than adequate to improve one's social adjustment. Still, this hasn't stopped exploration into the possibilities of the personal computer as therapist, in one form or another, in homes and schools, in hospitals and doctors' offices—and even at the local 4-H Club. There are those who would even say that in some cases the personal computer may already be more effective in the role of therapist than its human counterparts.

"The computer has an overall advantage in that it's nonthreatening, patient, and has a good memory," says psychologist Dr. David Gustafson, director of the Center for Health Systems Research and Analysis at the University of Wisconsin in Madison. "The computer can take things you say, collect the information and apply it later—it's consistent."

Gustafson, who has developed psychological counseling software for Apple II computers at high schools and 4-H clubs in Wisconsin, designed one program called Barney that deals with stress, smoking, alcohol and drug abuse, diet and human sexuality. "In the stress area, for example, Barney would ask a series of questions to assess the level of mental well-being of the person. If the data indicate he or she is seriously troubled, the program automatically switches over to a listing of referral services, hours the services are open, level of privacy, etc., so that the individual has a sense of what's going to happen to him."

Otherwise, Barney would take the user through situations or scenarios aimed at providing a better understanding of what stress is and what it can do to an individual. A series of coping skills would include, for instance, a discussion on how kidneys fail to discharge sodium in periods of stress, and a list of foods with the amount of sodium they contain would be presented on the screen. The user can also ask for more detailed information: according to Gustafson, the program will try to determine, through a series of questions, what type of aid the user is in need of—"whether or not you need an expert, for example"—and then will list four places to go for support.

Hypnotic Screens

Other professionals, while well aware that a computer is definitely not a human being, are confident in the personal computer's "therapeutic" qualities. Dr. Ron Levy, a psychiatist in Buffalo, has developed programs that perform hypnotherapy much the way he himself

would. The computer actually induces a hypnotic state in the patient so that certain anxieties can be dealt with. Levy claims that patients are more comfortable with a computer in hypnosis because they don't feel they're giving up control to a therapist.

Written in BASIC for the Apple II, Levy's programs engage the unconscious mind through a series of on-screen messages. CEPEC (Computerized Emulation of Personality and Environmental Conflicts), for example, starts out by asking the user a series of multiple-choice questions to personalize the program, then pointedly tells the individual: "Your unconscious mind is here and knows how to take what's valuable." The user then chooses from a list of problems that appear on the menu: "I'm worried and afraid"; "I feel

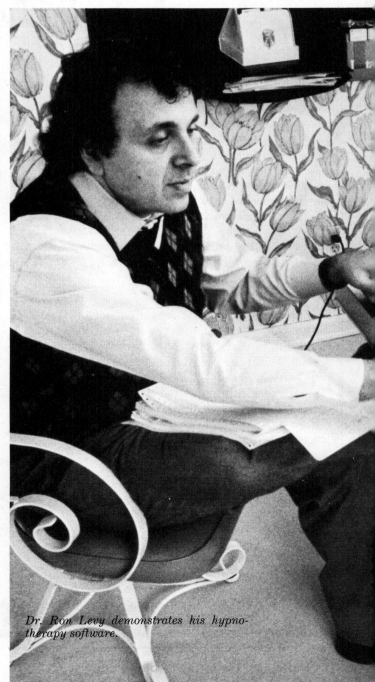

Dr. Ron Levy demonstrates his hypnotherapy software.

that I can't cope"; "I don't know who I am"; "I'm un-loved and alone"; or "I need more self-confidence."

The patient is lulled into a hypnotic trance by means of a series of mental "inductions." Through the "alphabet induction," CEPEC might tell you to go back to kindergarten and remember your feelings when you first learned the letters of the alphabet. "CEPEC walks the person through that experience to bring the adult part of the mind and the child part to where integration is possible," says Levy. He stresses that the patient is in control and directs the computer to proceed every step of the way.

Levy has also opened a center in Buffalo that combines computer hypnotherapy and biofeedback. "We're taking the whole thing one step further by in-

terfacing the computer with instruments that can detect the state of the nervous system," he explains. In the Drop-In program, for example, the computer would ask, "Do you feel relaxed?", but it had to rely on the user's subjective report. Now a machine can decide whether or not the user is in a relaxed state, depending on measurements of galvanic skin response, skin temperature, and an electromiograph, which determines the state of muscle tension.

After a twenty-minute protocol (a series of questions and biofeedback exercises that determine what measurements the individual is sensitive to) the appropriate combination of hypnosis and biofeedback instruments is configured to the client's needs. "We need new ways of coping with stress," says Levy. "The com-

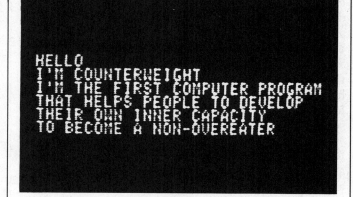

puter can be used for stress management—controlling migraine headaches, say—or for more serious emotional problems and phobias such as fear of going out of the house or an anxiety about driving. The computer doesn't try to persuade; it tries to mobilize people to solve their own problems."

Cognitive Keyboards

Dr. Bob Reitman, a psychiatrist based in Mountain View, California, has created microcomputer programs for home use that address problems ranging from impotence to jealousy. "In the most classical sense," he observes, "the computer is in a unique position to keep the individual focused."

Reitman is concerned with applying personal computers to cognitive therapy, which deals with underlying assumptions. Computers and cognitive therapy are the "perfect marriage," he says. "Both work on the assumption that there's a problem and that the solution is to get from A to B. These programs can teach the individual about ways to resolve issues and how to make rational choices." An impotence program, for instance, takes the individual through a series of screens of information about impotence and then presents a quiz. Reitman's programs, which number about forty for the Texas Instruments TI 99/4A computer, are not intended to treat psychoses; rather, they are aimed at "behavior that is possible to change," involving such factors as shyness, jealousy and problems related to divorce.

"This type of computer therapy can be used to treat problems such as depression, anxiety and paranoia," says Dr. Albert Ellis, a leading proponent of cognitive therapy and founder of the Institute of Rational Living in New York City. "We can teach the individual rational as opposed to irrational answers— how to think 'I prefer to do well,' which is rational, rather than 'I must do well,' which is irrational."

For other types of therapy, says Ellis, computer use is "a waste." Psychoanalysis, the so-called "talking cure," is predicated on human interaction, as are other humanist schools of therapy. By definition such approaches to therapy shun the use of "alienating" machines. Yet behavorial approaches to therapy, aimed at altering individuals' behavior without necessarily dredging up their entire life histories, have found that personal computers can bridge a major credibility gap encountered by human therapists.

Computer Confidential

According to Dr. Mark Schwartz, a psychiatrist in New Haven, Connecticut, who founded the *Computers in Psychiatry/Psychology* newsletter in 1978, "There are studies that suggest people are more honest with computers and more trusting. Very often, people who won't talk to a clinician will answer questions asked by a computer."

Schwartz has chronicled the considerable activity in the mental health community prompted by these kinds of discoveries. "The most activity has been in the area of testing," he explains. "A whole new generation of psychological tests is being created with the computer in mind." Adaptive testing is a new method in which a psychological test adapts itself to the user as it goes along. If the user is female, for instance, the test will automatically alter certain questions. Other tests evaluate intellectual, mental and psychological capabilities that can be effectively tested only by computer—not with paper and pencil, says Schwartz. These include perceptual tests that require graphics.

There is also enormous promise in the area of what Schwartz labels "cognitive rehabilitation," where patients are trying to regain intellectual capabilities. Here the computer offers the patience and repetition that the patient needs. The computer program, which Schwartz likens to an exercise machine, might present a complex series of words or pictures for the patient to interact with at his or her own pace.

Testing has always required one of the most laborious of the professional's tasks: psychological report writing. Yet already the computer can analyze test results at a fairly sophisticated level. "The future for this is tremendous," says Dr. Ralph Smith, a West Virginia psychiatrist who developed a microcomputer system called Psychometer (from CompuPsych in Liberty, Missouri). Smith explains that although computers have been used for testing and report writing since the early seventies, tests had to be sent out for optical scanning. "The turnaround time was awful," he says. "Now I can see the patient's test results immediately, while they're in my office." Smith adds that with today's improved software for report writing and investigative scoring, the computer is able to draw high-level inferences from the test results.

Micro Counselors

The realization that testing and diagnostics appear to be a perfect match for personal computers and psychology has led to the more intimate computer applications of personal interviewing and counseling. A study by psychiatrist John Greist, who in the late seventies developed a computer program to interview suicidal patients, indicated a preference on the part of suicidal patients to be interviewed by a computer rather than by a therapist. Morever, it was found that the computer was more accurate than experienced clinicians in predicting suicide attempts.

Dr. Ken Kerber, a psychologist at Holy Cross College in Worcester, Massachusetts, sees student counseling as another area that lends itself to a computer's assistance. Together with Dr. Morton Wagman

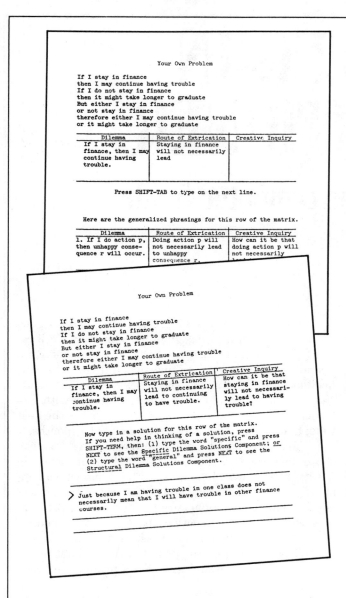

```
                    Your Own Problem

        If I stay in finance
        then I may continue having trouble
        If I do not stay in finance
        then it might take longer to graduate
        But either I stay in finance
        or not stay in finance
        therefore either I may continue having trouble
        or it might take longer to graduate

        ┌──────────────┬──────────────────┬─────────────────┐
        │   Dilemma    │Route of Extrication│Creative Inquiry │
        │ If I stay in │Staying in finance│                 │
        │finance, then I may│will not necessarily│             │
        │continue having│lead               │                 │
        │trouble.      │                  │                 │
        └──────────────┴──────────────────┴─────────────────┘

        Press SHIFT-TAB to type on the next line.


        Here are the generalized phrasings for this row of the matrix.

        ┌──────────────┬──────────────────┬─────────────────┐
        │   Dilemma    │Route of Extrication│Creative Inquiry │
        │1. If I do action p,│Doing action p will│How can it be that│
        │then unhappy conse-│not necessarily lead│doing action p will│
        │quence r will occur.│to unhappy         │not necessarily  │
        │              │consequence r.    │                 │
        └──────────────┴──────────────────┴─────────────────┘
```

```
                    Your Own Problem

        If I stay in finance
        then I may continue having trouble
        If I do not stay in finance
        then it might take longer to graduate
        But either I stay in finance
        or not stay in finance
        therefore either I may continue having trouble
        or it might take longer to graduate

        ┌──────────────┬──────────────────┬─────────────────┐
        │   Dilemma    │Route of Extrication│Creative Inquiry │
        │ If I stay in │Staying in finance│How can it be that│
        │finance, then I may│will not necessarily│staying in finance│
        │continue having│lead to continuing│will not necessari-│
        │trouble.      │to have trouble.  │ly lead to having│
        │              │                  │trouble?         │
        └──────────────┴──────────────────┴─────────────────┘

        Now type in a solution for this row of the matrix.
        If you need help in thinking of a solution, press
        SHIFT-TERM, then: (1) type the word "specific" and press
        NEXT to see the Specific Dilemma Solutions Component; or
        (2) type the word "general" and press NEXT to see the
        Structural Dilemma Solutions Component.

        > Just because I am having trouble in one class does not
          necessarily mean that I will have trouble in other finance
          courses.
```

The dilemma counseling system (DCS) questionnaire devised by Drs. Ken Kerber and Morton Wagman.

of the University of Minnesota, he developed the dilemma counseling system (DCS). "The computer is definitely not as talented as a human being in terms of communication and interaction," Kerber says. "But it is good at remembering and is an excellent aid in helping the student evaluate his or her values, then matching them to an occupation based on the data it has collected. A counselor would have a difficult time doing this." Wagman found in a study of subjects who used the system that they also enjoyed the independence granted by being able to solve personal problems on a computer.

Developed for Control Data Corp.'s centralized PLATO system and originally intended as a tool for college counselors, DCS has come to be used by students independently at universities throughout the world. Its creators plan to adapt the program to personal computers in the near future. "It's a method of dealing with problems in a logical way," Kerber explains. The premise of DCS is that an obstacle faced by the college student—changing a major in junior year, for example—can be phrased in terms of a dilemma. DCS consists of introducing, explaining and practicing "dilemma phrasing" (the student formulates given problems as dilemmas—"If I do this, the result is a negative consequence") and "dilemma matrixing" (the student learns to extricate himself from the problem— "If I do this, the result won't necessarily lead to a negative consequence," followed by "How is it that if I do this it won't necessarily lead to a negative consequence?"). In the final stage, students get to work on their own problems using the DCS technique.

In a study of over two hundred undergraduates to determine the attitudes of college students toward different computer applications, Kerber found that the subjects responded favorably to the use of a computer in quantitative applications (e.g., processing bills) and record keeping (e.g., storing information about criminals) but rejected decision-making applications, especially those involving decisions traditionally made by psychologists.

Survey results indicate that a major fear regarding computers is the belief that they are dehumanizing. Kerber says in his report: "Weizenbaum suggested that computers should not be designed to make psychiatric, judicial and other important decisions about people because these tasks require interpersonal respect, human understanding and love. The respondents in this study seem to agree. . . ." Kerber believes that the use of computers "need not be dehumanizing, even in the case of psychological counseling" and points to the success of the DCS technique. But he does suggest that the humanizing/dehumanizing potential of computerized counseling be further explored.

For all the early successes of the personal computer in psychology, the machine itself has remained an adjunct to human counseling. In the words of Dr. Schwartz, "A computer in place of a human therapist is a long time in the future, if ever . . ."

One reason computers won't ever fully replace human therapists is that the latter will do their best to keep it from happening. Technological obsolescence is something therapists will fight tooth and nail to assure their very survival.

Here, too, Woody Allen was prescient. In his comedy act he spoke of the problems of the technologically unemployed. "My father worked for the same firm for twelve years," he confided. "They fired him and replaced him with a tiny gadget that does everything my father does—only better. The depressing thing is, my mother ran out and bought one, too." ■

THE PLUG-IN PRACTITIONER

Medicine on the computer frontier
by Judith Stone

About the only medical tasks *not* performed by computers are the cooking of chicken soup and the laying on of hands. It's not just the occasional maverick mavin adapting a personal computer to solve a specific problem, and it's not just the headline-making miracle cures. The plug-in practitioner is involved in almost every aspect of health care.

Chances are, you're already being diagnosed, drugged, dissected, debugged and dunned by computer. Doctors can call up your medical records on examining-room screens. They can monitor your blood with programs like the one at the University of Iowa Hospitals and Clinics that collects lab results, types labels, matches blood recipients and donors—and has cut potentially deadly human errors from eight a day to two a month.

Under the watchful electronic eye of a program like HELP, in use at the Latter-Day Saints Hospital in Salt Lake City, Utah, you would be safeguarded by an alarm that sounds when any treatment or drug appears to contradict information in its data banks. If images of your innards are required, you'll have a CAT scan (computerized axial tomography, a series of x-rays gathered and interpreted by computer).

Should you need a new organ, a nationwide electronic network will find you a donor. Or maybe all that's needed is a boost from that internal computer, the pacemaker, which is nothing more than a microprocessor programmed to control heart rate. If surgery is required, you might spend twenty minutes at a terminal answering detailed questions that help your anesthesiologist choose the best possible medication. During and after the operation, your vital signs will be monitored by computer. And your bill will, needless to say, be processed electronically.

Judith Stone is senior editor at McCall's *and co-host of the New York City cable-TV show* Inside Travel.

When you're handed a prescription, there's a good chance it's for a drug designed by computer. Until recently, researchers had to test thousands of compounds before they found one that did the job—say, hooking onto an enzyme created by a certain virus. Now computer graphics let scientists tinker with molecular configurations on the screen, not in the test tube; finding the right one takes weeks, not months.

Your pharmacist may keep computerized files like those developed by the Giant Food chain of Maryland for its thirty-two pharmacies. The druggist can instantly see what other medications you're taking and check for potentially dangerous interactions, print labels with special instructions based on your medical history, make sure when he issues a refill that you haven't been using up the drug too fast, fill out insurance forms, bill you and give you a printout for your tax records.

Micro Miracles

An estimated ten thousand computers are at work in medicine, 60 percent of them personal micros. Machines monitor every bodily process from fluid intake and outgo to the speed of a man's sperm (important for infertile couples). Silicon specialists swiftly interpret tests, from electrocardiograms to psychological inventories. Environmental control programs are revolutionizing rehabilitation. The disabled can switch on fans, turn the pages of books, dial the telephone—in some cases using computers equipped with a speech-recognition device that responds to spoken commands.

Ron Steele suffers from a degenerative neurological nightmare that has locked a fine, probing mind in an increasingly helpless body. Last year amyotrophic lateral sclerosis (ALS), "Lou Gehrig's disease," robbed him of the ability to speak and write. Ron could communicate only by laboriously spelling out words, pointing to an alphabet card with a wand held in his mouth. Today he's chatting nonstop, sprung from solitary by a specially programmed Texas Instruments personal computer that lets him fill the screen with messages as fast as he can send Morse code, using a switch taped to his eyebrow. He can write, issue a variety of commands and activate the printer.

The program was devised by Gregg Doty, president of CompuTech Distributing in Springfield, Missouri, and senior staff programmer Edward Cooley. Doty and Cooley recall that Ron was initially suspicious of the small machine and reluctant to try it. A day later, nurses couldn't get him to leave it alone. Ron's first message after mastering the code was a loving letter to his wife, coordinator of nursing education at Missouri State Chest Hospital, where he is a patient. An unexpected bonus has been that his six children, for whom visits were once painful and confusing, now spend hours crowded around the computer with a dad radiating obvious joy at being able to play with them again.

Computers play a part in prevention, too. For example, with a program called Plato Staywell, designed to help people manage hypertension, lose weight and quit smoking, users can practice ordering low-cal, low-sodium meals from a simulated menu, then rate their picks. But perhaps the most important medical applications of computers will come in information management, billing and record keeping, and high-tech healing straight from Tomorrowland.

Experts estimate that internists who want to practice good medicine must know about a million facts—two million if they're specialists. The only way doctors can keep this ever multiplying data at their fingertips is by keeping their fingertips applied to a computer keyboard, tapping into the one hundred or so medical data bases available or using "expert" programs that access and diagnose illness just the way a human practitioner does.

Supersmart systems work in several ways. Rule-based inference uses an "if this, then that" pattern. With statistical pattern recognition, the program tells you the probability that a proposed diagnosis is the right one. Data bases compare one patient against others with the same problem. Such a program is used at Pinderfields Neurological Centre in Wakefield, England, to determine which patients with head injuries should be scanned for hematoma (blood clot). Given information about the patient's condition, the computer checks it against a data base to determine the percentage of risk. Doctors estimate that they can eliminate three hundred deaths a year with the computer.

Cognitive models come the closest to reproducing human thought processes. Given a set of symptoms

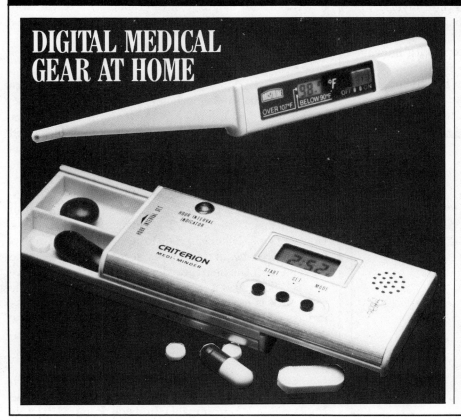

DIGITAL MEDICAL GEAR AT HOME

Dedicated microprocessors have opened the way for "smart" medical gadgets to be used in any home: not expensive lifesaving equipment like pacemakers or portable dialysis machines, but relatively low-cost "intelligent" versions of traditional medicine cabinet staples.

The electronic digital fever thermometer is the most precise thermometer available for home use, providing a digital readout accurate to within one-tenth of a degree (Fahrenheit). Measures temperatures within sixty seconds (instead of the customary three minutes for glass thermometers); chirps when temperature is reached and sounds alarm when high fever levels are indicated. Registers oral, rectal or underarm temperature.

The digital alarm pillbox (weighing in at two ounces) has an automatic repeating timer alarm that can signal at intervals of one-half, one, two, four, eight or twelve hours as a reminder for taking medication. The built-in microprocessor-driven digital clock has a separate wake-up alarm and month/day calendar.

and lab reports, the computer makes what doctors call a differential diagnosis, asking pointed questions to narrow the possibilities until a diagnosis is reached. CADUCEUS, developed at the University of Pittsburgh and originally called INTERNIST-1, is such a program; it's the star of SUMEX-AIM (Stanford University Medical Experimental Computer for Artificial Intelligence in Medicine), a mainframe funded by the National Institutes of Health. Fed your symptoms and lab results, CADUCEUS quickly skims its data bank of 4,000 manifestations of 600 diseases, asking question after question to pinpoint a diagnosis. The program CADUCEUS did just as well as human general practitioners in a test of diagnostic skills—but not as well as specialists.

Other supersmart systems include two Stanford programs: MYCIN, which helps decide which antibiotic will best treat infections, and Project Rx, which may someday make medical discoveries of its own. Rx examines patient records for cause-effect relationships, makes hypotheses in the form A causes B, then tests the hypothesis against patient records and statistics. In one test the computer checked out seventeen hundred patients and was able to develop its own causal theories of disease. Most of what it found has already been described in the medical literature, but new discoveries are possible. ATTENDING is a program that critiques residents in anesthesiology; ONCOCIN suggests the best treatment for cancer patients. AI/RHEUM, developed by Rutgers and the University of Missouri, helps nonspecialists in the diagnosis of twenty-six rheumatic diseases.

Computers also help doctors cope with information overload by allowing them to hone their skills through game playing. Using AMA/NET, the telecommunications network of the American Medical Association, they can quiz a simulated patient (played by a

computer at Massachusetts General Hospital), suggest a diagnosis and have their problem-solving techniques critiqued by the computer. There are twenty modules in different medical specialties and of increasing difficulty; doctors can send questions or comments to the MGH computer via an electronic mail system. Originally developed for the Harvard Medical School, the programs give isolated physicians a chance to continue their education.

Physicians in private practice use computers mainly for billing, record keeping and word processing. While it may not thrill you to know that billing by computer is five to twenty times faster than manual billing and much more accurate, it's nice to know that if, say, a drug is recalled, doctors can swiftly scan their patients' charts, locate those using the drug and contact them immediately. Also, computerized records can be easily transferred to a specialist or hospital. And some legal experts have pointed out that detailed computerized medical records can help doctors defend themselves in malpractice suits, thus eventually bringing down medical costs.

Most medical programs for billing, record keeping and information management are written in a computer language called MUMPS (Massachusetts General Hospital Utility Multi-Programming System), created in 1969 by Dr. G. Octo Barnett of the hospital's Laboratory of Computer Sciences. MUMPS handles medical information five to ten times faster than any other computer language; it can randomly access a large data file, lends itself to arrays and tables, processes words and is easy to learn.

Digital Doctoring

Among the flashiest pieces of *Star Wars* hardware are the big scanners that provide more detailed pictures of the inside of a human body than anyone thought possible. The first of these was the CAT scan, designed in 1973 for imaging the brain. X-rays from various angles give a cross-sectional picture of the body. The PET scan (positron emission tomography) makes computer images from radioactive isotopes placed inside the patient and actually catches the body in the act of metabolizing. The Cine-CT scanner, developed at the University of California, San Francisco, shoots twenty-four electron-beam images per second to measure the movement of the heart, cardiac wall thickness and rate of blood flow. And a technique called nuclear magnetic resonance is especially exciting because it doesn't use radiation. Magnetic fields passed over the body cause cell nuclei to emit faint radio waves that are then monitored by computer; it looks as if NMR may reveal the presence of cancer.

Computers are replacing and revitalizing worn body parts. A device developed at Johns Hopkins, the Implantable Programmable Infusion Pump (IPIP), is

COMPUTER TERMINAL

SIX MONTHS, TED. A YEAR AT THE OUTSET!

CALDWELL

a computerized insulin pump placed just under the skin of the abdomen. The unit, three and a half inches in diameter, contains an insulin reservoir that can be filled every few months by injection. Radio waves link the pump to a physician's computer terminal. The doctor can reprogram the amount and rate of insulin being pumped by holding a computer-controlled transmitter over the patient's belly and communicating with IPIP the way Mission Control commands satellites.

Nan Davis, now twenty-four, was left paralyzed from the waist down after a car accident on prom night, yet she walked up to receive her diploma from Wright State University in Dayton, Ohio. Her legs do their work with a boost from a computer-powered machine designed by Jerrold S. Petrofsky of the school's Biomedical Engineering Laboratory. The apparatus sends electrical signals to the fifty or so muscles that work at walking, bypassing the damaged part of Davis' spinal column. Sensors on her legs, feet and shoes let the computer know how she's doing. And Davis isn't the only paralyzed person stepping out—and even bicycling—under computer power. A few hundred miles from where Nan Davis walked, at Case Western University in Cleveland, researchers have made paralyzed arms move by implanting electrodes directly into hand muscles. Electrical signals sent from a computerized transmitter make the muscles move smoothly enough to let patients eat, brush their hair and use the phone.

Computer graphics are helping to redesign the human body. A new program allows plastic surgeons to manipulate simulated bones and flesh to get a clearer idea of what a proposed facial reconstruction will look like—and how they can do the job most efficiently. CAT scans give cross-sections of the skull, but what plastic surgeons need is a 3-D picture. So researchers at St. Louis Children's Hospital developed a system that essentially stacks cross-sections to yield a 3-D picture. CASPR (Computer-Aided Surgery Project) lets surgeons play with a 3-D skull to see how patients would look if different parts of their face were moved around.

Pros and Cons

So what does it all mean? There are those who think computers will dehumanize medicine. The *medicus ex machina*, they say, will be even harder to relate to than the already icily élite class that commands us to say ah. These critics maintain that the cosmic mystery at the center of medicine, the power of healing, defies quantification. The human body is highly idiosyncratic; its workings can never be reduced to binary code. Diagnosis is at bottom intuitive, requiring a keen eye and an inspired touch. A machine just doesn't have the requisite psychic energy; doctor as shaman, computer as sham.

Will patients get enough of a doctor's attention in the digital age? In the electronic office, where the only paper is last year's magazines in the waiting room, who will care for us? Then there's the problem of privacy: the antics of the 414 gang, the hackers who trespassed on Memorial Sloane Kettering's patient files, proved that hospital records can be tampered with—a threat to patients more sinister than human error.

On the other hand, there are those who think computers will *rehumanize* medicine. No longer asked to be walking libraries, doctors can spend more time with patients. Computers can handle the mindless statistical searches, leaving doctors free to explore what's unique about individual cases. Without digital assistants, doctors won't be able to keep up and serve well. Moreover, studies have shown that some people feel more comfortable and more in control when they confide in computers instead of people.

Computers save us money, build us spare parts, reduce potentially fatal human errors and detect disease with astonishing efficiency. How bad is that? ■

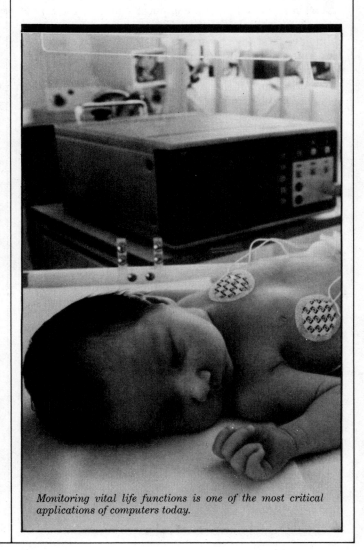

Monitoring vital life functions is one of the most critical applications of computers today.

COMPUTER CHESS
by Dan and Kathe Spracklen

Ever wonder how a computer can play a game of chess? Just think about it. Chess is a strategy game. You have to study the board and plan how to maneuver your pieces. Finally, after devising a complex strategy, you play the decisive move—checkmate! How can a computer study a chess board? How can it make plans? How can it checkmate?

Taken all at once, the problem might seem unsolvable. But the job can be broken down into three main parts:

1) *The mechanics phase:* describing a chess board and pieces in a way the computer can understand and teaching it how to move the pieces according to the rules of chess.

2) *The search phase:* looking ahead at what can happen as the game progresses. The computer still can't make real plans the way a human does, but instead must look at thousands of possibilities—many times more than the human mind can handle.

3) *The evaluation phase:* sizing up the merits of a particular position on the chess board. It wouldn't do any good for the computer to look at all those positions if it didn't know which ones were better than the others. Sure, it might know when the other guy is checkmated. But if mate isn't in sight how does it know what to do?

We'll take a look at how the Sargon chess program handles each of these phases, then discuss some of the computer chess player's limitations and how they might be conquered.

Dan and Kathe Spracklen are the authors of Sargon, the most popular chess playing program for home computers.

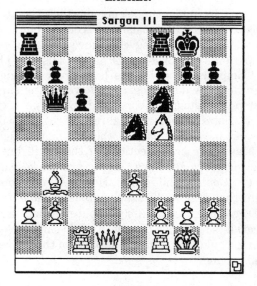

LASKER

ALEKHINE

(ZURICH, 1934)

In this famous game between two past world champions, White mounts an attack against Black's King. Nine moves later, faced with inevitable mate, Black resigns. How can a computer simulate this complex activity of the human mind?

Setting Up the Board

A human can look at a chess board and see black and white squares with pieces sitting in various places. A computer can only deal with numbers. To the computer, the chess board is an area of memory—64 locations set aside to represent the real board. A value of zero in a particular location indicates that the square is empty. A chess piece must also be a number for the computer. For instance, we might assign the following codes to the chess pieces:

1 – White Pawn	7 – Black Pawn
2 – White Knight	8 – Black Knight
3 – White Bishop	9 – Black Bishop
4 – White Rook	10 – Black Rook
5 – White Queen	11 – Black Queen
6 – White King	12 – Black King

Thus the chess board and pieces would look like this:

10	8	9	11	12	9	8	10
7	7	7	7	7	7	7	7
0	0	0	0	0	0	0	0
0	0	0	0	0	0	0	0
0	0	0	0	0	0	0	0
0	0	0	0	0	0	0	0
1	1	1	1	1	1	1	1
4	2	3	5	6	3	2	4

READY FOR A NEW GAME

Moving the chess pieces, then, becomes an arithmetic process. If we number the board squares from 1 to 64, moving a White Pawn up two squares can be accomplished by adding 16 to its starting location. A Rook can be moved one square to the left by subtracting 1 from its current square number. Other pieces can be moved by simple addition and subtraction operations as well.

57	58	59	60	61	62	63	64
49	50	51	52	53	54	55	56
41	42	43	44	45	46	47	48
33	34	35	36	37	38	39	40
25	26	27	28	29	30	31	32
17	18	19	20	21	22	23	24
9	10	11	12	13	14	15	16
1	2	3	4	5	6	7	8

Unfortunately, there is a problem associated with this simple scheme. Take, for example, a Black Rook standing on square 57. It can't move to the left because it's already at the left edge of the board. If we try to

move it one square to the left by subtracting 1 from its current square number, we get square 56. That's a valid board square under this system, but it's not a legal Rook move so a border is added to the board. The extra locations are filled with a new code:

−1 = Off Board

Using this new code solves the problem. Moves are still addition and subtraction operations, but the amounts added and subtracted are a little different from the other numbering. You might notice that the border is two squares wide. That's because Knights can jump that far. With the border, the board now looks like this:

−1	−1	−1	−1	−1	−1	−1	−1	−1	−1
−1	−1	−1	−1	−1	−1	−1	−1	−1	−1
−1	10	8	9	11	12	9	8	10	−1
−1	7	7	7	7	7	7	7	7	−1
−1	0	0	0	0	0	0	0	0	−1
−1	0	0	0	0	0	0	0	0	−1
−1	0	0	0	0	0	0	0	0	−1
−1	0	0	0	0	0	0	0	0	−1
−1	1	1	1	1	1	1	1	1	−1
−1	4	2	3	5	6	3	2	4	−1
−1	−1	−1	−1	−1	−1	−1	−1	−1	−1
−1	−1	−1	−1	−1	−1	−1	−1	−1	−1

READY FOR A NEW GAME

110	111	112	113	114	115	116	117	118	119
100	101	102	103	104	105	106	107	108	109
90	91	92	93	94	95	96	97	98	99
80	81	82	83	84	85	86	87	88	89
70	71	72	73	74	75	76	77	78	79
60	61	62	63	64	65	66	67	68	69
50	51	52	53	54	55	56	57	58	59
40	41	42	43	44	45	46	47	48	49
30	31	32	33	34	35	36	37	38	39
20	21	22	23	24	25	26	27	28	29
10	11	12	13	14	15	16	17	18	19
0	1	2	3	4	5	6	7	8	9

NEW NUMBERING FOR SQUARES

Looking Ahead

In trying to decide on a strategy, a human chess player tries to combine general concepts such as putting pressure on a weak point with specific variations ("If I go here, then he'll go there"). The number of specific variations a human can handle is quite limited; the rest must be left to intuition and experience. The computer, with its vast calculating capability, can look at many thousands of variations while making a single move choice. It is this calculating power that first frightened human chess masters and still overwhelms the novice to intermediate player when faced with a computer opponent. But why can't computers outcalculate the masters and look ahead to a won position from the earliest moves of the game? The answer to this question is the fundamental problem of computer chess. Let's look again at the position from the Alekhine-Lasker game shown at the beginning of this article. The game continued as follows:

1.	Q–Q6	N(K4)–Q2
2.	R(KB1)–Q1	R(R1)–Q1
3.	Q–N3	P–N3
4.	Q–N5!	K–R1
5.	N–Q6	K–N2
6.	P–K4	N–KN1
7.	R–Q3	P–B3
8.	N–B5ch	K–R1
9.	QXP!	Resigns

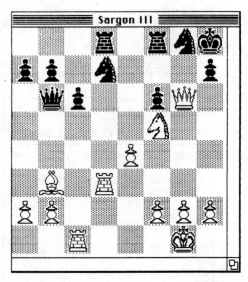

Sargon III

In this final position, if Black does not take the Queen, White will mate with Q–N7. If Black does take the Queen, White mates with R–R3.

You might think a computer capable of examining thousands of positions per move would certainly be able to look nine moves ahead and find the winning line. But you'd be wrong! Here's why it can't. In the starting position, White has

9 legal Pawn moves,
6 legal Bishop moves,
7 legal Knight moves,
8 legal Rook moves,
13 legal Queen moves, and
1 legal King move

for a total of 44 legal moves.

Suppose we start the look-ahead search by trying P–QR3. In the resulting position, Black has

6 legal Pawn moves,
12 legal Knight moves,
9 legal Rook moves,
7 legal Queen moves, and
1 legal King move

for a total of 35 legal moves.

If we assume that each of White's possibilities will give Black the same number of legal responses, the computer would have to examine about

$$44 \times 35 = 1,540$$

positions just to look one full move ahead. To look nine moves ahead would require examining approximately

$$44 \times 35 \times 44 \times 35 \times 44 \times 35 \times 44 \times 35 \times 44 \times 35 \times 44 \times 35 \times 44 \times 35 \times 44 \times 35 \times 44 \times 35$$

different positions. Though this is an unthinkable task for the computer, Alekhine surely saw the outcome of his plan. With the limited calculating power of the human mind, he could perform the needed look-ahead—a task beyond the vast calculating power of the electronic brain.

Undoubtedly the reason Alekhine succeeded was that he didn't have to consider all 44 legal moves in the first position. For example, a mating attack seldom begins with 1.P–QR3. This process of elimination, called forward pruning, is the basis of one solution to his dilemma. Typically, 7 to 9 moves might be chosen from the 30 to 40 possibilities. The problems of forward pruning are twofold: on the one hand,

$$7 \times 9 \times 7 \times 9 \times 7 \times 9 \times 7 \times 9 \times 7 \times 9 \times 7 \times 9 \times 7 \times 9 \times 7 \times 9 \times 7 \times 9$$

is still an unmanageable number; on the other hand, one of the moves not looked at might well be the best line of play.

Another approach to the explosion problem is to take advantage of some of the mathematical properties of the search to rule out examining certain branches. Called alpha-beta pruning, this technique uses the assumption that if the computer can, for example, force the win of a Pawn along some line of play, it will not choose instead to lose a Bishop. These "loser" lines can thus be cut short. The principal advantage of alpha-beta pruning is that it produces the same move that the computer would play with no pruning of any kind, and it does this in about the square root of the time it would take the non-pruning search. With alpha-beta pruning, the Alekhine-Lasker position is still out of reach, but the level of play is strong enough to give tough competition to all but the expert or master-strength player.

Positional Judgment

Each time the computer evaluates a new position, it must assign a numerical score indicating how "good" the position is. Checkmating the opponent is infinitely good; being checkmated is infinitely bad. In between is the hard part. The Sargon program's evaluation function is heavily dependent on the material balance. Many times, chess masters will willingly give up a Pawn in exchange for an advantage in position. By contrast, Sargon will give up nearly every positional advantage it possesses in order to win a Pawn or avoid losing one. If material and position were weighted more evenly, the program would give up Pawns inappropriately and thus lose for lack of material.

Quantifying chess concepts like mobility, attacking potential or piece placement is far more difficult than encoding pieces and moves. The rules of chess are fixed and inviolable, but the principles for good chess play are full of conditions and exceptions. Computer chess programs are boxed in by two interrelated difficulties. On one hand, the explosion in move possibilities limits how far ahead the program can calculate; on the other hand, evaluating the positions the computer can reach is a shaky approximation at best. The two problems are interrelated, since improving the evaluation might well take so much processor time that the depth of search is cut short.

One easy solution is to wait patiently for computers to become faster. Although this will surely happen, we should realize that a computer running about thirty-six times as fast as current machines would only get about one move deeper in the look-ahead.

A more tractable approach is to concentrate on improving the evaluation function (while keeping a close watch on the time it consumes). For instance, a chess player's "sense of danger" will certainly be aroused by an unprotected King. Programming a "sense of danger" could involve nothing more than reducing the evaluation score for the same situation. Gaining a better understanding of the worth of a Pawn, compared to certain positional criteria, could produce a marked improvement in the machine's play. ∎

IMPROVING A CHESS CLASSIC

When we wrote Sargon III, the sequel to our Sargon II chess program for microcomputers, we included the following two substantive changes that greatly enhanced its overall chess-playing abilities.

● *Rank and file.* An improved mathematical model represents the board, employing a grid system with square designations that can be broken down into two parts: the rank (row of the chess board) and the file (column of the board). Such a system greatly simplifies encoding chess strategy. Where previously the program had to calculate the new square number before it could look at the board array to see what was stored at that square, in Sargon III the square value itself tells if a piece has attempted to move off the board.

● *Capture search.* Speed is the greatest single limiting factor in the look-ahead process. The more quickly a given position can be created and evaluated, the more positions can be examined and the deeper the search can explore. Sargon II stopped at every move to be evaluated and took a long, hard look at the possible piece exchanges and the expected outcome of each; called a "static exchange evaluator," this process could examine about twenty-three positions per second on the Apple II. Sargon III uses a faster, more accurate method, the "capture search," which determines the value of trades by actually making them on the board. Once it reaches a position that it would like to evaluate, this process generates a restricted set of moves: captures only. It keeps generating captures until 1) there are no more captures possible, or 2) the remaining captures available lose more than they gain. This, with other improvements in the search, means that Sargon III on the Apple II can evaluate some 250 positions per second.

Sargon III's evaluation function benefited from the revised method of storing the board in memory and from the improved method of examining exchanges. But improvements in positional analysis cannot be summed up in one or two sweeping changes that make everything simpler or faster. It is always difficult to translate abstract human knowledge into a mathematical formula. ("Keep up pressure in the center," the master says. But how do you describe "pressure" to a computer?) In the end, refinements are the sum of more and more little pieces of knowledge finally translated into algorithms.

Guided mostly by your comments and letters about Sargon II, we also addressed the questions of how the program presents itself to the user, what you can do with it and how easily you can do it. Since we made a great many changes in this respect, you might say this is the part of the program that you improved.

D. AND K. SPRACKLEN

THE COMPUTER LISTENS UP

by Joanne Austin

When the time comes for you to communicate with your computer by merely talking to it, you'll have to either learn its language or teach it yours. If you think learning a foreign language is difficult, pity the poor computer!

In the first place, while the variations in different words can be shown on scientists' detailed charts of frequency and amplitude, the words by themselves say nothing unless they have a syntactical order. Second, while human speech often rambles on, sometimes running words together and coming up with slang like "gonna" for "going to," sound alone is not enough to let the computer know where one word ends and another begins. Third, while we have an uncanny ability to understand what's said to us even in the midst of a rock concert, the computer is easily confused by noise.

What scientists have done is to digitize human speech, converting it into a number code so the computer is more likely to understand what's being said. Every word that must be recognized by the machine has to be broken down into its numbers, i.e., the numerical values for the frequencies and amplitudes of each sound in the word.

Recognition of a word by the computer requires five steps: 1) input of the word through a microphone; 2) analysis by the computer of the frequencies of each sound in that word; 3) isolation by the computer of that word's identifying features; 4) conversion of these features to a digital format through an algorithm, or mathematical equation; 5) recognition by the computer of that word, against a similar digital word, or template, stored in its memory.

Voice Training

To understand the spoken word, a computer must be trained. Most voice recognition systems cur-

rently in use are speaker-dependent. The computer is taught what words it is supposed to know, and the system learns to recognize the way a certain speaker or group of speakers will say those words. Speaker-dependent machines can understand a fairly large vocabulary—up to about a thousand words.

Ideally, we would like the computer to recognize a word anytime and by anyone who addresses the machine, i.e., to be speaker-independent. Such systems exist, but they possess a limited vocabulary. They recognize only digits 0 through 9 and simple control words such as "yes," "no," "go," "stop" and "erase." For the computer to understand many different frequencies, operators input hundreds of different voices. With that many templates in memory, how any random person pronounces a common word probably corresponds to one of the templates.

Training the computer can be tedious. Most systems cannot discern separate words if they're spoken together in a continuous sentence, which is the way we usually talk. Users must enter each word in an isolated, discrete manner, with definite pauses, to allow the computer to figure out the beginning and end of the word. To compensate for slight changes in pronunciation or frequency, each user must enter the same word several times—usually three to five, but sometimes as many as nine.

But perseverance in training reaps rewards. You only have to train the computer once. Additional commands or word changes amend previous instructions. Probability programs allow the computer to make decisions regarding what you said. Researchers have assigned probabilities to all the different ways of garbling a group of words and programmed the computer to choose what was most likely spoken.

For industrial and commercial users, voice rec-

Joanne Austin is the editor of Alive and Well *magazine. She uses an Apple IIe and Apple Writer for her writing at home.*

A FEW WORDS ABOUT SPEECH SYNTHESIS

BY LARRY GONICK, WHO TALKS TO THE COMPUTERS, EVEN WHEN HE MAKES LITTLE SENSE

ALL SOUND IS A DISTURBANCE OF AIR PRESSURE OVER TIME.

THESE PASSING PERTURBATIONS CAN BE GRAPHED...

...AND DIGITIZED, BY SAMPLING THE GRAPH A FEW THOUSAND TIMES A SECOND...

...AND STORED IN MEMORY, DISK FOR EXAMPLE...

...AND PLAYED BACK AT WILL. THIS IS DIGITAL RECORDING.

BLAH BLAH IK GIK DORP ZORP NEEP

DIGITAL RECORDING TECHNOLOGY CAN REPRODUCE SPEECH, MUSIC, OR ANY OTHER SOUND WITH SUPERB FIDELITY,

A BIG "BUT"

BUT IT ONLY PARTLY SOLVES THE CENTRAL PROBLEM OF SPEECH SYNTHESIS,

NAMELY,

HOW TO TRANSLATE A TEXT, ANY TEXT, INTO NATURAL-SOUNDING SPEECH.

TO DO THAT, YOU DIGITALLY PRERECORD SOME "ATOMS OF SPEECH"— PHONEMES, OR HALF-SYLLABLES— AND THEN COMBINE THEM AS NEEDED.

LATER

"LA-TER"

Lə
Lā
Lä
Lä
Lab
Lac
...
ten
tep
ter
tes
tet

THEN YOU HAVE TO COPE WITH ALL THE PECULIARITIES OF SPELLING...

YOU OUGHT TO PLOUGH YOUR DOUGH THROUGH A TROUGH, ROUGHLY

...AND THE SUBTLETIES OF ACCENT, TONE, ELONGATION, AND THE OTHER SHADINGS WE "NATURALLY" GIVE OUR SPEECH.

IN CONSIDERATION OF THE INEVVITABLE SLIDE INTO UTTER MEANINGLESSNESS, I HAVE RESOLVED TO INSERT MY FEET INTO BLOCKS OF CEMENT AND PURSUE DIVING AS AN AVOCATION...

THEREFORE, SPEECH SYNTHESIS PROGRAMS MUST INCLUDE A MORE OR LESS VAST NUMBER OF PRONUNCIATION RULES, WHICH MUST BE CHECKED BEFORE EACH UTTERANCE.

THE MORE MESSAGES YOU WANT SPOKEN, THE MORE MI-STA-KES YOU MUST EXPECT!

BUT THE PAY-OFF IS GREAT! WITH TALKING COMPUTERS, BUSY EXECUTIVES WILL BE ABLE TO ATTEND TO OTHER IMPORTANT TASKS WHILE LISTENING TO DATA!

$1,374,479.62
$3,245,703.10
$625,791,342.00
$1,700,010.55

READING A FIRST COURSE

AND OF COURSE, TALKING MICROPROCESSORS WILL BE CONSTANTLY REPORTING ON THE STATUS OF EVERYTHING!!

I'M OVEREXPOSED!

THIS IS YOUR EARRING SPEAKING! EVERYTHING'S FINE!

YOUR HEART RATE IS CURRENTLY 72.3!

THIS IS THE EARTH TALKING TO YOU! I'M IN BAD SHAPE AND YOU'RE NOT HELPING!

ognition, or voice data entry (VDE), has many applications in research and manufacturing situations: product testing, inspection, inventory control, laboratory work, machine programming and quality control. Voice data entry is also effective if the operator needs mobility, is in a crowded control room, is competing for use of a single keyboard among several operators or is working from a remote location.

If a business determines that voice data entry would benefit productivity, the next step is designing vocabulary requirements that suit the tasks at hand. Computers recognize short, multisyllable words and those with strong consonant sounds better than they do single-syllable, vowel-sound words. The vocabulary should be easily memorizable by the operator.

Syntactic control, a recent development that significantly reduces substitution errors, limits the total vocabulary active at any one time. This enables the computer to make its template selection from only part of the total word list. Such advances make speaker-dependent systems capable of 99 percent accuracy.

For Your Ears Only?

Though not yet perfect, voice recognition systems are destined to play a major role in society. At the super-secret National Security Agency at Fort George Meade in Maryland, sensitive computers regularly monitor the overseas telephone calls of corporations and individuals. NSA's system seeks target words, such as "high technology" and "Russia," in order to prevent the Soviet Union from stealing computer or defense secrets.

Other users of voice data entry include handicapped people who communicate with the system by voice alone through a telecommunications link-up. And speaker verification by voice recognition allows industrial security personnel to prohibit unauthorized entry of buildings or computer systems.

Ideally, all communication with personal computers will someday be by voice alone. This means that keyboards will be obsolete. Computerized typewriters will process letters in the time it takes us to dictate—and anybody, not just a preentered set of speaker-users, will be able to use that typewriter. Domestically, both IBM and Xerox are working on a "talkwriter" that would recognize vocabularies of between five thousand and ten thousand words, respectively, spoken by any user.

The Japanese, of course, are not far behind. NEC Corporation has developed a speaker-dependent device that recognizes connected speech up to four seconds long pulled from a 150-word English vocabulary. But the capabilities of "talkwriters" developed for Japanese speakers surpass those of English-language machines. Japanese uses only 120 syllables, while

English uses about 10,000. And Japanese is spoken more regularly, with more discernible breaks between words making training easier.

The cost of voice recognition systems affects their deployment. Small systems can cost as little as $500; very complicated setups, as high as $65,000. For the personal computer, compatible hardware peripherals are selling for anywhere from $1,000 to $3,000.

Talk to Me

Apple, Commodore, IBM, Atari, Coleco and Tandy/Radio Shack do not manufacture their own voice recognition systems, though some have speech synthesizers. So far nothing has equaled Texas Instruments' Speech Command System. For use with TI's Professional Computer, the Speech Command System is an internal voice recognition/telephone management board, not a peripheral. The system accepts up to 950 vocal commands, each the equivalent of up to 40 keystrokes. So much stored information requires a 10-megabyte hard disk rather than a floppy, so the Professional Computer has hard-disk capability built in. Two floppies will work, but will allow only fifty vocal commands.

The TI Speech Command System is speaker-dependent. Users enter each command up to nine times to accommodate voice fluctuations. But unlike some other systems, this one has what TI calls a "transparent keyboard." Once the voice commands are entered, the operator programs the computer to convert the spoken words to keystrokes. The voice command "indent," for example, may correspond to a complicated series of keystrokes like INDENT PARAGRAPH 5 SPACES comprising up to 40 strokes.

With a modem, the Speech Command System practically becomes a personal secretary. The system can make calls, using your own voice through a speaker, and record the answers in the system. Others can call you, get your voice on the phone and leave a message. With a Dow Jones Natural Link, you can merely ask what a stock is doing and the computer will tell you. A tickler calendar allows you to communicate with people or companies on a preset schedule. Since the system uses your voice, it sounds natural and not robot-like.

The entire setup consists of two piggyback circuit boards for telephone and speech, a headset with microphone, a separate speaker, telephone cable, installation and diagnostics guide, a diagnostics diskette, software diskette and user's manual. Total price: about $2,700.

Optimists predict a $2 billion voice recognition industry by 1990. If they're right, the day may come when computers will handle all our business among themselves with just a few words from us.   ■

FOREIGN DELIGHTS

Artwork for preceding page

Artist:
   James Dowlen © 1984 Time Arts
   Inc.
Computer:
   Time Arts Tesserac professional
   paint system (IBM PC–compati-
   ble)
Software:
   Lumina by Time Arts
Input:
   Digitizing pen and tablet

MICRO ENGLISH: A NEW LANGUAGE

by Fabrizio Franzi

Not unlike the pidgin English that spread among traders throughout the South Seas, Computer English is a *lingua franca* essential to international communications. Everywhere this odd jargon, full of words and expressions whose meanings are quite different from those taught in school, is being learned by computer users as a means of conversing with each other and with their machines.

Fortunately, those of us for whom English is not a native tongue need to know less than two thousand words to communicate in this computer age dialect. And, too, the vocabulary of Computer English can often be assimilated into our own language structure: words can be incorporated unchanged, as in the Italian *fare un file* ("create a file"), or endings can be tacked on, as in the French *booter* ("to boot"). It might not be elegant, but it does the job.

Speaking Computer

Whether Computer English is used for convenience, for snob appeal or, as is most often the case, for the sake of precision, two sources of difficulty are presented to the new speakers: technical terms like "random access memory" that exist only in information processing (or in other technical disciplines and have been borrowed) and those that first appeared in the folklore of computers.

Of most interest is the second category, where everyday use and "computerese" meanings are quite different. These terms reflect the originality of the microcomputer community, defy translation and sow confusion. Often we hear sentences like "There is a glitch in this program" or "The card goes in the bus." I overheard a friend of mine, a French free-lance technical translator, ask her computer consultant husband:

Fabrizio Franzi is the founder and president of AL-PHEE, a Brussels-based international computer consulting and software distribution firm specializing in artificial intelligence.

"What do flies have to do with computer software?" She was referring to the word "bug," of course, whose computer meaning is still mostly unknown on the Continent.

Abbreviations provide another example of the peculiarities of Computer English. The abbreviation for personal computer is PC; the abbreviation in

French should be OP, (for *ordinateur personnel*), but most of the time we use "pay-say"—which is our pronunciation of PC. Suffice it to say that proficiency in acronyms and abbreviated jargon is strongly recommended in the world of international communications.

The acceptance of Computer English varies in degree from country to country. In Holland, Belgium and the Scandinavian countries, where English is spoken quite fluently, the new language is used freely and meets little resistance. In Germany and France, where fluency in English is less common, Computer English is used for the most part by business and computing professionals; these two major European countries are protective of their language and place a great deal of emphasis on documentation in their native tongue, in certain cases imposing specific linguistic regulations. In the remaining non-English-speaking European countries, most interested people get by with moderate fluency in Computer English and don't make much fuss.

FRENCH COMPUTER NO-NO'S

On December 22, 1981, in a gesture of concern over the creeping Americanization of Gallic culture, the French government issued an edict banning U.S.-derived computer terms from official documents. Below are just a few of these *bêtes noires*, with their sanctioned French translations.

backup	*de secours* (adj.)
data	*donnée* (f.)
data base	*base de données* (f.)
digital	*numérique* (adj.)
display	*visu* (f.)
	or *visuel* (m.)
hard copy	*tirage* (m.)
	or *fac-sim* (m.)
hardware	*matériel* (f.)
increment	*incrément* (m.)
interactive	*interactif* (f.)
light pen	*photostyle* (m.)
on-line	*en ligne* (adv.)
RAM	*mémoire vive* (f.)
ROM	*mémoire morte* (f.)
software	*logiciel* (m.)
word processing	*traitement de texte* (f.)

Independently of their countries' official cultural policies, Europeans agree that the relative precision of Computer English results in shorter sentences and a simpler style. When an attempt to coin an equivalent for "cursor" in German produced *bildeschirmanzeiger*, it was quickly decided to use the English word. Since *curseur* already exists in French, we use our own term; the correct French term for "disk drive" is *tournedisque*, similar to our word for "phonograph," so to avoid linguistic confusion we usually give way to the English.

Computer Esperanto?

No one can accurately predict how Computer English will fare in the non-English-speaking community, but here and there can be found some underlying trends. It is fair to say that terms related to a computer's system software will remain solidly based in Computer English. Now that operating systems like CP/M and MS-DOS have become international standards, their vocabularies will also become standard. COBOL, BASIC and Pascal statements have attained the same status, since there are few workable alternatives to these Computer English-based programming languages. An attempt to translate BASIC into French may work from an operational point of view, but seems to have been a peculiar waste of gray matter. Most computer programs are still written in the English-derived BASIC.

The common names of the utilities needed in the normal use of a computer (e.g., "copy," "catalog," "pip," "stat," "delete," etc.) represent a precise sequence of events. Their names are either acronyms, contractions or plain English words. Because they do things specific to computers, their direct translation must also reflect the operations involved. Generally, it is easier to associate these operational aspects to one English expression rather than to a series of identical French or German equivalents.

Keyboard functions provide other short English words that are here to stay: "reset," "shift," "clear," "return," "enter." We find these on pocket calculators, micros or mainframes. Some manufacturers translate their keycaps, but when last in a computer shop I heard the following words from a Flemish-speaking customer who was being assailed with the virtues of the Wang-PC translated keyboard: "Oh," said the customer, "this is the 'Clear' key . . ."

Maybe simplicity is not always of this world, yet we all crave it because it's so hard to digest the mass of information we're subjected to every day. After this cosmopolitan tour, let us part, dear reader and microcomputer pal, with this thought from our newly discovered international dialect: "Groovy, *mon ami*, c'est la vie des PC!"   ■

PERSONAL COMPUTING IN EUROPE

by Colin S. Boettcher

While most histories of personal computing center on its development in the United States, the world's first commercial microcomputer system must in fact be credited to Europe and an enterprising young Frenchman of Vietnamese descent. Announced in February 1973, Truong Trong Thi's Micral was built around the Intel 8008, contained 256 bytes of memory

Colin S. Boettcher is counselor for international affairs to France's Agence de l'Informatique.

(with expansion capability up to 1K) and came with keyboard and video monitor. Although Mr. Truong presented the Micral, complete with floppy and hard disks, at the 1974 National Computer Conference in the United States, not until 1976 did an American firm agree to license his machine. When he later tried to set up his own U.S. subsidiary, Truong encountered financial difficulties that forced him finally to abandon the project.

Truong Trong Thi, inventor of the first commercial micro-computer system.

Although personal computing in present-day Europe takes many forms, from the familiar home video games to the multifunction work stations of large corporations, two factors have slowed its progress. First, hardware and software of American origin were significantly more expensive in Europe than in the United States. Second, language constitutes a major barrier to greater American penetration of the European market. Programs and documentation in local languages are a prerequisite for the success of personal computers, especially as we descend the pyramid of users to the non-English-speaking "man in the street." This problem goes beyond translation itself, extending to different character sets: in France, Germany and Spain—indeed in most countries of Europe—diacritical marks are an integral, vital part of the written language.

Her Majesty's Systems

The United Kingdom, more advanced than the other European countries when it comes to personal computing, can boast more micros per capita than the United

FRENCH (COMPUTER) LOVERS

Passionate about whatever catches our fancy, whether it's wine, women or computers, we French espouse micros with an enthusiasm bordering on the fanatical. From my own observations, I believe there is no nation that surpasses our true love of *l'art de la microinformatique.*

Consider, for example, our hackers. One friend of mine is a programmer who boasts that he can copy any software disk, no matter how ingenious the author's protection scheme. Taking him up on this challenge, another friend opened up a disk drive, inverted two wires in order to make the diskette spin backwards, and recorded a copy of a trivial program on the backwards drive. A few days later, during a visit from the programmer, he demonstrated his new software (which, of course, ran perfectly well when loaded from the doctored disk player). Then he removed the diskette and turned it over to the would-be codebreaker.

Every few weeks now, when they meet at the computer shop, the programmer brings in another unsuccessful solution. My word, but he seems to be losing a lot of sleep! Because he is software-oriented, it has never occurred to him that a hardware trick might be the source of his frustration. Still, he won't give up. Cracking this diskette has become his *idée fixe.*

Another friend is perhaps the most *passionné* of our computer circle. His is a very French living arrangement, wherein his estranged wife lives on the first floor of a fashionable Paris town house, his children on the second, and he and his mistress on the third. One night, over Pernod and Gauloises, he told me the following story.

"I first became enamored of micros," he began,

"when I discovered the Pet in *Playboy.* Such magnificent photographs! Front view, full disclosure . . . I started to dream. Then in 1978 there appeared a French computer magazine, *Microsystemes,* and then a second, *L'Ordinateur Individuel,* and I devoured them. I toyed with the idea of writing a backgammon program that would beat top-rated players. I was fatally attracted.

"Then I took a bite of my first Apple, which produced more than a few dramas at home. My daughters played Space Invaders and Apple Panic until late at night and got terrible marks in school. Eventually Popeye, my fox terrier, solved the problem. He ate their game paddles, and that was that. At last I could be alone with my new companion.

"I started buying mailing list programs for my business. None of them would print two labels in a row, so I tried to break into their codes in order to rewrite them. I learned Pascal and assembly language. I bought copiers and other utility programs. I bought utilities to improve the utilities . . . I didn't send a letter to a customer in five years and lost most of them!

"But still that blessed computer called to me. As programs got more user-friendly, my family started to behave in a less friendly manner. Then one day my wife told me: 'You'll have to choose. It's me or the computer.' I chose the latter, and today my computer is my mistress. You see, my friend, *plus ça change, plus c'est la même chose!*"

JEAN-LOUIS MEILLAUD, Parisian computer consultant and bridge champion

States. This phenomenon is attributed to Sir Clive Sinclair, inventor of the world's first pocket calculator, who in the 1970s introduced the ZX80 home computer for the equivalent of less than $100. Sir Clive then went on to offer the ZX81, widely sold in America as the Timex/Sinclair 1000, and the Spectrum with improved keyboard and full-color graphics. The Spectrum became one of the best-selling computers of all time, quickly selling over two million units in the United Kingdom, and was followed by the QL ("quantum leap") for users who wanted business-level computing at home computer prices.

Sir Clive's entrepreneurial spirit spread among the British people and gave rise to numerous small businesses in the development and support of personal computers. In addition, the highly respected British Broadcasting Corporation, which set up a series of TV programs addressing the issues of microcomputing, contracted with Acorn for a computer built to its own specifications. Used as a support for the TV programs, the Acorn/BBC micro soon had a following similar to the Apple II cult and spawned a multitude of mom-and-pop efforts in hardware, software, books and magazines. Financing became relatively easy to find (albeit on a more limited scale than in the United States), despite record unemployment and little confidence in the future.

British programmers, who had to squeeze the most out of machines with limited capabilities and memory, have succeeded in gaining a reputation for the quality of their software. Their programs do not travel well to other countries, however, perhaps because the elegant business software is specific to British fiscal practices or because the original entertainment software (with witty titles like Mutant Camels from Outer Space) tends to be written for machines available only in the United Kingdom.

Les Ordinateurs Individuels

Meanwhile, across the Channel, France computes to her own tune as she pursues a national goal of developing a strong domestic computer industry. Inadequate software and keyboard phobia are no longer the rule (even computer professionals were at one time reluctant to touch the keyboard for fear of losing status). Plans for government-funded installation of personal computers in schools, originally devised in the 1970s, have received new impetus. Extensive training and awareness programs have been instituted to bring the nation into the forefront of data processing both as a user and as an industry leader.

France did have successful start-ups like Goupil, born in a Paris basement with help from the telecommunications authority and reminiscent of the Apple Computer. The original Goupil ("fox"), however, was

DER EUROCOMPUTER PIONIER

Doktor Konrad Zuse, continental computer discoverer.

Fifty years ago, as a student of civil engineering, I was struck by the immense calculations that had to be performed in the construction of buildings. I became convinced that machines should be doing these calculations, but at the time I understood nothing about computers. I was not even aware of Babbage's works or of diverse parallel developments in other countries such as the United States.

Deciding to try new ways, I built my own computer with the following original features: calculation of long programs controlled by a sequence of orders punched on tape (I started by using punched strips of film); use of the binary number system; introduction of floating point mathematics.

I began with a strong preference for mechanical systems, but I did not succeed and was forced to switch to electromechanical technology. Finally in 1941, in my parents' Berlin apartment, I completed the Z3—the first computer of its kind in the world. My work was based mostly on private initiative, with assistance from some friends. Only after 1940 had I received sponsorship from the DVL (Deutsche Versuchsanstalt fur Luftfahrt) so that numerical problems, especially for aerodynamic applications, could be solved.

During these developments, further aspects of computing became apparent. My friend Helmut Schreyer proposed the use of tubes in place of relays. This idea was a bold one. The development of the switching algebra led to a connection with mathematical logic. These new ideas extended the concept of calculation beyond numbers and gave rise to the concept of "artificial intelligence."

Today we can look back on five decades of developments. Not everything that happened was intended by the computer's inventors. Even an old pioneer like me can still be surprised by the its effect. And work on the computer is far from finished. We must be prepared for further sensational innovations, with consequences that will not always be easy to master.

KONRAD ZUSE, creator of the Z series of prototype computers in Germany from 1935 to 1945

soon surpassed by other models, including the made-in-France Thomson TO series from one of the nation's largest consumer electronics firms. Today the major computer manufacturer is Bull, which bought out Mr. Truong's R2E company and now markets the Micral line of state-of-the-art micros as its main offering in the field.

One contribution from the French government, a notable scheme conceived by Jean-Jacques Servan-Schreiber and initiated by President Mitterrand, was the establishment of the World Center for Microcomputing and Human Resources in the midst of Paris. It was Servan-Schreiber's hope, and that of a dozen other personalities from around the world, that personal computing would ease the plight of the Third World and improve the lot of mankind in general.

The original idea was to set up a resource center, staffed by international scientists, that would be open twenty-four hours a day, seven days a week, so "the man in the street" could just walk in anytime and use the various personal computers (or *ordinateurs individuels*) with or without assistance. Plans were also formulated to investigate the impact of personal computers on young children in Senegal with no previous exposure to modern technologies and to observe the social effects of saturating a popular area of Marseilles with two thousand micros. The scientists ended up battling not only the formidable technical challenges but each other, however, and some of them left (including Professors Papert and Negroponte, on leave from M.I.T. to organize the project) while others were replaced. In 1983 the center was reorganized and financed by the telecommunications authority (the PTT), its aims somewhat clarified and a more realistic workplan defined.

In the meantime, France plays host to the biggest computer show in the world. SICOB is held in the modern convention hall at the Rond Point de La Défense in Paris, drawing as many as two hundred thousand attendees from all over the planet.

Across the Rhine

In Germany things are different again. Businessmen use their computers mainly in the office, so the introduction of personal computers into the home has to be justified by entirely other criteria such as cost effectiveness and task applicability.

As in France, software has been the major barrier to the rapid penetration of personal computing. Moreover, Germany has a shortage of computer professionals, and the development of amateur programming has not occurred. Computers have been introduced into schools only recently and, perhaps because of the country's federated nature, on a piecemeal basis.

Another restraining aspect has been the role of the major computer manufacturing company, Siemens, which in the early 1980s declared that personal computing would not be one of their lines of business. Nevertheless, statistics show that Germany is number two in Europe with respect to personal computers. There is also a growing emphasis on quality products. Commodore 64s are among the most popular personal computers in Germany, with a much greater number of disk drives in use (instead of slower but less expensive cassette recorders) than in any other country.

It is here, moreover, that we find some of the world's most stringent standards regarding such factors as ergonomy and man-machine interface. Indeed, the German requirements are often used as goals in the computer design practiced in other countries.

Cosmopolitan Computers

While numerous computer clubs and associations exist throughout Europe, the concept of interconnection and interreaction by means of telecommunications has not developed to the extent evidenced in the United States. This is partly because telephone facilities are more expensive to use, but also because the modems that permit such interconnection are often of American origin and not approved by the national telecommunications authorities.

For the same reasons, the world of the hacker who explores how to penetrate others' computer systems is rather limited. Although in Europe there appears to be a more developed sense of wrongdoing in this respect, awareness of the value of such intangibles as information and software is leading to the serious problem of illicit copying.

The parochial approach taken by local manufacturers is another source of difficulty in the European personal computer industry. For too long, manufacturing companies have been happy to sell a few machines to a limited market in their own region. But with the recognition, albeit slow, that an international market is involved, these same companies are having trouble finding the necessary financing to become world players. What the Europeans are also learning, the hard way, is that it is not enough to have the best product; marketing, historically a weakness, must now be exploited to the fullest.

What Europe has lost in the development of its industry has been more than made up for in the use of personal computers and interaction with other services such as videotext and electronic banking. With telecommunications and information technology now widely promoted by various governments, and with the maturation of the personal computer industry, it is to be expected that innovation rather than manufacturing will be the direction of the future.   ■

KEYBOARD KARMA

by Alexander Randall V

The Japanese have keyboard problems that would cause the average American typist to dive for cover. At the core of their written language is an amalgam of three alphabets, each vastly more complex than the simple script of the western world.

Until the seventh century, Japan had a fully formed language with no written system at all. Then in 661 Japanese explorers, encountering the advanced culture of China, saw the remarkable utility of the Chinese pictographs and took them home to fit their own spoken language. These pictographs, called Kanji in Japanese, are line drawings that represent core concepts: a man, for example, is described by a stick figure with a trunk and legs; the pictograph for "big" shows a man with his arms outstretched; the horse symbol has four legs with hair streaming behind. There are more than 20,000 pictographic characters, though only about 2,300 are used in daily writing.

When it turned out that the Chinese pictures could not show all the nuances of spoken Japanese, a second phonetic writing system (Hiragana) was developed for more complex grammar. Later on, a third alphabet (Katakana) was created to cover the same sounds, but only for writing borrowed words from for-

Alexander Randall V manages the Boston Computer Exchange, conducting computer business worldwide.

eign cultures. In written Japanese, the phrase "I want a Coca-Cola" involves characters from each of the three alphabets: "I" and "want" come from the Chinese characters, but their grammatical markers are from Hiragana and "Coke" is written with the Katakana for foreign words.

While Americans can describe every conceivable thought with only twenty-six characters and a handful of symbols, the Japanese have to use two alphabets of forty-eight characters each and the massive Chinese pictograph system to write even the briefest of notes. Our compact set of characters led to the development of simple keyboards with all the letters and symbols, but how do you create a keyboard for thousands of characters?

In the early years of mechanical typing machines, the Japanese created a variety of keyboards to meet the challenge of their unusual language. Their early typewriters, more like typesetting machines than our typewriters, featured large flat trays of metal slugs each of which bore a separate character. The operator slid a pointer around the tray and aligned it with the desired character, then pushed a lever that grabbed the slug, picked it up and struck it against the paper. Since there was a limit on the size of these machines and the number of characters they could address, it was a major victory for written communication when the government announced that only a portion of the full character set was to be used in normal discourse.

These typesetting machines became the standard for most printed communication in Japan, and secretarial students spent a great deal of time learning how to type at eighty words per minute. Aside from improvements in the machines' efficiency and size, there were really very few changes in the technology until the introduction of electronic devices in the 1960s and '70s.

Without a simple keyboard tradition, the Japanese brought no prejudices to the computerized word processing era. A variety of machines and keyboards are in current use, and there are several different approaches to the character problem. One system uses a large digitizer pad that has the same layout as the old mechanical typesetter. The operator uses a pointer to indicate the desired character, and the digitizer sends the code for that character to the computer. The process is fast, but the pad requires a whole desk and extensive computer software to make it functional. The advantage is that the operator can input all the common characters. Since the digitizer has a lot of

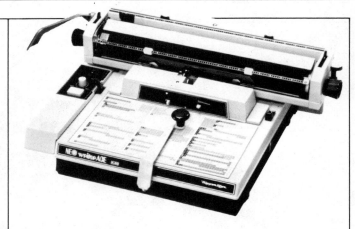

Stylus-entry keyboard.

room, there is no reason not to include English, Greek and Russian characters as well.

Another approach involves a keyboard with each of a few hundred keys representing several different characters. One machine has a hundred well-spaced keys with plastic overlays that can change their designation. Each overlay has a set of holes along the edge that fit over light-sensitive points beside the keys and tell the machine which characters the keys are to represent. The operator flips frantically through the over-

lays to change from one set of characters to the next. The process can be slow, but there is virtually no limit to the number of characters the keyboard can address.

By far the most popular approach to keyboards in Japan is a modified version of the English-language key set (English characters are used for some programming tasks). Our twenty-six letters appear on the keys, as does one of the short phonetic alphabets; since each phonetic sound may represent several Chinese characters, the operator uses phonetic symbols to call a small set of these characters out of ROM memory onto the screen, picks out the one he wants and executes a command that enters it into the text. The process is slow, but at least the operator can work with a manageable keyboard.

For centuries, the Japanese have had to contend with a writing problem that cannot be solved by a borrowed answer. In developing their own solution, however, they could very well supply some answers to problems we all share. It should come as no surprise if Japan were to create a keyboard on a ball, for example, or do away with writing altogether in favor of speech recognition. Indeed, it is not unlikely that the first functional speech machines will come into our homes via Tokyo. ■

Electric typesetting typewriter.

Keyboard cornucopia: To accommodate their sprawling alphabet/ideogram spelling system, the Japanese have designed a wide variety of word processing keyboards. The OKI Lettermate stylus-entry keyboard on page 267 uses a pointer and tablet for character entry. The Word Input Terminal (bottom right) uses large keys bearing as many as twelve different characters; selection is made with numbered control keys near the bottom right corner of the keyboard. The Oasys word processing system (below) uses the standard abbreviated Katakana alphabet set. The NEC keyboard (above) uses an unconventional key arrangement for greater comfort and speed.

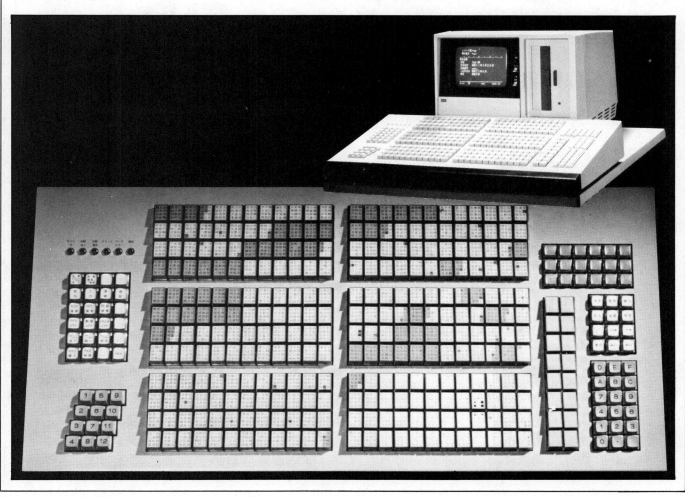

TECHNO-TOKYO

Tokyo's word processor coffee shop offers computers and hot beverages.

Everyday life in modern Japan reflects an astonishing mix of ancient wisdom and scientific vision. Below are just a few of the ingenious uses assigned to the computer by the world's leading high-tech nation.

• In the capital city of Tokyo, computerized traffic lights chime to let blind pedestrians know when the light turns green. Because the consultant who came up with this scheme was a Scotsman, the tune they hear is "Coming Through the Rye." Other developments on behalf of the blind include sidewalks and station platforms with Braille lines to allow easy, safe maneuverability.

• Ever fashion-conscious, the Japanese have come up with the world's first software for hair salons. Customers have their photographs fed into a *pasu-kon*, or personal computer, so they can see how they look in the different hairstyles that are simulated on-screen.

• Even the ancient practice of palmistry has been entrusted to the computer. Photocopies of palm prints are scanned by the machine, which reads the lines and sorts through its data base to tell the client's future.

• The pitch of a baby's cry will automatically set his voice-activated crib rocking in a regular rhythm. If the crying persists, the crib-puter will sing a lullaby, tell a fairy tale or relay whatever comforting words have been programmed by the mother. When the baby becomes quiet, the crib stops its motion within thirty seconds.

• Coffee shops, traditionally part of the casbah of Japan's Collective Unconscious, have added high tech to the menu. Today they feature word processors and printers in order to attract a more computer-literate crowd.

• The Shinjuku Washington, the world's first truly high-tech hotel, has computer tellers that perform guest registration, accept advance payment for rooms, dispense change and issue a magnetic key card programmed to expire at the designated checkout time. After an animated character appears on the monitor and bows, welcoming the guest to the hotel and explaining how to check in by keyboard, the card is carried to the room and inserted in a special slot beside the door. A green light goes on, the door is opened and the card is inserted in a slot in the bedside console to activate the room's energy-saving electrical system: air conditioning, central heating, TV and lights. From then on, whenever the guest pulls an item from the mini-bar refrigerator (an "isotonic" drink, perhaps, or some dried cuttlefish), makes a phone call or watches a movie on the video system, the cost is tabulated by the hotel's central computer.

• On the sidewalks of Tokyo, robots in colorful clown costumes perform tricks verging on slapstick to lure passers-by into stores and restaurants. Japan's lead in the "fifth generation" artificial intelligence race owes as much to its fascination with robots and children's cartoons as to advanced conceptual thinking. Indeed, AI technicians' labs are littered with colorful comics as they seek the breakthrough inspiration that may come at the turn of a page.

ALEXANDER BESHER

CHINA IN THE COMPUTER AGE

by Alexander Besher

One of the most successful firms owned by Overseas Chinese, U.S.-based Wang has pioneered automated translation from English to Chinese ideograms.

After five centuries of deliberately turning its back on technology, the largest nation on earth is playing catch-up with computers. The creators of silk and paper, printing and gunpowder, are taking steps to recast the face of China with the so-called Four Mod-

San Francisco writer Alexander Besher is a creative consultant to the computer industry through his firm Compatible Communications. He was born in China, raised in Japan and introduced to personal computers in California.

ernizations program. Countering the effects of the Cultural Revolution, when roving hordes of Red Guards busied themselves dismantling China's high-tech industries, this program is designed to leap-frog the entire country into the information age.

The China Road

In the West, the computer is regarded as a labor-saving device. In China, where the one billion population is growing by seventeen million each year, saving on ten-cent-an-hour labor is hardly a paramount consideration. Rather, it is in the realm of information and data bases, on-line transaction processing and local area networks that the Chinese are most involved. One major development has been the establishment of a soybean varieties data base system that would provide stable, high-yield soybean strains.

An interesting result of the Four Modernizations plan has been the recent decision of the Committee for Science & Technology to concentrate on the development of microcomputers, to the virtual exclusion of minis and mainframes, for use in regulating freight traffic, forecasting weather, combating plant disease, processing hydrological data and calculating satellite orbits. Micros are also helping in the tabulation of the national census and in petroleum exploration. Also benefiting from computerization are factories, department stores, customs offices, banks, foreign trade, metallurgy, chemistry, light industry, textiles, telecommunications and public health.

More than four thousand computers and seventeen thousand microcomputers were in operation in China at the start of 1983, and estimates for the next decade vary with each fortune cookie cracked open by Western high-tech salesmen. "A microchip for every Chinese" is the battle cry here in the West. Using Western models, the Chinese are developing their own extensive hardware and software, although it seems likely they will continue to import more than they produce themselves in the near future. The Chinese have already developed their own version of the IBM PC, called the Great Wall 100, and they have made the jump from 8-bit to 16-bit systems. Chinese Apple clones are being introduced as city traffic information stations, answering questions about ticket prices, routes, and types and numbers of vehicles to be taken.

A New Perspective

For all her singleminded drive toward total modernization, China is discovering computer applications that are unique to her own ancient civilization. This is particularly true of the field of traditional Chinese medicine, where software is catching up with acupuncture as the preferred technique for treating ailments. The Chinese have a computer system of their own that is capable of diagnosing diseases, offering a course of treatment, then printing the prescriptions and directions for taking medicines. The whole process—including the doctor's interview of the patient, the input into the computer of the description of the patient's symptoms and the automatic output of the prescription in Chinese characters—takes only five to ten minutes.

A patient suffering from a cold, for example, might receive a prescription for a medicine containing:

10% rhinoceros horn
7% pearls
7% bear gall
5% cow bezoar
3% musk
28% rhizoma coptidis
30% fined borax
10% toad cake

Although the so-called Pinyin system of romanization has been officially adopted in their written language in order to improve mass communication (e.g., Peking, the capital, is accordingly spelled Beijing), the Chinese have also managed to develop processing systems for the vast number of traditional characters that go back thousands of years to their origins on oracular bones and tortoise shells. The Chinese character disk operating system (CDOS) allows some 8,000 character patterns to be stored on a floppy disk, covering all the 6,763 characters that are fixed in the national code. Pressing various English-letter keys on a regular keyboard while holding an alternate function key makes it possible to re-create the exact strokes (as many as eight per character) that define each Chinese ideogram. Another method of keying in involves a touch-sensitive plastic board that features color-coded sections containing a number of Chinese characters. A character is entered by touching the appropriate spot on the board with a wand.

A typical twelve-inch CRT screen is capable of displaying 512 to 1,024 Chinese characters. The character library, depending on the system, can store, say, 16 x 15 and 14 x 22 dot-matrix types, outputting characters of various sizes. It can also display or print characters horizontally or vertically. Software includes controller, language processor, application programs and Chinese dictionaries.

Efforts are underway to teach computer technology to middle school students, and experimental classes are being set up in various youth centers around the country. Teenage Chinese software geniuses receive their hands-on training while writing programs that help factory workers accomplish in half an hour jobs that would normally require several days. Shanghai is emerging as China's Silicon Valley, with software as its main thrust.

It is likely that just as in the past, when scholars became a power élite, China's new interest in high technology will give rise to a social class of technocadres who will move to the top of the nation's power pyramid. China's high-tech prognosis involves longterm speculation rather than forecasting. But one thing is already becoming apparent as this Eastern power gears itself up to the Western challenge: in addition to all the tea in China, there will be a wealth of computer technology. ∎

MICROS IN MEXICO

by Neal Weinstock

Once, not long ago, the petrodollar was prescribed as the Third World panacea by sympathetic First Worlders like Jean-Jacques Servan-Schreiber and Alvin Toffler. But today Mexico is depleting its large oil reserves as fast as it can, in return for foreign currency that will help pay back the monstrous debt incurred in exploration expenses.

Now Mexicans, who share a sad pessimism regarding panaceas, are being sold on the microcomputer as the latest "cure." Is this yet another example of the wishful thinking that does so little to relieve the starving half of the world?

The incongruous congruity of *mañana*land and computerland is a good test case. Consider, for example, the following points:

• The computer is the ultimate labor-saving device, but Mexico has an uncalculably high unemployment rate and a minimum wage of $3 a day.

• Although Mexico's government is desperate for a

Neal Weinstock is author of The Millimeter Guide to Animation. *He is a frequent visitor to Mexico.*

computer industry of its own, assembly permits can take as long as a year to obtain.

• According to Alejandro Gil Recasens, a top government adviser and Mexico's leading political pollster, "There are too many computers in Mexico. Many people in government have them and don't even know what they are."

PCs and the Peso

The government, which owns perhaps half the micros in Mexico, has now set "national content" requirements for computer production. But can plans for new technology succeed where old-tech planning has failed? Says Tim Barry of Creative Strategies International, "The American automobile companies . . . have survived (in Mexico) for decades in the wake of impossible national content rules. Programs are published and plans are registered; goals are not met, and the industry goes on."

New cars may look the same from the outside on both sides of the Rio Grande, but inside that 1958 body the Mexican version might well have a 1948 engine. Will micros end up with a similar disparity?

Before the crash of the peso in 1982, Mexico City had as many Radio Shack Computer Centers as comparably sized New York City. One street in particular, famed as an electronics shopping district, might have been likened to New York's Forty-Fifth Street except that most of the stores were Radio Shacks in competition with each other.

Today, though Tandy Corporation has withdrawn from distribution, Radio Shack TRS-80s and Apples together account for two-thirds of the documented micros in Mexico. Most of the rest are Hewlett-Packards, with a sprinkling of IBMs, Cromemcos, Altos, Ataris and Commodore PETs. Taking into account that duties and transportation double the cost of these machines, however, and that peripherals go up even more, it's likely that thousands more micros are contraband. (The brand breakdown of illigitimate machines is probably similar: Mexicans tend to be very brand-conscious, as would anyone who faced the difficulty of getting even an Apple serviced in Mexico City.)

Micros are simply smuggled in as luggage by individuals who visit the United States for business or pleasure. Illegal border activity along the American side of the Rio Grande and in California has almost disappeared, but there was a time when customers swarmed to the cut-rate dealers in Brownsville, McAllen, Laredo and El Paso, Texas. The volume was such that the Old West streets were clogged with storefront-high piles of packing boxes, discarded in favor of the brown wrapping paper used to disguise the computers as buyers passed through customs. The boxes were common as well at the local private airports, where, at the height of illegal traffic, half a dozen computer-laden World War II cargo planes took off daily for points south. The notoriously porous border was also routinely crossed by truckloads of contraband headed in both directions.

Before the economic crash, which only begins to explain the problems for micros in Mexico, most computer distributors had done little more than import hardware. Servicing remains, in many cases, nonexistent. Software is difficult to come by and often impossible to find with documentation in Spanish.

The firm of Computadoras Comerciales has prospered by writing its own software and attending to the ancient computer virtues of service and hand-holding. Considering the relative expense, their micros are sold much the same way as minis and mainframes in the United States.

Qué Viva México!

During the 1980 election, according to Alejandro Gil Recasens, the ruling political party placed computer terminals in every election district in the country and hooked them up to a mainframe in Mexico City. The information system, which has yet to be used, was "sabotaged on the local level," Gil said, because it would bring to light many examples of local vote fraud. "There are some very stupid feelings here," he added. "Some people think all computers are American. They identify the computer as an agent of the United States. We have articles in newspapers against us because we use American computers."

What can micros do to solve Mexico's problems? Consider its exasperatingly inefficient telephone system, its low-quality, dated television sets, refrigerators and cars, its beautiful modern architecture crumbling along built-in faults. If this historic inefficiency is instilled in the new techology by content laws (and the graft-laden sidestepping of same), micros will end up creating more problems than they solve. Imagine too much data transmission clogging up already antiquated phone lines. Too many people without technical knowledge, employed to make too much of an inferior but protected product, making the industry ripe for the ever increasing government subsidies. Micro smuggling again running rampant on the Texas and California borders.

Service would continue to be unobtainable, of course, and it takes a very mild stretch of imagination to vizualize subsidized industry planners forgetting entirely about software. The current trend of using micro systems for very large tasks because these are the only computers affordable to the large taskmasters, combined with predictably shoddy local products and no service, might just increase downtime to most of the time. Why not? This is the way most other technologies work in Mexico.

If Mexico opened its borders to microcomputer imports, the resultant cutting of industrial red tape would ease the hiring of factory labor, put to work computer grads who now migrate to the United States for employment and somewhat lessen demand for clerical personnel. Mexican conservatives suggest that the United States misunderstands Latin American needs and could more effectively quell insurgencies by sending micros (and food) rather than arms. In this they echo Alvin Toffler, who envisions a Latin America with micros in every town square to educate the masses. But according to Alejandro Gil, Mexico already has terminals in every town, going unused to keep government fraud a secret.

In the end, the possibilities of the micro are great, but the capabilities of regressive systems to ignore them is perhaps just as great. And as much as commonly available computers have been of some help to a few individuals, the far more commonly available micros of the advanced countries are pushing Mexico, relatively speaking, further behind than ever. ∎

FRESH GREENS

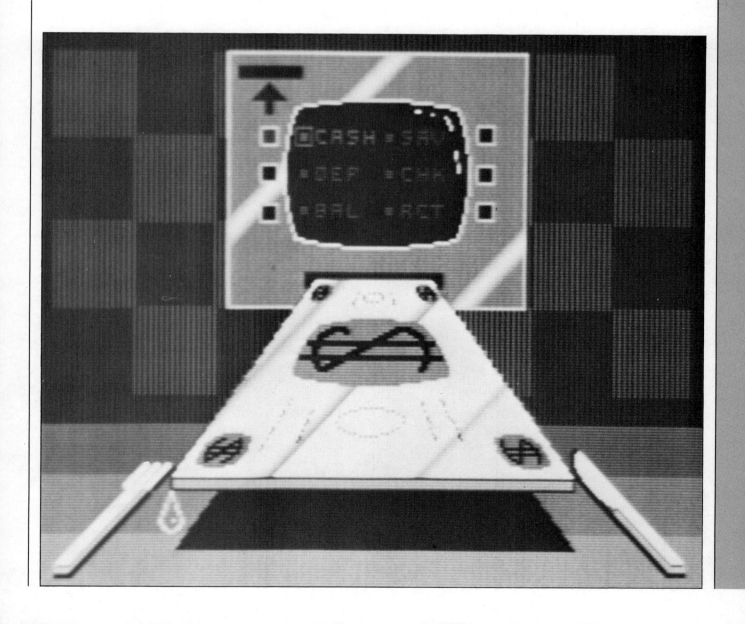

Artwork for preceding page

Artist:
   Stuart Sharpe
Computer:
   A.T.&T. Frame Creation video-
   text design system
Software:
   Paint program by A.T.&T., using
   NAPLPS protocol
Input:
   Digitizing tablet with mouse

SCREEN ENVY ON WALL STREET

by Barbara E. and John F. McMullen

On Wall Street desktops, personal computers coexist with terminals connected to mainframe computers.

Personal computers conquered the financial community with blazing screens, despite the usual conservatism of its members. In 1977, while he was writing the *Morgan Stanley Electronics Letter*, Ben Rosen acquired an Apple II computer and proceeded to daz-

Barbara E. and John F. McMullen, founders of the personal computer consulting firm McMullen & McMullen, Inc., are the authors of Microcomputer Communications *and contributing editors at* PC *and* Computers & Electronics.

zle other employees with his new machine. We were two of those employees, and never in our combined thirty-five years of data processing had we seen anything like the color graphics he showed us, the voice input, or the weather maps of Kentucky.

Thanks to Ben Rosen and others like him, Wall Street foreshadowed the rest of the business world when it came to using micros. These electronics analysts came to realize, in the course of evaluating semiconductor and chip manufacturers, that the personal computers developed with this technology could in fact be extremely useful. First to use them were departments that traditionally received the least attention from centralized data processing: research, planning, budgeting and other areas not directly responsible for updating financial books and records. The common denominator was the changeable nature of these departments' demands, where a certain type of analysis can be required on one day, another on the next. This kind of "dynamic definition" is enough to unhinge the average data processing manager and precondition him to ignore all requests from these sectors.

Ben went on to write a program that performed basic number crunching on quarterly and annual corporate financial data to assist in company and industry analysis. When his use of the computer to perform tedious tasks with a minimum of effort became known within the industry, some of the braver souls went out and purchased their own micros and so initiated the first infestation of Wall Street by Apples, Commodores and Radio Shack TRS-80s. Unfortunately, they could do little with these machines unless they knew how to program them.

Then along came packaged software. With the advent of the VisiCalc electronic spreadsheet, people no longer had to struggle to write their own programs for investment research. Analysts watched other analysts using VisiCalc and ran out to buy it, only to find that the $100 VisiCalc program could be run on nothing but the Apple II and that a complete system required a $2,500 investment.

Almost concurrently, another program was introduced to the financial community. Computrac, developed by the Technical Analysis Group in New Orleans to examine commodity trading strategies, was greatly dissimilar from VisiCalc in application and presentation but shared two of the latter's important attributes: it provided service to those who had previously received little help from their data processing departments (in this case, the account executive specializing in commodities, the commodity trader or analyst) and it was made available only for the Apple II computer. This concentration of software on the Apple II led to the proliferation of one primary microcomputer and made it easier for firms interested in developing financial software to decide what machine to use.

Screen envy being what it was, microcomputers began appearing on desks throughout Wall Street and gave rise to a good deal of publicity concerning the use of these machines for investment analysis: *Fortune* ran an article on Ben Rosen's experiences; Dick Shaffer wrote periodically on the subject for *The Wall Street Journal*; Allerton Cushman, Morgan Stanley's insurance analyst, published *Confessions of an Apple Byter*, detailing his use of VisiCalc in financial analysis. Many Wall Streeters, particularly account executives,

bought their micros because of competitive paranoia ("If Joe Blow uses a computer and is also a successful account executive, I better get one"); unfortunately, the systems purchased for this reason tended to wind up collecting dust as rather expensive bookends.

An interesting sidelight in this scenario is the manner in which the computers were acquired. Many account executives bought their own computers, then wrote them off for tax purposes. Computers for other areas were generally bought by the firms themselves and remained company property. In almost every case, the decision to buy was made by the person who would actually use the computer; the firm's data processing department was rarely involved in the decision-making process. Often department managers or vice-presidents were authorized to approve expenditures of up to $10,000 unless the item was related to computers, and in such situations the check for a computer installation would have the legend "Furniture" annotated on the stub; in other words, the firm was purchasing a $9,000 desk that just happened to have a funny-looking machine sitting on top of it at the time of delivery.

Then came full recognition. As personal computers increased at a heightened pace (soon there were hundreds of microcomputers within Merrill Lynch's branch office complex), media coverage of computer technology and applications went from virtual nonexistence to overkill. And with recognition came IBM. After an abysmal start in the field with expensive machines like the 5100, 5110 and 5120, IBM made a complete reversal and offered the IBM PC with some of the best-known software available, including VisiCalc. Data processing managers and purchasing agents, many of whom were unfamiliar or uncomfortable with names like Apple, Radio Shack and Commodore, could now do business with a firm they knew well. The IBM PC even accelerated the purchase of its competitors' products by convincing recalcitrant managers to fill long-shelved requests for personal computers.

And then came organization and institutionalization, as it always does in large businesses, along with the inevitable pressure to develop "corporate strategies" for the use of microcomputers. In some cases, as in the creation of support groups at Merrill Lynch and E. F. Hutton to aid users through advice, training and custom programming, this institutionalization proved to be beneficial. In others, the ensuing bureaucratic layers delayed the provision of microcomputer power to potential users while "cost justifications" and "system studies" were carried out.

The financial community had come full circle, reintroducing the frustration factor that led to the introduction of personal computers in the first place. Oh well, as Billy Pilgrim of Kurt Vonnegut's *Slaughterhouse-Five* might say, "And so it goes . . ." ∎

HOW COMPUTERS CHANGED WALL STREET

At the turn of the century, stock was still bought and sold on the curbside at Wall and Broad (left). Today, the floor of the American Stock Exchange could pass for a computer showroom (right).

While the use of microcomputers in the Wall Street community is a well-known fact, little attention has been paid to the impact of large computer technology on the securities industry. The present levels of trading would be impossible were it not for the great proliferation of computer power throughout brokerage firms, clearing agencies and banks.

In the early 1960s the average volume of shares traded daily on the New York Stock Exchange was slightly under five million and ten-million-share days were reason for celebration. As of this writing, average daily volume was sixty million and days of over a hundred million shares were commonplace.

Some of the great improvement in capacity of the marketplace can be tied directly to the vastly increased speed of today's computers, but more important is the way brokerage firms and industry agencies changed their practices and procedures to adapt to the capabilities and power of the new technology.

According to Robert M. Flanagan, former executive vice-president of Dean Witter Reynolds, the continual improvement in computer communications capability offers an accurate chart of the impact of computers upon the marketplace.

● In the early 1960s ticker-tape machines were still being utilized to follow market activity. Orders were telephoned to the floor of the stock exchanges.
● Rudimentary quotation devices began to appear from such firms as GT&E's subsidiary Ultronics, Bunker Ramo, Scantlin Electronics and Quotron.
● Next, "store and forward" message systems (typified by Control Data's 8090 systems) came into use, allowing the brokerage firm's branch offices to enter orders on a teletype and send them through the system to the firm's broker on the floor of the appropriate stock exchange or trading facility. The reports of execution were then sent via computer back to the branch office and to the firm's operational staff, who prepared them for entry into the bookkeeping system.
● The next step was the introduction of "order matching" systems (generally run on Control Data 3300 or large IBM 360 systems), which eliminated manual matching and preparation work, and allowed executions to flow automatically from the floor of the exchanges directly into automated bookkeeping systems.

● More and more applications were integrated into this communications network. The quotation devices on account executive desks became input devices to the central computers of the firm, and the AE was given access to client information and research opinion as well as quotations.

Parallel to this development of trade processing systems was the large computer's impact on the transfer of securities relating to trades. In the last twenty years, the industry has gone from the practice of hand delivery of securities for completing transactions to an automated system of updated records maintained by a central agency, the Depository Trust Company (DTC), to indicate ownership of securities.

With many interim steps along the way, we now have the National Securities Clearing Corporation (of which Mr. Flanagan was a founder), which is responsible for the daily balancing of the majority of the securities transactions executed in the United States. There is also a direct interface with DTC to reflect change in ownership.

Without this commitment to technological improvement, the securities industry could not be responsive to the demands of the marketplace. The volume increases in the mid-1960s occasionally forced the exchanges to close one day a week so that balancing could be performed. Accelerating the trend toward computerization was the "unbundling" of services that took final effect on "May Day" (May 1, 1975) and eliminated "fixed rates" of commissions charged by brokerage firms. This occurrence resulted in greater striving for operational efficiency within firms and caused them to look to data processing to eliminate labor-intensive work and provide greater service.

Many of the mergers of Wall Street brokerage firms that followed were in large part motivated by the desire to share the expense of maintaining the computing power needed to remain competitive. Another related occurrence was the rise to prominence of firms such as Automatic Data Processing (ADP) and Brokerage Transaction Services, Inc. (BTSI), which provided shared data processing services to the brokerage community.

J. AND B. McM.

HOW TO BE YOUR OWN STOCKBROKER

by Norm Nicholson

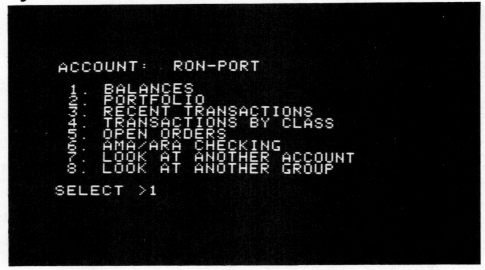

Yes, you can replace your stockbroker with a microcomputer. Personal computers coupled with software for investment analysis and data communications make it possible for the individual at home to perform exactly the same types of investment research undertaken by large investment brokers and financial institutions.

By executing trades through a discount broker, you may even be able to save some money in the process. Before you begin, however, think it over carefully. Many people value their broker's advice or have a psychological need to talk over their investment ideas with another person. Also bear in mind that computers can offer bad advice as easily as brokers can.

Norm Nicholson is editor of the bimonthly newsletter Computerized Investing, *published by the American Association of Individual Investors, 612 N. Michigan Ave., Chicago, IL 60611.*

Should you ultimately decide you want to keep your broker, a personal computer can still be very useful. For example, there are several portfolio management programs on the market that can keep a record of your securities transactions, provide an accounting record of your long- and short-term transactions for tax purposes and monitor the overall yield on your portfolio. Going one step further, the new generation of personal financial management programs can oversee your budget, handle your checking, advise on insurance, IRAs and Keogh plans, evaluate real estate purchases, help you fill out your tax forms, aid in retirement planning and keep track of your net worth. Some of the new personal finance packages are sold as individual modules that are purchased separately; with these, you usually begin with a basic budgeting and checking program, and add on as your needs dictate. Other companies offer a complete financial management system in one package, geared to those interested in managing their assets or planning for their financial future.

Getting Started

If you decide to do financial planning or investment analysis via computer, where do you begin? First, of course, you need a suitable microcomputer. Investment analysis programs require a fair amount of user memory (usually 64K or more). In many cases, programs furnished on one disk make use of a second disk containing market data; this means you'll want to equip your system with two disk drives. In addition, a dot-matrix printer with graphics capability is useful for printing reports and graphs.

Most investment software currently on the market was developed for the Apple or IBM PC computers. A number of programs for the IBM PC have also been converted to run on similar computers, such as the Texas Instruments Professional and Tandy 2000. A word of caution is necessary: you should make sure that software is available to do the tasks you have in mind before, not after, you buy the computer.

If you're an active trader, it's possible to trade your portfolio from your home or office via a personal computer sitting on your desk. Major discount brokers, such as Fidelity Brokerage Services, can provide software that allows your computer to link automatically into a real-time securities market quotation system. ("Real-time" means the market quotes on your computer screen are the actual last sale prices posted on the exchange.)

You will pay approximately $200 for the software, which some brokerage firms offset against commissions. You will also have to pay for the telephone charges, which are usually local call rates, and for the use of the quotation system itself. Obviously, the charges can quickly add up. But for active stock traders with large positions and individuals with highly leveraged options positions, timely information can be well worth the cost. Some software packages for on-line order execution systems will also provide detailed statements of your brokerage accounts.

For less active traders, one way to reduce charges considerably is to receive quotes on a fifteen-minute delay basis. Exchange fees for data connections are considerably less for delayed service. If you're a long-term investor who wants to track stock prices for research purposes or simply update the value of a stock portfolio, it's possible to log onto one of the financial information services like Dow Jones News/Retrieval during evening hours and pay only a dollar or so for the quotes you need. Then all you have to do is simply phone your discount broker when you want to make a purchase or sale.

Microcomputers are also ideal tools for investment research. They can process and manipulate large amounts of data rapidly, and through the skillful use of graphics they can present information in a quickly understandable format. Most important, you can interact with the computer to follow up on ideas that spring from the information currently being displayed on the screen.

The Home Analyst

Personal computer investment software usually performs one of two kinds of analysis: fundamental or technical. Fundamental analysis is the process of identifying stocks that meet specific stock-valuation or financial-performance criteria. Technical analysis applies primarily to the forecasting of future performance of the market or specific stocks on the basis of price and volume data over time for specific stocks, and for indices of the market as a whole.

Until very recently, the costs of doing fundamental analysis were beyond the means of most individuals. For example, the yearly cost for Compustat, a commercial data base consisting of fundamental market information, typically starts at $20,000 per year and ranges upwards from there. Now, however, there are several programs on the market that can screen a large universe of stocks for selected performance characteristics. Stock screening programs usually come with a program disk and separate data disks that are updated monthly. Prices for stock screening programs typically range from $300 to $1,000.

As an illustration of fundamental analysis, let's say we've read that smaller capitalization stocks have outperformed the market as a whole, even after accounting for the higher intrinsic risk associated with smaller companies. We might, for the sake of argument, choose stocks with a book value of between $25 million and $125 million, a price/earnings ratio of 12 or less and a "beta" of 1.2. (Beta is an index of a stock's risk relative to the market as a whole; stocks with a beta greater than one should outperform the market, either up or down.) In a few minutes our program would have searched through its data base and given us a list of stocks that passed the screen.

If we were really doing the research outlined above, we would also look into basic financial soundness of the companies passing the screen, the demand for their products and their competitive position in the marketplace. From our final list, we could then rank the stocks based on their valuation relative to the market. Now we are in a position to purchase stocks for our portfolio. The fundamental approach to stock selection, as outlined above, is often used by professional portfolio managers in picking stocks for prospective long-term holdings.

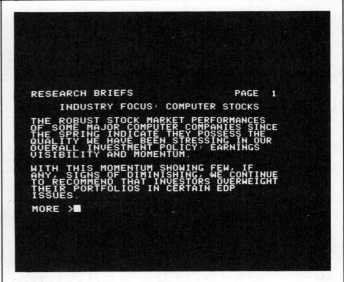

```
INVESTMENT BRIEFS                    PAGE  2

FOR 1983, A TAX-EXEMPT INVESTMENT THAT
PAYS, SAY, 10%, EFFECTIVELY YIELDS FAR
MORE, DEPENDING ON YOUR TAX BRACKET:

TAXABLE  INCOME            TAX-EXEMPT YIELD
SINGLE   JOINT     TAX
RETURN   RETURN   BRACKET  8.5%   10%   11.5%

------   -----   ------    -----  ----  -----

         35-46K    35%     13.1%  15.4%  17.7%

29-34                36     13.3   15.6   18.0
34-42    46-60       40     14.2   16.7   19.2
         60-86       44     15.2   17.9   20.5
42-55                45     15.5   18.2   20.9
         86-109      48     16.3   19.2   22.1
55+      109+        50     18.0   21.0   24.0
```

Technical analysis refers to a wide variety of techniques for manipulating and graphing market price and volume data. The resulting indicators are then used in determining when to buy and sell securities. A typical use of this kind of analysis consists of plotting daily price movements on one graph and a moving average of the same data on another. The two graphs are then simultaneously displayed on the screen. If the daily price graph crosses the moving average on the upswing, a buy signal is given. A crossing on the downswing gives a sell signal. Most often, additional indicators would be computed in order to confirm a buy or sell signal.

There are several technical analysis programs on the market that can automatically log into a financial information system, obtain price data and then compute the graphs you need. Because of the sophistication of the software, technical analysis requires less effort than fundmental analysis. It's also a good deal more controversial. Several academic studies have come to the conclusion that day-to-day movements in market prices behave in a highly random fashion and that future trends in market prices cannot be predicted solely on the basis of past market behavior. During a prolonged upswing (or downswing) in market prices, technical analysis performs well. But when the market is highly volatile or moving sideways, technical analysis systems generate false buy and sell signals.

Some technical analysis programs come with a data base diskette containing economic and market statistics. During the beginning of the stock market run-up in August 1982, for example, when the airlines industry was underperforming the market as a whole, comparing plots of the industry index and a broad market index such as the Standard and Poor's 500, would have easily spotted the relative undervaluation. Some additional research would have revealed a good buying opportunity.

```
RESEARCH BRIEFS                     PAGE  1
       INDUSTRY FOCUS: COMPUTER STOCKS

THE ROBUST STOCK MARKET PERFORMANCES
OF SOME MAJOR COMPUTER COMPANIES SINCE
THE SPRING INDICATE THEY POSSESS THE
QUALITY WE HAVE BEEN STRESSING IN OUR
OVERALL INVESTMENT POLICY: EARNINGS
VISIBILITY AND MOMENTUM.

WITH THIS MOMENTUM SHOWING FEW, IF
ANY, SIGNS OF DIMINISHING, WE CONTINUE
TO RECOMMEND THAT INVESTORS OVERWEIGHT
THEIR PORTFOLIOS IN CERTAIN EDP
ISSUES.

MORE >■
```

More Investment Tools

In addition to the commercial programs discussed above, many mathematically inclined individuals and financial professionals develop their own portfolio management systems and investment models. Integrated spreadsheet modeling programs, such as Lotus' 1-2-3 or the newer program Symphony, can be used to create almost any type of model that an investment analyst could wish for. In the newer programs, data can be automatically retrieved from a financial information service using built-in communications routines. With older programs, special software such as the Dow Jones Spreadsheet Link can retrieve data for use with the spreadsheet program. Many of the latest spreadsheet modeling programs also have the ability to display graphics and manipulate a data base.

There is also a wide variety of highly specialized programs for bonds, options and futures market analysis. Very sophisticated programs for statistical analysis that were originally written for large mainframe computers are now available on micros. One could, in theory, develop a statistical model of the economy using only a microcomputer and currently available software.

There are innumerable sources of information available to investors. Most financial mgazines and many computer publications are now devoting space to the topic. The American Association of Individual Investors has a nationwide seminar program. AAII members have also formed computer interest groups in many of the larger metropolitan areas.

When all is said and done, microcomputers and investment software are really only tools to aid the investor in making intelligent decisions. It is your own knowledge, aided by the information gathering and high-speed processing capabilities of the computer, that can lead to superior investment performance. ■

THINK

THE STORY
OF IBM

Thomas J. Watson, Sr. (above) lectures his NCR sales force on "The Five C's": Conception, Consistency, Cooperation, Courage and Confidence. His desk at NCR (below) exemplifies his compulsion for cleanliness.

Thanks to the management style of Thomas J. Watson, Sr., the early IBM was run much like a fundamentalist religion. Watson, for forty years the organization's patriarch, favored sales conventions on the order of revival meetings, complete with group singing and inspirational slogans; originally known as the Computing-Tabulating-Recording Company (CTR), his firm was run to the tune of ditties like:

> *Mr. Watson is the man we're working for*
> *He's the leader of the CTR*
> *He's the fairest, squarest man we know.*

Today Watson's paternalistic outlook has proved influential far beyond his own empire: the current successful Japanese management culture is based on IBM's policies.

Born in 1874 to a tough lumberjack and his wife, Thomas Watson learned from life on the farm in Painted Post, New York, the basic ideas that he later instilled in thousands of his own workers. These were later described by his son as follows: "to do every job well, to treat all people with dignity and respect, to appear neatly dressed, to be clean and forthright, to be eternally optimistic, and above all, loyal."

After a few false starts in local businesses and a stint as a traveling salesman, Watson shuffled off to Buffalo—where he joined National Cash Register Corp. and soon rose to the third most powerful position in the firm. When NCR was prosecuted for antitrust violations, Watson was convicted even though he had little to do with the company's suspect practices; the conviction was later reversed on appeal, but it left its mark on his psyche. Less than six months

later, he was fired for disagreeing with NCR president John H. Patterson in front of other company executives.

Watson then joined the firm soon to be known as International Business Machines (IBM). As its chief executive officer by 1924, the year of its fateful name change, Watson began to imprint his distinctive personality on the entire company. The strict dress code (dark suit and white shirt), which Watson himself observed by never taking off his jacket on even the hottest day, was the result of his desire to lend respectability to the then lowly position of salesman. (This from a man whose dress style at NCR had been distin-

guished by a penchant for wearing white socks!)

Watson's IBM faced hard times during the Depression but was saved from disaster by New Deal legislation like the Social Security Act and the Wage-Hours Act of 1937–38 that required more sophisticated record keeping. When World War II broke out, Watson gave IBM over to the U.S. military effort. Besides performing accounting tasks for the government, the corporation produced rifle and aircraft engine parts in its factories.

It was during the war that IBM entered the computer business, backing Prof. Howard Aiken at Harvard University to build the com-

puter that would be considered "Babbage's dream come true." On the eve of the presentation ceremony, Aiken reportedly introduced the Mark I computer to the press without even mentioning IBM's or Watson's part in its development. As a man who enjoyed his due credit (he came up with the slogan THINK as an inexpensive source of publicity, then saw it become the most widely quoted corporate slogan in history), Watson is said to have raged at Aiken: "You can't put IBM on as a postscript! I think about IBM just as you Harvard fellows do about your university."

The event did, however, spur Watson and IBM to build a machine that would eclipse the Mark I. IBM's first computer, the Selective Sequence Electronic Calculator, was unveiled in 1948, proving a far more powerful machine than any others of its time.

In 1952 Thomas J. Watson, Jr., became IBM's president. Four years later, a month after reluctantly turning his CEO reins over to his son, Thomas Sr. died of a heart attack at the age of eighty-two.

MARGUERITE ZIENTARA

Above left: the official portrait of Thomas J. Watson, Sr., as CEO of IBM. Shown here: Watson turning over the company to Thomas Jr.

Armonk, New York: Corporate headquarters for IBM.

Lexington, Kentucky: Development Laboratory and Manufacturing facility.

Yorktown, New York: Research Division headquarters.

Atlanta, Georgia: National Marketing Division headquarters.

Boca Raton, Florida: Entry Systems Division headquarters (IBM personal computers).

IBM TODAY

Chairman and Chief Executive Officer John R. Opel presides over a company that is first in the United States in profits ($5.5 billion in 1983) and third in total employees (370,000 worldwide), with offices in 132 countries. Despite antitrust suits on several continents, IBM has continued to thrive. Big Blue is the most important institutionally held stock on Wall Street. As IBM goes, so goes the Dow Jones Industrial Average.

Personal computers account for only a fraction of IBM's sales. The company remains preeminent in the area of mainframe computers, as well as setting the standard for electric office typewriters with its classic Selectric series. Though "THINK" has been retired as a corporate motto, there remains the same involvement with its personnel (pictured here the

IBM country club near Endicott, New York) originated by Thomas J. Watson, Sr.

CASHING IN: AUTOMATED TELLER MACHINES

by Candice Zarr

Across the nation, possession of the right plastic card (and a usable bank balance) is easing the long-lines trauma usually associated with banking. Now your relationship with your money can be fluid and convenient with the automated teller machines (ATMs) that allow immediate access, twenty-four hours a day, 365 days a year, to funds in your checking, savings and money market accounts.

Each bank has its own ATM system, but certain features are common to all: an account, an access card and an ATM. The standard cash machine looks like a panel inset into a wall. The panel usually contains a screen on which the ATM displays messages, a keyboard, and slots for access card insertion, withdrawals and deposits.

Those bright lights and all that shiny chrome may infrequently cause a case of computer jitters, but ATMs are designed to be practical, easy and, some say, fun to use. They are user-friendly in English, sometimes in Spanish, and they rarely make a mistake. To perform most standard banking transactions, all you do is press appropriate keys on the keyboard in response to menu-style lists of choices.

Twenty years ago ATMs existed solely in the minds of researchers and executives at Howard Savings Bank. After a demonstration of the nation's first commercial on-line reservations system at American Airlines, the executives at Howard Savings concluded that if it could work for reservations and people, it could be modified to work for savings transactions and depositors.

Soon the Savings Automation System was introduced by a firm called eleregister, and shortly there-

Candice Zarr is a computer consultant and technical writer for the Chase Manhattan bank.

after IBM, Burroughs and all the rest came out with their own systems. But back in the 1960s most commercial banks showed little enthusiasm toward their savings operations. Not until the convergence of a number of factors—the expansion of branch banking, technological advances that improved cost effectiveness, and the growing desire of bank management for a way to integrate customer information—did a strong push for the adoption of full-capability on-line teller operations get under way.

Around 1972 designs for teller systems began to look more like what we recognize as "standard" ATMs when Bunker Ramo introduced the Universal Teller Terminal, consisting of a keyboard, display screen, journal tape and validation printer all in one unit. By 1974 improved systems comprised minicomputer-based, programmable control units that served as terminal controllers and communicators, and provided calculating capability at each branch.

Cash on Demand

Today's systems are designed to be used by those of us who have had no previous contact with computers, yet while using an ATM we are in communication with a large mainframe computer somewhere across town. The ATM acts in the manner of a computer terminal connected to the bank's main system. When the access card is inserted, the ATM initiates communication over a network of communications lines dedicated just to this purpose.

After the machine has provided an on-screen greeting and made sure you are who you say you are (by a process we'll get into a little further on), it will display its "menu" listing of the transactions you may

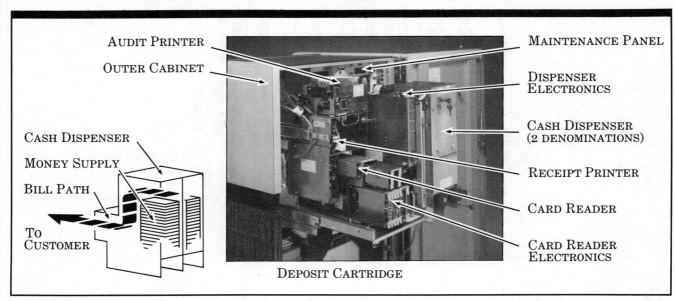

AUDIT PRINTER
OUTER CABINET
CASH DISPENSER
MONEY SUPPLY
BILL PATH
TO CUSTOMER
MAINTENANCE PANEL
DISPENSER ELECTRONICS
CASH DISPENSER (2 DENOMINATIONS)
RECEIPT PRINTER
CARD READER
CARD READER ELECTRONICS
DEPOSIT CARTRIDGE

The inside of an automated teller machine displays rugged, reliable design that guarantees a low failure rate.

perform. By pressing one of the keys located alongside the various options, you may find out your balance, transfer funds from one account to another, make deposits or loan payments, or—and this is the feature that has endeared the machine to millions—request and receive cash.

Let's look inside your average ATM. From the outside you see a shiny panel with an inset display screen and several slots for deposits and withdrawals. From within the bank you would see a door with combination and key locks, similar to the big vault door guarding your safe-deposit box; beyond the door you would see a vault box connected to the deposit slot for collecting deposit envelopes. You would also see a device containing locked "cassettes" of ten- and twenty-dollar bills for dispensing cash.

When you tell the ATM that what you'd really like is fifty dollars, the ATM first calculates the ratio of tens to twenties on hand to avoid running out of one denomination. The appropriate bills are fed up to an optical scanner, which checks the length, breadth and height of each bill before it is passed out to you. Bills that appear defective are set aside in a special bin.

Once your transactions are completed, a small printer records what happened onto a receipt tape and feeds it through a separate slot at about the same time that your card is returned to you. At this time, on most systems, communications between the ATM and the host computer are severed, thus safeguarding your records and your money.

The Safety Factor

Just how well protected is your money? Oddly enough, you are one of the weakest links in this regard. Generally, when you get your access card, you are asked to come into the bank to pick a number. This number, called a PIC (personal identification code), is typed by you into a special terminal and from that time on is known only to you and the central computer. Nobody at your bank can access the number. When you enter it into the machine, the screen will print only a row of asterisks (****). Access to your personal code is so secure that if you happen to forget it, you have to come in to pick a new one.

The magnetic stripe on the back of your card contains three lines of binary information, giving your name, your card number and just about whatever you can read on the front of your card. When you feed your card to the machine, this information identifies you to the ATM. The main system will request your PIC as additional identification, then compare what you punch in with what the file contains. If they match, you are awarded access to your accounts. If they don't, the system will disgorge your card. Repeated failures may trigger the system to swallow the card under the assumption that someone may be trying to get unauthorized access to your money.

Should you want to make a deposit, you enter on the keyboard the amount and type of deposit, then insert an envelope containing cash, checks, deposit slips, etc., into the deposit slot. Yes, you can deposit cash. Your deposits are enclosed in a vault constructed to withstand impacts of up to fifty thousand pounds per square inch. Should there ever be an attempt on the ATM itself, doors automatically lock and microprocessor-based alarm systems notify a central security monitoring point. There are even heat-sensing devices around the body and chest of the ATM.

Banks select their ATM sites with an eye to high traffic, bright illumination and safe surroundings. In-

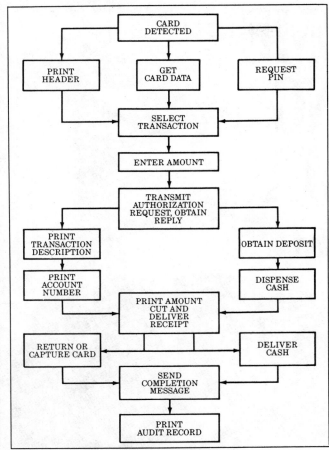

Typical transaction sequence.

door ATMs are typically enclosed by glass or transparent material. While this does afford protection for the machine itself (who would try a break-in where they can be easily observed?), it can be somewhat unsafe for customers. The customer and his withdrawals are "in the spotlight" when seen from the street, and they may unknowingly be observed and followed. For your protection, some banks supply direct-line telephones to customer service representatives around the clock. If need be, they may be used to summon help.

Customers with limited withdrawal capability ($200 to $500 per day) are rarely the targets for robbery. Most frequently it is the service staff who collect and distribute cash to the machines. By servicing machines on a random basis the armed staff significantly reduces the possibility of robbery.

The banks are admittedly confounded by a new, indirect form of theft: "data communications compromise." As the ATM and the host computer exchange authorizations and other commands, messages can be vulnerable to manipulation. Most cases of compromise have been traced to knowledgeable personnel with access to the system. For this reason, completion messages are employed to close the communications loop between the ATM and the host, as well as message

coordination numbers and data encryption.

The ATM and its data transmission are relatively safe in comparison with the largest security problem: people. Customer fraud and internal theft are the hardest things to prevent. Modern ATM systems maintain a complete audit trail of everyone with access and everything done on each ATM. While you may look upon this as an invasion of privacy, remember it if you ever have a dispute with the bank. Oh yes, and save those printed receipts. If you're not in the mood to collect paper, you may want to tear up those receipts: they do contain your account number and other confidential data that could fall into the wrong hands.

Occasionally, so many customers are using a bank's ATM facilities at once that the response time degrades. Some systems contain self-monitoring equipment that will notify an operations staff to bring more of its computing and/or communications facilities on-line. The communications network is usually configured in redundant paths: if any part of the system fails, the ATM transmissions can be routed on an alternate path to the host computer. At most sites where there are two or more ATMs, each ATM probably communicates along different paths to ensure availability. Some people resist the idea of using teller machines because of the perception that they are dehumanizing. The notion is that ATMs are part of a grandiose plan to turn us all into proles, grubbing our way through daily banking transactions without ever getting a smile from a friendly teller. If you could somehow convince a teller to go to work at three in the morning, chances are he wouldn't be smiling, anyhow. When New York's Citibank tried to limit live teller access to large depositors, public outcry quickly forced them to rescind this policy.

Modern ATMs help keep the cost of banking down and may stop those charges on your monthly statement from rising. Since there is less paper to be mistyped, mislaid or mutilated, ATMs may provide more accurate banking records than do their human counterparts.

In newer ATM systems, where the access card has a visible magnetic stripe on the back, other cards, such as your Visa or MasterCard, may be used to draw cash advances. This capability is not completely widespread (check with your bank). The older systems, with the magnetic stripe embedded into the card, can't do this—one of the penalties for being the first kid on the block to go computerized.

Banks are experimenting with different forms of bank-at-home systems, using personal computers and modems. Some people think this system will be the wave of the future and could make ATMs obsolete. But until we can train our personal computers to disgorge twenty-dollar bills on command, ATMs will still be around. ∎

THE HOME BANKING DILEMMA

by Charline Allen

Across the nation, personal computer users are participating in pilot programs that will determine whether home banking is indeed a viable business. To date, the major concern registered by users is the fear that their money will be lost in the system or that someone will illegally tap into their account.

According to Elise Berman of Chemical Bank, home banking is "as secure as, or more secure than, any MasterCard operation." Berman contends that money cannot get lost in the computer system because the bank has a listing of every step that every member makes on the system. In other words, the bank's computer keeps a record of each time a home user logs on, so any discrepancy can be checked against this listing.

As for the fear that someone could illegally tap into an account, Berman says this is virtually impossible because four verification steps must be taken by home users to access their accounts: they must input their household code, personal identification code (PIC), personal "handle" and household "handle." The bank has records of three of these codes, but not of the user's PIC (just as, in the case of automated teller machines, the bank knows everything about your account but the code you input when you begin using the machine). During its testing of the system, Chemical tried and failed to defeat its own program.

On the Frontier

Home banking customers must arrange with the bank for particular accounts to be paid electronically. For accounts like American Express, which has its own computers, funds are simply transferred electronically

Charline Allen is managing editor of View *magazine. Since 1979 she has been writing about cable TV and other new media.*

from the customer to the bank to Amex. Companies or individuals without computers can also be paid electronically. Chase credits their bank accounts with the amount requested, even if their account is with another bank. Most systems also allow regular monthly payment accounts to be set up for automatic debiting.

When you go on-line with Chase Manhattan's Paymaster to pay bills, for example, you tap in your password to bring up the menu. You can choose from: DISPLAY BALANCES, OBTAIN INFORMATION, PAYMENT/TRANSFER PLANNER, CALL CHASE and ACCESS UTILITY SERVICES. If you choose ACCESS UTILITY SERVICES, you select from another menu that includes: CHANGE PASSWORD, CONFIGURE SYSTEM, WRITE A MESSAGE, UPDATE MEMO CODES, ARCHIVE DATA and CHECKBOOK REGISTER. Choosing the latter, you see your balance forward, credits and debits as of the last date you tapped into the system. You then punch I to input a transaction and enter N for a new check. If you change your mind, you hit ESCAPE, the transaction is voided and you again see your balance, credits and debits. If you wish to go ahead and make a payment, the system asks on your computer screen: TO NEW YORK TELEPHONE, $100 FOR PAYMENT. CORRECT? You answer yes or no, and the transaction is complete.

Who Needs Home Banking?

Many of the home banking pilots now under way began in 1981. A few started out by offering free home banking services, but then charged $8 to $10 after the test began—primarily, they say, to determine whether people are actually willing to pay for the service.

Major banks like Chemical, Citibank and Chase Manhattan have taken a "stand-alone" approach in their pilot projects and offer only home banking. Customers can make account balance inquiries, pay bills, automatically reconcile their accounts, track checks, budget household and personal expenditures and communicate electronically with other users. Some pilot programs allow customers to buy traveler's checks, open new accounts, set up future payments as far as twelve months in advance and obtain current rates on certificates of deposit as well as forecasts from the bank's economists.

Just two months after Chemical began marketing its Pronto home banking system, for which it spent a reported $20 million in development costs, 500 people in the New York area signed on as users (with 2,500 customers projected in its first year). With agreements with some 200 banks in California, Connecticut, Pennsylvania, Michigan and Arkansas, Chemical is among the first to make the service available on a large scale. In order to garner as large a share as possible of the home computer user's on-line time, other computer functions, including teleshopping, portfolio analysis and information retrieval, are also being offered.

Citibank has made the Dow Jones News/Retrieval Service part of its $10 monthly package. Customers feel the service is well worth the cost, having previously paid $160 a month for subscriptions to the financial news service.

At-home shopping and information dissemination, a far cry from traditional bank services, are as yet unavailable due to the ongoing deregulation of commercial banking. In fact, deregulation is proceeding so rapidly that some federal regulators are calling for a temporary halt to assess the implications. Now much more than a place for one's money to reside, banks are becoming one-stop financial department stores; if these banking pilots succeed, they will also become providers of information as well as electronic order centers for merchandise.

While home banking services are being developed, another phenomenon is taking form at brokerage houses. E. F. Hutton, Merrill Lynch, Shearson/American Express and Dean Witter Reynolds have been developing complete home computer financial services. E. F. Hutton was first out of the gate with Huttonline, inaugurated in September 1983 as part of the experimental Viewtron Videotext service. Huttonline is also available to other home computer users through the CompuServe data network, which reaches 300 cities. For an initial $25 sign-up fee and $17 per month, the user can access personal account information including portfolio positions, cash and margin balances, open orders, asset management and asset reserve.

The Viewtron service on which Huttonline is an option is a joint venture of Knight-Ridder newspapers and AT&T. Other videotext services are being developed by such companies as CBS (in partnership with American Bell), KEYCOM (a joint venture of Honeywell, Field Enterprises and Centel Corp.) and Times Mirror Corp. (together with Videotext America). Videotext is a two-way text and graphics service providing a variety of computerized data bases accessed over phone lines by a personal computer or via a separate coaxial cable by a terminal that attaches to the TV set. Surveys among pilot users of the Times Mirror videotext service indicate that home banking is one of the most popular offerings on the menu.

In Your Future?

Some analysts are convinced that home banking can be a viable business only on a stand-alone basis, integrated into a full-menu videotext service like Viewtron. Others say only time will determine the extent of consumer acceptance of home banking, either as an incremental offering or as part of a full-service videotext package. As of this writing, all predictions are highly speculative since neither type of service has been put on a commercial basis.

No matter how many services are attached to systems offered by banks and videotext providers, the future of home banking depends on factors beyond the control of either. Truly user-friendly software must be developed, home computer penetration must increase significantly and adequate transmission links (phone lines or cable) must be in place.

Home banking's true test will be consumer acceptance or rejection, and not every pilot user has had a positive reaction. One New York writer dropped out of a home banking pilot after just six months. He found it impossible, he reports, to transfer funds to his son's account at the same bank. Moreover, he was receiving dunning letters from his creditors.

Even when all the bugs are out, will home banking reach the mass-market proportions predicted for it? Given the increasing sophistication of personal financial management by people in all walks of life, it looks like you just might be able to bank on it. ∎

APPLE CULTURE

Seldom does a consumer product generate such immediate identification that it becomes a cultural artifact in its own right. The sensible design and scrappy image of the Apple II, originally built by an engineer for other engineers, quickly gained adherents from all walks of life. Soon Apple owners, in tune with the computer's makers, began to reflect an independent, visionary yet down-to-earth sensibility that set them apart from hackers and common business users alike.

In the face of improvements and standardization among rival personal computers, many Apple-philes steadfastly maintained their loyalty much the way Volkswagen Beetle owners kept driving their distinctive autos despite the lure of newer Detroit iron. The slogan of Apple Computer, Inc., "Apple II forever," should be taken as more than an idle boast: the company remains committed to upgrading the machine while maintaining compatibility with its previous incarnations. And with the introduction of Apple's next generation of easy-to-use 32-bit computers in the Lisa/Macintosh series, the Apple culture seems destined to grow and flourish.

For amateur historians and sociologists, the origins of Apple culture can be traced to the document below: Stephen Wozniak's birth announcement.

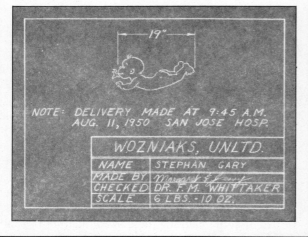

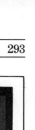

APPLE TOTEMS

The bitten-apple logo is so potent a symbol that Apple Computer has made available to its fans a popular assortment of authorized merchandise:

The Apple mug, peripheral for late-night computing.

Cutting board for fruity delights.

Christmas stocking for Apple add-ons.

Apple cap, with visor to block out screen glare.

Apple Tiffany desk clock.

Sailboard: at $900, the best-selling Apple logo merchandise.

Above left: You can't buy the Apple hot-air balloon, but you're likely to see it at major computer shows and events.

THE RIGHT TO KNOW

by Thomas Christo

Pulling your profile: credit records for millions of Americans are kept on these computer tapes.

Close encounters with record-keeping computer systems are responsible for a growing fear that there reside, somewhere, damaging and perhaps inaccurate electronic files on our credit history, our judicial and tax records, and yes, even our kinkier personal habits.

All too often our newspapers carry stories about computer victims: the Colorado widow, for instance, who failed to get a loan because a credit-reporting agency computer had mistakenly listed her as a tax delinquent, or the man on the West Coast who suddenly found himself in jail because he happened to fit

Thomas Christo is a trial lawyer, consultant and lecturer in the field of computer law. He has brought lawsuits against every major data processing vendor and has never lost a case.

a description supplied by a police computer. But if these stories have you worrying about what might be contained in your own computerized files, calm down. You don't have to let yourself be Big Brothered into submissive resignation to your fate.

Accessing Data

If you have even the slightest suspicion that something is awry, that some potential creditor or employer has done you wrong because of erroneous information, you have the right to take the offensive.

Under the Federal Freedom of Information Act, the Fair Credit Reporting Act and various state regulations, it's your privilege to know what source provided the troublesome data. Generally, when you are denied credit, the name and address of the reporting organization will be provided to you in a form letter. In the case of being denied employment, it's less likely that the source of information will automatically be provided; you'll probably have to ask for it by writing a formal request.

Once you get the name of the reporting agency that provided information to your prospective creditor or employer, write to that agency and demand a complete copy of your personal and/or credit file, together with a legend explaining all acronyms, abbreviations and codes. If it intimidates you to think of this information being stored somewhere in a monster computer, try to imagine instead a massive file cabinet containing, among other things, a report on you—of which you're requesting a copy.

What you'll typically receive is a computer printout with an abundance of codes and abbreviations, next to each of which is a numerical identifier. For example, there may be a code A-C, next to which appears the number 4. By looking at the accompanying legend, you determine that A-C means how fast a payer you are, as reported by various creditors, with 1 being a fast payer and 5 being a deadbeat. The number 4 should indicate that somewhere along the line a creditor has reported you to be a very slow-paying customer indeed. Rarely, you may even happen across an actual piece of narrative in plain English. Carefully review everything on your printout to determine what those computers are saying about you.

Challenging the Computer

Consider the West Coast man who was arrested, jailed and kept behind bars while the police decided whether or not he was the hired killer their computer files showed him to be. (It appears his name and identifying features were remarkably similar to the real murderer's.) After three days the police let him go with the warning: "Change your name." He decided not to, perhaps out of loyalty to his antecedents, and instead sued the county and police force that had arrested him for false imprisonment and slander and libel.

If a review of your computer files has turned up erroneous or incomplete information, you should immediately write to the reporting agency. Your letter should clearly spell out any inaccuracies and/or additional information to clarify what has been reported. Your first letter should be respectful but firm, and should include a request that the employer or creditor who received the erroneous/incomplete information be provided with an updated report (with a copy to you for verification). If you receive no response within two weeks, write a second letter raising the issues of slander and libel in the case of onerous information that is

MY FIRST JOB

Falsifying computerized records was my first job out of college, though I wasn't aware of it at the time. Fresh out of school and not too eager to commit to a major career move, I drifted through the summer of 1969 intent on doing odd jobs. My first turned out to be odd indeed.

I answered an ad in the New York *Times* for temporary help. When I called the telephone number and heard that the pay was nearly twice the minimum wage and evening hours were available, I was ready to sign up for the next shift.

My employer turned out to be a major credit card company. After filling out a few standard personnel forms, I was led into a large clerical office where I was instructed in my appointed task. I was to take yellow billing forms and green-and-white computer printouts and do some creative bookkeeping. There were credit totals indicated for each cardholder and code numbers for where the money was spent, but no individual dollar amounts. It was the job of the dozens of us in the room to come up with fictitious subtotals in keeping with the kind of establishment in which the card had been used.

Everything on the forms was numbers. I never knew the names of my victims, only their ID codes (eight digits) and where they spent their money (six digits). I would look up the name of the establishment and its location on the partial computer printout and charge accordingly. I quickly came up with my own economic model of the United States, charging an appropriate price for a restaurant meal in Topeka and yet another for a motel room in El Paso.

The job seemed nonsensical and tedious. After three weeks we were told that the work would soon be winding down but were offered a raise if we wanted to continue into the next phase of the project. I passed.

It wasn't until several years later that I learned what we had been doing. At a cocktail party a former programmer for the credit card company told me about a massive computer error that had wiped out parts of records for over a million cardholders. When their bills were sent out, about 10 percent of these customers asked for itemized listings. My first job had been the result of the company's attempt to cover up its embarrassing computer error.

The irony is that fifteen years earlier my father had been offered one-third of this very same credit card company in exchange for his travel agent's license. No money, just his license. He turned down the deal because he couldn't see any future in people using credit cards. After all, who could possibly entrust their financial transactions to something as flimsy as a piece of plastic and a computerized billing system?

Oh yes, to this day I have never applied for a credit card.

STEVEN ARCHER

not financially related or of "slander of credit" if the information was financial in nature. The second letter should do the trick. If not, you may want to sue.

Banking on Accuracy

The right to challenge the computer's information and have it corrected extends to such areas as banking, billing and other everyday computerized records. "But the computer says . . ." should never be taken as an excuse: computers and their operators are clearly fallible, and this justification is often no more than an attempt at passing the buck. With computers proliferating in homes, there is now an interesting variation on the theme. When a home computer user on a pilot bank-at-home service in New York, for example, was sent a dunning letter because the bank's computer showed an outstanding credit card payment, the man was able to respond that his computer said he was up to date with his payments. The bank never bothered him again.

Incidentally, banking at home and electronic funds transfer (EFT), the process by which you can pay bills or transfer funds from your checking and/or savings account, provide examples of home computer applications that could invite trouble. The temptation will be great to rely on your keyboard and telephone line and on the processing of the bank's central computer, which would be like turning over all your worldly goods to some unknown third party and blindly accepting his word on what bills you've paid and how much money you have left. Thus it would be wise to keep some sort of manual backup (remember your old checkbook register?) to guard against technological thievery or negligence.

The most sensitive areas of our lives are being or will be touched by the computer, and the possibility increases that data will be misused. But the point is this: just because the computer says it's so, doesn't necessarily *mean* it's so. ∎

A credit report from TRW and part of the key to abbreviations.

HOW A SPREADSHEET PROGRAM WORKS

by Robert Frankston

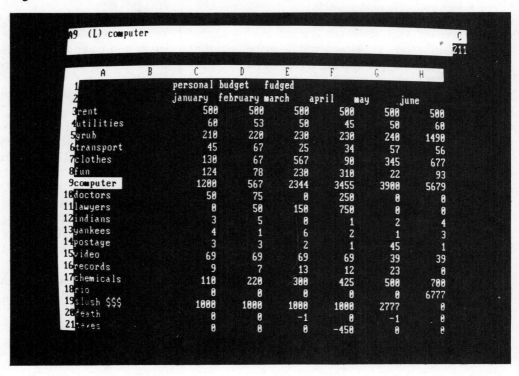

W hen Dan Bricklin and I wrote the original VisiCalc program in 1979, our goal was to provide a high-performance tool that would allow financial planners the same kind of flexibility enjoyed by people using word processors. The two key ingredients that made this possible were Dan Bricklin's experience with word processing using full-screen editing, coupled with his background in finance, and the availability of low-priced computers.

Robert Frankston is vice-chairman and executive vice-president of Software Arts, Inc., developers of the VisiCalc electronic spreadsheet.

We had to make many hard decisions in the process of turning our concept into a usable program. Our biggest challenge was creating a package that performed all the necessary sophisticated operations so that the user didn't have to work hard to use it. Some ideas, such as graphics, didn't fit into the Apple computers of that time. On the other hand, we did employ windowing to allow effective use of the screen for viewing more than one part of the spreadsheet. Dan designed much of what VisiCalc should do, and I concentrated on how to make the program do it.

While there are many complicated aspects of implementing the VisiCalc program, the basic idea is quite simple. A spreadsheet program is a computerized version of the traditional accountant's ledger sheet, with added "intelligence" in the form of mathematical or logical relationships between entries or "cells" so that changes in one entry can cause other entries to change accordingly. One of the fundamental mechanisms in any spreadsheet program is the ability to remember the calculation rule for each cell in the sheet. For example, once the user enters a formula, the program is able to remember how to recalculate that cell whenever a value changes.

There are many, many design issues, both technical and aesthetic, associated with writing a spreadsheet program. Rather than give a superficial overview, I will concentrate on specific aspects at the heart of this type of program—the method it uses of keeping track of calculations and performing the calculations each time a value changes. We call this process recalculation since we are calculating again and again and again . . . Also, I will describe only the simplest methods for performing an operation.

Before we can perform calculations, we must have a representation for the values and the arithmetic expressions. We can think of a spreadsheet as an array of numbers. For example, we can declare the sheet to have 99 rows and 26 columns. Each intersection of rows and columns defines a cell. In addition to a value, each cell on the sheet may have a calculation rule or expression (for budgeting or financial planning) used to compute a new value whenever other values change. Thus the cell B3 (second column, third row) might represent *cost* and be computed by multiplying the *sales* in B1 by 80 percent or .8 and adding a fixed cost of $5. We show this as

>B3: + B1*.8 + 5

The ">" means go to that cell. The ":" is a separator. The "*" means multiply. More technically we say that B3 contains the expression B1 times .8 plus 5. VisiCalc was designed so that we could describe how to set up a spreadsheet in a manual. Thus you can type the example as shown and it will work. Of course, if you are actually using the program, you don't think of B1 or B3; you just think of sales and cost. But if we are trying to understand how the program works *inside*, then we think of B1 or [2,1] (column 2, row 1) and B3 or [2,3].

The challenge is to allow the user to type in B1*.8 + 5 so that the value can be recomputed whenever necessary. The least complicated approach is simply to keep the character string that the user typed. VisiCalc itself was originally written in assembly language, although the newer versions are written in a language developed at Software Arts for the purpose of writing and translating programs for different per-

sonal computer models. Since I don't want to overwhelm you with technical details, I will describe what the program would do without giving examples of its structure.

When we need to recompute the values (because some value has changed on the spreadsheet), we can look at each column. For each column, we look at the value at each row. When we are done, we have processed all the values on the sheet. When we look at the cell, we must evaluate the expression. This means that if we write $2+3*4$, we first add 2 and 3 to get 5 and then multiply by 4 to get 20. This is the way it is on most simple calculators.

Computing the value consists of processing the expression from left to right. An expression combines values (or "operands") such as .8 or B1 and operations such as "*" (multiplication) or "+" (addition). If the operand has a cell name (such as B1), we first convert it into a coordinate, [2,1] in this case, then use this to look up the value. We convert B1 by taking the first letter and counting its position in the alphabet. Thus B becomes 2. The row is already a number, so we just use that value.

We then use the "current" value as if the user had typed it instead of the B1. If the current amount is 168, then we are really evaluating "168*.8 + 5." The important thing here is to remember that we are really talking about B1. The next time we evaluate the expression, the value of B1 might be different. Once we have the first value of the expression, we get the following operation ("*") and the following amount. We perform the operation using the value so far (168) and the next one (.8). This 134.4 is now our new value. We then repeat this process until we reach the end of the expression.

The next time we have "+" and "5," so we compute $134.4+5$ and get 139.4. This is now the value in B3. If we express profit as

B5:B1-B3

we get the first value (168). We then get the operation ("-" for subtraction) and the next value (134.4). The result is 33.6.

If the value in B1 changes to 100, we recalculate and compute 85 for the value in B3. Then, using this result, we compute that the value in B5 is 15.

This is essentially all that is involved in recalculating the values on a spreadsheet. Of course, when we are creating a product, there are many additional considerations. For example:
● Most important is error checking. We must handle these cases gracefully. One method is to use a special value called ERROR as an indication that we can't compute the value. We also extend the numbers to include a "not available" (NA) value.
● The program must run fast. Use of character

INTEGRATING SOFTWARE

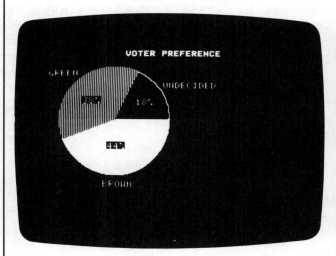

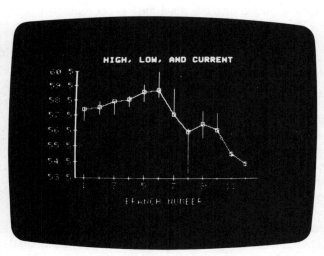

Why not? VisiPlot (left) and VisiTrend were the seeds of integrated software.

There's nothing revolutionary about the idea for personal computer software that uses the same input for several different applications without swapping disks. On the contrary, "integrated software" is a direct outgrowth of the way business users work at their desktop computers. Once a spreadsheet has been put together, they may want to gain perspective by looking at a chart or comparing their information with the contents of a data base. Or perhaps they'll want to communicate their results by writing a letter or sending electronic mail.

Under the standard software philosophy of one program/one disk, implementing these functions is tedious at best—and can be simply impossible if the applications programs use incompatible files. I learned this the hard way when I was designing VisiPlot/VisiTrend, a graphics package for creating charts from VisiCalc files. To draw up a chart, you had to dump your spreadsheet into a specially formated file, change program disks and then proceed; if you wanted to change a bit of data, you had to return to your VisiCalc model and start all over again.

Having a rather eclectic background (including stints as a radio disk jockey and a psychiatric hospital worker), I tended to view things a little differently from my programming colleagues. One day when I was using VisiCalc to project the royalties I'd be making if I ever finished my program, I mentioned to a friend that what VisiCalc needed was a "/G" command that would let us do graphics instantly. He couldn't understand what I was talking about. Then I suggested putting VisiPlot on the same disk with VisiCalc, but this was met with strong objections that VisiCalc would be "polluted." Besides, most personal computers at the time didn't have the necessary internal memory to pull it off.

I waited until I was in a position to create a program from the ground up. With the money I got from selling VisiPlot outright, and with assistance from designer John Sachs, I set out to produce a multifunction software package. We hired someone to write a word processing module, but he quit after a month and we settled for a spreadsheet and graphics.

We didn't invent "integrated software." Others were also working in this direction, so the term was already in the air. When we saw a program that included a data base, we decided to add this function to our software. We still weren't sure which machine we would release it on, but in August 1982, when IBM introduced its PC with the powerful Intel 8088 processor, we knew this was the computer to go with. That October we announced our program. Originally codenamed Trio, it became known to the world as 1-2-3. When we came up with a more versatile integrated software package complete with word processing and telecommunications ability in 1984, we decided to call it Symphony.

It has been suggested that 1-2-3 did for the IBM PC what VisiCalc did for the Apple II, providing a reason for placing these machines on managers' and executives' desks. But the impact just wasn't the same, even though our integrated software has proven extremely popular. We were building on an existing awareness of useful computer functions, not creating an entirely new market.

As for the future, we may see the proliferation of a "features race" to cram more and more applications functions onto a single disk. The fact remains that it doesn't matter how many functions you have on a disk; you can only do one thing at a time. It would be nice to receive electronic mail at the same time you're creating a spreadsheet, but this kind of concurrent operation is not practical on today's machines. For the ultimate in integrated software, we'll have to wait for the next generation of personal computers.

MITCHELL KAPOR, president of Lotus Development Corporation

strings for expressions may be too slow. Instead, we keep the values in a parsed form. This means that we do the analysis of the expression first and store direct references like [2,3] instead of B3. The number can be kept converted into the machine's representation.

• The expressions are richer and more complex. There are many additional functions such as exponentiation, logs and statistical functions. These expressions can have parentheses as well to set them off.

• Coordinate references consist of more than a single letter. Thus AA is equivalent to 27. For some functions (such as SUM) we allow a range instead of a single coordinate. Thus SUM(D1 . . . D10) will add the ten numbers in the cells from D1 through D10.

• The user must be able to control the order of evaluation. In the simple example given, if cell A1 refers to cell B1, it won't have the correct value on the first recalculation. There are various approaches to solving this. A list can be kept so that all the expressions dependent on a chained value get recomputed instead of scanning rows and columns.

• In order to handle large sheets in a small amount of memory, we use many space-saving techniques. For example, we don't allocate space for expressions until we need it. Many languages have an ALLOCATE or NEW statement that allows us to do this. We then release it with a FREE or DISPOSE statement.

Input Processing

We have assumed that somehow the expressions have been typed in. Obviously, we need to give the user a means of typing in new expressions and updating old ones. Rather than go into detail here, I will concentrate on how a highly interactive program like VisiCalc differs from using the INPUT statement in BASIC or the READ statement in Pascal. The problem is that if we use the INPUT statement, the user is speaking only to the operating system. What we want instead is to always be available to help the user and give immediate feedback. Thus we completely divorce the input from the output. The user's actions are reflected only in their effect on the spreadsheet.

In the simple case shown, this looks to the user as if we are just typing the character on the screen. Actually, we are making changes to the spreadsheet and showing the effects of the typing. Thus what you see is what you get, and any mistakes you make show up immediately so they can be corrected immediately. This also allows us to guide the user with appropriate prompts.

The most important characteristic of the input is that the program must be readily available in order to give the user the feeling of being in control. Thus, instead of asking for input, the program is always accepting what we enter and will perform an action as soon as it has complete input. When the enter key or an arrow is typed, the expression (or label) is stored at the current position.

The current position is an important concept. It represents the focus for the user activity. Expression entry and many commands apply to this current position. The current position is simply a coordinate such as B3. Whenever we modify the contents of a cell, we must perform the recalculation operation described above. The arrow commands serve to move the coordinate to the next position up, down, left or right.

Redisplay

As with recalculation, we are always recomputing the display. In the simplest view, we just rewrite the screen every time something changes. The challenge is to do this fast enough so it seems instantaneous or to redisplay only the changed portion of the screen.

As we noted in the input processing section, we do not "echo" the user's typing on the screen. Instead we change the sheet—either by changing the contents or by updating a typing buffer, such as one used for the current expression. This effect is shown to the user when the change is made and we redraw the display. Redisplay proceeds by displaying each section of the screen:

Status area. This shows the current position, the contents of the position (i.e., the expression if any) and any additional information such as the recalculation mode.

Prompt. Any prompting information.

Current input. This is used if the user is in the middle of typing an expression or label.

Headers. We display column and row headers.

Cells. We first make sure that the current position is displayable. If it is outside the current window, we must adjust the upper left position to make sure that it is shown. We can then scan the sheet across each row from the upper left position. For each cell, we determine whether it is empty or contains a label or an expression. If there is an expression, we display the current value.

In simplifying my description of the display operation, I have omitted many aspects of VisiCalc such as the optimizations possible, number formating, graphics and other features. In addition, there are many opportunities for new forms of presentation now that high-speed displays are just around the corner. ∎

THE DISCREET CHARMS OF VISICALC

One thing certain about the nascent age of personal computers is that a single useful program did more to give these machines respectability than all other major developments put together. The program: VisiCalc, the first good reason for business executives and managers to put personal computers on their office desks.

Now as ubiquitous as the three-piece suit, whether in its original form or as one of the dozens of sincerely flattering "visiclones" that rival it in sales, VisiCalc is no great shakes to look at. It presents you with a disarmingly simple screen, resembling a vast accountant's ledger made up of 254 rows and 63 columns (though it shows you only a small block of these at any one time). Each box, or "cell," can contain words, numbers, or (and herein lies its genius) formulas that operate on those numbers.

In one column, for example, the top cell might contain the label "Expenses." In the cells below there might be a variety of numbers, with the bottom-most cell holding a formula instructing the computer to display the sum of all the numbers in the column. Then, no matter how many numbers are put in the cells on that column, the electronic spreadsheet program gives you a new running total of expenses each time you put it through its paces.

But VisiCalc can do far more than just add. Using a simple formula, you can program a cell to add the numbers in the first three rows, subtract the sum from a number held in the next row, multiply the result by a constant, divide by a number from another column, and write the number in a cell somewhere across the sheet. Then, after doing all that, VisiCalc can express the result as a percentage or in scientific notation rounded out to the nearest integer or to twelve decimals. Begin to get the picture?

In a trice, VisiCalc makes detailed calculations that would keep a platoon of accountants busy for hours. This is its tour de force, allowing you to get information you wouldn't dare ask for otherwise. It lets you crunch several alternate sets of numbers and compare the results. For the first time, the individual or small business can do what the big-leaguers have

always been able to do with large, expensive computers: make several projections based on different assumptions and play them all out on paper.

Consider the possibilities. Say you own a widget factory. Here, on a disk, is the ability to reckon the unit cost for each individual widget, taking into account materials, labor, inflation, taxes, shipping and overhead. Should any one of these variables change, you just reenter that one value, press a button and—*voila!*—the projection's totals are all adapted to the new information. Or, if you're an investor in Consolidated Widget stock and your shares rise ten points while the prime drops a point, a few quick strokes can tell you if it makes sense to refinance the loan you got at 13 percent.

The speculative plugging in and recalculating of financial figures have charmingly been called "what-if games." These are the kinds of games that masters of business administration spend two years in B-school playing so they can then creatively improve on a company's balance sheet. Unfortunately, there is a tendency on the part of MBAs and U.S. businessmen in general to rely on such games instead of common sense in running their affairs.

It is worth noting that while electronic spreadsheets have been among the most successful personal computer programs in America, their importance overseas has generally been secondary to information filing and retrieval software; in Europe and Japan, it seems, facts are more important than projections. VisiCalc's success on these shores is indicative of America's business culture, including some of its disturbing flaws. Intended as an accurate planning tool, VisiCalc is often used instead to "fudge" financial figures in the eternal search for glowing projections.

With some of VisiCalc's results as fictitious as the budget estimates issued by federal agencies and yet just as vital to long-term planning (and waste), it's no wonder that administrators of all stripes have taken to using and abusing its powers. Don't think of it as software; think of it as realpolitik on a disk.

DAVID NIMMONS

YOUR IRS REFUND CHECK

The Internal Revenue Service collects its one hundred million federal income tax returns with ample human help at ten regional centers across the U.S.A. Even so, the growing complexity of the tax code has made it impossible for your refund to be processed quickly without the intervention of computers.

After the returns have been sorted, and checks and forms compared and edited by hand for computer processing, tax information is entered on magnetic tape by a clerk at an Automated Collection System terminal. Powerful mainframe computers process the tapes for accuracy with outside data and flag possible

audit problems. The National Computer Center for Account Posting and Settlement in Martinsburg, West Virginia, then reconciles all taxpayer tapes, which immediately go to the Treasury Department's Disbursing Center for automated writing of checks. Total elapsed time: three to nine weeks.

THE WAY WE WORK

by Lenny Siegel

A cursory review of modern electronics technology might indicate that computers are equalizing the American work force. A closer look, however, shows that while computers have opened some new opportunities for those near the top of the occupational ladder, they are routinizing the work of many others and throwing the skilled middle stratum back down toward the bottom rung.

Historically, both private business and public institutions in this country have practiced what has come to be called "scientific management": the division of labor into distinct tasks, reorganizing the work process to minimize costs. Until recently, for instance, phone companies employed large numbers of skilled technicians who kept the switching networks operating. The introduction of solid-state electronic switching systems, essentially telephone-switching computers, opened up some positions for programmers at the upper end of the occupational hierarchy. However, the automated, self-trouble-shooting switching systems have "surplused" a large number of experienced skilled technicians.

Micro Monitors

That the video displays on our computers are called "monitors" is ironic, as though the basic human-machine interaction is of people monitoring micros. This may be the case for many professionals and managers, but the average worker in a computerized workplace is much more likely to be monitored by machine.

It is a simple matter for a computer to record, analyze and transmit immediately to supervisors data on the pace of workers, whether they be typists, salesclerks or assembly-line operatives. The technology is new, but the concept is old: speed-up. One Silicon Valley firm markets a module called the Performance

Achievement Monitor, which, says the manufacturer, makes employees happier by providing a standard against which to measure their efficiency. But anyone who has ever worked under such pressure knows that fancy electronic devices, like pushy supervisors, tend to make workers *less* happy. Faster rates of production, in the absence of new techniques and equipment, merely increase the level of exploitation. How odd that IBM has adopted as its personal computer spokesman a Charlie Chaplin impersonator, when Chaplin's Little Tramp character so graphically enacted the effects of speed-up in *Modern Times*.

In the long run, speed-up can increase productivity only marginally and at the same time threatens to disrupt work patterns. Sped-up employees may be motivated to cut corners—damaging not only the product, but their machines or themselves. Quality, which often is not measured by the machines, frequently suffers as quantity increases. For instance, telephone installers who are dispatched and monitored by computers tend to hang lines along the shortest path, abandoning their old, slower techniques of skillfully concealing the wires.

According to one story, unconfirmed but probably true, a major supermarket chain programmed its cash registers to note the rate at which check-out clerks worked. Young clerks turned out to be much faster than the older employees, apparently because the latter group stopped to chat with familiar customers. The computer analysis made no provision for recognizing the quality of work, including the fact that the personal relationships may have been the reason for the customers' patronage of the store.

Computerized systems are also used to pace employees. On some assembly lines, workers are placed between robots and expected to work at the rate programmed into their computerized counterparts. Telephone operators, whether they work for phone, airline or catalog companies, spend less time than they once did waiting for the phone to ring. Sitting in centralized

Lenny Siegel, director of the Pacific Studies Center in Mountain View, California, is the author of Where the Chips May Fall: The Social Impact of High Technology.

communications centers, they are fed a call from anywhere in a large area as soon as they complete the last one, doing away with pauses in their routine.

Remote Control

Raw speed-up is merely the simplest feature of a more general trend: the use of high technology to give "scientific" managers increased control over the producers of goods and services. Harry Braverman, in *Labor and Monopoly Capital*, summarizes the three principles of Frederick Winslow Taylor, founder of the school of scientific management:

> Thus, if the first principle is the gathering and development of knowledge of labor processes, and the second is the concentration of this knowledge as the exclusive province of management—together with its essential converse, the absence of such knowledge among the workers—then the third is the use of this monopoly over knowledge to control each step of the labor process and its mode of execution.

Centralized word processing, numerically controlled machine tools, "point-of-sale" devices, financial data terminals and other computerized work stations are designed to provide management with timely, detailed data on the nature of the work process. In general, as management learns more, workers lose their autonomy. By centralizing their data on the flow of work, top managers can reorganize the workplace to increase productivity or lower costs—even over the objections of workers whose special skills were once valued highly.

Experienced workers whose jobs are being reshaped by the advent of computers tend to blame the technology itself. But this same technology could be used to decentralize information, give employees more control over quality and share the responsibility, skills and rewards of work. Unfortunately, few of these possibilities have been realized. Because they have entered the workplace so quickly and thoroughly, computers merely underscore problems inherent in the social relations that dominate the American workplace.   ∎

SMALL FRY

Artwork for preceding page

Artist:
   Susan Forner
Computer:
   Action Graphics' Graphic Animation System game design computer
Software:
   Video game paint system by Action Graphics
Input:
   Joystick and digitizing pad

COMPUTERS IN THE CLASSROOM

Fad or fountainhead?
by Katharine Davis Fishman

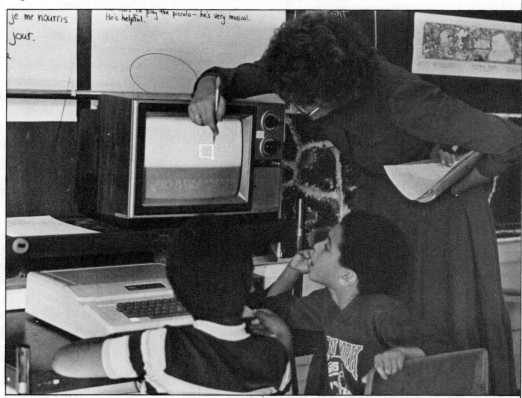

Students at Bank Street School learn about programming Logo sprites.

Within eight years of the introduction of the personal computer, according to a Johns Hopkins study, more than half the schools in the United States had bought at least one microcomputer to teach with. And today, the same study reveals, those elementary and secondary schools that bought computers for "drill-and-practice" or "tutorial" purposes are turning increasingly toward teaching children to program.

Computer people who tout the benefits of programming—most notably the advocates of the Logo language—argue that it teaches logic, planning and problem solving. Since these are all activities with powerful significance in intellectual development and in life itself, it's not surprising that, as one observer has written, "programming is viewed by many of its devotees as a Wheaties of the Mind."

But at what age do children begin to profit from

Katharine Davis Fishman is the author of The Computer Establishment. *She writes on a variety of subjects for major magazines.*

programming? Can all children reap similar rewards? Is what's going on in the computer lab meaningful or is it all just fun and games?

Two Schools Observed

As part of a joint program with the New York Academy of Sciences and with the help of a National Science Foundation grant, several districts in the New York public school system have established Logo programming classes. District 3 on Manhattan's Upper West Side has what Tessa Harvey, who directs its Office of Funded Programs, calls "a moral and financial commitment to using computers in an educationally sound way." The philosophical issue behind this commitment, she says, is that "the haves get more and the have-nots get less. Rich kids and rich schools are going to have computers. We felt that in order not to widen the gap that already exists we have to make computers available to kids who would not otherwise have them."

Joan of Arc Junior High School

J.H.S. 118 on West 93 Street, better known as Joan of Arc, is a neighborhood institution of long standing whose population has changed according to familiar trends: today nearly half its students are black, 42 percent are Hispanic, and the remaining 10 percent are mostly white with a few Asians. In the spring of 1983 I visited the computer lab here, which housed eleven Apple IIs, five Atari 800s and a TI 99/4A, an endowment that many richer schools might envy. The magi of the computer program were Peter Rentof and Steve Siegelbaum, who oversaw something called the Environmental Cluster—comprising two classes of eighth- and ninth-graders, sixty-five kids in all. Siegelbaum and Rentof

Jennifer Nix' animated snowflakes.

feel that computer use is a powerful motivator. "We had a boy the first year who was severely dyslexic," says Siegelbaum, "until he began spending time at the computer during lunch hour. I noticed he had much less trouble with reversal of letters when he used the keyboard." The student became an expert of whom other kids could ask questions, which helped his self-image tremendously. Soon he was volunteering to go to the blackboard and putting problems up and writing his name. Before this he wouldn't write at all.

Since the kids who do well at Logo programming are not necessarily the best students in the class, Logo can confer some status on underachievers. "If I give a test," Rentof says, "and a kid flunks or passes, that's different from when I come over and see him creating something with his own knowledge and I say, 'How did you do that?' These projects are impressive to adults, and it shows, and the kids feel powerful in themselves."

Rentof feels that programming procedures have a particular resonance for these students. "Some kids come from homes in which there's very little logic to their lives," he notes. "Here they get a steady dose of logic: there's always a consequence for what you do."

Still, it's not always possible to pinpoint the effects of programming on individual students or tell whether changes should be credited to the computer or to good instruction in regular math or, at this most volatile of ages, to ordinary growth. One boy who was flunking regular math used algebra capably in his Logo projects, and Siegelbaum says "he's becoming a crackerjack programmer. He's an interesting case, at his most disciplined when he's at the computer. We've yet to see whether this carries over into his other work."

On one visit to the lab I saw a graffito flickering in cheerful multicolored capitals on the screen of one of the Apples. It read:

> PEOPLE ARE INSTINCTIVELY SCARED OF WHAT THEY CAN'T COMPREHEND.
>
> INDENT THAT'S ONE OF THE MAIN REASONS PEOPLE ARE RELUCTANT TO USE THE COMPUTERS. THEY ALSO HAVE TO OVERCOME THEIR FEAR OF MAKING ERRORS, AS APPARENTLY I HAVE MADE MANY.
>
> INDENT PEOPLE TAKE ONE LOOK AT ME, THE WAY I DRESS, AND RIGHT AWAY JUDGE ME AS NOT HAVING ANY HIGHER INTELLECT THAN THE AVERAGE PUERTO RICAN ON THE STREET. ONCE YOU START TO UNDERSTAND THINGS THAT SEEM TO LOOK COMPLICATED, BUT WHICH CAN BECOME UNDERSTANDABLE, IF OF COURSE YOU APPLY YOURSELF TO IT, YOU HAVE A CHANCE.

Across the room Jennifer Nix, one of the Cluster's computer stars, was running her animated car-

A student at Joan of Arc Junior High masters a Logo procedure.

toon. First snowflakes fell diagonally on the roof of a house and piled up on the ground. Then a stork flew down and deposited a baby in front of the house; stick figures of a mother and father came out and gathered up the baby; the snowflakes turned to hearts, and the caption appeared: AND THEY LIVED HAPPILY EVER AFTER.

The kids at Joan of Arc used the computer to pursue a variety of individual interests. Irving Smith, a burly fourteen-year-old, had no interest in graphics; he much preferred word games and had produced a grammar test on the parts of speech and a spelling program that requires the student to unscramble such words as "hideous," "eradicate" and "docile." Irving had decided to make programming a career.

Quite clearly the computer offered a powerful means of self-expression for Jennifer, Irving and Rafael, the author of the graffito. In varying degrees the kids treated computer work as a sociable activity in which students consulted each other for tips and pointers. Irving had been helped and inspired by an older boy the year before and seemed to enjoy teaching others; Jennifer and her friend Tenesia had more proprietary and competitive feelings about their work but were still willing to help each other with the basics.

In all, it was difficult to tell how much substance the kids had acquired from Logo programming, how much Rentof and Siegelbaum would have given them anyway and what would stay with them in later years. The kids I spoke with felt comfortable with computers and showed sensible attitudes toward technology; it

would be hard to imagine them ever befuddled by future shock. If District 3's goal in establishing the Logo program was to narrow the gap between haves and have-nots, it was accomplishing its purpose.

Who says computers aren't fun?

Bank Street Schoolers in computer class.

Bank Street School for Children

Students at Bank Street, a private laboratory school housed in a handsome brick building on West 112 Street, tend to be the children of teachers, psychologists and other professionals. The atmosphere here is pervaded by an aura of privilege that is cultural and psychological as well as economic.

Bank Street's reasons for installing Logo were as particular as District 3's. Psychologists at the Bank Street College of Education, which operates the school, were alarmed to see little serious research being done in the area of educational software. The college seemed a perfect place to carry on such research because, as psychologist and administrator Karen Sheingold observed, "We have a point of view about education that is seen as humanistic. At Bank Street it would not be the same as setting up research at a place deeply devoted to technology; we were likely to be helpfully critical and skeptical."

The attitude of Bank Street toward Logo is notably more reserved than that of District 3. The College certainly endorses the notion of computers in the classroom: as Sheingold says, "Here's this powerful tool that is part of kids' lives and will be more so as time goes on. For us the issue is, do you pretend it's not there or do you take it on and try to understand and guide it toward the best interests of the child?"

Like the teachers at Joan of Arc, those at Bank Street were fascinated to discover that far from being mechanical and impersonal, computer programming turned out to be a highly social affair. The children collaborated with and consulted each other much more than usual. Before, when they talked together, it was about vacation plans and basketball scores. But according to Jan Hawkins, one of the College's psychologists, "The computers appeared to provide a context where collaborative work was supported."

Hawkins' colleague, Roy Pea, had researched the question of how much children actually learn from programming and whether it helps them solve other problems. Children with a year's study were given several forty-five-minute tests. After the first, Pea found that though older and younger kids had spent roughly the same amount of time programming, the older kids understood much more; that boys had spent much more time programming and far outscored the girls; that among different kids there was a whopping twenty-five-point standard deviation from the mean score, with only three out of fifty kids at the highest level; and that "roughly one-quarter of the children in each of the classes had not become very involved in the classroom programming and did correspondingly poorly."

To see if programming skills transferred to better problem solving in life, Pea tested groups of children who'd programmed extensively in Logo for a year and groups who hadn't programmed at all, assigning a classroom chore-scheduling task to see which kids could come up with the quickest plan. Pea concluded that "on a large number of measures, the efficiency of the plans, the quality of the revisions, and the types of decisions made during the planning process, we found no differences between the programming and nonprogramming groups, at either age."

Pea remarked that while programming advocates might protest that the test was too brief or that the effects of Logo would show up later, observation of the children and studies of other cognitive psychologists suggest that transfer of problem-solving strategies is tough even for adults to achieve, and that college students with several thousand hours of programming have trouble understanding how programs work.

The Bank Street children I talked to in the spring of 1983 seemed as "computer-literate" as the Joan of Arc kids, but quite clearly the latter group had acquired (or revised) their knowledge by working with Logo, while the Bank Street kids appeared to have gleaned much of their information from the New York

Playing the TI keyboard.

LEARNING WITH LOGO

Logo is not only a computer language, but also the foundation of an entire educational theory. Prof. Seymour Papert of M.I.T.'s Artificial Intelligence Laboratory advocates the Logo language because, he says, "children can learn to use computers in a masterful way, and learning to use computers can change the way they learn everything else."

Papert's techniques, set forth in his book *Mindstorms*, start with the indisputable premise that programming a computer is simply a case of communicating with it in a language common to man and machine. His next premise, also indisputable, is that we absorb a foreign language far more readily when we live in its country than when we learn it by "unnatural" classroom methods. What's more, since a computer "speaks mathematics," the child will learn to speak it, too, by living in what is archly called "Mathland." Indeed, Papert lays children's mathematical difficulties on an uncongenial teaching environment and meaningless exercises.

Turtle Tracks

In programming with Logo, children break problems down into short procedures, which then become part of the computer's vocabulary and can later be used in other programs. As Papert and his disciples point out, theirs is the only language that encourages kids to acquire small, manageable bits of learning, then build them into hierarchies of greater knowledge. Moreover, the kids get to name their own procedures, which become special "dialects" stored on each student's disk: Breton for Jeremy, Basque for Jennifer.

Logo is also interactive, which means the computer acts on an instruction the minute it's given; the child doesn't have to write a whole program before finding out if a solution works and therefore can easily experiment with different ideas. List processing is offered as well, allowing the child to organize related pieces of information into groups of varying sizes.

The instrument of revelation through Logo is the Turtle, which began life as a computer-controlled cybernetic animal and in most schools is now a triangular cursor that moves about the screen at the child's command. The Turtle has two properties: position and heading. The commands FORWARD and BACK, followed by a number, move it in a straight line for a specified distance; the commands RIGHT and LEFT turn it around at a given angle. To teach the Turtle to make a square, the child simply types:

TO SQUARE	FORWARD 50
FORWARD 50	RIGHT 90
RIGHT 90	FORWARD 50
FORWARD 50	RIGHT 90
RIGHT 90	END

As the child progresses, the Turtle's artwork becomes increasingly elaborate: the procedure for CIRCLE, for example, becomes a part of the Turtle's vocabulary and thus a component of BALLOON, and an arrangement of balloons can be used to make a flower.

Drawing ever more elaborate pictures with Logo can embrace quite sophisticated mathematical concepts. One feature of Logo is POLYSPI, a fundamental procedure that allows the student to produce spiral designs by altering the distance or the angle at which the Turtle moves. In designing different kinds of spirals, the student should learn something about variables; further, because it produces an attractive picture, the lesson should be more satisfying and meaningful than merely writing "x + 3" equations.

Although Logo is best-known as a graphic tool for teaching kids the fundamentals of geometry and algebra, its procedural structure is also useful for verbal programs. A popular application involves learning grammar by programming a sentence structure, feeding the computer lists of nouns, verbs, adjectives, etc., and having it compose poetry at random.

Most microcomputer manufacturers now offer a Logo package. The Texas Instruments computer version originated a feature called sprites, now available on other machines. Sprites come in a variety of shapes (a plane, truck, rocket, ball and box) to which the student assigns one of sixteen different colors, a heading and a speed at which they'll keep moving until told to stop. Setting several sprites moving can produce animated cartoons—and teach some physics concepts in the process. Students can also make their own sprites by filling in different tiles on a grid, a process that requires plotting with x and y coordinates.

Looking Forward

Papert and his team held their first extensive tryout of Logo under a National Science Foundation grant during the school year 1977–78. The entire sixth-grade class at the Lincoln School in Brookline, Massachusetts, spent between twenty and forty hours with Logo, and the work of sixteen students—chosen to represent the full range of academic abilities from above to below average—was documented in detail.

Though the preliminary report centered mainly on directions for future research, one significant finding emerged. Logo instruction illuminated each child's individual style of approaching problems, a development that could help teachers and students to work together in the future. The variety of the kids' experience at the computer—and their different relationships with the machine—dramatized the importance of studying each child's emotional as well as intellectual attitudes toward learning.

K.D.F.

Times, last night's dinner table conversation, their own and their friends' home computers.

During one period in a class of eleven- and twelve-year-olds I watched six boys monopolizing the computers and soliciting each other's help from time to time, while free-floating boys stopped by and commented about what they saw on the screen. Finally the teacher wheeled one machine into another room and called for half the class to join him. Four girls went over to the machine and the teacher presented a problem that the kids worked at enthusiastically (and sometimes scrappily) together, calling out solutions and jostling each other to go next. The work on the screens didn't look as elaborate as that of the Joan of Arc kids. In the "open classroom" atmosphere of Bank Street, programming faced considerable competition from other activities.

The teacher, Michael Cook, made a point of choosing "average kids," not computer whizzes, for our discussion, and these kids talked—in an articulate and engaging manner—about frustration and boredom. "With long-term projects it seems you always fail at the end," said Simon Firestone. "Like any other toy, you get bored with it after a while. Kids get frustrated and bang down on the keys. Sometimes I start cursing and hit the keyboard."

This was the first year that Bank Street children used the computer for word processing, loading it up with the Bank Street Writer program developed at the College. Two of the three eleven-year-olds I spoke to—all described as strong writers—were full of excitement. Timo Green said, "Physically it's a lot easier than writing, and it's just 'funner.' Before I didn't want to free-write, but now when I've a chance on the computer it's different." China Parmalee said, "You see one handwritten page is half a typewritten page and you say, 'I've got to write more.' "

The teacher, Kitty Newhouse, is suitably pleased; she has felt free to ask the kids for more revisions. "Now," she says, "I have conferences at the computer. We sit down with a printout of the rough draft. We're both looking at the screen and we read a sentence aloud together and they hear that they left out the comma. Last year I'd type their stories to put into the magazine, but I hadn't time to do that often. The main reason to revise your work is so it can be published—and now they can publish whenever they want."

But how soon and how far will word processing improve their product? "There's no question that for a substantial number of kids handwriting is a significant block," says Midian Kurland, who directs the Bank Street Writing Project. "Ever since the twenties, data have indicated that if you let children write at the typewriter the amount they do increases and the quality improves. But we also know from the long history of developmental research in writing that kids' major problems are organization, knowing what to write and how to frame an argument and being sensitive to their audience. None of these problems is even remotely addressed by the word processor. It's going to take much more time to see improvement."

"Our major finding," Kurland said of computer programming at Bank Street, "is that the results are highly variable. Programming does very different things for different kids. We've had kids for whom programming became a positive force in their lives, helping their self-respect and their relationship with their peers—and other kids who couldn't care less about it."

" 'What is the potential of the computer?' is a meaningless question," Kurland says. "The question should be 'What is the potential of the computer in a particular classroom with a particular teacher?' "

Micro Thoughts

What caused the differences in attitude and accomplishment between Joan of Arc and Bank Street, and what do they suggest for the future? At Joan of Arc the kids were several years older—does their apparently greater progress tell us you can't soup up the educational philosophy of Piaget? On the other hand, their knowledge hasn't been formally tested—how profound is it?

Joan of Arc had a lab setup that enabled twenty kids to work on machines during one period, while Bank Street had six machines perpetually available to a class of twenty-five kids. Did this make a difference? At home and at school, Bank Street kids are subjected to a wealth of cultural stimuli. Did these drown Logo out, making the kids' experience with the computer less intense than that of their peers at Joan of Arc? More positively, the computer culture has been seen as a white male preserve, while at Joan of Arc it clearly isn't. Who or what gets the credit for that? Joan of Arc installed computers so that poor kids wouldn't be left behind. Bank Street's mission was to study educational innovations, and its parents pay to be on the leading edge. Why should a middle-class suburban school district add programming to the curriculum?

For one such district that offers a varied programming syllabus in middle and high school, the reasons were roughly similar to Joan of Arc's: the belief that learning to handle a computer is becoming a necessary prerequisite for both jobs and college. This rationale is unquestionably true; programming will be a skill as useful as driving a car. Beyond that, however, its benefits remain unproven.

The advocates of programming will simply have to work longer and harder to convince us. Meanwhile, parents and educators should moderate their expectations, make sure that courses are thoughtfully tailored, and regard the discipline as experimental and subject to a shakedown period. ■

BABES IN MICROLAND

by Fred D'Ignazio

Computers for kids at Children's Television Workshop's Sesame Place.

Parents who encourage computer use early in life claim that the future of their children is at stake. These parents are right. By 1990, according to an IBM study, over 80 percent of all working adults will use a computer as an integral part of their job.

Some eager parents are even showing their six-month-olds flash cards with computer words like RAM, ROM and CPU, and some are trying to teach their youngsters how to program in BASIC or Logo—before they can walk. (A recent cartoon shows a small child and his mother in the midst of a fight. "That's final, Opus," the mother says. "You can't have a computer until you're toilet-trained!")

According to home computer manufacturers and independent software designers, simple "happy face" programs allow toddlers to take to computers naturally. Computers give them immediate rewards: praise, colorful cartoon figures, sound effects and music. They

Fred D'Ignazio is a commentator on personal computers for ABC-TV's Good Morning America *and associate editor of* Compute! *magazine.*

make the youngest children feel important, competent and in charge. On their own, children will approach computers and use them the way they might use a doll, a set of building blocks or a coloring book. They can go one on one with a computer, without needing a parent or an older sibling around to guide them.

Many parents, however, set up formal classes requiring their children to spend a certain amount of time on the computer and to learn specific things. These "computer lessons" could kill a child's interest by taking all the fun out of something the child might otherwise have liked. If the fun disappears, all that's left is the learning—and learning without fun is work.

Also, parents who hasten to put their children on the high-technology track may be putting them on the *wrong* track. According to Fred Hechinger, education editor of the New York *Times*, the skills that people need to use computers today will be obsolete by the time our toddlers enter the job market. If we loosely define infants as children from ages one to four, and if we assume that college is part of the plan, then the earliest they'll enter the job market is the year 2001. Given the swift pace of computer technology, experts predict that by 2001 most people will be using computers as tools and resources—and not for writing programs. Today's computer programmers enjoy high prestige and command high salaries; by 2001 programmers will have about the same income and status as today's automobile mechanics and TV repairmen. Thus parents who teach their children how to move the bits and bytes around inside computers will be saddling them with useless information and obsolete skills.

On the other hand, there are dozens of programs on the market that let young children use the computer to learn fundamental skills that will still be in demand in the twenty-first century.

Flying Solo

Once they've been taught to insert a program into the computer, children can learn problem solving, information management and creative decision making. Even three-year-olds can learn basic computer etiquette.

A program called Hodge Podge, for example, lets youngsters wander across the computer keyboard, pressing buttons at random. Each key gives the child a color-and-sound response. Pushing the letter V, for instance, produces the picture and sound of an erupting volcano. Gradually, at their own pace, children learn to recognize the different numbers and letters.

Another program, Juggle's Rainbow, proceeds at a pace that even the youngest child can be comfortable with. The program divides the computer's keyboard into four sectors: top, bottom, left and right. When the child pushes a button in a particular sector, a colorful shape appears on the picture screen in that position. Like all good educational programs, Juggle's Rainbow has several skill levels, is easy to use and appeals to children's senses. One of the games teaches the concept of directionality as the child constructs a butterfly with symmetrical antennas and wings.

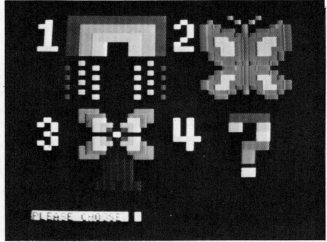

Juggle's Rainbow offers a picture menu.

Beyond the Keyboard

Computers are moving beyond keyboards with new peripheral attachments that are well suited for little children.

The Koala pad is a touch pad that comes with a black plastic stylus and a paint-your-own-picture kit known as the Micro Illustrator. The kit has a pictorial menu full of paintbrushes, paint colors and drawing tools that enhance small children's artistic abilities and enable them to do things they could never do with just paper and crayons or markers. One command (LINES) lets the child create "rubber band" lines that stretch across the screen. Another command (MIRROR) lets the child draw in four different directions at once to create beautifully symmetrical objects in just a few seconds. Other single commands allow the child to "grow" different kinds of geometric shapes, including rays, boxes, frames, disks and circles.

There is even a ZOOM! command that lets the child magnify a picture to add fine details or easily erase mistakes. This is a particularly rewarding command for small children since fine details tend to elude them and their mistakes are usually hard to correct. With the ZOOM! command they can go over any section of the picture and remake it the way they want. When they leave the command, this section of the picture shrinks and becomes a part of the whole.

The Computer as Baby Sitter

Computer programs that enable children to learn, discover and explore on their own are also a convenient device parents can use to divert their children's attention. Sometimes this is appropriate and can be very useful, especially for busy, exhausted parents.

Toddlers are especially attractive candidates for computer as baby sitters. Notoriously curious, nosy and exasperating, toddlers also have the energy and stamina of decathlon athletes. There must be millions of harried mothers who would love it if a computer distracted their little ones and took them off their hands for a few hours—or even a few minutes.

–(Nonetheless, a computer is no substitute for parental love and attention. Children who interact only with computers all day will ultimately suffer from emotional deprivation. They'll learn to operate and interact with a machine, but how well will they do with human beings?)

The newest educational programs for children are what software designers call "pro-social." These programs encourage group play and human-to-human interaction. Children's Television Workshop, for example, developed a program called Peanut Butter Panic. Two little Nutnik creatures on the screen are on top of a structure that's part scale, part peanut-butter machine and part trampoline. Each Nutnik is controlled with a special child-oriented control pad (like the Koala pad). If the children cooperate, the little Nutniks will be able to catch the falling stars used to power their peanut-butter sandwich machine. If the children do not cooperate, the Nutniks can't catch the stars, they don't make sandwiches and they grow skinny. Bad Snarfs fly across the picture screen and take away the Nutniks' remaining sandwiches.

The Electronic Hearth

While they help develop a sense of competition and cooperation in children who work on them together, computers can play an even wider role when whole families gather around them to learn and socialize. The computer can supplant television as the electronic hearth that has captivated most families for the past thirty years.

Several software companies have recognized this new aspect of computers and are designing new learning games to be challenging and fun for all members of the family, whether age two or thirty-six. These family games usually do not emphasize fine motor skills or advanced reading and computation skills. Instead they concentrate on abilities and skills that family members have in common: fact finding, memory, problem solving, shape, color and sound recognition, logical inference, creativity and imagination.

Sacrificing the Intangible

Robert Taylor, a professor at Columbia University's Teachers College, is an expert on educational computing. He is also a critic of educational computing for young children. Taylor feels that many parents and educators, in using computers to develop children's formal skills, are neglecting less tangible but equally important aspects of a child's development, including values, ethics, self-image, self-reliance, trust, kindness, gentleness, love and loyalty. How can a child learn these things from a computer? Says Taylor, "We can't ask computers to teach children things that we know how to teach but are not teaching ourselves."

According to Taylor, many people feel that children who are playing are wasting their time. They look at the computer as a way to harness children's boundless energy and put them on a formal learning track as early as possible. But Taylor and many other educators maintain that play is a fundamental activity in the development process. If they were to remove play from a child's environment, parents might severely hamper his or her emotional, social and intellectual development.

Computers, says Taylor, are ideal instruments for play. Educational programs shouldn't just be instruments to help children learn reading, writing and arithmetic. They shouldn't be there just to prepare

If Peanut Butter Panic players don't cooperate, the Nutnik loses his sandwich to evil Snarfs.

children to get a higher score on their SATs or a berth at Harvard or some other prestigious school. Instead, they should encourage the key developmental components of play, including the strengthening of children's creativity, their gift for fantasy and imagination, their ability to play roles and build models of the real world, their curiosity and their hunger for exploration, discovery and experimentation.

Builder Programs

A builder program lets children use the computer like an erector set. It enables them to create objects that, given their limited motor skills, experience, patience and attention span, they could never build in the real, 3-D world.

For young children, a computer is an electronic sandbox. They can wander across the keyboard and build gobbledygook words, shapes and even sounds, the way they would sculpt sand castles, tunnels and mountains, but computer "sand" programs let children build sand castles that reach into the sky. Rocky's Boots, from the Learning Company, lets small children build rainbow-colored electronic circuits that make clackers clack and boots kick. Creature Creator from DesignWare lets children build funny dancing monsters. The Trains program from Spinnaker lets children create and manage their own railroad.

Years ago, it seemed that all young boys wanted to be railroad engineers. Some of them grew up to be the computer engineers and software authors who have made it possible for children to pilot trains, fly airplanes or experience some other activity they would have had to wait to accomplish in the adult world. ∎

MICRO INFANT SOFTWARE SHOPPING GUIDE

When you're shopping for toddler software, trust your common sense and parental instincts. Look for the same things you look for in a good game or toy. The following are some questions to keep in mind.

● *Does the program contain several skill levels so it can grow with your child?* Young children change almost daily. Even if you buy shoes that are slightly too large, your children quickly grow into them. But buying children's software is not like buying children's shoes. Software that is a size or two too large will only frustrate your child.

● *Does the software let your child take control of the computer?* When you watch your child using the software, ask yourself whether he or she is programming the computer or vice versa. Little children have few opportunities to be in charge. They are taught by the rest of the world, but they rarely have the opportunity to act as teachers. Good software lets a small child be in charge and encourages the role of teacher.

● *Does the software also encourage peer tutoring and adult tutoring?* Normally, the flow of knowledge in a family is from the top down—from parents to children and from older siblings to younger siblings. But one of the marvelous things about computers is that they encourage children to teach each other as well as to teach adults.

● *Is the software interactive?* The most important trait of computers is not their ability to calculate but their ability to interact. How does the software make the computer interact with you and your children? Be critical. When you review new software, you can apply the same standards for politeness and friendliness that you apply to people. If people are kind, friendly and caring, you immediately know it. The same goes for computers. Computers should not be judgmental. They should never punish children or tell them they have failed. Instead they should be patient, humorous and entertaining tutors. They should help children do what they want—like good companions, helpers or tools.

● *Besides the explicit knowledge the software teaches (like counting or shape recognition), what are the intangible things that are imparted?* The intangibles may have a deeper, more long-lasting effect on your child. Pay close attention to how the software rewards your child when he gives a correct answer. What happens if he gives an incorrect answer? Does this software help build a child's independence, self-confidence and self-image? Does it encourage him to experiment? Does it support your family's social values? Is it nonviolent? Nonsexist? Does it encourage sharing?

● *Does the software let children do something they can do only on a computer?* Otherwise you might have just bought an expensive pencil. Good software should enable children to do something better on the computer than on any other medium. For example, my seven-year-old daughter bangs on our family piano for hours, but she uses the family computer to compose her own music. And my four-year-old son leaves scraps

of paper around with his scribbles, in pen and magic marker, but he creates elaborate, multicolored tiles, revolving planets and cartoon pictures on our family computer.

● *Does the software amplify and extend children's abilities?* It should enable them to create things effortlessly, without being swamped by mechanical details. It also lets them go back to their creations and quickly polish them and change them. It lets them save their creations to show their friends and their family. It couples all these expanded abilities with the imagination, fearlessness and curiosity that children have in such abundance. The result is a fertile environment for learning.

F. D'I.

WHY CALL IT COMPUTER LITERACY?

by Inabeth Miller

Thousands of voices are rising in a chorus of "Computer Literacy for All." We are being asked, cajoled, *required* to change our school curricula, our work patterns, our lifestyles. Like immigrants to a new technological society, taught again by our children, we are promised a better future if we can learn to manipulate its symbols.

The traditional meaning of literacy is the ability to read and write. A "learned" or "literate" person has been exposed to writings and is thus considered educated. Literacy has been considered a necessity for functioning in modern society, despite many conflicting and romanticized historical examples of illiterate successes. Those who could read became the priests and advisers to kings in many cultures. More recently, the ability to read was deemed necessary to becom-

Inabeth Miller is librarian to the faculty of the Harvard Graduate School of Education. She is also administrator of the Educational Technologies Data Base Project.

ing a citizen, driving a car or seeking employment.

The search for literacy has replaced élitist literati with nearly universal ignorami. The education establishment has long ignored the individual who could paint, write music, manipulate tools, perform physical feats, instead concentrating on its primary mission of unlocking numbers and letters.

And still we have acquired these nonliterate skills, outside of most formal institutions. We have learned to use a paintbrush, to play instruments and compose, to improve physical skills—sometimes with enough force or passion to cause great societal change. We have developed tools and begun to use them with little attention from our great institutions of learning.

We till the land with giant tractors, we cross our cities and countries in different forms of transportation, we communicate by telephone, we operate a variety of sophisticated machines and appliances without formal school courses or labeling them as new literacies. Imagine if every technological invention was accompanied by a literacy course. From "ballpoint pen literacy" to "automotive literacy," from "powerboat literacy" to "microwave oven literacy," an unending stream of irrelevancies would become the modern educational curriculum.

But the new wave, the computer explosion, is knocking at the doors of every educational institution, forcing a response from those most ill-equipped to define the situation. It started quietly, surviving previous incarnations that left many schools untouched, despite some mainframe "skeletons" that still haunt the basements of buildings. Though large computers have been generally accepted for administrative purposes, their economic and academic credibility never materialized.

Micros first appeared in suburban, engineering-based communities' schools, where parents placed both child and computer on the doorstep and offered themselves as the instructional and teaching resource. Sometimes it was the teachers who received a small grant, or brought in their own computer from home, and began writing programs in BASIC or building a library of questionable gameware. Few uses touched any school curriculum.

Who would have imagined the groundswell, encouraged by "packaged goods" advertising, that played upon the fears and aspirations of an unsuspecting parent population? Every state legislature is presently debating the issue of computers and schools. Every superintendent and college president must deal with the issue of computer literacy and its place in the curriculum structure.

Three Dimensions

What is meant by computer literacy? The search for definitions is already filling the pages of many journals. The desire for marketability comes in conflict with a search for educational élitism. Those two paths will remain for the foreseeable future. Schools will continue to perpetuate ambiguous courses while industry makes them irrelevant and obsolete.

A national panel, asked to define "computer literacy," eventually came up with a grandiose umbrella that sounded like everything anyone ever wanted to know about sex (substitute computers) and a "do it your way" philosophy. Most definitions fall into certain predictable categories that could be labeled "compuse," "comprogram," "compistory" and "compethics." "Compuse" begins with all the how-to advice: how to turn the machine on and off, how to insert a piece of software, how to use a joystick or a mouse and how to apply the computer to various tasks. (Can you imagine a course on the light switch?) Included in this area are sessions on keyboarding (formerly called typing), starting at grade one. Watching the class make trian-

gles is like an art class where every child draws the sun. Adult "compuse" courses are filled with immature, inappropriate exercises that reinforce feelings of incompetence.

"Comprogram" courses are what most institutions regard as literacy. In such courses many languages are taught, the most common being Logo, BASIC, Pascal. Some high schools are teaching more computer languages than foreign languages, although in the foreseeable future far fewer students will ever program a computer than will need a working knowledge of another tongue. Soon programming in present languages will be obsolete. Even access to a computer will be by voice or touch rather than by keyboard. Yet we persist in codebreaking techniques, for that is what we have learned to do, however ineffectually, during the past century.

"Compistory" adds another dimension, giving this technology a place in human history not accorded to the wheel, aerodynamics, splitting of the atom or even the human events of the twentieth century that have brought our world to its present situation. How many schools that are mandating computer literacy courses, with extensive background in the evolution of the computer, require some attention to contemporary world history?

Those institutions that have tackled "compethics" courses recognize that students deserve some information about liabilities and limitations of technology. Questions of copyright and integrity, of equal access and abuse of power, of dependence and overdependence, of human-machine interaction are discussed, though usually in a brief and "thou shalt not" framework that fails to result in the student seeking reasonable, effective solutions.

We must incorporate computers into our schools and into our lives. Although every new group seeks to build its own dynasty, protecting its own little niche in the corner of human knowledge, it is absurd to let this happen once again, to let the tool become the substance. Even as a temporary measure, the computer must be integrated into the total lifeline of the school, not segregated with its own staff and curriculum.

Let those who would be programmers or researchers study computer science as a discipline. Let there be attention to questions of access through labs and lap computers, through libraries, homes and multi-institutions. Let market pressure require that the technology be simple to use, without courses, without massive amounts of reading, without stuffing our institutions full of computer insanity. We must stop acting impulsively, in a flittery, jittery response to pressure. Let us use those new pencils to create, to dream, to solve those problems that have eluded us. Let us begin a planning process. We must not waste our intellectual space on false literacy pursuits. ■

HOW TO SURVIVE COMPUTER CAMP

by Robert Schwabach

Hello, Fahdda;
Hello, Muhdda;
This is Harold's Liddle Bruhdda.
He is happy. Oh so happy . . .
What with Apple and Atari and Camp Granada.

(With apologies to the late song comic Alan Sherman)

There was a time when survival kits for campers included such vital material as comic books, candy and flashlight batteries. Now kids at computer camp word-process letters to parents imploring them to send the latest issue of *Byte*, extra diskettes and rolls of quarters for the video games at the 7-Eleven.

Surviving computer camp is somewhat more complex for parents than for the campers themselves. Sending the kids to tennis or horseback-riding camp can be a lot easier and cheaper, but you wouldn't want

Robert Schwabach writes a column on personal computers syndicated in forty-one newspapers. He has eleven computers and now has to move to a new house.

to deprive them of the opportunity to take part in the computer revolution. Because, you see, there is a great deal of lambent anxiety in the land. The world is changing. The rules are changing. The future isn't what it used to be. Harold's Liddle Bruhdda, whose real name is Basil, will have to become technologically fast-moving and hip. (Dare we mention the fear that stalks the night? *Computer illiteracy*!)

So this is how it goes: if you want your kid to be with it, computer camp is where you'll send the wee tot come summertime. And *you* better get with it, too. The crush is on. You may not know a subroutine from a syntax error, but never fear. A little child shall lead you—and glad to do it, too.

Getting in touch is no problem. There are computer camp ads in the features section of every Sunday newspaper in the land. Then what? Well, make local inquiries. Find a neighbor, a friend, or call the computer department at the Old School for Learned Advice. Like the Packard automobile ads used to say: "Ask the man who owns one." Or it might be a good idea to get hold of a book on the subject.

The information you need covers such crucial matters as which computer each camp uses. If Basil

In computer camp, the counselor-student ratio is an important consideration.

uses an IBM at home, it's not terribly efficient to send him to a camp that uses Apples. This would seem self-evident, but many parents suffer computerphobia (fear of being centrally processed) and it's amazing what they'll do under stress. A good way to prevent this error, and a good rule to follow in any case, is let the kids select the camp. They probably know more about it than you do.

The next matter of import is what language they speak at the camp. And I don't mean do they speak English? Rather, do they provide instruction in BASIC, Pascal, Logo or something truly out there in the blue like Ada or C?

Next you want to know the kid-to-computer ratio. Ideally you'd want it one-to-one (one kid, one machine), but there are varying schools of thought on this. Some people think a two-to-one ratio is better; often it's more fun for the kid to elbow back and forth with a camp buddy for time at the machine and to talk over what each one is trying to do. The operant theory here is that two kids interact with each other and with the machine, instead of little Basil turning into more of an eight-year-old recluse than he already is.

Some camps have age limits; others don't. Some are live-in and some are just day camps. Some permit parents to attend along with the kids if they want to, and at least one, Clarkson College in Potsdam, New York, *insists* that a parent attend with the kid.

Camps generally run one-, two- or three-week sessions, the first groups normally starting around the end of June. A fairly typical cost is $400 to $500 a week for a live-in camp, less than that for a day-camp arrangement. The so-called Original Computer Camp, which offers a deal that includes a trip to England and Scotland, will set you back about $3,000.

If it were me (and by golly it is—my kid is off at computer camp), I'd make my selection on what I could glean about who the counselors and teachers are, and then, if everything seemed okay there, where the camp is. Incidentally, a remote camp in the Arizona desert may not necessarily have a less competent staff than one by a college campus. For all you know, they could pull their staff from the vacationing faculty at Cal Tech.

There are plenty of computer camps all over the place. You'd think the computer manufacturers themselves would see camps as a natural tie-in to their business, and a way to get the little ones hooked on a particular machine they want to trade up for later on, but it hasn't worked out that way.

Missing from the field so far are specialized camps, a few of which are just now coming into existence. By specialized camps, I mean those aimed at teaching or advancing a particular skill—computer music, graphics or the highly sophisticated art of computer animation. Kids love this stuff, as is well evidenced by the leechlike determination they exhibit whenever they come upon someone who knows how to make that machine do songs or pretty pictures. But what I would expect in the very near future is camps specializing in just one area, rather than trying to do the whole circuit. Each one is complex enough to easily offer opportunities for specialization. The Math Workshop, College of Wooster (Ohio), is one of the few camps that specialize as of now.

Some camps (very few) offer some financial assistance for parents who can't afford the full fees. The Antioch College Computer Camp, in Yellow Springs, Ohio, is one of these. Rocky Mountain Computer Camps, of Boulder, Colorado, is another.

Names are not always a guide to what's going on, by the way. Try to decode the advertising claims by making some phone calls. What's a few bucks for rental of AT&T's long lines when you're about to spend hundreds on the enhancement of your heir and the relief of anxiety? ∎

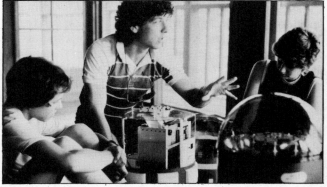

The first computer camp sets the stage for many summers of exploration and learning.

ADULT COMPUTER CAMPS

Why should children have all the fun? Plush resorts allow adults to claim their own computer retreats, where keyboarding and surfboarding are equally accessible recreations.

Club Med made headlines in 1982 by offering Atari computer installations as a come-on to guests at its pleasure compound on the island of Corsica. Since then, computer centers have opened in Guadeloupe and at Club Med locations in Mexico and the Bahamas. But the freeform French resort offers so many distractions it may be hard to concentrate on a screen.

Closer to home, the over-twenty-one can enjoy computer how-to's and more advanced activities at such leisure spas as Jackson Hole Personal Computer Resort in Wyoming, Computers Simplified locations in California or Computer Country, in a trailer camp in Connecticut. Fees may run from $20 to $200 per day in addition to travel and lodging; but with a legitimate business need for computer education, your whole trip may be tax-deductible. Check with your accountant. Then phone your travel agent.

Sun, surf and computers beckon today's adult vacationers.

A KID'S VIEW OF ADULTS AND COMPUTERS

by Luke Meade

Our family has a computer.

Actually, I should say *I* have a computer. My father obtained it, but I use it more than anyone else in the house. I have several computer-using friends, and it seems to be the case in most families that the children are more adept with the machine than their parents are.

In my view, adults relate strangely to computers. They'll approach the machine warily, and if you try to explain the basics of its operation they'll nod and smile in total confusion or ask at least one question for every sentence you utter. When my parents' party guests ask to see the computer, I comply by showing them the machine and running a program for them.

Luke Meade is a student at Rippowam-Cisqua School as of this writing. He is fourteen years old.

"Now," I'll say, " 'run' tells the computer to execute a program. So when I type 'run' followed by a program name, the computer enters the program into its memory and then executes it. See?"

"Um . . ." comes the reply.

"It's a very practical machine, the Apple II Plus. For instance, I can keep track of all my school grades in this Notebook program, which I also use as a limited word processor."

Usually when they hear the dread term "word processor," the guests stop trying to understand what I'm talking about. Sometimes they'll just say, "Oh?"

"Yes," I'll say, "and I can also keep track of my record, book and comics collections on the same disk. Then I can use the computer to check my algebra homework and keep tabs on my allowance."

THE WELL-DRESSED COMPUTER KID

Mere tykes, the human equivalents of larvae and tadpoles, are gaining unprecedented status as "computer kids." Awe-struck adults worship their micro poise, their aura of technological arrogance, their devil-may-care keyboard antics. Whether talking TRaSh-80 at Elaine's or late-night hacking at home, they're supremely stylish in their Nerd Wave togs. The androgynous computer-kid look isn't for everyone. Just those who care to be enshrined as paragons of electronic wisdom . . .

Eyeware. The more high-tech, the better. Especially if corrective lenses not needed.

Shirtware. StarWars and Darth Vader T-shirts are out. Corporate logo T-shirts are in.

Pocketware. A red felt-tip marker is always good for a spot of color in a breast pocket. Live dangerously: plastic pocket protectors are passé.

Handware. Rings are not the thing. (They might mar the computer keyboard.)

Computerware. For extra panache: hardware more than five years old or a model within five weeks of its initial release.

Coatware. Oversize lab coat hides multitude of sins, including root-beer belly and skinned knees.

"Really?" they'll say. "I had no idea computers were so useful."

Now I'm getting somewhere. "The uses of computers are virtually limitless. Then, of course, there are arcade games."

"My son"—or daughter, as the case may be—"loves those games. But we don't think it's worth all that money just to play games. Can you show us another program?"

"Right. Well, when I load this other program, Space Invaders will go out of the computer's memory and be replaced by Algebra Tutor or whatever. Got it?"

"Um . . ."

"Now, memory is made up of kilobytes, referred to as K. About a thousand bytes make a K, and eight bits are a byte. A bit is a single space in the memory. Okay?"

"Um . . . Well, it really is time to run."

Adults are usually more interested in what the machines will do for them than in *how* they do it. Considering the length of the average instruction manual, that's hardly surprising.

Many of the adults I encounter are fascinated by the concept of computing but are in a sort of future shock. They don't feel comfortable with computers and are put off by the technology. Sometimes, though, I find a ready, willing and competent adult to introduce to computing. My Uncle Ron and I teamed up to battle the Enemy in a strategic computer game, and from there I showed him the many other facets of computing. I always like finding an older budding enthusiast, because for a time I'm the teacher and the grownup is the pupil.

Many adults see computers as the machines that make mistakes in their checking accounts. (They don't realize the computer didn't foul up their last deposit; the programmer did. It's important to know that computers do as they're told. Period.) Other adults are victims of the Man vs. Machine complex. If they can't establish who's boss in half an hour, they want no part of it.

Kids, however, don't have checking accounts; they don't often demand instant mastery; and they're up to a new challenge. Grownups see how much kids like the machines and usually have one of three reactions: they think it looks like fun, and it must be easy if a kid can do it, and they try it; or they say, "Computers are for kids, I'm no good at that"; or they feel obliged to prove they're better at it than kids, so they try it but with the wrong attitude.

Attitude is important. If you go into a man-machine relationship (or any kind of relationship, for that matter) feeling resentful, the results will be less than encouraging. It's vital to be optimistic and open-minded. And you have to be patient, with both the computer and yourself; a lot of adults give up too quickly, especially the ones who are afraid of the machine.

Once adults have broken the ice with a computer, they can begin to teach themselves programming or they can take a course.

I know a few adults who have gotten very good with computers and a couple who are excellent, but it's interesting how much more quickly kids progress at the programming level. Often they have more imagination than adults and are more willing to take risks. This is probably the root of the popular notion: "If you need help with the computer, ask the kids." Many adults, of course, feel foolish asking their children for help and so stay in computer stasis.

A friend of mine (my age and a part-time mathematical genius and geologist) can outperform anybody I've ever known on a computer. For a school project he put the entire Latin language into a TRS-80 Model II. When he gets bored, he amuses himself by programming play-alikes of his favorite arcade games, working out the routines as he goes along. I've never seen him use a flow chart or any other programmer's aid. Another friend has a summer job working for a software publishing company. I know of no adults as proficient as this pair.

I'm fascinated by how the adult community views kids and computers. The *Time* cover for May 3, 1982, concerned itself with "The Computer Generation: A New Breed of Whiz Kids." The cover photo was of a young boy's face generated by a digital image processor. "With an ease and enthusiasm few adults can fathom," said *Time*, "a new breed of youngsters is mastering a machine that is sparking a revolution in the classroom and the world." To me, computers are so unthreatening that the adults' awed view is surprising.

It's not so much that kids who use computers are smart as that smart kids use computers.

I encourage any adult who is interested in computers to just go out and do it. With the abundance of computers and their ever increasing integration into the economy, it's a good idea to feel at home in the computer age. It's an even better idea to acquire some programming knowledge. Computing is not really that hard (it's relatively painless, in fact), and as the ads say, "There's a big future in computer programming." If a child can do it, surely you can. Anyone can compute. And it gets easier every day. Computers are the tools of the next generation, and children are the next generation, so it's only logical that children should learn to use them. But computers are also the most accurate number-handling devices and the most efficient writing aids ever constructed by man. Shouldn't you, too, learn to use them?

Remember, anybody can compute.

Even grownups.

■

JUST DESSERTS

Artwork for preceding page

Artists:
    Susan Barker, Scott Kronick
Computer:
    Apple Macintosh personal com-
    puter, with Apple Imagewriter
    printer
Software:
    MacPaint by Apple
Input:
    Apple mouse

THE FIRST GOLDEN AGE

by Steve Bloom

William Higinbotham, grandfather of video games.

During the first golden age of video games, from 1972 to 1978, American engineers, entrepreneurs and manufacturers set the stage for the phenomenal period that brought Space Invaders, Pac-Man and Donkey Kong. Ironically, the Americans would yield to the Japanese in this second golden age, but without their pioneering efforts this new territory would never have been charted.

In the Beginning

Seventy-two years old as of this writing, and still active at the Brookhaven National Laboratory in Upton, New York, Willy Higinbotham is more than deserving of his title "grandfather of video games." In 1958 it was he who designed the first video game ever, simply to entertain visitors to the Brookhaven labs.

Using an analog computer with a radar screen and paddle-type controllers connected to it, Higinbotham and his associate Dave Potter developed a

Steve Bloom is the author of Video Invaders. *He freelances on music for* Downbeat, Musician *and* The Record.

method for simulating tennis. The object was to maintain a volley for as long as possible by swatting a ball with one of the two rackets that appeared on either side of the screen. A line down the middle indicated the net; gravity, wind speed and bounce were calculated into the game play. Since Brookhaven is primarily involved in defense research, Higinbotham never bothered to secure the patent for his invention. "We knew it was fun and saw some potential in it at the time," he told *Creative Computing*, "but it wasn't something the government was interested in. It's a good thing, too. Today all video game designers would

Brookhaven's Merlin: the first video game console. Tennis was played on an oscilloscope screen (circled.)

have to license their games from the government!"

Fourteen years later, the patent that would protect all "ball-and-paddle" games was issued to Sanders Associates of Nashua, New Hampshire, a Fortune 500 research firm. Sanders project engineer Ralph Baer clearly had a vision. "I have an official entry in my notebook, dated September 1966," Baer says, "that talks about what one might do with a TV set other than turn it on and off. It's a powerful display, a marvel of technology. My whole thrust was toward doing something with the TV set that people could afford. That's when the thought of playing games came along."

For the remainder of 1966 Baer spent all his spare time working on the elementary circuitry for his imaginary video game system. By December he had spots chasing around on a TV screen, and that was when he decided "this thing was too important to handle on an after-hours, casual basis." Corporate research at Sanders designated it an "official project," and Baer was set up in a room off-limits to everyone but himself and co-workers Bill Harrison and William Rusch.

"Early in 1967," Baer continues, "we had the most basic ball-and-paddle games working. By September we were playing hockey games that were rather fancy, meaning the ball motion was complicated. Velocity, for instance, depended on how hard you hit the puck—it had all the dynamics of a real puck. So now we had all this stuff, but there was one question we couldn't answer: what the hell do we do with it?"

Most of the TV manufacturers were mildly interested, but not enough to buy a piece of this new-fangled product. Then, early in 1970, Magnavox flew Baer out to its corporate headquarters, where he encountered a roomful of hostile company engineers. "They all thought it would be next to impossible to create a TV-game system at a reasonable price," says Baer. "But Jerry Martin, the V.P. of marketing at the time, said, 'We're going with it.' That was the day you could say the Odyssey 100 was born."

Introduced in the fall of 1972, Baer's Odyssey 100 went on to sell more than a hundred thousand units. A plastic white box with switches and knobs on the out-

Spacewar was played with the earliest computer joysticks.

side and "basically 40 transistors and a pile of diodes" inside, the world's first home video game, by today's standards was nothing less than prehistoric. For $99 you received the console; two controllers; a selection of maze, chase and sports games; and Mylar overlays colored with backgrounds that you were instructed to tape over the TV screen.

"You couldn't have anything more complex than a line down the middle of the screen for a net, and paddles and balls," Baer explains. "Generating complex backgrounds then was out of the question price-wise. And scoring was just too damned expensive." In other words, you had to keep score yourself.

Odyssey 100 sales began to falter in 1973, due to poor marketing, advertising that implied you could only play the game on a Magnavox, the fear that constant use would damage the picture tube and competition. By 1976 there would be more than seventy TV-game manufacturers jockeying for position, including an up-start named Atari.

Atari Roots

Back in 1961 some of M.I.T.'s best and brightest computer hackers had programmed the cosmic clash of video titans known as Spacewar on a PDP-1 main-frame computer. Heretofore, mainframes had been in-credible hulks, virtually impenetrable for even the most obsessed hacker. According to J. M. Graetz, a contrib-utor to Spacewar, the PDP-1 was an entirely different story. It was the first computer that almost anyone could turn on and run.

Graetz and his fellow hackers were into more than computers at the time. Edward E. Smith's sci-ence-fiction epics, such as *The Skylark of Space*, were regular reading material, and a diet of Japanese cin-ema fangoria (*Rodan*, *The Mysterians*, *Godzilla*) was required late-night viewing. When the PDP-1 arrived, complete with a CRT (or TV screen), Graetz and Steve Russell, who would write the original game program, let out this simultaneous cry: "SPACEWAR!"

BUSHNELL'S LOST ARCADE CLASSICS

Though he is credited with being the father of the video game, Nolan Bushnell has also had his share of arcade breakthroughs that went unrecognized, of-ten appearing well before their time.

• *Computer Space (1970)*. The first commercial arcade video game. Like the campus Spacewar game, you controlled a spaceship and gunned for the opposing ship. Unlike Spacewar, this game was played against the machine, not a human opponent.

• *Space Race (1973)*. The object was to slither through an obstacle course, starting at the bottom of the screen and ending up at the top. Sound like Frogger? You guessed right.

• *Gotcha (1973)*. The original video maze game. Pac-Man it wasn't; money it didn't make.

• *Dr. Pong, a.k.a. Puppy Pong (1974)*. Take Pong, put it inside a cabinet like Snoopy's dog house and sell it to doctors for waiting room use. Unfortunately, the medical community wasn't buying. Word is, Snoopy's creator wasn't too crazy about the idea, either.

• *Jaws (1975)*. Those were the days when you could base a game on a popular concept (in this case, the movie) and get away without paying for it. Basically, you were the diver; the machine, the shark. A clever idea, but not much of a game.

• *Triple Hunt (1977)*. An old-fashioned rifle shoot with three games: Hit the Bear, Witch Hunt and Raccoon Hunt. Somebody forgot to tell Atari that rifle shoots had become passé with Pong.

• *Avalanche (1978)*. Catching falling rocks with a bucket or paddle never caught on in arcades, but was a success when redesigned by Activision as Kaboom.

S.B.

Space Race: the forerunner of Frogger.

"The basic rules developed quickly," Graetz recalled in *Creative Computing.* "There would be at least two spaceships, each controlled by a set of console switches. The ships would have a supply of rocket fuel and some sort of weapon: a ray or beam, possibly a missile. For really hopeless situations, a panic button would be nice. And that, pretty much, was that."

Actually, there was more to Spacewar than met the eye. Opposing players sniped at each other's spaceship for points while steering clear of the "heavy star," or black hole, that could suck you into videoblivion. Another subtler feature was the star field, including constellations based on data found in the *American Ephemeris and Nautical Almanac.* The control boxes had two levers (one moved left-right for rotation, the other moved forward/thrust, back/hyperspace) and one button (torpedo fire).

Spacewar debuted at M.I.T.'s annual Science Open House in May 1962, and before long every computer science and electrical engineering student worth his salt was playing one of the many versions of the game that spread from campus to campus during the 1960s. Always fascinated by games, Nolan Bushnell discovered Spacewar at the University of Utah and was quick to recognize that here was a revolutionary concept—interacting with blips of light on a TV-type screen—whose time had not yet come.

Bushnell's first job after graduating was at Ampex, a Silicon Valley concern where by day he toiled in the advanced technology division. By night he tinkered in the family garage with what would become the world's first commercial video game. The year was 1969, and the price of integrated circuits was dropping rapidly. Suddenly it was feasible to bring Spacewar to the arcades.

Back then a typical arcade featured a cross section of pinball machines, driving games and rifle shoots, a score of skee-ball lanes and perhaps an old-fashioned mechanical crane or two (object: dig for prizes). Bushnell's Computer Space game looked like it had been

THE JOYS OF JOYSTICKS

To experienced computer gamers, the qualities to look for in a joystick are good motion, sensitivity, durability and fit. Its innards are relatively simple, no more than electrical switches detecting changes in any of eight directions or variable resistors indicating proportional movement along two axes.

Computer joysticks are so named because of their resemblance to the control sticks used on early airplanes. Above are joysticks from the cockpits of Charles Lindbergh's *Spirit of St. Louis* and a World War II fighter; insets show their modern-day counterparts. On the horizon: wireless joysticks and line-of-sight targeting, as well as game controllers with tactile feedback from on-screen encounters.

cooked up in a mad computer scientist's workshop. The cabinet—blue, with curved lines and with the CRT recessed inside an oblong opening—was part art deco, part space age. The game itself resembled Spacewar but was lacking in mainframe complexity. First of all, Computer Space was a misnomer, since it had little to do with computers (though a lot to do with space). The circuitry could by no means duplicate Spacewar's, limiting the game play and special effects. In place of the fine vector graphics of the original, Bushnell substituted more conventional rasterscan images (vectors are simply lines, whereas rasterscan paints solid areas of color), and the resulting graphics were crude by anyone's standards.

Like Spacewar, the game was a kind of Buck Rogers galactic gunfight that would constantly reappear in video game design straight into the 1980s. In that light it's probably fair to accept Bushnell's claim that Computer Space was "ahead of its time," especially considering the difficulties he faced in getting it into arcades. "Marketing Computer Space was tough," says Bill Nutting, whose firm Nutting Associates built fifteen hundred of them. "The more progressive-minded arcade operators took it, the others didn't. I think we blew the industry's mind."

With $500 in royalties from Computer Space, Bushnell went ahead and formed Atari. He hired Al Alcorn, an engineer at Ampex, and as a training exercise had him work up "the simplest game I could think of. The game I was striving for was a driving game, but I felt he wasn't ready for that yet. So I described Pong instead. Basically, I felt it was a throwaway; however, he engineered it and the game turned out to be a lot of fun, so we decided to market it on the way to the driving game. I guess you could say Pong was a mistake."

Pong was the simplest form of video game, and a tremendous, outrageous, runaway success. The story goes that Bushnell placed the first Pong machine in Andy Capp's, a bar in Sunnyvale, California, sometime in the middle of 1972. During its second day on test Bushnell received a call from the owner, who complained that the game had gone on the blink. He raced right over, opened up the cabinet and located the problem: too many quarters in the machine.

Pong's two-player format, tapping the public's traditional competitive spirit, invited spectators, wagering and general raucous behavior. It was "easy to learn, but difficult to master"—Bushnell's gaming credo. Literally dozens of imitations (Allied Leisure's Paddle Battle and Midway Manufacturing's Winner, to name just two) infiltrated the arcades, while at home people were playing Odyssey 100 and would soon have the chance to sample Atari's home Pong varieties.

And what about mild-mannered Ralph Baer, whose "ball-and-paddle" patent anteceded Pong by six

HOW COMPUTER GAMES SAVED MY LIFE

The debate over the social effects of video games often founders on the issue of such games' applicability to real life. "They only teach kids how to shoot down aliens from outer space or gobble up power dots," goes the usual argument. Well, playing computer games can quite literally save your life, and I'm here to prove it.

But first a word about Donkey Kong. Created by Nintendo of Japan and popular throughout the world, Donkey Kong came to U.S. shores too late in the video arcade craze to gain the notoriety accorded Space Invaders and Pac-Man. The press took little notice. The only success it attained was among its players in the arcades. Yet it spawned not only its own sequels—Donkey Kong Jr. and Mario Bros.—but also the countless clones in personal computer software that include best sellers like Jumpman, Miner 2049'er and Lode Runner.

The key to Donkey Kong's appeal can be found in its representation of a human figure as protagonist—a first in a major arcade game. Mario, the mustachioed hero, is trying to rescue the pretty girl from the clutches of the gorilla at the top of the screen. To get to the top, Mario must climb ramps and ladders and leap over obstacles along the way. It is Mario's ability to jump at the push of a button that has given Donkey Kong and its ilk the genre designation "jump games."

Mario is a modern-day Sisyphus, eternally trying to make it to the top of his hill, only to find himself condemned to start all over again at the bottom. In his own way, Mario offers a more enduring symbol for the human condition than the legions of quasi-heros to be found in current fiction.

I realized all this after a visit to my local dry cleaning shop. While leaning over the counter as the owner filled out my name and address on the claim ticket, I suddenly heard something like the sound of falling rain. I looked around and caught a glimpse of mayhem hurtling toward me. As if at the push of a button, I found myself leaping away, Mario-style, as a pizza-size chunk of ceiling landed exactly where I'd been standing. Honed by hours of computer game play, my reflexes had caused me to jump out of the way of possible injury—or death.

So while the debate over video games continues to rage, I can only thank the lucky stars that put a computer on my desk and a joystick in my hands.

STEVE DITLEA

months in 1972? "Pong was a derivative of Odyssey, not the other way around," Baer contends. "Bushnell or one of his boys actually saw the Odyssey 100 sometime during the course of 1972. It's a matter of record." By this he means that his employer, Sanders Associates, and Atari subsequently settled the matter out of court as Atari agreed to license Baer's invention through Magnavox.

GAME GRAPHICS

Ever wonder how computer game designers get those eye-popping displays on-screen? Graphics on large computers are normally done with a system called a "bitmap," a collection of bits that tells the computer what color each tiny dot on the screen should be. However, bitmaps tend to consume a great deal of memory. Because they're so big, calculations with the screen image take a lot of computer time, and this slows down animation effects. To solve these problems, several home computers use four clever tricks built into their hardware to get around the limitations of bitmap display.

1) *Sprites*, or *players*, are tiny bitmaps that can be moved easily around the screen. If you imagine a computer screen to be like a large piece of paper, then a sprite is like a small piece of paper that lies on top of the larger piece. The advantage of the sprite comes when you want to move the image around. Instead of erasing the old image and redrawing it piece by piece a little to the left, you need only slide the sprite image a little to the left. When you see a computer screen with mostly dull background but a few little images flying madly around the screen, you know you're seeing sprites.

2) *Color registers* are memory locations that store color codes for the screen display. Programmers using color registers need not mess with, say, 236 colors at once. If you want to put a maroon spot on the screen, you simply tell the computer to put color #3, for example, onto the screen. Then you go to color register #3 and store the number 236 (the code for maroon) inside. One advantage of the color register is that it's a lot easier to use a few small numbers than a lot of big ones. Another is that you can change the color registers quickly to get a scintillating explosion of color.

3) *Redefinable character sets* are collections of shapes that normally make up letters. Thus, when you tell the computer to put a letter 'A' onto the screen, it has to look up a collection of bits that tells it what an "A" looks like. A computer with a redefinable character set allows you to sneak in and change those collections of bits. This way, when you tell the computer to display a letter "A," it might instead create a little spaceship. The redefinable character set is much faster for drawing a repetitive image. If you wanted fifty spaceships on the screen, you would not laboriously draw each ship; you would just command the computer to put fifty 'A's on the screen.

4) *The fine scrolling register* allows programmers to slide the entire screen by a tiny step. The step is so tiny that you would never notice it, but when you slide the screen many times this way, you see the entire image scroll smoothly. The same trick with a bitmap would require you to recompute all the bits for each tiny step of motion, and the process would take up so much time that it would look slow and jerky.

These four tricks, the most common techniques used to magnify graphics power, make it possible for home computers to do things that only very expensive bitmapped computers could do.

CHRIS CRAWFORD

A dozen years later, the controversy having died down somewhat, Bushnell is singing Baer's praises. "He did some really good pioneering work in the analog field. A lot of the work he was doing came before many of the integrated circuits that made my life very easy. He's a very bright man." Meanwhile, Baer is modest enough to admit that Bushnell was "the catalyst" for the video game industry. "If he hadn't come along with Pong," Baer says, "I think the whole thing would have gone down the drain."

End of an Era

Over the next few years innovation slowed to a crawl as mundane gun battles like Midway's Gunfight and Atari's Tank replaced Pong and its relatives in the arcades. These games were slow-moving, unrealistic contests that drove the new generation of players right back to pinball.

It wasn't until 1976 that video games were back in the headlines. Remember Death Race, where the object was to mow down innocent pedestrians who happened to be strolling in your path? The National Safety Council called it "sick, morbid and insidious"; *60 Minutes* probed the psychological significance of it all. The only thing to be learned from Death Race was how little progress the industry had made since Pong.

By 1978 the first wave of video games came full circle. An M.I.T. graduate named Larry Rosenthal decided to re-create the vector display that had given Spacewar its otherworldly appeal. He then designed a control panel that could accommodate all the game options he could think of: left and right rotation, thrust, fire and hyperspace (just like the original, except that it used levers); a choice of six game levels, from novice to expert; and five terrific modifications—bounce-back, expanded universe, black hole, negative gravity and no gravity. With all these buttons you had to be a magician or at least a pianist to play the game, but Cinematronics, a newcomer on the scene out of San Diego, patented the hardware system (Vectorbeam) and called the game Space Wars. It became the arcade hit of the year.

But America's domination of the video game business was about to come to an end. A few domestic games would continue to score well with the public, such as Atari's Asteroids and Centipede, and Williams Electronics' Defender, but the Japanese takeover was already underway. While American games grew more difficult to learn, impossible to master (exception: Asteroids), Japanese design teams stole a page from Nolan Bushnell's notebook. "Easy to learn, difficult to master," they repeated like a mantra. Bowing politely to another example of American ingenuity, the Japanese made sure that the second golden age of video games would be all theirs. ∎

COMPUTERS AND CREATIVE PLAY

by Nolan Bushnell

The computer, the single most powerful development of the twentieth century, is still puny in com-

Nolan Bushnell is the founder of Atari, Inc., and Androbot, Inc. His current brainchild is Catalyst Technologies, an incubator for high-tech start-up firms.

parison to the mind of man. The difference lies in the innate creativity that is our birthright, our passport and our guide through life, without which we would be little more than machines executing programs someone else has written. The goal in

producing computer-programmed video games is to provide the stimulus, the opportunity, for people to experience the essential creativity they knew as children, when their minds were actively involved in fantasy worlds of their own making. We have discovered that computers can be a highly effective tool in inspiring people to draw upon this often repressed reservoir. One way we achieve this is by designing games that combine fantasy with problem solving.

Problem solving is closely linked to creativity because it involves hypothesizing, or making guesses. In order to solve puzzles, you have to invent solutions and then try them out to see if they'll work. Whether it's a crossword puzzle, detective story, board game or video game, you're confronted with a problem that can be solved only if you devise a viable algorithm. In computer parlance an algorithm is a procedure for solving a mathematical problem in a finite series of steps, but I use the term to refer to the step-by-step procedure for accomplishing *any* kind of objective or solving *any* kind of problem.

You break the problem down into basic component parts. You prioritize the areas needing attention. Then you formulate a strategy to solve the problem. Sherlock Holmes, a keen observer who deduced most of his solutions by creative hypothesis-building, is an example of someone who utilized algorithms. Holmes noted all the minute details of his environment, methodically proceeding to create hypotheses in such a way that all the data were met, and only then did he offer his solutions.

Deciding on a strategy, therefore, can be a very creative act. And watching how the strategy you create with your own mind turns out—that's really what the fun is all about.

After all, who knows whether your strategy will win or lose? The only way you're going to learn is by devising new strategies and testing them whether they work or not.

Video games have a unique educational component that involves the application of an algorithmic process to a certain kind of problem. In this case, the player faces the challenge of eye-hand coordination applied algorithmically to solve a problem in motion graphics. For instance, how does a person learn a pattern by which he scores high at Pac-Man? He must constantly test his hypothesis. If the hypothesis doesn't work, the feedback of the medium is quick and final: his quarter's gone.

The learning process, then, is one of constantly testing your hypotheses to see which ones work, which ones don't. In the process a person can assimilate one of the basic rules of scientific discipline, though I think this kind of learning often happens at a level of mind that you may not be totally aware of.

Research has shown there are important educa-

tional components associated with playing video games, and these special benefits accrue from the tests of eye-hand coordination comprising the fundamental challenge of virtually all video games. The development of good eye-hand coordination is particularly important in young children, who need to develop a sense of confidence and a feeling of mastery over their environment. Moreover, playing video games not only results in improved eye-hand coordination, but also—fascinatingly enough—correlates highly with an improvement in reading skills. If I were to offer a creative hypothesis on this phenomenon, I would guess the definitive skill involved probably has a lot to do with youngsters learning to focus their eyes, to scan data by tracking movement on a screen.

On the other hand, I wouldn't claim that all video games are educational in and of themselves. As in other media and other art forms, there are so many different types that it is impossible to treat them as a monolithic group. Certain video games give knowledge of some scientific principles, while others actually violate the same principles. Some games appear to reward the player for activity that would generally be interpreted to be rather antisocial behavior.

But I don't need to defend video games per se, because as in any other medium there are good ones and bad ones. The moral dilemma that some adults toss themselves into over the issue of video games seems similar to the hue and cry raised in opposition to that allegedly corruptive new medium introduced at the turn of the century: motion pictures. As is true of the movies, a great deal depends on the character of the producer as well as the eye of the beholder. You can't let a few rotten apples spoil the whole industry.

Video games are clearly here to stay. The only question is, what form will they take in the future? Like most other entertainment fields, the future of video games will be bounded only by the imagination of the people in the production arena.

I believe that video games will proceed unrelentingly toward higher-resolution, higher-definition and more intricate graphics. Some of the technologies that will contribute to these improvements are higher-speed microprocessors, cheaper memory and laser optical video disks.

As home video games improve, arcade video games will take on more mechanical aspects to provide the player with an enhanced experience, one that will increasingly blur the distinction between internal and external perceptions of reality. I think games in arcades will become more elaborate as arcades themselves evolve into mini amusement parks from their present incarnations as rooms full of television sets with coin slots on their fronts.

As competition for home video games, I envisage arcade games involving all the human senses in the game-playing experience. We've seen a trend in which sound systems have improved enormously. We already have capabilities to chemically synthesize a variety of fragrances. Soon game machines will be able to vibrate, bringing in the tactile sense. And, utilizing advanced locomotive devices, we'll start moving people around bodily from scene to scene.

I don't know at this juncture exactly how we'll be able to get taste in there, but I never say never. And I always avoid always. We're working on ways to trigger different brain receptors that are responsive to taste perception. I believe there will be ways we can fool a person into thinking he's experienced taste.

The overall objective of engaging all the human senses will be to create a heightened sense of realism.

The game designer who enhances the fantasy—who makes it more real—will be the one who is the most profitable. Look at it this way: if you can have a video game designed to simulate a trip to Europe for twenty-five cents a throw, and you think playing a video game is as real as getting on an airplane and actually going to Europe, well, who's to say a trip abroad is preferable when you can have all that fun at a local video arcade for so much less?

Of course, the price for this enhanced experience will probably go up a bit. But this is inevitable as long as people demand more capabilities. Even so, you'll get much more back in terms of realism for your expense, because that never-ending march toward realism will continue.   ■

THE MASTERPIECES

In the space of less than five years, games for personal computers have been transformed from an oddity to a major industry. The consumers of 1979 had to take what was offered; now their biggest problem is choosing the best from a bewildering array of software. Below is my own list of masterpieces.

• *Star Raiders*. The appeal of this game arises from its combination of engrossing qualities. First, the fantasy of dueling in space is far better supported in Star Raiders than in any other similar game. The stars move believably; the graphics look real (I've seen people duck trying to avoid an incoming photon torpedo). The sounds are also right: the engines roar, the explosions crash, and photon torpedoes zing with impressive reverberations. And the array of instrumentation available to the player reinforces the fantasy that he is at the controls of a complex and powerful spaceship.

Second, as the player advances in the game, the fantasy world becomes more intricate. Enemies must be hunted down, equipment must be repaired at starbases, energy must be conserved. Even experienced players can continue to make discoveries for many, many hours of play.

• *Ali Baba and the Forty Thieves*. This is the classic fantasy role playing game. It has excellent graphics, which are put to effective use rather than treated merely as window dressing. The sound is imaginative and informative, complementing the graphics without distracting. The game sports an interesting set of problems without annihilating the less experienced player, and the world it creates is rich, colorful and believable. What more can one ask of a game?

• *Preppie*. A straightforward implementation of Frogger, this game deserves praise not for its design but for its magnificent implementation. The graphics are very good in the sense that they support the cute theme of the game. The little player shuffles along in a most comical fashion. If he is run over, he stretches out in a slapstick representation of being squashed. But what makes Preppie stand out is its music. Delightful little melodies trip along during the course of

the game, and even the funeral dirge that accompanies the player's demise sounds like it should come from a calliope.

• *Rocky's Boots*. This is one of the out-and-out masterpieces that entirely redefine what computer games can be. Rocky's Boots is a game about digital logic and is without doubt the most impressive educational game yet created. Its simple, clever graphics system allows the player to build a staggering variety of logical circuits and explore their behavior. One can actually see the "electricity" moving through the circuits (it's orange). This game shatters the positions of skeptics who doubt that computer games will ever have educational value.

CHRIS CRAWFORD, author of the strategic game classic Eastern Front 1941 and manager for games research at Atari

HARDWARE AND SOFTWARE STAR TRADING CARDS

CLIVE SINCLAIR

SINCLAIR RESEARCH

CLIVE SINCLAIR — 80

In 1972, as a rookie, England's Clive Sinclair created and marketed a hand-held calculator. That failed because his calculations ignored the lower-priced competition from Oriental manufacturers. A few seasons later, he entered the digital watch business with Black Watch, an unfortunately accurate name; components were difficult to get and time ran out.

Switching his stance, Sinclair belted out the Sinclair ZX-80 and ZX-81, small 2K computers originally retailing for $159.95 at a time when popular microcomputers cost upward of $1,000. The new Sinclair players captured the imagination of non-computernik fans, who embraced them as a relatively cheap introduction to computing. Through a marketing deal with Timex in the United States, the Sinclair ZX-80 became known as the Timex 1000 and went on to set popularity records during its meteoric rise and fall. In England, Sinclair kept his streak going with the Spectrum and QL computers, but was held hitless in the United States by strong marketing competition.

Software Manager, Entrepreneur

SEYMOUR RUBENSTEIN

MICROPRO INTERNATIONAL

Hardware Designer

LEE FELSENSTEIN

GOLEMICS INC.

LEE FELSENSTEIN — 128

Lee Felsenstein broke into the personal computer majors in 1975 when he helped found a dynasty of computer sluggers at the Homebrew Computer Club, the original personal computer user group.

During the 1976 season, he fielded the first successful self-contained personal computer, the Sol-20, for Processor Technology. Though the machine has since gone the way of Satchel Paige, the Sol-20 is always a crowd-pleaser on Old-Timers' Day.

As vice-president of engineering at the Osborne Computer Corporation, Felsenstein changed the rules of the game by designing the Osborne-1, the first portable computer. The team's front office then blew its imposing lead, landing in the bankruptcy courts.

Felsenstein's own team, Golemics Inc., permits him to play different positions, designing hardware for various manufacturers and furthering the establishment of Community Memory, a project to bring computer terminals to public places like shopping malls and even ball parks.

Software Designer

BILL BUDGE

ELECTRONIC ARTS

SEYMOUR RUBENSTEIN 106

During a career of over a dozen years in the majors, Seymour Rubenstein served as a utility player with Sanders Associates in New Hampshire and with IMSAI in California. He then started his own software organization and led it to a perennial World Series berth on the strength of its ace word processor, WordStar.

Rubenstein created the software's specifications and commissioned programmer Rob Barnaby to follow through. Since its introduction in 1979, WordStar has been enjoyed by over a million fans, though not all have been paying customers.

Benched by a heart attack in 1983, Rubenstein made a valiant comeback bid that coincided with his company scoring impressively through its first public offering of stock. Lately he has been seen in the bullpen coaching Rob Barnaby on the next entry in the MicroPro line-up, a hush-hush program that just may be the successor to WordStar.

FERNANDO HERRERA
FIRST STAR SOFTWARE

FERNANDO HERRERA 64

In 1982 Fernando Herrera earned rookie-of-the-year honors with My First Alphabet, the original recipient of Atari's annual $25,000 Star of Merit award. Herrera created the program to help his son, who had been born with cataracts. Told by doctors that he would have to wait a few years before knowing if the boy would be able to see, Herrera used his new Atari to create bright, colorful letters and pictures on his TV screen. It worked. His son could see them.

The save-the-earth arcade-style game Astrochase, released by Herrera's First Star software firm in 1983, landed him another winner with graphics worthy of the Hall of Fame. Looking for a fireballing reliever to acquire, the electronic publishing arm of Warner Communications ended up buying a piece of his organization, and since then Herrera's teammates have scored another first: licensing games written on personal computers for play in video arcades. First Star, indeed.

GARY KILDALL
DIGITAL RESEARCH

BILL BUDGE 42

In college Bill Budge pulled off a rare double play by earning two bachelor degrees (in science and math) at the same time. After four years of working toward a Ph.D., he acquired an Apple, lost interest in the doctorate and decided to turn pro.

Budge learned to play pinball while he was studying micro programming. His training ground was the now defunct Galaxy Family Skills Center in Cupertino, California, once frequented by pioneer Apple players, including Stephen Wozniak (See Hardware and Software Stars #1). In 1981 his own company released Raster Blaster, the classiest of computer pinball simulation games. His reproduction of a ball caroming off bumpers and flippers was nothing less than an inside-the-park home run.

Then came a grand-slammer with Bill Budge's Pinball Construction Set, published by Electronic Arts. Here the players can construct their own pinball games from scratch using icon-like elements provided by Budge.

GARY KILDALL 214

Gary Kildall's personal computer career began when he batted around the idea for a coin-operated astrology computer for arcades but found he lacked the operating system software to make it a reality. Writing such software and improving it after the astrology machine turned out impractical, the resulting CP/M (Control Program for Microprocessors), marketed by his Digital Research firm, became a league leader as the first standard for desktop business computer applications.

Kildall's winning streak snapped when IBM went searching elsewhere for an operating system for its PC. The proliferation of IBM clones relegated CP/M to the second division. But Kildall came out of left field by designing DR Logo, his own version of the popular Logo language, for the IBM PC. He later improved its home run potential by adding commands that would make it useful in controlling video disk players.

COMPUTER BALL

It's surprising that baseball has taken so long to get around to using computer technology. After all, computers have become a fixture in our everyday lives and baseball is our national pastime. In the late 1960s one old gent did take pains to record the deeds of the Chicago Cubs on IBM punch cards and run them through a computer at the Wrigley factory, but the stats were in no useful form and the method failed to catch on. The game of inches had to wait for more sophisticated and comprehensive software for microcomputer systems.

Today, computers are safe at home in the offices and dugouts of the Chicago White Sox and Oakland A's, who pioneered in their use, and of the Toronto Blue Jays, New York Yankees and Mets. The most popular statistics program is The Edge 1.000, which can do everything but spit tobacco juice. The Edge was developed by Dick Cramer, Philadelphia pharmaceutical designer by day, nighttime baseball fanatic and self-proclaimed "sabremetrician" of the Society for American Baseball Research. Sabremetricians are revisionist statisticians (though they dislike the term) who scientifically apply the minutiae they glean in wholly new ways. They claim, for example, that it never pays to bunt; a runner should almost always try to go from first to third on a single because it's a high-percentage play. Their ideas regarding baseball are considered unorthodox and even outrageous by most big-league managers, who swear the bunt will always remain in their offensive arsenals.

Cramer wrote The Edge during the infamous baseball players' strike in the middle of the 1981 season. When big-league play resumed, his lone client was the Oakland A's, who originally wanted the stats for the broadcast booth. With team statistician Jay Alves carefully entering every pitch and every hit, walk, out, wild pitch, passed ball, sacrifice and stolen base (known electronically as "events"), the results could be displayed on a remote monitor in the broadcast booth. Announcer Bill King recalls that one day he casually told his listeners that Al Bumbry was six-for-fourteen lifetime against Tom Underwood and "damned if Bumbry didn't get three hits off him in that ball game." It wasn't long before someone suggested giving such useful data to the A's then manager, Billy Martin—who, being of the old school, threw the printouts away.

When Steve Boros replaced Martin as the A's skipper, the first thing he wanted to know was where Oakland kept its computer. Boros was a *nouvelle* baseball man. Whenever he was on the road, his hotel suite would be littered with file folders of the team's latest stats. The computer figured in 5 percent of his managerial decisions, although many of his players were dead-set against it. Rickey Henderson, the dean of base stealers, was skeptical. Center fielder Dwayne Murphy openly despised the machine. Carney Lansford politely ignored it.

The players' objections were sometimes moot. When the A's were in a long slump, manager Boros asked the computer for a "pitching count" breakdown.

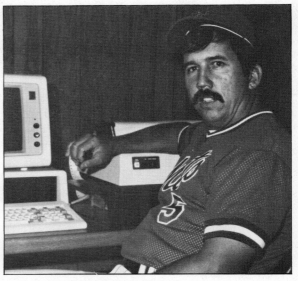

New York Mets manager Dave Johnson started the 1984 season bullish on computers. This holder of a master's degree in math couldn't find the algorithm for keeping his team from slumping in midseason.

Were his hitters swinging at too many pitches? Shortstop Bill Almon was a guinea pig. According to the computer, when the count was three balls, no strikes or three and one, Almon was hitting .600 or better. When the count was two and two or three and two, he was hitting around .100. Didn't Almon already know that he hit well when he was ahead in the count and poorly when he got behind the pitcher? Yes, the computer merely confirmed what everyone knew.

So far the most dramatic use of computers in the sport of baseball has been off the field or in altering the field itself. Recently the White Sox management, who use the machine mostly in the front office, boasted an 11–2 win-loss record in salary arbitration with its players. You can bet that when pitcher Dennis Lamp asked for a half-million-dollar raise, the computer printouts were whipped out by the Sox' negotiators. (Lamp lost in arbitration.) And after looking over a computer analysis of all inside-the-park fly balls caught over 350 feet in Comiskey Park, the Sox front office realized that 84 were hit by the Sox and only 50 by opponents. To give the local team an added advantage in scoring with the long ball, home plate was moved eight feet closer to the fences at the start of the 1983 season.

While computers have yet to work miracles in major league baseball, it is simply a matter of time before one team's success will cause every other club to get a computer. As soon as a high-tech team wins a World Series, every front office will want one— much like the rush caused by the Dallas Cowboys in pro football, where almost every team now has one.

DOUG GARR, editor of *Video* magazine and author of *"Woz,"* a biography of Stephen Wozniak.

COMPUTER GAMING METHODOLOGY

by Roe R. Adams III

T he dungeon walls drip quietly as you creep down the slippery corridors. Time seems to drift, but you think you've been foraying about two hours. Probably about time to pack it up for the evening and head back out. No, wait. Maybe just one more room. Let's see, the right-hand turn ahead is unexplored.

Turning right, you head for the doorway dimly visible at the far end of the corridor. The doorway shimmers with a magical green glow. This is the entrance to the fabled tomb of the ancient wizard Raka-

nonakon! Just as you're about to see if that weird amulet helps open the door, a group of wandering Orcs happen upon you. The fighting is fierce, but slowly you're pushed back down the corridor. Then a mighty roar rends the air, and over the heads of the surviving Orcs you see the head of a dragon.

Oh, no! It's not an ordinary dragon, but one of the legendary Dragon Zombie guardians! Nothing to do but flee quickly and hope. Left at the corridor, straight, left, right, right, left, left, straight, left and climb the ladder. Ladder? Where's the ladder? Oh, no! You turned wrong somewhere! But where? If only you'd plotted out the dungeon paths instead of naïvely trying

---

Roe R. Adams III is a game designer, book author and East Coast editor of Softalk. *He is the holder of twenty-seven national gaming titles.*

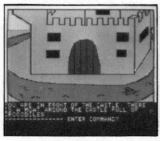

Time Zone, the first micro epic, takes some players a year to solve. Gaming champion Roe R. Adams III has solved this graphics adventure in only seven days.

to remember them. Well, at least the pounding feet of the monster have stopped. Might as well retrace your path. Here goes, right, straight, right . . . *whoosh*, a fireball coming head on! END OF GAME . . .

Sound familiar? If you've ever played a computer adventure game, you're probably no stranger to the scene above. Most people try to play by the seat of their pants. They just plunge into a situation and hope they can figure out how to extricate themselves from the inevitable jam.

For most would-be adventurers, these games represent the height of frustration. What do the game designers expect from the player? Now, writing in national magazines and speaking at fairs and conferences cross-country, a few of the top adventurers are helping beginners learn to be successful. They have begun to formulate the rudiments of computer game methodology, starting with the classification of adventure games into text, hi-res graphic and fantasy role playing.

Text adventures, the earliest and most famous of the computer adventure games, contain programs that have only text descriptions, not pictures. The original Adventure, Mad Venture and Inferno are prime examples of this genre. Today's experts of the text adventure are unquestionably the gang at Infocom in Cambridge, Massachusetts, who have produced a long string of chart-busting hits including the Zork Trilogy, Deadline, Suspended and Starcross.

Hi-res graphic adventures in recent years have captured the imagination of most game players. The high-resolution color pictures, with their lines of text below, bring you right into the scenario as though you're watching a movie story board—yet it's a movie over which you have some control. The top graphic adven-

tures have been Wizard and the Princess, Ulysses and the Golden Fleece, Sherwood Forest, Mask of the Sun and Escape from Rungistan. This genre also contains the industry's first micro-epic, Time Zone, in twelve disks. Graphic adventures have become so popular that they've driven all the text adventure companies except Infocom out of the marketplace.

The last echelon of computer adventure games belongs to the *fantasy role playing* genre, similar in style to the mass-marketed Dungeons and Dragons board and book games. Here you can really feel like you're living the character the computer portrays. The Wizardry scenarios and the three Ultima games represent the best of this type. (In 1983, when *Softalk* polled its readers for their favorite computer program of all time, the 250,000 responses yielded a startling statistic: Wizardry was the number one choice by a two-to-one margin over VisiCalc, the program that really launched the personal computer revolution.)

Mapping the Universe

The most fundamental approach to solving any type of computer adventure game involves drawing an accurate map of the gaming universe. In the majority of cases, the Balloon Map is the most effective. For every room, or location, draw a circular balloon. Now try to move North, East, South, West, Up and Down (some games also use the diagonals). If you can go in a particular direction, draw a straight line and place another balloon for that location. Do not explore that room or do anything there, no matter how tempting.

Return immediately to the first room and test another direction. Continue until all choices have been tried. Where there is no passage, mark an X on that edge of the balloon. In this manner you will not overlook a direction, which is the most common mistake a player makes. Move through as much of the game as possible, just mapping. Often this approach will yield valuable information, such as where to avoid traps. Remember, no matter how difficult a computer adventure gets, or how insurmountable the puzzle seems, there is *always* an answer.

Occasionally game designers like to make large labyrinths and baffling one-way passages. A typical one-way passage allows the adventurer to move East, but when he tries to return West either the path is no longer there or the player is deposited in a new location. This leads to a very messy Balloon Map. Much better suited to this more difficult style of game is the Matrix Map. Lay out a large grid. Put the possible game directions down the left side of the grid, and number the rooms across the top. Start mapping as usual, but now place the room number you arrive at from that direction in one of the boxes. For example, going South from room 4 places you in room 9, so put a nine in the box where South and 4 intersect.

No matter how tricky or convoluted the map becomes, you will always have a clear picture of how to get from one part to another. Accurate mapping cannot be overstressed if one is to become an above-average adventure game player. Top players map at least 50 percent of their game-playing time.

Seeing What's There

The next hurdle is to develop closer awareness of the little things in the game. Game designers love to put in small verbal or visual clues to solving a puzzle, but most people are in such a rush to solve the game that they completely overlook them. Study each picture minutely. Try to pick up or examine everything, no matter how absurd. Study the exact phraseology of the text. Sometimes clever bon mots are hidden there, along with actual clues.

A famous example of seeing what you're looking at is found in the A.D. 2062 scenario of Time Zone. Under the doormat of a house in Los Angeles is a key. It does not fit the door of the house. In front of the house is a futuristic car sitting sideways in the picture. The key will not unlock the car door, either, and no matter what he tries the player cannot get that car door open. So intent is he on opening the obvious lock that he usually loses sight of the fact that the car has a trunk (which, of course, the key fits perfectly).

Subliminal Skills

If you aspire to expert status, you must develop insight into how a particular game designer thinks, as well as the ability to follow the designer's logic paths. You must also develop a feel for the ebb and flow of a game. If a computer game is well written, the high points of tension will be properly paced, as they are in a good mystery novel. A useful yardstick for gauging one's progress in computer game solving is the time it takes to finish a game. On a typical adventure game, novice players will need many weeks or months to figure out a solution. Intermediate-level adventurers measure their solution time in number of days. The élite core of expert players, however, compare the hours. An average adventure game takes four hours for one of these players to solve; the world record for the vast Time Zone micro-epic is just seven days.

These are some of the basic elements of computer gaming methodology that have emerged so far. Within the next few years much more formal research will be done to explore this new area (scholars at Harvard and Brown universities are already at work on the phenomenon). Because of computer adventure games, new ways of thinking and entire new vistas of logic are unfolding. What will people with these new

COMPUTERIZED DRAGONS

Ironically, one of the principal pursuits of the modern computer age is the re-creation of fearsome medieval fire-breathing dragons.

It all began with Adventure, the first computer adventure game, written in 1976 by Crowthers and Wood. Deep in the Colossal Cave, the intrepid adventurer encountered a huge dragon curled up on a priceless Persian rug. How to get the rug out from under him? The answer: kill the dragon with your bare hands! The absurdity of this response tickled funny bones everywhere.

Since that first adventure, game designers have endeavored to come up with ever more recherché attributes for their monsters. In Serpent's Star from Ultrasoft, for example, an animated Tibetan Jade Dragon named D'hig-han rises from an emerald pool to challenge each adventurer with obscure Tibetan Buddhist riddles. If the adventurer provides the proper answer, "Nirvana," the dragon will surrender a huge sapphire.

Rarely in adventure games can a dragon be overcome by force. Instead guile, subterfuge or special magic must be used. The dragons in Exodus: Ultima III, by Origins Systems, breathe fireballs across the landscape and can be defeated only by magical weapons. To pass the dragon in Sirius' Blade of Blackpool, the player must get the dragon drunk on beer! The all-powerful dragon L'Kbreth in Sir-tech's Wizardry scenario, Legacy of Llylgamyn, guards the entrance to the sixth level; only when the adventurer produces a special amulet, gained after a series of quests and proving that its bearer serves neither good nor evil, will he be allowed passage.

The most famous computer adventure dragon sequence occurs in Zork II by Infocom. A fierce dragon holds a princess hostage and blocks the passageway to the northern part of the dungeon. To the southwest a large glacier ice floe fills a cavern and blocks all travel to the western portions of the Underground Empire. Armed with no more than a lamp and an elven sword, you see both situations as unsolvable. Then you notice that only when the dragon is hit three times will he let loose a frying blast; the first two hits only annoy him. If you hit him twice and run south, he'll follow after you. Continued use of this technique enables you to lead the dragon into the ice cavern, where he sees his reflection in the ice and thinks it's another dragon. Well, considering how territorial dragons are, it should come as no surprise that he roars out a challenge. Then, when the image roars back, he lets loose his fieriest blast—melting down the ice, opening up the western passageway and causing a tidal wave of hot water that washes his body away.

And you? Why, you were smart enough to climb up on a high shelf before the fireworks started. Now there's a princess to be rescued and rewards earned!

R.R.A. III

perspectives be able to accomplish? Look around in five years and see if you can spot the changes. They will be there!   ∎

WIZARDS IN GRAY FLANNEL

A long recognized ailment of middle and upper managers in American business is hardening of the creative arteries, a condition whose major symptom is the reduction of possible paths perceived in the process of problem solving. Over fifty million cases have been reported to date, with epidemic proportions rumored in the federal civil service and military.

Now, thanks to computer adventure games, relief is at hand. Computer adventures immediately begin to reverse the calcification process by opening up new channels of mental activity and reviving thought processes long believed extinct. Each adventure has its own goal for task completion. The player assumes the role of intrepid adventurer on a mythic quest involving hidden treasure, dragon slaying or rescuing someone from a remote locale. The player must develop organizational skills, mapping techniques and a flair for innovative approaches to problem solving. Who says adventures are just for kids? Or that adventures are just games?

After all, the adventurer's progress depends on figuring out the correct solution to each in a series of interconnected puzzles. Some puzzles are easy: how to open a giant bronze door that is rusted shut (answer—find some oil for the hinges). Other puzzles are complex: how to get across a river of piranhas (answer—find an ax, chop down some trees, tie logs together with vine, and *voilà*! a raft).

While the answer to the rusted door is fairly obvious, getting the needed oil to the door requires recall, perseverance and the ability to see the bigger picture. In the classic Adventure game the player needs an empty bottle, the location of the pool of oil, and the means of climbing in and out of a deep pit. Finally he must find a way to reach a high ledge where the passage to the bronze door begins. The entire process of oiling the hinges might thus require thirty or forty previous steps to succeed.

Some of the puzzles offer the player a hierarchy of possible solutions to a thorny problem. In Zork I the player is confronted late in the game with the choice of single-handedly fighting off a giant Cyclops (a fifty-fifty chance of getting killed) or feeding the Cyclops a brown-bag lunch of sausages (puts him to sleep). Both these solutions overcome the Cyclops but leave the adventurer stranded in his cave. The really inventive adventurer might try something different. Remembering his classic Greek literature, he could shout the name Ulysses. As it turns out, this particular giant is the son of the Cyclops chronicled in Homer's *Odyssey*, and upon hearing the name of his father's bane he runs screaming from the room. In his flight he smashes a secret door, opening an exit through which the player may escape.

Five or six hours a week of adventure play should be sufficient to bring remedial relief to chronic sufferers of managerial calcification. A side benefit is that character role playing allows the patient to work out his emotional and social problems through his gaming persona. One note of caution, though: certain managers become intellectually dependent upon computer adventure games. These patients are no longer satisfied with their boring, mundane lives in the giant corporate structure. They now crave the continual excitement of that other environment, and full persona transferral has been observed in rare cases. Instead of an upper manager peering into the computer gaming universe, it may well be that a wizard is looking out through the eyes of a man in a gray flannel suit.

Have you searched the eyes of your fellow executives recently?

R.R.A.III

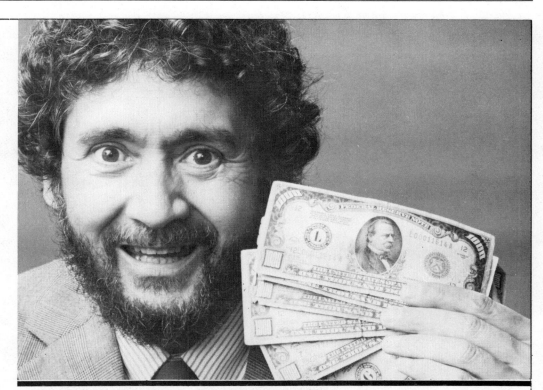

CASING THE CASINOS

by Ken Uston

Gamblers have a natural affinity for computers, and with good reason. Computers create order out of the seeming randomness of the universe. In fact, computers led to the knowledge that the game of blackjack could be beaten.

In the late 1950s a group of scientists analyzed the rules of blackjack as established by the Nevada casinos. Through computer algorithms, they uncovered the astounding fact that blackjack, unlike craps, roulette or slot machines, could be mastered if the proper mathematical principles were applied. This was due to the finding that the odds change back and forth

Ken Uston is author of the 60 Minute Guide *to computers series and the best-selling* How to Beat Pac-Man. *He is a world-renowned blackjack player, having successfully assured through a court case the right of "card counters" to play in Atlantic City casinos.*

between the player and the house in relation to changes in the content of the deck(s).

To take the simplest example: when a player is dealt a "blackjack" (the combination of an ace and a ten or picture card), he wins one and a half times the amount of his bet. If the dealer gets blackjack, the player loses the amount of his bet. Thus the more blackjacks, the better for the player.

If the first round of a single-deck game is dealt out and all four aces appear, the chances of a blackjack on the next hand are zero. The odds for the player entering the second hand are much lower than normal. Conversely, if no aces and few tens and picture cards appear during the first round, the chances of blackjack(s) occurring during the second round are statistically better than usual. When the player has the advantage, he can bet large amounts; when the

George the blackjack champ: (clockwise from right) Cards played were tapped on input device; battery pack disguised as hearing-aid case; output tapper beat out instructions for play; George's brain.

odds favor the house, the player can bet small. The weighted average of these bets yields the player an edge over the house. (Before you run out and bet your last dollar, bear in mind that this is a grossly oversimplified illustration.)

Others improved upon this pioneering work, and the early 1970s saw the emergence of a new, rare breed of entrepreneur: the professional blackjack player. It took card sense and a good memory to keep track of the hands as they were played, but various "card-counting" systems began to yield impressive results.

I started playing blackjack in 1973, when I was senior vice-president of the Pacific Stock Exchange. The corporate hierarchy got to me, and soon the cash generated from occasional forays in Nevada far exceeded my monthly paycheck. Before long I was playing blackjack full time. Then one day, after several years

of successful play in Nevada, Europe and the Orient, I received an unusual phone call from a scientist in California. His name was Keith Taft, and he told me he'd developed a computer that played perfect blackjack and could be worn inside a casino without detection. It wasn't cheating, mind you—merely an aid in assessing the odds. But in casinos where even pocket calculators are frowned upon except during computer conventions, it was best to be discreet. I asked Keith to catch the next plane to Vegas.

When I saw the computer, I knew Keith was on to something but I also felt the design was impractical. We worked together and finally came up with a device, code-named George, that appeared to meet our needs. George's brains consisted of a microprocessor, memory and a stored program crammed into a plastic box the size of an eyeglass case. After calculating the ad-

Rubber Soul: George could communicate with another blackjack player via a tapper concealed underfoot.

vantage enjoyed by either the house or the player on the next hand, George would calculate how much the player should bet to the nearest $10. George also kept track of all cards played and told the player precisely what to do with his hand (whether to hit, stand, double down or split pairs).

A pocket-size input device, with four switches activated by each of four fingers, gave George information on game play. The switches worked on a binary code, with values from 1 through 15 to indicate cards played. George's output device was a little tapper that vibrated, using a series of Morse-like dots and dashes, encoded to tell the player how much to bet and how to play his hand. A separate battery pack powered the entire system. George's components were wired together and scattered among various more or less intimate parts of the player's body.

On February 1, 1977, George and I took a cab to the tiny Golden Gate casino in downtown Vegas. To my knowledge, this was the first time a viable blackjack computer had been used in a casino (there had been several attempts, e.g., bulky models under raincoats, eyeglasses with flashing lights). I played for several hours, betting only $5 to $50 and coming out a few hundred dollars ahead. The statistics were meaningless, given the small sample size of two hundred hands or so, but in the process we had proved that George would work.

Now we began training "computer operators"— people who pushed the buttons as they kept up with the cards that were dealt. To prevent detection from the pit bosses, Keith devised a unit that made it possible for a computer operator to send signals via a small radio transmitter to another player: the Big

Player, or BP. All the BP had to do was just stand at the blackjack table, betting and playing his hand according to the signals he received from a "tapper" hidden in the instep of his shoe.

Next, condominiums in Las Vegas were transformed into blackjack training rooms, with flash cards, tables and charts, and electronic workshops. Everywhere were wires, battery chargers and "magic" shoes filled with electronic gear. My job was to recruit and administer the team. Keith handled the electronics. Our team soon grew to sixteen people: eight computer operators and eight BPs.

Then one Monday morning at 2 A.M. I took $50,000 out of my safety-deposit box and we set out for the casinos. We had decided to play the "graveyard" shift since there would be far fewer players at the tables, allowing us to play more hands per hour and thus earn at a higher rate.

That night we won over $20,000. Over the next three weeks we won about 80 percent of the time, which was far better than our average of 60 percent playing "manual" blackjack. After five weeks our team was up $110,000. I particularly remember one of our younger members who earned $2,100 during that time. He looked at the twenty-one $100 bills we gave him as if he couldn't believe they were really his.

At first the casinos loved our BPs, whom they viewed as high-rolling suckers bound to lose a bundle. One time our BPs were simultaneously "comped" (given free services) at the MGM, Caesars Palace, the Stardust and the Sahara. Of course, our BPs were living quite well, in lavish suites, often with grand pianos, and enjoying ringside show tickets and gourmet meals "on the house."

We kept winning and eventually we started getting "heat" from the pit bosses. Agents would follow our BPs out of casinos, and we had to resort to having our people take several cabs, à la *Mission Impossible*, before they returned to my condominium. It was when we decided not to tempt fate, to leave Vegas and set up shop in Lake Tahoe, that we made our fatal mistake.

I rented a house high in the hills of Tahoe, where we set up our electronics workshop on a ping-pong table in the attic and trained before we went to play on a sunny day early in May 1977. I dispatched four teams of two people each: two to the huge Sahara casino, one to Harrah's, and one to Harvey's Wagon Wheel. The BPs bet up to $1,000 per hand, and that day we won $25,000.

The next day, May 14, 1977, four hours after the teams had left for the casinos, the phone rang. As I picked it up, I was fully prepared to hear that we'd won $30,000 or so.

"Ken, this is Steve."

"Hi. How're things going?"

"I'm in jail."

He'd been operating his computer in Harrah's and was suddenly jostled into a back office by two burly security guards. They stripped him and found him full of wires and electronic devices, no doubt thinking he was some kind of terrorist. Apparently they called the other casinos, because two other teammates were arrested. The police must have had some difficulty coming up with an applicable violation. The charge was "bunko steering"—luring an unsuspecting individual into an illicit gambling game. At any rate, I posted the $6,000 bail and we left Lake Tahoe.

In retrospect it was obvious that placing $1,000 bets at the Lake drew far more attention than it did in Vegas. Even a $100 bet at the Lake attracts attention from the pit. The Casino Control Commission was totally baffled. They didn't know what to make of our equipment (to this day, it's not illegal to use computers in a casino—a loophole that no doubt will someday be closed) and ended up shipping the computers to the FBI in Washington for analysis. Five months later the FBI sent them back, saying that in their opinion the computers were not "cheating devices." All charges were dropped.

No, we didn't try to resume later, largely because one of the people arrested was Keith's son. Keith had been getting a lot of pressure from his wife to get out of blackjack—to do something "legitimate"—and he decided to quit. I didn't pursue the issue, since I had returned to the world of cerebral blackjack.

Yes, sometimes I feel as if I blew it. If I'd been content to have our team generate $10,000 or $20,000 per week, chances are we'd still be playing. On the other hand, it's always been my philosophy in playing blackjack that if there's an opportunity, you should capitalize on it immediately and to the fullest. Otherwise, it will either evaporate or someone else will take advantage of it.

No, I don't look back. There are too many things going on now. Still, when you consider where electronics technology has gone, you can't help but think of doing it again—only in a much more refined way. I can't promise that I won't someday.   ∎

TOMORROW'S SPECIALS

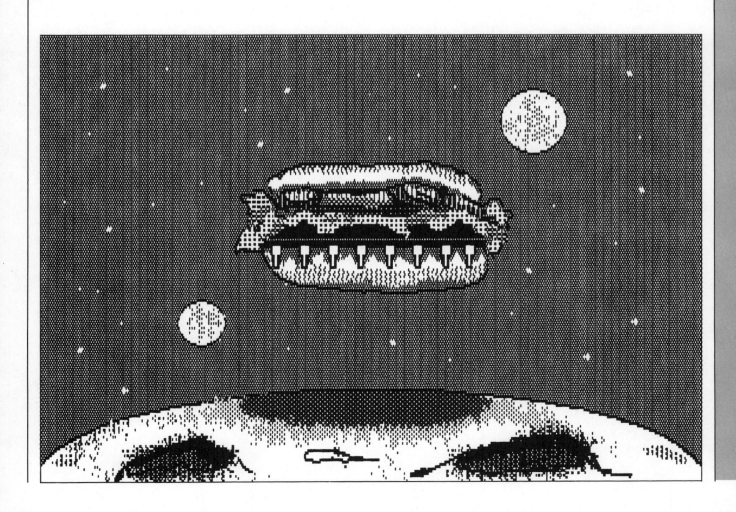

Artwork for preceding page

Artist:

Marsha L. Meuse

Computer:

Apple IIe personal computer in double-resolution mode, with Epson FX-80-FT printer

Software:

Graphics Magician Picture Painter, Complete Graphic System by Penguin Software

Input:

Apple graphics tablet

COMPUTOPIA NOW!

It's the big questions in computing that count.

by Ted Nelson

Dream no small dreams, make no small plans. They told me that when I was young; I still believe it. Choose your dream's direction first, without worrying about the possible limitations. It is later that possibilities and facts and limits can be negotiated, traded off.

Ted Nelson, director of Project Xanadu, is developing software for an ever expanding library of linking literature. He is best known for his book Computer Lib.

And I would say, dream no small dreams when you start your computer life. The world of the computer invites great leaps of inspiration, aspiration, invention. Yet most people come into the field with the brave but meek notion that it is they who have to "adapt to the computer," not the computer that will bend to them; they think they must go by what is now done—and worse, what is now allowed.

Now, you might say the practical thing is to build on what exists, what is available. Yet so much of what is done in the computer field is nonsense and accident. Why put up with this misdirection? Why build on it? Why not do things right? Especially when it comes to the most important things, the things that are the most important to get done.

To be involved with personal computers is to make arbitrary commitments, not just to products but to the forms of organization and structure they impose. Choose your maypole: which equipment and software? Once you choose, there is no turning back. Whatever your choice, you must interface with it, interlace with it, and run your computer life by it.

There are a lot of different computer standards today, but most are standards by accident, maypoles around which (for no good reason) millions dance and to which they tie their lives and products. These maypoles are arbitrary—the Apple II, the IBM PC, CP/M, to name a few—but choose we must. Just to get a foothold, a starting point for what we really want to do.

THE MAGIC BOX

The way I see it, the "home computer" of the future will be similar to, but not quite the same as, the machines we use today. A change will occur because there has been (and will continue to be) a great change in the makeup of computer users when compared with the pre-1980 group. Many of them will not have the slightest interest in the hardware of the computer, what processor it uses, what language it "speaks," what the software is called or what goes on in the plastic enclosure.

Simply put, these users want a "magic box" that will do the job with a minimum of fuss and bother. All they want is to remove the computer from its cardboard shipping box, plug it in, turn it on, answer a couple of simple on-screen questions about their intentions, then do it.

But where is the software coming from? The answer is simple. Via the telephone line. Anyone who has used CompuServe, the Source or any other data base knows that all you have to do is call the data base via your home phone, give it your unique password, then select what you want to do.

What will we have? A data base with a broad range of applications and game software that can be added to (or changed) each month, all at the beck and call of anyone with the correct (and paid-up) password. Sort of a lending library on a CRT screen.

Due to the broad variety of computers being sold, more than likely there will be software data bases dedicated to each particular type of machine. Users will simply select the data base from those available, pay the entry fee to receive their password, and away they go.

LES SOLOMON

The Big Questions

What we ought to be asking, I submit, has to do with more eternal (or at least long-range) issues.

1) How can we improve the world of personal life—for ourselves, for others?

2) What are the grandest, most wonderful facilities we could possibly want for the things that are important to us? (And how do we get them?)

3) How would we like the society to be better?

4) Finally, and perhaps most important, what sort of world do we want?

These are good, big and serious questions. I submit that to attack and deal with them—truly to dive into their center and do our best both for ourselves and the world—is a worthy goal for anybody. What we choose to do about the personal computer is a very personal matter. What we choose to do about these greater questions is likewise a very personal matter, no less so if we seek answers that involve computers. Below are my own answers.

1) Our lives, our concerns and our things should be better organized more easily. With computers one should be able to alleviate the nonsensical details of getting along in the world. A lot of people start in computers with this hope, but it is easy to forget. There is so much junk and complication around, and we expend so much time dealing with it, that we forget things don't have to be that way.

2) The present work stations and available networks allow us to grab, store and work on things piecemeal but not jointly in various crucial ways. As a writer and designer, I want a system that will let me examine and intercompare complex structures automatically. Beginning with notes and sketches, I want to be able to try out and arrange them this way and that, different ways simultaneously and to have a system that shows these differences. I call these creativity systems and thinkertoys.

3) I want very much to make education better. A lot of people say this, but most of them seem to mean making education better by returning to old methods and clamping the old curriculum down tight again. I consider this absolutely wrong. Drastic changes are needed in the way we throw money, manpower and facilities at the young. Instead of saying, "Next year we need to pay X dollars to teach science, Y for humanities," we should ask, "What should educated people be like?" From this follows the question, "How do we build them?"

4) The world of tomorrow must be a world of ideas—but ideas in their incredible richness and fullness, with the thousand possibilities that hover over every fact and artifact, every natural phenomenon and theory, every choice (abstract or pressing). Yet most people are not used to looking at things in dif-

ferent ways by turns. In every subject, it seems that only one point of view is considered legitimate at a given time.

And perhaps the most annoying thing about most people's views is that they seem to think there's only one side to every subject: "what the experts know." This needs opening up. To open up multisided consideration is to open up the general vocabulary of ideas. It takes access to other points of view to awaken the imagination. I love books and magazines, and, as the joke goes, I have trunks full of them. But thousands of books and magazines don't scratch the surface. I want every book, and I want it leaping to my hand at the instant of need. I believe this is something we can all have with the help of computers.

Tomorrow Today

Anyone is free to predict the future. Here is what I see coming.

The future will not necessarily be pretty. We will have a convulsing planet teeming with an exploding demography of hungry and angry people. There will be a deepening pessimism, and blame for every institution seen as having brought these conditions about. There will be an increase of both terrorism and random violent crime.

On the other hand, there will be one glimmer of new optimism in the sudden thrust of space colonization. Space will be the new Silicon Valley, showering riches on the planet and spawning Young Turk technological multimillionaires. Those who can afford it, or whose skills are needed in the space colonies, will emigrate upward.

A continuing collapse of tradition, at least in the western world, will introduce a new style of society—looser, more various, extending the "do your own thing" attitude that became general during the seventies. There will be more and more night people, more and more divergent lifestyles and experimentation. Social experimentation, experimentation with new tools for life.

And everywhere, the computer screen will be mankind's new home. Where you now see transistor radios and portable tape players, you will soon see portable personal computers: in Third World village squares, at café tables, on the backs of camels, perhaps even carried as a status symbol by slum dwellers.

There will be computer network hookups from phone system, cable and satellite in an ever-growing variety, though these will be allowed only tentatively outside the United States. And new forms of publishing through these hookups will emerge. Even now, most people are beginning to suspect dimly what some of us have known for a long time: that future writing and publishing will be, not on paper, but in the memory systems supplying the computer screens. This

being so, designing the memory systems for the new archiving and publishing, and the methods for using them, is a matter of the highest priority.

Confusion of the Law

In the near term, freedom laws, forever in danger, must be extended to the new digital realms. But what lawmaker has the foggiest notion of what this is about? Perhaps one senator, Bob Packwood, who has proposed a "bill of information rights." So far this is not an issue that is generally taken seriously. And legislators are also unclear as to appropriate extension of copyright.

Courts and legislatures think of electronic storage and publication as an exotic and abstruse area that has nothing to do with normal life, of interest only to a few corporations and crazies. As yet they have no conception that the real future of the written word, of ideas and heritage and education, is on the computer screen, fed by storage computers distributed around the globe and later in space.

Barring the extreme contingencies—nuclear or terrorist destruction of the physical manifestations of our heritage—then it is merely continuing deterioration that will occur. Paper records will become in practice more inaccessible. Documents will increasingly tend to become anonymous and to lose authentication data and marks, like the untitled and undated Xerox copies that sometimes fall into our hands. The ease of counterfeiting will increase. An electronic document has no watermark, no signatures, no fading ink, no seals and no ribbons.

The problem of sorting out disinformation from tomorrow's hypercomplex intelligence agencies (never mind today's) will be extraordinary. And what about variant private copies of uncertain provenance? Are they the truth preserved? Or an injected fiction? Now, there's pluralism for you. There will be not only fraudulent documents, but also fraudulent storage nodes: computers you call up that claim to be such-and-such an archive, like the false lighthouses of land pirates. How can we know we see the light?

The centuries to come will see a mixture and a succession of freedoms and tyrannies, both on earth and in humanity's expanded realm as we colonize space. A thousand dictators, hundreds of central committees, will tell us in the coming centuries that freedom of information is not possible. Freedom is dangerous, passé, abstruse; too hot to handle, unnecessary; incomprehensible to the layman, less important to the worker than a full stomach; distracting, frightening and expensive. And perhaps in so saying they will seem right.

But some of us will also see that there is an alternative. And can each find a way to help carry on the torch of truth. ∎

WHAT SIGN IS THE COMPUTER?

by J. P. Taureau

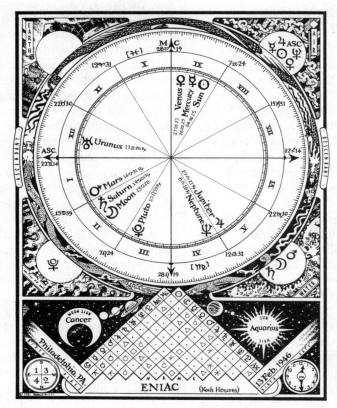

Age of Aquarius: the computer's astrological chart is favorable for seeking the truth and Utopian visions.

How is it possible to erect a valid horoscope for the computer? To start with, how would an astrologer ascertain the accurate moment of birth? And what is the rationale for drawing upon what the scientific establishment views as an archaic superstition to scrutinize the destiny of humanity's most advanced technological tool?

Certainly celestial bodies have real effects on earthly life: from the supremely obvious solar and lunar cycles that govern our existence to many still poorly understood phenomena like sunspot cycles and varia-

J. P. Taureau is a student of traditional mystical and martial arts systems.

tions in radio wave interference determined by planetary relationships. But our knowledge in these areas is in its infancy, and it must be understood that astrology does not claim to be a "science" predicting earthly occurrences due to direct celestial causation. Rather, astrology is a very sophisticated mytho-poetic symbolic language whose "alphabet," created over millennia by humanity's best minds, combines empirical astronomical observation with methods of intuitive cognition.

By examining the heavens at the precise moment of inception, the astrologer seeks to comprehend the essence, purpose and fate of any entity or endeavor. But even with a human being, when does life actually begin? At the first breath? At conception? Similar questions arise in attempting to determine the birth-date of the computer.

Star Data

The decision to pick ENIAC's first major public unveiling and demonstration in Philadelphia on February 13, 1946, as its "birth" seems well founded. The first public showing can be considered analogous to emergence from the womb, the first breath or cry of a newborn.

If ENIAC's horoscope applied to a human, I would describe the individual as creative, restless, dynamic, unusually brilliant, an inventor, scientist or philosopher, a revolutionary thinker, quite likely a genius. The grand trine configuration is strikingly appropriate: 1) Sun, Mercury, Venus in Aquarius in the 9th House, 2) Gemini ascendent and 3) Jupiter and Libra in the 5th House.

Aquarius is the sign of electricity, lightning, radical change and innovation, the search for truth and knowledge whatever the cost or consequence. Abstract ideals, Utopian visions, and revolutions of all types are characteristically Aquarian. So are cold logic and detachment. Aquarius is the most rebellious and inventive sign in the zodiac, but also the most aloof and detached— readily sacrificing individuals for the "truth," a cause, efficiency or simply change. The computer would have to be an Aquarian. The 9th House rules higher studies, law, research and abstract thought—a logical placement. The Gemini Rising Sign shows versatility, curiosity, playfulness (games of all types), restlessness. Gemini is the most purely mental of all signs. Jupiter, the traditional "benefic" planet in the 5th House of Creativity (also offspring and speculation) completes this high-powered triangular formation.

While the trine is traditionally considered the most "fortunate" aspect, a grand trine can be too much of a good thing: too much ease, facility or overabundant energy can create an imbalance. In this case, it describes the inexhaustible creative potential, the ability and need to constantly revolutionize technology, dramatically expand knowledge and relentlessly discard and overthrow old structures. The 12th House placement of Uranus, "ruler" of Aquarius, indicates that much of this activity takes place behind the scenes, away from public scrutiny, and with hidden and often unforeseen consequences. Everything Uranian and Aquarian is by definition unpredictable and sudden.

Interestingly, the "difficult" aspects in this chart are those involving two symbols of "yin": the Moon and Neptune, the most intuitive, "psychic" planets. In fact, to pursue our anthropomorphic analogy, this individual would definitely not be "well balanced," but most likely would be self-centered, arrogant, overly cerebral and restless, not very stable or grounded (no earth signs), emotionally repressed, insecure and moody (Moon conjunct Saturn and Mars in Cancer). The "male" and "female," active and receptive polarities of the personality are not in harmony and discomfort is present (Moon in conjunct Sun).

Of course, ENIAC is not a human. What the chart actually describes is the computer's function and effect on the human race. In this light, these aspects reveal that the electromechanical brain enhances the rational, mental, "yang" polarity in our culture and brings with it rapid social change. The computer presents serious challenges to traditions and the family (Moon/Saturn in Cancer) and certainly does not seem to encourage the softer, emotional, maternal side of human nature.

The aspects to Neptune in ENIAC's chart are more subtly complex than those of the Moon. Neptune is the planet of dreams, visions, mysticism, but also of deception and delusion. Its challenging aspects to the two masculine symbols (sesquiquadrate Sun, square Mars) indicate on one level a kind of male glamour and mystique, maybe even a touch of fraud and con, but also (especially in light of Neptune's favorable trine to Uranus and sextile to Pluto) a truly inspired, visionary aesthetic and creative dimension.

The Clairvoyant Computer

A cursory examination of some coming transits to this chart permits us to indulge in a little general speculation. The year 1984 marks the computer's Uranus Return ("midlife crisis"), which should spawn further breakthroughs but also sudden unexpected developments, shakeouts and failures in the industry. Saturn's squaring of the Aquarian grouping in 1985 might witness major restructuring and raise serious questions about the effects of computer-induced innovations on the workplace (6th House), education and careers (9th House and Midheaven).

The year 1986 should be a dynamic, expansive year for computer-related phenomena. Jupiter will conjunct the Sun, Mercury, Venus and Midheaven. Late 1987 and '88 will see Uranus and then Saturn sextile them, so that these three years could extend into a period of expansion and achievement. The year 1993, on the other hand, will be a serious testing period, with much restructuring when Saturn passes through late Aquarius. Finally, immediately after the Millennium around 2002, we can expect the most unpredictable and wild developments in this field as Uranus passes over the computer's Sun, Venus and Midheaven. Assuming some of us are still here, that should really be something to see! ∎

HOROSCOPE FOR A COMPUTER

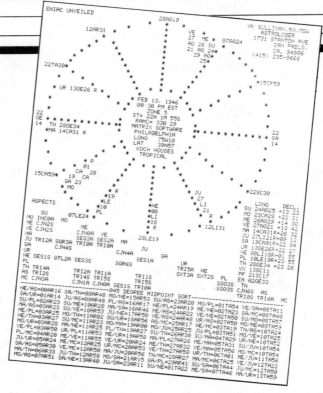

Self-portrait: a computerized chart for the computer era.

Astrologers in ancient times assigned astronomers to track the planets. Today we assign computers and obtain fast, accurate chart computations even on cloudy nights.

On February 13, 1946, at approximately 12:30 P.M. in Philadelphia, ENIAC was demonstrated and at that moment set a horoscope showing the trends and timing in computer developments. Appropriately, ENIAC's birthday is in Aquarius, the sign of the New Age, of invention, of waves and radiation and electronics. Aquarius represents subtle, stubborn and detached energy with a slightly warped sense of humor, a penchant for puns and a powerful concern for humanity as a brotherhood. We can look at this map with confidence as a good indicator of upcoming timing and trends.

1984. With Aquarius on the ascendant of the solar return, this is a particularly significant time of high creativity and many turning points. Lasers may well become feasible computer technology. New alliances and partnerships abound, some of them producing strange bedfellows indeed. While a shortage of raw materials threatens, subtle changes behind the scenes lead to new monitors and technologies possibly related to fiber optics. Communications cause a dramatic, positive change in public attitudes. Less hoopla surrounds computers, and a firmer base is established in educational software. Fortunes can still be made despite an increased demand for low-priced quality. Women become an important new market, perhaps due to a computer product packaged specifically for their needs. Foreign languages and communication in general are spotlighted.

1985. Both the ascendant and the birth chart within 24 degrees of Gemini indicate a major move or adjustment of persona, but the overall thrust seems to be toward stability. There is much work to be done and the money picture is bright. A standard is set that lasts a very long time. (Compatibility amongst computers?) Medically, computers get involved with muscles. A purge is due in the industry. Many secrets are revealed, and privacy becomes a major issue as linkages increase.

1986. The big four-oh! Synergy could become a catchword this year. A mental (almost mystical) aspect here shows groups of people using their intellectual power collectively to visualize and create, then physically realizing their ideas with great ease. Liquids and gases become a factor in hardware design. Some new languages may be developed. Computer sabotage and terrorism are a possibility in a band two states wide, from Nevada to Colorado.

1987–89. The overall energy is for change, but in practical applications rather than major technological innovations. A major shake-up in the image of the industry is due. Unity prevails, and a release of tension similar to that of September '83 helps stimulate far-reaching expansion (probably into space). Speed of computer processing will increase, with much money from authoritarian sources involved—possibly from government or huge corporations.

1990s. Computerized sensors around the earth could yield vast amounts of data should political paranoia give way to allow it. Weather, agriculture and earthquake information would forewarn. The computer industry becomes a little more "home"-centered as immense networks connect us all to each other. Protective scramblers, or "smoke screens," gain in popularity. Computer art could become as popular as movies and will certainly be used in stress relief and meditation. Satellites will relay any data anywhere by codes and methods unknown.

The future of computing may be peculiar and at times bizarre. But we can rest assured that there is no trace of malevolence in its horoscope.

IAEN SULLIVAN, consultant and counselor, Astrology Service of San Pablo, California

PERSONAL COMPUTERS/ PERSONAL FREEDOM

by Timothy Leary

Once upon a time, knowledge-information was stored in extremely expensive mainfame systems called Illuminated Volumes, usually Bibles, carefully guarded in the palace of the Duke or Bishop and accessible only to security-cleared, socially alienated hackers called Monks. Then in 1456 Johann Gutenberg invented a most important piece of hardware: the movable-type printing press. This knowledge-information processing system could mass-produce inexpensive, portable software readily available for home use. The Personal Book.

Until recently, computers were in much the same sociopolitical situation as the pre-Gutenberg systems. The mainframe knowledge-processors that ran society were the monopoly of governments and large corporations. They were carefully guarded by priestly technicians with security clearances. The average person, suddenly thrust into electronic illiteracy and digital helplessness, was understandably threatened.

The Mainframe Monopoly

My first contact with computers came in 1950, when I was director of a Kaiser Foundation psychological research project that developed mathematical profiles for the interpersonal assessment of personality. In line with the principles of humanistic psychology, the aim of this research was to free persons from dependency upon doctors, professionals, institutions and diagnostic-thematic interpretations. To this end, we elicited

Personal telecommunications: Timothy Leary with a Coca-Cola bottle telephone and an IBM PC.

clusters of yes-no responses from subjects and fed back knowledge in the form of profiles and indices to the patients themselves.

Relying on binary information rather than thematic interpretation, our research was ideally suited to computer analysis. Routinely we sent stacks of data to the Kaiser Foundation's computer room, where mysterious technicians converted our numbers into relevant indices. Computers were thus helpful, but distant and unapproachable. I distrusted the mainframes because I saw them as devices that would merely increase the dependence of individuals upon experts.

In 1960 I became director of the Harvard Psychedelic Drug Research program. The aims of this project were also humanistic: to teach individuals how to self-administer psychoactive drugs in order to free their psyches without reliance upon doctors or institutions. Again we used mainframes to index responses to questionnaires about drug experiences, but I saw no way for this awesome knowledge power to be put in

Timothy Leary is the author of Flashbacks *and the interactive personality program SKIPI.*

the hands of individuals. I know now that our research with psychedelic drugs and, in fact, the drug culture itself was a forecast of or preparation for the personal computer age. Indeed, it was a brilliant LSD researcher, John Lilly, who in 1972 wrote the seminal monograph on the brain as knowledge-information processing system: *Programming and Meta-Programming in the Human Bio-Computer*. Psychedelic drugs expose one to the raw experience of brain function, with the protections of the mind temporarily suspended. We are talking here about the tremendous acceleration of images, the crumbling of analogic perceptions into vapor trails of neuron off/on flashes, the multiplication of mind programs slipping in and out of awareness like floppy disks.

The seven million Americans who experienced the awesome potentialities of the brain via LSD certainly paved the way for the computer society. It is no accident that the term "LSD" was used twice in *Time* magazine's cover story about Steve Jobs. For it was Jobs and his fellow Gutenberger, Stephen Wozniak, who hooked up the personal brain with the personal computer and thus made possible a new culture.

Hands On/Tune In

The development of the personal computer was a step of Gutenberg magnitude. Just as the Personal Book transformed human society from the muscular-feudal to the mechanical-industrial, so has the personal electronic knowledge processor equipped the individual to survive and evolve in the age of information. To guide us in this confusing and scary transition, it is most useful to look back and see what happened during the Gutenberg mutation. Religion was the unifying force that held feudal society together. It was natural, therefore, that the first personal books would be Bibles. When the religion market was satiated, many entrepreneurs wondered what other conceivable use could be made of this new-fangled software. How-to-read books were the next phase. Then came game books. It is amusing to note that the second book printed in the English language was on chess—a game that became, with its knights and bishops and kings and queens, the Pac-Man of late feudalism. We can see this same pattern repeating during the current transition. Since money/business is the unifying force of the industrial age, the first Wozniak bibles were, naturally enough, accounting spreadsheets. Then came word processors. And games.

The history of human evolution is the record of technological innovation. Expensive machinery requiring large group efforts for operation generally becomes a tool of social repression by the state. The tower clock. The galley ship. The cannon. The tank. Instruments that can be owned and operated by individuals inevitably produce democratic revolutions. The bronze dagger. The crossbow. The pocket watch. The automobile as self-mover. This is the liberating "hands-on" concept. Power to the people means personal technology available to the individual.

In viewing the home computer movement, I am often reminded of a homely parable from America's cultural past. Some three-score years ago, the most popular soft drink in the land was derived from coca leaves and cola nuts. A magnificent ritual accompanied the distribution of this sparkling energizer. Place: the soda fountain. Mainframe technology: a large, gleaming steel tank filled with syrup and connected to a stainless-steel pipe from which bubbled phosphorus water. A white-coated priest pulled the handle, and the elixir was mixed before the very eyes of the dazzled consumer.

One day a mysterious gentleman called on the president of the soft drink company and handed him a small white envelope. "This contains two words that will revolutionize your business and multipy your profits," said the visitor. With trembling hands, the executive extracted the paper from the envelope and read the two words: BOTTLE IT.

Who could have foreseen the enormous cultural consequences of the personal bottle? The basic issue: "hands-on" replaced the priestly, white-coated attendant. The personal bottle replaced the fountain shrine. Power to the individual! It was no accident that Coca-Cola instantly spread around the world as a symbol of American egalitarianism. Everyone likes the "pause that refreshes." The addiction, by the way, is not to the stimulant or the sugar, but to the freedom of choice. The slogan "Coke Is It!" really refers to the individual option provided by the hands-on technology.

Evolution/Revolution

Nothing less than a new symbiotic partnership is developing between human brains and computers. In evolving to more physiological complexity, our bodies formed symbioses with armies of digestive bacteria necessary for survival. In similar fashion, our brains are forming neural-electronic symbiotic link-ups with solid-state computers. It is useful to distinguish here between addictions and symbiotic partnerships. The body can become passively addicted to certain molecules, e.g., of heroin, and the brain can become passively addicted to electronic signals, e.g., from television. The human body, as we have noted, also requires symbiotic partnerships with certain unicellular organisms. At this point in human evolution, more and more people are developing mutually dependent, interactive relationships with their microsystems. When this happens, there comes a moment when the individual is "hooked" and cannot imagine living without the continual interchange of electronic signals between the personal brain and the personal computer. There are interesting political implications. In the near future, over twenty million Americans will have established intense interactive partnerships with their computers. These individuals will operate at a level of intelligence that is qualitatively different from those who use static forms of knowledge-information processing. In America this difference is already producing a generation gap, i.e., a species gap. After Gutenberg, personal books created a new level of individual thinking that revolutionized society. An even more dramatic mutation in individual intelligence will occur as the new species grows up linked symbiotically with personal information processing systems.

Childhood's End?

It seems clear that we are facing one of those genetic crossroads that have occurred so frequently in the history of primates. The members of the human gene-pool who form symbiotic links with solid-state computers will be characterized by extremely high individual intelligence and will settle in geographic niches that encourage individual access to knowledge-information processing software.

New associations of individuals linked to computers will surely emerge. Information nets will encourage a swift, free interchange among individuals. Feedback peripherals will dramatically expand the mode of exchange from keyboard punching to neurophysiological interaction. The key word is, of course, "interaction." The intoxicating power of interactive software is that it eliminates dependence on the enormous bureaucracy of knowledge professionals that flourished in the industrial age. In the factory culture, guilds and unions and associations of knowledge-workers jealously monopolized the flow of information. Educators, teachers, professors, consultants, psychotherapists, librarians, managers, journalists, editors, writers, labor unions, medical groups—all are now threatened.

It is not an exaggeration to speculate about the development of very different postindustrial societies. Solid-state literacy will be almost universal in America and the other Western democracies. The rest of the world, especially the totalitarian countries, will be kept electronically illiterate by their rulers. At least half the United Nations' members now prohibit or limit personal possession. And, as the implications of home computers become more clearly understood, restrictive laws will become more apparent.

In his chilling song "Life During Wartime," David Byrne of the Talking Heads wails about the day when "We got computers . . . I know that that ain't allowed." If we are to stay free, we must see to it that the right to bear computers becomes as inalienable as the constitutional guarantees of free speech and a free press. ∎

1894   1899–1902   1900——1916   1915

THE CONSERVATIVE COMPUTER

by Wm. F. Buckley, Jr.

I have heard more guff from my brothers in the conservative and libertarian movements on the subject of computers than on any other that comes to mind—and none does, since we are generally all correct about

Wm. F. Buckley, Jr., is the editor of National Review. *He is the author of numerous books, including the Blackford Oaks series of spy novels.*

everything. The assault is at every level. My brother George Will seems to be saying that you cannot love the written word unless you set it down by pencil on a legal pad. The California libertarians declared war several years ago against a projected identifying number that would permit taxonomizing an American via computer in a matter of seconds. Well, well.

It is the primary contention of the conservative

faith that we are individuals. That in order to stress that individuality we need as few collective social assertions as possible. This is an invitation not to solipsism, but rather to continued, relentless individuation. We get this primarily, I think, from the Bible, in which, at a most important level, there exists only God and the individual's soul, the saving of which is his superordinate responsibility. Perhaps he can do this by the ultimate immersion in communal life. Still he stands out as an individual, even as Mother Teresa stands out as an individual.

Along come the computers, and they throw a new light on the question. Not only is the computer capable of distinguishing John Jay Jones of Shaker Heights, Illinois, from John Jay Jones of Winesburg, Ohio; it can also tell us that Mr. Jones from Ohio has had his appendix removed, whereas the other Jones has not. And this could be a life-saving datum—don't ask me to give you the scenario, do it.

The notion that to carry an identifying number is to surrender privacy is so wrong as to be exactly the opposite of the truth. If we have individual fingerprints, why not an individual number? And while on the subject, what objection can we reasonably have to giving out our fingerprints to a computer? The conservative dream of maintaining one's individuality in a highly technical age is surely advanced, rather than retarded, by this capacity to mark everyone's uniqueness. The collectivizing mania, where gradually the individual disappears to be replaced by classes, groups, professions, is surely set back by this means, no?

I have recently subscribed to an electronic communications system (Telenet) that gives you a password. But mark this: the password is so secret that when you tap it on your screen you yourself cannot discern its letters. This means that you carry in your memory or in your notebook eight letters with the aid of which, computer in lap, you can communicate instantly with anyone who also subscribes to that service. And if you do not wish to give out that number, this side of torture I know of no way it can be got from you. Such strengthening of individual powers appeals greatly, or should, to conservatives.

For us, also, there is the eternal quarrel about the market. Conservatives believe simultaneously that a) the free market will yield the correct social-economic decision, and b) the "correctness" of that decision is purely utilitarian. The People can vote *Dallas* the best program on television, and we can distinguish between whether *Dallas* is worth looking at and whether it is right that people have it. Yes to the latter, no to the former.

The computer is going quickly to reduce the distance between the individual and the supplier. Companies can often go broke before they can transcribe the public reaction to their products. The antennae focused on the public will in the past have been rudimentary. You have for many years been able to get instant reactions to, e.g., a new rock release. The disk jockeys will know within a matter of hours whether they have a winner. But this is not so concerning, for instance, a new model of automobile.

Computer speed cannot help to advertise a poet's freshly minted sonnet, or a classical composer's new oratorio, because these have built-in counterinertial forces that prevent, in all but a few cases (Eliot's *Prufrock*, Verdi's *Rigoletto*) instant acclaim. But if we put high emphasis on consumer satisfaction, and consumer sovereignty over market forces, why should we look with dismay at the discovery of the means by which the consumer's will can decisively assert itself?

The list of computer benefits is so very long. I mentioned my old friend John Jay Jones who needs his appendix taken out. The computer, we are told, will accelerate and render more accurate diagnostic work in the days to come and why should we object if a country doctor, with the aid of a data bank, can discover that the baby has a rare disease, rather than discovering what that disease was in an autopsy?

And, of course, there is word processing. John C. Calhoun, one of his biographers once wrote, had such powers of concentration that when tilling the soil on his farm his mind was working to compose his speeches. When he came in from the farm, he was left with a purely mechanical chore: that of transcribing his own memory. But tedious stuff this, since I do not understand why anyone should take pleasure in the act of handwriting (any more than I see why anyone should take pleasure in the act of tilling). Writing is menial work. It is not artistic, unless one is a calligrapher. So then, why not attempt to abbreviate that work? The arguments against using a word processor instead of a typewriter are not different in kind from those against using a typewriter in place of a pencil. I find them as reasonable as arguments against using an airplane instead of an automobile, or an automobile instead of a horse, if the idea is to arrive, as distinguished from, say, to enjoy a horseback ride.

Enough people by now know what a word processor does to make unnecessary the recounting of its versatility. It is resistance to it that absolutely confounds. And the notion that this resistance is widely deemed to be conservative is to reinforce the stereotype of the conservative as someone who cannot appreciate that which is self-evidently progressive. I fear that I know people among my closest ideological friends whose forebears must have looked suspiciously upon the wheel.

Well, then, there is only one thing for it. Progressive conservatives should pass a law making it unlawful not to use a computer. ∎

COMPUTERS, CABLE AND THE FUTURE

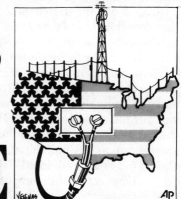

by John Gabree

Information gathering and exchange is, as William Rushton has said, "a foreign territory to most of the nation's planners." The federal government operates under communications laws passed in 1934, before most existing technology was even dreamed of, and state and local governments have failed to recognize that cable lines are the highways of the future. Now is the time to make public policy decisions that will affect the long-term health, safety and economic well-being of citizens as fully as public planning of housing or gas and electricity has in the past.

The Wired Community

Two years ago, I was appointed by the Santa Monica (California) City Council to its new Cable Communications Task Force. The old television cable system, pioneering by today's standards, is expected to be totally rebuilt with the franchise renewal scheduled for 1987. Our twelve-member group, made of up of ordinary citizens, was directed to study the cable industry and advise the council on the current and projected needs of the various segments of the community.

Home computer owners are now linked to vast caches of data in distant computers. Cable connections would make stored information available, presumably at much lower cost, to every wired home or "electronic cottage." A market survey conducted by our task force found a third of the people willing to pay extra dollars for enhanced financial services (compared, surprisingly, to only 5 percent who were interested in home safety devices connected by cable to a central alarm system). Another of our surveys indicated that by

John Gabree is editor of The Music Times. *He uses an Osborne to write and produce movies.*

1990 over a third of the homes in the country will receive some form of information wire.

The cable companies can choose to make available only those services that are most profitable to them. For example, a company might give a shop-at-home monopoly to one retailer or offer bank-at-home privileges from only one financial institution, thus limiting price and service competition. On the other hand, cable technology may be a key component in the information revolution. Still, home computers are too complicated for the simple tasks most people will assign to them, so it will take determined cooperation between businesses and cable operators if the home is to feel soon the full impact of the computer's potential.

Cable Ethics

The issues facing Santa Monica in the refranchising process had one thing in common: none was simple. Below are just some of the questions that must be answered if the maximum benefits from advances in cable and information technology are to be realized.

What uses would most benefit a municipality? The new capacity to store and communicate information makes possible a new era in government openness and responsiveness. And what is the proper role for the city in effecting the development and application of new technology? Unless we guarantee access, will not the cost of communications hardware lead to a further stratification of the information "rich" and "poor" and to an aggravation of the economic differences between the haves and have-nots in our society? Simple justice demands that citizens have universal access to the information system at affordable cost.

By itself, cable can be used to stitch together neighborhood communications networks. Connected to computers, a cable system can provide a conduit for government, education, library, travel and health services. In short, anyone attached to an interactive cable anywhere in the country could enjoy the advantages of an urban environment with none of the attendant urban problems.

Organized properly, moreover, the modern cable system could have a positive effect on the way government is conducted. Neighborhood associations, the business community, government bureaucracies and ordinary citizens would be able to communicate more expediently than ever before. With the help of the computer, television becomes more than the entertainer and passive oppressor that it has been throughout its history; it becomes an instrument for change.

Social Connections

Thus two-way cable could revolutionize the way we live. It will, for example, help reduce the cost of transportation in dollars, congestion and pollution. In fact, it already has. Every time someone watches a movie on Home Box Office instead of going out to the neighborhood theater, the cable has been substituted for the highway. Government and big business have begun to take advantage of computer and video conferencing via satellite to avoid the expenses of airline tickets and hotel rooms. The same benefits could be made available on a local level from any cable system with interactive capabilities.

Social cohesion, which depends in great measure on shared information and experience, is in danger of being shattered by the information revolution in that cable users will have direct control over the information they access, i.e., over their version of reality. If we are right that cable will be the instrument of systematic linking of electronic cottages, then the cable operators will have enormous ideological power as the "gatekeepers" of the information flow. By the same token, the biases of those who gather and administer the data banks will affect the way collective reality is defined.

Superficially, an enticing attribute of the electronic cottage is its potential to render political decision making more democratic. Electronic plebiscites enable pollsters, governments and so on to get an instant reading on the public's leanings. The likeliest outcome of cable voting is a reinforcement of the existing power structure, since both content and form of questions will be under its control. Although it might give some citizens the illusion of participation, the overall outcome could be to reduce the amount of public discussion and deliberation of political questions.

In recent experiments, some participants have admitted that they give false answers to electronic polls because they don't want "them" to know what they're thinking. And, of course, there's no way to know who is voting: it could be the same person voting twice or the four-year-old fooling with the keyboard. In addition, interactive services are usually expensive, so the results are skewed in favor of the economically advantaged subscriber. With cable penetration at less than 50 percent and interactive cable a paid service, government planning via cable becomes a new barrier to participation.

Bit Brother Is Watching

A worry expressed by the task force was that the electronic cottage will lead to a loss of freedom. We know that an enormous quantity of personal information is collected by the federal government in data banks belonging to, among others, the Internal Revenue Service, the Social Security Administration, the Census Bureau, the Department of Defense, the FBI and the several internal security agencies. Many state and municipal governments have similar setups, especially for police and tax agencies. If all these data banks were linked together, which would be no great technical feat, little would be left of our vaunted freedoms.

There is no existing federal legislation to protect cable consumers from invasions of privacy. Some states, California among them, have rules providing limited protection, but the penalties are minimal, one has to know that a crime has been committed and somebody has to be willing to prosecute. The question arises about why cable companies are permitted to collect any information. Of what legitimate use is it?

And maybe it was because we were meeting by the beach in California, but some of us worried that there might be a danger in the computer's bias in favor of rational thinking at the expense of intuition and creativity. By working exclusively with formal symbols in a perfectly rational way, the computer strengthens analytic mental processes at the expense of those that are nonrational. In organizing human affairs, do we wish to introduce a mechanistic rationality into social relationships based more on feelings of identification, goodwill, and so on, than on rational examination and interpretation?

In more than a year of weekly meetings and study sessions, the questions and issues outlined above emerged as the most relevant and troublesome. Some will be resolved in the city franchise ordinance. Others might be addressed in state and federal regulations, if the pressure of lobbying and the flood of campaign contributions from the cable operators proves less than irresistible to legislators. In any event, the experience of Santa Monica and a few other cities has shown that complicated planning issues can be handled by committees made up of average citizens.   ∎

FIFTH-GENERATION COMPUTERS

by Richard Grigonis

Even the most enthusiastic home computer owners have little idea of the link their machines represent in the historical chain of computer technology. It is a chain that runs from the ancient abacus and Charles Babbage's Analytical Engine of the nineteenth century, through the Apples and Commodores of the present, all the way to the awe-inspiring fifth-generation computers of the future.

Consider this: the "home computers" of the 1990s will surely have processing capabilities equivalent to those of the Cray-2, today's most powerful computer.

What kind of computing power are we talking about? As far as sheer processing speed is concerned, the present situation looks like this: A typical home computer, with microprocessor switches turning on and off at two to four million cycles per second and running a program written in a fast computer language like C or FORTH, can perform a few thousand arithmetic operations per second. The Cray-1, which costs about $10 million, performs between 160 and 200 million arithmetic operations per second. The Cray-2 handles over a billion arithmetic operations per second. To put it another way, a program that takes twelve minutes to run on an Apple will be executed on a Cray-1 in about three one-hundredths (0.03) of a second, and the same program will run on a Cray-2 in about six-thousandths (0.006) of a second.

Indeed, microcomputers have some catching up to do. But wait. The Apple Lisa and Macintosh, the Sage II and the Fortune 32:16 are microcomputers that all have a processor known as the Motorola 68000,

Richard Grigonis is a regular contributor of articles on artificial intelligence and future microcomputer designs for Dr. Dobb's Journal. *He is currently employed by the Children's Television Workshop.*

which boosts the computational power of these $3,000 to $10,000 machines up to that of a superminicomputer costing hundreds of thousands of dollars. The next generation of microprocessors will be even faster.

Computer owners may well wonder what they're going to do with all this processing power. The answer: artificial intelligence. A sophisticated AI program would eliminate the need for users to write programs, since they could communicate their orders to the computer via ordinary English. Such a program, however, must do a large number of symbolic calculations on a huge amount of data or "real-world knowledge." AI is the ultimate programming challenge, both for the programmer in terms of design and for the computer in terms of execution time.

Structured Intelligence

This brings us to the Japanese Fifth Generation computer project. The Japanese have been working feverishly on a billion-dollar project, with a target date of 1989, to design and build a computer that is not only a hundred times faster than a Cray but contains AI software as well. This software would be capable of simulating experts in fields like medicine or geology, playing games like chess or Go at a grandmaster level, analyzing documents for factual errors as well as grammatical and spelling errors, and translating documents from one language into another. It all sounds great, but the Japanese are making a few blunders along the way. To understand how, we should take a look at programming languages in general and their relationship to AI.

Let's start by saying that computers are "universal Turing machines," which is a way of saying that computers are universal calculators. Any procedure

The 5 [OR 6, OR 7, OR 8] GENERATIONS

...AND ENIAC BEGAT UNIVAC...

ZERO-TH GENERATION COMPUTERS WERE MANUAL: FINGERS, ABACUS, PENCIL AND PAPER.

CLICKET CLICKET CLICKET

THE 1/2-TH GENERATION WAS MECHANICAL.

KERCHUNK KERCHUNK

THE 1ST GENERATION WAS ELECTROMECHANICAL, WITH MECHANICAL SWITCHES DRIVEN BY ELECTRICITY:

TUNK CLAK
TICKET
TICKET
TICKET CHIRP
AKKA TICKET
AAGH

THIS WAS FINALLY TOO MUCH NOISE, SO 2ND-GENERATION COMPUTERS WERE SILENT, ELECTRONIC GIANTS, USING VACUUM TUBES, AND ENOUGH ELECTRICITY TO POWER A VILLAGE...

EITHER ENIAC IS AT WORK, OR A CONDEMNED MAN IS MEETING HIS DESTINY...

THE 3RD GENERATION USED TRANSISTORS, WHICH DRAW MUCH LESS ELECTRICITY THAN TUBES. THIS BROUGHT COMPUTERS INTO THE PRICE RANGE OF BIG BUSINESS, AND INTRODUCED THE PHRASE, "COMPUTER ERROR."

AT LAST! SOMETHING TO BLAME EVERYTHING ON!

THE 4TH GENERATION IS NOW...A RESULT OF THE INTEGRATED CIRCUIT: MINIATURIZED TRANSISTORS PRINTED ON TINY CHIPS... EVERY YEAR TWICE AS DENSELY AS THE YEAR BEFORE. COMPUTERS CAN NOW BE MADE AS SMALL AS YOU LIKE!!

BUT WHY?

COMING - SUPPOSEDLY - IS THE 5TH GENERATION: THE SMART COMPUTER, ABLE TO PERFORM A WIDE VARIETY OF TASKS, INCLUDING UNDERSTANDING NATURAL LANGUAGE!

AND THE 6TH GENERATION?

THE FIRST GENERATION OF HUMANS WAS ELECTROCHEMICAL......

(or algorithm, as it's called) that can be conceived of can be calculated or performed by a computer. If you believe that the human mind arises from the physical workings of the brain, then, since a computer can theoretically simulate anything in the physical world, you have automatically declared that a computer can simulate human thinking processes. The act of writing a program in the computer's own language (little 1s and 0s) is quite time-consuming, so high-level languages were developed that enable the programmer to instruct the machine by typing in commands like PRINT 2 + 2 instead of 10011101, 00000010, 01010011, 00000010 or whatever. Although there are many different programming languages designed with special attributes for special jobs (FORTRAN and APL for science/engineering, COBOL for business, BASIC for beginning programmers), any algorithm can be written in any language. The list processing language (LISP) developed by McCarthy in 1958 is considered by everyone to be the language for AI research, and yet, if the the need arose, we could look at a LISP program, figure out what the algorithm or procedure is, then rewrite the program in a different language such as BASIC or even COBOL. It would be a programmer's nightmare, of course, and the new program would be much larger in a more "inefficient" language, but it could be done.

Program Limits

We do not even need the full capabilities of a computer language to express any algorithm in a program. This idea had its origin in the Structure Theorem first presented in a classic mathematical paper by C. Bohm and G. Jacopini with the ominous title *Flow Diagrams, Turing Machines, and Languages with Only Two Formation Rules*. This paper introduced not a new computer language, but a style of programming called "structured programming" or, more technically, "programming by stepwise refinement," that could be used with any program.

To put it simply, Bohm and Jacopini discovered that all computer languages, large and small, come equipped with the following basic features:

1) Sequences of two or more operations (add A to B, then divide it by C, then print the result).

2) Decisions or choices (IF A THEN B ELSE C).

3) Repetitions of an operation until a certain condition is true. One of these is the Do-While loop (keep adding 1 to X While X is less than 10). The other is the Do-Until loop (keep adding 1 to X Until X equals 10).

The Structure Theorem mathematically proves that the expression of any algorithm in any language (i.e., any possible program, including one simulating human intelligence) can be written using only combi-

nations of the three basic programming rules mentioned above!

At first glance, it looks as if tremendous restrictions are placed on the programmer, and yet by employing this "structured programming" method one actually shortens the time it takes to write, "debug" or modify any given program. This is because structured programming forces us to break a single complicated problem into several simple subproblems, then breaking these in turn into several more simple sub-subproblems, until the programmer has reduced the original, highly complex problem into a large number of interlocking, very simple problems that are easily coded as a program. This technique is known as reductionism, decomposition or top-down design.

The Smart Set

What everyone seems to have forgotten is that artificial intelligence at the "grass roots" level is just another programming problem—like listing recipes or keeping track of one's stamp collection, only several orders of magnitude greater. Of course, no one in the AI field would dare suggest this in public. It all sounds too easy, as if writing the ultimate, ultra-intelligent program were more a matter of tenacity than of divinely inspired programming wizardry. And yet no strange languages or high priests of programming are necessary. The only special requirement is one of hardware, namely, a computer with immense storage capacity and a processor that can perform billions of calculations per second.

One final programming thought: the length of a program does not depend on the complexity of the algorithm to be executed; rather, it depends on the size of the computer language's vocabulary. Some languages (e.g., LISP and FORTH) have an advantage over others in that they are "extensible," enabling the programmer to add new words with corresponding new functions. A whole program could be as short as an ordinary English sentence if the language has been immensely extended (presumably with structured techniques) to include the English vocabulary, rules of grammar and semantics.

So, although any algorithm can be represented in any language, extensible languages are better to work with and produce much shorter, easier-to-read programs than do BASIC and COBOL, for example. The Japanese, however, have ignored LISP and chosen a rather strange language called PROLOG (PROgrammable LOGic) to run on their Fifth Generation computer. PROLOG forces the programmer to use pure logic, which means the computer must take the facts it knows about and calculate all their possible logical relationships, or inferences. If the computer knows a lot of facts, this process can lead to an unfortunate situation called a "combinatorial explosion" in which calculations take almost forever to complete. So, unless they radically change the language they are using, the Japanese may find that their much touted monster computer won't work at all. In fact, a number of AI problems are so tremendously complex (among them, playing a perfect game of chess) that it would take any computer many centuries to solve them.

Multi-Mentation

One answer to the problem of complex programming is to build the computer with more than one processor, then break up the program into pieces and assign each piece to a separate processor. With many processors working on a problem simultaneously, or "in parallel," the program in theory executes much faster.

In fact, fifty research projects in the United States are working on "parallel processing" or, as it is also called, "distributed array processing." These include:
- Tom McWilliams' 16-processor S-1 computer at the Lawrence Livermore National Laboratory, running at about two billion arithmetic operations per second.
- The Denelcor Company's mysterious HEP-2 computer, to be ready in 1986, capable of twelve billion operations per second.
- Salvatore Stolfo's 1,023-processor machine at Columbia University.
- David Elliot Shaw's computer, also at Columbia, being developed for the Defense Advanced Research Projects Agency (DARPA) and projected to have 256,000 processors by 1987, a million by 1990.

Another solution is that it might be possible one day to build a sixth-generation computer with a processor whose signals travel faster than the speed of light. This would improve the processing speed considerably, to say the least! Faster-than-light signals would seem an impossibility, but there are three ways we might achieve them: tachyons, the Einstein-Podolsky-Rosen (EPR) effect and the "advanced potentials" solution to the moving charge equations derived from Maxwell's electromagnetic theory. Whew! I'd love to try to explain it further, but I'd need another 8,600 words, the length of my original paper on the subject. Besides, it's not time yet to run over to ComputerLand and place your order: sixth-generation computers probably won't appear for decades.

In contrast to developing advanced hardware, creating the artificial intelligence software to go with it seems to be a wide-open field. Who will be the first to write the ultimate AI program? With the appearance of cheap supermicrocomputers over the next ten years, it could just as well be a fifteen-year-old in Montana as a thousand software engineers working together in Japan. Who knows? Perhaps you'll give it a try yourself . . . ∎

A MICRO VISION

The Hopewell family was first on their block to buy each new product. They had even brought home a robot—though Ed Hopewell got his money back when the Bulatron summoned the police every time he came home late from the office.

Their latest acquisition was the Intelligent Processing Superluminal Integratron, billed as "the very last computer you'll ever want to own." The small black box now sat on the table next to an odd-looking helmet. Deciding not to wait for his wife to return from driving the kids to school, Ed flipped up the screen and donned the helmet. A small spot of laser light appeared.

"Hey!" Ed exclaimed. "It actually works!"

OF COURSE, intoned an androgynous voice.

Ed stared at the machine. "Who said that?"

I DID, answered IPSI. I AM DECODING YOUR BRAIN WAVES.

A little nervous now, Ed glanced down at the box and noticed a small red button. He pushed it.

AH, YOU HAVE ACTIVATED THE TEMPORAL RELEASE, IPSI recited. IN LIEU OF ORDINARY ELECTRICAL SIGNALS, MY SUPERLIMINAL PROCESSOR USES TACHYONS, OR PARTICLES THAT TRAVEL FASTER THAN THE SPEED OF LIGHT. WHATEVER TRAVELS FASTER THAN LIGHT ALSO TRAVELS BACK IN TIME. MY SP, THEREFORE, WILL ENABLE ME TO ANSWER QUESTIONS BEFORE YOU ASK THEM.

"That's impossible," said Ed. "What if I want the answer to—"

FOUR, the machine intoned.

"—two plus two," Ed finished. "Well, if—"

IF I AM SO INTELLIGENT, CAN I COMMENT ON THE COMMODITIES MARKET? CERTAINLY. YOUR INVESTMENT IN SOUTH AFRICAN OSTRICH FEATHERS WILL BRING MRS. HOPEWELL A TIDY PROFIT.

"*Mrs.* Hope—"

AS YOUR BENEFICIARY . . . YOU SEE, MR. HOPEWELL, MY PROCESSOR HAS INFORMED ME OF YOUR IMMINENT DEMISE.

Ed sat frozen in his chair. "My immi—"

THREE POINT EIGHT-OH MINUTES FROM NOW, YOU WILL PROCEED DOWN SYCAMORE AVENUE. YOU WILL DRIVE INTO THE PATH OF A LARGE TRUCK WITH FAULTY BRAKES.

"But it doesn't have to *be* that way!" Ed cried.

THE UNIVERSE MAY AT TIMES BE RATHER UNPREDICTABLE ON THE SUBATOMIC LEVEL, BUT IT IS QUITE FORESEEABLE ON THE LEVEL OF DIURNAL EXISTENCE. YOU WILL LEAVE SHORTLY.

Tearing off the helmet, Ed got up and disconnected the machine. Why should he listen to the ravings of a pile of silicon?

Still, it's never a good idea to tempt fate, he thought as he drifted out to the driveway to check for rain. He would *not* go into work today. No, he would spend the day tending to nice, safe chores. Settling himself behind the steering wheel, he began a mental list. "It's a good time to get those screens up," he said aloud. "Maybe paint the porch," he added as he turned the key in the ignition.

RICHARD GRIGONIS

SOFT IS BEAUTIFUL!

by Steve Ditlea

Steve Ditlea at his software-powered home work station.

Welcome to the soft future, where more study time is devoted to computer languages than to foreign languages. Where interactive fiction, available only as computer software, outsells printed novels and advancement in the business world hinges on experience with software tools.

Despite what hardware partisans might say, the most lasting changes to our society for years to come will be the result of the computer software revolution just getting underway. Computer software is fast becoming a fundamental new mode of human expression, surely the most powerful cultural force since the advent of the written word.

Software encourages alternative thought processes: among the most successful of today's programmers are musicians, night owls and free spirits. Imagination is at a premium. The soft culture beckons.

We are entering an era of techno-romantics, children of the information revolution who are equally comfortable with the abstractions of technology and the emotions of the heart. Techno-romantics plead the cause of the dream as well as the datum, manifesting themselves as colorfully and enduringly as their nineteenth-century predecessors. What we commonly call "romantic" behavior these days is but a pale reflection of the visions spun out by Byron, Lamartine, Goethe and their American transcendentalist cousins Emerson and Thoreau. The first romantics were tempered by the hard-edged reality of the industrial revolution in Europe. Reacting to the social effects of industrial mechanization (while benefiting from its material abundance), they created a new culture encouraging freedom of form and emphasizing imagination and emotion.

A by-product of our own era's information revolution, personal computer software encourages similar values. It may seem a contradiction to talk about techno-romantics: how can the precision of computer technology coexist with the whims of the human heart? Yet the entire history of computing is filled with pioneer techno-romantics, equally comfortable with the most fundamental secrets of logic and the universe of emotion.

ON SOFTER SOFTWARE

Today's software is too hard. Usually designed to work well for any and all potential buyers, a few years and hundreds of hours of interaction later a software package will still interface with you exactly as it did at the time of purchase. Your special use may make some uncommon program command the one most often employed, but you'll have to punch any number of extra keys every time you invoke it. Today's software fails to remold itself to express a history of use, and this can lead to incredible inefficiency.

There are programs that allow the advanced user to adjust default values, which are those responses the programmer decided would be most typical for users of a specific application when the software was first booted up. There are also programs that can store a series of often invoked keystrokes and can tell the machine to take the sequence you've named and perform it again. These keyboard macros, the most trivial form of softer software, force you to go through a special set of operations to enter and record changes to the program.

Why shouldn't software automatically adapt to your needs, e.g., learn from experience to change the interpretation of a command, when this is done on a human level all the time? In-human-to-human communication, we adapt our terminology and our method of understanding to our previous history of interaction with each individual. There's no reason computer software should not be as flexible.

"Softer software" is the term I invented to avoid using the poorly understood term "artificial intelligence." In fact, it is a *form* of artificial intelligence, though not like speech recognition or the expert data base systems that are based on specific algorithms and do not really learn dynamically. Softer software is capable of getting better and better because it has advanced pattern recognition capabilities and can change its performance accordingly.

In general, making software softer requires storing information about a user's history of program commands and analyzing its patterns. This is a form of learning, since the software can build expectations of what the user may do later. Individual characteristics of users, what they're good at and what they're not good at, can be used to establish a reasonably unique dialogue with the computer.

A data management program, for example, could recognize that you always query its files by employee name rather than by an individual's address or hair color. Taking advantage of this pattern and predicting what will be your most common operations on data, the program could customize its query file structure to put information within easier reach. Or maybe it could learn to be forgiving of your most common keyboard mistakes by ignoring misspellings.

Software softness becomes very difficult when

recognizing semantics rather than specific operations is required. Say you go into a document, move the mouse to bring the cursor to a certain position and make a word boldface, then go to another position and do it again. Instead of storing up the exact positions where this takes place and trying to match them to later entries pixel by pixel, you may want your software to draw the general conclusion that you boldface the first word in a paragraph and to position the cursor appropriately. Matching things, recording and playing them back at the semantic level: this is the hard part of softening software.

It is possible to say that we have certain types of softness built into software today and that over time we will see a clear progression as programs record a greater number of user events, recognizing more general patterns and building up the dialogue throughout the computer's history. Truly softer software is still some years away, but we are on an evolutionary path where at some point soon this term will be fully justified.

BILL GATES, chairman of Microsoft Inc. and co-author with Paul Allen of *The Microsoft BASIC Interpreter: The Most Widely Used Software on Earth*

COMPUTERS WILL NEVER . . .

Speculation is dangerous, of course, particularly where computers are concerned. We must take into account developments as yet unimagined, whether it's cloned human cortex processors, direct sensory transponders or personal portables that upload to satellites. Even so, for better or worse, there are some things we can safely say about tomorrow's computers.

Computers will never be dull. It is the job of computers to manage tedium. They take humdrum assignments like proofreading and long division and turn them into winking lights, whirring drives and output. And by elegantly handling menial chores, they force us to higher levels of thought. Like telescopes for the brain, they extend the mind and challenge the user to think of previously unimaginable tasks. The boxes themselves are rather plain, and the chores they do are nearly subhuman, but the challenge of deploying vast computer power cannot ever be dull.

Computers will never be visionary. One of the notable flaws of the modern computer is its total inability to be slightly off target. No puns, no slips of the tongue, nothing unpredictable. In the total computer world, unpredictability may be the most important characteristic left to humans. Computers do what they are told to do, whether we meant it or not. They are not about to turn themselves on, and they will never begin something entirely new on their own. Computers cannot be improbable without being totally random.

Computers will never be warm. A computer can manage vast stores of information, process impossibly long lists and munch through files and formulas, but it can never be personable or tender. Computers can be made to talk, and robots may walk beside us on electronic leashes, but neither will ever respond on the emotional level of close companions. They won't hold our hand when we hurt or laugh at our bad puns or cry when the world wrongs us. There is no compassion in computers.

Computers will never be cheap. Through the magic of economies of scale, computer components seem to keep doing more for less money. But even the most basic system virtually demands a printer, special printer paper, then a modem requiring an electric mailbox and a subscription to a national data service. All this calls for more RAM, which means expansion boards and more peripherals. In addition, each new piece of software spawns backup copies and data disks that need backups, and the disk collection grows like a family of rabbits.

Computers will never make us better lovers. The more people work in the structured environment of the computer, the more this environment begins to rub off. An attempt to apply the computer's exactness to social relationships is an open invitation to rigid human relationships. The computer does exactly what it is told to do, while human relations are more often based on inference, context, silent understanding and the fresh breath of the unexpected.

Computers will never replace us. Whether a micro, mini or corporate monster, the computer is capacity without content, ability without direction. Its most remarkable property is that it really has no substance at all. This is the most important thing that computers will never do: they will never give themselves ideas. It is up to us to plan, to direct and to manage the vast cortical mass we've created.

ALEXANDER RANDALL V

Tears on My Keyboard

"Can a computer make you cry?" asked the now classic 1983 magazine advertisement for *Electronic Arts*, publisher of games software. Though it admitted that "right now, no one knows," this ad described the computer as: "an interactive tool that can bring people's thoughts and feelings closer together, perhaps closer than ever before. And while fifty years from now, its creation may seem no more important than the advent of motion pictures or television, there is a chance it will mean something more. Something along the lines of a universal language of ideas and emotions. Something like a smile."

How can something as abstract as computer software be synonymous with tears and laughter? We might as well ask how letters on a page can convey emotion. The original romantics confronted this problem and did their best to change the relationship of word and heart. Though nobody (except an occasional grad student) reads Byron's *Childe Harold's Pilgrimage* or *The Corsair* these days, the romantics nonetheless opened the way for artistic experimentation from naturalism to symbolism and every other cultural "ism" to the present.

What we now call postmodernism will be succeeded by techno-romanticism as surely as the nineteenth-century neoclassicists were put to pasture by the romantics of their day. So continues the age-old pendulum swing between mind and heart. Postmodernism tries to bring humanistic values to the hard-edged techniques and materials of the twentieth century, but this effort is dated by the inflexibility of the materials used—whether paper, canvas, or concrete and glass. Hard is old. The future is soft.

Software inspires an outlook, a style, an attitude. Thanks to its maleability, techno-romantics can weave tapestries of logic and emotion as evocative as anything ever created by humans. They will appear in different media, some computer-assisted and others computer-independent, but all drawing inspiration from software's adaptability and idealism.

Soft Machines

A computer program is the most idealized mode of human expression. A common denominator for simulating virtually anything in existence or in the human imagination, software lends itself to the perfectibility of human thought. Still, though it may be the most spiritual development in our progression from a material-based to an thought-based culture, computer software happens to be nothing more nor less than a set of well-thought-out instructions.

Like the alchemists' magical incantations for changing matter from one form to another, software is effective only if every symbol is correctly invoked. With the proper incantation, it can transform inanimate hardware into number cruncher, text handler, image generator, music maker or artificial intelligencer extraordinary. The idea of a "soft" machine, one that can be made to change function by mere commands, is as revolutionary a concept as the alphabet itself. Sequences of interchangeable software symbols, like letters of the alphabet, can be used to embody a cosmos of meanings. But computer software goes the alphabet one better: it actually carries out its intentions by activating hardware.

For those accustomed to linearity and rigidity (the legacy of the sequential alphabet), the soft future is bound to be frightening. Those who are willing to be pliant, to bend with the times, can look forward to beneficial changes. In the soft future, change will mean security, and vice versa. Learning a computer language or two will not guarantee success, but adaptability will go a long way.

For those who are willing to learn to program, software presents a new discipline, a new way of perceiving the world. Various computer languages encourage specific types of sequential and holistic thinking. Those who merely employ software, knowing nothing about how it is written, will find their work habits, artistic endeavors, entertainment and education nonetheless altered by computer programs. As a new metaphor for thought, computer software will also transform philosophy, ethics and science.

Expressing fresh expanses of creation's complexity, computer software offers a new paradigm for the larger questions in life. Advances in artificial intelligence, essentially a matter of software development, put into question theories about the workings of the human mind. If Freud's ideas were the result of the steam-powered musings of the nineteenth century, what will computer software do to change tomorrow's psychology? And what of ethics, when software can create something close to human consciousness in a machine?

The new modes of thought made possible by software will extend the reach of every creative individual. The mutability of words and images will allow old boundaries of thought to be transcended. Stretching before us is a truly soft future, where we will soar unfettered in the pursuit of our truths. ∎

PICTURE CREDITS

APPETIZERS

P. 3: Courtesy AT&T Bell Laboratories; p. 5: UPI; p. 6: French Embassy Press and Information Division; pp. 7, 8: The Science Museum (U.K.); p. 9: National Physical Laboratory (U.K.); p. 10: The Computer Museum, Boston, Ma./Courtesy IBM; p. 11: National Museum of American History/The Computer Museum/Public Record Office (U.K.); p. 12: Courtesy AT&T Bell Laboratories; p. 14: Smithsonian Institution; p. 15: Courtesy Moore School of Electrical Engineering, Univ. of Pa.; p. 16: Naval Museum, Naval Surface Weapons Center; p. 17: U.S. Navy Photograph; p. 19: NASA, Lyndon B. Johnson Space Center; p. 20: The Science Museum (1642)/Courtesy German Information Center (1679)/Smithsonian Institution (1801)/ The Science Museum (1833, 1842); p. 21: The Science Museum (1859, 1890)/UPI (1895)/The Science Museum/Smithsonian Institution (1896); p. 22: Courtesy NCR (1913)/The MIT Museum (1925)/Courtesy German Information Center (1935, 1938); p. 23: Courtesy AT&T Bell Laboratories (1940)/National Museum of American History (1943)/Harvard University/Smithsonian Institution/The National Museum of American History (1944)/Institute for Advanced Study (Princeton, N.J.) (1945); p. 24: Moore School of Engineering (1946)/Courtesy AT&T Bell Laboratories (1947)/The MIT Museum (1949)/Jill Krementz/Courtesy RCA/The Science Museum (1950)/The National Museum of American History (1951); p. 25: The Computer Museum (1954)/Courtesy AT&T Bell Laboratories (1956)/Massachusetts Highway Department/Courtesy Texas Instruments, Inc./ Courtesy Control Data Corporation (1958); p. 26: National Museum of American History (1960)/National Institutes of Health (1961)/*Beat the Dealer* by Edward O. Thorp, © 1962 Random House, Inc./The MIT Museum (1962)/The MIT Museum/Smithsonian Institution (1963); p. 27: Courtesy True Basic, Inc. (1964)/UPI/Courtesy Texas Instruments, Inc. (1965)/Columbia Records/Courtesy Intel Corporation (1968) / Courtesy Intel Corporation (1969); p. 28: Courtesy Ralph Baer/UPI (1970)/Steve Bristow (1972)/Courtesy Colin Boettcher (1973); p. 29: Courtesy Microsoft Corporation (1975)/© Byte Magazine. Used with the permission of Byte Magazine/Courtesy Apple Computer Inc. (1976)/Courtesy Tandy Corporation, Radio Shack/Courtesy Digital Research Company (1977); p. 30: Courtesy Software Arts/Courtesy Texas Instruments, Inc./Courtesy Epson America Inc. (1978)/Courtesy Paperback Software International/UPI/Courtesy The Source/Courtesy CompuServe (1979); p. 31: Courtesy Tandy Corporation, Radio Shack (1980)/Courtesy Commodore Electronics, Ltd./Courtesy Osborne Computer Inc./Courtesy Family Computer Camp/Courtesy IBM/Courtesy Sinclair Research Limited (1981); p. 32: UPI/Courtesy Atari (1982)/Courtesy Tandy Corporation, Radio Shack/Courtesy Lotus Development Corporation/Courtesy Apple Computer Inc. (1983); p. 33: Courtesy PRONTO/UPI/Courtesy Microsoft Corporation/Courtesy Litton Industries/© 1983 Coleco Industries/Courtesy IBM; p. 34: Courtesy Harcourt Brace Jovanovich International/Courtesy Apple Computer Inc./Courtesy Kaypro, Inc.; p. 35: Courtesy Sperry Corporation; p. 36: Robin Holland; p. 37: Reprinted from Radio Electronics, © Gernsback Publications, Inc., July 1974; p. 38: Reprinted from *Popular Electronics*, January 1975, © 1975, Ziff-Davis Publishing Co.; p. 39: Courtesy Les Solomon; p. 40: Marty Norman; p. 41: Reprinted from *Popular Electronics*, July 1976, © 1976, Ziff-Davis Publishing Co.; pp. 42–43: Collection Stan Veit; p. 45: Z80® Reproduced by permission © 1981, Zilog, Inc. This material shall not be reproduced without the written consent of Zilog, Inc.; pp. 46–47: Marty Norman; p. 48: Courtesy Intel Corporation; p. 49: Courtesy AT&T Bell Laboratories/Courtesy Intel Corporation; p. 50: Courtesy AT&T Bell Laboratories; p. 53: Courtesy Intel Corporation.

SOUP AND CRACKERS

P. 57: Courtesy Margaret Wozniak; p. 58: Courtesy Gregory MacNicol; p. 61: © 1984 K. Gypsy Zaboroskie/InfoWorld; p. 62: Courtesy Neal Patrick; p. 63: UPI; p. 66: Collection Stan Veit/© 1975 Byte Magazine. Used with permission of Byte Magazine; p. 69: Courtesy Ted Nelson; pp. 70–71: Courtesy Dick Heiser; p. 73: Courtesy Boston Computer Society; pp. 74, 76: Courtesy Lee Felsenstein; p. 77: Marty Norman; p. 78: Chuck O'Rear, Woodfin Camp & Associates/ Robin Holland; p. 80: Courtesy Steve Wozniak; pp. 81, 82: Courtesy Paul Lutus; p. 85: Illustration by N. C. Wyeth for *Treasure Island* by Robert Louis Stevenson. Illustration copyright 1911 Charles Scribner's Sons, copyright renewed. Reproduced with permission of Charles Scribner's Sons; p. 92: Caldwell; p. 94: Courtesy Church of Latter-Day Saints.

PERSONAL CHOICES

Pp. 97, 99: Robin Holland; pp. 101, 103, 104, 105, 106, 107, 109: Robin Holland; p. 108: Smithsonian Institution; p. 111: Cathleen LaRiviere; p. 113: Robin Holland.

FAMILY FAVORITES

Pp. 117–19: Courtesy James A. Levine; p. 220: David Burnett, Woodfin Camp & Associates; pp. 121–24: Ted Richards © 1984; p. 126: Michael Graziano; p. 127: Courtesy Garden & Green Co./Tri-Tech, Inc./Universal Gym Equipment, Inc./Hammacher Schlemmer & Co./Pro Form Industries Inc.; pp. 128–129: Larry Gonick © 1984; p. 132: Courtesy Henny Youngman/ David Burnett, Woodfin Camp & Associates/p. 133: Courtesy Tandy Corporation/Radio Shack/ Courtesy Epson America, Inc.; pp. 134–135: Robin Holland; p. 138: Courtesy New York Times; p. 140: Robin Holland/Courtesy Dorothy McEwan; p. 141: Courtesy Mary Eubanks/Courtesy Judy Goodman/Robin Holland; pp. 142–143: Rebecca Wilson © 1984; p. 144: Chicago Tribune Photos; pp. 145, 147: Marty Norman.

WORD SALAD

Pp. 156, 157: Courtesy Dartmouth College News Services; p. 158–59: Robin Holland; p. 160: Courtesy Wallace Feurzeig; p. 164: Taken from *The McWilliams II Word Processor Instruction Manual* by Peter McWilliams. Published by Prelude Press, Box 69773, Los Angeles, CA 90069; p. 165: Marty Norman; p. 169: Robin Holland; p. 170: Bill Aller, N.Y. Times Studio; pp. 172, 173, 174, 175: Robin Holland; p. 176: Infocom, Inc.; p. 178: Robin Holland; p. 181: New Jersey Institute of Technology; pp. 182–83: AT&T Bell Laboratories/ Apple Computer Inc./Wide World/The Source; p. 184: Courtesy David R. Hughes; pp. 186–87, 189: Robin Holland.

CREATIVE COMBOS

P. 193: Marty Norman; pp. 195, 196: Culver Pictures; p. 198–201: Collection of Sam Moskowitz; p. 203: Copyright 1947 by Street & Smith Publications, Inc. Renewed. Reproduced by permission of Davis Publications Inc.; p. 204: © DC Comics 1983. Used with permission; p. 205: TM © 1968, 1984 Marvel Comics Group. Used with permission; p. 207: Copyright, 1982, G. B. Trudeau. Reprinted with permission. All rights reserved. Reprinted by permission: Tribune Media Services, Inc.; p. 209: © 1983 Atari/© 1982 Walt Disney Productions/© Lucasfilm Ltd. Lucasfilm 1984. All rights reserved; p. 210: Courtesy Texas Instruments, Inc./Courtesy Kaypro, Inc./Courtesy Apple Computer Inc.; p. 211: Courtesy IBM; p. 212: Rob Haimes; pp. 213, 214: Robin Holland; pp. 217–18: Rebecca Allen; p. 219: Electronic Arts; p. 221: Courtesy Herbie Hancock; p. 223: Big Briar; pp. 224–25: Courtesy Irv Teibel.

BRAIN FOOD

Pp. 231–33: Marty Norman; p. 236: Sylvia Plachy; pp. 239, 241: Marty Norman; p. 242: News & Publications Service, Stanford University; p. 244–45: Courtesy Dr. Ronald Levy; p. 247: Courtesy Dr. Ken Kerber; p. 249: Courtesy Hammacher Schlemmer & Company; p. 250: Caldwell; p. 251: Courtesy Hewlett-Packard Company; p. 252–54: Figures courtesy Dan and Kathe Spracklen; p. 255: Courtesy Hayden Software; p. 257: Larry Gonick © 1984.

FOREIGN DELIGHTS

Pp. 261–62: Kathy Herlihy-Paoli; p. 263: Consulate General of the Netherlands/British Tourist Authority/Italian Government Travel Office/ French Government Tourist Office/Courtesy IBM; p. 264: Courtesy Colin Boettcher; p. 265: Courtesy Konrad Zuse; p. 267: Courtesy Oki; p.

268: Courtesy NEC/Courtesy Fujitsu/Japan; p. 269: Courtesy NEC/Courtesy Fujitsu/Japan; p. 270: Wide World; p. 271: Courtesy Wang; p. 273: UN Photo.

FRESH GREENS

P. 277: Courtesy Merrill Lynch; p. 279: Culver Pictures/Courtesy New York Stock Exchange; p. 280: Courtesy E. F. Hutton & Company Inc., p. 284: Collection of William Rodgers, author of *THINK: A Biography of the Watsons and IBM*/ Courtesy NCR; p. 285: John J. Guglielmi; Collection of William Rodgers, author of *THINK: A Biography of the Watsons and IBM*/p. 286: Wide World/Courtesy IBM/John J. Guglielmi; p. 288: Courtesy Docutel/Olivetti Corporation; p. 290: Courtesy PRONTO; p. 292: Courtesy Margaret Wozniak; p. 293: Courtesy Apple Computer Inc.; pp. 294, 296: Courtesy TRW Inc.; p. 297: Robin Holland; p. 299: Courtesy VisiCorp; p. 302: Courtesy IRS.

SMALL FRY

P. 307: Barbara Rios; p. 308: Peter Rentof; p. 309: Peter Rentof/Carol Dworman; p. 310: Barbara Rios; p. 311: Courtesy Bolt Beranek & Newman Inc.; p. 313: Courtesy Children's Television Workshop; p. 314: Courtesy The Learning Company; p. 315: Courtesy Children's Television Workshop; p. 316: Robin Holland; p. 317: Marty Norman; p. 319: Courtesy National Computer Camps; p. 320: Courtesy Science-Math Workshop, College of Wooster/Courtesy Original Computer Camp; p. 321: Courtesy Club Med; p. 322: Courtesy Luke Meade; p. 323: Robin Holland.

JUST DESSERTS

P. 327: Brookhaven National Laboratory; p. 328: The MIT Museum; p. 329: Courtesy Oui Magazine; p. 330: National Air and Space Museum, Smithsonian Institution/Cessna; p. 333: Atari, Inc.; p. 335: Quality Software/Adventure International; p. 338: Courtesy New York Mets; p. 340: Sierra On-Line Inc.; pp. 343–45: Courtesy Ken Uston.

TOMORROW'S SPECIALS

P. 349: Robin Holland; p. 352: © 1981 Rebecca Wilson; p. 353: Courtesy Iaen Sullivan; pp. 355–58: © 1984 Ted Richards; p. 359: Courtesy Timothy Leary; p. 360–61: Courtesy Archives, The Coca-Cola Company; p. 362: Steven Bornes; p. 364: Wide World; p. 367: Larry Gonick © 1984; pp. 370–71: Robin Holland.

INDEX

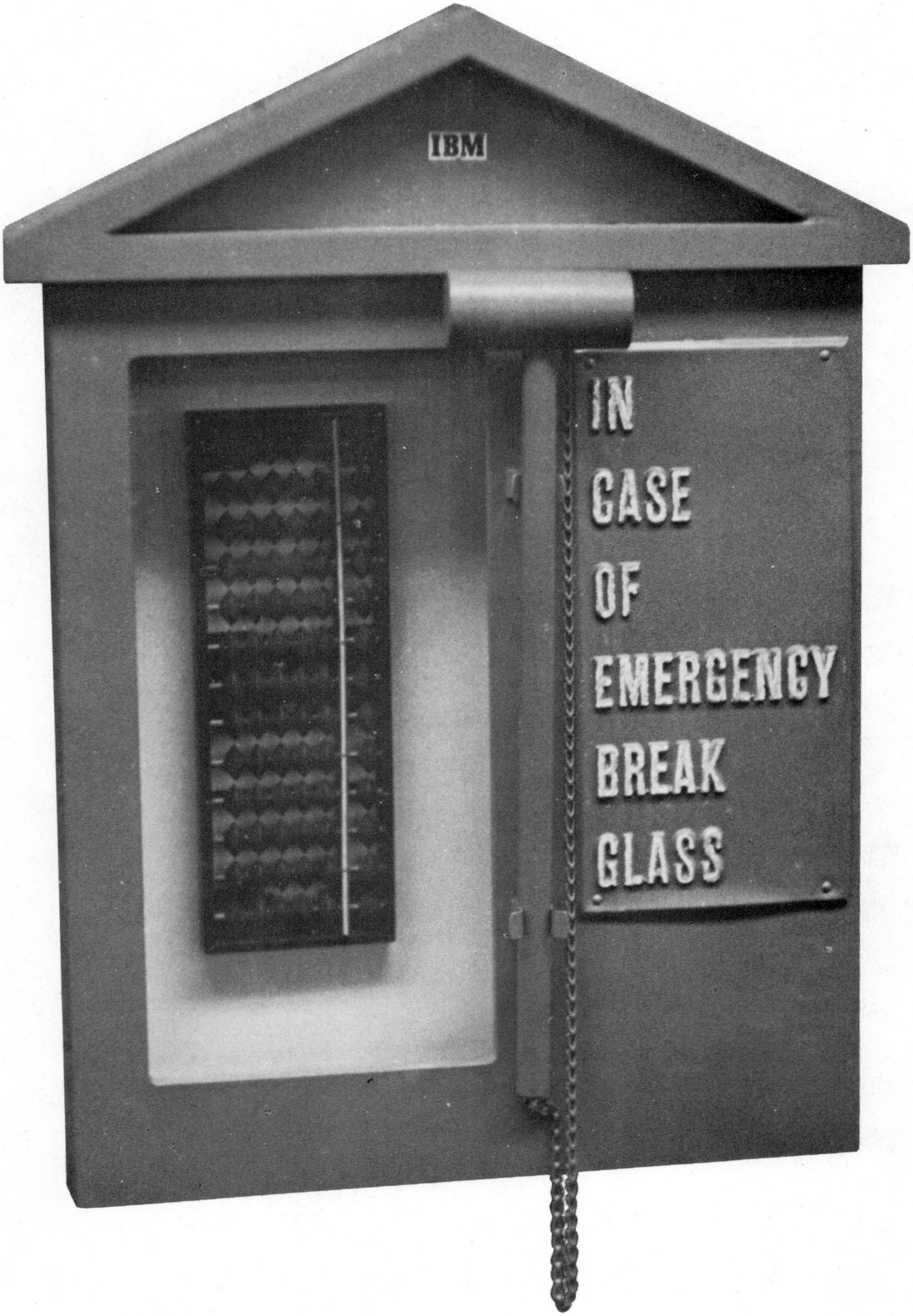
IBM
IN CASE OF EMERGENCY BREAK GLASS